Volume II

THE BOOK OF PRIVILEGES ISSUED
TO CHRISTOPHER COLUMBUS
BY KING FERNANDO AND QUEEN ISABEL

1492–1502

Geoffrey Symcox
General Editor
UCLA

M. J. B. Allen
Philip Levine
Norman J. W. Thrower
Edward Tuttle
UCLA

Luciano Formisano
UNIVERSITY OF BOLOGNA

*Publication of this volume was made possible
by the generous support of the*

NATIONAL ENDOWMENT FOR THE HUMANITIES
Washington, D.C.

COMITATO NAZIONALE PER LE CELEBRAZIONI DEL V CENTENARIO DELLA
SCOPERTA DELL'AMERICA
Rome

SOCIEDAD ESTATAL QUINTO CENTENARIO
Madrid

Published under the auspices of the

UCLA CENTER FOR MEDIEVAL AND RENAISSANCE STUDIES

Volume II

THE BOOK OF PRIVILEGES ISSUED
TO CHRISTOPHER COLUMBUS
BY KING FERNANDO AND QUEEN ISABEL
1492–1502

Helen Nader

Editor and Translator

Luciano Formisano

Philologist

Wipf & Stock
PUBLISHERS
Eugene, Oregon

Wipf and Stock Publishers
199 West 8th Avenue, Suite 3
Eugene, Oregon 97401

The Book of Privileges Issued To Christopher Columbus
By King Fernando and Queen Isabel 1492-1502
Edited by Nader, Helen
Copyright©1996 UCLA Center for Medieval and Renaissance Studies
ISBN: 1-59244-675-2
Publication date 4/28/2004
Previously published by University of California Press, 1996

SERIES PREFACE

The Repertorium Columbianum is a collection of contemporary sources relating to Columbus's four voyages, and the interpenetration of the hitherto separate worlds that resulted from them. This multivolume series will provide in readily accessible form the basic documents that are the starting point for research into this pivotal moment in world history; they form the indispensable tools for all scholarly inquiry into the encounter. The series provides accurate editions of the essential texts in their original languages, for the use of specialists, while at the same time making them available to students and scholars in related fields through parallel translations into modern English.

The Repertorium Columbianum was originally conceived by the late Professor Fredi Chiappelli, former director of the Center for Medieval and Renaissance Studies at the University of California, Los Angeles. The series is respectfully dedicated to his memory. He intended it to be an up-to-date, greatly expanded version of the Raccolta Colombiana published on the occasion of the Columbian quatercentenary in 1892. He laid down the basic lines of editorial policy that are being followed in these volumes, in an approach that blends philological and historical methodologies. Because of the dual approach, the editing of most volumes is an interdisciplinary undertaking among specialists in the field represented by the source materials in that volume. A final, cumulative index volume will enable users of the series to make connections and trace thematic linkages among the wide variety of documentary materials that the series contains. The Repertorium's scope is generally limited to sources from the period between Columbus's first voyage and the Spanish conquest of Mexico in 1519–1521, although certain volumes, by their nature, may extend the chronological range of the series beyond these dates.

Since 1892 historical perspectives on the Columbian encounter have shifted, and the techniques of philological analysis have made enormous strides. The Repertorium's presentation of the sources reflects these changes. Centennial commemorations such as the Columbian quincentenary serve to remind us of the way in which scholarly methods and concerns have altered over the intervening years; they are occasions for taking stock of the past century's achievements, for seeing how interpretations have changed, for scrutinizing new material that has come to light, and for charting the course for future research. These are the purposes that inform the editorial policy of the Repertorium Columbianum. It seeks to sum up what has been achieved in the field of Columbian studies over the past century, to throw new light on the encounter and its immediate aftermath, to collect in a standardized format the essential materials for research, and to suggest lines of inquiry for the years ahead.

The original Columbian ventures were international in conception and execution, and in this same spirit the Repertorium Columbianum is an international undertaking. The contributing scholars and the members of the editorial board are drawn from both sides of the Atlantic, and the costs are being borne with the help of generous funding from the United States National Endowment for the Humanities, the Italian Comitato Nazionale per le Celebrazioni del V Centenario della Scoperta dell'America, and the Spanish Sociedad Estatal para la Ejecución de Programas del Quinto Centenario. The administrative and editorial work for the series is being performed by the UCLA Center for Medieval and Renaissance Studies, under whose auspices these volumes will appear. As general editor it is my pleasant duty to acknowledge a profound debt of gratitude to the three government sponsors, without whose generous and enlightened support this project would have been impossible.

Geoffrey Symcox
General Editor

The Virgin of Good Winds. On either side, officials of the House of Trade. In the center, the figure on the left is presumed to be Christopher Columbus. In the foreground, ships of the early sixteenth century. Native Americans shiver in the background. Painted by Alejo Fernández for the chapel of the House of Trade about 1505. Alcázar Real, Seville. (From the collections of the Patrimonio Nacional)

CONTENTS

Chapter 3.2: Fernando and Isabel Organize the Royal
Enterprise of the Indies   118

PREFACE

THIS EDITION

Scholars studying the Columbus voyages and their consequences require an understanding of the privileges with which the Catholic kings Fernando and Isabel established the relationship between ruler and colony. Historians especially are interested in tracing the evolution of motives and perceptions among Europeans such as Fernando, Isabel, and Columbus, who had the power to formulate policy toward the American Indians and the American environment. For studies in these areas, documentary evidence is indispensable. As historians, we best understand the statements of intent in chronological order, as they developed in the context of new information from the Americas and changed perceptions in Spain. The editions of the *Book of Privileges* previously available cannot provide this understanding, even to those fluent in Spanish.

The greatest obstacle to historical study of the *Book of Privileges* has been its intractable disorder. This difficulty became apparent to me after I had translated the documents and was attempting to write introductory essays for them. In order to explain what documents at the beginning of the collection referred to, I had to cite documents that had been issued earlier but were located near the end of the codex. For my own convenience (and sanity) in writing the introductions, I temporarily rearranged and renumbered the documents in chronological order.

This new arrangement proved helpful and made sense out of many puzzles. Before this present edition, the documents had always been published in no chronological or thematic order. They were edited and translated just as Columbus presented them to the Seville notaries for copying in 1498 and 1502. Columbus had placed on top of the pile those documents most important to him personally, but the authors of the privileges, King Fernando and Queen Isabel, had a different set of priorities. These are important considerations to keep in mind if one is interested in Columbus's assessment of his privileges; Luciano Formisano addresses this issue in his philological commentary in this volume. The text makes two different kinds of sense, either in the order in which it survives, or in the order in which the documents were written. We have opted to present the text in both orders. In the first half of this edition we provide an English translation of the documents in their correct chronological order, which shows them as a continuous historical narrative of the monarchs' enterprise and Columbus's privileges. In the second half we present the documents in the order in which Columbus left them. (A Table of Correspondences between the two numbering systems begins on p. xxvi.)

By arranging the documents in rough chronological order, the first half of this edition of the privileges reveals the evolution of royal policy as the monarchs received and absorbed new information about the American environment and natives, and changed their earlier evaluations of the admiral's abilities as an administrator of the colonies. In 1492, Fernando, Isabel, and Columbus all assumed that they were negotiating terms for a relatively familiar world, Asia, made up of large cities and centralized empires and monarchies. The monarchs authorized Columbus to negotiate with the rulers he would encounter and named him their viceroy and governor general of lands he would discover en route that were not under the jurisdiction of other rulers. The monarchs' jolting realization that the lands were not in Asia and that all of what Columbus had encountered could become theirs begins to appear in the 1497 documents and becomes clear in those added to the 1502 codices. This changing perception on the part of the monarchs was masked and flattened by the chaotic and nonchronological arrangement of the documents in previous editions.

Too strict a chronological arrangement would have introduced another type of historical anachronism. The documents that Columbus considered so important were copies of the early fifteenth-century grant of the admiralty of Castile as a hereditary office. That sequence of documents reflected Columbus's priority in 1498—to secure confirmation of his legal right to bequeath his offices to his son Diego Colón. He had been promised this privilege in the 1492 Capitulations, but the granting of hereditary royal office violated the fundamental laws of the Castilian monarchy. Enrique III's grant of the admiralty of Castile to Alfonso Enríquez in 1405 and Juan II's subsequent confirmations provided the legal precedents Columbus sought for the heritability of his office as admiral of the Ocean Sea.

Chronologically, the admiralty of Castile documents are the earliest in the *Book of Privileges,* but they did not enter the Columbus story until much later than most of the other documents. They came into Columbus's possession in late 1497, and when we read them in their proper place we can see how they clarified and focused Columbus's demands. When the monarchs in 1492 promised Columbus privileges and powers equal to those of the admiral of Castile, they certainly did not know the specifics of their ancestors' grants. Reading the admiral of Castile's privileges for the first time in late 1497, Columbus must have hardened his resolve to press for every jot and tittle of the Capitulations, and more. His acquisition of a copy of the admiral of Castile's privileges was the precipitating event that inspired Columbus to commission copies in early 1498. Thus, he must have realized even before embarking on his third voyage that he and the royal council would engage in a prolonged legal duel.

I have followed the basic principle of the Repertorium Columbianum project to render each document into modern plain English. While avoiding literal exactness, I have tried to be sensitive to the original linguistic character of the sources, carefully considering Castilian social, political, intellectual, religious, and moral realities as they affected the language. I have tried to avoid anachronistic representations of the Castilian monarchy and of the encounter between Europeans and native Americans. It should be noted that one of the tenets of the Repertorium Columbianum project is to view language as conditioned perception in the reporting of both old and new realities.

In attempting to achieve these formidable goals, I confronted what at first seemed insoluble problems of legal prose style and vocabulary. Help came from the guidelines of the legal profession itself. Most of the documents in this volume were written in the jargon-laden and repetitive prose of any legislation or executive orders drafted by bureaucrats. Little would have been gained by transforming such Spanish into the equally tortured English prose of modern lawyers. To avoid this pitfall, which has plagued earlier translations of the *Book of Privileges,* I adopted the norms recommended by the American legal profession for the drafting of legislation (Dickerson 1986). In trying to find modern vocabulary for archaic expressions without going to the other extreme of erasing their legal implications, I have been guided by modern Spanish-English legal dictionaries.

I also faced serious historical problems in translating the *Book of Privileges.* The first is the same one that the Spanish law courts took years to untangle—the meaning, intent, and precedents of the Spanish original. The documents span one of the most turbulent and innovative periods in the history of the Castilian monarchy. As a result, the secretaries who composed and dictated them were innovating—inventing, borrowing, and adapting terminology and concepts to fit bewilderingly rapid changes in the structure and needs of the royal government. Some of the titles and offices that Fernando and Isabel granted to Columbus, for example, were their own creations: they appointed the first Castilian viceroy in 1484 and the first captain general in 1492. The nineteenth-century translations did not incorporate these changing formularies of the fifteenth century.

Spanish names and signatures were also changing in the fifteenth century. Spelling varied riotously before Castilian orthography was standardized in the eighteenth century, and clerks spelled names in a variety of forms, even in the same document. Signatures are of little help in deciphering spellings of names. During the reign of Fernando and Isabel, government officials were adopting rubrics—logos—instead of signing their names. Many of those who continued to sign usually did so with just first name(s) and office, or with office alone. I use the modern spelling of the names and have added accent marks, which were not used in the fifteenth and sixteenth centuries.

I use the Castilian forms for personal names, including those of the royal family. For many years American reference works have employed inconsistent norms for Fernando and Isabel. Instead of listing the queen's name as Elizabeth, its English equivalent, they use Isabella, its Italian form. The king's name has no ready English equivalent and, instead of using the Italian form Ferrando or Ferrante, most of them use Ferdinand, a truncated Latinization. American readers readily adapt to the Spanish names Fernando, Isabel, Juan, Diego, Luis, which are already familiar as place-names in California and the southwest. European scholars have long used these Castilian forms in their research publications and now American scholars are beginning to use them in publication for a broader audience. The recent *Christopher Columbus Encyclopedia* (Bedini 1991), which is intended for school libraries, uses Fernando and Isabel, and Peggy Liss's recent biography of the queen is entitled *Isabel the Queen* (Liss 1992).

Columbus and his family hispanized their names when they moved to Spain. His brothers Giacomo and Bartolomeo Colombo became Diego and Bartolomé Colón. His legitimate son may have been baptized Diogo in his native Lisbon, but all written references to him in Spain name him Diego Colón. The name of Columbus's illegitimate son is both Fernando and Hernando, since initial F and H were identical in the handwriting of the period. I use Fernando, to conform to the name of his homonym the king. Columbus himself is called Cristóbal Colón in the *Book of Privileges* and other Spanish documents. He signed with his title, "the admiral," and a Latin form of his first name, "Christoferens," or a rubric whose meaning has not been deciphered. The documents from Italy signed by members of the Columbus family—transcriptions of more than 100 are extant in an early seventeenth-century edition, including three attested or signed by Christopher himself—were written in Latin, the usual language for business documents there. The Latin nominative form of the family name, Columbus, has become standard in America, with the English form of his first name, Christopher.

Tracking down all the variants of these names in the archival and printed sources has required several years of research, and still I have not been able to identify all. A majority of the persons mentioned in Columbus's privileges were members of the royal staff, either working in Spain to expedite the financing, authorization, and provisioning of the Columbus fleets or posted to the Americas by the monarchs to serve as members of Columbus's staff. The most abundant sources of information about these persons have been various sections of the Archivo General de Simancas, national depository for the fifteenth- and sixteenth-century royal archives. Unless otherwise noted, my identification of persons in the *Book of Privileges* and their biographical data are based on manuscripts in AGS Registro General del Sello.

ACKNOWLEDGMENTS

This book is the product of the expertise, labor, and generosity of many colleagues and institutions. The late Fredi Chiappelli conceived the series and asked me to translate this volume. His colleague Ted Cachey generously shared his copy of the rare 1823 translation and his own preliminary survey of the manuscripts. The National Endowment for the Humanities provided crucial financial support in the form of a Translation Fellowship.

Professor Luciano Formisano supplied in timely and machine-readable fashion a thoroughly reliable text based on the Genoa Codex. My talented graduate students Liz Lehfeldt, Roland Pearson, and Kristy Wilson carried out the early research identifying codices and personnel. Generous and expert curators and librarians assisted me in identifying and assessing the codices and manuscripts conserved in special libraries in the United States: Joel Silver, Lilly Library, Indiana University; Rosemary Plakas, Rare Books Division, Library of Congress; Norman Fiering, Director, The John Carter Brown Library; and William Frank, The Huntington Library.

In the final stages of the project, Linda Martz provided invaluable advice on the identity of persons from the city of Toledo. Peggy Liss guided me through the various portraits of the royal family. Arthur Field and Fred McGinniss advised me on the Latin of the papal chancery, rescuing me from several solecisms in translation. Any infelicities that have crept back in are my own, of course. My immensely capable research assistant David Stark kept the project progressing through a marathon final year of revisions, checking, reassessing, and polishing. Spanish archivists and staff have been unstintingly generous with their expert assistance. I have been especially fortunate that the present Director of the Reading Room at the Archivo General de Simancas, Isabel Aguirre Landa, is the compiler of the most recent catalog (volume 16, covering the last half of the year 1499) of Registro General del Sello. In the true spirit of academic cooperation, she has helped me answer research questions that only her thorough acquaintance with this section could resolve.

Helen Nader

LIST OF ILLUSTRATIONS

ABBREVIATIONS

Introduction, Translation, and Notes

ACA   Archivo de la Corona de Aragón, Barcelona

AEA   *Anuario de Estudios Americanos*

AGI   Archivo General de Indias, Seville

AGS   Archivo General de Simancas

AHDE   *Anuario de Historia del Derecho Español*

AHN   Archivo Histórico Nacional, Madrid

AHR   *American Historical Review*

AUH   *Analecta Universitatis Hispalensis*

BRAH   *Boletín de la Real Academia de la Historia*

CSIC   Consejo Superior de Investigaciones Científicas

DHEE   *Diccionario de historia eclesiástica de España.* Ed. Quentín Aldea et al. 4 vols. Madrid: CSIC, 1972

EEHAS   Escuela de Estudios Hispano-Americanos en Sevilla

HGCM   Gutiérrez Coronel, Diego. *Historia genealógica de la casa de Mendoza.* Ed. Angel González Palencia. 2 vols. Madrid: CSIC, 1946

Pleitos   *Pleitos colombinos.* Ed. Antonio Muro Orejón et al. 5 vols. to date. Seville: EEHAS, 1964–1989

RAH   Real Academia de la Historia

Raccolta   Italy. R. Commissione Colombiana. *Raccolta di documenti e studi pubblicati dalla R. Commissione colombiana pel quarto cente-*

nario dalla scoperta dell'America. Rome: Ministero della Pubblica Istruzione, 1892–1896

RHA *Revista de Historia de America*

Philological Commentary and Transcriptions

Bustamante *Libro de los Privilegios del Almirante Don Cristóbal Colón (1498).* Ed. Ciriaco Pérez Bustamante (Madrid: Real Academia de la Historia, 1951), 2 vols.

Davenport Francis G. Davenport, "Text of Columbus's Privileges." *AHR* 14.4 (1909): 764–776.

Nuova Raccolta Ministero per i Beni Culturali e Ambientali. Comitato Nazionale per le Celebrazioni del V Centenario della Scoperta dell'America. "Nuova Raccolta Colombiana" (Rome: Istituto Poligrafico e Zecca dello Stato, 1988 ff.)

Raccolta See Raccolta, cit. Without specification of Part and volume: *Il Codice dei Privilegi di Cristoforo Colombo edito secondo i manoscritti di Genova, di Parigi e di Providence.* Ed. L. T. Belgrano and M. Staglieno (Raccolta, cit., Parte II, vol. II).

Stevens Christopher Columbus, *His Own Book of Privileges, 1502.* [Photographic Facsimile of the Paris Codex], with transliteration and translation by George F. Barwick . . . , The Introduction by Henry Harrisse. The whole compiled and edited with preface by Benjamin Franklin Stevens (London: B. F. Stevens, 1893).

Varela-Gil Cristóbal Colón, *Textos y documentos completos.* Edición de Consuelo Varela. *Nuevas Cartas.* Edición de Juan Gil (Madrid: Alianza Editorial, 1992).

TABLE OF CORRESPONDENCES BETWEEN FORMISANO'S AND NADER'S
NUMBERING OF DOCUMENTS

FORMISANO	NADER	NADER	FORMISANO
0	65	1	II.ii
I.i	40	2	III.ii.1
I.ii.1	41	3	XXXI
I.ii.1.1	42	4	II.i
I.ii.1.1.A	43		III.i
I.ii.1.1.a	44	5	III.ii.2
I.ii.1.1.b	45	6	XXXV
I.ii.1.1.a′	46	7	XXVII
I.ii.1.1.B	47	8	XXVIII
I.ii.1.2	48.1–10	9	XXIX
I.ii.2	48.11–13	10	XXXIII
II.i	4	11	XXVI
II.ii	1 (= 49)	12.1	IX.i
		12.1–17	IX.ii
II.iii	50	13	XXXII
III.i	4	14.1	XXXVI.i
		14.2–3	XXXVI.ii.1
		14.4–15	XXXVI.ii.1.1
		14.16–19	XXXVI.ii.2
		14.20–22	XXXVI.iii
III.ii.1	2	15	XXXIV
III.ii.2	5	16	XVIII
III.iii	51	17	XIX
IV	35	18	VI
V	33	19	XXI
VI	18	20	VIII
VII	25	21	XXII
VIII	20	22	XII
IX.i	12.1	23	XIII
IX.ii	12.1–17	24	XIV
IX.iii	34	25	VII
X	26	26	X
XI.i	27	27	XI.i
XI.ii	28	28	XI.ii
XII	22	29	XV
XIII	23	30	XX
XIV	24	31	XVI

FORMISANO	NADER	NADER	FORMISANO
XV	29	32	XXV
XVI	31	33	V
XVII	38	34	IX.iii
XVIII	16	35	IV
XIX	17	36	XXIII
XX	30	37	XXIV
XXI	19	38	XVII
XXII	21	39	XXX
XXIII	36	40	I.i
XXIV	37	41	I.ii.1
XXV	32	42	I.ii.1.1
XXVI	11	43	I.ii.1.1.A
XXVII	7	44	I.ii.1.1.a
XVIII	8	45	I.ii.1.1.b
XXIX	9	46	I.ii.1.1.a$'$
XXX	39	47	I.ii.1.1.B
XXXI	3	48.1–10	I.ii.1.2
		48.11–13	I.ii.2
XXXII	13	49	II.ii
XXXIII	10	50	II.iii
XXXIV	15	51	III.iii
XXXV	6	52	Addtl. Doc. 2.A.2
XXXVbis	69	53	Addtl. Doc. 2.A.1
XXXVI.i	14.1	54	Addtl. Doc. 2.B.1
XXXVI.ii.1	14.2–3	55	Addtl. Doc. 2.B.2
XXXVI.ii.1.1	14.4–15	56	Addtl. Doc. 2.C
XXXVI.ii.2	14.16–19	57	XL
XXXVI.iii	14.20–22	58	Addtl. Doc. 3
XXXVII.i	67	59	XXXVIII
XXXVII.i.1	61	60	XXXIX
XXXVII.i.2	63	61	XXXVII.i.1
XXXVII.i.3	62	62	XXXVII.i.3
XXXVII.i.4	64.1–14	63	XXXVII.i.2

FORMISANO	NADER	NADER	FORMISANO
XXXVII.ii	64.15-18	64.1-14	XXXVII.i.4
		64.15-18	XXXVII.ii
XXXVIII	59	65	0
XXXIX	60	66	(no text)
XL	57	67	XXXVII.i
XLbis	70	68	(no text)
		69	XXXVbis
		70	XLbis
		71	(no text)
		72	(no text)
		73	Addtl. Doc. 1.C

Addtl. Docs.	
1.A	(no trans.)
1.B	(no trans.)
1.C	73
2.A.1	53
2.A.2	52
2.B.1	54
2.B.2	55
2.C	56
3	58
4	(no trans.)

INTRODUCTION

Helen Nader

GENERAL INTRODUCTION

THE SIGNIFICANCE OF THE *BOOK OF PRIVILEGES*

In the *Book of Privileges* the Spanish monarchs laid the legal foundations on which the Kingdom of Castile justified its exploration, conquest, and colonization of the Americas. King Fernando and Queen Isabel by these writs instructed their business partner Christopher Columbus to engage in commerce with Asia and authorized him to claim for Castile the land he explored. In 1492 they assumed that that land would be on the Asian mainland or its offshore islands. As the monarchs issued further authorizations and concessions to Columbus from 1493 to 1502, they authorized Columbus to claim this land by various means: by treaty with local rulers, by effective occupation through colonization, or by military conquest in just war. These justifications, though modified over the centuries by interactions between native American and European civilizations, are still the legal foundation of American governments and societies.

The legal and political concepts embodied in the royal decrees, writs, and warrants were the common stock of European civilization, venerated as the cultural heritage that linked Renaissance society to the ancient Greeks and Romans. The point has been extensively studied by Lewis Hanke and is neatly summed up in the title of one of his works, *Aristotle and the American Indians* (Hanke 1970). Tensions and conflicts soon erupted out of the volatile mixture of the royal intentions expressed in the *Book of Privileges,* Columbus's personal objectives, and the self interest of native Indians and Spanish colonists. Yet, eventually, all adopted the concepts laid out in the *Book of Privileges* as weapons in their pursuit of possession and control of American land and peoples. Within a century after the first Columbian voyage, astute Indian communities in central Mexico were citing these legal precepts to claim the same tax-free status as neighboring Spanish towns (Gibson 1952). When Portuguese, French, and English conquerors and colonists displaced the Spaniards as the principal exploiters of native American lands and peoples in the early seventeenth century, they used these same legal arguments. In some cases, these latecomers justified their actions by accusing the Spaniards of failure to fulfil the precepts embodied in the *Book of Privileges.*

After early experiments with treaties and conquest, the monarchs favored effective occupation as the principal means of establishing legal possession. Beginning in 1497, Fernando and Isabel instructed Columbus to colonize the Americas and authorized him to establish a government that would assure an orderly and productive replica of the Castilian homeland while integrating the native Indians as loyal subjects of the crown. At the time, these objectives were not seen to be inherently contradictory or inappropriate for the Americas.

From 1498 on, most parties to the conflicts tried to justify and explain their own actions by harking back to the *Book of Privileges:* Columbus in his letters and memoranda (Columbus 1984, 1989); Bartolomé de Las Casas on behalf of the Indians (Casas 1986); Gonzalo Fernández de Oviedo from the perspective of the Spanish colonists and officials (Fernández de Oviedo 1959); Andrés Bernáldez and Fernando Colón in defense of the admiral (Bernáldez 1962, and Colón 1959). When applied to indigenous civilizations of the western hemisphere, European legal precepts encountered a variety of responses, ranging from open resistance to opportunistic imitation. The *Book of Privileges* shaped the Encounter by defining the relationship between the Americas and the Castilian government.

THE AUTHORS OF THE *BOOK OF PRIVILEGES*

Fernando and Isabel

The normative force exerted by the *Book of Privileges* through the centuries is due to the legislative skill of the authors, the most able monarchs of their age, Fernando, King of Aragón (ruled 1479–1516) and Isabel, Queen of Castile (ruled 1474–1504). During their long reigns, these partners in government and marriage expanded and reshaped the Spanish realms. Before issuing these privileges to Columbus, they won a civil war in Castile, fought wars against Portugal to the west and Granada, the last Muslim government on the Iberian Peninsula, to the south. They expanded their influence through diplomacy as well, negotiating the return of the counties of Roussillon and Cerdagne from France to Aragón in 1492, and arranging marriages for their five children that, eventually, made future generations of Spanish monarchs rulers of Portugal, the Netherlands, and the Holy Roman Empire.

Adept in war and diplomacy, they and their staffs had also developed formulae and rationales for the conquest and governance of lands and people previously unknown to Europeans. At the end of the war with Portugal, the Spanish and Portuguese monarchs agreed on a division of the Atlantic into separate spheres of exploitation: in the Treaty of Alcáçovas (1479) Castile received the only inhabited islands thus far encountered in the Atlantic, the Canary Islands, while Portugal received everything south and east of the Canaries, including the west coast of Africa. When Fernando and Isabel drew up contracts in the 1480s with individual Spaniards for the purpose of conquering the

Canary Islands, they faced and resolved many of the same problems that they would address in their contracts with Columbus.

Christopher Columbus

During the time that the monarchs were negotiating terms with Alonso de Lugo for the conquest of La Palma, one of the most important of the Canary Islands, Christopher Columbus (1451–1506) was already a salaried member of their staff. Though Columbus was an Italian, born and raised in Genoa, his point of view broadened during his career as a seafaring import-export merchant. He married a Portuguese woman with close connections to the Portuguese royal court, and he and his wife's relatives took refuge in Castile when their noble patrons in Lisbon were killed by the Portuguese king. Columbus joined the staff of one of Spain's great seafaring entrepreneurs, the duke of Medinaceli, and the duke introduced him to the Castilian royal court.

Although the monarchs did not respond initially to Columbus's proposed voyage west to Asia, they recognized his talents as a businessman, whose navigational skills, business experience, and political loyalties could serve them well. His business affairs had put him in touch with a vast network of Genoese and Florentine bankers and merchants in Andalusia, yet moving between the business community and the court whetted his ambitions to enter higher levels of society. He had been in the royal encampment at the siege of Málaga, called there specifically by Queen Isabel just before Castile's final assault on the Muslim port city. There, the queen had reinstated the high admiral of Castile in his offices and estates (he had been banished from the kingdom after an indiscreet public quarrel) and Columbus had the opportunity to learn of the high status and great wealth enjoyed by the holder of this hereditary office.

By the time Castile had completed its war against Granada in January 1492, Columbus knew Fernando and Isabel, had defined what he wanted from the monarchs, and understood how they contracted with private persons to carry out government policy abroad. In late 1491, he again presented his proposal for a westward voyage to Asia and then waited while the monarchs submitted the proposal to their counsellors for debate. Once Fernando and Isabel agreed to sponsor the voyage, they turned the negotiations over to their chancery staffs and thus set in motion the process for drafting the capitulations and other royal documents that comprise the *Book of Privileges*.

The first royal document, the Santa Fe Capitulations, was exceptional in several ways, particularly because it was processed through the Aragonese rather than the Castilian chancery and because its implementation was contingent on the outcome of the voyage. Although the monarchs had agreed to sponsor the Columbian voyage, the specific terms remained to be worked out. Contemporary sources tell us that Columbus's terms were not initially acceptable to the monarchs, because he demanded too much. Both sides appointed personal representatives; Columbus appointed Friar Juan Pérez, prior of the Franciscan monastery at La Rábida and parish priest of Palos; Fernando and Isabel delegated the king's secretary, Juan de Coloma. Pérez and Coloma arrived at an agreement, which Coloma drafted point by point. The design of this draft suggests that Coloma used it as an *aide-mémoire* to make a verbal report to the monarchs. As Fernando and Isabel approved each section, Coloma wrote under it "It pleases Their Highnesses," and signed his name in testimony. The registrar of Fernando's chancery, Juan Ruiz de Calcena, made a clean copy for Columbus, which the monarchs signed in their usual form "I, the King" and "I, the Queen." Calcena added his signature below. In this rather informal state, the Santa Fe Capitulations were completed on 17 April 1492.[1]

Columbus immediately asked the monarchs to confirm their intention to confer royal offices on him should the voyage prosper. The Castilian chancery drew up this confirmation, which is called the Granada Capitulations, and the monarchs signed it on 30 April 1492. This document drafted and registered by the Castilian chancery was a model of the process by which most of the items in the *Book of Privileges* were issued by Fernando and Isabel.

The Chancery

The rest of the royal documents in the *Book of Privileges* were drafted in the Castilian chancery with the normal formulae and procedures for documents issued by the royal council. Most of the formularies had been developed in the mid fifteenth century by the chancery of Isabel's father, Juan II of Castile. Isabel refined details of the chancery's operations, without significant deviation from her father's procedures. Over the course of the century, for example, the chancery had adopted paper as its official medium, abandoning vellum and parchment except for ceremonial items. Instead of depending only on the original documents retained by the secretaries who drafted them, they added a chancery register in which the staff recorded the text *(minuta)* of documents drafted by all the secretaries. The chancery continued to travel with the ambulatory royal court except when the monarchs were in Andalusia on campaign against the Kingdom of Granada (1481–1492) and during royal sojourns in Catalonia. At these exceptional times, Fernando and Isabel appointed governors for northern

[1]Spain's pre-eminent Columbus scholar, Antonio Rumeu de Armas, has devoted a whole book to the textual and procedural anomalies of the Santa Fe Capitulations. He notes that Coloma normally would have made a record *(minuta)* of the text in the chancery register immediately, but the record is not in its correct chronological place. He attributes the discrepancy in part to the need for secrecy and in part to the more urgent nature of another project that Coloma was carrying out for Fernando in 1492. Coloma was at the time Fernando's representative to France in negotiations for the return of Roussillon and Cerdagne, traveling between the royal court besieging Granada and the negotiations at the French border. Having come to Granada to report to the monarchs in early April, he returned immediately to the north, carrying the Santa Fe Capitulations with the rest of his official papers, as was the custom for royal staff members. He apparently did not have a chance to record the agreement in the Aragonese chancery register until months later, after Columbus had returned from his first voyage and was preparing his second (Rumeu de Armas 1985).

Castile and divided up the royal council and chancery. One team of the royal council and chancery based itself with Isabel in Córdoba. The other team based itself in Valladolid, Burgos, or Olmedo, and had a permanent chancery with its own special secretary.

Fernando and Isabel called on this highly professional staff to compose the variety of documents that would mobilize royal staff, subjects, and resources throughout the Kingdom of Castile. The two highest offices, high chancellor of the great seal and high chancellor of the privy seal, were sinecures held by high aristocracy who were often employed in military campaigns or embassies and not resident at the court.[2] For the working staff, which traveled with the monarchs on their peregrinations throughout the two kingdoms, Isabel had developed in her chancery a skilled and loyal corps of clerks and secretaries who could perform at all levels of drafting and issuing executive orders.

These men were educated right in the heart of the royal bureaucracy as adolescent apprentices in the households of royal secretaries (Nader 1979: 141–142). Those who displayed outstanding talent, and a willingness to spend the rest of their lives traveling, took the oath of vassalage to the queen and thus became *continos,* members of the royal staff and household. They began at the bottom of the bureaucratic ladder as clerks of the royal chamber, taking dictation, entering texts in the chancery's registers, and making fair copies. The able rose through the ranks of the rotating offices in the chancery, such as deputy registrar and deputy chancellor. Finally, the truly exceptional crowned their careers as one of several secretaries to the queen, with the impressive salary of 100,000 maravedís per annum in addition to per diem allowances, chancery fees, and royal gifts (Escudero 1969).

The Process

Of all the chancery staff who participated in drafting the documents in the *Book of Privileges,* none played such a prominent role as the queen's secretary, Fernán Alvarez de Toledo, who composed most of the Columbian documents from 1492 through 1497. He was privy to the monarchs' discussions with Columbus and composed the substantive portions of the documents in consultation with Fernando and Isabel. Once his staff of secretaries and clerks had added the usual opening and closing formulae, made a fair copy, and proofread it, Fernán Alvarez submitted it to the monarchs for their signatures and signed it himself, certifying that he had ordered it written at the command of the monarchs (as opposed to documents that might be issued by one of the royal institutions such as the treasury or, beginning in 1503, the House of Trade in Seville).

---

[2]Isabel's high chancellor of the great seal was Sir García Fernández Manrique, marquis of Aguilar; her high chancellor of the privy seal was Sir Rodrigo de Mendoza, at that time lord of the town of Jadraque and son of the archbishop of Toledo, Pedro González de Mendoza.

After the king and queen and their chancery staff signed, the chancery sent the documents to the royal council, an advisory body to the queen. There they were scrutinized by the queen's legal counsel, Dr. Rodrigo Maldonado de Talavera. He reviewed the text to make sure that the documents did not violate Castilian law. If the text was satisfactory, he wrote "Approved" on the back of the page and signed his name. If he found legal fault with the document but could not persuade the monarchs to change it, he wrote "Approved in form" or "Reviewed" and signed it. As we shall see, Maldonado disapproved of conferring hereditary royal office on Columbus from the very beginning, foreseeing all the tangled legal arguments that would be played out in the *Pleitos*. Maldonado sent the signed document back to the chancery, where the deputy registrar recorded it in the chancery register and the deputy chancellor embossed it with the royal seal.

Despite all these reviews, the document that issued from the chancery was not necessarily final. Signed and sealed decrees that sketched out royal policy and writs mandating that whole classes of royal officials and subjects throughout the realm should implement the new policy were both amended before the chancery issued warrants ordering specific persons to carry out single acts. Once a document was issued, both parties had a chance to study it and seek changes. Twice, in 1493 and 1497, Columbus asked for confirmations of the Capitulations and received them, with additional prefaces, appendixes, and theoretical justifications. Several documents issued in early April 1497 to prepare for Columbus's third voyage returned to the chancery in late April for clarification, emendation, or the addition of further details that had not been included in earlier issues. All parties further scrutinized and discussed the new version and sent it back to the chancery, which issued greatly expanded and revised versions of several documents in May and June.

The process reveals close cooperation between Columbus and the monarchs, as well as the consultative nature of the Castilian royal government. Many paragraphs in these documents reveal the royal couple responding readily to the admiral's suggestion about financial matters. Several documents show emendations or additions explicitly describing Castilian customs for distribution and cultivation of land and the Spanish traditions of local self-government—instructions that would not have been necessary had Columbus been a Spaniard.

In matters related to Columbus's offices and revenues, the documents display the divergence of opinion between the royal legal counsel, who consistently disapproved alienating the regalia of royal office on constitutional grounds, and the monarchs, who overrode Maldonado's objections. In their eagerness to gain Columbus's services, the monarchs were willing to concede vast royal powers and privileges never before granted as hereditary property to anyone outside the royal family.

MANUSCRIPTS AND PREVIOUS EDITIONS

Christopher Columbus selected the documents in this collection and had them copied in two stages. From 1492 through 1497, he had accumulated many decrees, warrants, and writs issued to him by the Spanish monarchs, Fernando and Isabel. He carried these documents with him on his first two voyages, but the dangers of this practice became evident in La Isabela harbor in 1495; in June a hurricane destroyed three of his four ships; in October another hurricane destroyed the newly arrived resupply fleet. On 16 December 1495, the clerk of the city of La Isabela, Rodrigo Pérez, explained why Columbus had asked for a copy:

> because the admiral intended to send this instrument and capitulation to the kingdoms of Castile, and since they would have to sail on the ocean for many days and a long time because of the great distance from this city to the kingdoms of Castile and because there are great dangers at sea, it might happen that the ship or ships on which these documents were traveling could be lost.[3]

With this, one of the earliest public documents drafted by Europeans in the Americas, began the tangled tale of Christopher Columbus's efforts to preserve his most precious possession, the privileges issued to him by King Fernando and Queen Isabel. When he returned to Seville in 1496, Columbus followed the lead of Castilian military leaders who wanted their valorous deeds recorded for posterity; he dined with a local writer of history, the priest Andrés Bernáldez, gave him an interview, and loaned him the documents related to the first two voyages. Bernáldez duly incorporated the Columbian voyages in his history of the reign and thus safeguarded the historical record independently of the documents themselves (Bernáldez 1962).

Dangers at sea, it would transpire, were not the most serious threat to Columbus's privileges. Although his collection of royal confirmations held the royal lawyers at bay, a new threat to his jurisdiction came from a wider front. Disgruntled colonists returned from La Española with complaints about his administrative ineptitude, while other captains eagerly sought licenses to explore the routes he had opened. With every new danger, the admiral requested and received more detailed assurances and confirmations from the monarchs.

Columbus received royal permission to copy a group of older documents that set legal precedents for his office of admiral. These had been issued by earlier Castilian rulers to the admirals of Castile. Neither Columbus nor the monarchs knew the specifics of those early grants when they negotiated the 1492 capitulations, but what Columbus learned from them in 1497 impelled him to preserve them from the dangers that had become apparent in the highly competitive and politicized enterprise of the Indies. Retrieving his documents from Bernáldez in Seville, he commissioned copies of these, the newest instructions for the third voyage, and the earlier privileges granted to the admiral of Castile.

---

[3]The Isabela copy is now AGI, Patronato, legajo 295, doc. 2, according to Muro Orejón 1951: 3. I have consulted the photograph in the Library of Congress, Manuscripts Division, Ac. 369A, Box I.

Shortly before departing from Spain on his third voyage in 1498, Columbus commissioned notaries in the city of Seville to make copies of about twenty-five royal and notarial documents. These included the decrees in which the monarchs appointed him admiral and governor of the Indies, their writs instructing him to establish a colony of Spanish settlers on the island of La Española, and the earlier grants to the admirals of Castile. These loose copies, with their notarial certificates, were completed in Seville in March 1498. Columbus carried unbound copies with him on his third voyage, as well as some new originals issued for the voyage. This was the first of many copies commissioned by Columbus. Each has had its own separate fate or good fortune in the past five hundred years.

In the newly established city of Santo Domingo on the island of La Española, the admiral commissioned copies of four of the new originals. Santo Domingo's clerk, Diego de Alvarado, copied them on 4 December 1498, on paper different from the Seville copies. Columbus added the four new documents (11, 7, 8, and 9) and Alvarado's notarial certificates (55 and 56) to the Seville copies. This collection of about 35 documents became known as the Veragua Codex. Since the new documents he copied were royal grants of power over officers and settlers, scholars believe that his purpose was to leave a copy in Santo Domingo with his lieutenant governors, his brothers Diego and Bartolomé Colón, and to keep the originals with him as he carried out further explorations (Davenport 1909). He may also have wanted to create an heirloom for his son by commissioning a deluxe copy on vellum. If the Washington Codex was started with this intent, Columbus must have later decided that it was inadequate for his purposes, since it lacks the notarial descriptions and declarations typical of the other codices.

The Veragua Codex was inherited by Columbus's son Diego Colón and became a living document, the focus of nearly three centuries of litigation between the Castilian monarchy and Columbus's descendants, the dukes of Veragua. It was cited and copied as evidence in the Columbus family lawsuits—*Pleitos*—against the monarchy during the sixteenth century.

Columbus and his brothers returned to Spain in 1500 under indictment on charges of misfeasance in their administration of the colony on La Española. The monarchs exonerated Columbus but did not reinstate him as admiral and viceroy. Instead, they authorized him in 1502 to carry out further explorations without going to La Española. Before embarking on this fourth and final voyage, Columbus added more documents to the collection of originals and commissioned four copies of this expanded version, which he called his *Book of Privileges*. The additions included a royal mandate ordering restitution of his property, Columbus's open letter of complaints about his treatment by the monarchs, and legal opinions as to Columbus's rights to a share of the royal profits from the Indies and his rights and privileges as admiral. The Seville notaries finished copying this full set of about seventy documents on 22 March 1502.

The title that Columbus chose for his collected documents, *Book of Privileges,* was customary in Castile. City council secretaries recorded royal writs in the city council minutes and safeguarded the original writs in separate volumes entitled *Royal Privileges*. While Columbus may not have known these particular volumes, he was by 1502 enmeshed in the Genoese business community of Seville, which had commissioned a notarized collection of Castilian royal writs a decade earlier. These were forty-seven documents issued by Castilian rulers from 1251 to 1491 giving special status to the Genoese businessmen in Seville as a corporation. When the Seville city clerk, Bartolomé Sánchez de Porras, copied the collection into a single volume in 1491, he gave it the title *Book of Privileges of the Genoese Nation*.[4]

Columbus sent two deluxe, parchment copies of his *Book,* bound and cased, to Genoa (Genoa and Paris Codices). The Genoa and Paris Codices have different covering letters and supplementary materials because, although Columbus sent them to the same person in Genoa, he entrusted them to separate carriers who departed from Seville at different times. Columbus deposited a third codex of the full collection in the monastery of Las Cuevas in Seville, along with the original documents (not extant), and left a fourth codex, on paper, for his business agent in the Indies, Alonso Sánchez de Carvajal. The fates and locations of the third and fourth codices are not known.[5]

In 1504 and 1505 Columbus instructed his son Diego, who was at the royal court, to persuade King Fernando to restore Columbus's offices of admiral and viceroy. He ordered Diego to copy specific documents from the *Book of Privileges* as the basis for his claims. The documents copied by Diego in 1505 comprise the Providence Codex at the John Carter Brown Library.[6] After his father's death in 1506, Diego brought suit against the monarchy to claim as heritable property the revenues and offices granted to Columbus in the 1492 Capitulations. He submitted copies of the Veragua Codex as evidence. The courts ruled partially in Diego's favor on 5 May 1511, and the king instated him as viceroy and governor general of La Española, where Diego had organized a colonizing expedition in 1509 and established residence with his wife and children.

Diego objected to the limitations imposed by this ruling, which confined his governorship to the island, where he had to share jurisdiction with a royal judge. In 1512, he sued for the admiralty's full judicial cognizance, powers of appointment, and income.

The crown attorney argued that the office of admiral could not be hereditary, but Diego submitted depositions from participants in the Columbus story. The deponents included such luminaries as the royal counsel who had certified the legality of most of the privileges, Dr. Rodrigo Maldonado de Talavera; Columbus's brother Bartolomé Colón; and the admiral's business agent, Alonso Sánchez de Carvajal.

[4]González Gallego 1974.

[5]Heers believes that the copy Carvajal took to La Española remained there, in the Columbus family residence in Santo Domingo, and that Las Casas used it there (Heers 1981: 364).

[6]Though the Providence Codex was once described as the Santo Domingo codex copied by Diego de Alvarado in 1498, it contains extracts of a royal letter issued in 1501. Furthermore, the selection of documents dovetails with Columbus's instructions to Diego in 1504 and 1505 (Nader 1992).

Impatient with the judicial process, Diego made a direct appeal to the new king, Charles V, probably in 1518. Documents in the Huntington Library (Huntington Codex) appear to have been selected to persuade the new monarch that Columbus's offices of admiral and viceroy were hereditary and should be inherited in full by his son Diego.[7] To sweeten the argument, Diego made an offer that Charles could not resist. He gave the new ruler 10,000 ducats to help defray the costs of Charles's election as Holy Roman Emperor. Not surprisingly, Diego received a favorable ruling from the king himself on 22 May 1520.

The litigation then began to focus on another issue, the extent of territory over which the admiral could hold jurisdiction. The crown attorney claimed that the grant extended only to those places that Columbus had discovered himself. As Diego's claims and the crown's counterclaims followed one another with conflicting interpretations of portions of the privileges, the courts admitted evidence from an ever widening range of eyewitnesses and experts to define ever smaller segments of the text. The crown's argument was based on a strict reading of the 1492 contract and on depositions given by captains who carried out authorized voyages of discovery up and down the South American coast between 1495 and 1503, known as the Andalusian Voyages. Their firsthand descriptions of events, topography, flora, and fauna are an invaluable source of information for the history of early European exploration of the Americas.

Although these accounts are self-interested, they shed light on how participants in the Columbian voyages understood the *Book of Privileges*. The witnesses were attempting to claim discoveries for one side or the other in order to preserve for themselves a share of the revenues and positions granted in royal exploration contracts. They were well aware that their own royal concessions had been modeled on the monarchs' 1492 Capitulations with Columbus and that their rewards would depend on the court's interpretation of *The Book of Privileges*.

After Diego's son, the third admiral Luis Colón, died in the late sixteenth century leaving no legitimate male heirs, the litigation changed from questions of the meaning and extent of the privileges to disputes over who should be the rightful heir of the Columbus family titles and fortune. Although Columbus had many direct female descendants, he had placed all his titles and property in a heritable trust (39) in which he stipulated that collateral male descendants, even in Italy, should inherit before direct female descendants. This inspired a great number of spurious claims by Italian men named Colombo, each of whom submitted cooked-up genealogical charts and forged documents to the Spanish courts.[8] The courts found in favor of the dukes of Alba,

---

[7]I am indebted to Dr. William Frank for bringing these documents to my attention and supplying me with an excellent photocopy of the text and related materials including Meisnest (1949).

[8]Belgrano and Staglieno believed that the parchment codex (now Washington Codex) purchased by Edward Everett in 1818 had been presented to the Council of the Indies in 1583 by Baldassare Colombo in his claim to be the heir of Christopher Columbus. They did not explain how Everett purchased in Florence a codex submitted to a council in Spain or why Baldassare would have presented an unnotarized copy as legal evidence (Belgrano and Staglieno 1894, preface).

Spanish descendants of a Columbus granddaughter. For over a century, the Columbus family title of duke of Veragua was held by the dukes of Alba, but in 1796 the royal law courts ruled that the earlier ruling had been in error (the seventeenth-century claimant had been descended from an illegitimate son) and awarded the title to the current heirs of Columbus's legitimate female descendants, the Colón y Carbajal family.

During these two centuries of litigation when no one and everyone possessed the Columbus family archive, many papers disappeared and others were damaged by rain and fire. But the French despoliation of local treasures during the Napoleonic invasions sparked patriotic reactions in Italy and Spain, while revolutionary Americans began looking for their new nation's non-English origins. These patriotic motives inspired new interest in the Spanish documents as historical artifacts rather than as legal evidence.

Genoa's resident Columbus historian, Giovanni Batista Spotorno, published the first modern compendium of Columbus documents, including the *Book of Privileges* (Spotorno 1823). Spain's indefatigable naval historian, Martín Fernández de Navarrete, began transcribing and publishing documents from state and private archives, including some of the original royal writs and warrants (now lost) from which the *Book of Privileges* had been transcribed (Navarrete 1825–1837). An American consul in Spain, Washington Irving, published a highly imaginative biography of Columbus that has misled generations of American schoolchildren and serious scholars (Irving 1828; Russell 1991). The tireless American in Paris, Henry Harrisse, skeptically scrutinized documents and artifacts throughout Europe to establish a severely reduced corpus of authentic documentary sources (Harrisse 1866) and to demonstrate beyond doubt the Genoese origins of Christopher Columbus (Harrisse 1884). The duchess of Alba in 1892 and 1902 published transcripts of previously unpublished Columbus autographs and related papers from her family archive that somehow had escaped transfer to the Veragua archive in 1796 (Berwick 1892 and 1902).

Over a number of years from the early 1920s through 1944, an indomitable American researcher, Alice Bache Gould, published the names and biographical data of Columbus's crew on the first voyage (Gould 1984). In addition to this work, which has rightly been described as the "greatest piece of Christopher Columbus scholarship in the 20th century" (Provost 1991: 78), Gould also discovered in the Spanish archives two registered copies of the Columbus heritable trust, for which Columbus had received royal permission in late 1497 (39). Their edition and publication by a Spanish legal historian demonstrated the authenticity of a major document in the *Book of Privileges* on which Harrisse had cast considerable doubt (Altolaguirre 1926).

The removal of this last shadow on the privileges made them more valuable than ever to bibliophiles and historians. In 1915, the duke of Veragua, Sir Cristóbal Colón y Aguilera, had offered the manuscripts for sale. The Library of Congress made microfilm and photographic copies, apparently with an eye to a possible purchase. When a New York firm, the Central Union Trust Company, offered to buy them, the Spanish government purchased the Columbus manuscripts in the Veragua archives in 1926. The papers, including the Veragua Codex, were exhibited at the Ibero-American

Exposition in Seville, and deposited in 1930 in the AGI in Seville, making them available to qualified researchers for the first time. In 1951, Ciriaco Pérez-Bustamante published a meticulous edition of the Veragua Codex as an aid to the preparation of a published edition of the *Pleitos*—a project still in progress (Pérez-Bustamante 1951: LIX–LXI).

While the Veragua Codex was a living document repeatedly consulted for litigation in Spain, the Paris and Genoa Codices had remained safe but unused in Genoa. Columbus had sent them to Genoa's ambassador to Spain, Nicolò Oderico, and both codices remained in his family until 1670. In that year, Lorenzo Oderico presented the two parchment codices to the Republic of Genoa in exchange for a promise of preferment to government office (72). There they remained until 1808, when Napoleon's armies shipped one (Paris Codex) to France.

The other codex that Columbus sent to Genoa was hidden during the chaos of the Napoleonic invasion and could not be found during an 1812 search of the archives. In 1816, the Republic learned that the Genoa Codex was in the possession of the patrician Michelangelo Cambiaso and bought it in the sale of his estate. The manuscript was moved to Turin when Genoa was incorporated into the kingdom of Sardinia (1815), but it was returned to Genoa in 1821 and was entrusted to Giovanni Spotorno for study and editing. Spotorno published his edition of the *Book of Privileges* in 1823, whereupon the Genoa Codex was placed in a specially constructed monument in Genoa's city hall, where it remains today.

English and Spanish translations of Spotorno's edition followed in 1823 and 1867. A new edition of the Genoa Codex, incorporating the latest historical research and philological methods, was published in 1894 by L. T. Belgrano and M. Staglieno. It has been the standard edition ever since.

The Paris Codex, like much else that Napoleon expropriated, remained in Paris, unnoticed and unstudied until Harrisse located it in the archives of the Ministry of Foreign Affairs. In 1893, Harrisse and Benjamin Franklin Stevens brought out a deluxe edition, a photographic reproduction of the entire manuscript with facing page transcription and English translation. The transcription and translation were done by an American lawyer in Paris, George Barwick. He drew heavily on the anonymous 1823 English translation of Spotorno's edition of the Genoa Codex, the only transcription at the time. Apart from scattered translations of individual documents, or rather portions of documents, Barwick's has been until now the most recent English translation of the *Book of Privileges* (Stevens 1893).

The Washington Codex has the most obscure provenance of all the manuscripts. It was bought by the American Edward Everett in Florence in 1818 but was believed lost in a nineteenth-century fire that gutted the Everett house in Boston. About 1900, the codex was found jammed behind the drawer of a desk that had survived the fire. The Library of Congress bought the codex from Edward Everett's son William in 1901 (Davenport 1909). The Washington Codex, written on vellum, comprises the same 35 documents in the Veragua Codex, with the addition of the papal bull *Dudum siquidem* dated 26 September 1493. This bull is written in an Italian hand on paper folded as a letter and stitched into the front of the codex. The Washington Codex bears several indications of haste in copying and, lacking the usual notarial certificates, must be considered incomplete.

The manuscripts are bound together by strong paleographical resemblances. Except for the inclusion or exclusion of one or more notarial certificates, there are no substantive differences; this is just as we would expect from official copies collated and corrected by Castilian notaries. All are written in the standard cursive hand of early sixteenth-century Castilian clerks. The Veragua, Providence, and Huntington codices are written on paper with watermarks typical of Spanish manufacture in the fifteenth and early sixteenth centuries. The Paris, Genoa, and Washington codices are on parchment, a material no longer the norm for Castilian legal and official documents during the reign of Fernando and Isabel. This circumstance, along with their illuminated initial letters, leather bindings, and, in the case of Genoa and Paris, leather cases with silver locks, indicates that they were intended as family heirlooms or gifts rather than legal documents.

SCHOLARSHIP ABOUT THE *BOOK OF PRIVILEGES*

Since the final settlement of the Columbus family's lawsuits in the eighteenth century, the collection has suffered scholarly neglect. Philologists were not interested in an apparently inchoate collection noted only for its legal formulae and repetitive style. Historians chose not to engage with the diversity of contradictory messages from one document to another. Broad concessions to Columbus seem to alternate with limitations on or revocations of those concessions. Profit motives dominate some stipulations, only to be followed by declarations of religious purpose or instructions for good government. Few scholars of any persuasion were attracted to documents issued by the Spanish monarchy. Interest has focused instead on Christopher Columbus himself, regarded until very recently as a heroic or sympathetic figure. Historians studied portions of the *Book of Privileges* as incidental to the story of America or as evidence of Spanish ignorance, incompetence, or ill will toward the Genoese explorer who gained another world for Castile.

In the twentieth century, scholars have made excellent philological editions and historical studies of three documents in the *Book of Privileges*: the Santa Fe and Granada Capitulations and the papal decree *Inter caetera*. These modern studies have established the historical precedents for the present translation and edition. The most important problems in the *Book of Privileges* developed within days of the Santa Fe Capitulations and proved to be of enduring significance. The monarchs attempted to clarify their intentions by issuing the Granada Capitulations, in which they invoked their absolute power to grant royal offices to Columbus as hereditary possessions. By violating the Castilian constitution, the Capitulations gave rise to a continuing debate in the royal council about the nature and legality of royal concessions to Columbus. The monarchs attempted to find a compromise between the offices and income they had promised to Columbus and the law of the land upheld by their legal advisers. The tension between these irreconcilable objectives led to the extensions and limitations of the Capitulations, which occupy most of the space in the *Book of Privileges.*

The second problem arose relatively late in the Columbian saga, during the preparations for the third voyage in 1497, and marked a turning point in the history of Spanish America. Again, the dispute arose out of efforts to find legitimation for Castile's American enterprise. The Spanish monarchs in 1493 appealed to Pope Alexander VI, asking him to legitimate Castile's sovereignty over the western Ocean Sea, which Castile already claimed by virtue of treaty and effective occupation. The papal chancery balked at claiming temporal authority in the Americas. Instead the decree issued by the papal chancery, *Inter caetera,* granted Castile sovereignty on the basis of religion; the papacy tried to transform the enterprise of the Indies from a commercial venture grounded in the civil law into a missionary endeavor. *Inter caetera* introduced religious motives into the American enterprise for the first time by basing papal legitimation on conversion of the natives to Christianity. Isabel and Fernando never made conversion of the Indians an important aspect of their instructions to Columbus; of the 40,000 words in the *Book of Privileges,* only about 500 refer to religion. But fifty years later, effective implementation of *Inter caetera* flared into a burning dispute within the Spanish world. It became the basis for the famous controversy, personified in the debates between Bartolomé de Las Casas and Juan de Sepúlveda, over the nature of Spain's Indian subjects and the monarchy's responsibility for converting them to Christianity.

Columbus's obsession with these documents sheds considerable light on the man's character. In recent years there has been a tendency by scholars to stress the mystical millenarian side of Columbus's thought (Watts 1985; West in Columbus 1991). Columbus's repeated requests for royal confirmations that guaranteed his economic, political, and social privileges, and his relentless hunt for new documents that could provide historical precedents for his privileges point to another Columbus, the Columbus "who reveals himself to be greedy, wise, and crafty in the science of acquiring and preserving wealth" (Gil and Varela 1986, "Cuentas": 109).

Columbus's pursuit of profit fit perfectly into the policies of the Spanish monarchs. Recently scholars have attempted to connect Franciscan millenarianism to the Columbian project at the royal court (Milhou 1983). The documents issued to Columbus by Fernando and Isabel, however, reveal that the monarchs adopted religious objectives only grudgingly after reception of the papal decree *Inter caetera.* At the beginning, Fernando, Isabel, and Columbus united in pursuit of economic wealth and political power. When no profit accrued in the first five years of the enterprise of the Indies, the partners became rivals, still sharing the same motive but now competing for shares of a smaller pie. Even Columbus's resort to arguments based on conversion and his suggestion of conquering Jerusalem seem to have served as "a form of penance, when his conscience was uneasy and his confidence low" (Fernández Armesto 1991: 109).

INTRODUCTION TO PART 1: THE FIRST VOYAGE

CHAPTER 1: CREATING THE ENTERPRISE OF THE INDIES

1. Santa Fe Capitulations.

After Fernando and Isabel conquered and occupied Granada early in 1492, they agreed to Columbus's proposal to sail west toward Asia on a commercial and exploratory voyage. On 17 April 1492, in the town of Santa Fe, they drew up a memorandum of intent to form a business partnership with Columbus. This royal commitment to Columbus is known as the Santa Fe Capitulations.

In the Santa Fe Capitulations, Fernando and Isabel promised Columbus five major concessions:

1.2. Commission as admiral.
1.4. Commission as viceroy and governor general.
1.6. Right to one-tenth of all gold, precious stones, and merchandise the monarchs acquired from his admiralty.
1.8. Jurisdiction over lawsuits arising from commerce in his admiralty.
1.10. Right to invest up to one-eighth of the costs of all vessels outfitted for commerce in his admiralty and to keep up to one-eighth of the profits.

Every one of these concessions aroused controversy within the royal court and, later, between the monarchs and the Columbus family. The concessions of the Santa Fe Capitulations were so extraordinary and innovative for Castile that during the next fifteen years Columbus repeatedly found it necessary to request confirmations, adjustments, and interpretations. The royal responses to his requests comprise the bulk of the documents in the *Book of Privileges*.

While we cannot dismiss personality conflicts as a source of some of the controversy, these did not emerge until late in Columbus's relations with Fernando and

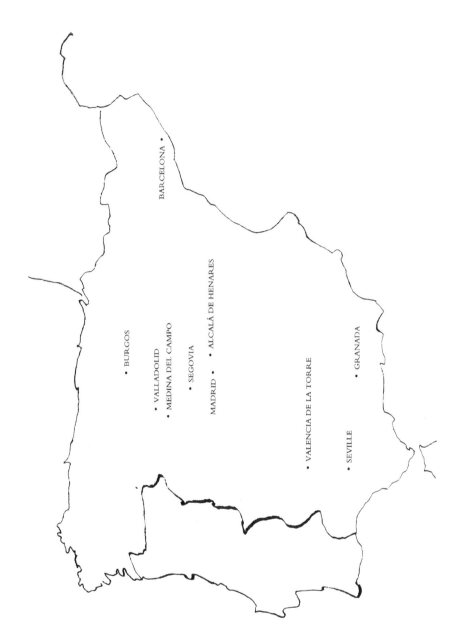

Map of Spanish cities and towns where Fernando and Isabel issued writs to Christopher Columbus.

Isabel, as we will see in the documents issued to Columbus after his return from his third voyage in 1500. Even before the first voyage, however, when the monarchs personally expressed the greatest confidence and warmth toward Columbus, the legal implications of their concessions required explication and close definition.

Castile's history during the previous half-century—a period of bitter economic rivalry with Portugal in the Atlantic and frustration with Granada's dominance of the North African trade—had whetted the monarchs' appetite for economic expansion. They wanted to establish direct commercial relations with Asian rulers and, if possible, to acquire islands off the Asian mainland as trading posts and supply stations. In their eagerness to have Christopher Columbus's services for this enterprise, Fernando and Isabel agreed to the sweeping terms of the Santa Fe Capitulations.

One aspect of the capitulations that may seem surprising is the apparent lack of interest in converting native peoples to Christianity. Contrary to popular and scholarly impressions of Castilian goals in the Columbian voyages, religious motives are absent from the royal documents issued for the first and second voyages, including the capitulations. The first mention of a religious purpose for the Columbian voyages occurs in the papal decrees of demarcation dated May and June 1493. These papal decrees reached Spain after Columbus had already left on his second voyage to the Americas. Even after the papal decree of demarcation in 1493 imposed a religious motive on the Castilian voyages, the royal documents refer to missionary activity only in passing, almost as an afterthought to please the papacy. From the beginning, the Columbian voyages were inspired by economic aspirations.

The Santa Fe Capitulations established a business partnership between the monarchs and Columbus. The investment and distribution clauses of the Capitulations were standard in commercial partnerships of the fifteenth century. The three partners agreed that Fernando and Isabel would provide two ships and their crews and in return receive nine-tenths of the profits; Columbus would provide his management *(mano)* and expertise *(ingenio)* and receive one-tenth of the profits. If Columbus wanted to invest money in the enterprise, he could supply up to one-eighth of the cost of outfitting the voyage and receive one-eighth of the profits.

The partnership was formed for the purpose of a commercial voyage to Asia, which Europeans at that time called the Indies. Everything that we call Asia today was called India by fifteenth-century Europeans. They applied the name Asia only to that part of the Asian continent that had once been part of the Roman Empire, which we today call Asia Minor and the Near East. They used the plural—Indies instead of India— because maps often showed the Asian continent to be made up of three Indias. These were India Sinus (China); India Magna or India Mayor (between the Ganges and Indus Rivers); and India Parva-Ethyopis, from Calicut on the southwest coast of India to East Africa, including Persia, the Arabian Peninsula, and the Indian Ocean (Rumeu de Armas 1972: 21). Spanish merchant shippers previously did not have direct access to Asian markets; they traded with Asia through middlemen. These were either Muslim merchants based in the Kingdom of Granada or Italian merchants based in trading posts throughout the eastern Mediterranean. Fernando and Isabel had just eliminated the Muslim middleman by conquering the Muslim seaport of Málaga. They now prepared to expand Spanish commerce directly into Asian markets by sailing west and thus circumventing the Italian middleman (Heers 1957).

All three partners—Fernando, Isabel, and Columbus—for different reasons, wanted more than the usual business partnership, however, and this resulted in extraordinary concessions to Columbus. Fernando and Isabel wanted to acquire possession of any islands (and perhaps a trading station or two on the Asian mainland) that Columbus might find. For this purpose, Columbus had to have royal authority to take possession and govern on behalf of the Castilian monarchy. Thus the monarchs promised Columbus the hereditary offices of admiral, viceroy, and governor of all he discovered.

The partners may have modeled these terms on the example of Portugal, whose royal family during the previous fifty years had sent ships to explore the west coast of Africa. Columbus revealed personal knowledge of the Portuguese slaving and gold trade in Guinea or West Africa and the Cape Verde Islands. Fernando and Isabel were well informed about how their Portuguese rivals financed their Atlantic ventures as royal monopolies and claimed sovereignty over islands and trading posts. Castilian rivalry with Portugal in the Atlantic equalled in intensity Aragon's rivalry with France in the Mediterranean . . . and rivalry invites imitation.

At their most optimistic, Fernando and Isabel hoped that Columbus would outdo the Portuguese by reaching the fabled cities of the Asian mainland. Once there, he would acquire from the ruler jurisdiction over some piece of the mainland where the Spaniards could establish a trading station, just as the Portuguese king had done at St. George of the Mine on the West African coast. With this possibility in mind, the monarchs issued to Columbus a Latin letter to the presumed ruler of China, the Grand Khan, and letters of introduction in triplicate to unknown rulers whose names and countries were left blank.

Despite these optimistic gestures, the monarchs had committed themselves to a highly speculative venture. The voyage would attempt to cross the Ocean Sea, whose great expanse from Europe to Asia was conceived at the time to be broken by numerous small islands. No one had imagined an Ocean Sea almost devoid of islands or a continent blocking the way to Asia, though scientists for centuries had posited the existence of a southern continent, the Antipodes, balancing the Arctic in the north. The true obstacle to such a journey, according to scientists of the day, was distance; they knew that Columbus underestimated the earth's circumference. Most thought he also exaggerated the size of the Asian continent in order to propose a narrow Ocean Sea.

Fernando and Isabel expected, at a minimum, that the expedition would find a large number of islands that had not previously been claimed by European powers. These could be developed as supply stations and trading posts for the Asian trade. Yet few islands had been discovered in the western Ocean sea, despite many exploratory voyages by Portuguese and other mariners. Columbus loaded the ships for the first voyage with European trade goods traditionally sold to Asia, especially wool cloth, but if Columbus did not encounter unclaimed islands or the Asian mainland, the voyage would be a commercial failure.

The Capitulations were contingency contracts; they would take effect when and if Columbus succeeded in finding previously unknown islands. Until then, Columbus and the monarchs committed themselves to a highly speculative venture. These circumstances and concerns shaped the language and style of the capitulations. Fully aware of the speculative nature of the venture, the royal secretaries phrased the capitulations to emphasize their contingency quality. The Santa Fe and Granada Capitulations did not specify the destination of the first Columbian voyage; neither document mentions Asia or China. This silence in the Capitulations about destination fuelled nearly a century of debate about the monarchs' intentions.[9]

Recent textual scholarship, however, has established the authenticity of key documents that support the "destination Asia" motive. The most important statement about the destination was made by Columbus himself in his journal entry of 21 October 1492: "But I am still determined to go to the mainland and to the city of Quinsay and to give Your Highnesses' letters to the Grand Khan and ask for a reply and return with it" (Columbus 1988).[10] The royal letters that Columbus wanted to deliver to the ruler of Asia were a recommendation and a safe conduct issued by Fernando and Isabel in Granada on 16 and 30 April 1492. In their letter of recommendation of 16 April, the monarchs themselves stated that they were sending Columbus "to the region of India by way of the Ocean Sea."[11]

These statements by Columbus and the monarchs about their own motives are supported by another contemporary witness, Columbus's first patron in Spain, the duke of Medinaceli. In March 1493, the duke wrote to his uncle, Pedro González de Mendoza, cardinal of Spain, announcing the news of Columbus's safe return from his first voyage. In this letter to one of the queen's senior advisers, the duke recalled that, years before, Columbus had proposed a voyage "to discover the Indies" and the duke had recommended Columbus to the queen, who placed her accountant Alonso de

[9]A lifetime of research by Henry Vignaud led him to conclude that the motives for the first voyage were to find new islands, not Asia (Vignaud 1905, 1920, 1921). That theory was first systematically criticized by Emiliano Jos in his university lectures, which, though only recently published, formed a new generation of Columbus specialists convinced that Columbus, Fernando, and Isabel all intended the voyage to reach China, if possible (Jos 1980). More recently, the monarchs' letter of introduction to the Grand Khan has been used to document the "destination Asia" conclusion (Rumeu de Armas 1985).

[10]The journal survives only as the *Diario,* an extract made by Bartolomé de Las Casas. Early in the century much doubt was cast on the authenticity of the document, but recent comparisons between thirteen other documents extracted or transcribed by Las Casas with their originals preserved in the collections of the duchess of Alba have demonstrated the fidelity and accuracy of Las Casas's copies (Rumeu de Armas 1985: 159, n. 296).

[11]"Mittimus in presenciarum nobilem virum Christoforum Colon, cum tribus carauelis armatis, per maria Oçeana ad partes Indie . . ." (Rumeu de Armas 1985: 94).

Quintanilla in charge of the project. Quintanilla, according to the duke, evaluated it and agreed to send Columbus "to search for the Indies" (Navarrete 1825–1837, 2.31).

Columbus's proposal to reach Asia within six to eight weeks, however, flew in the face of the geographical knowledge of the time. When Fernando and Isabel turned to their royal counsellors for advice, Dr. Maldonado recommended against the project, because, as he later testified: "Everyone agreed that what the admiral was saying could not possibly be true" (*Pleitos*, 3.390). Everyone at court knew that Columbus underestimated the circumference of the world.

The monarchs' desire for profit, however, triumphed over science. They listened to a wealthy banker on Fernando's payroll, Luis de Santángel, who made a speech that, Las Casas reports, convinced Fernando and Isabel to accept Columbus's project. Santángel's speech says nothing about Asia but simply argues that backing him would be a cheap gamble (Las Casas 1951, bk. 1, chap. 32). No one could say with certainty what lay between Europe and Asia. The only way to find out was to take a risk by sending a voyage west by sea.

Their risk made sense to their generation, which lived in a unique moment of European business history. World events that shaped the mentalities and motives of Fernando, Isabel, and Columbus emerge clearly in the recent study by William D. Phillips, Jr. and Carla Rahn Phillips (Phillips and Phillips 1992). During the Middle Ages, Europeans had carried on maritime commerce with Asia regularly. Genoese businessmen leased space on cargo carriers and accompanied their merchandise on board ship to the Black Sea. On the Asian shores of the Black Sea, Genoese merchant consortia had acquired from local rulers jurisdiction over a few ports and their surrounding territory, as well as a number of islands in the straits and the eastern Mediterranean. The consortia owned and ruled these territories, where they built warehouses. Arriving Genoese businessmen unloaded their goods for sale to Central Asian and Central European merchants, who traveled hundreds of miles between inland trading centers transporting merchandise by pack animal. The ships stayed in their trading ports for months, even years, while the Genoese merchants sold their merchandise— almost entirely heavy wool cloth manufactured in various parts of Europe—and bought highly valued merchandise from the Asian businessmen—most notably spices, precious stones, silk cloth, and slaves. All of this frequent exchange between European and Genoese merchants began to shrink during the fourteenth century, as political turmoil in Central Asia made overland trade routes dangerous. By the early fifteenth century, Italian governments watched helplessly as their consortia lost one island and trading post after another to Ottoman expansion. During the 1470s, Genoa lost its last islands in the eastern Mediterranean; only the Republic of Venice continued to trade directly with Asia, having negotiated a monopoly with the Ottoman rulers of the Levant.

To the generation of Fernando, Isabel, and Columbus, which had witnessed these events as young adults, the earlier period of regular trade with Asia, by sea and through European trading posts on the Asian mainland and islands, seemed a Golden Age.

Their Portuguese cohorts had taken the lead in finding a new sea route to the south around Africa and, by the terms of the Treaty of Alcáçovas in 1479, had acquired a monopoly on that route. For Isabel, who had gained uncontested sovereignty over Castile by that treaty, there could be only one other route to Asia—west across the Ocean Sea.

It is not necessary to guess at what went on in the monarchs' minds when they drafted the Capitulations in 1492. They stated their motives clearly, and these motives coincided perfectly with those of Columbus and the rest of their generation. At best, the monarchs hoped that Columbus would make a treaty with the Grand Khan ceding to Castile enough territory to establish a trading post on the Asian mainland. After the return of Bartolomeu Dias in December 1490, none could doubt ultimate success by the Portuguese, only the timing (Fonseca 1987). If Columbus by sailing west could reach Asia before the Portuguese did by sailing south, then Castile would preempt its rival by negotiating a monopoly on commerce between Europeans and Asians on the mainland. Failing that, Fernando and Isabel expected Columbus to take possession of islands along the way that would serve as supply stations on a later route to China.

The monarchs' motives for not specifically stating Columbus's Asian destination in the Santa Fe Capitulations also stemmed, I believe, from more mundane considerations. In order to shorten the sailing distance, already recognized at court as dangerously overextended, Columbus required a stopover at the Canary Islands for fresh water and food. The Castilian monarch had agreed in the Treaty of Alcáçovas to give prior notice whenever Castilian ships planned to cross Portuguese waters in order to sail to the Canaries. Now, in their race to be first, Fernando and Isabel would not want to take a chance on being denied Portuguese permission. Columbus had long since divulged his project, but the timing, ultimate destination, and route of this particular voyage remained secret even from the crew in order not to alert the rival nation. The queen ordered the town of Palos to supply Columbus with two caravels in payment of a fine for trespass of Portuguese waters that some citizens of Palos had committed in previous years. Now these same lawbreakers set sail on the queen's payroll to trespass in Portuguese waters between the west African coast and the Canary Islands.

The royal secretaries registered the Santa Fe Capitulations and the letters of recommendation and safe conduct in the Aragonese rather than Castilian chancery records, a circumstance that has raised some questions about the monarchs' respective responsibilities for the decision to sponsor Columbus's first voyage. Nineteenth-century pride in the enterprise of the Americas led writers from the Crown of Aragon—Aragonese, Catalans, and Valencians—to claim that Fernando alone made the decision to send Columbus and, consequently, that the enterprise of the Americas must have been an Aragonese venture. Castilian historians countered, arguing that the monarchs deliberately registered the crucial texts in the Aragonese chancery in order to keep the voyage secret from Portuguese spies who naturally focussed their attention on the Castilian chancery (Rumeu de Armas 1985). The placement of the records, however, does not require some grand motive as explanation. The monarchs had asked Juan de Coloma,

Fernando's secretary, to negotiate with Columbus's agent Juan Pérez. Coloma also drafted the letters of recommendation and safe conduct. From his own notes, Coloma normally entered in the Aragonese chancery register the records of all texts he redacted. He did so with these Columbus documents as well (Rumeu de Armas 1985).

The original document issued to Columbus in Santa Fe disappeared from the Columbus family archives sometime after 1526. Nevertheless, we know its terms because the monarchs confirmed, expanded, and updated the capitulations as soon as Columbus arrived at court in Barcelona after his first voyage. Columbus commissioned two transcripts of the original. The copy made on 16 December 1495 by Rodrigo Pérez, clerk of the city of La Isabela on the island of La Española, disappeared from the family archives in the early nineteenth century. The second copy (recently identified in AGS, RGS) was made by the royal chancery in the city of Burgos on 23 April 1497 (Rumeu de Armas 1985). Columbus twice included this Burgos transcription of the Santa Fe Capitulations in his *Book of Privileges* (49 and 58).

Without the original document, we cannot know exactly how much the chancery amended or rephrased the language of the original. An obvious addition appears in the form of paragraph 1.1, which has several indications of having been written after the fact: it alludes to the first voyage as already completed, calls Columbus "sir," and refers to his imminent departure on the second voyage.

The monarchs did not add "destination Asia" to these updated copies of the capitulations. Spanish scientists did not believe Columbus's claim that the island of La Española lay close to Asia—the voyage had been too short. As Peter Martyr, a member of Isabel's intimate circle, wrote in May 1493, the monarchs did not believe him either (Ramos 1981, 1982).

2. Granada Capitulations.

The most controversial aspects of the partnership agreement provided that the monarchs would appoint Columbus as hereditary admiral of the Ocean Seas, once he returned from successfully discovering islands and mainlands previously unknown to Europeans. The monarchs, worried about potential Portuguese claims to their islands, insisted that Columbus be invested with this military and governing authority over his discoveries.

Columbus wanted these as hereditary offices, however, not just as lifetime appointments. Columbus was perhaps inspired to make this demand by the example of his Portuguese in-laws. His wife's father, Bartolomeu Perestrelo, had been one of the three discoverers of Madeira and its satellite island of Porto Santo. While Perestrelo's colleagues received hereditary governorship of Madeira in partnership, Perestrelo became hereditary governor of Porto Santo. This demand presented serious legal difficulties for Fernando and Isabel, and may have caused the serious opposition of the royal council, which was dominated by lawyers. The granting of hereditary offices, especially to foreigners, went against royal policy; Castilian law prohibited the monarchs from permanently giving away or selling any portions of the royal domain or any royal office. At first the monarchs hesitated, but because Fernando and Isabel wanted to gain legal possession of any islands Columbus might find in the Atlantic, they acquiesced to his demands.

The monarchs intended to settle and develop these islands in the Portuguese manner. In their African ventures the Portuguese had introduced an innovation particularly appealing to the Castilian monarchs; their trading post was a monopoly of the royal family. The Castilian monarchs decreed that there would be only three shareholders in the enterprise of the Indies, they and Columbus. In contrast to the large number of merchants permitted to trade in the Italian trading posts, the royal trading post on La Española operated as a company store and the enterprise of the Indies remained a royal monopoly until 1504.

Castile's claims to legal possession of islands and mainland would be strongest, however, if Columbus were a royal official, not just the monarchs' business partner. Royal office would give him legal authority over the personnel on land, in addition to his command as admiral in navigable waters. A compromise would benefit all the partners, even if the monarchs had to bend the law.

In Granada on 30 April 1492, the monarchs issued a writ appointing Columbus to the royal offices he had requested, a document known as the Granada Capitulations. In the Granada Capitulations, Fernando and Isabel decreed that Columbus would be their hereditary admiral of the Ocean Sea. Equally significant, they appointed him viceroy and governor of any islands or mainland he discovered. Because the monarchs and royal chancery took the precaution of phrasing both the Granada and Santa Fe Capitulations as contingency grants, these concessions became operative only when Columbus discovered and took possession of any islands or mainland in the name of the monarchs.

Throughout the negotiations and preparations, the purpose and destination of his voyage were state secrets. Fernando and Isabel maintained strict security, issuing sketchy orders to the fleet's outfitters and officers. If the monarchs had made public their intention of sailing west to Asia, spies would have reported the news immediately to Castile's rival, Portugal. Instead, the monarchs concealed their agreement with Columbus and took the precaution of describing the fleet's destination in the vaguest possible terms—"certain parts of the Ocean Sea" or "parts of the Ocean Sea in the direction of India."

Royal clerks recorded the Granada Capitulations in the registers of the Castilian chancery and Columbus received the original. He took the original Capitulations with him on the voyage, together with the letters of introduction.

Fernando and Isabel immediately issued orders implementing their part of the contract. Columbus did not include these royal orders in the *Book of Privileges,* probably because they did not refer to him as "sir." He did keep them safe, however, and the orders survive in the family archives of Columbus's descendants. They have been published several times (Navarrete 1825, vol. 2; Berwick 1902). Fernando and Isabel ordered local merchants and outfitters to sell supplies and equipment to Columbus at reasonable prices, ordered government officials not to collect royal taxes on the sales, and extended these same exemptions to Columbus's purchases for his own needs and investment in the voyage. To help speed the preparations, they sent a royal staff member, Juan de Peñalosa, to the coast to act as their business agent in purchasing and transporting supplies and equipment.

Columbus left Granada on 12 May 1492 and went directly to Palos, where he turned over to the Palos town council responsibility for implementing the royal writs. Palos was a small fishing port of about 300 households in the late fifteenth century. Still a young town—it had been settled only about a century earlier—Palos did not yet have a town hall. Instead the town council conducted its business in the parish church. Here Columbus and the town council performed a ritual familiar to every Castilian citizen; Columbus presented the royal writs to the municipal judge on duty that day. Traditionally, the judge would kiss the royal document and, holding it over his forehead, swear on behalf of the town to obey it. Then the town crier read the document out loud. The town clerk recorded the ritual in the town council minutes, listing as witnesses Columbus and the parish priest, Friar Juan Pérez, who was also prior of the local Franciscan monastery of Santa María de La Rábida.

Contrary to popular belief, Columbus did not have ships built for the voyage. The monarchs ordered the town of Palos, whose seagoing citizens had been convicted of an infraction by the royal appeals court, to pay the penalty by providing Columbus with two caravels (Manzano 1988). The town council chartered two caravels, *Pinta* and *Niña,* from the town's leading merchants, both members of the Pinzón family. Columbus persuaded the shipowners to captain their own ships and recruit Palos seamen and apprentices as crew for the voyage. He also went to Seville and its seaport, Sanlúcar de Barrameda, and chartered a Basque cargo carrier *(nao), Santa María,* from its owner Juan de La Cosa. Columbus apparently leased and outfitted *Santa María,* as his share of financing the voyage, with money invested by a Florentine merchant in Seville, Juanoto Berardi (Varela 1988: 35–58).

These preparations for the first voyage were begun at the worst possible time of year for provisioning a fleet. By the time Columbus left Granada in mid May, the previous year's wheat supply would have been almost depleted, while the new crop would not be harvested until June and threshed until July. Until the end of the summer, market prices would remain high for the wheat necessary to make the ship's biscuit (unsalted, twice-baked bread) that would comprise the staple food during the journey.

Columbus had calculated that the voyage west would take six weeks to reach Asia. He expected to find islands all along the way but could not count on finding food there, because experience had shown that most Atlantic islands were not inhabited. He had to provision the ships as if the fleet would not get fresh supplies before reaching its destination. Furthermore, he knew the example of the Portuguese captain Bartolomeu Dias, whose voyage of exploration south along the west coast of Africa had lasted two years. Thus, Columbus's ships would be provisioned for one year. The amount of wheat required to prepare ship's biscuit for ninety men over such a long journey must have strained the resources of the Andalusian countryside that summer.

As ships, provisions, and equipment were collected in Palos at the end of the summer, Fernando and Isabel issued orders providing security for the families of the crew and admiral. The monarchs ordered that, for the duration of the voyage, the Palos seamen's private property would not be seized and sold to pay court-ordered damages and fines. Finally, the monarchs made a magnificent gesture of confidence and favor toward Columbus; they appointed his son Diego as a page in the household of their own son, Prince Juan, with an annual allowance of 9,400 maravedís for his clothing and maintenance. Diego probably stayed in Seville, however, with his aunt, Violante Moniz, and her husband and did not go to court until after Columbus returned from the voyage.

The fleet left the port of Palos on 3 August 1492. Columbus himself captained the flagship *Santa María,* while Martín Alonso Pinzón commanded *Pinta,* and his brother Vicente Yáñez Pinzón captained *Niña.* They put in to the Canary Islands for repairs and additional provisions on 9 August, and sailed from there on 9 September (on the Pinzones, see Manzano 1988).

After making landfall somewhere in the Bahamas at dawn on 12 October, Columbus explored the coasts of many islands, naming and taking possession of a number of them, including Juana (modern Cuba) and La Española (modern Haiti and the Dominican Republic). On Christmas Day, *Santa María* ran aground off the north coast of La Española, leaving insufficient ship's provisions or space for all the crew. Columbus salvaged enough timbers and planking to construct a palisaded trading post, which he named La Navidad. Then, on 4 January 1493, he set sail for the return voyage to Spain, leaving behind thirty-nine men in La Navidad.

3. Letter from Fernando and Isabel Inviting the Admiral to the Court at Barcelona.

Near the end of the return voyage *Niña* and *Pinta* were separated by a violent storm that lasted several days. *Pinta* made port at Bayona on the north coast of Spain, while Columbus aboard *Niña* sought safe harbor in Portuguese ports. On Friday, 18 February, *Niña* dropped anchor off Santa María, the smallest of the Azores Islands. Here Columbus showed his credentials to the local officials and replenished his food and water supplies. On 4 March, after surviving an even worse storm, *Niña* dropped anchor next to a Portuguese warship in Lisbon harbor. Once again, Columbus showed his credentials, this time to the master of the warship, who was none other than the discoverer of the Cape of Good Hope, Bartolomeu Dias.

On 8 March, Columbus had an interview with the Portuguese king, João II. While the Portuguese would not have believed Columbus's claim to have reached Asia, they had reason to question the fleet's route, because in 1479–1480 an accord had divided up the fishing and trading rights in the Atlantic into Portuguese and Spanish zones. King João released Columbus after he was satisfied that *Niña* had not traveled to his trading post in Africa. From Lisbon, Columbus sailed directly to Spain, reaching Palos on 15 March and, leaving most of the crew to happy reunions with family and friends, traveled to Seville with his Indian captives, exotic souvenirs, and some of the remaining crew.

Columbus must have sent word from Lisbon to Fernando and Isabel of his successful journey and safe return. The monarchs, who were visiting Fernando's Aragonese domains, immediately sent him the following letter summoning him to the royal court in Barcelona. According to the terms of the Granada Capitulations, the moment Columbus had taken formal possession of any island in the name of Fernando and Isabel he became admiral of the Ocean Sea as well as viceroy and governor of the islands. A transformation had taken place; Christopher Columbus, a commoner in the 1492 royal documents, by virtue of his accomplishments, had become Sir Christopher Columbus. Fernando and Isabel received Columbus with joy and honor when he finally arrived in Barcelona, having traveled overland from Seville. Now that the enterprise had become a reality and Columbus had fulfilled the terms of the contract by actually discovering and taking possession of islands, both the monarchs and their admiral rushed to formalize their agreements and prepare a return voyage.

4. Preface to 1493 Confirmation of the Granada Capitulations.

5. Appendix to 1493 Confirmation of the Capitulations.

Once Columbus arrived in Barcelona, where the court was in residence, he asked the monarchs to elevate the Granada Capitulations from a simple writ of grant to a charter of privilege that would be permanently binding on all Spaniards. During March 1493 the Castilian royal staff redrafted both capitulations, incorporating Columbus's new titles. They also upgraded the relatively informal writs of grant *(cartas de merced),* to official and permanent status as charters of privilege affixed with a lead seal *(cartas de privilegio emplomadas).*

Columbus, the monarchs, and the chancery all recognized that more than the documents themselves needed to be confirmed. The Granada Capitulations' concession of hereditary royal office to Columbus and his descendants violated the Castilian constitution. Extraordinary arguments from philosophy, religion, and precedent were needed to justify the terms of the Capitulations, and the chancery's lawyers and secretaries supplied these in the form of a preface and an appendix. Principles of monarchical government were at stake, however, and the royal legal counsel, Rodrigo Maldonado de Talavera, approved the Granada Capitulations in form only, without approving the content.

The principal difficulty arose from those clauses of the 1492 Capitulations granting to Columbus royal offices and governing powers as hereditary possessions. While Columbus had negotiated hard to win these extraordinary powers, the monarchs hesitated because these administrative concessions violated the very nature of monarchy.

Monarchies developed in Europe on the premise that the royal domain belonged to the royal family as a function of the monarch's judicial and military responsibilities, carried out for the welfare of the entire realm. Although monarchs could temporarily delegate royal power and use income from the royal domain to reward proxies, they could not permanently alienate royal functions or domains. To give away the monarchy's military and judicial functions as hereditary offices violated this fundamental tenet of monarchical government.

The Castilian chancery staff attempted to overcome these difficulties by expanding and reinforcing the Capitulations. First, the Castilian royal secretary, Fernán Alvarez de Toledo, drafted a preface stating that Fernando and Isabel were acting of their own free will. Then he composed an extensive postscript confirming the royal intention to make these grants in perpetuity as hereditary private possessions and justifying this permanent alienation of royal offices and income by employing arguments from philosophy, scripture, and Roman law.

These elaborate appeals to reason, religion, and authority, however, never assured Columbus. After all, any arguments that could be employed as justification for violating the fundamental constitution of the monarchy could just as deftly be deployed at some future date to justify abrogating the Capitulations themselves. Before departing on each of his four voyages to the Americas, Columbus requested and received confirmation of the Capitulations, and he included nearly all these reconfirmations in his *Book of Privileges* for safekeeping.

The Granada Capitulations went through several bureaucratic steps in their transformation from writ of grant to charter of privilege. After royal clerks wrote out the documents from Fernán Alvarez's dictation, Fernando and Isabel signed with their usual signatures: "I, the King," and "I, the Queen." Next, Alvarez signed the documents and passed them on to the chancellor, Pedro Gutiérrez, who waived the chancery's usual fees and then sent the documents on to the royal legal counsel, Rodrigo Maldonado de Talavera. Maldonado checked the text to make sure that it conformed to Castilian legal norms in both form and content. He approved the Capitulations, signed his name in Latin on the back, and passed the documents on to the registrar, Alfonso Pérez. It was Pérez who recorded the Capitulation in the Castilian chancery registers, signed below Maldonado's signature on the back, and gave it to Columbus. In this new form, the Capitulations became public decrees for the first time, binding on all royal subjects and citizens of the realm.

INTRODUCTION TO PART 2: THE SECOND VOYAGE

CHAPTER 2.1: FERNANDO AND ISABEL DEFINE
COLUMBUS'S AUTHORITY AND JURISDICTION

6. Warrant to the Admiral and Juan de Fonseca to Outfit a Second Voyage.

The discoveries of Columbus's first voyage focused Castilian objectives for the second voyage. The monarchs wanted to relieve the unfortunate crew left behind at La Navidad immediately. At the same time, they wanted to establish their claims to sovereignty over the islands that Columbus had explored and claimed for them. Finally, they wanted to reward and honor Columbus for his accomplishments in their behalf, even though the first voyage had resulted in a financial loss. These multiple objectives, together with the monarchy's usual lack of finances in the 1490s, inspired a flurry of royal writs and warrants shaping, organizing, and defining the next phase of Spanish exploration in the Americas, the inchoate and tragic second voyage.

Despite Columbus's assurances that the native people were meek and peaceful, Fernando and Isabel perceived that La Navidad faced dangers. The thirty-nine Europeans Columbus left behind there carried the usual seamen's tools—knives, short swords, and axes—with which they could guard their supplies and equipment within the palisade. When European provisions began to run low, however, the men would become vulnerable. European coins had no monetary value in the local barter economy. The crew would have to barter for native food by offering European goods of little value for Caribbean islanders except as novelties; most of the European merchandise Columbus had taken on the first voyage had consisted of wool cloth. The crew in La Navidad could not afford to trade their European tools and equipment, which, though highly desirable to the island people, who had no metal tools or glass, were also essential to the crewmen's survival.

Within a month of Columbus's return to Spain, the monarchs instructed him to organize another transatlantic crossing. In addition to relieving La Navidad, the monarchs wanted Columbus to develop commerce with Asia. Although the first voyage had not yielded a profit, all good things seemed possible in the still unknown Americas. Fernando and Isabel commissioned Columbus to find and claim more islands, reach the coast of the Asian mainland, and establish business relations with Asia. Columbus and many other Europeans were fascinated by Marco Polo's reports on Central Asia, China, and Japan. European readers mistakenly projected a continuity in Asian government over the centuries from Polo's experience to their own days, and the monarchs had anachronistically addressed a letter to the Grand Khan, whom Marco Polo had described as the ruler of the Asian continent. For profitable business, they thought it necessary to develop La Navidad into a fully stocked royal trading post. They also wanted to lay effective claim to the islands by having Castilian citizens establish a town and produce their own food by cultivating the land.

The monarchs placed the responsibility for equipping and organizing the voyage in the very capable hands of Columbus and the newly ordained archdeacon of Seville cathedral, Juan Rodríguez de Fonseca. On 20 May 1493 the monarchs commissioned Fonseca to form a fleet in Cádiz and then to station himself in Seville, where he could organize the provisions and equipment and forward them to Columbus, who was collecting and outfitting the fleet in Cádiz harbor. Fonseca proved to be a superb administrator and soon was supervising all government contracts, fleet outfitting, emigration, and navigational matters concerned with the Americas. For the rest of his life, Fonseca was entrusted with responsibility for supervising the European side of Spain's transatlantic trade. Columbus continued to command the voyages themselves and was responsible for managing commerce and colonization in the Indies. The two worked together amicably and efficiently to prepare a massive second voyage.

Cádiz harbor could accommodate many oceangoing ships and the port was easily defended. At the time, military defense was a primary consideration, because Fernando and Isabel were worried about the possibility of a Portuguese attack. The duke of Medina Sidonia, commander of the coastal defenses, had reported that the Portuguese king was organizing a large fleet, destination unknown. In addition to the monarchs' concern that the Portuguese might be preparing to seize forcibly some of the islands Columbus had claimed for them in the Caribbean, the possibility also existed that the Portuguese fleet could attack Cádiz or the Castilian fleet as it left the harbor.

The excitement generated by Columbus's report about the Americas attracted hundreds of the scientifically curious and venturous. About 1200 men were on board when the seventeen ships departed during September 1493. Spanish farmers and artisans, carrying their tools, seeds, and seedlings, went as colonists to the new Castilian territory. Hundreds of Italian and Spanish merchants now wanted to invest in contracts with Columbus. His boyhood friend Michele da Cuneo and his youngest brother Diego came from Savona, Italy, to embark on the voyage. A handful of American Indians, the five or six survivors of the nine islanders whom Columbus had seized and brought to Spain six months earlier, had learned to speak Spanish and had been baptized. Columbus now brought them as passengers, intending that they should return to the Caribbean with him to act as translators. They all jumped ship as soon as the fleet arrived off the coast of La Española, however, and were never found again. The monarchs sent the first Christian priests to America, Mercedarian clergy led by Friar Bernal Buyl, to minister to the spiritual needs of the new settlement. Other passengers who would later play distinguished roles were the Seville physician Dr. Chanca; shipowner turned cartographer Juan de La Cosa; Francisco and Pedro de Las Casas, father and uncle of Bartolomé; and Juan Ponce de León and Alonso de Hojeda, businessmen turned explorers.

Fonseca and Columbus chartered these seventeen ships of various types and capacities from private owners, and probably several belonged to the duke of Medinaceli. Medinaceli had been Columbus's first patron in Spain, had introduced him to the royal court, and first reported Columbus's return from the first voyage. In his letter to the monarchs announcing Columbus's return, he wasted not a minute in asking the monarchs to designate his port across the bay from Cádiz, Puerto de Santa María, as the port of embarcation for future voyages to the Indies.

Everything we know about the preparations for the second voyage indicates a close and harmonious understanding between the Spanish monarchs and their admiral of the Ocean Sea. Columbus and Fonseca together selected the settlers and merchants who were allowed to embark. Columbus himself drafted the specifications for the voyage, which the monarchs issued as a royal warrant in Barcelona on 29 May. The warrant specified the conduct of the voyage, the order of departure, the organization of the fleet, its course, and proceedings on arrival (Parry 1984, 2:71–75).

Isabel, Fernando, and Columbus all had the same hopes for the second voyage: to establish a permanent Castilian trading post on the island of La Española. Through this base, all commerce with Asia would be conducted. Here Columbus would collect the gold he still hoped to find and provide manpower for further exploration.

Until the colony on La Española could bring in its first crops and breed its own plow stock, European crops and animals were needed to supply food and textiles. One ship carried a herd of pigs in its hold, which Columbus intended to breed for meat. The monarchs granted the contract for provisioning the fleet to Columbus's business associate in Seville, Juanoto Berardi, a Florentine slaver who had loaned Columbus the money for his share of the expenses for the first voyage. They commissioned Berardi to lease and equip a cargo carrier of between 100 and 200 toneladas and to acquire and pack for shipping between 200,000 and 300,000 pounds of ship's biscuit (Gil and Varela 1984: 226–230). From February 1494 through the fall of 1496, the monarchs and Fonseca commissioned four separate resupply fleets to provision the Spanish colony on La Española.

The royal plan followed the model of their Portuguese rivals in Africa. Fernando and Isabel intended the royal trading post of La Navidad to function as a company store. Columbus would manage the store as the monarchs' business partner, stocking it with European goods supplied by merchants in Spain and native goods acquired by Spanish merchants on the islands. If all went as planned, Spaniards on La Española would have to buy all their European equipment and manufactured goods from this company store. In this royal monopoly, Portuguese in inspiration and abhorrent to every Spaniard, lay the seeds of Columbus's failure as viceroy and governor.

7. Writ Ordering Captains and Mariners to Obey the Admiral As Captain General.

Fernando and Isabel intended the Spaniards at La Navidad to be salaried employees of the crown, as completely subject to Columbus's authority as the military force they also sent on the voyage. Among their first documents for this voyage (7), they confirmed Columbus's appointment as admiral, viceroy, and governor, and iterated that these offices should be hereditary in perpetuity. They further specified and clarified the prerogatives and authority that had been implied in the offices granted to Columbus in the Granada Capitulations.

For the second voyage, the monarchs insisted on sending a contingent of cavalry. They were not trying to overwhelm the native peoples with a display of force; rather they intended to defend Spanish sovereignty should the Portuguese intrude in Castile's western route to the Indies. Columbus, on the other hand, thought there was a greater danger from the French, whose ships were attacking Spanish commercial vessels in and near the strait of Gibraltar. Outfitting one of his ships to accommodate the twenty horses became one of the more time-consuming aspects of the preparations, and Columbus's resentment of the cavalry commander's authority over this armed band only fueled the admiral's hostility toward a military force he seemed to think unnecessary. Ironically, a year later Columbus himself would order the cavalry to attack the natives in the highlands of La Española, over the objections of the cavalry officers (Ramos 1979, 1982).

8. Authority to the Person Whom Columbus Appoints to Act in His Absence to Grant Decrees and Charters, Embossing Them with the Royal Seal.

9. Writ Giving to the Admiral the Sole Right of Appointing His Officers.

In defining Columbus's authority, the monarchs also defined the type of government they were establishing for the Spanish colonies. In a significant departure from Europe's mixture of private (feudal or seigneurial) and royal governments, the monarchs placed all their new territory in the royal domain. All inhabitants of the Americas, both Spaniards and native Americans, would be royal, not seigneurial, subjects. Columbus, his proxies, deputies, and successors were to issue orders and decrees in the names of Fernando and Isabel, not in their own names or in the name of some seigneurial lord, and to emboss these orders with the royal seal. Columbus alone would appoint his officers, with the approval of the monarchs.

CHAPTER 2.2: FERNANDO AND ISABEL ADJUST TO
THE REALITY OF THE AMERICAS

Despite Columbus's glowing descriptions of the islands in 1493, his first report to Fernando and Isabel during the second voyage convinced them that the Caribbean environment could not support a European society without major compromises. Antonio de Torres, who commanded the return fleet of twelve ships that left La Isabela harbor at the beginning of February 1494 and arrived in Seville in March, brought with him twenty-six Indians and about 30,000 pesos of gold. Yet the report he carried from Columbus revealed the harsh realities of the Americas: the natives, soil, and climate were hostile. All the admiral's expectations from the islands were disappointed: he found no cities, no money economy, no metal tools or ores. Instead he had his hands full coping with the natives and colonists of these islands from which he had hoped for so much.

The plans that had seemed reasonable in Spain in the glow of Columbus's reports on the first voyage proved impractical in the unexpectedly harsh environment of the Caribbean. The first sign of the disasters to come appeared as soon as the second voyage, after a long and stormy delay off the coast of La Española, landed on the island. The admiral and his crew and passengers were horrified to find all thirty-nine men left behind at La Navidad dead. Columbus moved the site of the royal trading post away from the Indian settlement, but the new Spanish city he founded, La Isabela, floundered.

Within days of disembarking there, more than one-fourth of the Europeans fell ill, and many of those died. Contrary to Columbus's assurances, the natives were not all friendly, and the admiral found himself engaged in wars of conquest with the very people he had promised would accept the sovereignty of Fernando and Isabel. The city council of La Isabela, which convened its first meeting on 24 April 1494, was helpless to avert the impending collapse of the colony. The European crops that the Castilian farmers planted near La Isabela—wheat, barley, grapes, olives, cotton, fruits, legumes, and vegetables—failed to mature in the tropical climate, and the food and feed supplies brought from Seville suffered an alarming rate of spoilage in the heat and damp. Columbus refused to issue provisions from the stock he kept in the fortified royal warehouse. In desperate hunger, some Spaniards tried to farm farther away from La Isabela, while others moved to island villages and went native.

The demographic consequences for this and future Spanish colonies were appallingly apparent to the royal court in Castile. The modern popular notion that Europeans were immune to bacterial and viral infections is both biologically and historically incorrect. The monarchs could see that Europeans in the Americas died in large numbers from disease, warfare, and shipwreck. Of the ninety crew and officers on the first voyage, thirty-nine died in La Navidad during 1493. Meanwhile, of the 1200 crew, staff, and passengers on the second voyage, dozens had died within weeks of disembarking, despite the heroic care of Dr. Chanca. Columbus reported to the monarchs that every contingent of Spaniards who went into the interior of the island came back with yellow complexions and seriously ill. He himself almost died and he suffered serious aftereffects from his illness for the rest of his life.

During 1494, Columbus organized La Española into the classic European trading post, with tragic consequences for the native Taino population and political disaster for Columbus. The colony received reinforcements and new supplies when Antonio de Torres returned from Spain in fall 1494 with a resupply fleet of four caravels. The plan formed in Spain had been to keep the caravels in port until Columbus loaded them with American merchandise to sell in Spain, but by early 1495 he had found nothing of value—except the natives. Columbus rounded up 1200 war captives and selected 500 for sale in Spain. He might yet be able to make enough money to satisfy the monarchs and his own creditors, especially Berardi to whom he still owed 100,000 maravedís from the first voyage. Torres's return fleet became ships of death; instead of following the northerly route, he sailed south and wasted weeks in becalmed waters. By the time he corrected course and reached the Madeiras, 200 of the enslaved Indians on board had died. Fonseca put the survivors on sale in Seville as soon as they disembarked in April 1495. But the queen put a halt to the sale.

The queen's moratorium on the sale of enslaved Indians remained in force for the rest of her life, and most later rulers confirmed it for centuries. This does not mean that Spanish rulers rejected slavery. The Spanish policy in the Americas did not derive from some humane impulse; rather it fit the ethical norms of the day. Nearly every civilization known to historians, anthropologists, and archaeologists practiced slavery for centuries, from prehistoric times up to the twentieth century. Yet no society enslaved its own people. All of them regarded slavery as an evil, a sort of living death, employed as the only alternative to killing war captives. Fernando and Isabel themselves had enslaved the entire Muslim population of the newly-conquered city of Málaga in 1487 and sold the enslaved Muslims throughout the western Mediterranean. But it was one thing to sell Muslims taken captive in war, quite another to enslave the queen's willing subjects, as Columbus had described them. Columbus claimed a legal pretext for enslaving them as prisoners captured in "just war." Yet the monarchs knew from other sources that the natives of La Española had risen in revolt against intolerable treatment. To make the idea of enslaving Indians more palatable to the monarchs, Columbus proposed to limit slave hunting to the Caribs, whose supposed cannibal habits, as he described them, excluded them from human society. The Spanish monarchs remained firm, and the royal policy against enslaving the monarchy's Indian subjects remained the law (Rumeu de Armas 1969).

The royal policy did not end enslavement of the native population. Columbus continued to enslave natives on La Española and sent more to Spain during the third voyage. Las Casas wryly observed that Indian slaves were "the principal crop of the Admiral, with which he expected to cover the expenses" of the monarchs. Other Spanish explorers also sent enslaved Indians to Seville, always claiming they were cannibals or had been taken prisoner in just war. All told, between 1495 and 1500 some

2,000 Indians were enslaved and sent to Spain from the Antilles, Venezuela, and Central America (Sued-Badillo 1983). In Spain, a court of law reviewed the case of each enslaved Indian. Those judged to have been unlawfully enslaved were ordered shipped home. Their number in Spain must have been quite small—a dozen enslaved Indians appear in the notarial registers of Seville between 1492 and 1504, most of them under the age of fifteen (Franco Silva 1980). The monarchs' intentions towards the Indians may have been humane, as some have claimed, but their judicious policies did not protect the Indians from the cruel rapacity of men whose greed for profit contributed to the destruction of native civilization (Fernández Armesto 1991: 138).

10. Letter from Fernando and Isabel in Reply to the Admiral's Letters Delivered by Antonio de Torres.

11. Mandate Ordering the People in the Indies to Obey the Admiral As Viceroy and Governor.

12. Permission for Other Persons to Make Voyages of Discovery and for Spanish Settlers to Colonize the Island of La Española.

Repeated assurances from Fernando and Isabel that they still had confidence in Columbus's administrative and navigational leadership nevertheless revealed that the monarchs recognized the mounting problems. For the moment they insisted on maintaining the agreed organization of the colony as a trading post and supply station, with all colonists in the employ of the monarchy. In response to the many complaints by returned settlers about the Columbus brothers' administration, they issued a direct order for all Spaniards in the Indies to obey the admiral. In recognition of the obvious need to increase the flow of European provisions, they improvised a plan for Fonseca to send more frequent resupply fleets under the command of other captains.

CHAPTER 2.3: DIVIDING THE OCEAN SEA

13. Letter from Queen Isabel Sending the Admiral a Transcript of His Log Book and Inquiring about a Sailing Chart She Had Asked Him to Prepare.

With the presumed success of the first voyage, Fernando and Isabel immediately took measures to secure legal claim to the newly discovered islands. The monarchs wanted public acknowledgement of Castilian sovereignty over the Indies. Publicity was essential. For this, they extracted relevant passages from the journal Columbus had kept during his first voyage and the letters he had sent to them and their treasurer Luis de Santángel from Lisbon and Palos in which he described the climate, people, flora, fauna, and mineral resources of the newly claimed Spanish islands. A royal treasurer, Gabriel Sánchez, organized the excerpts in the form of a letter from Columbus, the famous *First Letter from America,* which was published in Castilian in Barcelona. The only surviving exemplar of the first printing belongs to the New York Public Library. It is written in the Castilian language, not in Catalan as Fernando Colón mistakenly catalogued it. Isabel sent Columbus's journal back to him, with a request for a sailing chart (13), but these documents arrived after Columbus had already sailed for the Indies and had to wait until the admiral's brother, Bartolomé Colón, arrived in La Isabela with a resupply fleet of three caravels in April 1494.

A courier carried the *First Letter* to Rome, where an Aragonese priest, Leander del Cosco, translated it into Latin for publication throughout Europe. The monarchs publicized their claims by having the Latin version of the *First Letter* printed in Rome, Basel, Antwerp, and Paris. These claims were further publicized by an Italian verse version of the letter printed in Florence, and a German language version printed in Strasbourg (Ramos 1986). Thus, by 1499, the reading public in most west European capitals had been exposed to Castile's claims as first European explorers, settlers, and governors of an island previously unknown to Europeans, the island Columbus had named La Española.

All of this publicity laid the groundwork for gaining clear legal title to the Indies for Castile. Rather than exacerbate disputes with Portugal, the monarchs turned to the only international court of appeals in Christendom, the papacy. No doubt they felt confident of success, since the newly elected pope was a Spaniard, the notorious Cardinal Rodrigo Borgia, who had been their ally for the last twenty years. During the next months, the new pope issued a series of decrees (bulls), granting sovereignty over previously unknown islands and continents in the Indies to Castile.

With this appeal to the papacy, Fernando and Isabel forever changed the nature of the enterprise of the Indies. The papal decrees rested legal title to islands and continents squarely on the imperative to convert the native people to Christianity. Fernando and Isabel, by seeking legitimation from the church, changed the nature of European government in America from its purely commercial Spanish, Italian, and Portuguese origins to an enterprise infused with the religious objectives of the church. The admiral in America did not yet know about the conditions imposed on the enterprise by the papal decrees, but he would have approved heartily.

14. Papal Decree Granting Castile Sovereignty over the Indies.

Scholars believe that the papal decree *Inter caetera* included in the *Book of Privileges* was written in June but predated 4 May in response to a request from Fernando and Isabel. According to this interpretation, the monarchs were dissatisfied with the wording of the papal decree *Inter caetera* dated 3 May, and asked for a revision. The two *Inter caetera* decrees are as near identical as two manuscripts can be except for one significant difference: the geographical extent of the sovereignty granted to Castile. The 3 May decree granted dominion to Castile over islands and continents discovered by Castilians up to *(usque)* the Indies, while the 4 May decree, by granting dominion over islands and continents toward *(versus)* the Indies, does not imply a limit.[12]

This interpretation that the monarchs were dissatisfied with the 3 May decree is supported by the differing fates of the two manuscripts. The 3 May decree was recorded in the pontifical register, and the original draft was sent to the Spanish monarchs, but it was never copied in its day and was always kept strictly secret. The 4 May decree, in contrast, was issued with the full formality of the papal curia and recorded in the papal register, probably on 28 June. The monarchs received the decree while they were still in Barcelona. Because the decree directly affected the Asian aspirations of Portugal, once again on poor terms with Castile, Fernando and Isabel kept the decree secret. In July, they ordered a copy made for Columbus. The 4 May decree was copied in Barcelona by papal notaries on the staff of the city's bishop, Pedro Garcias, and predated 19 July 1493 (García Gallo 1957–1958; Giménez Fernández 1944a). Antonio de Torres carried it to Columbus in La Isabela, and it has been frequently reproduced and used by historians since the sixteenth century as the source text of the decree of demarcation.[13]

15. Letter from Fernando and Isabel Promising Great Rewards to the Admiral, Requesting Information about the Indies, and Sending the Terms of the Treaty of Tordesillas.

By the time the monarchs sent a copy of the papal decree to Columbus, he had already departed on his second voyage. Columbus received the decree (14) and other royal letters concerning the demarcation (13 and 15) while in the Indies and later included them in his *Book of Privileges* compiled in Seville in 1502. The monarchs informed him of their negotiations with the Portuguese leading to the Treaty of Tordesillas and asked him to cooperate with Portuguese captains to establish the location of the demarcating line. Despite the discouraging reports they received with every returned fleet, the monarchs still trusted Columbus to establish the boundaries of their new overseas empire.

The weather Columbus had praised as balmy and healthful revealed itself to be hostile. The two hurricanes of 1495 destroyed all but one of Columbus's ships in La Isabela's harbor and the return fleet brought by Juan de Aguado in late September. An unusually large sea wave immediately following the first hurricane flooded the Spanish town and its farm fields, contributing to the shortage of food for those who remained. Most of the passengers had returned to Spain on the resupply fleets commanded by

---

[12]The originals of both *Inter caetera* decrees are in AGI, Seville, Patronato I-I-I.

[13]The authoritative English translation of both *Inter caetera* decrees by Frances Davenport, made from the originals in Seville, has been an indispensable guide for this translation (Davenport 1917: 61–78). See also a new printing of Davenport's translation (Parry 1984, 1:271–74). I wish to thank Arthur Field and Fred McGinniss for their expert and generous assistance with the Latin text.

Torres. But Columbus and the colonists were left stranded knowing that Torres was not scheduled to return until 1497.

With the colony in despair, Columbus managed to build a ship, nicknamed *India,* out of the timbers and rigging salvaged from the hurricane wreckage. Such unforeseen disasters—Europeans had never before experienced hurricanes—ended all Columbus's hopes for realizing a profit on the second voyage. With little to show for two years of explorations, planting, and mining, and with a royal moratorium on the sale of the natives he had enslaved, Columbus departed from La Isabela in March 1496 with no profits from which to pay his creditor Berardi. On *Niña,* lone survivor of the hurricanes, he led *India,* the first sailing ship built in the Americas, back to a momentous confrontation with his critics and supporters in Spain.

By the time the admiral returned to Seville in June 1496, the realities of the Caribbean had become apparent. Columbus could not know then that these realities would continue to decimate every Spanish expedition and settlement for the next century, but he certainly knew that the signs were ominous for the future of his colony. Only the monarchs' confidence in him personally could persuade them to adjust the financial terms of the failed business partnership and authorize further expeditions and colonies.

INTRODUCTION TO PART 3: THE THIRD VOYAGE

When Fernando and Isabel received Columbus on his return from the second voyage, everything had changed. From 1497 through 1500, Fernando and Isabel were preoccupied by the possibility that the succession to their thrones might suddenly become a matter of conflict.[14] In these circumstances, the problems of the new colony on La Española could not be their primary consideration, especially since they had to sift through many conflicting opinions about the solution. By mid 1497, they and their counsellors concluded that, if Castile was to retain its foothold in the Indies, it must establish a viable colony on traditional Castilian norms of repopulation, make the royal monopoly profitable as a supply station as well as a trading post, and restructure the partnership with Columbus.

After the dismal financial failure of his first and second voyages, Columbus anxiously solicited further concessions and guarantees from Fernando and Isabel. Still confident in the admiral's abilities as explorer and navigator, the monarchs responded to his requests and suggestions as generously as they had in documents related to the first two voyages. At the same time, the monarchs could not ignore reports from royal staff who had made trips to La Española from 1493 through 1496. These reports had been critical of Columbus's administration as viceroy of the colony, giving credence to complaints from returning colonists. The monarchs wanted to reduce the friction between their viceroy and the colonists, without impairing Columbus's power to defend the colony from the Portuguese.

To achieve these goals, the royal chancery drew up a very large number of documents, impressive in their quantity and important for their wealth of details. Once a

[14]The marriages that the monarchs had arranged for their children were, one by one, ending in tragedy. They were devastated by the death of their only son Prince Juan on 4 October 1497, the stillbirth of Juan's daughter a few months later, the death in childbirth of the monarchs' eldest child, Isabel, queen of Portugal, on 23 August 1498, and of her infant son, Miguel, heir to the Portuguese, Aragonese, and Castilian thrones, in 1500. The monarchs' second daughter Juana, archduchess of Austria and duchess of Burgundy, became heiress to the Castilian and Aragonese thrones, but her mental stability was questionable (Azcona 1964).

document was drafted and Columbus and the monarchs had a chance to study it, both parties sought changes. Thus, several documents issued in early April 1497 were returned to the chancery in late April for clarification or emendation of certain stipulations or the addition of further details that had not been included in earlier drafts. All parties further scrutinized and discussed the new version and sent it back to the chancery, which issued greatly expanded and revised versions of several documents in May, June, and July.

The process reflects the close cooperation between Columbus and the monarchs, as well as the consultative nature of the Castilian royal government. Many paragraphs in these documents reveal the royal couple responding readily to the admiral's suggestions based on his knowledge of the Americas. Fernando and Isabel in turn gave Columbus detailed instructions on how to organize a new town, based on their knowledge of Castilian customs of municipal self-administration and distribution of private property. The documents for this voyage also display a divergence of opinion between the royal legal counselors, who opposed heritable alienation of royal offices, such as admiral and viceroy, on constitutional grounds, and the monarchs, who were willing to concede vast royal powers and privileges to Columbus. Antonio Rumeu de Armas has suggested that the generous financial privileges and confirmation of the royal offices that the monarchs granted to Columbus in late summer 1497 were inspired by their desire to reach India before the Portuguese. Their alarm was awakened by news from Portugal; on 8 July 1497, Vasco de Gama sailed from Lisbon commanding three ships—*S. Gabriel, S. Rafael,* and *Bérrio*—en route around Africa to India. Establishing Castile's sovereignty over the western Ocean Sea became crucial.

Columbus, according to Rumeu, argued that the papal grant extended all the way west to Calicut, on the southwest coast of India, which he believed to be just over the horizon from La Española. If Columbus was right, and Da Gama traded in India, the Portuguese would be violating the papal decree *Inter caetera* and the Castilian-Portuguese Treaty of Tordesillas. More than ever the monarchs needed Columbus's services as admiral to fight off the Portuguese threat militarily (Rumeu de Armas 1972).

Thus the royal instructions for the third voyage reflected deep tensions in the royal objectives: favorable terms to attract colonists yet more explicit authority for Columbus to govern them, a more profitable royal monopoly yet expanded privileges to Columbus as their business agent in the Indies, peaceful governance of the native and European residents yet increased military forces. The colony established by the terms of these instructions, with their norms of local democratic self-government, became the political model for Spanish and later European settlement of the Americas. The economic and financial provisions most energetically sought by Columbus denying free trade to the colonists doomed his colonial administration to failure.

INTRODUCTION TO CHAPTER 3.1: COLONIZING THE
AMERICAS

The most detailed and innovative documents (16–24) concerned the voyage's major objective, to colonize the island of La Española. To their already existing claims based on first discovery, treaty with local rulers, and conquest, Fernando and Isabel now added the most widely respected of all justifications for sovereignty, effective occupation through colonization.

The monarchs' first concern was to base their legal claims on the establishment of self-sufficient and self-governing towns on La Española. To establish such towns, it was necessary to guarantee conditions favorable enough to attract and keep settlers from Castile. Fernando and Isabel instructed Columbus to grant the settlers land and local self-government along the traditional lines of Castilian frontier settlements.

With this plan for colonial towns, the Castilian monarchy instituted a significant innovation in European maritime enterprise. In 1492, the monarchs had anticipated establishing trading stations, the customary form of overseas possessions for European states. A trading station was simply a mercantile exchange, where businessmen could collect and store their merchandise and engage in currency exchanges until the fleet returned to the home country. They usually had some kind of fortification or walled perimeter to control the transit of people and goods. In the Italian trading stations along the Black and Aegean seas the merchants could buy familiar foods such as wheat, barley, and domesticated animals in the local markets. In the Atlantic, the Portuguese found it necessary to bring farmers on salary to cultivate the land and provide food for the trading stations.

Columbus had carried out the royal intentions during the second voyage, managing his city of La Isabela as if it were a Portuguese trading station with salaried farmers cultivating the land and supplying the trading post with European foods. The farmers who had gone on the second voyage had encountered devastating natural disasters, including epidemic, crop failure, and hurricane. These salaried employees had watched most of the food crops fail to bear fruit. By 1497, the monarchs concluded that Castilian farm towns would replace the salaried farmers.

Fernando and Isabel drew on centuries of Castilian experience in establishing new towns. In the Castilian tradition of populating uninhabited land between Christian and Muslim Spain, the first task was recruitment of settlers (16). Typically, a land surveyor assessed the carrying capacity of the land, then determined the optimal number of households. Experience since 1492 had demonstrated that the optimum for the island of La Española was not very great.

The 1497 instructions reveal lowered expectations for the European population of La Española. On the second voyage, the crown had paid salaries to over 1200 people, but most of them died of epidemic disease in the Indies or returned to Spain on resupply fleets. In the spring of 1497, fewer than 300 Spaniards remained on the island.

The monarchs concluded that the optimum size of the colony would be no more than 330 households (16).

Fernando and Isabel planned traditional Castilian towns of farmers, vegetable gardeners, tradesmen, and craftsmen. They expected fifty to sixty farmers and gardeners to produce enough food for the Spanish settlements, though they gave Columbus authority to reapportion the occupations and ranks of the 330 colonists if he found it necessary (18.3). Columbus wanted to take more colonists, and the monarchs later agreed he could take as many as 500 as long as the salary and maintenance for the extra 170 persons came from the Americas (19). Recruiters had great difficulty in finding people willing to go as colonists, however. The many dangers and political disadvantages of La Española had become public knowledge with the reports of the disaffected returnees from the second voyage. The admiral delegated the recruitment of farmers to Diego de Escobar, who recruited twenty-eight farmers, nearly all from the region of Jerez de la Frontera. Columbus asked for and received royal permission to recruit felons convicted by royal appeals judges (22–24). Their death sentences would be commuted at the end of ten years' unpaid service in the Americas under Columbus's supervision.

Even this extralegal measure, however, which required the monarchs to employ their absolute royal power in order to overturn the sentences of their own appeals courts, garnered only ten convicts, of whom four were gypsies. In the end, the third voyage carried only a portion of the colonists that had been projected.

The monarchs assumed that the Spanish farmers on La Española would be able to provide enough food for the whole colony. Until the first crops could be harvested, Fernando and Isabel would pay the colonists and supply them with plow animals, seed, and rations from the royal storehouse in La Isabela (17). Fernando and Isabel instructed Columbus to introduce plowing and animal husbandry near the new settlement (18.5). They ordered Columbus to divide up the land into farm fields and house lots, distribute these equitably to the colonists, and preserve the commons and stubble free of fencing (21). The terms were the same as in Castile. Columbus was to distribute seed and plow stock to the farmers on loan until the first crops were harvested. The farmers were permitted to sell their grain and vegetables on the open market to the other colonists and ships returning to Spain. Columbus had the power to establish maximum prices in order to protect consumers.

The royal instructions were redrafted and refined through the spring and summer of 1497 (20). Now that the harvest had begun in the south of Spain, Isabel and Fernando found the grain supplies promised in more general terms in 18.5–6. New articles in the writs specified sources of the Spanish grain Columbus had been ordered to distribute to colonists as provisions and to farmers as seed (20.5).

In late July, Fernando and Isabel issued the final version of their instructions for establishing farm communities in the Indies. To their earlier instructions, they added more specific stipulations about the conditions under which farmers would receive title to the land they cultivated (21.1). These residency and improvement requirements were standard in Spain and later throughout Spanish America. They were the precedent for our own homestead laws in those parts of the western United States acquired in the Mexican-American War.

The royal instructions still left much of the colonizing process undefined. They did not define the form of governance that Columbus should establish in the new towns, but any Spaniard would have understood how a Castilian settlement should be governed. By taking this knowledge for granted in a foreigner, Fernando and Isabel opened the way for Columbus's failure as an administrator.

Fernando and Isabel anticipated following the Castilian tradition of establishing many small settlements rather than one large one. They instructed Columbus to establish a second Spanish settlement on La Española on the other side of the island near "the gold mine" (18.4). In fact, there was no mine. In 1496, while Columbus was in Spain, Spaniards discovered gold on the south side of the island of La Española, near the Ozama River. They were washing a great deal of sand and dirt, panning for gold nuggets in the river and stream beds. A gold rush developed, depleting the population of La Isabela. The miners formed a squatter settlement near the mouth of the Ozama River, and Columbus's brother and lieutenant governor, Bartolomé Colón, moved there from La Isabela. When Columbus returned to La Española, he authorized the squatter settlement rather than forming a new one, and named it Santo Domingo. The city of Santo Domingo quickly eclipsed La Isabela, became the administrative headquarters of the Spanish Caribbean, and is still the capital of the Dominican Republic.

Probably the most significant and long-lasting departure from Castilian tradition appeared in these instructions for establishing new towns. Fernando and Isabel decreed that no one in the Americas could exercise private legal jurisdiction over their property. In other words, no seigneurial domains could be established; all of the Americas were to be in the royal domain (21.1). For this reason, the monarchs gave inordinate powers to their viceroy Columbus: he could issue writs, warrants, and decrees in their name with their seal; he could appoint persons to fill vacancies in the royal staff and military on the islands; he was to decide who would receive royal gifts in cash and other valuables; and he could appoint the royal appeals judge *(alcalde mayor)* for the island. Thanks to this decision by Fernando and Isabel not to delegate their royal powers to anyone except the viceroy, Spanish America throughout its colonial history remained an empire without seigneurial domains.[15]

Royal intentions for the founding of many small towns and cities would prove successful in the Americas: by 1515 there were twenty-seven Spanish cities and towns on the four major islands of the Caribbean. This successful innovation was almost undermined, however, by the determination of the monarchs to make money from the colony. This objective and the discovery of gold, together with Columbus's inept

---

[15]The monarchs' grandson Charles V made two exceptions; he granted the noble titles and seigneurial domains of marquis of the Valley of Oaxaca to Hernando Cortés and duke of Veragua to Luis Colón.

handling of his power over the colonists, produced serious shortages of food, clothing, and tools by 1500 (Ayala 1965). Though the extensive powers the monarchs gave Columbus seemed appropriate for a trading station in 1498, they gave rise to so much conflict between Columbus and the colonists that the monarchs finally ended the royal monopoly and instituted free trade in 1504.

The monarchs wanted the Americas to be profitable, and if not that, then at least self-sufficient. For that reason, and because all their Castilian revenues were already committed to other expenses, the monarchs planned that the wages of the colonists and crews and other colonial expenses would be paid from Indies revenues. They addressed this instruction (17) to the royal treasurer in Seville responsible for receiving and disbursing royal revenues from the Americas, Bernardo Pinelo.

The monarchs directed the treasury to pay wages only on the presentation of vouchers and payrolls drawn up by Columbus and validated by the royal accountants in the Indies. By means of this process, Columbus acquired total power of the purse over the colonists, staff, and military in the Indies. The colonists on the roster were to be paid from royal revenues derived from the Indies (18.8). All those who went to the Indies without being on the royal payroll were to be paid wages by Columbus and other private employers.

The payment schedule also depended on Columbus. Only when and if Columbus delivered valid rosters and vouchers would the money be issued by the royal treasurer in the Americas (18.6). This system built in prolonged delays in the payment of wages; Columbus would issue rosters and vouchers after satisfactory performance of duties, royal accountants in the Americas would audit and record the accounts, and the royal treasurer in Santo Domingo would then authorize payment. These delays and the total control of the payroll by Columbus created real economic hardship for the colonists.

The writs for the third voyage also contained the first royal mention of converting the native Americans to Christianity (18.2) and instructed Columbus to delegate this responsibility to the clergy on the island. The monarchs gave no specific funding or instructions for the priests. For the Spanish colonists, tradition should have been sufficient to guide the establishment of parish churches in the Spanish towns. For the conversion of American natives, there was no tradition to draw upon. There were no mission churches in Spain. The monarchs did not develop further instructions for converting native Americans, though they repeated the order several times in the *Book of Privileges*. During the next fifty years, the issue of how the conversion of native Americans should be carried out became one of the most controversial in the history of Spanish America.

Fernando and Isabel explicitly gave Columbus the power to implement his privileges as viceroy and admiral. Among the most lucrative were his power of preferment to offices, which they authorized him to distribute to the colonists at his discretion (18.9). In two of the earliest examples of case law in the Americas, the monarchs created new laws for the disposition of property belonging to deceased lawbreakers

(18.10), and decreed that the probate of estates of those deceased in the Indies be carried out according to Columbus's suggestion (18.12). In a gesture of the highest confidence in their viceroy, they authorized Columbus to take with him equipment necessary for minting in order to coin money from American gold according to royal mint regulations (18.14).

One of the very few powers of government that the monarchs entrusted to someone other than Columbus was taxation. They had decreed that Spaniards going to the Americas as colonists would be tax exempt (hidalgos), but they wanted to collect taxes from the native Americans (18.15). At the administrative level, the monarchs arranged for taxes in America to be collected as in Castile. They appointed a tax collector and receiver who would keep five percent of what he took in (18.16).

Beyond this superficial similarity with the Castilian tax system, the monarchs designed taxation in the Americas to adapt what they believed were the major characteristics of native society to the royal purposes. Conquered people were traditionally required to pay to the Spanish monarchs the same taxes they had previously paid their native rulers. The monarchs applied this principle to the conquered Kingdom of Granada, for example, and extended it to the Americas. Since these native taxes did not fit into the customary nomenclature of Castilian taxes, the chancery used the generic term "tribute."

In fifteenth-century Castile, ordinary citizens "served" the monarchy by paying a royal per capita tax, the *servicio*. The Cortes of Castile voted for the *servicio* and allocated the tax according to the population of each municipality. Each municipal council raised its allocated tax from municipal revenues rather than from individual taxpayers. After the municipal councils delivered the taxes to the Cortes's tax receivers, these ad hoc officials remitted the money to the royal treasury (Nader 1990).

The monarchs knew that the natives did not have municipal councils; Columbus had said so in his *First Letter* when he described the natives as "without self-government" (*sin regimiento*). Five hereditary caciques ruled the island of La Española when Columbus first arrived there. The caciques and other hereditary and religious leaders lived off the labor and goods produced by a servile class, known in the Caribbean as *naborías*.[16]

Although Columbus at the beginning established friendly relations with one or two caciques, Fernando and Isabel were determined that there should be no hereditary rulers in the Americas other than themselves. Having the caciques collect royal taxes from their traditional subjects would have strengthened the caciques' authority, so the monarchs sought another means of tax collection. The monarchs and Columbus decided that native Indians should be subject to an annual per capita tax (18.15) and that they should pay it individually. When the monarchs decided to collect taxes from the

[16]The same term was applied to the preconquest taxpayers of modern Mexico. In Peru they were called *yanaconas*.

native Americans, they effectively transformed the Indians into royal subjects rather than subjects of the caciques.

Native economy did not fit the Spanish system of taxes in another important aspect; Spaniards paid royal taxes in cash, but native Americans did not use money. They paid taxes to their caciques and religious leaders in the form of goods and services. Traditional native payments to caciques included some essential foods, such as casaba bread and chili peppers, but also decorative goods such as feathered regalia, not useful to Europeans, and religious and war items that Spaniards actively sought to discourage. To the Spaniards on La Española, payments in cassava and other food supplies seemed the most valuable tribute, especially after hurricane tides flooded and salted their crop land in 1495.

For Columbus, the Taino tribute system had little value. Only cotton thread, of all the traditional tribute goods, satisfied Columbus's obsession to find merchandise he could sell for a profit in European markets. Columbus led the monarchs to believe that some Tainos had already become her subjects and had agreed to pay taxes to her (18.15), and he had devised a new tribute system that the monarchs authorized. Columbus anticipated only one difficulty with the tax system: how to keep track of which Indians had paid. In a civilization like that of the Caribbean Tainos, in which writing was not used, written records of tax payments would not suffice. The monarchs authorized Columbus and the royal tax collectors to issue brass and lead tokens as evidence of tax compliance. These tokens could only have come from Spaniards because natives did not work these metals.

In focusing on record keeping, Columbus once again revealed his powers of self-deception; he misjudged or disregarded the effects of his policy on the native population. The tribute system that Columbus established on La Española required every Taino over the age of fourteen to supply a hawk's bell of gold every three months or, in areas without gold, a bushel of cotton thread. The system was in Las Casas's words, "impossible and intolerable," because there was no way that the quotas could be met.

The native population had never mined gold; they collected nuggets uncovered by natural erosion. Once the Tainos turned over to Columbus their stock of found nuggets and worked ornaments, neither they nor the Spaniards knew how to find gold veins or exploit them. When, in 1496, Alonso de Hojeda found evidence of gold in the central plain of La Española, and other Spaniards later found gold in the Ozama River near the south coast, the colonists abandoned La Isabela to move to the gold fields—America's first gold rush. They also forced the native population to move to these areas for several months each year to dig for gold, thus disrupting Taino patterns of family life and food production. Even this did not produce the results Columbus had expected, since no one had expertise in panning or mining for gold. Samuel Eliot Morison, a great admirer of Columbus, called the results of his tribute policy "hell on Hispaniola." The destruction of Indian society and the indescribable hardships suffered by the Taino laborers contributed to the disappearance of the native population of the Antilles, yet made no visible impression on Columbus's conscience.

INTRODUCTION TO CHAPTER 3.2: FERNANDO AND ISABEL ORGANIZE THE ROYAL ENTERPRISE OF THE INDIES

In 1497, when Columbus and the monarchs were planning and organizing the third Columbian voyage, their business partnership still held a monopoly on all commerce in the Indies. The monarchs still hoped to make a solid profit from the Indies, not just on the gold they now expected to receive from the newly discovered gold fields around Santo Domingo but also from the royal enterprise of the Indies. They placed new emphasis on the royal storehouse as a company store. To improve the profitability of the enterprise, the monarchs and Columbus in 1497 imposed regulations to keep their costs down and assure their control over the sale of provisions, equipment, and clothing to colonists and royal employees on La Española.

First, the monarchs took measures to control the cost of the food they promised for one year to colonists and royal employees on La Española. They issued a writ (25) requiring merchants in Spain to sell provisions to Columbus at normal prices and ordered municipal councils to enforce these price limits on Indies-bound supplies sold in their marketplaces. Because the monarchs still held a monopoly on sales in the Indies, only the royal enterprise stood to benefit from this order.

Next, the monarchs exempted from royal taxes Indies-bound merchandise, which, of course, belonged to their partnership with Columbus and its subsidiaries. They ordered (26) that the goods that Columbus and Fonseca were buying as stock for the royal trading post on La Española would not be subject in Seville or Cádiz to royal import tax, sales tax, or fees. In their determination to acquire merchandise at the lowest possible price, Fernando and Isabel further exempted (27) their Indies-bound purchases from all local and municipal taxes—excise, transit, customs, tithes, and admiralty. The royal treasury, which must have winced at losing these steady tax revenues for the sake of high risk ventures, postponed the drop in treasury income by issuing a memorandum that the tax exemptions would go into effect at the new year (28).

The monarchs also tried to minimize transport costs, one of the significant expenses of international commerce. They ordered (29) their factors on the coast, if necessary, to lease ships forcibly and impress the ships' owners into the royal service for the duration of the voyage. The monarchy's power to command the ships and services of seamen was by no means peculiar to Castile, but the peninsular customs carried specific compensations. Although they served under duress, the owners received charter fees, and they and the seamen received salaries and enjoyed tax exempt (hidalgo) status. The monarchs ordered the treasurer (30) to pay officers' salaries and the wages of seamen, colonists, and soldiers upon presentation of muster rolls and pay vouchers signed by Columbus.

Once the fleets reached La Española, Fernando and Isabel expected the colonists to subsist on supplies from the royal storehouse. They ordered royal officials to acquire the wheat and barley for the colonies at the least expense to the monarchy by taking grain from the royal tithe barns (31). Knowing that the market value of European goods would be very high in the colonies, they authorized Fonseca, Columbus, and the royal council to set maximum prices on La Española for the benefit of the colonists (32).

INTRODUCTION TO CHAPTER 3.3: ROYAL
AUTHORIZATION FOR THE COLUMBUS FAMILY
BUSINESS IN THE INDIES

While Fernando and Isabel wanted profits from the royal monopoly, they recognized that their profit was still the product of Columbus's management and expertise. The monarchs appointed arbiters to negotiate a settlement of profits and losses from the first and second voyages (33). They agreed to pay him a lump sum in lieu of the one-eighth, which he had never received because it was a fraction of a profit that had not been realized. During 1498, 1499, and 1500, Columbus would receive only the one-tenth of the enterprise and whatever profits he made on his own investments (35).

The monarchs attempted to safeguard Columbus's interest (his share of the royal profits and his possession of royal offices) and extend them to his brothers and sons, without cost to the royal treasury. Columbus wanted the enterprise of the Indies to be a family business. Fernando and Isabel confirmed Columbus's appointment of his brother Bartolomé Colón as lieutenant governor of the Americas (36).

They reconfirmed the provision of the Capitulations that had made Columbus the only partner or agent of the monarchy in the enterprise of the Indies (34). Columbus requested this writ in order to revoke an earlier writ (12) designed to send resupply fleets to him on La Española. Fonseca and the monarchs had taken advantage of 12 to send exploratory voyages under the command of other captains. With this new confirmation Columbus expected his authority over all voyages of exploration to the Indies to be safe, but the monarchs sent more exploratory voyages—the Andalusian voyages that mapped the west coast of South America—beginning in 1499, when they had determined to replace him.

Two royal writs issued in the first round of negotiations for the third voyage, on 23 April 1497, were to have long-term repercussions for both the monarchy and the Columbus family. Fernando and Isabel authorized Columbus to commission copies of the royal privileges held by the high admiral of Castile (38) and they gave him permission to establish one or more trusts in favor of Sir Diego Colón, "your legitimate eldest son, or any of your heirs and children" (39). The writ allowed him to include in this trust any property, goods, and heritable offices that he had received from the monarchy. Monarchs who gave away portions of the royal domain or royal offices regarded the law of partible inheritance as a hindrance to their largesse. In order to retain some power of influencing the beneficiaries of their largesse, the monarchs required the beneficiaries to place these royal grants in a heritable trust (*mayorazgo*), of which the monarchs were the trustees. By this means, the monarchs maintained the fiction that they were not really giving away the royal patrimony—just loaning it out forever.

Heritable trusts circumvented inheritance law by exempting from partition all property in the trust. Parents could not exclude a legitimate child from a fair share of the inheritance, except for extraordinary crimes such as attempted murder of a parent, nor could a parent donate more than ten percent of the estate as charitable and religious bequests. After the parents' deaths, the children partitioned the parental estate among themselves, under the supervision of municipal judges.

In order to confirm that the monarchs intended their will to prevail over the law, the royal chancery invoked the principle of royal absolute power. Beginning with King Juan II, royal writs granting permission to establish heritable trusts invariably justified royal abrogation of inheritance laws by using the phrases "by our own initiative, with full knowledge, and making use of our royal absolute power" (*propio motu, cierta sciencia, et poderio real absoluto*) (39.2). Here, the monarchs invoked the full formula of royal absolute power, permitting Columbus to circumvent the laws of inheritance. As usual in the *Book of Privileges,* when Fernando and Isabel invoked their royal absolute power to violate the law, the royal legal counsel, Dr. Rodrigo Maldonado de Talavera, withheld his approval. Maldonado did not even "approve in form"; he simply wrote "in form" and signed his name. Columbus wrote up a draft defining the principal he would place in the heritable trust and designating Diego as the first beneficiary. Columbus finished the draft in Seville on 22 February 1498, in the midst of his preparations for the third voyage. He listed the offices and revenues he had received as heritable property from the monarchs: the offices of admiral of the Ocean Sea and viceroy and governor of the islands and mainland he had discovered, with their salaries and revenues, the one-tenth of all movable property the monarchs acquired from there, and the right to invest one-eighth of the Indies commerce and receive one-eighth of its profits. At no time did Columbus mention how much the principal of the trust might be worth in cash. This was typical of the founding documents of heritable trusts; the capital assets were listed, but the income was expected to grow from year to year.

His statement of motive is of particular interest to Columbus scholars, because it is the only place in which the admiral describes himself as a native of Genoa: he establishes the trust to immortalize the services he performed for Their Highnesses because, although "born in Genoa, I came to serve them here in Castile" (Columbus 1984: 192). He submitted a copy of his draft to the monarchy, which issued the official deed of trust on 28 December 1501 (Altolaguirre 1926).

Columbus placed the usual restriction on this trust: the beneficiary could not touch the principal but had full use and possession of the income. Columbus also imposed some restrictions that later led to great confusion and litigation about the inheritance of the trust. He stipulated that any collateral male descendants would inherit the trust before direct female descendants could. This restriction was made necessary by the fact that the admiralty was a military office and, therefore, could not be exercised by a female, just as Queen Isabel could not exercise the office of master of a military order and granted these masterships to King Fernando. As a consequence of this stipulation, Columbus's female heirs in Spain at the end of the sixteenth century had to cooperate with the law courts in searching through Italy for any collateral male heirs—a search that predictably inspired a multitude of false claims and forged Columbus family genealogies. Columbus's attempt to perpetuate the family name by restricting the heritable trust to male heirs had a deleterious effect on the reputation of the Columbus family. By the end of the sixteenth century, the law courts, satisfied that there were no collateral male descendants in Italy, named Columbus's direct female descendants in Spain as the Columbus family heirs, but by then a great deal of misinformation about Columbus's ancestors and origins had been spread about. An erudite lawyer, Giulio Salinero, citizen of the city of Savona, where the Columbus family lived during the 1470s, copied notarial documents regarding Columbus and his family. We are very fortunate that he published these Latin documents, because just seventy years later the Genoa notarial archives burned in a fire set off when King Louis XIV's navy bombarded the city. Salinero's transcriptions of the notarial documents, plus a notarial document found and published by Ugo Assereto in 1904, still constitute today the entire corpus of documentary evidence of Columbus's family and youth (Raccolta 2.2, 1896).

With this trust Columbus exempted his royal offices and income from the laws of inheritance. Castilian inheritance law strictly required that all legitimate children must receive equitable shares of their parents' estate. The rule of primogeniture that prevailed in some parts of France and England did not exist in Spain. The modern misconception that many Spanish emigrants to the Americas were younger sons who had no chance to inherit is the product of two powerful strains in modern writing about Spanish colonial history: misreading of fifteenth-century law by false analogy with modern law, and a Victorian prudishness that did not permit authors to describe some of the conquerors as what they were, bastards and juvenile delinquents.

A standard reservation in royal permissions to establish heritable trusts stipulated that the trust could be revoked if the founder or any succeeding beneficiary were found guilty of heresy (39.5). This actually happened to the Columbus family trust: in the 1530s, the third admiral Luis Colón was found guilty of the heresy of bigamy. He was condemned to military service at a North African post, where he died. Before departing for Africa, Luis and the emperor Charles V negotiated a compromise settlement of the Columbus trust: Luis agreed to relinquish the royal offices of admiral, viceroy, and governor (thus effectively ending the heritable trust), in return for lordship (*señorío*) over Veragua (modern Central America), and the title duke of Veragua. The monarchy assumed responsibility for paying his heirs an annuity (Schoenrich 1949–1950).

INTRODUCTION TO CHAPTER 3.4: COLUMBUS
DISCOVERS NEW PRIVILEGES AS ADMIRAL

When Fernando and Isabel gave Columbus permission to make copies of the privileges of the high admiral of Castile, they gave him the key to an unsuspected treasury of wealth and power. When they had issued the Granada Capitulations, in which they promised to give him privileges equal to those of the admiral of Castile, they may not have been aware of how much of the admiral's vast wealth derived from his royal office: anchorage, lading, and sailing fees, taxes on maritime and riverine imports and exports, and one-third of royal maritime profits and privateering on the high seas.

Columbus learned of all this and more when he read the privileges that had been issued to the admirals of Castile by Castilian kings during the early fifteenth century. The admirals of Castile possessed judicial cognizance over all cases arising at sea, on navigable waters, in ports, or as a result of commerce in those places. They had the power to assess court fees, impose fines, and convict and execute sentences, including the death penalty. Furthermore, the admiralty of Castile had been granted to the founder of the Enríquez dynasty in 1405 as a hereditary office.

This permanent alienation of a royal office had been made during the reign of Isabel's grandfather, Enrique III, in circumstances so extraordinary that it had been necessary to demand the agreement of the aristocracy and church hierarchy, who endorsed the privilege by signing in a circle around the great seal. Every generation of admiral thereafter requested reconfirmation from succeeding monarchs.

These privileges of the admiralty of Castile probably inspired Columbus to make the copies of royal documents now known as the Veragua and Washington Codices in Seville in 1498 (*Pleitos* I.xvii). He began the collection with copies of the admiral of Castile's original grant and several later confirmations.

INTRODUCTION TO CHAPTER 3.5: FERNANDO AND
ISABEL CONFIRM THE CAPITULATIONS

Before leaving Burgos to organize his third voyage to the Americas, Columbus requested and received reconfirmation of the Santa Fe and Granada Capitulations. These repeated the originals (1 and 2) and the addenda that had been granted in Barcelona in 1493 (4 and 5). Now, the royal chancery expanded the legal justification for alienating a royal office (49, 50, and 51). In addition to the earlier arguments from natural law and religion, the new prefaces and appendixes invoked the royal absolute power. These documents were one more futile attempt by Fernando and Isabel to assure Columbus of the binding power of their extralegal grants to him in the Capitulations. All of these coveted grants and promises led Columbus to commission notaries to make copies in Seville in early 1498.

In order to carry out these instructions for colonization, Columbus began recruiting military and seamen in the area around Seville and sent public criers to Galicia,

Vizcaya, Burgos, Guadalajara, and Toledo to announce the offer of free land and citizenship. The largest contingent of recruits, however, came from Andalusia, recruited by Diego de Escobar in Jerez de la Frontera. Escobar paid and supplied twenty-eight men from Jerez, most of them farmers who enrolled on 4 February 1498.

The monarchs' carefully thought out plans for the colony began to fail even before embarkation. A comparison of his projected recruits in 1497 and the actual musters of the ships carrying the colonists in 1498 shows a serious shortage of colonists in all categories except the military:

Category	Projected 1497	Muster 1498
Military officers	40	20
Enlisted men	0	57
Able seamen	30	15
Ship's apprentices	30	6
Gold miners	20	1
Unskilled workmen	100	50
Artisans	20	18
Farmers and gardeners	60	28
Women	30	6

In the end, the fleet carried ten convicted murderers, of whom four were gypsies, as well as four of the admiral's servants, two clergy, an artilleryman, and a tambourine player. Two of the gypsies were women (Catalina de Egipcio and María de Egipcio), and two of the Castilian women who went as passengers are known to us: Catalina de Sevilla, wife of noncommissioned officer Pedro de Salamanca, and Gracia de Segovia, apparently single (Gil and Varela 1986: 3–20).

Columbus sent two caravels directly to La Española under the command of the fleet's marshal Pedro Fernández Coronel. These two ships carried a decidedly military group of passengers: eight noncommissioned officers, forty-seven enlisted men, six more men of unknown occupation but armed, and twelve farmers. The composition of the passenger list indicates that Columbus intended this contingent to make war on the Indians and enslave them to work in the mines.

Columbus departed from Seville on 30 May 1498, commanding three ships and following a southern route to find mainland China. He made landfall off Trinidad Island and a few days later off the coast of Venezuela. The crew and officers knew that this was not Asia, because the people were very similar in culture and society to those on La Española and very different from their expectations of China. There were no cities, no sailing ships, no money or metal tools. They knew that it was a continent, however, from the volume and force of river water pouring into the ocean at the delta of the Orinoco River. They understood that these rivers must drain a very large body of land.

This was probably the most disillusioning moment of Columbus's life. He was already physically ill and had to send someone else ashore to perform the ritual of taking possession in the name of Castile. Columbus consoled himself for this great disappointment by speculating that the continent, which he believed to lie south of India, was the source of the four great rivers of the Earthly Paradise. He then turned north to explore the coast of Central America, and proceeded to La Española without further delays. He arrived in Santo Domingo on 31 August 1498.

The ships of the third voyage that had gone directly to La Española to begin the process of colonization suffered even worse fortune. Their supplies had begun to spoil even before they reached La Española, and they found the island, which had been governed by Bartolomé Colón during the admiral's absence, in turmoil. Spaniards were scattering all over the island, looking for gold and food. More than one hundred had tried to establish their own Spanish settlement without the permission of Bartolomé and many more had "gone native" and refused to return to Spanish settlements. Columbus commissioned more copies of his privileges from the notary of the city of Santo Domingo before proceeding to carry out further explorations, leaving his brother once again to quell the mounting resistance to his governance.

Fernando and Isabel, as usual, received reports from returning ships about matters in the colony. By early 1500 they knew that drastic changes were necessary in the administration and provisioning of La Española. They appointed Francisco de Bobadilla as interim governor of the island, with the power to investigate and audit the administration of the Columbus brothers. Bobadilla arrived in the Americas in the fall of 1500. As his fleet entered Santo Domingo harbor, he could observe a horrifying sight—gallows hung with the bodies of executed Spaniards. Bobadilla arrested Columbus and his two brothers and sent them back to Spain on 1 October 1500. They arrived in Seville on 25 November 1500—after one of the longest Atlantic crossings in the Columbian years—and were immediately released on their own recognizance (Incháustegui 1964).

INTRODUCTION TO PART 4: THE FOURTH VOYAGE AND AFTER

The documents related to the fourth voyage differ significantly from the rest of the *Book of Privileges,* because most of them were not issued by the royal chancery. Columbus wrote some himself and commissioned others from lawyers in Granada and notaries in Seville. In contrast to the rest of the documents, these provide important and unique insights into the admiral's point of view. Heavily laden with self-pity and recriminations, the letters and petitions in this group have been widely cited to argue that hostility had always existed between Columbus and the Spanish court. The documents must be read with great care to avoid anachronism, however, because they are the products of Columbus's circumstances after returning from the third voyage.

Columbus and his brothers were arrested by the new governor, Francisco de Bobadilla, and sent back to Spain for the royal council and monarchs to dispose of the case. On the passage back from Santo Domingo, Columbus composed an open letter to a sympathetic person at the royal court, Antonio de Torres's sister Juana de la Torre (57). In this missive, which he distributed in several copies, he presented his own point of view on what had happened on La Española. The letter is one of the few places in which Columbus speaks openly about himself and his motives. He accuses the colonists of disobedience, charges Bobadilla with malicious lies, and implies that the monarchs have broken their promises.

Columbus was referring to the 1497 renegotiation of the Capitulations, by which he received only the one-tenth of the enterprise and whatever profits he made on his own investments for three years. He was lobbying for restitution of his authority, property, and reputation. The monarchs ended his arrest immediately, of course, but they did not reinstate Columbus in his offices. Instead, they abrogated the provision of the Capitulations that had made Columbus the only partner or agent of the monarchy in the enterprise of the Indies; conditions during the second voyage had demonstrated that Columbus and his suppliers could not provide enough merchandise and provisions to sustain a colony. Many more contractors were needed and they had to travel to the Indies on a regular, frequent schedule without waiting for the admiral to finish his explorations and return to lead the fleet.

Queen Isabel, exhausted by recent personal and political tragedies, spent over a year in residence in the city of Granada. Columbus moved to Granada and remained there throughout 1501. He solicited a legal opinion arguing that the Capitulations were a binding contract. His lawyer further argued that Columbus deserved an even greater share of the profits from the Indies than stipulated in the Capitulations, because in the Capitulations the monarchs had promised him privileges and prerogatives equal to those of the high admiral of Castile (58, 59, 60). But the monarchs did not reinstate him in his royal offices. On 3 September 1501, Fernando and Isabel appointed a man of unimpeachable integrity, Nicolás de Ovando (Lamb 1977), to replace Bobadilla as governor of La Española.

In late 1501 Fernando and Isabel relented on the financial terms of Columbus's case. They reinstated Columbus's privilege of investing one-eighth of the voyages to the Indies (62) and ordered the restitution of property that Bobadilla had confiscated from him and his brothers (61, 63). While Columbus continued his legal battle for reinstatement in office, he and his business agents were actively engaged in the enterprise of the Indies. Columbus could once again bestow on his business associates the privilege of doing business in the Indies—still a royal monopoly. Four Genoese merchants in Seville formed a partnership with Columbus, giving him a munificent cash advance for his expenses while in Granada and investing heavily in the fleet organized to carry Ovando to his new post. The Genoese provided the capital and the merchandise, which, it transpired, was mostly heavy wool cloth. When Ovando's fleet arrived in Santo Domingo on 15 April 1502, the royal agent there, Monroy, complained that the merchandise was unmarketable in the tropical climate.

In early 1502, Fernando and Isabel partially restored Columbus's authority as admiral. They instructed Columbus to make a fourth voyage, for exploration of Veragua (Central America) in search of a route to Asia (64). However, they did not restore his full privileges. They withheld from him any authority over the colonies already established and forbade him access to the island of La Española. Although the monarchs had revoked 12 in 1497, in September 1502, Fernando and Isabel contracted with two Spaniards to resupply the island of La Española, without involving Columbus in outfitting the fleet. Meanwhile, they promised, they would reevaluate the privileges of the admiralty of Castile as the model for the admiralty of the Ocean Sea. Columbus returned to Seville, where his fleet of three ships was being outfitted and provisioned. In early 1502, he commissioned copies of the most recent royal writs of restitution (61–63) and instructions for the fourth voyage (64).

Columbus took extraordinary measures to safeguard his privileges for future generations. In January 1502 he commissioned deluxe, parchment copies of the full set of documents, adding to the 1498 Veragua Codex the instructions for the fourth voyage, the royal orders for restitution and reinstatement, the royal permission to establish a heritable trust, the papal decree of demarcation (14) and royal writs for earlier voyages that he had not included in the 1498 redaction (3, 6, 7, 8, 9, 10, 11, 13, 15, 19, 21, 30, 32, 36, 37, 39). This full set of royal writs, warrants, and letters, together with his own additions produced in Granada, and the notarial certificates comprise the final version of *The Book of Privileges*. Columbus sent two bound and cased parchment copies to his friend in Genoa, Nicolò Oderigo, formerly Genoese ambassador to Spain. At the same time, he sought fame and recognition from his native city, asking the Bank of St. George to accept a donation for the purpose of reducing the government-fixed price of bread in the city (68). The city of Genoa acknowledged receipt of the two transcriptions, now Genoa Codex and Paris Codex. The letter from Genoa arrived in Seville after Columbus set sail on 11 May 1502 and was delivered to Diego.

When Columbus came into the harbor of Santo Domingo on 29 June 1502, the new viceroy and governor, Nicolás de Ovando, followed royal instructions to the letter and denied him anchorage. Ovando's predecessor Bobadilla departed Santo Domingo about the time of Columbus's arrival, on the ships that had brought Ovando. Bobadilla's fleet, carrying a year's accumulation of gold dust, gold nuggets, returning colonists and their native wives, and the profits of the Genoese, was destroyed by a hurricane in the Mona Passage. The only ship to survive and reach Spain safely was the vessel carrying Columbus's share of the gold.

Columbus rode out the storm in the lee of the island, then proceeded to Central America, searching for a route to Asia. He tried to establish a new trading post on the Central American coast, but the natives were so hostile that he was forced to abandon the site, leaving one ship stranded on a sand bar. Though he was able to rescue the crew, the two remaining ships got only as far as Jamaica before becoming totally unseaworthy. He blamed this on the quality of the construction, but today we know that wooden ships had a very short life in Caribbean waters—an average of six years—due to the ravages of the dreaded teredos mollusk, popularly known as the shipworm. Marooned on Jamaica for over a year, Columbus was rescued through the heroic efforts of his lieutenant Diego Méndez and a crew of native Jamaicans, who paddled two days and nights against the current from Jamaica to Cuba to summon help from Santo Domingo.

On 12 September 1504, Columbus returned to Seville broken physically but rich. His agent Alonso Sánchez de Carvajal had taken care of his gold and his accounts in Spain and Santo Domingo. His Genoese partners in Seville, headed by Franco Catanio, took most of the financial damage from the 1502 hurricane. Catanio spent the next ten years trying to clear the accounts of the partnership, as news trickled in about the loss of individuals, ships, and cargo. While his partners floundered in a sea of losses, Columbus was receiving regular shipments of his share of the gold and profits from the Indies.

Wealthy but disgruntled, Columbus was newly angry because at the beginning of 1504 the monarchs ended the royal monopoly and established free trade between Spain and the Indies. Columbus would still receive one-tenth of the royal profits, but his right to finance one-eighth of all voyages became null. Although he wanted to make his case directly to Queen Isabel, he was too ill to make the trip north before she died in November. All through the end of 1504 and early 1505, Columbus kept up a barrage of letters to his son Diego at Fernando's court in the northern city of Toro. Columbus ordered Diego to protest free trade as a violation of the Capitulations and instructed him to make copies of specific sections of the *Book of Privileges* as evidence for his arguments (Nader 1992).

By the time Columbus died in Valladolid, on 6 May 1506, Diego had already learned how to make use of the *Book of Privileges*. Throughout his life, Diego would commission copies as supporting evidence in his petitions to Fernando, to Fernando and Isabel's grandson and successor Charles V (Huntington Codex), and to the royal appeals court in the *Pleitos*.

TRANSLATION OF THE TEXTS

Helen Nader

PART 1

THE FIRST VOYAGE

CHAPTER 1

Creating the Enterprise of the Indies

1

Santa Fe Capitulations
Santa Fe, 17 April 1492
Confirmation
Barcelona, 28 March 1493

[1] The things requested and that Your Highnesses give and grant to Sir Christopher Columbus in partial reward for what he has discovered in the Ocean Seas[1] and will discover on the voyage that now, with the help of God, he is to make on the same seas in the service of Your Highnesses, are the following:

[2] First, Your Highnesses, as the lords you are of the Ocean Seas, appoint Sir Christopher Columbus from now on as your admiral on all those islands and mainland[2] discovered or acquired by his command and expertise in the Ocean Seas during his lifetime and, after his death, by his heirs and successors one after the other in perpetuity, with privileges and prerogatives equal to those that Sir Alfonso Enríquez, your high admiral of Castile, and his other predecessors in the office held in their districts.

[3] It pleases Their Highnesses. Juan de Coloma.[3]

[4] Also, Your Highnesses appoint Sir Christopher your viceroy and governor general in all those islands and any mainland and islands that he may discover and acquire in the seas. For the governance of each and every one of them, he will nominate three persons for each office, and Your Highnesses will select and appoint the one most beneficial to your service, and thus the lands that our Lord permits him to find and acquire will be best governed to the service of Your Highnesses.

[5] It pleases Their Highnesses. Juan de Coloma.

[6] You wish him to have and take for himself one-tenth of all and any merchandise, whether pearls, precious stones, gold, silver, spices, and any other things and merchandise of whatever kind, name, or sort it may be, that is bought, exchanged,

Queen Isabel of Castile. Anonymous painting. (The Royal Collection © 1993 Her Majesty Queen Elizabeth II)

King Fernando of Aragón. Anonymous painting. (The Royal Collection © 1993 Her Majesty Queen Elizabeth II)

found, acquired, and obtained within the limits of the admiralty that Your Highnesses from now on bestow on Sir Christopher, deducting all the relevant expenses incurred, so that, of what remains clear and free, he may take and keep one-tenth for himself and do with it as he pleases, reserving the other nine-tenths for Your Highnesses.

[7] It pleases Their Highnesses. Juan de Coloma.

[8] Should any lawsuits arise on account of the merchandise that he brings back from the islands and mainland acquired or discovered, or over merchandise taken in exchange from other merchants there in the place where this commerce and trade is held and done, and if taking cognizance of such suits belongs to him by virtue of the privileges pertaining to his office of admiral, may it please Your Highnesses that he or his deputy, and no other judge, shall be authorized to take cognizance of and give judgment on it from now on.

[9] It pleases Their Highnesses, if it pertains to the office of admiral and conforms to what the admiral Sir Alfonso Enríquez and his other predecessors had in their districts, and if it be just. Juan de Coloma.

[10] On all vessels outfitted for trade and business, each time, whenever, and as often as they are outfitted, Sir Christopher Columbus, if he wishes, may contribute and pay one-eighth of all that is spent on the outfitting and likewise he may have and take one-eighth of the profits that result from such outfitting.

[11] It pleases Their Highnesses. Juan de Coloma.

[12] These are authorized and dispatched with the replies from Your Highnesses at the end of each article. In the town of Santa Fe de La Vega de Granada, on the seventeenth day of April in the year of the birth of our savior Jesus Christ one thousand four hundred and ninety-two.

I, the King
I, the Queen

[13] By command of the king and queen. Juan de Coloma.
[14] Registered. Calcena.[4]

2
Granada Capitulations[5]
promising to confer on Columbus the offices of admiral, viceroy, and governor of
the islands and mainland he might discover and the title of sir
Granada, 30 April 1492

[1] Sir Fernando and Lady Isabel,[6] by the grace of God king and queen of Castile, León, Aragón, Sicily, Granada, Toledo, Valencia, Galicia, the Balearics, Seville, Sardinia, Córdoba, Corsica, Murcia, Jaén, the Algarve, Algeciras, Gibraltar and the Ca-

nary Islands, count and countess of Barcelona, lords of Vizcaya and Molina, dukes of Athens and Neopatria, counts of Roussillon and Cerdagne, marquises of Oristano and Goceano.[7]

Because you, Christopher Columbus, are going at our command with some of our ships and personnel to discover and acquire certain islands and mainland in the Ocean Sea, and it is hoped that, with the help of God, some of the islands and mainland in the Ocean Sea will be discovered and acquired by your command and expertise, it is just and reasonable that you should be remunerated for placing yourself in danger for our service.

Wanting to honor and bestow favor for these reasons, it is our grace and wish that you, Christopher Columbus, after having discovered and acquired these islands and mainland in the Ocean Sea, will be our admiral of the islands and mainland that you discover and acquire and will be our admiral, viceroy, and governor of them. You will be empowered from that time forward to call yourself Sir Christopher Columbus, and thus your sons and successors in this office and post may entitle themselves sir, admiral, viceroy, and governor of them.

You and your proxies will have the authority to exercise the office of admiral together with the offices of viceroy and governor of the islands and mainland that you discover and acquire. You will have the power to hear and dispose of all the lawsuits and cases, civil and criminal, related to the offices of admiral, viceroy, and governor, as you determine according to the law, and as the admirals of our kingdoms are accustomed to administer it. You and your proxies will have the power to punish and penalize delinquents as well as exercising the offices of admiral, viceroy, and governor in all matters pertaining to these offices. You will enjoy and benefit from the fees and salaries attached, belonging, and corresponding to these offices, just as our high admiral enjoys and is accustomed to them in the admiralty of our kingdoms.

[2] With this our writ or its transcript certified by a public clerk, we order Prince Sir Juan, our most dear and very beloved son, and the princes, dukes, prelates, marquises, counts, masters, priors, and commanders of the orders;[8] royal councillors, judges of our appellate court, and judges and any other justices of our household, court, and chancery;[9] subcommanders and commanders of our castles, forts, and buildings;[10] all municipal councils, royal judges, corregidores, municipal judges, sheriffs, appeals judges, councilmen, parish delegates, commissioned and noncommissioned officers, municipal officials, and voting citizens of all the cities, towns, and villages of these our kingdoms and domains and of those that you may conquer and acquire;[11] captains, masters, mates, warrant officers, sailors and ship's crews;[12] and each and every one of our subjects and citizens now and in the future,[13] that, having discovered and acquired any islands and mainland in the Ocean Sea, once you or your designated representative have performed the oath and formalities required in such cases, from then on you shall be accepted and regarded for the rest of your life, and your sons and successors after you forevermore, as our admiral of the Ocean Sea and viceroy and governor of the islands and mainland that you, Sir Christopher Columbus, discover and acquire.

Sepulcher of Prince Juan (1478–1497). Domenico Fancelli, late fifteenth century. Marble. Convent church of Santo Tomás, Avila. (Arxiu Mas)

[All these officials and people] shall put into effect everything pertaining to these offices, together with you and the proxies you appoint to the offices of admiral, viceroy, and governor. They shall pay and cause to be paid to you the salary, fees, and other perquisites of these offices. They shall observe and cause to be observed for you all the honors, gifts, favors, liberties, privileges, prerogatives, exemptions, immunities, and each and all of the other things that, by virtue of the offices of admiral, viceroy, and governor, you should receive and that should be paid to you fully and completely, in such a way that nothing will be withheld from you. They shall not place or consent to place hindrance or obstacle against you in any way.

[3] For with this writ we grant to you from now on the offices of admiral, viceroy, and governor as a hereditary right forevermore, and we grant you actual and prospective possession of them, as well as the authority to administer them and collect the dues and salaries attached and pertaining to each of them.

[4] If it should be necessary for you, and you should request it of them, we command our chancellor, notaries, and other officials who preside over the table with our seals to give, issue, forward, and seal our letter of privilege with the circle of signatures,[14] in the strongest, firmest, and most sufficient manner that you may request and find necessary. None of you or them shall do otherwise in any way concerning this, under penalty of our displeasure and a fine of 10,000 maravedís for our treasury on each person who does the contrary.

[5] Furthermore, we command the man who shows you this writ to summon you to appear before us in our court, wherever we may be, within fifteen days of having been cited, under the same penalty. Under this same penalty, we command every public clerk who may be summoned for this purpose to give the person showing this writ to him a certificate to that effect, inscribed with his rubric, so that we may know how well our command is obeyed.

[6] Given in our city of Granada on the thirtieth day of the month of April in the year of the birth of our Lord Jesus Christ one thousand four hundred and ninety-two.

I, the King

I, the Queen

[7] I, Juan de Coloma, secretary of the king and queen our lords, had this written at their command.

[8] Approved in form: Rodericus, doctor.[15]

[9] Registered: Sebastián de Olano.[16] Francisco de Madrid, chancellor.[17]

Letter from Fernando and Isabel inviting the admiral to the court at Barcelona
Barcelona, 30 March 1493

The King and the Queen

[1] Sir Christopher Columbus, our admiral of the Ocean Sea and viceroy and governor of the islands that have been discovered in the Indies. We have seen your letters and were very pleased to learn about what you wrote to us in them and also that God has given you such a good ending to your efforts, guiding you well in what you began, by which He and we will be well served, and our kingdoms will receive great benefit. May it please God that, besides serving Him in this, you will also receive because of it many favors from us that, rest assured, will be conferred on you as your services and labors merit.

[2] We wish you to continue and carry forward what you have begun, with the help of God, and thus desire that you return immediately, because it is to our service that you hurry your return as much as possible in order to supply everything needed on time.

[3] As you know, summer has begun and the season for the return trip already may be passing. Therefore, see if there is anything that can be procured in Seville or other places for your return to the land you have found. Write to us by way of this courier, who must return immediately, so that the necessary provisioning can be done while you are on the way here and back. Thus, everything will be ready by the time you leave.

[4] From Barcelona, on the thirtieth day of March, in the year ninety-three.

I, the King
I, the Queen

[5] By order of the king and queen. Fernán Alvarez.[18]

[6] and on the back it said: "By the king and queen, to Sir Christopher Columbus, their admiral of the Ocean Sea, viceroy and governor of the islands that have been discovered in the Indies."

4

Preface to 1493 confirmation of the Granada Capitulations
Barcelona, 23 May 1493

[1] In the name of the Holy Trinity and Eternal Unity, Father, Son, and Holy Spirit, three persons in one divine essence who lives and reigns forever without end,

and of the Most Blessed Virgin, glorious Saint Mary, our lady, His mother, whom we accept as sovereign and advocate in all our affairs; in honor and reverence to her, to the most blessed apostle, lord Saint James, light and mirror to all the lands of Spain, patron and guide to the kings of Castile and León, and to all the other saints of the entire celestial court. Although man cannot completely know what God is, however great his knowledge of the world may be, yet he can know Him by seeing and contemplating His wonders and the works and acts that He has done and does every day, since all works are done by His power, governed by His wisdom, and maintained by His goodness.

[2] And thus man can understand that God is the beginning, middle, and end of all things, and that in Him they are comprehended; and He maintains each one in that state which He has ordained for them, and all have need of Him and He has no need of them, and He is able to change them whenever He may choose, according to His will; and it is not in His nature to change or alter in any manner.

[3] He is called King over all kings, because from Him they derive their name and by Him they reign, and He governs and maintains them, who are His vicars, each one in his own kingdom, appointed by Him over the nations to maintain them in justice and worldly truth.

[4] This is fulfilled in two ways, one being spiritual, as the prophets and saints revealed, to whom our Lord gave the gift of knowing all things accurately and causing them to be understood. The other way is by nature, as was shown by the philosophers who were knowledgeable about things rationally.

[5] For the saints declared that the king is appointed on the earth in place of God to execute justice and give to each his due, and therefore he was known as the heart and soul of the people; and just as the soul is in man's heart, and by it the body lives and is maintained, so justice is in the king, which is the life and sustenance of the people under his dominion; and just as the heart is one, and all the other parts receive their unity from it in order to be a body, even so all those of the kingdom, no matter how many they may be, are one, because the king must be and is one, and therefore they must all be one with him in order to follow and help him in the things he has to do.

[6] The philosophers reasoned that kings are the head of the kingdom, because, as from the head proceed all the senses by which all parts of the body are commanded, just so by the commandment that proceeds from the king, who is lord and head of everyone in the kingdom, must all be commanded and guided, and obey it.

[7] So great is the authority of the power of kings, that all laws and rights are subject to their power, because they do not hold it from men but from God, whose place they supplant in temporal matters: to which, among other things, chiefly pertains to love, honor, and protect their peoples, and among others he should nobly single out and honor those who deserve it for the services they have rendered; and therefore the king or prince has, among other powers, not only the power but also the duty to confer favors on those who deserve them for the services they have rendered him and for the goodness that he finds in them.

[8] According to the philosophers, justice is among virtues appertaining to kings

and it is the virtue or truth of things by which the world is better and most righteously maintained; it is like a fountain from which all rights flow. Justice endures forever in the will of just men and, never failing, gives and apportions to each equally his right, and contains in itself all the principal virtues. From it proceeds very great utility, because it causes everyone according to his status to live in peace and harmony, without fault or error. The good are made better by it, receiving rewards for the good they did, and others are reformed and amended.

[9] This justice consists of two principal parts: the one being commutative, which is between one man and another, the other distributive, in which are obtained the rewards and remunerations for good and virtuous works and services that men perform for kings and princes or for the public welfare of their kingdoms.

[10] Because, as the laws declare, to give rewards to those who well and loyally serve is something that is very becoming to all men but especially to kings, princes, and great lords who have the power to do it, it is their particular privilege to honor and exalt those who serve them well and loyally, and whose virtues and services deserve it. In rewarding good deeds, kings show that they are discerners of virtue and likewise administrators of justice.

[11] For justice does not exist solely to correct the wicked but also to reward the good. Moreover, another great utility proceeds from it, because it encourages the good to be more virtuous and the wicked to reform themselves. If kings did not [reward the good], the contrary could happen.

[12] Because, among other rewards and remunerations that kings can give to those who well and loyally serve them, is the honor and exaltation of them above others of their lineage, and ennoblement, decoration, and honor of them, as well as the conferral on them of many other benefits, gifts, and favors. Therefore, considering and mindful of this, we desire, by this our charter of privilege or by its transcript certified by a public clerk, that all people from henceforth shall know that we, Sir Fernando and Lady Isabel, by the grace of God king and queen of Castile, León, Aragón, Sicily, Granada, Toledo, Valencia, Galicia, the Balearics, Seville, Sardinia, [Córdoba], Corsica, Murcia, Jaén, the Algarve, Algeciras, Gibraltar, and the Canary Islands, count and countess of Barcelona, lords of Biscay and Molina, dukes of Athens and Neopatria, counts of Roussillon and Cerdagne, marquises of Oristano and Goceano, have seen a writ of grant signed with our names and sealed with our seal, made in this manner:

[Here was inserted a new copy of 2, the Granada Capitulations.]

Appendix to 1493 Confirmation of the Capitulations
Barcelona, 28 May 1493

[1] Now, because it pleased our Lord that you should find many of those islands, and because we hope that with His help you may find and discover other islands and mainland in the Ocean Sea in the region of the Indies, and because you appealed and asked as a favor that we confirm for you our writ that is incorporated above and the grant contained in it, so that you, your sons, descendants, and successors, one after the other and after your days, will be empowered to hold the office of admiral, viceroy, and governor of the Ocean Sea, islands, and mainland that you have thus found and may discover from now on, with all those faculties, privileges, and prerogatives that the admirals, viceroys, and governors of our kingdoms of Castile and León, past and present, have enjoyed and enjoy; and so that you may be compensated by all the dues and salaries pertaining and belonging to these offices, as used by and paid to our admirals, viceroys, and governors, or that we should command provision be made for you in that regard according to our grant. [2] Mindful of the risk and danger in which you placed yourself for our service in going to seek and discover these islands, and that to which you will now subject yourself in going to seek and discover other islands and mainland, by which we have been and hope to be greatly served by you, and in order to confer benefit and favor on you, with this charter we confirm to you and to your sons, descendants, and successors, one after the other, now and forevermore, the offices of admiral of the Ocean, governor, and viceroy of the islands and mainland that you have found and discovered, and also of other islands and mainland that are found and discovered by you or by your expertise from this time forth in the region of the Indies.

[3] It is our wish and command that you and, after your days are ended, your sons, descendants, and successors, one after the other, shall have and hold the office of our admiral of the Ocean that is ours, which begins at a boundary or line that we have caused to be marked between the Azores and Cape Verde Islands from north to south, from pole to pole, in such a manner that all that is to the west of this line is ours and belongs to us.[19]

Therefore we make and create you, your sons, and successors, one after the other, our admiral of the islands and mainland discovered and to be discovered in the Ocean Sea in the region of the Indies. We give you actual and prospective possession of all the offices of admiral, viceroy, and governor forevermore, and the power and faculty to exercise the office of our admiral in all things at sea, in the form and manner and with the same prerogatives, privileges, rights, and salaries as our admirals of the seas of Castile and León exercised and exercise, enjoyed and enjoy.

[4] In order that colonists may be better governed on all the islands and mainland

that are and may be discovered from now on in the Ocean Sea of the region of the Indies, we give you such power and authority as to enable you, as our viceroy and governor, to exercise in person and through your proxies, judges, sheriffs, and other officials that you may appoint for that purpose, the legal jurisdiction, both civil and criminal, high and low, with authority to make and enforce the laws.

You can remove or withdraw these officials and appoint others in their places whenever you desire and see that it is to our service. They shall have the power to hear, despatch, and decide all suits and cases, civil and criminal, that may occur and be brought on the islands and mainland and to have and collect the fees and salaries customarily belonging and pertaining to those offices in our kingdoms of Castile and León. You, our viceroy and governor, shall have the power to hear and take cognizance of all and any of these cases that you desire, in first instance, on appeal, or in direct complaint, and to investigate, decide, and dispatch them as our viceroy and governor.

You and your officials shall have the power to make any investigations relevant to cases in law and in all other matters pertaining to the offices of viceroy and governor that you, your proxies, and the officials whom you may appoint for that purpose may perceive to be expedient for our service and for the execution of our justice.

[5] All of which you and your officials have the power to do, execute, and carry out to due and effective completion, just as these officials would and could do if they had been appointed by us. But it is our favor and wish that you cause these writs of appointment to be drafted, expedited, and dispatched under our name, saying "Sir Fernando and Lady Isabel, by the grace of God king and queen of Castile, León, etc.," and that these should be embossed with our seal, which we command be given to you for the islands and mainland.

[6] We command all citizens, residents, and other persons who are now and in the future may be on the islands and mainland to obey you as our viceroy and governor of them. Those who travel on the seas described above shall obey you as our admiral of the Ocean Sea. All of them shall comply with your writs and orders, and join with you and your officials to execute our justice, and shall give and cause to be given to you all the consideration and help that you ask of them and may need, under the penalties that you may impose; which penalties we, with this writ, impose and consider as imposed on them, and which we give you the power to execute on their persons and property.

[7] Likewise, if you consider it expedient for our service and for the execution of our justice that any persons should be required to leave, not enter, or not remain in the Indies [sic] and mainland, and that they should come and appear before us, it is our wish and command that you shall have the power to order it in our name and make them leave there. By this writ we command them to execute immediately and implement this without having recourse to or consulting us about it and without any other writ or order from us, notwithstanding any appeal or petition that they might make or initiate against your order.

[8] For all of these and any other things fitting and pertaining to the offices of our

admiral, viceroy, and governor, we give you full and complete power, with all its incidentals, dependencies, windfalls, appurtenances, and connections. If you so desire, we order our chancellor, notaries, and the other officials who preside over the table with our seals, to give, issue, pass, and seal for you our charter of privilege with the circle of signatures, as strongly, firmly, and sufficiently as they can and as you may need. None of you or they shall do otherwise in any way, under penalty of our displeasure and a fine of 10,000 maravedís for our treasury on each person who might do the contrary.

[9] Furthermore, we command the man to whom this our writ is shown as a summons to appear before us in our court, wherever we may be, within fifteen days of having been cited, under the same penalty. Under this same penalty we command every public clerk who may be summoned for this purpose to give the person showing this writ to him a certificate to that effect inscribed with his rubric, so that we may know how well our command is obeyed.

[10] Given in the city of Barcelona on the twenty-eighth day of the month of May in the year of the birth of our Lord Jesus Christ one thousand four hundred and ninety-three.

I, the King

I, the Queen

[11] I, Fernán Alvarez de Toledo, secretary of the king and queen our lords, caused these to be written at their command.

[12] Pedro Gutiérrez,[20] chancellor.

[13] Fees for seal and registry: none.

[14] On the back: "Approved, Rodericus doctor; Registered: Alfonso Pérez."[21]

PART 2

THE SECOND VOYAGE

CHAPTER 2.1

Fernando and Isabel Define Columbus's Authority and Jurisdiction

6

Warrant to the admiral and Juan Rodríguez de Fonseca to outfit the second voyage
Barcelona, 24 May 1493

[1] Sir Fernando and Lady Isabel, by the grace of God king and queen of Castile, León, Aragón, Sicily, Granada, Toledo, Valencia, Galicia, the Balearics, Seville, Sardinia, Córdoba, Corsica, Murcia, Jaén, the Algarve, Algeciras, Gibraltar, the Canary Islands, count and countess of Barcelona, lords of Vizcaya and Molina, dukes of Athens and Neopatria, counts of Roussillon and Cerdagne, marquises of Oristano and Goceano.

To you, Sir Christopher Columbus, our admiral of our islands and mainland that by our order have been and will be discovered in the Ocean Sea in the region of the Indies, and to you, Sir Juan de Fonseca,[1] archdeacon of Seville and member of our council, greetings.

[2] You are informed that we have decided to order a fleet of several ships formed and sent to the Indies, both to secure jurisdiction over these islands and mainland, of which possession has been taken in our name, and to discover others. In order to form this fleet, outfit it with equipment and stores, and provision it with all things needed and appropriate, we will appoint and delegate persons necessary to be responsible for it and get it started.

Trusting that you will protect our best interests by doing well, faithfully, and diligently what we order you to do, we command that this our warrant be given to you for this purpose.

By this warrant we order that you go to the cities of Seville and Cádiz, and any other cities, towns, villages, and seaports of their respective archdiocese and diocese that you consider appropriate, and cause to be leased and bought, and you yourself may buy and lease, any ships, cargo carriers, caravels, and vessels that you think will suffice and are appropriate for this fleet, from any person or persons. If you are not able to

Bishop Juan Rodríguez de Fonseca, donor of the painting, kneels at the left hand of Our Lady of Compassion. Flemish school, about 1505. Palencia Cathedral. (Javier y Tomás Foto)

obtain them in this way, seize them, even though they are leased to other persons, with as little damage as possible.

[3] We order the owners to give, transfer, sell, or lease these cargo carriers, ships, vessels, and caravels to you, for which you will pay them the price at which they were bought or leased for you, according to the contracts and agreements they make or negotiate with you. Once these cargo carriers, ships, caravels, and vessels have been bought and leased, you can outfit, equip, and supply them with arms and munitions, also provisioning them with weapons, ammunition, supplies, and cannons; soldiers and seamen, sails and rigging,[2] and any masters of trades that are necessary whom you see and believe are competent.

[4] You may take ships from any places, vessels wherever you find them, paying their owners the reasonable prices they should expect to receive for them. Likewise, you may compel and oblige any masters of any trade that are deemed necessary for going on this fleet to do so. They will be paid the reasonable wages and salary that they ought to have.

So that you can issue any guarantees in our name that are both appropriate and necessary for the purpose of all that has been described, and [5] so that you can make good on all the guarantees, penalties, imprisonments, executions, auctions, and sales of goods that are suitable and necessary, with all their incidentals, dependencies, attachments, and appurtenances, we give you full power by this our warrant.

It is our wish and command that a description and account of all this be kept so that, when we wish to send for it, it may be entered in our books kept by our chief accountants. Anything relating to this fleet shall be done and approved by Juan de Soria, secretary of Prince Sir Juan, our most dear and very beloved son, who will go as our deputy chief accountant, and by his authority and in no other manner.

[6] It is our wish and command that everything relating to the purchase of arms, munitions, provisions, and other things; the leasing of ships; and other expenses of this fleet, shall be done and approved by our clerk's deputy, whom we now appoint for this fleet, together with Juan de Soria, deputy of our chief accountants. Likewise, so that there shall be no fraud or deception in the wages paid to the personnel who go in this fleet, it is our desire that the muster and appointments of these personnel be made in the presence of our clerk's deputy, and that by his warrant, signed with his name, the admiral and Sir Juan de Fonseca shall authorize the payment of all that has been described. This deputy of our chief accountants shall sign these vouchers because he is responsible for their records and accounts. Whoever has to make a payment shall not pay anything without a warrant or pay voucher from the admiral and Sir Juan de Fonseca, signed by this deputy chief accountant.

[7] Should it be necessary for you to have preferment and aid in order to do, carry out, and implement all or any part of this, with this our warrant we command any municipal councils, royal judges and governors, municipal judges, sheriffs, councilmen, commissioned and noncommissioned officers, masters of trades, and voting citizens; masters of ships and vessels; and any other persons required by this, to give

preferment and aid to you well and fully, and not to obstruct or oppose you in any way, under pain of our displeasure, loss of their offices, and confiscation of all their property for each person who does the contrary.

[8] Furthermore, we command the man who shows you this warrant to summon you to appear before us in our court, wherever we may be, within fifteen days of having been cited, under the same penalty. Under this same penalty, we command any public clerk summoned for this purpose to give the man who shows this warrant to you a certificate to that effect inscribed with your rubric, so that we may know how well our command is obeyed.

[9] Given in the city of Barcelona on the twenty-fourth day of the month of May in the year of the birth of our Lord Jesus Christ one thousand four hundred ninety-three.

I, the King
I, the Queen

[10] I, Fernán Alvarez de Toledo, secretary of the king and queen our lords, had this written by their order.

[11] And on the back it said: "Registered in form. Rodericus, doctor; Pedro Gutiérrez, chancellor; and sealed."

7

Writ ordering captains and mariners to obey the admiral as captain general

Barcelona, 28 May 1493

[1] Sir Fernando and Lady Isabel, by the grace of God king and queen of Castile, León, Aragón, Sicily, Granada, Toledo, Valencia, Galicia, the Balearics, Seville, Sardinia, Córdoba, Corsica, Murcia, Jaén, the Algarve, Algeciras, Gibraltar, the Canary Islands, count and countess of Barcelona, lords of Vizcaya and Molina, dukes of Athens and Neopatria, counts of Roussillon and Cerdagne, marquises of Oristano and Goceano.

To all and any captains, masters, owners, boatswains, and seamen of cargo carriers, caravels, and other vessels; and to any other persons of whatever status, be they our vassals,[3] subjects,[4] or citizens,[5] to whom the contents of this letter pertain or could pertain, and every one of you to whom this writ or its transcript certified by a public clerk may be exhibited, greetings.

[2] You are informed that we have ordered Sir Christopher Columbus, our admiral of the Ocean Sea and our viceroy and governor of the islands and mainland of that Ocean Sea in the region of the Indies, to go as our captain with some cargo carriers, caravels, and other vessels to the islands and mainland that are in that region of the Indies discovered and to be discovered.

[3] For that purpose, with this writ we order all and each of you masters, captains, owners, boatswains, and crews of these ships, caravels, and other ships and all the crews that may sail on them, to accept and regard Sir Christopher Columbus, our admiral, viceroy, and governor of the Ocean Sea, as our captain general of these ships, vessels, and caravels. You shall obey and accept him as our captain general, and do, carry out, and put into effect all and every part of what he orders and commands you to do on our behalf, in the manner, as soon as, and with the same punishments that he orders on our behalf, without making any excuse or delay, as well and fully as if we personally had ordered you to do it; because with this writ we make him our captain general of these ships, caravels, and other vessels, and give him power and authority to order and govern as our captain general and to execute on their crews any punishments that they may receive and incur for not carrying out and obeying his orders.

[4] It is our wish and command, however, that neither our captain general, Sir Christopher Columbus, our admiral, viceroy, and governor, or any of you should go to the mine[6] nor engage in the trade that the most serene king of Portugal, our brother,[7] has with it. Our desire is to observe and have our vassals, subjects, and citizens observe what we have negotiated and agreed[8] to with the king of Portugal about the mine. We order you to implement this, under penalty of confiscation of your property for our treasury.

[5] Given in the city of Barcelona on the twenty-eighth day of the month of May in the year of the birth of our Lord Jesus Christ one thousand four hundred ninety-three.

I, the King

I, the Queen

[6] I, Fernán Alvarez de Toledo, secretary of the king and queen our lords, had this written at their order.

[7] And on the back of the writ was written this: "Agreed: Rodericus, doctor. Registered: Alfonso Pérez; Pedro Gutiérrez, chancellor."

8

Authority to the person whom Columbus appoints to act in his absence to grant decrees and charters, embossing them with the royal seal
Barcelona, 28 May 1493

The King and the Queen

[1] By virtue of the power that we ordered given and give to you, Sir Christopher Columbus, our admiral of the islands and mainland that have been and will be discovered in the Ocean Sea in the region of the Indies, and our viceroy and governor of

those islands and mainland, you may have to issue writs and decrees that will have to be written and expedited in the islands and mainland in our name in the form "Sir Fernando and Lady Isabel, etc." These shall be embossed with our seal, which we command you to take for this purpose.

It could happen that you might not be on the islands and mainland because it is proper for you to discover other islands or mainland or do other things for our service. Consequently you would have to leave a proxy to administer and provide for the matters of the islands and mainland in your absence, which he cannot administer. Neither is he empowered to issue writs and decrees in our name, without first having our authority to that effect.

For this reason, by this writ we give authority to the person whom you designate to remain on the islands and mainland in your absence, so that he may issue and expedite any business and cases that come up, giving writs and decrees in our name and embossing them with our seal, as you would do if you were present in the islands and mainland, by virtue of our powers that you have.

[2] We order all this granted by this writ signed with our names.

[3] Done in Barcelona on the twenty-eighth day of May in the year ninety-three.

I, the King
I, the Queen

[4] By order of the king and queen. Fernán Alvarez.

[5] And on the back it said: "Agreed."

9
Writ giving to the admiral the sole right of appointing his officers
Barcelona, 28 May 1493

The King and the Queen

[1] The contract that we ordered made with you, Sir Christopher Columbus, our admiral of the Ocean Sea and our viceroy and governor of the islands and mainland of the Ocean Sea that are in the region of the Indies, stipulates among other things that you may nominate three persons for each governmental office necessary on those islands and mainland, and we will choose and appoint one of them to the office.[9]

Because this contract cannot be observed due to the imminence of your departure for the islands, however, we trust that you, our admiral, viceroy, and governor, will make these appointments in a trustworthy manner, in our best interests, and for the good government of the islands. Therefore, by this writ we give you power and authority to fill the governmental offices on the islands and mainland with such persons, for such period, and in such form and manner as seems best to you, for as long as it is our wish and command.

To those whom you appoint, we give power and authority to occupy their offices, according to and in the form and manner that will be described in the commissions that you will issue for those offices.

[2] Done in the city of Barcelona on the twenty-eighth day of May in the year one thousand four hundred ninety-three.

I, the King
I, the Queen

[3] By order of the king and queen. Fernán Alvarez.

[4] Agreed.

CHAPTER 2.2

Fernando and Isabel Adjust to the Reality of the Americas

10

Letter from Fernando and Isabel in reply to the admiral's letters delivered by
Antonio de Torres
Medina del Campo, 13 April 1494

The King and the Queen

[1] Sir Christopher Columbus, our admiral of the Ocean Sea and our viceroy and governor of the islands newly found in the region of the Indies.

We have seen the letters that you sent us with Antonio de Torres,[10] which gave us much pleasure, and we give many thanks to our Lord God who has done so much good by having guided you in everything.

[2] We deeply appreciate and regard as a great service what you have done and accomplished there with such good order and planning that it could not have been done better. And also we have listened to Antonio de Torres and received all that you sent us with him. We would not have expected anything less from you, considering the goodwill and affection that have been and continue to be demonstrated by you in matters of our service.

[3] You can be certain that we consider ourselves well served by you and obliged to confer on you favors, honor, and wealth as your great services require and obligate.

Because Antonio de Torres was delayed in arriving until now, and we had not seen your letters, which for security reasons he brought with him [instead of sending them ahead], and because of haste for the departure of these ships that are now leaving, to which, as soon as we were informed of it here, we ordered dispatched under guard all the things that you mentioned in your report from there, as completely as could possibly be done without delaying [the ships]. The same will be done and executed along with everything else that he brought to be done, when and as he says. There is not time to respond to you as we wish, but, when he [Torres] goes, God willing, we will respond to you and order the provisioning of all that is necessary.

[4] We have been angered by the things done against your wishes there [in the Indies], which we now order corrected and punished.

[5] On the next voyage from there, send back Bernal de Pisa,[11] whom we have written ordering him to prepare for immediate departure. The person whom you and Friar Buyl[12] designate to replace [Bernal de Pisa] should understand that the appointment is only until someone is commissioned here, since, due to the imminence of the ships' departure, it was not possible to appoint someone for this now, but on the next voyage, God willing, a person appropriate for the job will be appointed.

[6] From Medina del Campo, on the thirteenth of April, ninety-four.

I, the King
I, the Queen

[7] By order of the king and queen. Juan de la Parra.[13]

[8] And on the back it said: "By the king and queen, to Sir Christopher Columbus, their admiral of the Ocean Sea and their viceroy and governor of the islands newly found in the region of the Indies."

11

Mandate ordering the people in the Indies to obey the admiral as
viceroy and governor
Segovia, 16 August 1494

[1] Sir Fernando and Lady Isabel, by the grace of God king and queen of Castile, León, Aragón, Sicily, Granada, Toledo, Valencia, Galicia, the Balearics, Seville, Sardinia, Córdoba, Corsica, Murcia, Jaén, the Algarve, Algeciras, Gibraltar, the Canary Islands, counts of Barcelona, lords of Vizcaya and Molina, dukes of Athens and Neopatria, counts of Roussillon and Cerdagne, marquises of Oristano and Goceano. To each and all of you, the commissioned and noncommissioned officers, officials, voting citizens, and any other persons of whatever status or condition you may be, who by our order have gone, are going, and will go from now on to the islands discovered by our command and still to be discovered in the Ocean Sea in the region of the Indies, greetings.

[2] You know that Sir Christopher Columbus, our admiral of the Indies in the Ocean Sea, is our viceroy and governor of them by virtue of our letters of appointment that we gave him. Because it is our will and command that the admiral should have the post of viceroy and governor to occupy and exercise in the islands, and that everyone should obey and implement all that he orders on our behalf and believes to be in our service, we order all of you to carry out, execute [his orders], and cooperate with him, doing and carrying out all that he orders you to do on our behalf. Do this as if we commanded it in person, under pain of whatever penalties he imposes or orders imposed in our name, which we impose and consider imposed with this our writ.

In order for him to carry out these penalties against anyone who does the contrary, we give full power to the admiral, Sir Christopher Columbus, or to his proxy, so that no one shall do otherwise in any way, under pain of our displeasure and a fine of 10,000 maravedís for our treasury from everyone who does the contrary.

[3] Done in the city of Segovia on the sixteenth day of the month of August, in the year of the birth of our Lord Jesus Christ one thousand four hundred ninety-four.

I, the King

I, the Queen

[4] I, Fernán Alvarez de Toledo, secretary of the king and queen our lords, had this written by their order.

[5] And on the back of the letter was written: "Registered: Alfonso Pérez; Pedro Gutiérrez, chancellor."

12

Permission for other persons to make voyages of discovery and for Spanish settlers to colonize the island of La Española

Madrid, 10 April 1495

[1] Sir Fernando and Lady Isabel, by the grace of God king and queen of Castile, León, Aragón, Sicily, Granada, Toledo, Valencia, Galicia, the Balearics, Seville, Sardinia, Córdoba, Corsica, Murcia, Jaén, the Algarve, Algeciras, Gibraltar, and the Canary Islands, count and countess of Barcelona, lords of Vizcaya and Molina, dukes of Athens and Neopatria, counts of Roussillon and Cerdagne, marquises of Oristano and Goceano.

At the time that Sir Christopher Columbus, our admiral of the Ocean Sea, went by our command to discover land in the Ocean Sea, a contract was made with him. Later, when the first voyage returned, by the grace and help of God our Lord, from having discovered and explored the Indies and mainland, we confirmed and approved the contract and agreement that we had drawn up with him, giving him certain privileges and grants stipulated in that contract and in other letters and privileges. Now, Sir Christopher, our admiral of the Ocean Sea, has reported to us that we should issue a writ stipulating the following terms:

Sir Fernando and Lady Isabel, by the grace of God king and queen of Castile, León, Aragón, Sicily, Granada, Toledo, Valencia, Galicia, the Balearics, Seville, Sardinia, Córdoba, Corsica, Murcia, Jaén, the Algarve, Algeciras, Gibraltar, and the Canary Islands, count and countess of Barcelona, lords of Vizcaya and Molina, dukes of Athens and Neopatria, counts of Roussillon and Cerdagne, marquises of Oristano and Goceano.

We have been informed that certain persons who are citizens and residents of various cities, towns, villages, and ports of our kingdoms and dominions, our subjects and citizens, wish to go and discover more islands and continents in the region of the Indies in addition to the islands and continent that have already been discovered by our command in that part of the Ocean Sea. Likewise others want to go and live and reside on the island of La Española, which has already been discovered and found by our command, if we would give them permission to do so and help maintain them for a certain time. But they have not done so because of the prohibition we placed on anyone going to the Indies except with our permission and command, under certain penalties. In view of all this, we believe that it would be a service to God our Lord if they discovered lands and islands and traded on them, and if we allowed them to settle on the already discovered island of La Española, because through contact with them the inhabitants of those lands could become aware of God our Lord and be brought to our holy Catholic faith.

Also, for our service and for the benefit and welfare of our kingdoms and dominions and of our subjects and citizens, we agree to order that permission be given and by this letter do give and concede permission to our subjects and citizens so that they may go to those islands and continent and discover and trade on them, under the following conditions and according to the following provisions and stipulations:

[2] First, all the ships going to the region of those islands in any manner described in this our letter must depart from the city of Cádiz and not from any other place. Before leaving, they must appear before our appointed officials or representatives there, so that those going to the Indies can be known. They must implement and observe in all instances what is stated in this our charter.

[3] Any persons wishing to go live and reside on the island of La Española without being on our payroll can go and come freely. There they will be free and tax-exempt, paying no dues at all. They and their heirs and successors shall possess as their own property the houses they build, the land they plow, and the fields they plant there on the island, where they will be apportioned land and sites for this purpose by the persons whom we will appoint to do this. The persons who live and reside on the island of La Española in this way, without receiving a salary from us, shall be given maintenance for one year.

[4] Furthermore, we desire and it is our favor that anyone going to the island of La Española with the permission of our officials authorized for this purpose may keep for themselves one-third of any gold they find and acquire on the island, provided it is not by barter. The other two-thirds shall be ours and must be brought to our official on the island.

[5] In addition to this, those going with permission may keep for themselves all the merchandise and any other things they find on the island, giving us or our delegated official one-tenth of it, except for gold, of which they must give us two-thirds. All transactions on the island of La Española must be carried out in the presence of our officials, paying to our agent there two-thirds of the gold and one-tenth of everything else they acquire.

[6] From now on, for as long as it is our will and pleasure, any of our subjects or citizens who wish to do so can go to discover islands and continents in the vicinity of the Indies and to trade on those already discovered and any others except the island of La Española. They can buy from the Christians [on La Española] any property and merchandise except gold.

[7] They can and may do this with any ships they want, as long as they leave our kingdoms from the city of Cádiz and present themselves to our officials there because they must allow on board each ship one or two persons from there who shall be appointed by our officials, before whom they must present themselves. Moreover they must carry our cargo free of charge, up to one-tenth of their carrying capacity. Our cargo shall be unloaded on the island of La Española and turned over to the person or persons whom we have commanded to receive what is sent and take charge of it.

[8] We desire and it is our pleasure that these people may keep nine-tenths of whatever they find on the islands and continent, while the remaining one-tenth shall be ours. This they must render to us at the time they return to our kingdoms, in the city of Cádiz, where they must put in first and pay it to the person in charge of receiving it for us. After paying, they can go home or wherever they choose with what they have brought back. Before leaving the city of Cádiz, they must guarantee that they will comply accordingly.

[9] Any persons wishing to take provisions for the island of La Española or any other islands in the Indies that may be settled by our command can transport and sell them freely at prices they negotiate with the buyers there, who will pay them either in merchandise or in whatever else they may have there. If they sell all or part of these supplies to our officials there for provisioning our employees there, the officials must pay them there or else give them vouchers for payment to be made here.

[10] We guarantee that with these vouchers they will be paid, provided that the ships carrying the provisions had left from the city of Cádiz, presented themselves to our officials, and without charge carried the cargo we sent to the island up to one-tenth of their carrying weight. They are obliged to pay us one-tenth of what they brought back from there, having been traded according to the stipulated terms and, on their return, they must come to the city of Cádiz to pay it.

[11] Also, because we have granted to Sir Christopher Columbus, our admiral of the Indies, the right to invest in one-eighth of the cargo of all ships going to the Indies, it is our will that, for every seven ships going to the Indies, the admiral or his representative may load one for the purpose of trade.

[12] We order that all and every part of this writ shall be enforced and observed in its entirety. In order to make it known to all, we order that it be announced publicly in the plazas, markets, and other usual places in the cities, towns, villages, and ports of Andalusia and other suitable parts of our kingdoms, and that a transcript of this writ shall be given to any persons who wish it.

[13] We order given and do give this our writ, signed with our names and embossed with our seal.

[14] Given in the town of Madrid on the tenth day of the month of April in the year of the birth of our Savior Jesus Christ one thousand four hundred ninety-five.

I, the King

I, the Queen

[15] I, Fernán Alvarez de Toledo, secretary of the king and queen, our lords, had this written by their command.

[16] Agreed: Rodericus, doctor.

[17] Registered: Doctor; Francisco Díaz, chancellor.[14]

CHAPTER 2.3

Dividing the Ocean Sea

13

Letter from Queen Isabel sending the admiral a transcript of his log book and
inquiring about a sailing chart she had asked him to prepare
Barcelona, 5 September 1493

The queen

[1] Sir Christopher Columbus, my admiral of the Ocean Sea, viceroy and governor
of the islands newly found in the Indies. With this courier I am sending you a transcript
of the book that you left here. The transcript is behind schedule because it had to be
written secretly, so that neither those who are here from Portugal nor any others
should find out about it. For this reason and so that it could be done more quickly, it
is in two handwritings, as you will see.

[2] Certainly, according to what has been discussed and seen here, every day this
business is recognized to be of great quality and importance. You have served us well
in this, and we are greatly indebted to you. Therefore we trust in God that, besides
what has been agreed with you about what has to be done and implemented fully, you
should receive from us increasing honor, favor, and wealth, as is reasonable and as your
services and merit deserve.

[3] Right away send me the navigation chart that you were supposed to make, if it
is finished, and for my service speed your departure so that, with the grace of our Lord
it may take place without any delay, for you know how crucial it is to the success of the
business. Write and inform us about everything there, and we will advise and inform
you of everything here that is necessary.

[4] No agreement has been made in the business of Portugal with those who are
here. Although I believe that the king will reach an agreement in it, I'd like you to
think the contrary so that you would not fail or cease to take the proper precautions,
and so that you would not be deceived in any way.[15]

[5] From Barcelona, on the fifth day of the month of September in the year ninety-three.

I, the Queen

[6] By order of the queen. Juan de La Parra.

[7] And on the back it said: "By the queen, to Sir Christopher Columbus, her admiral of the Ocean Sea and viceroy and governor of the islands newly found in the Indies."

14

Papal decree granting Castile sovereignty over the Indies

Rome, June 1493

[1] In the name of God, amen. This is a transcript well and faithfully copied from a document written on parchment in the Latin language, embossed with a red wax seal, placed in a wooden box, tied with a green silk ribbon, and apparently certified and signed by a certain papal notary, the content of which, word for word, is as follows.

[2] Pedro Garcias,[16] by the grace of God and the apostolic see bishop of Barcelona, royal judge and councillor. To each and everyone who sees, reads, and hears this public document, eternal health in the Lord and prosperous success.

[3] By these [letters] we inform you and whoever of you there may be that we had in our hands, held, felt, viewed, and diligently inspected the apostolic letters of the most holy father in Christ and of our Lord, Alexander the Sixth,[17] by divine providence pope, with his genuine leaden bull hanging from it by red and saffron colored silk ribbons in the custom of the Roman court. [We inform you] that they are indeed whole and entire, not corrupted, crossed out, or in any part suspect but free of every kind of suspicion, as they appeared, whose contents and tenor follow word for word.

[4] Alexander, bishop, servant of the servants of God, to the illustrious sovereigns, our very dear son in Christ, Fernando, and to our very dear daughter in Christ, Isabel, the king and queen of Castile, León, Aragón, Sicily, and Granada, greetings and apostolic benediction.

[5] Among other works well pleasing to the Divine Majesty and dear to our heart, this assuredly ranks highest, that in our times especially the Catholic faith and the Christian religion be exalted and everywhere increased and spread, that the health of souls be cared for, and that barbarous nations be overthrown and brought to the true faith. Since we have been called to this holy chair of Peter by the favor of divine clemency, although of unequal merits, recognize that, as true Catholic kings and princes, such as we have known you always to be, and as your illustrious deeds now known to nearly the whole world declare, you not only eagerly desire but with every

Pope Alexander VI. Il Pinturicchio. Fresco in the Borgia Apartments, Vatican Museum. (Art Resource)

effort, zeal, and diligence are laboring to that same end, disregarding hardship, expense, danger, and even the shedding of your blood. We also recognize that you have long dedicated to this purpose your whole will and all your endeavors—as witnessed in these times with so much glory to the Divine Name by your recovery of the Kingdom of Granada from the tyranny of the Saracens. We therefore are rightly persuaded and consider it our duty, of our own accord and applauded by others, to grant you those things by which, with daily effort, you may be more heartily enabled to carry forward your holy and praiseworthy purpose pleasing to immortal God, for the honor of God himself and the spread of the Christian rule.

[6] Indeed, we have learned that for a long time you had intended to seek out and discover certain islands and continents, remote, unknown, and not hitherto discovered by others, so that you might bring their residents and inhabitants to the worship of our Redeemer and the profession of the Catholic faith. Having been up to the present time engaged in the siege and recovery of the Kingdom of Granada, you were unable to accomplish this holy and praiseworthy purpose. But finally, as was pleasing to the Lord, the kingdom having at last been regained, you wish to fulfill your desire. You chose our beloved son, Christopher Columbus,[18] a man assuredly worthy and of the highest recommendations and qualified for so great an undertaking. You furnished him with ships and men equipped for that purpose, not without the greatest hardship, danger, and expense, to make diligent quest for those remote and unknown continents and islands, through the sea where hitherto no one had sailed.

[7] They at length, with divine aid and with the utmost diligence sailing in the sea, discovered certain very remote islands and even continents that hitherto had not been discovered by others. A great many peoples reside there, living in peace, and, it is reported, going unclothed, and not eating meat. Moreover, as your envoys think that these same peoples living on those islands and mainland believe there to be one God, the Creator in heaven, and seem sufficiently disposed to embrace the Catholic faith and be trained in good morals, it is hoped that, were they instructed, the name of the Savior, our Lord Jesus Christ, would easily be introduced to these continents and islands.[19]

[8] To that end, on one of the principal islands, Christopher has already caused a well equipped fortress to be established and built. There he has stationed some Christians who came with him as a garrison and to search for other remote and unknown islands and continents. Gold, spices, and a great many other precious things of various kinds and qualities are found on the islands and mainland already discovered.

Therefore, after earnest consideration of all matters, especially the exaltation and propagation of the Catholic faith, as becomes Catholic kings and princes in the manner of your kings of shining memory, you have endeavored with the favor of divine clemency to make subject these continents and islands, their residents and inhabitants, and to bring them to the Catholic faith.

[9] Fully commending to the Lord this your holy and praiseworthy purpose, we desire that it be duly accomplished and that the name of our Savior be carried into

those regions. We most earnestly exhort you in the Lord and by your reception of holy baptism, which binds you to the apostolic commands, and by the bowels of the mercy of our Lord Jesus Christ, strictly enjoining that, since with eager zeal for the true faith you plan to equip and dispatch fully this expedition, your purpose and duty are to lead the peoples dwelling in those islands and countries to embrace the Christian religion. At no time let either dangers or hardships deter you from this, with the stout hope and trust in your hearts that Almighty God will further your undertakings.

[10] In order for you to undertake such a great project with more freedom and boldness by being endowed with our apostolic favor, of our own accord and not at your initiative or at the request of anyone to us on your behalf, but from our own pure liberty and certain knowledge, and from the plenitude of our apostolic power, the authority of Almighty God conferred on us in blessed Peter and the vicarship of Jesus Christ, which we hold on earth, by these decrees we give, grant, and assign forever to you, your heirs, and successors, the monarchs of Castile and León, all islands and continents found and to be found, discovered and to be discovered toward the west and south of a line to be drawn from the Arctic pole, namely the north, to the Antarctic pole, namely the south, whether these continents and islands to be found are in the direction of India or toward anywhere else, found by your envoys and captains, together with all their dominions, cities, forts, towns, and villages, and all rights, jurisdictions, and appurtenances. This line is to be distant by one hundred leagues west and south from whatever of the islands that are called in Spanish "the Azores and Cape Verde" or any territory that was in the effective possession of any Christian king or prince before the Christmas just past, from which the present year one thousand four hundred and ninety-three begins.[20]

We make, appoint, and invest you, your heirs, and successors as lords of them with full and free power, authority, and jurisdiction of every kind, with this proviso however, that by this our gift, grant, and assignment rights acquired by any Christian prince in effective possession of those islands and mainlands prior to this past birthday of our Lord Jesus Christ, are not understood to be withdrawn or taken away.[21]

[11] Moreover we command you, in virtue of holy obedience, to employ all due diligence, just as we also promise. We do not doubt that for the sake of your utmost devotion and royal greatness of soul you will appoint worthy, God-fearing, learned, skilled, and experienced men to these continents and islands to instruct their inhabitants and residents in the Catholic faith and train them in good morals.

Furthermore, under penalty of automatic excommunication[22] to be incurred by the very nature of the deed itself should anyone contravene this, we strictly forbid all persons of whatsoever rank, even imperial and royal, or of whatsoever estate, level, order, or condition, to go for the purpose of commerce or any other reason to the islands or continents, found and to be found, discovered and to be discovered, west and south of a line from the Arctic pole to the Antarctic pole, without the special permission of you, your heirs, or your successors.

Whether the continents and islands found and to be found lie in the direction of India or toward any other quarter, this line will be one hundred leagues west and south of the islands commonly known as the Azores and Cape Verdes, notwithstanding any apostolic constitutions, ordinances, and other decrees to the contrary.

We trust in Him from whom empires, governments, and all good things proceed, that your hardships and endeavors soon will attain the most felicitous result, to the happiness and glory of all Christendom, should you, with the Lord's guidance, pursue this holy and praiseworthy undertaking.

[12] Because it would be difficult, however, to have these decrees sent to every desirable place, with similar accord and knowledge we wish and command that two copies of them shall be made, signed by the hand of a suitably commissioned public notary and embossed with the seal of any ecclesiastical officer or ecclesiastical court. These copies are to receive the same respect when exhibited in or out of court, or anywhere else, as would be given to these originals.

[13] Let no man infringe or with rash boldness contravene this our commendation, exhortation, requisition, gift, grant, assignation, ordinance, deputation, decree, mandate, prohibition, and will. Should anyone presume to attempt this, he is informed that he will incur the wrath of Almighty God and of his blessed apostles Peter and Paul.

[14] Given at Rome, at St. Peter's, in the year of the incarnation of our Lord one thousand four hundred and ninety-three on the fourth of May in the first year of our pontificate.

[15] Gratis by order of our most holy lord, the pope.

June. For the referendary, A. De Mucciallis.

For A. Consenino, L. Podochatharus, D. Gallectus.

Registered in the apostolic office. Amerinus.

[16] These letters indeed having been diligently inspected by us, as is said above, at the request of the honorable Alfonso Alvarez de Toledo,[23] staff member of the Spanish royal household, were signed by the public notary by force of this clause at the end of these apostolic letters: "But because it would be difficult for the present letters to be taken to all the places expedient, we wish and with similar initiative and knowledge decide that to the copies of those letters, signed by the hand of a public notary commissioned for this task and furnished with the seal of some person ordained as an ecclesiastical official or of an ecclesiastical court, complete credence be shown in court, outside court, and anywhere else, as would be shown the original letters, were they exhibited or displayed."

[17] We have ordered these letters be copied, transcribed, and rendered public, deciding and wishing that thereafter full credence be shown to this public transcript or copy in each and all places opportune, and that this transcript itself engender confidence and be explained as if the original letters themselves were to appear, be brought forth, and presented. On each and every one we have inserted our customary authorization and in an equal manner we both insert this authority on the decree through these documents and for the more ample and clearer proof of these matters we have thought to affix our seal to these documents together with the rubric and signature of the notary below who is applying himself to this task.

[18] These proceedings took place at Barcelona, in the house of our residence, in

our chamber, on Friday, the nineteenth of the month of July, in the 1493rd year from the birth of the Lord, in the first year of the pontificate of the same most holy Father in Christ, our lord Alexander the Sixth by divine providence. Present in this place were the venerable and prudent men Nicolo Pillicer, canon of our church of Barcelona, and Petro Joanne Vayo and Michele Ginnous, clerics, priests, chaplains, and our familiars, witnesses called and requested for these matters.

[19] And I, Alvar Pérez del Villar, canon of the holy church of Compostela, apostolic notary, secretary to the most reverend Sir Diego,[24] bishop of Seville, together with the above-named witnesses, was present at these matters of the apostolic letters inserted above while they happened, were dealt with, and stated for presentation, reception, requisition, viewing, and introduction of the decree, copying, and all other individual matters. I saw, heard, and took notes about all and each of these matters as they occurred. From these notes I have drawn up, by order of the said lord bishop, the present instrument, which was written faithfully by another while I was occupied with other business. I have copied and collated with the originals these apostolic letters inserted above. It agrees word for word; and for the trustworthiness and testimony of each and all of the things described above, I, having been asked and requested, have signed them with my customary and usual rubric and name.

[20] This transcript was corrected and collated with the original document that it was copied from, by me, the undersigned notary, in the most noble and loyal city of Seville, on Thursday, the thirtieth day of the month of December in the year of the birth of our Lord Jesus Christ one thousand five hundred and two.

[21] The witnesses who were present and saw it corrected against the original were the honorable and distinguished men Gómez Nieto, clerk, Martín de Ayamonte and Juan González Contero, citizens of the city of Seville, all summoned and requested for this purpose. Ruiz Montana, notary.

[22] I, Pedro Ruiz Montana, clerk of Córdoba, papal notary public,[25] together with these witnesses, was present at all and everything contained in this parchment document from our most holy Father, and saw and heard it, and had it faithfully copied by someone else while I was occupied with other business, and I countersigned it with my accustomed rubric in testimony of the truth, as requested and required. Pedro Ruiz Montana, notary.

Letter from Fernando and Isabel promising great rewards to the admiral, requesting information about the Indies, and sending the terms of the Treaty of Tordesillas
Segovia, 16 August 1494

The King and the Queen

[1] Sir Christopher Columbus, our high admiral of the islands of the Indies.

We have seen your letters and the reports you sent us with Torres and have been very pleased to learn of all that you wrote us in them. We give many thanks to our Lord for all of it because we hope that, with His help, your business will be the means by which our holy Catholic faith is augmented. One of the things that has pleased us the most about this is that it was conceived, begun, and accomplished by your command, work, and expertise. It seems to us that all of what you told us at the beginning could be achieved has turned out to be true, for the most part, as if you had seen it before telling us. We trust in God that what remains to be discovered will continue in the same way, which would oblige us to confer favors on you in a way that will leave you very satisfied.

[2] Having seen all that you wrote to us, it is a great joy and a delight to read [your letters] because you talk about things at such great length. Nevertheless, we desire that you write us something more about how many islands have been found up to now. Of those islands you have named, what name has been given to each, because in your letters you give the names of some but not all of these, the names that the Indians call them, how far it is from one to the other, all that you have found on each one of them, including what [the Indians] say is on them, and also what has been harvested from that which was sowed after you went there, because the season has passed when all sown crops ought to have been harvested.

[3] Most of all we want to know what the weather is like there in all the months of the year, because it seems to us from what you describe that there is a great difference between the seasons there and here. Some wonder if in one year there are two winters and two summers. Write us about all this for our benefit and send us as many falcons as can be sent from there, and specimens of all the types of birds that are and can be collected there, because we want to see all of them.

[4] Regarding the things that you requested in your report to be ordered and sent from here, we are ordering everything to be provided, as you will learn and see from what Torres takes with him. In order to know how you and all the people there are doing, and so that everyone can be provided on a daily basis with whatever is needed, we would like, if you agree, that every month one caravel should come from there and another should go from here, now that affairs with Portugal have been settled and ships will be able to come and go safely. Think about it and, if you think it should be done, do your part there and write us explaining how you think sailings should be dispatched from here.

[5] Concerning the relations that you should establish with the people you have there, we approve of what you have begun up to now. This is how you should continue to proceed, giving them the most satisfaction possible but not giving them any license to exceed the things they are supposed to do and what you order them to do on our behalf.

No one from here can give valid orders or amend anything regarding the settlement you established there. We would take your advice and opinion about it if we were there and all the more so while absent. For this reason we delegate all to you.

[6] As for all the other things contained in the report that Torres brought, answers to those things that are suitable for you to know are given in its margins, to which we refer you.

[7] Regarding matters with Portugal, a valid treaty has been signed with their ambassadors that seemed to us the least disadvantageous. We are sending you a transcript of the terms that were made, so that you may be well informed in detail. Consequently, it is not appropriate to elaborate on it here. Nonetheless, we order and charge you to observe it fully, causing it to be observed by everyone, just as stipulated in the articles.

[8] It seems to us that the line, or border, that is to be made is an extremely difficult matter requiring great wisdom and trust. If possible, therefore, we would like you to locate it yourself and establish it with those who are to be involved on behalf of the king of Portugal. If it is very difficult for you to go do this, or if it would interfere with what you are there for, see if your brother [Bartolomé Colón] or someone else there knows about this, and instruct them very well in writing, orally, drawing, and by any means that they could best be informed. Then send them here by the first caravel that sails, because on its return trip we will send others from here for the time that has been agreed on.

Whether or not you do this yourself, write us at great length with everything you find out about it and what you think should be done for our information, so that everything can be arranged to the fulfillment of our service. Do this in such a manner that your letters and those whom you send come quickly, so that they can return to where the line is to be made before the time expires that we have agreed on with the king of Portugal, as you will see by the agreement.

[9] From Segovia, on the sixteenth of August, ninety-four.

I, the King
I, the Queen

[10] By order of the king and queen. Fernán Alvarez.

[11] And on the back it said: "By the king and the queen, to Sir Christopher Columbus, their high admiral of the islands of the Indies."

PART 3

THE THIRD VOYAGE

CHAPTER 3.1

Colonizing the Americas

16

Authority for Columbus to take 330 colonists on the royal payroll

Burgos, 23 April 1497

The King and Queen

[1] By this writ we give permission and authority to you, Sir Christopher Columbus, our admiral of the Ocean Sea, to take on our payroll up to 330 persons to reside in the Indies, of the following occupations in this manner: 40 noncommissioned officers, 100 infantry and day laborers, 30 able seamen, 30 midshipmen, 20 gold miners, 50 farmers, 10 vegetable gardeners, 20 masters of all trades, and 30 women, for a total of 330 persons. You shall pay them salaries according to the instructions that we are issuing. If it is necessary to make adjustments by increasing the numbers of some of these occupations and staff and reducing others, you may do so as you think most beneficial to our service, as long as there are not more than 330 persons total.

[2] Done in the city of Burgos on the twenty-third day of the month of April in the year one thousand four hundred ninety-seven.

I, the King
I, the Queen

[3] By order of the king and queen. Fernán Alvarez.

[4] Agreed.

Sancho de Matienzo, canon of Seville Cathedral and comptroller of fleet outfitting in Seville, 1497–. Detail of a painting by Alejo Fernández for the funerary chapel that Matienzo constructed in the church of his hometown Villasana de Mena at the end of the fifteenth century. The painting was destroyed in a 1936 church fire. (Arxiu Mas)

17

Writ for payment of wages on the admiral's warrants
Burgos, 23 April 1497

The King and Queen

[1] Our treasurer[1] of the treasure and things that belong to us from the islands and continent discovered and placed under our sovereignty in the Ocean Sea in the region of the Indies.

We order that, from the gold, merchandise, and other things acquired in the Indies, you shall pay the persons who are entitled to receive from us any salary, wages, or other money for the hiring of ships, crews, and other things necessary for the housing and settlement of people going to the Indies on salary and wages, and whatever is owed to people who have served us in the past.

Pay these according to the rosters, writs, and vouchers you receive signed by Sir Christopher Columbus, our admiral, viceroy, and governor of the Indies, or his proxy and by the officials of our chief accountants in the Indies.

[2] With their vouchers and rosters, and with the letters of payment from private parties, we order you to receive on account, disburse, and pay these sums that the admiral and officials release to you, and you shall not do otherwise.

[3] Done in the city of Burgos on the twenty-third day of the month of April in the year one thousand four hundred ninety-seven.

I, the King
I, the Queen

[4] By order of the king and queen. Fernán Alvarez.
[5] Agreed.

18

Instructions to Columbus for colonization of the Indies
Burgos, 23 April 1497

[1] Sir Christopher Columbus, our admiral, viceroy and governor of the Ocean Sea.

In our opinion, the things that must be done and implemented, with the help of God our lord, above and beyond that which, by another of our writs,[2] you and the bishop of Badajoz must provide for the settlement of the Indies and continent discovered and placed under our sovereignty, of those islands and mainland still to be discovered in the region of the Indies in the Ocean Sea, and of the people who, by our command, are already there and will go to live there in the future, are the following:

[2] First. When, God willing, you are in the Indies you shall endeavor with all diligence to encourage and lead the natives of the Indies to serve us and remain benignly under our sovereignty and subjection in peace and order, and especially to convert them to our holy Catholic faith. They and those who are going to live in the Indies shall be administered the holy sacraments by the monks and priests who are already there and those going now, so that God our lord may be served and their consciences may be satisfied.

[3] Item. From now until we order further, 330 persons may go with you, whom you shall choose with such qualifications and professions as stipulated in the instructions. If it seems to you that some of the instructions should be adjusted, however, by adding to some occupations and professions while reducing others, you or your proxy can do so, as you think will contribute to our service as well as the welfare and advantageous governance of the Indies.

[4] Item. When, God willing, you are in the Indies, you shall establish another settlement or fortress on the island of La Española, on the other side of the island from the one already in existence, near the gold mine in the place and form that seems best to you.

[5] Item. Near this new settlement or the one that is already established or in some other location that seems well situated to you, establish and introduce plowing and animal husbandry,[3] so that the persons who are or will be residing on the island can sustain themselves better and more economically.

In order best to accomplish this, give to the farmers now going to the Indies up to fifty cahices of the wheat and barley being sent there, on loan for sowing, and up to twenty yokes of oxen, mares, or other plow stock. Farmers who receive the grain shall plow, sow, and obligate themselves to return [an equivalent amount of] grain to you at harvest time in addition to paying the tithe on what is harvested.

The farmers may sell the remaining grain to the Christians for as much as they can, provided that the prices do not cause undue hardship for those purchasing it. If the latter should occur, you, our admiral, or your representative must set and enforce a maximum price.

[6] Item. The 330 persons going to the Indies must be paid their wages at the rate that has been paid up to now. Instead of the maintenance that they are usually given, they must be provided with some of the grain that we are ordering sent there: to each person one fanega of wheat every month and 12 maravedís per day to buy other necessary food. This is to be issued to them by you, our admiral, or your proxy, and the agents of our chief accountants in the Indies. Our treasurer in the Indies shall pay them according to your roster, vouchers, and writs in the stipulated manner.

[7] Item. If you the admiral believe that it would be advantageous to our service if the total number of persons were increased from 330, you may do so up to a total of 500 persons, on the condition that the wages and food of these extra persons are paid

from any merchandise and valuables acquired in the Indies, without our ordering provisions for them from elsewhere.

[8] Item. The persons who remain in the Indies shall be paid the wages owed them according to the roster, in the manner stipulated. Those who are not on the payroll are to be compensated for their service as appears best to you, and those who have worked for others likewise.

[9] Item. The posts, salaries, and wages of commanders and other principal persons and officials who live and serve there ought to be remunerated according to what seems proper to you, our admiral, taking into consideration the qualifications of each person and what work each has done and will do. In addition to this, when, God willing, the means to bestow favors in the Indies exists, we shall issue further instructions on how to do so. These shall be awarded by our officials, who will be notified to issue and pay them in the prescribed manner.

[10] Item. When the heirs of the abbot Gallego and Andrés de Salamanca who died in the Indies appear, they should be paid the value of the casks and barrels that were used and confiscated from them for having gone to the Indies contrary to our prohibition.

[11] Item. Concerning the settlement of estates for those who die in the Indies, it seems to us the procedure should be observed that you described in a section of your report to us, which is as follows:

[12] "Many foreigners and citizens have died in the Indies, and I ordered, by virtue of the powers that I have from Your Highnesses, that they should draw up wills and that these should be executed. I gave responsibility to Escobar, citizen of Seville, and Juan de León, citizen of La Isabela, faithfully to discharge all this by paying what the deceased owed, if their executors had not paid it, as well as recovering all their property and wages. All this must be recorded by magistrates and public clerks. Everything accumulated should be placed in a chest with three locks:[4] the executors will have one key, a monk another, and I the third. The money of the deceased shall be placed in this chest and remain there for up to three years, so that the heirs will have time to come for it or send to claim it. If they do not claim it in this time, it should be distributed in good works for their souls."

[13] Likewise, it seems to us that the gold obtained in the Indies should be minted and made into coins of Granada excelentes as we have ordered in these our kingdoms, in order to avoid the making of counterfeits from this gold in the Indies.

[14] In order to coin the money, we order that you take the persons, dies, and tools necessary, for which purpose we give you complete power, with the condition that the money coined in the Indies conforms to the ordinances that we now order to be made about the coining of money. The craftsmen who do the coining must observe these ordinances, under the stipulated penalties.

[15] Item. It seems to us that the Indians who have agreed to pay the ordered tax should wear a token of brass or lead that they can hang from the neck. The design or mark on this token should be changed each time one pays, so that it will be known if

someone has not paid. Every time persons are found on the island without this token hanging from the neck, have them arrested and given some light penalty.

[16] Because it will be necessary to appoint a diligent and trustworthy person to collect and receive the tribute, it is our wish and command that . . .⁵ should have this office. From the tribute and merchandise that he receives, collects, and causes to be paid, he shall take and keep for himself five pesos, medidas, or libras per hundred, which is one-twentieth of what he is to receive and cause to be collected and received.

I, the King
I, the Queen

[17] By order of the king and queen. Fernán Alvarez de Toledo.
[18] Agreed.

19
Permission and authority for Columbus to increase the number of personnel to 500
Burgos, 23 April 1497

The King and the Queen

[1] By this writ we give permission and authority to you, Sir Christopher Columbus, our admiral of the Ocean Sea, so that, if you consider it advantageous to our service that more people should be taken on the payroll besides those we have already ordered to go and reside in the Indies, you may take and keep up to a total of 500 persons, for the period and manner that seems best to you, so long as the wages and provisions for these extra people are drawn from merchandise and other valuables acquired in the Indies, without our ordering provisions for them from elsewhere.

[2] Done in the city of Burgos on the twenty-third day of the month of April in the year one thousand ninety-seven.

I, the King
I, the Queen

[3] By order of the king and queen. Fernán Alvarez.
[4] Agreed.

20

Instructions to Columbus and Antonio de Torres about colonists, supplies, and
provisions
Medina del Campo, 15 June 1497

The King and the Queen

[1] Sir Christopher Columbus, our admiral of the Ocean Sea, viceroy and governor
of the mainland and islands of the Indies, and Antonio de Torres, of our staff.

It seems to us that the following things should be obtained and sent, with the help
of our lord God, to the Indies for the governance and maintenance of the people who
are already there and will be going to do things there for the service of God and our
selves:

[2] First, on this next voyage and for as long as we order, 330 persons shall go to stay
in the Indies of the sort, qualities, and occupations listed below, including in these 330
those persons already living there in the Indies.[6]

[3] These same 330 persons are to be chosen by you our admiral or by your proxy
and are to be distributed in this way: 40 noncommissioned officers, 100 enlisted men,
30 able seamen, 30 midshipmen, 20 gold miners, 50 farmers, 10 vegetable gardeners,
20 masters of all trades, and 30 women, for a total of 330 persons.[7]

[4] They are to go and stay in the Indies as long as they wish, so that if some people
who are in the Indies want to come back, there will remain 330 counting those already
there and those now going. But if it seems to you, the admiral, that it is good and
advantageous for this business[8] to change the number of persons, decreasing the numbers of some occupations and substituting others in their place, you may do so as long
as the number of persons in the Indies does not exceed 330.

[5] For your maintenance and that of your brothers, other officials, important persons who will be going with you to stay in the Indies, and the 330 persons, in order to
plow and sow and for the care of the animals that you are taking there, you may have
and transport 550 cahices of wheat and 50 cahices of barley[9] obtained from the grain
belonging to us as the royal share of the tithes of this past year of '96 in the archdiocese
of Seville and the diocese of Cádiz, in accord with the vouchers for it that we order to
be issued.

[6] Send to the Indies the tools and equipment that you judge suitable for plowing
in the Indies, and also appropriate mattocks, hoes, sledgehammers, and crowbars.[10]

[7] Likewise, the oxen and mares that are already in the Indies shall be increased up
to the number of twenty yokes of oxen, mares, and donkeys whichever you the admiral think best for plowing in the Indies.[11]

[8] Also, it seems to us that it would be good to purchase an old cargo carrier[12] to
transport as much of the provisions and things as can fit in it, so that its decking,
timbers, and nails could be used for the new settlement to be established on the other

side of the island of La Española near the mines. But if taking this ship does not seem a good idea to you, the admiral, then it shall not be sent.

[9] Furthermore, 50 cahices of flour and up to 1,000 quintals of biscuit should be taken to the Indies as provisions until water- and horse-mills[13] are constructed. Take some millstones and other milling equipment from here to build these.

[10] Two field tents costing up to 20,000 maravedís shall be taken to the Indies.

[11] It seems to us that whatever other supplies and provisions may be necessary to take to the Indies for outfitting and clothing those who are going to stay there should be arranged in the following way:

[12] Some solvent citizens should be found, such as those with whom you the admiral claim to have tentatively contracted, for loading and transporting to the Indies these supplies and the other things needed there. Pay them in advance, using the money that we have ordered released for this purpose, provided they post surety bonds for the money thus received.

[13] They shall use this money for buying supplies, loading them, and transporting them to the Indies at their own expense, while the risk of loss at sea will be ours. After arriving there, God willing, they must sell these supplies: an azumbre of wine for fifteen maravedís, a pound of bacon or salted mutton for eight maravedís, and the other supplies and dried beans at the prices you the admiral or your deputy set, so that they will make a profit and not lose on this, and the people will not be cheated.

[14] Out of the money that these persons receive from selling supplies in this way, they must reimburse our treasurer in the Indies the money that you gave them in advance and that they in turn used for buying supplies, so that the treasurer can use it to pay the wages of the people. But if the people take these supplies on credit against their wages, they should receive them on account, giving collateral and signing receipts for what they have received so that the treasurer and accountants can deduct it from their wages. Persons having obliged themselves to act and perform in this way shall be given cash as you see fit.

[15] Monks and priests of good character should be recruited for the Indies to administer the holy sacraments to those who will be staying there. They also should try to convert the Indian citizens[14] to our holy Catholic faith. For this purpose, they should take whatever equipment and items are required for celebrating the divine liturgy and administering the holy sacraments.

[16] Also, a physician, a druggist, and a herbalist must go, and some instruments and music books for the amusement of the people who are going there to stay.

[17] Furthermore, we now order the release of a fixed sum of money for the voyage that you the admiral are now making at our command. Spend this in accord with the budget signed by the high commander of León, our chief accountant;[15] by Doctor Rodrigo Maldonado, of our council; and by Fernán Alvarez, our secretary.

[18] Because we order you to observe, fulfill, and implement all that is described above, by which you will be doing our pleasure and service, we give you full power with all its incidentals and rightful perquisites and responsibilities.

[19] Done in the town of Medina del Campo on the fifteenth day of June in the year of our lord Jesus Christ one thousand four hundred and ninety-seven.

I, the King
I, the Queen

[20] By order of the king and queen. Fernán Alvarez.

[21] Agreed: Rodericus, doctor.

21

Authority to Columbus to apportion land among the colonists in the Indies
Medina del Campo, 22 July 1497

[1] Sir Fernando and Lady Isabel, by the grace of God king and queen of Castile, León, Aragón, Sicily, Granada, Toledo, Valencia, Galicia, the Balearics, Seville, Sardinia, Córdoba, Corsica, Murcia, Jaén, the Algarve, Algeciras, Gibraltar, and the Canary Islands, count and countess of Barcelona, lords of Vizcaya and Molina, dukes of Athens and Neopatria, counts of Roussillon and Cerdagne, marquises of Oristano and Goceano.

Some people, already having established residency on the island of La Española and other islands, have petitioned us to order given and allocated on these islands land on which they can sow grains and plant vegetables, cotton and flax, grapevines, trees, sugar cane, and other plants, and construct houses, flour mills, sugar mills, and other structures useful and necessary for their living, which is to our service and useful for the general welfare of the islands' residents.

Therefore by this writ we give permission and authorize you, Sir Christopher Columbus, our admiral of the Ocean Sea and our viceroy and governor on that island, to give and distribute the land, commons, and water in all the municipal territories of the island to those who now and in the future live and reside there. Give and allocate land and water as you think appropriate to each, considering his status and service to us and the condition and quality of his person and lifestyle. You shall survey and set boundary markers for what you give and distribute to each one, so that each will have and possess his own private property held in legal and just title, to use, plant, plow, and utilize, with the right to sell, give, donate, exchange, trade, alienate, encumber, and do with and on as he wishes and sees fit.

Require such persons to establish and maintain residency by occupying their own houses on the island of La Española for the next four years continuously, counting from the day that you give and turn over to them the house lots and farm land. They must build houses and plant the vines and gardens on the island in the manner and quantity that you deem fit, with the condition that over the land, commons, and water that you give and allocate, the owners cannot claim or exercise any civil or criminal jurisdiction.

They cannot exempt, post, or close off anything except what they have fenced in with a wall. Everything else unfenced, once the produce and harvest is collected from it, is to be common pasture and free to all.

[2] We reserve for ourselves the brazilwood[16] and any gold, silver, and other metals found in those lands. Furthermore, the persons to whom you give and distribute these lands cannot load or unload there or on any other part of those lands any metal, brazilwood, or any other things belonging to us and that must be loaded and unloaded by our command.

They may only sow, gather, transport, and profit from the harvest of grain, seeds, trees, vines, cotton fields, and whatever they sowed and harvested in their fields.

[3] We desire and order that no one occupy or embargo in whole or in part, or impede in any way the land that you give and distribute to the people in the manner described. Rather, the people shall be allowed to freely keep, possess, use, and benefit from their land as stipulated in our writ.

[4] Any person who does otherwise shall incur our displeasure and a fine of 10,000 maravedís for our treasury.

[5] Given in the town of Medina del Campo on the twenty-second day of the month of July in the year of the birth of our savior Jesus Christ one thousand four hundred and ninety-seven.

I, the King

I, the Queen

[6] I, Juan de la Parra, secretary of the king and queen our lords, had this written by their order.

[7] And on the back of the writ it said: "Agreed: Rodericus, doctor; Fernán Ortiz, for the chancellor.[17] Registered: Doctor."[18]

22

Writ allowing persons guilty of certain crimes to settle on La Española, at their own expense, with a prospective pardon
Medina del Campo, 22 June 1497

[1] Sir Fernando and Lady Isabel, by the grace of God king and queen of Castile, León, Aragón, Sicily, Granada, Toledo, Valencia, Galicia, the Balearics, Seville, Sardinia, Córdoba, Corsica, Murcia, Jaén, the Algarve, Algeciras, Gibraltar, and the Canary Islands, count and countess of Barcelona, lords of Vizcaya and Molina, dukes of Athens and Neopatria, counts of Roussillon and Cerdagne, marquises of Oristano and Goceano.

To the members of our royal council, judges of our appellate court, judges and sheriffs of our household, court, and chancery; all the municipal councils, judges, councilmen, commissioned and noncommissioned officers, masters of trades, and voting citizens of all the cities, towns, and villages of our kingdoms and dominions, whether in the royal domain or in the domains of ecclesiastical lords, military orders, lay lords, or any other persons; our subjects both native born and naturalized who are affected by and involved in what is described in this our writ; and to any of you shown this writ or its transcript certified by a public clerk, greetings.

[2] You are informed that we have ordered Sir Christopher Columbus, our admiral of the Ocean Sea, to return to the island of La Española and other islands and mainland that are in the Indies, and engage in their conversion and settlement, because God our lord is served by this, and His holy faith increased, and our kingdoms and domains expanded.

To that end we have ordered several ships and caravels outfitted to transport there certain people on our payroll for a fixed time, as well as supplies and provisions for them. Since that will not be enough to carry out the settlement as it should be done for the service of God and ourselves unless other people go at their own expense to remain, live, and serve there, and, wanting to provide for this as well as for the conversion and settlement, and to treat our subjects and citizens with mercy and piety, we order this our writ issued in this way.

[3] To this end, by our own initiative and with true knowledge, we desire and order that all and any persons, men and women, our subjects and citizens, who, before the date of the publication of this our writ, may have committed any murders, injuries, or other crimes, regardless of their nature and gravity—except the crimes of heresy, lese majesty, sedition, treason, perfidy, murder by ax, fire, or arrow, counterfeiting, sodomy, or export of money, gold, silver or other prohibited things—may go to serve their sentences on the island of La Española and work there at their own expense, doing whatever the admiral tells and commands them to do for us.

Those who merit the death penalty will serve for two years, while those who merit lesser penalties not involving death although possibly the loss of a limb shall serve for one year.

They are to be pardoned of any crimes and misdemeanors, of whatever nature, quality, and gravity except the stated cases, that they committed before the date of the publication of this our writ if they present themselves before Sir Christopher Columbus, our admiral of the Ocean Sea, and a public clerk, between today, the date of this our writ, and the end of the coming month of September, in order to go with the admiral to the island of La Española and other islands and mainland in the Indies, and serve there for the entire time as ordered by the admiral, in fulfillment of our service.

If, after presenting themselves, they go to the islands and mainland, serve continuously for the full stated time, and bear a warrant signed by the admiral and certified by a public clerk attesting that these delinquents have served on the islands or any one of them for the full term, they shall be pardoned.

[4] With this writ, by our own initiative and true knowledge, we pardon all their misdemeanors committed before the publication of this our writ. From then on, they cannot be indicted for these crimes or any one of them, and proceedings cannot be brought against them or their property by our criminal judges or for any civil or criminal penalty by private parties, either officially or otherwise. The sentences already given against them cannot be executed either against their persons or their property. With this our writ, we revoke the sentences and make them null, void, and without effect, once the service is completed.

[5] We order the admiral of the Indies and any other persons who are in the Indies on our behalf to allow those who have served their term to come back freely, as this our writ stipulates, and not to detain them in any way.

[6] With this writ we order the members of our royal council, judges of our appeals court, judges of our court and chancery; all royal and other judges of all cities, towns, and villages of our kingdoms and domains, to put into effect and execute this letter of pardon and remission and each and every part of it.

In implementing and executing it, they are not to proceed against those who have served their term in the Indies for any crime they may have committed, except in the stated exceptions, at the request of any party, officially or otherwise, and they are not to execute sentences against their persons or property for those crimes.

[7] If any proceedings are brought or sentences given against them, they shall be revoked and voided, because by this writ and with true knowledge, we revoke, suppress, and annul them from now on. We restore the delinquents to their good name and to the place and status they occupied before they committed their crimes.

[8] In order that this shall become public knowledge and no one can claim ignorance, we order that it be publicly announced in plazas, markets, and the usual places. No one shall do otherwise in any way, under penalty of our displeasure and a fine of 10,000 maravedís for our treasury from each person who does the contrary.

[9] In addition, we command the man who shows you this our writ to summon you to appear before us in our court, wherever we may be, within fifteen days of having been cited, under the same penalty. Under this same penalty we command every public clerk who may be summoned for this purpose to give the person showing him this writ a certificate to that effect inscribed with his rubric so that we may know how well our command is obeyed.

[10] Given in the town of Medina del Campo on the twenty-second day of the month of June in the year of the birth of our Savior Jesus Christ one thousand four hundred ninety-seven.

I, the King
I, the Queen

[11] I, Fernán Alvarez de Toledo, secretary of the king and queen our lords, had this written at their command.

[12] Agreed: Rodericus, doctor.

[13] Registered: Doctor; Francisco Díaz, chancellor.

23

Order to royal judicial officers that persons liable to banishment may be sent to La
Española
Medina del Campo, 22 June 1497

[1] Sir Fernando and Lady Isabel, by the grace of God king and queen of Castile,
León, Aragón, Sicily, Granada, Toledo, Valencia, Galicia, the Balearics, Seville, Sar-
dinia, Córdoba, Corsica, Murcia, Jaén, the Algarve, Algeciras, Gibraltar, and the Ca-
nary Islands, count and countess of Barcelona, lords of Vizcaya and Molina, dukes of
Athens and Neopatria, counts of Roussillon and Cerdagne, marquises of Oristano and
Goceano.

To all royal and municipal judges, sheriffs, and any other justices of all cities, towns,
and villages in our kingdoms and domains who may be shown this our writ or its
transcript certified by a public clerk, greetings.

[2] You are informed that we have ordered Sir Christopher Columbus, our admiral
of the Indies in the Ocean Sea, to return to the island of La Española and other islands
and mainland in the Indies, to undertake their [conversion and] settlement. To that
effect we ordered that he be given cargo carriers and caravels to carry specific people
on our payroll for a fixed time, with supplies and provisions for this. But because these
people will not be enough to accomplish the settlement in fulfillment of God's service
and ours unless other people go to stay, live, and serve at their own expense, we agreed
to order this writ issued to all of you for this reason.

[3] When any persons from our kingdoms, either male or female, have committed
crimes for which they merit exile to an island, hard labor, or service in mines, according to the laws of our kingdoms, we order you to exile them to go, stay, and serve on
the island of La Española doing the things that our admiral of the Indies orders them to
do for the term that they are to stay on the island and work in the mines. You may
condemn and exile to the island of La Española all other persons who are guilty of
misdemeanors not carrying the death penalty but who justifiably could be given a
sentence of exile to the Indies, depending on the nature of the offense, where they
must stay, doing what the admiral orders for the time that seems appropriate to you.

[4] From now on, sentence to go to the Indies those whom you have already
convicted and are holding prisoner. Send them under guard and safe escort to one of
the jails at our appeals courts of Valladolid or Ciudad Real, or to the royal jail in
Seville. You shall remand those whom you send to the appeals courts to the judges of
those courts, while those whom you send to the royal jail in Seville should be re-
manded to our royal judge there, at the expense of the condemned if they have property, and if they do not, the costs are to be paid from the money collected as fines by
our treasury.

[5] We order our judges to do and execute this as instructed, and that the councils

of all cities, towns, and villages of our kingdoms give them all the help and assistance they may need for this. If any other persons have committed or do commit crimes or misdemeanors for which they should be exiled from our kingdoms, you shall exile them to the island in the following manner: those who ought to be exiled from our kingdoms permanently, you are to exile to the island for ten years, and those who should be exiled from our kingdoms for a fixed term shall be exiled to the island for half of the term they would have had to be outside our kingdoms. None of you shall do otherwise in any way, under pain of our displeasure and a fine of 10,000 maravedís for our treasury on each person who does the contrary.

[6] Furthermore, we command the man who shows you this our writ to summon you to appear before us in our court, wherever we may be, within fifteen days of having been cited, under the same penalty. Under this same penalty, we command every public clerk who may be summoned for this purpose to give the person showing him this writ a certificate to that effect, inscribed with his rubric, so that we may know how well our order is obeyed.

[7] Given in the town of Medina del Campo on the twenty-second day of the month of June in the year of the birth of our Savior Jesus Christ one thousand four hundred ninety-seven.

I, the King

I, the Queen

[8] I, Fernán Alvarez de Toledo, secretary of the king and queen our lords, had this written at their command. Sir Álvaro.[19]

[9] Agreed: Rodericus, doctor.

[10] Registered: Doctor; Francisco Díaz, chancellor.

24

Order to the royal judge of Seville to receive such prisoners and deliver them on board.

Medina del Campo, 22 June 1497

The King and the Queen

[1] Count of Cifuentes,[20] our chief standard bearer and royal judge[21] in the city of Seville.

We are writing the judges of our kingdoms to order that, if they have to exile people to islands or outside our kingdoms, they should sentence them to exile on the island of La Española and send them to our jail in Seville.

[2] To this end, whenever our presidents and judges of our appeals courts in Valladolid and Ciudad Real or other royal judges or justices[22] of our kingdoms send you

some of these convicts, we order you to accept and imprison them under secure guard until you deliver them to our admiral of the Indies in the Ocean Sea. In his absence, deliver them to the person we appointed to be in charge of supplying the Indies and to the person appointed for this purpose by the admiral. These officials will send for the convicts at the time they have ships ready to sail for the Indies.

[3] At that time, deliver the prisoners to them on board the ships in the city of Seville or in the city of Cádiz, wherever the ships are ready to sail. Deliver the prisoners under guard and safe escort before a clerk and witnesses, receiving acknowledgment and guarantee from the ships' masters that they will indeed take the prisoners under secure guard and escort until delivering them to the admiral or the person he appoints to receive them on the island of La Española, and that they will take sworn testimony of how they transported, delivered, and left them on that island.

[4] You shall pay the expenditures incurred until they are delivered to the ships from the property of the convicts; and if they do not have property, pay it from the money collected as fines by our treasury; and do not do otherwise.

[5] Done in the town of Medina del Campo on the twenty-second day of the month of June in the year ninety-seven.

I, the King
I, the Queen

[6] By order of the king and queen. Fernán Alvarez.

CHAPTER 3.2

Fernando and Isabel Organize the Royal Enterprise of the Indies

25
Order for provisions for the Indies at customary prices
Burgos, 23 April 1497

[1] Sir Fernando and Lady Isabel, by the grace of God king and queen of Castile, León, Aragón, Sicily, Granada, Toledo, Valencia, Galicia, the Balearics, Seville, Sardinia, Corsica, Murcia, Jaén, the Algarve, Algeciras, Gibraltar, the Canary Islands, count and countess of Barcelona, lords of Vizcaya and Molina, dukes of Athens and Neopatria, counts of Roussillon and Cerdagne, marquises of Oristano and Goceano.

Our chief judge, members of our council, judges of our appellate court, judges and sheriffs of our household, court, and chancery; all the royal judges, municipal judges, sheriffs, and any other justices of all the cities, towns and villages of these, our kingdoms and domains; to each and every one of you in your respective posts and jurisdictions to whom this letter or its transcript certified by a public clerk is exhibited, greetings.

[2] You are informed that for the settlement of the islands and continent discovered and placed under our dominion in the region of the Indies in the Ocean Sea, it will be necessary to buy in these our kingdoms merchandise, food, provisions, tools, equipment, casks, bottles and other things for transport there. These will be bought by the person placed in charge or designated by us and by Sir Christopher Columbus, our admiral of the Ocean Sea.

[3] We have received a report that the persons who have the merchandise and other things decline to sell them in order to charge more, which would be to our disservice. Our wish and command is that these things shall be purchased at the prices they usually are worth. To that end, we order you to sell things at reasonable prices to our personnel and the admiral's, who will be buying to provide housing and provisions for the Indies and for the voyage there, just as they are usually priced among the citizens of

cities, towns, and villages, without inflating the price. You shall not do otherwise under penalty of our displeasure and a fine of 10,000 maravedís for our treasury from each one who contravenes this order.

[4] Furthermore, we command the man who shows this writ to any of our magistrates who are required to execute and fulfil it to summon you to appear before us in our court wherever we may be, within fifteen days of having been cited, under the same penalty. Under this same penalty, we command every public clerk summoned for this purpose to give the person showing him this writ a certificate to that effect, inscribed with his rubric, so that we may know how well our command is obeyed.

[5] Given in the city of Burgos on the twenty-third day of the month of April in the year of the birth of our lord Jesus Christ one thousand four hundred ninety-seven.

I, the King
I, the Queen

[6] I, Fernán Alvarez de Toledo, secretary of the king and queen our lords, had this written at their command.

[7] Agreed: Rodericus, doctor.

[8] Registered: Alonso Pérez; Francisco Díaz, chancellor.

26

Remission of taxes and tolls on exports to and imports from the Indies

Burgos, 23 April 1497

[1] Sir Fernando and Lady Isabel, by the grace of God king and queen of Castile, León, Aragón, Sicily, Granada, Toledo, Valencia, Galicia, the Balearics, Seville, Sardinia, Córdoba, Corsica, Murcia, Jaén, the Algarve, Algeciras, Gibraltar, and the Canary Islands, count and countess of Barcelona and Cerdagne, marquises of Oristano and Goceano.

To you, our import tax collectors, tax receivers, tax farmers, inspectors, collectors, and other persons who have charge of collecting and receiving in cash, collateral, or any other form, the revenues, import taxes, and sales taxes in the cities of Seville and Cádiz, in this present year of the date of this our writ and in the coming years for as long as we wish, each and every one of you, greetings.

[2] You are informed that our wish and command is that all the provisions and other things that are loaded for shipping to the Indies by our command and that of Sir Christopher Columbus, our admiral of the Ocean Sea in the region of the Indies, and likewise what is transported from there to these cities here and their ports, do not have to pay import, sales, or any other tax on the first sale, this year or from now on for as long as it is our wish and command.

[3] We order each and every one of you to observe and comply with the content of our writ. In observing and complying you may not demand or levy any excise, sales, or any other taxes at all for the first sale, or for the loading and unloading of any merchandise, provisions, or other things that are being loaded for the Indies or unloaded having been brought from the Indies on the word of our officials, admiral, and other persons who are in charge of this loading and unloading in both or either of these cities and ports, this year and from now on as long as it is our wish and command.

[4] If you do not implement this, we order any of our judges to compel and obligate you to do so. None of you shall do otherwise in any way, under penalty of our displeasure and a fine of 10,000 maravedís on each person who does the contrary. Furthermore, we command the man who shows you this our writ to summon you to appear before us in our court wherever we may be, within fifteen days of having been cited, under the same penalty. Under this same penalty, we command every public clerk summoned for this purpose to give the person showing him this writ a certificate to that effect, inscribed with his rubric so that we may know how well our command is obeyed.

[5] Given in the most noble city of Burgos on the twenty-third day of the month of April in the year of the birth of our Lord Jesus Christ one thousand four hundred and ninety-seven.

I, the King
I, the Queen

[6] I, Fernán Alvarez de Toledo, secretary of the king and queen, our lords, had this written at their command.

[7] Agreed: Rodericus, doctor.

[8] Registered: Alfonso Pérez; Francisco Díaz, chancellor.

27

Further remissions of taxes and tolls on Indian exports and imports

Burgos, 6 May 1497

[1] Sir Fernando and Lady Isabel, by the grace of God king and queen of Castile, León, Aragón, Sicily, Granada, Toledo, Valencia, Galicia, the Balearics, Seville, Sardinia, Córdoba, Murcia, Jaén, the Algarve, Algeciras, Gibraltar, and the Canary Islands, count and countess of Barcelona, lords of Vizcaya and Molina, dukes of Athens and Neopatria, counts of Roussillon and Cerdagne, marquises of Oristano and Goceano.

To all royal and municipal judges, sheriffs, councilmen, commissioned and non-commissioned officers, masters of trades, and voting citizens of the cities of Seville and Cádiz, and the towns, villages, and ports of their respective archdiocese and diocese;

and you the tax farmers and receivers, excise tax agents, transit tax collectors, customs agents, tithe collectors, and others who now and in the future are responsible for collecting and receiving in cash, collateral, or any other form, the revenues of the sales, excise, transit, and admiralty taxes in these cities and towns, greetings.

[2] You are informed that for the settlement of the islands and continent discovered and placed under our dominion now and in the future in the Ocean Sea in the region of the Indies, it will be necessary to bring merchandise and other things from there for sale in our kingdoms, and to transport from here to the Indies provisions, supplies, and other things needed both for commerce and for the subsistence and provisioning of the people there, and their dwellings and farms.

[3] It is our wish and command that such goods brought to these our kingdoms from the Indies not pay any dues or sales tax for the first sale, and that those who buy goods to send and transport to the Indies for the purveyance and sustenance of the people there not pay any excise, customs, transit, admiralty, nor any other loading tax.

We order this our writ given for this purpose. By this writ we order each and all of you, every time you bring and unload any goods from the Indies to these our kingdoms, that, for as long as it is our wish and command, you shall allow these goods to be unloaded freely without charging high or low excise, customs, admiralty, transit, or any other taxes, nor sales tax on the first sale of things that are brought from the Indies, if you are shown a warrant signed by Sir Christopher Columbus, our admiral of the Indies, or his proxy, and by the persons who are posted to the Indies by us or our chief accountants in our name, because those things are going to be shipped from the Indies for these our kingdoms.

[4] You shall allow to be freely loaded, for as long as it is our wish and command, anything being taken to the Indies for the purveyance and sustenance of the people there, without demanding or levying any fees for high or low excise, customs, admiralty, transit, or any other taxes. Implement this whenever you are shown a warrant signed by Sir Christopher Columbus, admiral of the Indies, or his proxy, and by the person posted in the city of Cádiz by us or by our chief accountants to handle the things from the Indies.

[5] If anyone unloads goods being sent here from the Indies without exhibiting a letter from the admiral or his proxy and the persons posted to the Indies by us and our chief accountants; or loads goods being sent from here to the Indies without a warrant from the admiral or his proxy and the persons posted to Cádiz by us and our chief accountants certifying that those things are being loaded for shipment to the Indies, they shall be confiscated.

[6] By this writ we give power and authority to the persons that we or our chief accountants appoint for this purpose in the city of Cádiz, or the person that the admiral for his part has appointed there, to confiscate merchandise and other things shipped from the Indies or loaded for transport there without having displayed these properly signed warrants. They shall hold the goods as security until we order what is just and what it is our wish and command to do with them.

[7] We order these agents and officials to make sure that what is loaded for the

Indies is transported there and not elsewhere. The officials in the Indies, likewise, must make sure that whatever is shipped from the Indies is unloaded in these our kingdoms and nowhere else, and is presented to the officials that we and the admiral of the Indies have appointed in the city of Cádiz to prevent fraud or deceit. We order you, our judges, to do and implement this for as long as it is our wish and command.

[8] In order to bring this to the notice of everyone so that no one can claim ignorance, we command that this our writ be announced in all the plazas, markets, and other usual places of these cities of Seville and Cádiz, and the ports of this region. We order our chief accountants to make a transcript of this our writ and that they register and record it in their books, countersigning this original on the back and returning it to Sir Christopher Columbus, our admiral of the Indies.

From the tax farming contracts that [the tax farmers and receivers] make for our excise, sales, transit, customs, and other royal taxes, they shall deduct what is contained in this our letter from now on, for as long as it is our wish and command. Any of you who contravenes this in any way will incur our displeasure and a fine of 10,000 maravedís for our treasury.

[9] Furthermore, we command the man who shows you this writ to summon you to appear before us in our court, wherever we may be, within fifteen days of having been cited, under the same penalty. Under this same penalty, we command every public clerk summoned for this purpose to give the person showing him this writ a certificate to that effect, inscribed with his rubric, so that we may know how well our command is obeyed.

[10] Given in the city of Burgos on the sixth day of May in the year of the birth of our Savior Jesus Christ one thousand four hundred and ninety-seven.

I, the King
I, the Queen

[11] I, Fernán Alvarez de Toledo, secretary of the king and queen our lords, had this written at their command.

[12] In form, agreed: Rodericus, doctor.

[13] Registered: Alfonso Pérez; Francisco Díaz, chancellor.

28

Treasury office memorandum to crown officers that these regulations will take effect on 1 January 1498
Burgos, 6 May 1497

[1] Royal and municipal judges, sheriffs, councilmen, commissioned and noncommissioned officers, masters of trades, and voting citizens of the cities of Seville and

Cádiz and the towns, villages and ports of their archdiocese and diocese; tax farmers and receivers, collectors of excise, transit, and customs taxes, and tithe collectors; and others mentioned in this writ from the king and queen our lords.

See that this writ from Their Highnesses is implemented in its entirety, as Their Highnesses stipulate in it. All merchants going from Andalusia or any other ports enjoying this tax exemption to the Indies must guarantee that they will adhere to the testimony and word of the admiral or his proxy and of the person designated for this purpose by Their Highnesses or their chief accountants. Also the permissions and warrants that must be taken to or brought from the Indies concerning goods sent and brought must be signed both by the admiral or his proxy and by the person designated by Their Highnesses and their chief accountants, not just by one of them.

[2] What is described in this letter may not be received on account in cash or any other form by the tax farmers and chief tax receivers, excise agents, and other persons who have charge of collecting and receiving the revenues that belong to us in this archdiocese of Seville and diocese of Cádiz, not this year or in the future, for as long as it is the wish and command of Their Highnesses that it remain in effect. Although this writ says that this tax exemption is to be observed from this year on, let it be understood that it will go into effect the first day of January of the coming year of ninety-eight, from then on and not before.

[3] Treasurer Juan López, Fernán Gómez, Juan Hurtado, Montoro, Luis Pérez, Pedro de Arbolancha.

29

Warrant for the seizure and leasing of vessels required for the Indies

Medina del Campo, 22 June 1497

The King and the Queen

[1] It will be necessary to charter some cargo carriers, caravels, and other ships for the colonization of the islands and mainland discovered in the Ocean Sea, in order to take provisions to the people who are and will remain there, and to discover other lands and bring back any merchandise found there. If the masters and owners decline to lease their ships or if they ask higher charter rates than they usually charge and should fairly receive, it would be a disservice to us, damaging and disrupting the voyages that must be made to the Indies. Therefore, if our admiral of the Indies cannot find the ships he needs or, finding them, the [owners] do not want to go with him, and he asks you for some ships, caravels, and other vessels for these voyages, we charge and order you to inspect the ships and vessels necessary, arranging with their owners to charter them at reasonable prices that seem fair to you and requiring that the owners

and masters go with their ships while creating as little trouble and financial loss as possible to the parties involved. By this writ we give you complete authority to do this.

[2] Done in the town of Medina del Campo on the twenty-second day of the month of June in the year one thousand four hundred ninety-seven.

I, the King
I, the Queen

[3] By order of the King and Queen. Fernán Alvarez.

30
Mandate for reimbursement of cash advances made by Columbus to the colonists
Burgos, 9 May 1497

The King and the Queen

[1] Our chief accountants and your proxies and officials. Sir Christopher Columbus, our admiral of the Ocean Sea, has reported to us that he loaned to people in the Indies sums of money that he says should be deducted from the wages and per diem that those people are supposed to receive from us. He asked us to order you to pay him the money that those people are supposed to receive from us.

[2] To that end, we order you to release the money to our treasurer or his deputy in the Indies, so that the admiral can be reimbursed from the wages the treasurers are supposed to pay to the persons who owe money to the admiral, provided that the admiral or his representative demonstrate to you in a sufficiently legal manner that he is owed this money by those people.

[3] Done in Burgos on the ninth day of May in the year ninety-seven.

I, the King
I, the Queen

[4] By order of the king and queen. Fernán Alvarez.
[5] Agreed.

31
Delivery order for wheat for the Indies from the royal tithe barns
Medina del Campo, 22 June 1497

The King and the Queen

[1] Judges of confiscated and prohibited goods, tithe and excise collectors, and guards in the archdiocese of Seville and the diocese of Cádiz, individually and collectively.

From the grain that we have in the archdiocese and diocese as a result of the two-ninths of the tithe belonging to us, we order you to allow and freely give consent for Sir Christopher Columbus, our admiral of the Indies, or the person he sends bearing a writ signed with his name, to take and transport by sea 550 cahices of wheat and 50 cahices of barley as provision and supplies for the islands of the Indies.

[2] You shall allow him to transport this grain within the next five months, counting from the date of this our writ, on any roads he desires provided that on every main road he register himself in the presence of a municipal judge, two of you, and a clerk, recording on the back of this writ what he is taking, because he cannot take more than these 550 cahices of wheat and 50 cahices of barley.

We order you not to demand or levy any export or other taxes on this grain. It is our wish and command that he not pay any, because this grain is ours and we are ordering it taken for matters of our service.

[3] We order you to do and implement this, without raising any obstacle or opposition, and without contravening it, under pain of our displeasure and a fine of 10,000 maravedís for our treasury on each person who does the contrary.

[4] Done in the town of Medina del Campo on the twenty-second day of the month of June in the year ninety-seven.

I, the King
I, the Queen

[5] By order of the King and Queen. Fernán Alvarez.
[6] Agreed.

32
Authority to the bishop of Badajoz and the admiral to contract for provisions
Alcalá de Henares, 23 December 1497

The King and the Queen

[1] Reverend father in Christ, the bishop of Badajoz;[23] Sir Christopher Columbus, admiral of the Ocean Sea; and members of our council.

We saw your letter in which you say that up to now nothing has been acquired as supplies for the Indies because no one has been found to fulfill the contract at the prices set forth in the instructions that you, the admiral, have. You say that supplies cost more there than they were priced here, and since this is so, we order and charge you two together to investigate and find solvent citizens to contract for it. Set the price that you think ought to be paid, keeping in mind the value of the supplies.

If you do not find such persons, provide for this as seems best to you. We give you full authority for this, so that you, the admiral, are not delayed for departure.

[2] Done in the town of Alcalá de Henares on the twenty-third day of the month of December in the year ninety-seven.

I, the King
I, the Queen

[3] By order of the King and Queen. Fernán Alvarez.
[4] And on the back it said: "Agreed."

CHAPTER 3.3

Fernando and Isabel Authorize the Columbus Family Business in the Indies

33
Order for representatives chosen by the crown and Columbus to ascertain his share
of the profits
Medina del Campo, 30 May 1497

[1] Sir Fernando and Lady Isabel, by the grace of God king and queen of Castile, León, Aragón, Sicily, Granada, Toledo, Valencia, Galicia, the Balearics, Seville, Sardinia, Córdoba, Corsica, Murcia, Jaén, the Algarve, Algeciras, Gibraltar and the Canary Islands, count and countess of Barcelona, lords of Vizcaya and Molina, dukes of Athens and Neopatria, counts of Roussillon and Cerdagne, marquises of Oristano and Goceano.

At the time that Sir Christopher Columbus, our admiral of the Ocean Sea, went to discover the islands and mainland that, by the grace of God our lord, he found and were discovered by him in the Ocean Sea in the region of the Indies, it was agreed with him that he should keep for himself a specific share of whatever might be found.

Now, so this may be better and more completely observed and fulfilled, we have been asked on his behalf to order that all the business and things that should be done and provided in these our kingdoms pertaining to this business with the Indies must be done by one or more of our knowledgeable personnel holding our power of attorney and attending to it jointly with Columbus or whoever holds his power of attorney. Thus, they can better ascertain what becomes of the expenses in this business, as well as the profits and benefit, so that he can be paid his share under our contracts with him, or by virtue of the grants we gave him, or else that we should make some other arrangement for this matter.

We agreed and by this our writ order the persons holding our mandate or responsible for carrying out these grants and contracts from now on to do so by dealing directly with the person or persons that the admiral or whoever holds his power of attorney appoints or nominates for this purpose and in no other manner.

[2] Let it be understood that the admiral of the Indies will delegate and appoint a person or persons who will attend to this on his behalf or with his power of attorney, and we shall be informed when such persons are delegated and appointed by the admiral to administer this business on his behalf. We command you to issue this writ to that effect signed with our names and embossed with our seal.

[3] Given in the town of Medina del Campo on the thirtieth day of the month of May in the year of the birth of our lord Jesus Christ one thousand four hundred and ninety-seven.

I, the King
I, the Queen

[4] I, Fernán Alvarez de Toledo, secretary of the king and queen our lords, caused this to be written by their order.

[5] On the back of this writ it said: "In form, approved. Rodericus, doctor. Registered. Alfonso Pérez; Francisco Díaz, chancellor."

34

Revocation of the permit of 10 April 1495 (document 12)
Medina del Campo, 2 June 1497

[1] The admiral, Sir Christopher Columbus, claims that our writ [of 10 April 1495] and everything stipulated in it is prejudicial to the grants he holds from us and to the powers we gave him. He has appealed and asked us as a favor to provide some remedy for this, if we please.

[2] It never was and is not our intent or desire that Sir Christopher Columbus, our admiral of the Ocean Sea, should be harmed in any way, or that anything should violate or infringe on the contracts, privileges, and grants that we made and conferred on him; rather, we intended to confer on him additional favors in view of the services he has done for us. By this writ, if it is necessary, we confirm and approve the contracts, privileges, and grants we made with the admiral, it being our wish to order that all of them be observed and implemented in their entirety for him by everyone.

[3] We firmly prohibit that anyone should ever dare to contravene or infringe on them or any part of them in any way, under the stated penalties. If their content and form is in any way detrimental to this writ that we order issued and included above, we revoke it. It is our wish and command that it shall have no effect at any time or in any way be prejudicial to the admiral or what we have decreed and confirmed.

[4] We order this given, signed with our names and embossed with our seal.

[5] Given in the town of Medina del Campo on the second day of the month of June in the year of the birth of our Savior Jesus Christ one thousand four hundred ninety-seven.

I, the King
I, the Queen

[6] I, Fernán Alvarez de Toledo, secretary of the king and queen, our lords, had this written by their command.

[7] Agreed: Rodericus, doctor.

[8] Registered: Alfonso Pérez; Francisco Díaz, chancellor.

35

Settlement of Columbus's share of expenses and profits, negotiated by the representatives appointed under authority of document 33 above
Medina del Campo, 12 June 1497

The King and the Queen

[1] The capitulation and contract that by our command was made and signed with you, Sir Christopher Columbus, our admiral of the Ocean Sea in the region of the Indies, stipulates that you are entitled to a specific share of what might be acquired and brought back from the Indies, subtracting first the costs and expenditures that have been and will be incurred, as is more fully contained in the capitulation. Because until now you have directed your efforts at discovering more land in the region of the Indies, little profit has been received from them, although some costs and expenses have been recovered. Because our desire and intent is to confer favors on you, by this writ we wish and command that no part of the costs and expenses thus far incurred in the business relevant to the Indies shall be demanded of you nor for expenses incurred in that leg of this voyage, which we now command to be formed and equipped for the Indies, before you arrive at the island of La Isabela Española.[24] You are not obliged to contribute anything to the costs and expenses beyond what you invested at the time of the first voyage.

This is granted on the condition that you not request or keep anything at all of what has been brought back from the islands in payment of the one-tenth or the one-eighth that you, the admiral, are supposed to have from the movable goods of the islands or on any other account. We make a gift to you of what you have already received from us.

[2] You, the admiral, claim that your one-eighth should be deducted first from whatever is acquired from now on in the islands, then from the remainder should be deducted the expenses and after that the one-tenth. By the order and contents of the

capitulation it seems that first the expenses should be deducted and then the one-tenth and afterwards the one-eighth. How this is to be done has not been ascertained thus far. Nonetheless, it is our pleasure, in order to bestow favor on you, the admiral, that for [the next] three years your one-eighth shall be deducted first before any costs, next the expenses shall be deducted, and of what remains one-tenth shall be deducted for you, the admiral.

After this period of time has lapsed, however, the one-tenth, costs, and one-eighth all shall be deducted as stipulated in the capitulation. By virtue of this grant conferred on you for this period, no further sums shall be given to or deducted for you, other than what you are owed according to the capitulation. Rather, it shall resume in force and vigor as soon as the term has expired.

[3] Done in the town of Medina del Campo on the twelfth day of June of ninety-seven years.

I, the King
I, the Queen

[4] By order of the king and queen. Fernán Alvarez.
[5] On the back of this letter it said: "approved."

36

Appointment of Bartolomé Colón as interim governor of the Indies
Medina del Campo, 22 July 1497

The King and the Queen

[1] Sir Fernando and Lady Isabel, by the grace of God king and queen of Castile, León, Aragón, Sicily, Granada, Toledo, Valencia, Galicia, the Balearics, Seville, Sardinia, Córdoba, Corsica, Murcia, Jaén, the Algarve, Algeciras, Gibraltar, the Canary Islands, count and countess of Barcelona, lords of Vizcaya and Molina, dukes of Athens and Neopatria, counts of Roussillon and Cerdagne, marquises of Oristano and Goceano.

It is reasonable for kings and princes to honor, exalt, and bestow favors and graces on their subjects and citizens, especially those who well and loyally serve them. Recognizing and considering the many, good, and loyal services that you, Sir Bartolomé Colón,[25] brother of Sir Christopher, our admiral of the Ocean Sea, viceroy, and governor of the islands newly found in the Indies, have performed, are still performing, and that we expect you will continue performing for us in the future, we considered it good. It is our wish and command that from now on you should entitle yourself interim governor of the islands newly found in the Indies.

You can use, exercise, and carry out on those islands all the things that other governors of these our kingdoms can do. You should keep, enjoy, and have accorded to you all the honors, graces, favors, privileges, and prerogatives that are due and should be accorded to our other governors of these our kingdoms in their districts and outside them, according to the laws promulgated by us in the Cortes of Toledo[26] and other laws of our kingdoms.

[2] By this our writ or its transcript certified by a public clerk, we order the most illustrious Prince Sir Juan, our most dear and very beloved son, and the princes, prelates, dukes, marquises, counts, governors, magnates, masters, priors, commanders and subcommanders of the military orders; members of our council, judges of our appeals courts, judges, sheriffs, and any interim justices of our household, court, and chancery; all the municipal councils, judges, councilmen, commissioned and noncommissioned officers, masters of trades, and voting citizens of the cities, towns, and villages of these our kingdoms and domains; our admiral, viceroy, and governor of the islands; and the citizens, residents, and other people who are on them whether by contract or in any other way, that from now on they shall entitle, call, accept, and recognize you as governor of the islands and mainland, according to you all the honors, privileges, prerogatives, and immunities that by our laws should be accorded you. The fees and salaries incidental and inherent to the office of our governor shall be remitted to you fully and sufficiently in such a manner that you shall not lack anything.

By this our writ we create and make you interim governor of the islands and mainland only recently found and discovered in the Indies, and install you in the office, its administration, and exercise. We order that you not be prevented or impeded either in the whole or part of it.

[3] If you desire our charter of privilege for this we order our chancellor, notaries, and all other officers who preside at the table of our seals to give, pass, and seal it for you. None of them shall do otherwise under pain of our displeasure and a fine of 10,000 maravedís for our treasury on each person who does the contrary.

[4] Furthermore, we order any man who is shown this our writ as a summons to appear before us in our court wherever we may be within fifteen days of having been cited, under the same penalty. Under this same penalty, we order any public clerk summoned for this purpose to certify that this writ has been displayed to him by inscribing his rubric, so that we may know how well our command is obeyed.

[5] Given in the town of Medina del Campo on the twenty-second day of July in the year of our Lord one thousand four hundred and ninety-seven.

I, the King

I, the Queen

[6] I, Juan de la Parra, secretary of the king and of the queen our lords, had this written at their command.

[7] And on the back of the charter it said: "Agreed: Rodericus, doctor; Fernando Ortiz, for the chancellor. Registered: Doctor."

37

Authority for Columbus to draw on royal profits and assets in the Indies to pay
wages and other expenses
Alcalá de Henares, 23 December 1497

The King and the Queen

[1] By this writ we give permission and authorize you, Sir Christopher Columbus,
our admiral of the Ocean Sea and member of our council, to pay the persons who have
been, are, and in the future may be among the number of people staying in the Indies
in accord with the instruction that you have from us, and to the personnel and owners
of ships transporting supplies and other things to the Indies, all the money that they are
owed for wages, per diem, and freightage, having been verified first.

This shall be paid here by the bishop of Badajoz and you, and in the Indies by you
and our deputy chief accountants residing there, giving to each what he justly deserves
and is owed. Pay them from any merchandise and other things acquired in the Indies
so that the pay or vouchers given them are signed by our deputy chief accountants and
recorded in our books, for which we give you full power.

[2] Done in the town of Alcalá de Henares on the twenty-third day of the month of
December in the year one thousand four hundred ninety-seven.

I, the King
I, the Queen

[3] By order of the king and queen. Fernán Álvarez.
[4] Agreed.

38
Warrant to Francisco de Soria
Burgos, 23 April 1497

The King and the Queen

[1] Francisco de Soria, lieutenant of our high admiral of Castile. We order you to
give and have given to Sir Christopher Columbus, our admiral of the Ocean Sea, an
authorized transcript faithfully rendered of any writs or grants, privileges, and confirmations that the high admiral of Castile has for his office of admiral, by virtue of which
he and others for him collect the dues and other things belonging to him by virtue of
his office.

We order this because we have conferred on Sir Christopher Columbus the same grants, honors, prerogatives, exemptions, taxes, and salaries in the admiralty of the Indies that our high admiral has, holds, and enjoys in the admiralty of Castile.

[2] Execute and implement this as soon as you are notified by this warrant, without any excuse or delay. If you do not implement or execute this, we order our royal judge and the other judges of the city of Seville to compel you to do so, and they shall not do otherwise.

[3] Done in the city of Burgos on the twenty-third day of the month of April in the year ninety-seven.

I, the King
I, the Queen

[4] By order of the king and queen. Fernán Álvarez.

[5] Agreed.

39

Permission for Columbus to establish a hereditary trust

Burgos, 23 April 1497

[1] Sir Fernando and Lady Isabel, by the grace of God king and queen of Castile, León, Aragón, Sicily, Granada, Toledo, Valencia, Galicia, the Balearics, Seville, Sardinia, Córdoba, Corsica, Murcia, Jaén, the Algarve, Algeciras, Gibraltar, and the Canary Islands, count and countess of Barcelona, lords of Vizcaya and Molina, dukes of Athens and Neopatria, counts of Roussillon and Cerdagne, marquises of Oristano and Goceano.

You, Sir Christopher Columbus, our admiral, viceroy, and governor of the Ocean Sea, asked as a favor that we bestow on you our authority to form and establish out of your goods, subjects, properties, and heritable offices one or two hereditary trusts serving as an enduring memorial of you, your family, and lineage, and so that your descendants may be honored.

Having seen this and considered that it is reasonable for kings and princes to honor and elevate their subjects and citizens, especially those serving them well and loyally, and because creating such hereditary trusts honors the royal crown of these our kingdoms and is to their welfare and benefit; and in consideration of the many good, loyal, great, and continuous services that you, Sir Christopher Columbus, our admiral, have done and continue to do every day, especially in discovering and bringing under our power and domain the islands and mainland that you discovered in the Ocean Sea; and principally because we hope that, with the help of God our Lord, it will redound greatly to His service and to our honor, as well as to the welfare and benefit of our kingdoms; and because it is hoped that the Indian peoples of the Indies will be converted to our holy Catholic faith, we approved it.

DESCENDANTS OF CHRISTOPHER COLUMBUS

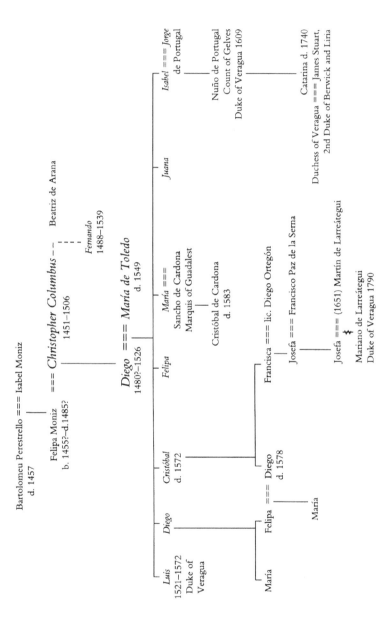

Italic type = lived or traveled in the New World

With this writ, by our own initiative, with true knowledge, and our royal absolute power, of which we desire to make use and do use as king, queen, and lords recognizing no temporal superior, we give you permission and authority so that you can make one or more hereditary trusts, whenever and as often as you wish and think best, either by simple contract and bequest in your lifetime, or as a donation inter vivos, or by your last will, testament, codicil, or any other method you wish, by means of one or more documents, as often and as seems best to you.

You may revoke, bequeath, amend, add to, remove from, decrease, and increase these trusts one or more times as often and in any way convenient for you. This hereditary trust or trusts can be made in favor of Sir Diego Colón, your legitimate eldest son, or any of your heirs and children that you have now and in the future, and, in the absence of any children, favoring one or two of your relatives, or other persons you want to name.

You may include in this trust any subjects, jurisdictions, buildings, properties, heritable offices, mills, and pasture lands that you hold from us by right and inheritance and of all the above everything you possess now and that you are entitled to have, and may acquire from now on, whether by grant and gift, or by renunciation, purchases, trades, exchanges, permutations resulting from any other honorific or lucrative titles, or by any other manner, whatever the cause or reason may be.

[2] You are authorized to establish this hereditary trust or trusts entirely at your own desire and of your own free will and disposition encompassing your possessions and things, fully and completely without any diminution at all, or any part or parts of them, so that these possessions, things, and any part of them shall remain inviolably as a hereditary trust for Sir Diego Colón, your son, for your children and descendants, and for whomever else you want, with the conditions, limitations, obligations, encumbrances, and promises, institutions and substitutions, modes, rules, penalties, and submissions that you wish and find appropriate, and with any ordinances, orders, pacts, and covenants, according to and in the form and manner that you will, order, dispose, and confer, by one or more documents.

[3] Having mentioned and manifestly stated each and every clause of the hereditary trust written here as if every word had been deliberately chosen, we, by our own initiative and with true knowledge, choose to and do make use of our absolute royal power for this purpose. Therefore, we laud the trust and approve, confirm, and impose our royal decree and authority in all and every part of it. We order that all of it shall be valid and observed for you, in whole and in part, inviolably, in the present and forevermore, even though the trust, in whole or in part, may contradict both the spirit and letter of a specific law, and its content and form may be such that it will be necessary to make specific and special mention of it in this our writ, which otherwise cannot be understood due to its vague nature. It shall be observed as well and effectively as if each item, part, and article of it had our approval, permission, and command, according to and in the form your stipulations describe.

[4] It is our wish that all this be done even if your other children, heirs, and other

relatives, both lineal and collateral, may be deprived of their legitimate inheritance and allowances belonging to them, or if Sir Diego Colón, your son, or any others whom you might make beneficiaries of the hereditary trust, legacy, or augmented share, should receive and have a very great and notable excess of what, by rights and municipal laws, you are allowed to bequeath to them in your last will and testament and as a donation inter vivos or in any other way.

[5] It is our wish and favor that the possessions you will include and place in your hereditary trust or trusts can never be lent or divided, that the persons whom you make beneficiaries of the trust or who get it by virtue of your stipulation, cannot sell, give, donate, alienate, divide, or detach it. It cannot be lost or forfeited for any debt he may owe or for any other reason or cause, or for any offense, crime, or excess he may commit, except crimes of lese majesty, sedition, or heresy.

[6] We desire and it is our wish that this be obeyed, notwithstanding the laws stipulating that hereditary trusts cannot have effect even if they are made by virtue of any writs and rescripts that have been given about it; and likewise notwithstanding any laws, constitutions, codes, edicts, uses, customs, proceedings, and actions, be they common or municipal, given by the kings our ancestors that contradict it. None of the laws and codes stipulating that any act prejudicial to a third party or contradicting good use and custom to the detriment and injury of some party shall have effect; and including the law that says prohibitive codes cannot be revoked, the laws that say charters given against law, constitution, and code must be obeyed but not implemented, even though they may contain within themselves mitigating clauses and other binders and exclusions; as well as the law that says a party's right to defense is guaranteed by natural law and cannot be removed or revoked, and that valid laws, constitutions, and codes cannot be revoked, except by the Cortes, nor can any other thing, effect, quality, force, or mystery that may contradict what is described above, even if it is urgent, necessary, enforcing, or of any other type.

Because, by our own initiative, with true knowledge, and by virtue of our royal absolute power, of which we wish to make use as monarchs and sovereign lords not recognizing any temporal superiors, having considered it to be expressed, declared, recorded, and written here as if each word had been deliberately chosen, we dispense, abrogate, rescind, delete, and remove any objection or argument and all other obstacles or impediments touching on this and that could pertain to this our writ and its contents. We supply any defects and any other matters of fact and law, substance, or formality that may be necessary and advantageous for its validation and corroboration.

[7] We order the most illustrious Prince Sir Juan, our most dear and very beloved son, and the princes, prelates, dukes, counts, marquises, and magnates; masters, priors, commanders, and subcommanders of the military orders; commanders of castles, fortresses, and houses; members of our royal council, judges of our appeals court and its chancery; judges and sheriffs of our household, court, and chancery; and to all the royal and municipal judges and sheriffs, toll and tithe judges, municipal councilmen, commissioned and noncommissioned officers, masters of trades, and voting citizens of all

cities, towns, and villages in these our kingdoms and domains, now and in the future, to observe this grant that we confer in its entirety, according to what is stipulated in it.

You may not contravene or violate it or any part of it, at any time, in any way, or for any cause or reason. You shall implement, execute, and carry out to the proper extent and effect the stipulations required by this heritable trust, legacy, and augmented share, according to and in the form and manner expressed in every clause contained in it, without waiting for or expecting any other writ or mandate from us, or a second or third opinion.

[8] This we order our high chancellor, notaries, and other officials presiding over the table with our seals to issue, pass, and seal our charter of privilege, as best and most sufficiently you need. None of you shall do otherwise in any way, under penalty of 10,000 maravedís fine payable to our treasury on the person who does the contrary.

[9] Further, we command the man who shows you this writ to summon you to appear before us in our court, wherever we may be, within fifteen days of having been cited, under the same penalty. Under this same penalty, we order any public clerk who may be summoned for this purpose to give to the person displaying this writ to him a certificate to that effect, inscribed with his rubric, so that we may know how our command is obeyed.

[10] Given in the city of Burgos on the twenty-third day of the month of April in the year of the birth of our Lord Jesus Christ one thousand four hundred ninety-seven.

I, the King

I, the Queen

[11] I, Fernán Álvarez de Toledo, secretary of the king and queen our lords, had this written by their order.

[12] And on the back of the letter was written the following: "In form: Rodericus, doctor. Registered: Alfonso Pérez, and sealed."

CHAPTER 3.4

Columbus Discovers New Privileges as Admiral

40

Warrant to Francisco de Soria to deliver to Columbus a copy of the privileges and
confirmations of the admiral of Castile

Burgos, 23 April 1497

The King and the Queen

[1] Francisco de Soria, lieutenant of our high admiral of Castile.

We order you to give and cause to be given to Sir Christopher Columbus, our admiral of the Ocean Sea, an authorized transcription faithfully rendered of any writs of grants, privileges, and confirmations that the high admiral of Castile has for his office of admiral by which he and others for him collect dues and other things belonging to him by virtue of his office.

We order this because we have given Sir Christopher Columbus the same gifts, honors, prerogatives, liberties, dues, and salaries in the admiralty of the Indies that our high admiral has, holds, and enjoys in the admiralty of Castile.

[2] Implement this as soon as you are notified by this our warrant, without any excuse or delay. If you do not implement it, we order our royal judge and the other judges of the city of Seville to compel you to comply; and neither you nor they shall do otherwise.

[3] Done in the city of Burgos on the twenty-third day of the month of April of the year ninety-seven.

I, the King
I, the Queen

[4] By order of the king and queen. Fernán Álvarez.

41

Notarial description of the following document
Burgos, 23 April 1497

[1] This is a transcript of a document written on paper, and inscribed and signed by a clerk and public notary. Its content is as follows:

42

Notarial declaration of the following document presented for confirmation on behalf of Admiral Fadrique Enríquez
Valladolid, 5 July 1435

[1] In the town of Valladolid, where the court and chancery of our lord king are staying, Tuesday, the fifth day of July, in the year of the birth of our lord Jesus Christ one thousand four hundred and thirty-five, before the lords judges of the lord king, who were making reports in the palaces and houses of lord Sir Gutierre de Toledo,[1] bishop of Palencia, judge of the chancery court, in the usual palace and place where they are accustomed to hold public audience and give opinions. In the presence of us, Juan Martínez de León and Pedro García de Madrigal, clerks of the lord king and his chancery court and his public notaries in his court, kingdoms, and dominions, and in the presence of the witnesses written below, Gonzalo Fernández de Medina appeared before the lord judges and declared himself to be the representative here in the lord king's court on behalf of the lord admiral, Sir Fadrique.[2] He had read to us clerks a charter of privilege from the lord king, endorsed by members of the royal court, written on parchment, signed with the king's name, and sealed with his lead seal hanging from silk threads. The content is as follows:

43

Juan II acknowledges his charter appointing Alfonso Enríquez as admiral of Castile, document 48 below

[1] Sir Juan,[3] by the grace of God king of Castile, León, Toledo, Galicia, Seville, Córdoba, Murcia, Jaén, the Algarve, and Algeciras, and lord of Vizcaya and Molina.[4]

To all the prelates, masters of the military orders, dukes, counts, and notables; all members of my council and judges of my appellate court; judges, notaries, justices, other officials of my court and chancery and of my household and precinct; governors, chief judges, knights, and officers; and all the municipal councils, councilmen, municipal judges, sheriffs, toll, tax, and ecclesiastical judges, provosts, and any other justices and officials of the most noble city of Seville and all the other cities, towns, and villages of these my kingdoms and dominions; sea captains, my fleet outfitter, commanders and boatswains of my galleys; masters, sailors, navigators, and any other persons who sail by sea or river; all other persons of whatever status, condition, rank, or dignity that they may be who may or could be affected by the following, or whoever is shown this my charter of privilege or an authorized transcription of it signed by a public clerk, greetings.

[2] This is to inform you that I have seen a charter of privilege endorsed by the members of the royal court, sealed with my hanging lead seal, written on parchment, issued by my order to Sir Alfonso Enríquez, my uncle[5] and high admiral of the sea. Its content is as follows:

44

Juan II acknowledges his charter appointing Alfonso Enríquez as admiral of Castile

[1] In the name of God the Father, Son, and Holy Spirit, who are three persons in one true God who reigns forevermore; and of the Most Blessed Virgin, glorious Saint Mary, his Mother, whom I revere as my lady and advocate in all my affairs; and in honor and service to the most blessed apostle Saint James, light and mirror to all the lands of Spain, and patron and guide of the kings of Castile, my ancestors, and me; and [in the name] of all the saints of the entire celestial court.

It is natural that all who serve kings well and with pure motives, exerting great toil and effort, should receive an equally great reward as a great comfort and consolation for their efforts; and also it is good for kings to reward those who serve them well, both to do as kings ought and to set an example so that whoever knows or hears of it might more willingly serve them. The king who does so should consider three things: first, what gift he gives; second, to whom he is giving it and whether that person deserves it; and third, what good or harm he might receive by giving it.

To this end, I am mindful of this and take it into consideration, as well as the many and good services that you, Sir Alfonso Enríquez, my uncle and high governor of the seas, performed for the lord King Juan[6] of illustrious memory, my grandfather (may God reward him with holy paradise); and [the services that you did] for the lord King Enrique,[7] my father and lord (may God have mercy on him); and the services that you have done and are doing daily for me and for your lineage; and the relationship that I have with you.

Because of who you are, and in order to reward you for all these things, I wish by this privilege to make known to all men, present and future, that I, Sir Juan, by the grace of God king of Castile, León, Toledo, Galicia, Seville, Córdoba, Murcia, Jaén, the Algarve, and Algeciras, and lord of Vizcaya and Molina, have seen a letter from the lord King Enrique, my father and lord (may God have mercy on him), written on paper, signed with his name, sealed on the back with his seal, and drawn up in this manner:

45
Charter from Enrique III appointing Alfonso Enríquez admiral of Castile
Toro, 4 April 1405

[1] Sir Enrique, by the grace of God king of Castile, León, Toledo, Galicia, Seville, Córdoba, Murcia, Jaén, the Algarve, and Algeciras, and lord of Vizcaya and Molina.

In order to reward you, Sir Alfonso Enríquez, my uncle, for the many, loyal, and notable services that you did for the lord King Juan, my father and my lord (may God have mercy on him), and [the services you] have done and are doing daily for me, I make you my high admiral of the sea, just as the Admiral Sir Diego Hurtado de Mendoza,[8] deceased, used to be.

You shall have the admiralty with all the income, dues, and jurisdiction that belong to it in any manner, as Sir Diego Hurtado and the others who have been admirals until now most fully had them.

[2] With this my charter I command all the prelates, masters, counts, notables, and commissioned and noncommissioned officers; all the municipal councils and judges, sheriffs, toll, tax, and ecclesiastical judges, provosts, and any other judges of my most noble city of Seville and of all the other cities, towns, and villages of these my kingdoms and dominions; sea captains, my fleet outfitter, commanders and boatswains of my galleys, masters, seamen, navigators, and all other persons who travel and sail by sea that any and all of them are to accept and obey you, Sir Alfonso Enríquez, as my high admiral of the sea in all things pertaining to the admiralty.

I order them to remit and cause to be remitted to you in full all the income and dues that they owe you pertaining to this office, so that nothing at all owing to you is diminished, as well and completely as they used to accept, obey, and remit to the admiral Sir Diego Hurtado and to the other admirals before now.

[3] By this my charter I give you all my full power so that you can exercise the civil and criminal jurisdiction pertaining to the admiralty office in whatever manner in all

the laws of the sea. I give you my power both to issue letters of marque and to judge all lawsuits that may arise at sea, in ports, and in their territories as far as the tide reaches and ships navigate.

You the admiral have the power to appoint your judges, sheriffs, clerks, and officials in all the towns and villages of my kingdoms that are seaports, and preside over and resolve all the criminal and civil suits that may arise at sea and in the tidal basins of rivers. You shall appoint them in the same way and as fully and completely in the city of Seville as my previous admirals did.

[4] By this my charter I command the members of my council, judges of my appellate court, judges of my royal court, and all the other judges of the towns and villages that are seaports in my kingdoms, that they shall not presume to preside over nor resolve these lawsuits, nor disturb you or the officials you will appoint in your jurisdiction to preside over the suits for you in the prescribed manner.

[5] For this I command my high chancellor, notaries, clerks, and any other officials who are in charge of my seals, to give, issue, and seal for you my strongest, firmest, and most encompassing charters of privileges, with the safest guarantees that may be necessary, as they were given to the other admirals who were your predecessors or whichever of them held it most completely. None of you shall do otherwise in any way under pain of my displeasure.

[6] I hereby command that you be given my charter signed with my name and sealed with my privy seal.

[7] Given in the city of Toro on the fourth day of the month of April, year of the birth of our Lord Jesus Christ one thousand four hundred and five.

[8] I, Juan Martín, chancellor of the king, caused this to be written at his command.

I, the King

[9] Registered.

46
Juan II confirms the appointment of Alfonso Enríquez as admiral of Castile
Valladolid, 17 August 1416

[1] Now, Sir Alfonso Enríquez, my uncle and my high admiral of the sea, has asked me as a favor to confirm for him the writ of the king, my father and my lord, may God have mercy on him, and the favors contained in it. He asked me to command that every detail of the writ be observed and fulfilled by ordering that my charter of privilege written on parchment and sealed with my hanging lead seal be given to him, so that he can better and more fully enjoy the office of admiral and the favors contained

in the writ of the lord king, my father. Moreover, he asked that he may be paid all the admiralty revenues and dues that should be his. He also asked to have all the admiralty's jurisdictions, franchises, privileges, and liberties that belong and should belong to him as fully as my other admirals, his predecessors, held them and that are contained in the writ of the lord king, my father and my lord (may God have mercy on him).

[2] I, the lord King Juan, in order to confer favor and grace on Sir Alfonso Enríquez, my uncle and my high admiral of the sea, am pleased to confirm for him the writ of the king, my father, and the favors contained in it. I command that these favors contained in the writ shall be valid and observed fully, faithfully, and completely.

[3] By this my privilege and by its transcription signed by a public clerk, copied by authority of a royal or municipal judge, I command all prelates, masters, priors of the orders, and counts, magnates, commanders, subcommanders, commissioned and non-commissioned officers; members of my royal council; judges of my appellate court, and judges and sheriffs of my royal court; all municipal councils and judges, sheriffs; toll and tax judges; provosts; commanders of castles, forts, and houses; any other justices, officers, and magistrates of the most noble city of Seville and of all the other cities, towns, and villages of these our kingdoms and dominions; sea captains, commanders, boatswains, bargemen, masters of cargo carriers and galleys, my fleet outfitter, sailors, navigators, all seamen, rivermen, fishermen, boatmen, and all others who travel in my fleet or on any other ships that travel from now on, of whatever status or rank they may be, that you and they regard and receive Alfonso Enríquez, my uncle, as my high admiral of the sea everywhere in my kingdoms and dominions.

I command that you work in conjunction with him in the administration of the admiralty's civil and criminal jurisdiction, and appear in response to his citations and summonses or those of whom he may appoint in his place, as faithfully and completely as you used to do with any and all of the admirals who served in the time of the kings from whom I descend, and also in the writ from the king, my father and lord (may God have mercy on him).

I command that you remit and have remitted to him all the revenues and dues that pertain to the admiralty in any way and for whatever reason, and that you obey and carry out his command as my high admiral of the sea as you would do for me in my own presence.

[4] Furthermore, I approve and order that, if any persons do anything at sea, in a river, or elsewhere for which it may be necessary to try or punish them, or if they are disobedient to Sir Alfonso Enríquez, my uncle, or to the officers he may appoint in his place at sea, in a river, or on land, the admiral may order them tried and impose on them any punishments they deserve according to the law.

[5] I agree that, of all the profits that my high admiral has or makes in my fleet or at sea, I shall have two-thirds, and the admiral shall have one-third when he goes in person with the fleet, even though the fleet or part of it separates from his command or goes without his command. I also agree that, of the profit accruing from galleys that I

order outfitted for profit apart from a fleet, I shall have two-thirds and the admiral one-third.

[6] I agree and order that, of all the galleys, ships, galliots, vessels, and boats that will be outfitted elsewhere, in which I am entitled to one-fifth [of the profits], I will keep two-thirds of this fifth, and the admiral one-third of it. I ordain that for each one that the admiral outfits by my command, he can take with him four persons under arrest and charged with crimes punishable by death or brought to the city of Seville or any other ports in my kingdoms and dominions. For every ship at sea or about to sail, my admiral personally can invest one-third of the cost of outfitting.

[7] I ordain that my admiral shall have full jurisdiction over his admiralty, sailings, and cases civil and criminal in all ports and of these my kingdoms and domains, whether these are seaports or not, including the city of Seville,[9] with all powers and dues pertinent to the admiralty office. He and those whom he appoints in his place shall have and exercise full civil and criminal jurisdiction in all the seaports and their towns and villages, both issuing letters of reprisal and trying all those lawsuits that might arise at sea and on the river, as well as in the ports, towns, and their villages, as far as the salt water reaches and ships navigate. The admiral may appoint judges, sheriffs, clerks, and officials in all towns and villages that are seaports in these my kingdoms and domains to preside over and resolve all criminal and civil cases arising at sea or on the river in the tidal basin.

[8] I command the members of my council and the judges of my appellate court, of my royal court, and of all the towns and villages of the seaports in my kingdoms, not to meddle in, preside over, or resolve those cases. They shall not trouble my admiral or the officials whom he may appoint in his place to try the cases under his civil or criminal jurisdiction. I strictly forbid anyone to dare oppose or contravene the writ of the lord king, my father and my lord (may God have mercy on him), or to break or diminish the favors, exemptions, and liberties stipulated in it and in this my privilege, now or in the future.

Anyone who does the contrary, opposes, or contravenes any part of this shall incur my wrath and forfeit to me two thousand Castilian doblas of fine gold and true weight in penalty for every violation, and to my high admiral or his representative double all the resulting damages and losses that he may have suffered. Furthermore, I shall have recourse to their persons and property for this purpose.

[9] I command the justices and each one of you in your places and jurisdictions to seize the property of those who contravene or oppose this, or who try to do so, up to the same amount of two thousand doblas for each violation. You shall keep [the doblas] so that I may do with them whatever I desire and shall compensate my high admiral or his representative for double all the damages and losses that he may have received as a result of these violations.

[10] Every time that someone fails to do and implement this, I command the person to whom this privilege or its authorized transcription is displayed to summon you, the municipal councils, to appear before me wherever I may be. You shall send in person

your authorized representatives and one or two of the officials of every city or town where this might occur, with the power to represent the rest of your fellow officials, within fifteen days of having been summoned, under the stipulated penalty, to state the reason why you have not executed my order. I command, under the same penalty, that any public clerk summoned for such purpose shall deliver, to the person presenting this decree, a certificate marked with his rubric, so that I may know in what manner my order is obeyed.

[11] I command you to give to Sir Alfonso Enríquez, my uncle and my high admiral of the sea, this privilege written on parchment, bearing the circle of signatures,[10] and sealed with my lead seal hanging by silk threads.

[12] Given in the town of Valladolid on the seventeenth day of August in the year of our lord Jesus Christ one thousand four hundred and seventeen.

[13] And I, the lord King Juan, reigning together with the lady Queen Catalina,[11] my mother, lady, guardian, and regent of these my kingdoms, and with the lady Princess Catalina, my sister, in Castile, León, Toledo, Galicia, Seville, Córdoba, Murcia, Jaén, Baeza, Badajoz, the Algarve, Algeciras, Vizcaya, and Molina, grant this privilege and cosign it.

[14] The prince, Sir Juan,[12] cousin of the lord king and his high steward, cosigns.

[15] Sir Enrique,[13] his brother, cousin of the lord king and master of Santiago, cosigns.

[16] The prince, Sir Pedro,[14] his brother, cousin of the lord king, cosigns.

[17] Sir Luis de Guzmán,[15] master of the military order of Calatrava, cosigns.

[18] Sir Pedro, lord of Montealegre, vassal of the king, cosigns.

[19] Sir Luis de La Cerda,[16] count of Medinaceli, vassal of the king, cosigns.

[20] Sir Pablo,[17] bishop of Burgos, high chancellor of the king, cosigns.

[21] Sir Lope de Mendoza,[18] archbishop of Santiago, high chaplain of the king, cosigns.

[22] Friar Sir Alfonso,[19] bishop of Santiago, cosigns.

[23] Sir Juan,[20] bishop of Segovia, cosigns.

[24] Sir Diego,[21] bishop of Cuenca, cosigns.

[25] Sir Gonzalo de Zúñiga,[22] bishop of Palencia, cosigns.

[26] Sir Diego Gómez de Sandoval,[23] royal judge of Murcia [sic], cosigns.

[27] Sir Juan Ramírez de Arellano,[24] lord of Los Cameros, vassal of the king, cosigns.

[28] Sir García Fernández Manrique,[25] lord of Aguilar, vassal of the king, cosigns.

[29] Iñigo López de Mendoza,[26] lord of La Vega, vassal of the king, cosigns.

[30] I, Juan Fernández de Palencia, clerk of the king, had this written by his command in the tenth year that the lord king reigned.

[31] Fernandus, bachelor in laws; Alfonsus: registered.

47

Amplification of charter appointing Alfonso Enríquez admiral of Castile
Segovia, 6 June 1419

[1] And now Sir Alfonso Enríquez, high admiral of the sea, has asked me as a favor to confirm to him the privilege of favor contained here, and to command that it be observed in its entirety.

[2] I, King Sir Juan, in order to confer grace and favor to Sir Alfonso Enríquez, my uncle and my high admiral of the sea, having considered the relationship that he has with me, as well as the many, good, and notable services that he performed for King Sir Juan, my grandfather, and for King Sir Enrique, my father and my lord (may God have mercy on him), and does for me daily, approved it.

[3] Therefore of my own volition and full knowledge, it is my wish and command to confirm for him this privilege and all the favors in it. I issue it for him now again in its entirety, according to and in the manner contained in the privilege. He can exercise the office of admiral with all the justice, jurisdiction high and low, civil and criminal, with law making and enforcing authority, and with each and all the other things contained in the charter of privilege incorporated above. He also may avail himself of it, as may those whom he appoints as his proxies, both within my court, chancery, household, and precinct, and outside them. He and those whom he appoints as his proxies shall have the power to perform each and all the other things contained in the charter of privilege incorporated above. These things I now grant and confer with the same free and plenary jurisdiction, power, and complete authority as I myself have.

[4] By this my charter of privilege or its transcription signed by a public clerk and copied by authority of a magistrate or judge, I firmly forbid that anyone from now on dare act or proceed against him or the privilege in order to violate or diminish anything stipulated in it. Anyone who does so, or acts or proceeds against all or any part of the privilege, will incur my anger. Moreover, he shall pay me the fines stipulated in the privilege incorporated above, and [pay] to Sir Alfonso Enríquez, my uncle and my high admiral, or to his representative, all the resulting damages and losses. He also must pay a penalty of 10,000 maravedís to the treasury of Sir Alfonso Enríquez, my uncle and my admiral. I desire, and it is my wish and command, that anyone who contravenes or attempts to contravene what is contained in this my privilege or any part of it, by that very fact itself shall become liable for this penalty of 10,000 maravedís. I confer this as a favor on Alfonso Enríquez, my uncle and my high admiral, or on whomever he may designate.

[5] To this effect, I command all prelates, masters of the orders, commanders, sub-commanders, dukes, counts, and magnates; members of my council and judges of my appeals court; judges, notaries, sheriffs, justices, and other officials of my court, chancery, household, and precinct; my royal governors, appellate judges, and commis-

sioned and noncommissioned officers; all municipal councils, royal and municipal judges, sheriffs, toll, tax, tithe and other judges and officials of the most noble city of Seville and of all the cities, towns, and villages of these my kingdoms and domains; sea captains and outfitter of my fleet, commanders and boatswains of my galleys, masters, seamen, navigators and any other persons who travel and navigate by sea; and all other persons, of whatever status, rank, lineage, or dignity they may be, who may see this my letter of privilege or its transcript signed as mentioned, to observe and fulfil, and cause to be observed and fulfilled to Sir Alfonso Enríquez, my uncle and my high admiral of the sea, or to whoever he designates to receive it for him, this privilege and all the favors contained in it, in all things fully and completely, and in the manner stipulated. They are not to oppose, contravene, nor agree to oppose or contravene, all or part of it at any time or for any possible reason, under pain of incurring my displeasure and the penalty stipulated in the charter of privilege on any person by whose fault it might remain undone and unfulfilled.

[6] I command the high chancellor of my privy seal, members of my council; judges of my appeals court, royal judges, and notaries; chief accountants; and my officials and clerks who preside over the table with my seals,[27] that if, with respect to any or all of these things, my admiral or those he may appoint in his stead demands from them my writs, charters of privilege, or any other documents, to give them to him and deliver, issue, transfer, and seal them as securely, sufficiently, and completely as they are able and as they may find necessary so that all and every clause and item may be executed. Neither you nor they shall contravene it, under the stipulated penalty. If, because of you or them, it remains undone and unfulfilled, I command the person who exhibits to you this my charter of privilege or its authenticated transcript to summon you to appear before me in my court. Within fifteen days of having been summoned, municipal councils must send representatives, and officials and other individuals must appear in person, under the stipulated penalty, each to explain why you did not fulfil my command. I command every public clerk summoned for this purpose immediately to give the person who exhibits this charter a certificate inscribed with his rubric, so that I may know how my command is obeyed.

[7] I order given to my admiral, my uncle, this my charter of privilege, written on parchment, signed with my name, endorsed, and sealed with my lead seal hanging by silk threads.

[8] Given in the city of Segovia on the sixth day of June in the year of our savior Jesus Christ one thousand four hundred and nineteen.

I, the King

[9] I, King Juan, reigning together with the lady Queen María, my wife,[28] and with the lady Princess Catalina, my sister, in Castile, León, Galicia, Toledo, Seville, Córdoba, Murcia, Jaén, Baeza, Badajoz, the Algarve, Algeciras, Vizcaya, and Molina, grant this privilege and confirm it.

[10] Prince Juan, cousin of the lord king, prince of Aragón, master of Santiago, cosigns.

[11] Prince Pedro, cousin of the lord king, cosigns.

[12] Sir Alfonso Enríquez, uncle of the lord king, high admiral of the sea, cosigns.

[13] Sir Ruy López Dávalos,[29] constable of Castile, royal governor of Murcia, co-signs.

[14] Sir Luis de Guzmán, master of the military order of Calatrava, cosigns.

[15] Sir Luis de La Cerda, count of Medinaceli, vassal of the king, cosigns.

[16] Sir Juan Alfonso Pimentel,[30] count of Benavente, vassal of the king, cosigns.

[17] Sir Pedro, lord of Montealegre, vassal of the king, cosigns.

[18] Sir Lope de Mendoza, archbishop of Santiago, chief chaplain, cosigns.

[19] Sir Rodrigo de Velasco,[31] bishop of Palencia, cosigns.

[20] Sir Pablo, bishop of Burgos, high chancellor of the king, cosigns.

[21] Sir Alfonso,[32] bishop of Sigüenza, cosigns.

[22] Sir Juan, bishop of Segovia, cosigns.

[23] Sir Juan,[33] bishop of Ávila, cosigns.

[24] Sir Alvaro,[34] bishop of Cuenca, cosigns.

[25] Sir Fernando,[35] bishop of Córdoba, cosigns.

[26] Sir Gutierre Gómez, administrator of the church of Palencia, high chancellor of the queen of Castile, cosigns.

[27] Sir Rodrigo,[36] bishop of Jaén, cosigns.

[28] And I, Juan Fernández de Guadalajara, caused it to be written by command of the king our lord.

[29] Fernandus, bachelor in laws. Registered.

48
Certificate of collation of the authenticated copy of decree, confirmation, and amplification of decree appointing Alfonso Enríquez admiral of Castile
Valladolid, 12 November 1489

[1] After this charter of privilege of the lord king was presented and read, Gonzalo Fernández, representing the lord admiral, explained to the lords judges that the lord admiral intended and found it necessary to send this charter of privilege and to present it in various places where it would serve the lord king and the welfare of the subjects and citizens of his kingdoms and domains, and for the care and preservation of the admiralty and the admiral's affairs. But it is feared this charter of privilege could be lost or damaged, either by theft, fire, water, or any other unexpected dangers that might befall, resulting in a disservice to the lord king and great damage to the lord admiral.

Therefore he asked the judges, in the best manner and form he could and by right of their office should, to grant permission to us, Juan Martins and Pedro García, clerks, so that the two of us working together as public officials could copy and cause to be copied from the original writ and privilege of the lord king, one or more transcripts, as many as might suffice and be necessary for the admiral Sir Fadrique, and that we should deliver them inscribed by each of us and faithfully collated with the original charter of privilege. The transcripts of the lord king's charter of privilege, which we shall give to the lord admiral or his representative on his behalf, are to be inscribed with our rubrics.

[2] To make them more secure and valid, he asked the lords judges to give and bestow their decree and authorization so that all transcripts that we clerks deliver so inscribed will avail and obtain credence wherever they appear, in litigation and otherwise, in the same manner that the original charter of privilege would avail and obtain credence upon being placed in evidence.

[3] The lords judges, having seen the request, took the original charter of privilege in their hands and inspected, tested, and examined it. On this occasion they did not find it either torn, broken, cancelled, or interpolated, nor any part of it dubious or suspicious, but rather free of all defect. Therefore, they declared, ordered, and gave license to us, Juan Martíns de León and Pedro García de Madrigal, clerks, as public officials jointly to make or cause to be made from the original of our lord king's charter of privilege one or two transcripts or as many as might suffice and be necessary for the lord admiral, and deliver them to him inscribed with our rubrics and collated with the original charter of privilege. The lords judges declared that they bestowed their authorization and decree on the transcript or transcripts that we deliver to the lord admiral, to the degree and in the best manner and form that they could and should by law, so that the transcript or transcripts that we deliver duly inscribed should avail and obtain credence wherever they might appear, whether in or outside litigation, as completely as the lord king's original charter of privilege would avail and obtain credence.

[4] Witnesses who were present: licentiate Juan López de Miranda and bachelor [of arts] Diego Muñoz, judges of the hidalgos,[37] and bachelors [of arts] Luis Rodríguez, Fernand Matheos, Alonso López de Sevilla, and Luis González de Córdoba, clerks of the lord king.

[5] Then Gonzalo Fernández, in the name of the lord admiral, requested us clerks to give him this transcript of the lord king's original charter of privilege, with its authorization and decree, for the security and protection of the admiralty and the admiral's affairs. This was done and occurred on the day, month, and year written above, in the presence of the witnesses.

[6] We, Juan Martíns de León and Pedro García de Madrigal, clerks, by virtue of the license and command given and delivered to us by the lords judges, both of us together complying with the authorization and decree bestowed by them, caused this transcript of our lord king's original charter of privilege to be written and copied. We collated it word by word with the original charter of privilege, in the presence of the witnesses below, who were present at the collation and saw, heard read, and collated this transcript with the original charter of privilege.

[7] Witnesses who were present and summoned to the collation are the following:

Francisco Martíns de Villa Anpando, clerk of the appellate court, and Andrés de Valladolid and Fernando de Medina, son of Juan de Medina, employees of Juan Martíns de León.

[8] A deletion in a place where it says "wherefore great reward" has been written in above the line; and where it says "and written" between lines; and where it says "my" and "written" between lines; and where it says "any ship" and where it says "at sea"; and between lines where it says "said"; and crossed out where it says "public which for"; and between lines where it says "of" and where it says "of Orgaz"; and written and crossed out where it says "notable content"; and written between lines where it says "me" and where it says "Juan López" let this be no prejudice thereto.

[9] I, Juan Martíns de León, clerk and public notary, having been present with Pedro García de Madrigal, clerk, along with the other witnesses who were present before the lords judges, by command and license of the lords judges, together with Pedro García, clerk, caused this transcript of the lord king's charter of privilege, with its authorization, to be written and copied on these three and one half sheets of parchment. This sheet bears my rubric, and my name is written at the bottom of each page. I collated this transcript with the lord king's original charter of privilege together with Pedro García, clerk, in the presence of the witnesses mentioned in this document, who were present at the collation. To that effect, I inscribed my rubric here, like this, in testimony of the truth. Juan Martíns

[10] I, Pedro García de Madrigal, clerk and public notary, having been present, with Juan Martínez de León, clerk, before the lords judges, together with the other witnesses who were present, by command and license of the lords judges, together with Juan Martíns, clerk, caused this transcript of the lord king's charter of privilege, with its authorization, to be written and copied on these three and one half sheets of parchment. On this sheet I made my rubric, and my name is written at the bottom of each page. Having collated this transcript with the original charter of privilege from the lord king together with Juan Martíns, clerk, in the presence of the witnesses mentioned in this document, who were present at the collation. To that effect, I inscribed my rubric here in testimony of the truth. Pedro García.

[11] This transcript was collated with the original document, from which it was copied, before the witnesses who were present, on Friday, the thirteenth day of the month of November, in the year of the birth of our savior Jesus Christ one thousand four hundred and eighty-nine.

[12] Witnesses who were present at the reading and collation of this transcript copied from the original document: Alfonso de Valle and Diego de Mesa, judges; Nuño de Mendoza, Fernando de Esquivel, and Juan de Montanos, clerk of the king our lord; and others.

[13] I, Gonzalo García de Villamayor, clerk of our lord king and his public notary in this court and in all the courts of his kingdoms and dominions, was present together with the witnesses to collate this transcript with the document from which it was copied, which I caused to be written. I inscribe my rubric here in testimony. Gonzalo García, clerk of the king.

CHAPTER 3.5

Fernando and Isabel Confirm the Capitulations

49
[original placement of 1, Santa Fe Capitulations]

50
New preface to confirmation of the Granada Capitulations
Burgos, 23 April 1497

[1] Because you, Sir Christopher Columbus, our admiral of the Ocean Sea and our viceroy and governor of the mainland and islands, have asked us as a favor, in order more completely to observe the charter of favor to you, your children, and descendants, we confirm and approve it for you and command that you be given our charter of this privilege or of whatever our favor may be. We are mindful of all this and the many good, loyal, great, and continuing services that you, Sir Christopher Columbus, our admiral, viceroy, and governor of the islands and mainland discovered and to be discovered in the Ocean Sea in the region of the Indies, have performed and that we hope you will perform for us, especially in discovering and bringing into our power and under our dominion the islands and mainland, principally because we hope that, with the help of God our Lord, it will redound to His great service and our honor, as well as to the good and benefit of our kingdoms and domains. Hoping that, with the help of God, the Indian inhabitants of the Indies will be converted to our holy Catholic faith, we approved it. By this our charter of privilege or its signed transcript, of our own initiative, with true knowledge, and by our royal absolute power,[38] which we choose to exercise in this instance, we confirm and approve, in the present and forevermore, for you, Sir Christopher Columbus, your children, grandchildren, descendants, and heirs, our charter incorporated above and the favors stipulated in it. We wish and command, and it is our favor and grace, that it be observed and guaranteed to you,

your children, and descendants, now and in the future inviolably, according to and in the form and manner stipulated. If necessary, again we bestow on you this favor and firmly forbid that any person dare to oppose you or contravene it or any part of it, so as to violate or diminish it at any time or in any manner.

[2] We command the prince Sir Juan, our most dear and very beloved son, and the princes, dukes, prelates, marquises, counts, and magnates; masters, priors, commanders, and subcommanders of the military orders; members of our royal council; judges of our appellate court, judges, sheriffs, and any other justices of our household, court, and chancery; commanders of the castles, forts, and houses; and each and all municipal councils, royal judges, corregidores, municipal judges, sheriffs, toll, tax, and tithe judges, as well as other justices of all the cities, towns, and villages of these our kingdoms and domains, to observe and cause to be observed this our charter of privilege, its confirmation, and the writ of favor contained in it.

They shall not oppose or hinder you contrary to its content and form, or attempt to do so, at any time or in any manner, under the stated penalties.

[3] We order that you be given this our charter of privilege and its confirmation, written on parchment, signed with our names, and sealed with our lead seal hanging by colored silk threads. We order our chancellor, steward, notary, and other officials who preside over the table with our seals to emboss, issue, and pass it.

[4] All of which we desire as stated in the articles above and contained in this our confirmation. It is our wish and command that it be observed and executed accordingly. None of you or them shall oppose it in any manner, under penalty of our displeasure and a fine of 10,000 maravedís for our treasury on each person who does the contrary.

Further, we command the man who shows you this writ to summon you to appear before us in our court, wherever we may be, within fifteen days of having been cited, under the same penalty. Under this same penalty, we command every public clerk who may be summoned for this purpose to give to the person showing this writ to him a certificate to that effect, inscribed with his rubric, so that we may know how our command is obeyed.

[5] Given in the city of Burgos on the twenty-third day of the month of April in the year of the birth of our lord Jesus Christ one thousand four hundred and ninety-seven.

I, the King

I, the Queen

[6] I, Fernán Álvarez de Toledo, secretary of the king and queen our lords, caused this to be written at their command.

[7] Antonius, doctor. Registered. Doctor Rodericus; doctor Antonius; doctor Fernand Alvarez; Juan Velázquez.

[8] And on the back of the charter of privilege was written the following: "Without chancery and without fees, by order of Their Highnesses."

New confirmation of Columbus's appointment as admiral, viceroy, and governor
Burgos, 23 April 1497

[1] You, Sir Christopher Columbus, our admiral of the Ocean Sea and our viceroy and governor of the mainland and islands, have asked us as a favor, in order better and more completely to guarantee the charter of favor to you, your children, and descendants, to confirm and approve it for you. We command that you be given our charter of this privilege or of whatever our favor may be. We, mindful of all this and considering the many, good, loyal, great, and continuing services that you, Sir Christopher Columbus, our admiral, viceroy, and governor of the Indies [*sic*] and mainland discovered and to be discovered in the Ocean Sea in the region of the Indies, have done and that we hope will do for us, especially in discovering and bringing within our power and under our dominion the islands and mainland. Especially we hope that, with the help of God our lord, it will redound greatly to His great service, our honor, and the good and benefit of our kingdoms and domains. We approve it especially because we hope that the Indian inhabitants of the Indies will convert to our holy Catholic faith. By this our charter of privilege or its signed transcript, at our own initiative, with true knowledge, and invoking our royal absolute power,[39] which we wish to exercise in this instance, we confirm and approve this our charter incorporated above and the favor contained in it now and forevermore for you, Sir Christopher Columbus, and for your children, grandchildren, descendants, and heirs. We wish and command, and it is our favor and grace, that it be observed and guaranteed to you, your children, and descendants inviolably, now and forevermore, fully and completely, according to and in the form and manner stipulated.

[2] If it is necessary, again we bestow on you this favor and firmly forbid any person or persons to dare to oppose or contradict you in any part of it by infringing or violating it at any time or in any manner. To this end, we command Prince Sir Juan, our most dear and very beloved son, and the princes, dukes, prelates, marquises, counts, and magnates; masters, priors, commanders [and subcommanders] of the military orders; members of our council, judges of our appellate court, judges, sheriffs, and any other justices of our household and court and chancery; commanders of castles, forts, and houses; all municipal councils, royal judges, municipal judges, sheriffs, toll, tax, and other justices of all the cities, towns, and villages of these our kingdoms and domains to observe and cause to be observed this our charter of privilege, confirmation, and writ of favor. You shall not oppose or hinder it contrary to its content and form, or attempt to do so, at any time or in any manner, under the stated penalties.

[3] We order that you be given this our charter of privilege and its confirmation, written on parchment, signed with our names, and sealed with our lead seal hanging by colored silk threads. We order our high chancellor, notary, and other officials who

preside over our seals, to emboss, issue, and pass it. None of you or them shall do the contrary in any manner, under penalty of our displeasure and a fine of 10,000 maravedís for our treasury on each person who does the contrary.

[4] We command the man who shows you this our writ to summon you to appear before us in our court, wherever we may be, within fifteen days of having been cited, under the same penalty. Under this same penalty, we command every public clerk who may be summoned for this purpose to give to the man showing this writ to him a certificate to that effect, inscribed with his rubric, so that we may know how our command is obeyed.

[5] Given in the city of Burgos on the twenty-third day of the month of April, in the year of the birth of our savior Jesus Christ one thousand four hundred and ninety-seven.

I, the King
I, the Queen

[6] I, Fernán Alvarez de Toledo, secretary of the king and queen our lords, caused this to be written at their command.

[7] Rodericus, doctor; Antonius, doctor; Fernán Alvarez; Juan Velázquez; Antonius, doctor. Collated.

[8] And on the back of the privilege it said: "Registered. Doctor."

52

Notarial description of royal documents copied in Seville

15 March 1498

[1] In the most noble and most loyal city of Seville on Saturday, the fifteenth day of the month of March in the year of the birth of our savior Jesus Christ one thousand four hundred and ninety-eight, the most magnificent lord Sir Christopher Columbus, high admiral of the Ocean Sea, viceroy and governor of the islands and mainland of the Indies for the king and the queen our lords, and their captain general of the sea, appeared in person in these houses where he is living, which are in this city in the parish of San Bartolomé, before me, Martín Rodríguez, public clerk of the city, and the other clerks of Seville who were present there.

The lord admiral presented to the clerks two charters of privileges from the king and queen our lords, written on parchment, sealed with their lead seal hanging from colored silk threads, and signed with their royal names, the names of members of their council, their chief accountants, and other officials. He also presented other writs signed with their royal names and embossed on the back with their red wax seal, and other decrees from Their Highnesses signed with their royal names. These privileges, writs, and decrees will be written below and named.

[2] The admiral declared that he was worried that, if he had to carry them by sea to the Indies and elsewhere, they could be damaged by fire, water, other accidents, or just by being carried around, with the result that his rights would perish and Their Highnesses would be ill served, because these privileges, writs, and decrees pertain to the service of Their Highnesses.

Therefore he asked us clerks to copy a transcript, or two or more, of the privileges, writs, and decrees, correcting them well and faithfully against the originals, in a manner that would lend credence for the preservation of his rights as lord admiral.

[3] The privileges, writs, and decrees, one after the other, are these that follow:

53
Notarial corrections of transcripts copied in Seville
15 March 1498

[1] This transcript was copied from the decree of Their Highnesses and compared with the original document from which it was copied in the presence of the public clerks of Seville, who signed and inscribed their names in testimony in the city of Seville.

[2] This transcript was copied from the decree of Their Highnesses and compared with the original document, in the presence of the public clerks of Seville, who signed and inscribed it with their names in testimony, in the city of Seville, on the fifteenth day of the month of March, year of the birth of our savior Jesus Christ one thousand four hundred ninety-eight.

[3] It is crossed out where it says "and public notary"; and where it says "that you may give and cause to be given to Sir Christopher"; and where it says "of this I order give to you the said"; and between lines it says "and in him"; and crossed out where it says "and chancery and household and precinct"; and where it says "the which said"; and where it says "whoever may travel and navigate by sea and all the other persons of whatever status and condition and privilege and dignity they may be who see this my charter of privilege or a transcription of it, marked as it is, shall observe"; and where it says "subject of the King"; and where it says "admiral," avail and let this not prejudice it [RUBRIC].

[4] I, Diego de la Bastida, clerk of Seville, am witness to this transcript [RUBRIC]. [5] I, Juan Fernández, clerk of Seville, am witness to this transcript [TWO RUBRICS]. [6] I, Martín Rodríguez, public clerk of Seville, caused this transcript to be written and here make my mark [SEAL] and I am a witness [TWO RUBRICS].

Further notarial corrections of transcript copied in Seville
15 March 1498

[1] This transcript was corrected and collated with the two privileges, writs, and all the other decrees incorporated in the originals, from which they were copied, in the presence of the public clerks of Seville, who signed and marked them with their names in witness. Done and copied in the city of Seville on this day, month, and year.

[2] Words are written over the lines where it says "eight," and "members of his council" and "of his," and "if the contrary should occur," and "islands that," and "large," and "mos" and "we order Prince Sir Juan," and "which is shown," and "and appurtenances," and "and after your death," and "would have" and "in" and "the cargo," and "with" and "sir" and "dri," and "nor admirably," and "of that" and "and tithe-paying and others," and "for which" and "are against them" and "re" and "that wheat" and "that might do the contrary."

[3] And in the decree addressed to Francisco de Soria, there is written above a line of ink "persons asked us" and "our"; avail and let this not prejudice it.

[4] I, Diego de la Bastida, clerk of Seville, am witness to this transcript [RUBRIC].

[5] I, Juan Fernández, clerk of Seville, am witness to this transcript [RUBRIC].

[6] I, Martín Rodríguez, public clerk of Seville, had this transcript written and here inscribe my sig[SIGNET]net, and I am a witness [TWO RUBRICS].

55
Notarial description of the documents copied in Santo Domingo
4 December 1498

[1] In the town of Santo Domingo, which is in the Indies on the island of La Española, Tuesday, the fourth day of the month of December, year of the birth of our Lord Jesus Christ one thousand four hundred ninety-eight, in the lodgings in this town of the most magnificent lord Sir Christopher Columbus, high admiral of the Ocean Sea, viceroy, and governor of the islands of the Indies and mainland[40] for the king and queen our lords and their captain general of the sea, which are in this town of Santo Domingo. The lord admiral appeared before me, Diego de Alvarado,[41] public clerk of the king and queen our lords, and then the lord admiral presented before me, the clerk, some writs of the king and queen our lords, written on paper and embossed on the back with their red wax seal, and other decrees from Their Highnesses, signed with their royal names, which letters and decrees will be written and named below.

[2] He said that if he had to carry or send them by sea to the kingdoms of Castile or other places, he feared that they could be damaged or destroyed by fire, water, or other accident, or they could get lost in transit, with the result that his rights would perish and Their Highnesses would be ill served, because these writs and decrees related to the service of Their Highnesses. For that reason, he said that he asked me, the clerk, to make a transcript, or two or more, of the writs and decrees, correcting them against the originals well and faithfully so that they would obtain credence for the preservation of the rights of the lord admiral. [3] These letters and decrees, one after the other, follow:

56
Notarial corrections of transcript copied in Santo Domingo
4 December 1498

[1] This transcript of Their Highnesses' original writs and decrees was done and copied in the town of Santo Domingo on Tuesday, the fourth day of the month of December in the year of the birth of our Lord Jesus Christ one thousand four hundred ninety-eight.

[2] Witnesses who were present to see, read, and collate the original writs and decrees with the transcripts, which are correct and collated: Pedro de Terreros,[42] Diego de Salamanca, Lope Muñoz.

[3] And I, Diego de Alvarado, clerk and public notary, was present at all this together with the witnesses, and by order of the lord admiral copied these transcripts from the original writs and decrees, which are correct and collated. To that end, I here inscribe my sig[SIGNET]net, thus, in true testimony.

Diego de Alvarado
public clerk[RUBRIC]

PART 4

THE FOURTH VOYAGE AND AFTER

CHAPTER 4.1

Columbus Makes His Case for Restitution of His Privileges

57
Copy of an open letter from Columbus to Lady Juana de La Torre,[1] governess of
the household of Prince Juan of Castile
late 1500

[0] Transcript of an open letter[2] that the admiral wrote to the governess of Prince
Juan (may he be in glory), in the year 1500, while he was returning from the Indies
under arrest.

[1] Most honorable lady. If my complaint about the world is new, its habit of
mistreatment is very ancient. A thousand battles I have fought, resisting them all until
now when neither arms nor intelligence have availed me. [2] With cruelty it has cast
me into darkness.[3] [3] Faith in the Creator of all men sustains me, however; His help
has always been very ready. Once, not long ago, when I was feeling overwhelmed,
with His right arm He raised me up, saying: "O man of little faith, rise, for I am; do not
be afraid."

[4] I came with such sincere love to serve these princes and have performed services
the likes of which have never been heard of or seen before.

[5] Of the new heaven and earth[4] that our Lord made, as Saint John writes in the
Apocalypse, after having spoken through the mouth of Isaiah, I was made the messenger and showed the place.

[6] All were incredulous except the queen, my lady, whose intelligent spirit and
great strength prevailed, making her heiress of all as a dear and most beloved daughter.

[7] The possession of all this I went to take in her royal name. Everyone sought to
make amends for their ignorance by overlooking their own little knowledge by speaking of impediments and costs. Her Highness approved it, nonetheless, and supported it
as much as she could.

[8] Seven years passed in discussions and nine in the execution, [9] during which
many notable and memorable things occurred that no one had foreseen at all.

[10] I have arrived and continue in such a condition that there is no one so vile that he does not think of insulting me. Virtue, however, will reward in this world those who do not consent to this.

[11] If I were to steal the Indies or the land that lies in their vicinity, which everyone is talking about now, from Christendom and give it to the Muslims, I could not be shown greater enmity in Spain. [12] Who would believe such a thing where there was always such magnanimity?

[13] I would have abandoned this business had it been fair to the queen, but the strength of our Lord and of Her Highness urged me to persevere. In order to relieve the queen somewhat of the suffering that death was inflicting on her then,[5] I undertook a fresh voyage to the new heaven and world that had remained concealed until then. If this voyage is not held in such high esteem there as others to the Indies, it is no wonder, because it seemed to come about as a result of my expertise.

[14] The Holy Spirit inflamed Saint Peter, and with him another twelve who all fought here. Their efforts and troubles were many, yet finally they won a victory over all.

[15] I believed that this voyage to Paria would pacify the situation somewhat, what with the pearls there and the gold[6] strike on La Española. I ordered the people to collect and fish for pearls, and agreed with them that I would return and pay them at the rate of one-half fanega. If I did not write about this to Their Highnesses, it was because I first wanted to arrange the same with the gold.

[16] This turned out for me just like a lot of other things. I would not have lost them or my honor if I had looked out for my own good and allowed La Española to be lost, or if my own privileges and agreements were observed. Likewise, I say the same about the gold that I had collected because, with the many resulting deaths and labors, only by divine virtue could the business have been brought to perfection.

[17] When I left Paria [and sailed to La Española], I found almost half of the people on the island in rebellion. They have fought me as if I were a Muslim up to now, while the Indians have harassed me seriously on the other flank.

[18] Then Hojeda[7] came and tried to seal my fate. He said that Their Highnesses were sending him with promises of gifts, exemptions, and pay. He attracted a great following, for on the whole of La Española there are few except vagrants, and none with a wife and children.

[19] This Hojeda harassed me greatly. When it was necessary for him to go, he left saying that he would return soon with more ships and people, and worse, that when he had left Spain, the royal person of the queen, our lady, was near death.

[20] Meanwhile, Vicente Yáñez[8] arrived with four caravels. There was mutiny and suspicion but no injuries resulted. [21] The Indians mentioned many other [ships] in the vicinity of the Cannibals and in Paria. Later another rumor surfaced of six more caravels that a brother of the appellate judge[9] was bringing, it was said with malicious intent.

[22] This occurred at the end, after all hope was lost of Their Highnesses sending a

ship to the Indies,[10] and we did not expect it of them, because it was widely rumored that Her Highness was dead.

[23] At that time, a certain Adrián[11] tried to rebel again, but our Lord did not allow his evil intentions to succeed.

[24] I had promised myself not to touch a hair on the head of anyone. I lament to say that with him I could not keep my pledge as I had hoped, because of his ingratitude. I would not have done less to my brother, had he tried to kill and steal the jurisdiction that my king and queen had given me in trust.

[25] This Adrián, as will be proved, had sent Sir Fernando to Jaraguá to gather some of his followers, but there ensued an argument with the judge, from which a deadly discord arose but did not succeed. The judge arrested him and some of his supporters and the case was such that he would have executed them had I not intervened. They were imprisoned while awaiting a caravel in which they could leave the island. [26] The news I mentioned previously, about Hojeda, made them lose hope that he would return again.

[27] For six months I had been ready for the return trip[12] to Their Highnesses with the good news about the gold and eager to flee from governing dissolute people who do not fear God or the king and queen and are full of defiance and malice.

[28] I only needed six hundred thousand [maravedís] to pay the people, and for this there were four million and some more from tithes after discounting the royal third from the gold.

[29] Many times before my departure I asked Their Highnesses to send someone there at my cost to take charge of justice. After I found the judge in rebellion, I again asked Their Highnesses for some staff, or at least a servant, with letters, because my fame is such that, were I to build churches and hospitals, these would be known as dens for thieves.

[30] Finally, when they appointed someone, it was exactly the opposite of what the business required. May it succeed because it was done at their specifications.

[31] I was there two years without the power to win an appointment either in my favor or for those who went there, but this one carried a full chest's worth. Only God knows if they will all redound to their service. Already, to begin with, there are exemptions for twenty years,[13] which represents one generation of a colonist, and one person alone can gather five marks of gold in four hours, of which I will speak at more length later.

[32] If it pleased Their Highnesses to disabuse of a rumor those who know my troubles, it would be an act of charity, because people's lies do me the most harm and as a result my great service and preservation of their estate and lordship have not benefitted me. I would be restored to honor and it would be talked of everywhere, because this business is such that daily it will be increasingly recognized as more wonderful and held in high esteem.

[33] Meanwhile, when Commander Bobadilla[14] came to Santo Domingo, I was in La Vega,[15] while the interim governor[16] [Bartolomé Colón] was in Jaraguá, where this

Adrián had made himself leader. By then, however, all was calm, the land rich, and all at peace.

[34] The day after he arrived, [Bobadilla] created himself interim governor, appointed officials, pronounced sentences, and announced exemptions from gold restrictions, tithes, and all other things in general for twenty years, which, as I say, is a generation. He also announced that he would pay everyone, even though they may not have served fully until that day. Furthermore, he gave notice that he planned to send me and my brothers back to Spain in irons, as he did, and that I could never return there, and neither could anyone of my lineage, saying a thousand dishonest and discourteous things about me.

[35] All this occurred the day after he arrived, as I said, while I was absent far away and unaware of him or his arrival.

[36] [Bobadilla] wrote and sent some signed blanks from Their Highnesses, of which he had brought a quantity, to the judge[17] and his company, with grants and lifetime lordships. I was never sent a letter or messenger, and he has failed to do so up to this very day.

[37] Consider, your grace, what someone in my position must have felt seeing someone who tried to steal the lordship from Their Highnesses and has done so much evil and harm honored and favored while the person who preserved the lordship at such peril is degraded!

[38] When I learned of this, my first thought was that this would be like that incident with Hojeda or one of the others. I restrained myself, however, on learning from the friars[18] that Their Highnesses were sending him. [39] I wrote him that his arrival was welcome and that I was prepared to sell off what I had and go to the court. I also said he should not be hasty in granting exemptions because I would soon turn over this and the governance to him peacefully, and I also wrote the same to the monks. [40] None of them replied to me. Rather, [Bobadilla] made as if to prepare for war. I hear that he gave twenty-year exemptions to those who went there, if they swore to accept him as governor.

[41] As soon as I learned about these exemptions, I pretended to agree to such a great error so that he would be content although he had no need or cause to give vagrants what would have been too much even for someone bringing his wife and children. I proclaimed by word and in letters that he could not make use of his provisions, because mine were stronger, and I showed them the exemptions that Juan Aguado brought.[19]

[42] I did all this to gain time so that Their Highnesses would be apprised of the state of the land and have time to issue new orders about this that would be to their service.

[43] Granting such exemptions in the Indies is folly because it is very lucrative for the citizens who have established residence there. They have been given the best lands at little cost, and these will be worth two hundred thousand [maravedís] at the end of four years when their residency requirement is completed, without their having turned over so much as a spade.[20]

[44] I would not carry on this way, if the citizens were married, but there are not six among them who do not intend to get what they can and go back as soon as possible. It would be good if [the Indies] were settled by honorable people from Castile whose identities and professions are known.

[45] I had agreed with the citizens' request that they pay one-third of the gold and the tithes. They accepted this as a favor from Their Highnesses. I reprimanded them, however, when I heard that they were not paying it. I expected that the commander would do likewise, but he did the contrary.

[46] He turned them against me by saying that I wanted to deprive them of what Their Highnesses had given them. He tried to get them to turn their backs on me, which he did, and then he persuaded them to write to Their Highnesses asking them never again to make me responsible for the island's governance. (Ironically, I had asked the same for me and my family as long as there was no other town.) Furthermore, he ordered investigations of me and my brothers for misdeeds, the likes of which have never been heard of in hell.

[47] I trust in our Lord, who rescued Daniel and the three boys with such knowledge, force, and disposition as He had, if it should please Him and be His desire.

[48] I might have known how to remedy all this and the rest of what has been said and happened since I have been in the Indies, if my disposition were such that it allowed me to seek my own advantage and if it seemed just to me. The upholding of justice and the augmentation of Their Highnesses' lordship has, however, prevented me from seeking redress until now, when so much gold has been found.

[49] There is a difference of opinion about which is more profitable: to steal or to mine. A hundred castellanos are as easily obtained for a woman as for one field, and this is very widespread. There are plenty of merchants who go around looking for girls; from ages nine to ten they are esteemed now, although for those of all ages a good price must be paid.

[50] [I say that the impact of lies from the discontented has hurt me more than my services have benefitted me, which is a bad example for the present and future. I swear that a quantity of men who have gone to the Indies and since returned to Spain not deserving even so much as water in the eyes of God and the world, now want to go back and are being given permission.]

[51] I told the commander he did not have the authority to do this. Even though I went along with what he wanted, I did it to gain time until Their Highnesses could be informed about the land, reconsider their commands, and order done what would be most beneficial to their service.

[52] He alienated all of them from me. From what he has done and his manners it appears that he came as my enemy and a very rabid one at that. It is clear from what has been said that he spent a lot in order to obtain this post. [53] I do not know anything more about this except what I have heard. I never imagined an investigative judge would allow rebels and other persons either without good faith or unworthy of it to act as witnesses against the person who governs them.

[54] Were Their Highnesses to order a general investigation carried out there, I tell you that it would be a miracle if the island did not sink.

[55] I think that your grace will remember how, when a storm drove me without sails to Lisbon, I was falsely accused of having gone there in order to give the Indies to the king [of Portugal]. Later, however, Their Highnesses learned the contrary and that all had been said out of malice.

[56] I may not know much, but no one would consider me so stupid as to think that, even if the Indies had been more bountiful, I could have sustained myself without the help of a ruler.

[57] Even if this were true, where could I have found better protection and assurance of not being expelled from [the Indies] altogether than in the king and queen our lords, who have raised me from nothing to so much honor and are the most exalted princes, by sea and land, in the world.

[58] They believe that I have served them and continually reserve more privileges and favors for me. Were anyone to deprive me of them, Their Highnesses would compensate me, with interest, as was seen with Juan Aguado, when it was ordered that I be accorded great honor. As I have already said, Their Highnesses received service from me and have placed my sons in their own household as pages,[21] which could never have happened with another ruler, because where there is no love, everything else ceases.

[59] I have spoken out this way against a malicious lie and against my will, because it is something that should not be contemplated even in dreams. Commander Bobadilla's manners and actions indicate that he wants his malicious conduct and actions seen favorably. With one arm tied behind my back, however, I will show him that his little knowledge and great cowardice, along with his uncontrolled greed, have made him fail in this regard.

[60] As I have already said, I wrote to him and the friars and then immediately set out completely alone, because all the people were with the governor, but also to remove all cause of suspicion.

[61] He, having learned of this, threw Sir Diego [Colón] in jail as a prisoner, chained with irons, and did the same with me when I arrived, and then to the [interim] governor when he came. I have never spoken to him again, and neither has he consented that anyone speak to me about it. I swear that I cannot understand why I should be held prisoner.

[62] He made it his first order of business to seize the gold, which had not been measured or weighed yet. In my absence, he said that he would pay the people from it. According to what I heard, he paid himself first and then sent new procurers to collect ore in the mines.

[63] Of this gold I had set aside certain samples, enormous nuggets, like the eggs of geese, hens, pullets, and of many other shapes, which some individuals had gathered in a short time. These would have pleased Their Highnesses and helped them to comprehend the business when they received a quantity of large stones full of gold. He pock-

eted this for himself first thing so that Their Highnesses would not highly regard this business before he feathered his own nest, which he is in great haste to do.

[64] The gold that is ready for smelting disappears at the fire, while some chains that weighed up to twenty marks have never been seen again!

[65] I have been greatly harmed in this matter of the gold, even more so than with the pearls, for not having brought it to Their Highnesses.

[66] The commander soon put into effect everything that he thought could hurt me. As I have already said, with six hundred thousand [maravedís] I could pay everyone without robbing anyone, and I had collected more than four million in tithes and fees without counting the gold.

[67] He made some very generous gifts that are outrageous, though I think he began by giving himself the first share. Their Highnesses will find out about it there when they order his audit, especially if I am in on it.

[68] He does nothing but say that a great sum is owed. In fact, that is just what I have said and probably not as much. I have been greatly distressed in having an investigator sent with authority over me who knows that, if the judicial inquiry that he sends back is very negative, he will probably remain there as governor.

[69] Our Lord would have been pleased if Their Highnesses had sent him or another person two years ago. [I know] that by now I would already be free of scandal and slander, and my honor would not have been taken from me, nor would I have lost it. God is just and will make known why and how things happened.

[70] They are judging me there as if I were a governor who went to Sicily or a self-governing city or town where the laws can be observed fully, without fear of losing everything. As a result, I am receiving great harm.

[71] I should be judged as a captain who traveled all the way from Spain to the Indies to conquer a most bellicose people, with customs and sect very opposed to ours, who live in mountains and wilderness not in fixed towns as we do. There, by divine will, I have put another world under the sovereignty of the king and queen, our lords. Consequently, Spain, once considered poor, now is the richest.

[72] I should be judged as a captain who up to the present day has maintained arms at the ready without rest for a single hour, of the type appropriate to gentlemen of conquest, not of letters, unless they were Greeks or Romans, or other moderns, of which there are so many and such noble ones in Spain. For, otherwise, I receive great harm, because in the Indies there was no town or settlement.

[73] The door is already opened for gold and pearls, and a quantity of all—precious stones, spices, and a thousand other things—can definitely be expected. Nothing worse will befall me, by the name of our Lord, because now the first voyage should be compensated by the business from Arabia Felix[22] to Mecca, as I wrote to Their Highnesses courtesy of Antonio de Torres in reply to [their query about] partitioning the sea and land with the Portuguese. Later, as I put in writing at the monastery of La Mejorada,[23] this would extend to Calicut.

[74] The news about the gold that I earlier promised to relate is that on Christmas

day, while I was very afflicted, under attack by the evil Christians and by Indians, to the point of leaving all and escaping life if I could, our Lord miraculously consoled me and said: "Exert yourself, do not be discouraged or afraid: I will provide for everything; the seven years limit on gold are not over yet, and in that and the rest I will give you remedy."

[75] That day I learned that there were eighty leagues of land and, in each promontory, mines. It now appears, however, that it is all one mine. [76] Some people have picked up 120 castellanos' worth in a day, others 90, and even as much as 250, [others] from 50 to 70. In many other cases, from 15 to 50 is considered a good day's work, and many people do it. The average is from 6 to 12, and anyone who gets less is not contented.

[77] It also appears that these mines are like others, yielding more some days than others, probably because the mines are new and so are the miners.

[78] It is commonly believed that even if all of Castile were to go there, no matter how stupid a person might be, he would obtain no less than one or two castellanos' worth daily. Now this is doubly true. It is true that some people employ an Indian, but the business remains entirely in the hands of Christians.

[79] Look at what discretion Bobadilla exercised. To give all four million of tithes for nothing, without cause or being instructed, and without first having notified Their Highnesses! And this is not the only damage.

[80] I know that my errors have not been done for evil purposes, and I think that Their Highnesses will believe the same as I have said, and I know and see that they deal mercifully with those who maliciously do them disservice. [81] Therefore, I believe and hold most certain that their compassion will be much better and abundant toward me, who [am their creature] and fell into disservice through ignorance and under duress, as they will learn in full later. They will look at my services and recognize more and more that they have benefited greatly. Everything will be weighed in the balance, just as the holy scripture tells us, the good together with the bad on the day of judgment.

[82] If they still insist that another person should judge me, which I do not expect, and that it should be by audit of the Indies, I very humbly beg them to send there two individuals of conscience and honor, at my expense. I think these will easily discover that five marks of gold can be found in four hours. In either case, it is very important that they provide for this matter.

[83] The commander, on arriving at Santo Domingo, lodged in my house just as he found it. He appropriated everything as his own. He is welcome, because perhaps he needed it (although no corsair ever did this to a merchant!).

[84] I have a major complaint about my documents. They have been taken from me, and not one of them has been retrieved from him. Those that would have benefited me the most in my acquittal are the ones he has best kept concealed. Behold the just and honest inspector he is!

[85] They tell me that all the many things that he may have done are within the

letter of the law, if not its spirit. God our Lord is present with his forces and knowledge, as always, and in the end punishes ingratitude resulting from injuries in each instance.

58
(Repetition of document 1, the Santa Fe Capitulations)
[Paris Codex]

The Capitulation[24]

[1] The things requested and that Your Highnesses give and grant to Sir Christopher Columbus in partial reward for what he has discovered in the Ocean Seas and will discover on the voyage that now, with the help of God, he is to make on the same seas in the service of Your Highnesses, are the following:

[2] First, Your Highnesses, as the lords you are of the Ocean Seas, appoint Sir Christopher Columbus from now on your admiral on all those islands and mainlands discovered or acquired by his command and expertise in the Ocean Seas during his lifetime and, after his death, by his heirs and successors one after the other in perpetuity, with all privileges and prerogatives equal to those that Sir Alfonso Enríquez, your high admiral of Castile, and his other predecessors in the office held in their districts.

[3] It pleases Their Highnesses. Juan de Coloma.

[4] Also, Your Highnesses appoint Sir Christopher your viceroy and governor general in all those islands and any continents and islands that he may discover and acquire in the seas. For the governance of each and every one of them, he will nominate three persons for each office, and Your Highnesses will select and appoint the one most beneficial to your service, and thus the lands that our Lord permits him to find and acquire will be best governed to the service of Your Highnesses.

[5] It pleases Their Highnesses. Juan de Coloma.

[6] You wish him to have and take for himself one-tenth of all and any merchandise, whether pearls, precious stones, gold, silver, spices, and any other things and merchandise of whatever kind, name, or sort it may be, that is bought, exchanged, found, acquired, and obtained within the limits of the admiralty that Your Highnesses from now on bestow on Sir Christopher, deducting all the relevant expenses incurred, so that, of what remains clear and free, he may take and keep one-tenth for himself and do with it as he pleases, reserving the other nine-tenths for Your Highnesses.

[7] It pleases Their Highnesses. Juan de Coloma.

[8] Should any lawsuit should arise over merchandise that he brings back from the islands and mainland acquired or discovered, or over merchandise taken in exchange

from other merchants there in the place where this commerce and trade is held and done, and if taking cognizance of such suit belongs to him by virtue of the privileges pertaining to his office of admiral, may it please Your Highnesses that he or his deputy, and no other judge, be allowed to take cognizance of and give judgment in it from now on.

[9] It pleases Their Highnesses, if it pertains to the office of admiral and conforms to what the admiral Sir Alfonso Enríquez and his other predecessors had in their districts, and if it be just. Juan de Coloma.

[10] On all ships outfitted for trade and business, each time, whenever, and as often as they are outfitted, Sir Christopher Columbus, if he wishes, may contribute and pay one-eighth of all that is spent on the outfitting and likewise he may take and keep one-eighth of the profits that result from such outfitting.

[11] It pleases Their Highnesses. Juan de Coloma.

[12] These are authorized and dispatched with the replies from Your Highnesses at the end of each article. In the town of Santa Fe de La Vega de Granada, on the seventeenth day of April in the year of birth of our savior Jesus Christ one thousand four hundred and ninety-two.

I, the King.
I, the Queen.

[13] Juan de Coloma.
[14] Registered. Calcena.

59
Anonymous legal opinion about Columbus's rights under the Santa Fe Capitulation
Granada 1501

[1] Opinion about what does, can, and should belong to the lord admiral, viceroy, and governor of the Indies by authority of the king and queen our lords, is the following.

[2] It seems very clear from the agreement made with Their Highnesses and signed with their royal names that Their Highnesses issued and conceded to the admiral of the Indies all the privileges and prerogatives that the admiral of Castile has and possesses; to whom, by his privilege, seems to belong one-third of all that is acquired. Consequently the admiral of the Indies should have one-third of all that has been acquired from the islands and mainland that he has discovered and that still remain to be discovered, because *relatum me est in referente*. He also should have one-tenth and one-eighth, as it seems to say in the third and fifth articles of the agreement.

[3] If anyone should try to argue that the one-third conceded to the admiral of

Castile should be understood as the movable goods acquired at sea and that, because these islands are land, a third of them do not belong to the admiral because they are immovable, even though they were acquired by sea, to this the admiral responds and declares that it is obvious in this article in which the admiral of Castile is named admiral of the sea, by reason of which he is issued one-third of what is acquired by sea, because otherwise he is not given jurisdiction or office; and it would be very inconvenient and unreasonable to give him a share outside his office, as the saying goes, *"quia propter offitium datum beneficium"* (because the benefit is and must be in respect of the office, and not outside it).

[4] But the admiral of the Indies has been constituted and appointed, according to the content of this article, as admiral not of the sea but expressly of the Indies and mainland discovered and to be discovered in the Ocean Sea. For this reason one-third of these islands and mainland that have been acquired in the exercise and conduct of his office of admiral most justly belongs to him, and that is how one should understand and interpret the admiral of Castile's privilege and the article that refers to it. For it is manifest that everything should be understood *secundum subiectam materiam et secundum qualitatem personarum.* Drawing any other conclusion, the privilege and article would have no benefit for the admiral of the Indies, because if he does not receive a third of the Indies, of which he is admiral, and if he is not considered admiral of the [Ocean] Sea, he could not receive what is acquired by sea because it would be outside his jurisdiction and office, so that this article and constitution would not be advantageous. Such a reading is not admissible, because every word written in a contract must be operative and should not be interpreted as superfluous. This is even more true in this case of such importance, benefit, and glory for Their Highnesses, acquired at very little cost and no danger to their honor, persons, or property, but with the greatest danger, as was commonly known, to the admiral's life, and not without much cost to him. For this reason alone one-tenth would be regarded as a very paltry share by itself (not to mention the one-eighth, which belongs to him by virtue of his pro rata share of the costs). What a very small share it would be for such a great service, so tiny a favor that what the sacred laws say is very appropriate: *"quia benefitia principum sunt latissime inter-petranda."* The favors granted by princes should be understood at their broadest and most encompassing, especially from most excellent and high princes such as Their Highnesses, from whom the broadest favors are more to be expected than from others.

[5] Therefore, this one-third, although seeming minimal, belongs to the admiral. We see this in partnerships made between merchants in which the expertise and intelligence of one partner is held and reputed in such high esteem that as much share belongs to him as to another who invested money if, as a result of the former, a profit results, even though the money itself came from the latter. Much more so in this case of the admiral, who has exercised admirable and incredible expertise at great cost and danger to his person and those of his brothers and staff. Because of this there is all the more reason for him to have one-third of all, as was truly the intention of Their Highnesses. To realize that this is the truth, we have only to see that Their Highnesses

are giving five-sixths to those who are going to the Indies, and to those who receive less than five-sixths, four-sixths and the governance of land without any danger, the route having been opened, secured, and clarified to all.

[6] As confirmation of what I say, as stipulated in many privileges of the admiral of the Indies, the admiral was ordered by Their Highnesses to acquire not cargo ships, vessels, or anything from the sea, but specifically islands and mainland, as it clearly says in the privilege's eleven pages. The privilege could more aptly be called a grant, because at the top of the first page and beginning of the privilege, it says: "and because you, Christopher Columbus, are going by our command to discover and acquire islands and mainland, etc." Well then, if the acquisition had to be islands and mainland, then necessarily the one-third must be from the acquisition, and if the one-third is from the acquisition, then clearly one-third of the islands and mainland acquired belong to the admiral. Undoubtedly we must believe that if at the beginning the admiral had asked for a larger share, it would have been granted to him, since everything was his acquisition and something completely unexpected, unknown, and beyond the fame and domain of Their Highnesses. Therefore, those who argued against this are answered fully and clearly; one-third of the Indies and mainland justly and clearly seems to belong to the admiral.

[7] The one-tenth is clearest in relation to the one-eighth, which is also very clear.

[8] If anyone should argue the contrary, saying that he should not have one-eighth of the merchandise and goods sent and brought on the ships that have gone on to explore and those that went to las Perlas and other parts of his admiralty while he was on the island of Española in service to Their Highnesses, saying that the admiral contributed nothing to their outfitting, it is answered that he was not notified, asked, or advised of the departure of those ships at the time of the departure. Because by law the ignorant can plead ignorance of a fact by reason of lack of opportunity, ignorance without any doubt is a legitimate excuse and deserves full restitution. Thus it could be deduced and said in this case that the admiral could satisfy the requirements by contributing his share now. He cannot be found culpable, but rather those who have not notified him as they were obligated, etc.

60
Explication of Columbus's rights and privileges under the five articles of the Santa Fe Capitulations
Granada, 1501

[0] The explanation of what does, can, and should belong to the admiral of the Indies by virtue of the agreement and treaty that he made with Their Highnesses,

which is the title and right that the admiral and his descendants have to the islands and mainland of the Ocean Sea, is this that follows.

First Article

[1] First, by the first article Their Highnesses made him their admiral of the islands and mainland discovered and to be discovered in the Ocean Sea, with the same privileges and in the same form as the admiral of the sea of Castile has and holds in the administration of his admiralty.

[2] For the interpretation of this, it is to be noted that the admiral of Castile holds as his privilege one-third of what is acquired or that he might acquire at sea. For this reason, the admiral of the Indies ought to have one-third of them and of what is acquired on them.

[3] Although the admiral of Castile has one-third of only what is acquired at sea, the admiral of the Indies should have one-third of all that is acquired on them [the Indies].

[4] The reason is because Their Highnesses ordered him to acquire islands and mainland, and they specifically entitled him admiral of them, and from them he should be rewarded, as the person who is their admiral and acquired them at great risk against the predictions of everyone.

Second Article

[1] With the second article Their Highnesses made him their viceroy and governor general of all these islands and mainland, with the authority to nominate all the officers of government, except that Their Highnesses can appoint one out of the three [nominated by the admiral]; and later Their Highnesses granted him a new favor of these offices in the years 1492 and 1493 by a published privilege, without that condition.

[2] The interpretation of this is that to the admiral belong these offices of viceroy and governor, with authority to appoint all the officials in the offices and magistracies of the Indies, because Their Highnesses in reward and payment for the effort and expense that the admiral made in discovering and acquiring the Indies, granted him these offices and governance with this authority.

[3] It is very clear that at the beginning the admiral was not disposed, nor would anyone have been, to undertake such risk and venture, if Their Highnesses had not promised him offices and governance in reward and payment of such an enterprise.

[4] Their Highnesses justly promised these to him, because it was with these that the admiral, rather than anyone else, did them such notable, advantageous, honorable, and exalted service.

[5] Very little honor, or almost none, did the admiral receive, although he would have received payment if Their Highnesses had appointed someone superior to him in

that land that he won at such great pains. For such just reasons was he provided them, that these offices and governance justly belong to the admiral.

[6] Now the admiral, while peacefully exercising these offices in the Indies in the service of Their Highnesses, has been deprived of the possession of them unjustly and against all reason and law, without having been summoned, heard, or convicted, from which the admiral suffered very great harm and great dishonor to his person and loss of his property. According to this article, clearly it seems unjust for the following reasons:

[7] Since the admiral could not be deposed or deprived of his offices because he never committed or did anything against Their Highnesses, by what law should he lose his property? Even if there were allegations, God forbid, then first the admiral would have had to be cited, called, heard, and convicted by law.

[8] In deposing him without due process, the admiral suffered great injury and a great injustice was done to him, and even Their Highnesses could not do these by right.

[9] Because Their Highnesses gave him these offices and governance of the land in satisfaction of the service and expense that the admiral gave in acquiring it, from this he got just return and perpetual title to these offices. Since he was unjustly deposed from them, the admiral, before anything else, should be reinstated in these offices as well as in his status and estate.

[10] As for the damages he has suffered, the admiral says they are very large, because with his expertise were found and discovered in the Indies much gold, pearls, spices and other things of great value. The admiral swears and declares the quantity of the profits, and by right he should receive satisfaction.

[11] Satisfaction for this should be made to him by whoever unjustly dispossessed him of all his property, because he, according to divine and human law, is obliged to do it as the person who exceeded the limits of the power of Their Highnesses.

[12] Satisfaction and restitution of these offices, possessions, and honors to the admiral should be made all the sooner in proportion to how unjust it was to have been dispossessed of them.

[13] For it is absolutely incredible and not worthy of credence that Their Highnesses should consider it good that a man so expert, who from such a distant land came to do such notable and exalted service for Their Highnesses as he did with his expertise and person, service deserving a most gratifying reward, should be destroyed at every turn because of envy and malice, when by reason he should be so joined in love with Their Highnesses and so established in their magnanimous affections that the admiral and the whole world would believe that no detractors could make him a stranger to meriting great favors, much less to inflame the heart[s] of Their Highnesses so as to make him lose what he so deservedly and meritoriously possessed. Consequently, the admiral always expected to serve and did serve Their Highnesses, procuring with his ingenuity the present profit of the Indies and governing through his offices for their settlement and increase.

[14] Which is something that no one else would or will do, because, apart from having forsaken all if he had not governed in the distant past, those who now govern with greed in order to take advantage during their term will not provide for the future as the admiral would. He, who has a perpetual annuity from the Indies, has ruled well and protected the Indians, which are the wealth of that land, and reformed and subdued its lordship, all without regard for [reward in the] present in expectation of honor and profit in the future.

Third Article

[1] With the third article Their Highnesses granted him one-tenth of all that is bought, found, and acquired within the borders of the admiralty, after deducting expenses.

[2] This is understood in such a way that the admiral is to have one-tenth of what is acquired and found in all the Indies and mainland of the Ocean Sea by any persons, whether for the profit of Their Highnesses or any other persons to whom they have made a grant for any or all of it, deducting the expenses that these persons or Their Highnesses have paid in it.

[3] And Their Highnesses cannot legally in prejudice to this one-tenth make a grant of all or any part of the profit from the Indies to any person, without first having to pay and paying one-tenth of the whole to the admiral.

[4] Their Highnesses, in making such grants, abrogate or discredit the one they already made to the admiral, leaving his just reward badly diminished or dismembered.

[5] Because the grant of this one-tenth was made to the admiral prior to the first discovery of the Indies, and it was given and conferred to help reward and compensate as such service merited, the one-tenth is therefore the principal source of his net profit.

[6] Even if Their Highnesses by agreement, stipulation, or any other manner were to give one-half or any other share to any persons who were disposed to the work and cost of such profit, the admiral would also possess one-tenth of the results before the share of such persons were deducted, just like the principal of Their Highnesses, because the one and the other is the true, principal gain and result of his admiralty of the Indies.

Fourth Article

[1] By the fourth article Their Highnesses conceded to the admiral civil and criminal jurisdiction in any lawsuits pertaining to the Indies. He can preside over them here in the regions and places comprised by the jurisdiction of the admiral of Castile, it being just.

[2] To interpret the jurisdiction that the admiral has, he says that this is his judicature, because it is one of the principal privileges and practically an arm of the body of his status as admiral, without which this admiralty could be ruled only with great difficulty. In fact, it would remain sterile, because this judicature is the principal force that honors, animates, and sustains all the other parts of the body of this admiralty.

[3] Such cognizance belongs to him in the ports and bays here, as well as on the specific islands and mainland where he is the admiral. If he were to have this judicature only there without including the cases emanating from here, then his jurisdiction would be almost nothing, because the parties are citizens of this land, and all of the trade and business come from it. Those who go to the Indies go only to engage in commerce, and the legatees and contracts of the companies that engender the lawsuits on their return remain here, even when such lawsuits proceed from business and commerce that took place within his admiralty.

[4] The other, that, although this article did not have to expressly make mention of this judicature at the moment that Their Highnesses established this office of admiralty and made a grant of it to the admiral with the same privileges as the admiralty of Castile, together with this admiralty they granted him this judicature with its comprehensiveness, because the admiral of Castile has as principal pre-eminence of his admiralty the judicature of all civil and criminal lawsuits that occur in it, which includes all the ports and bays of this land, even if they are outside his admiralty.

[5] As regards whether it was conferred justly, the admiral says that Their Highnesses, as monarchs and sovereign lords having absolute power in everything, justly could confer it on him, to whom alone belonged this appointment.

[6] And Their Highnesses, in conferring this office on the admiral with this comprehensiveness, did no injustice to anyone, nor involved their interest, because this admiralty, its judicature, and the islands and lands where it is instituted, are new and miraculously found, joined with, and brought to the dominion of Castile.

[7] The other, that the lawsuits emanating from this admiralty because of the great distance and separation of the land where it is instituted, and being so far from the confluence of tides of this land, must be very separate, divided, and distant from suits touching here, and by separating and dividing the cognizance from these no harm follows to any jurisdiction.

[8] It is very clear that, by virtue of their sovereign power, Their Highnesses bestowed such a dignity justly and without harm to anyone, involving no injustice. Two adversaries naturally cannot rule one subject; rather they avoid and distance themselves from each other. So by understanding one, we come to know the quality of the other. It is concluded, therefore, that this conferral is just.

[9] Also from the character of the admiral does this appointment proceed justly, because the quality of these Indies being unforeseen and unknown to everyone, of necessity there had to be appointed here a judge of certain experience in order to administer their justice. Well, who could have experienced them more, or possessed more accurate knowledge of the quality of their lawsuits, than the admiral who has

lived on them continuously and miraculously with his great acumen and knowledge of the sea, running great risks to deliver them from the sea itself?

Fifth Article

[1] With the fifth article Their Highnesses concede to the admiral the power to contribute one-eighth of any outfitting that is done for trade and business in the islands and mainland of his admiralty, and also to receive one-eighth of what may result from this outfitting.

[2] The true interpretation of this is that the admiral must have one-eighth of any goods that in any way are obtained in the Indies, whether by Their Highnesses' officials or by any other persons, deducting his pro-rated one-eighth share of the cost.

[3] It was in the first fleet, from which the Indies resulted, that is, the profit that proceeds from them, that the admiral contributed his one-eighth, and even up to one-half, of the cost; from which he acquired perpetual title to this one-eighth, the result of that outfitting being eternal.

[4] The other is that at the beginning he obviously went to acquire islands and mainland, which are not movable goods. This cannot be expected to bring a profit, if one-eighth of what is movable from there is not understood as the true result and purpose of such an outfitting.

[5] Although the admiral did not bring back movables from the Indies, the result and profit from the first outfitting was that he placed these islands and mainland under the power of Their Highnesses as their own, which likewise is understood to have empowered and given to Their Highnesses all the movables that at that and any other time may be obtained from them; for from then on Their Highnesses could send whomever they might wish for all of it, as for their own property, without contradiction.

[6] Another reason is that, because he contributed to the first fleet, the admiral did not acquire a perpetual right to this one-eighth. Their Highnesses necessarily must outfit in order to employ the fleets of the Indies; therefore, they cannot legally prohibit him from contributing to the cost of these fleets and taking one-eighth of the product. The fleets must be continuous in order for the profits of the Indies to be perpetual, of which one-eighth belongs to him perpetually.

[7] Although it is said that only one-eighth of the net profits on merchandise belongs to him, because as it states in the article about trade and business, that is understood to mean "merchandise," the truth is that generally one-eighth of all the movable goods from the Indies belongs to the admiral, because these words "trade," "business," include all types of goods that are had in any way and time.

[8] For the word "trade" is the astuteness or diligence that is employed to accomplish the purpose of business, and finally dealings or relationship that the admiral was to have with the possessors of the Indies who were going to profit by accomplishing his

purpose, which was to acquire them. Because he did acquire them, what results from them is what justly should be divided as the true result of such business.

[9] This other word "business" derives from "business" which means "not idle," *quia "negotium" est quasi "nega otium,"* so that its interpretation is general for any sort of thing; and by it is comprised any sort of movable thing that may be found in the Indies.

[10] Because this word was not an error and had a clear meaning of "merchandise," and because the admiral gained the Indies and mainland, especially La Española, more by gifts of merchandise than by force of arms, these Indies and all the things in them justly can be called "marketable," and from that "merchandise," because from "to market" is derived the word "merchandise."

[11] The other, that, even if the admiral had had to acquire the Indies by force of arms after Their Highnesses expressly had sent him to trade, he still would not have lost his one-eighth from them because of this, because the movables that may be found in them, such as gold, pearls, spices, and other things, pure and principally are merchandise; for any movable good that can be bought (except that which is consecrated) must be called "merchandise," according to the laws that say *"quod omnia sunt in conmertio nostro."*

[12] Also, that however the objective of the outfitting had to be achieved, which was the gaining of the Indies, one-eighth belonged to the admiral, because the profits of the sea and its cases are diverse, accidental, unpredictable, and unexpected. Thus, whatever remains from them to be divided is just as likely to have been carved out by force as untied by art. This is the common way of all outfitters, of which there are countless examples.

[13] For it is very clear, if some merchants outfit as partners only for the trade of merchandise and happen to agree with the owner that he can contribute some part of the outfitting because he also must have a share of the results, that, if beyond merchandise some city, cash, or enemy ship should be won, then part of the profit belongs to him also, as he by right had to have from the merchandise, because although it was gained apart from merchandise it obviously had to be the result of the outfitting.

[14] If by chance an agent of another company doing business in some kingdom becomes a great favorite of the king of that land, serving him with loans or by selling him merchandise at a lower price, and the company should be disbanded afterwards, and that king in consideration of the friendship should grant him something, he is obligated to divide it completely with his partners as a true profit acquired as a result of the partnership, although a long time may have passed since it was dissolved, because everywhere it is thus adjudicated and thus stipulate the laws of these kingdoms of Your Highnesses.

[15] In Portugal recently something similar happened to a Florentine, the agent of a large Florentine company that, for having served the king of that land very well with loans and other things from his merchandise, was required to give his partners a share of a grant that the king gave him in consideration of his friendship with him personally,

after the accounts were balanced and the partnership dissolved, as a true result emanating from it.

[16] Even that ship owner Lercar, to whom Their Highnesses gave a grant in consideration of the service he performed in transporting the archduchess[25] and in partial satisfaction of the carrack that he lost on the banks, was required by the court in Genoa to give a share to his partners as a legitimate return, and all that was left for him was what belonged to him as owner of a share.

[17] Take the case of a son who is given a gift by some great friend of his father. Even though all other presents are considered the son's private property, this should be considered part of his parental inheritance because the outcome proceeds from the father; and many other things occur constantly that would support this point.

[18] But leaving this aside, it is sufficient that from all this it is deduced that to the admiral belongs one-third of the Indies and mainland in addition to the one-eighth and one-tenth of all the movable goods on them and within his admiralty that are found, at any time, by any persons, and in any way as a legitimate result of his first fleet, even though he may not have contributed to the others. On this matter enough has been said in another document.[26]

[19] It remains to be said that Their Highnesses granted to the admiral all these offices just as the admiral of the sea of Castile holds them; he could appoint the sheriffs and clerks or order them to serve in his name. Since this is so, he also could delegate them and keep the revenues, just as a knight does to whom Their Highnesses may have granted a position or an office. This is seen in a great many cases in Castile in which they take the revenues and make a staff member do the job, or subcontract it to someone and give him a specific share of the revenue. So he begs Their Highnesses to give him relief and let him use his offices and receive the benefit, for thus was it by agreement and favor.

CHAPTER 4.2

Vindication

61
Writ ordering restitution of property to the admiral and his brothers
Granada, 27 September 1501

The King and the Queen

[1] We decree and order that the following must be done in matters of property pertaining to Sir Christopher Columbus, our admiral of the Ocean Sea.

[2] First, regarding his contribution of one-eighth of the merchandise that we order sent to the islands and mainland now and in the future, should the admiral put up one-eighth of such merchandise or its equivalent, then after deducting the costs and expenses, he shall keep for himself one-eighth of the profits obtained from this merchandise, in accord with the stipulations of the capitulation made with him about this.

[3] Commander Bobadilla took for himself some gold, jewels, and other movable, semi-movable, and real property that the admiral had on the island of La Española. Because those comprised the product and revenue of these Indies, we order that above all else [the admiral] shall be reimbursed costs, expenditures, and wages that were owed during the time that the admiral last went to the Indies in the year ninety-eight, counting from the time he arrived on the island of La Española, and should have been paid from these things that were taken from him. Although financial responsibility for the Indies belongs to the admiral according to the capitulation, nevertheless it was understood that [these expenses] should be paid from what was acquired from the Indies. Whatever remains after having paid all these expenses should be divided into ten shares, of which nine will be for us and the tenth for the admiral. From these nine-tenths we agreed to pay the wages, costs, and expenses until that voyage when the admiral went to the island of La Española in the year ninety-eight, because we granted him exemption from his share of those expenses. The admiral shall pay from his one-tenth what it has been verified that he owes personally to some people as admiral.

[4] Concerning the livestock that have been sent from there, according to the capitulation, the costs and expenses for this were to be at our cost, while the admiral was to have one-tenth of what remains. In consideration of this, it is our pleasure to order that he shall be credited with one-tenth of the gross of these livestock and any calves they have produced. The remaining nine-tenths belong to us. (Stet where "that" is crossed out on this page).

[5] We order that all his personal and household furnishings and supplies of bread and wine that Commander Bobadilla took from him, or their fair equivalent, shall be returned and restored to him without our taking any portion of it at all.

[6] Among other things that Commander Bobadilla took from the admiral was a certain quantity of stones from the gold field that contained some gold. We order our governor[27] of these islands to take a sworn statement from Commander Bobadilla about how many and what sizes they were and make him restore them so that they can be divided and distributed in the stated manner.

[7] We order that the admiral should receive restitution for two mares with their colts, which the admiral bought from a farmer in the Indies, and two horses that the admiral owned: one that he bought from Gorbalán,[28] and the other that he had from the mares that Commander Bobadilla took from him, or their fair equivalent, without our receiving any portion of this at all.

[8] The admiral says that he was harmed by not being permitted to appoint the captains and officers of the ships that we are ordering to go to the island of La Española, which he claims he should have appointed according to the capitulation. Although the present captains and officers have already been appointed by our order, we say that in the future we will order that they be appointed in accord with the capitulation.

[9] We declare and order that from now on the admiral can take from the island of La Española 111 hundredweights of brazilwood representing his one-tenth that he is entitled to have from the 1,000 hundredweights of brazilwood that by our command are to be given yearly to the merchants with whom a contract has been signed. By our contract with these merchants, their share is exempted from what the admiral is to receive during the term contracted with the merchants and afterwards the one-tenth shall be reserved for the admiral.

[10] The admiral claims that Commander Bobadilla has paid some back wages and other things on the island of La Española to some persons who were not owed wages or anything else, as may be seen in the books of the officials and can be proved and demonstrated. We order that, although the commander made payments to persons not owed wages or anything else, the admiral is not obligated to continue paying them.

[11] Commander Bobadilla took from the admiral's brothers a certain quantity of gold and jewels that had accrued to them by virtue of governing the Indies. All of this shall be divided into ten shares, of which the admiral shall receive one, while the remaining nine shares belong to us. As for the furnishings, supplies, fields, and houses that the Columbus brothers had, and the gold received from having sold their things, if it is proved that this was the case, and although we have the right to some of this, we

give it all to [the Columbus brothers] as a favor so that they may dispose of it as their own private property.

[12] It is our wish and command that the admiral have on the island of La Española someone in charge of his treasury to receive what he is supposed to have. This person shall be Alonso Sánchez de Carvajal,[29] of our household staff. On behalf of the admiral, Alonso Sánchez de Carvajal shall be present with our auditor to watch the smelting and stamping of the gold that is acquired on the islands and mainland. He and our agent shall be responsible for buying and selling this merchandise. We order our governor, accountant, judges, and officials who now and in the future may be on the islands and mainland, to implement and enforce all of this according to our wish and command. Alonso Sánchez de Carvajal shall supply whoever displays the proper power of attorney from the admiral with that portion of the gold that belongs to him in payment of the one-tenth of the island, net, as well as the one-eighth of the profit from merchandise whose cost he demonstrates that the admiral financed.

[13] The admiral had subcontracted the offices of sheriff and clerk for the island of La Española for a specific time. We order that the cash and whatever revenues and value these offices have generated shall be divided into ten shares, after first having paid the costs and expenses of these officials: nine shares shall be for us and one share for the admiral. Whoever received the office of clerk was not obligated to pay a fixed price for it. We order that whenever he wishes to leave this office he should appear with all he has acquired, so that it can be divided in this way. (Stet where it says "by him," which is crossed out on this page).

[14] The books and documents that were taken from him shall be returned to him. If any of them are needed for business, a transcript certified by a public clerk shall be copied and the originals returned to him.

[15] Concerning the lease and supplies, Carvajal shall profit from all of it according to and as our other officials do.

[16] We order you, our governor, accountant, and other officials, judges, and personnel of the islands and mainland to do and implement all and every part of this as stipulated. In implementing it, give and turn over to the admiral, his brothers, and his representative these things without creating any impediment or doing the contrary.

[17] Done in Granada on the twenty-seventh day of September in the year one thousand five hundred and one.

I, the King
I, the Queen

[18] By order of the king and queen. Gaspar de Gricio.[30]

62

Warrant to Jimeno de Briviesca to give the admiral a list of merchandise for the
Indies
Granada, 27 September 1501

The King and the Queen

[1] Jimeno de Briviesca.[31] We have ordered a contract drawn up with Sir Christopher Columbus, our admiral of the Ocean Sea, stipulating that he may supply one-eighth of all the merchandise taken to the Indies and receive one-eighth of the profits, as you will see from our agreement with him, signed with our names.

To this end, we order you to give him a written account of all the merchandise that we now order taken to the Indies, so that, if he wishes, he can finance one-eighth of it.

[2] Receive this [share of the supplies] in our name from the admiral or whoever has his power of attorney and give him a receipt for it. You may accept it either in cash or merchandise, whichever he or his representative prefers. If it is paid in cash, keep the full amount of money yourself, so that you can pay it to whomever we order. Post an account of all transactions in the books you keep, so that what is to be shared from the profits can be verified there, and do not do otherwise.

[3] Done in Granada on the twenty-seventh day of the month of September in the year one thousand five hundred and one.

I, the King
I, the Queen

[4] By order of the king and queen. Gaspar de Gricio.

63
Warrant to the commander of Lares, Nicolás de Ovando, to implement the
restitution of property
Granada, 28 September 1501

The King and the Queen

[1] Commander of Lares, our governor of the Indies.

We have decreed and ordered the procedure that must be taken in what has to be done with Sir Christopher Columbus, our admiral of the Ocean Sea, and his brothers concerning the things that Commander Bobadilla took from them, and about the procedure that has to be taken in supplying the admiral with the one-tenth and one-eighth that he is entitled to have from the movable goods of the islands and mainland of the Ocean Sea, and from the merchandise that we will send from here, as you will see in the declaration and mandate signed with our names that we have ordered given. To this end we order you to comply with the declaration and have the admiral's goods turned over to him. Supply him with what belongs to him according to this explanation and reinstate the admiral and his brothers, or their representative, with all of it. If the gold and other things that Commander Bobadilla took from them have been spent or sold, we order you to pay for them immediately. Pay from our treasury whatever was spent in our service but whatever Commander Bobadilla spent on himself, pay from the goods and estate of the commander, and do not do otherwise.

[2] Done in Granada on the twenty-eighth day of the month of September in the year one thousand five hundred and one.

I, the King
I, the Queen

[3] By order of the king and queen. Gaspar de Gricio.

64
Royal instructions for the fourth voyage
Valencia de La Torre, 14 March 1502

The King and the Queen

[1] Sir Christopher Columbus, our admiral of the islands and mainland that are in the Ocean Sea in the region of the Indies. We have seen your letter of the twenty-sixth of February, the other letters you sent with it, and the reports you gave us. You say that on this voyage you are making you would like to go by way of La Española. Regarding your request to go by way of La Española on this voyage we have already told you that, because it is not reasonable to lose any time on this voyage you shall go by this other route no matter what the circumstances may be. On the return, God willing, if you consider it necessary, you can put in to [La Española] for a short time. As you see, it will be best, however, that when you return from the voyage you are now making, we should be informed immediately by you in person about all that you found and did there. With your opinion and advice we can provide for [La Española] what best suits our service along with necessary things from here for trade.

[2] By this we are sending you instructions concerning what, our Lord willing, you will do on this voyage. In response to what you say about Portugal, we wrote what is appropriate to the king of Portugal, our son.[32] We are also sending you our letter that you say is needed for his captain, in which we inform him of your departure for the west and that we have learned of his departure toward the east. If you should encounter each other along the way, you are to treat each other as friends and as it is reasonable

to treat captains and personnel of kings with whom we have such close relations, love, and friendship, telling him that we have ordered you to do the same. We will make sure that the king of Portugal, our son, writes a similar letter to his captain.

[3] In response to your request that we permit you to take your son Sir Fernando[33] with you on this voyage, and that his allowance should be given to Sir Diego, your son, we are pleased by it.

[4] In response to your desire to take one or two persons who know Arabic, we are pleased by it, provided that it does not delay you.

[5] In response to your answer about the share of the profit to be given to the people who are going with you on these ships, we say that they must go in the same manner as the others have gone before.

[6] It was agreed that the 10,000 pieces of coin that you spoke of should not be made for this voyage until more is seen.

[7] As you will see, we have already ordered that the powder and artillery you requested be provided.

[8] In regard to what you had said about not being able to talk to Doctor Angulo[34] and licentiate Zapata[35] because of your departure, write us about it at length and privately.

[9] As you know, because we are traveling and you are about to depart, nothing can be done in regard to the rest of what is contained in your reports and letters about you, your sons, and brothers until we establish residence somewhere. If you were to wait until then, the voyage you are now going on would be ruined. With everything necessary for your voyage already arranged, it is therefore better that you should leave immediately without any delay and leave your son[36] in charge of soliciting what is contained in these reports.

[10] Be assured that your arrest hurt us a great deal. Of this you can be sure, for clearly everyone recognized it, because as soon as we learned of it we ordered it corrected. You know the favor with which we always have ordered you treated. Now we are even more disposed to honor and treat you well. The favors that we have done for you shall be observed fully according to the form and content of our privileges that you have, without any contradiction, and you and your sons shall enjoy them, as is reasonable. If it should be necessary to confirm them again, we will confirm them, and we will order your son placed in possession of all of it.

[11] Furthermore, it is our desire to honor you and give you grants, and we will take care of your sons and brothers as is reasonable. All this can be done if you depart on time, leaving your son in charge; and so we beg you not to delay your departure.

[12] From Valencia de la Torre, on the fourteenth day of March in the year five hundred and two.

I, the King

I, the Queen

[13] By order of the king and queen. Miguel Pérez de Almazán.[37]

[14] And on the back of this writ was written the following: "By the king and

queen, to Sir Christopher Columbus, their admiral of the islands and mainland that are in the Ocean Sea in the region of the Indies."

[15] This transcript was collated with the original declarations, decrees, and letters from which it was copied in the presence of the public clerks of Seville, who inscribed and signed it with their names in testimony, in the city of Seville on the twenty-second day of the month of March in the year of the birth of our Savior Jesus Christ one thousand five hundred and two.

[16] I, Gómez Nieto, clerk of Seville, am witness.

[17] I, Alonso Lucas, clerk of Seville, am witness.

[18] I, Martín Rodríguez, public clerk of Seville, had this transcript written and here inscribe my ru★★★bric, and am a witness.

CHAPTER 4.3

Columbus Safeguards his Privileges for Future Generations

65
Notarial declaration of the transcription made for Columbus of the first 63
documents
Seville, 5 January 1502

[1] In the most noble and most loyal city of Seville on Wednesday the fifth day of the month of January, in the year of the birth of our savior Jesus Christ one thousand five hundred and two, at about the hour of vespers, in the residence of the lord admiral of the Indies, which is in this city in the parish of Santa María, in the presence of Estevan de La Roca and Pedro Ruiz Montero, municipal judges of this city of Seville for the king and queen our lords, and in the presence of me, Martín Rodríguez, public clerk of this city of Seville, and of the witnesses written below, who were also present, there appeared in person the most magnificent Sir Christopher Columbus, high admiral of the Ocean Sea, viceroy and governor of the islands and mainland. He showed these judges certain writs, privileges, and decrees from the king and queen our lords, written on paper and parchment, signed with their royal names, sealed with their lead seals hanging from colored silk threads and with red wax on the back, and countersigned by certain officials of their royal household as each writ came before them. The contents of these writs, one after the other, are as follows:[38]

66

Covering letter from Columbus to Nicolò Oderigo[39] in Genoa accompanying the
Book of Privileges
Seville, 21 March 1502

Sir.

The loneliness in which you have left us cannot be expressed.

I have given the book of my documents to Sir Francesco di Rivarola,[40] so that he may deliver it to you, with another transcript of the open letters. I beg you to be so good as to write to Sir Diego informing him of your receipt of the book and the place in which you will keep it.

Another book like this one will be finished and sent to you in the same manner by Sir Francesco. You will find a new document in it.[41] Their Highnesses promised they would give me all that belongs to me and place Sir Diego in possession of everything, as you will see.

I am writing to Sir Juan Luis[42] and to my Lady Catalina. That letter is going with this one.

I am ready to sail at the first sign of good weather, in the name of the Holy Trinity, with much equipment. If Gerónimo de San Esteban comes, he must wait for me and not burden himself with anything, because they will take from him whatever they can and then leave him bare. Let him come here, and the king and queen will receive him until I return.

May our Lord have you in his holy keeping.

Done on 21 March in Seville, 1502.

At your command.

.S.

.S.   A   .S.

X   M   Y

Christoforo FERENS[43]

67

Notarial declaration of the transcription of documents 61 through 64
Seville, 22 March 1502

[1] This is a transcript well and faithfully copied from [one explication (61), two writs (62, 63), and an open letter (64)] from the king and queen our lords, written on

paper and signed with what appear to be their royal names; the contents of which, one after the other, are as follows.[44]

68

Letter from Columbus to the directors of the Bank of St. George in Genoa
Seville, 2 April 1502

Most noble gentlemen.

Although my body is here, my heart is still there.

Our Lord has conferred on me the greatest favor he has ever conferred on anyone since David. The fruits of my enterprise are already apparent and would be even more so if the darkness of the government did not overshadow them.

I am going back to the Indies in the name of the Holy Trinity, with the intention of returning immediately. Because I am mortal, I leave my son Sir Diego to pay you there a perpetual annuity of one-tenth of all the revenue that will be received,[45] as a contribution to the republic's provisions of wheat, wine, and other edibles. If this one-tenth amounts to anything, keep it; if not, receive the good will that I have.

I entrust this son of mine to you.

Sir Nicolò de Oderigo knows more about my affairs than I do, and I have sent him a transcript of my privileges and a letter so that he will safeguard them both. I would be pleased if you inspected them.

The king and queen, my lords, want to honor me more than ever.

May the Holy Trinity keep your noble persons and augment your magnificent office.

Done in Seville on the second day of April of 1502.

The high admiral of the Ocean Sea, viceroy, and governor general of the islands and mainland of Asia and the Indies, for the king and queen my lords, their captain general of the sea, and member of their council.

.S.

.S.   A   .S.

S   M   Y

Christoforo FERENS

69

End of the notarial declaration
Seville, 30 December 1502

[1] Having presented [the documents] before the judges in the manner stated, the lord admiral told the judges that, because he had to take and present these original privileges, decrees, and writs to many regions and places appropriate to his rights, he was worried that in taking and presenting them they could be lost or torn, or some accident might happen to some or all of them. In order to avoid these inconveniences he asked the judges together to look at and examine these privileges, writs, and decrees that he presented before them. They ordered me, the clerk, to copy or have copied one or more transcripts, as necessary. By their authority and judicial decree they confirmed these transcripts so that they would have full credence wherever they appeared, just as the original privileges, writs, and decrees signed with their names are valid and have credence.

Signed and inscribed with a rubric by me, the clerk, they ordered them issued to guarantee his rights. [The admiral] said that, if it were necessary, he implored the noble office of these judges to certify all of it.

[2] Then the judges, having considered this request, took the original writs, privileges, and decrees in their hands and read each and every one of them. Seeing that they were whole and not torn, cancelled, or suspicious in any way that would invalidate them, but rather free of all defect and suspicion, they unanimously ordered me, the clerk, to copy and have copied one or more transcripts of these writs, privileges, and decrees that the lord admiral might need and request of me, and to give and transfer them to him, signed with their names and signatures, and inscribed with my rubric. The judges certified each and every one of the documents by their authority and decree so that they would be valid and have credence before the law and apart from it, when and wherever they might appear, as well and fully as the original writs, privileges, and decrees would, if they were presented.

[3] The lord admiral said that he wanted all of this recorded and certified in order to guarantee his rights. To that purpose I gave him this, which is signed by each and every one of these judges, and signed and certified by me, the public clerk. It was done, copied, corrected, and collated with the originals in the city of Seville on the stated day, month, and year.

[4] It is crossed out where it says: "I make you my high admiral of the sea and it is my desire and pleasure that from now on you shall be my high admiral of the sea, just as the late Admiral Sir Diego Hurtado de Mendoza used to be and that you should have the admiralty"; and where it says "and others and I"; and where it says "and not on our payroll, as stated," it shall be valid to them and not impeded.

Ruiz Montero, judge
Estevan de La Roca, judge

[5] I, Gómez Nieto, clerk of Seville, was present at the authorization and mandate of the judges, and I am a witness.

[6] I, Juan Fernández, clerk of Seville, was present at the authorization and mandate of the judges, and I am a witness.

[7] And I, Martín Rodríguez, public clerk of Seville, was present at this authorization and here inscribe my rubric ★★★ and I am a witness.

70
Columbus's inventory of the originals and transcriptions of his privileges
Seville, December 1502

Inventory

[1] The originals of these privileges, writs, decrees, and many other letters from Their Highnesses and other documents relating to the lord admiral are in the monastery of Santa María de las Cuevas in Seville.

[2] Also in this monastery is a transcribed book of these privileges and letters, similar to this one.

[3] Alonso Sánchez de Carvajal took another transcript, written on paper and authorized, to the Indies this year 1502.

[4] Another transcript on parchment, like this one.

71
Covering letter from Columbus to Nicolò Oderigo in Genoa
Seville, 27 December 1504

Honorable sir,

When I departed on the voyage from which I have just returned, I spoke to you at length. I believe that you remember all this well. I thought that I would find your letters and someone with a personal message from you when I arrived. At that time, I also left with Francisco de Riberol a book of transcripts of writs and another one containing my privileges in a brown leather bag with silver locks, and two letters for the Bank of Saint George, to which I contributed one-tenth of my income in order to reduce taxes on wheat and other provisions. There is no news about any of this.[46] Sir Francisco says that everything arrived there safely. If so, it was discourteous of those gentlemen of Saint George not to have replied, nor have they increased their treasury. This is all exemplified in the proverb: "He who serves everyone serves no one."

I left another book of my privileges like this in Cádiz with Franco Catanio,[47] bearer of this letter, so that he would forward it to you also, placing both in safe keeping where you think best. A letter I received from the king and queen my lords at the time of my departure is copied in it. You can see that it is very favorable, although Sir Diego was not given possession as had been promised.

While in the Indies, I wrote to Their Highnesses about my voyage,[48] sending it by three or four routes. One came back into my hands, so I am sending it sealed to you along with the supplement of the voyage in another letter, for you to give with the other letter of advice to Sir Juan Luis, to whom I am writing that you will be its reader and interpreter. I am anxious to receive letters from you describing the project in which we are engaged.

I arrived here very ill. While I was ill, the queen my lady died (may she rest with God), without my seeing her. I still cannot tell you how my affairs will turn out. I believe that Her Highness will have provided well for them in her will, and the king my lord is well disposed. Franco Catanio will tell you the rest at length.

May the Lord keep you in his care.

From Seville, the 27th of December, 1504.

The high admiral of the Ocean, viceroy, and governor general of the Indies, etc.

72
The Republic of Genoa acknowledges receipt of the two codices from Lorenzo Oderico
Genoa, 10 January 1670

1670. January 10.

The magnificent Lorenzo Oderico[49] presented to the Most Serene Colleges two books. Each contained an authenticated copy on parchment of the privileges granted by King Fernando and Queen Isabel of Spain, his wife, to Christopher Columbus, a Genoese, in remuneration of his famous actions in the conquest of the New World. He gave these books with the hope that their Most Serene Lordships may be pleased to have the books preserved in the public archives as a worthy memorial of such an illustrious compatriot, at the same time accepting them as a token of the affection and zeal that the magnificent Oderico entertains for the public service.

The Most Serene Colleges accepted the books and voted to indicate their favor by ordering that a public testimonial be drawn up in favor of the magnificent Oderico, recommending him to the Most Serene Colleges as well as the two councils on any occasions when he might aspire to office on the mainland or Corsica. They hope that due regard will be paid to the zeal and affection that the magnificent Oderico displayed in presenting these books and that it may be possible to suitably gratify him on such occasions.

Greetings.

73

Inventory of the Genoa Codex

Genoa, 1670

Jesus

Inventory of the writs, privileges, decrees, and other documents in this book

NOTES ON THE TRANSLATION

Helen Nader

NOTES ON THE TRANSLATION

1.   1.1 OCEAN SEA   Europeans believed that the Ocean Sea stretched directly from Western Europe to the coasts of China and India. They believed many islands were scattered across the Ocean Sea, and they also assumed that logically there must be an Antarctica to match the Arctic. They had no idea that two continents, North and South America, blocked the direct sea route to Asia. Not until long after Balboa's first sighting of what he called the South Sea, and Magellan's traverse of what he called the Pacific Ocean, did Europeans distinguish between the Atlantic and Pacific Oceans and abandon the name Ocean Sea.

2.   1.2. MAINLAND   When the monarchs used the term "mainland" (tierra firme), they were hoping that Columbus would be able to establish Castilian sovereignty on some portion of the Asian coast. In this, they were trying to imitate the Portuguese, who in 1480 acquired permission from local rulers in west Africa to establish a trading post under Portuguese sovereignty, the fortress they called São Jorge da Mina.

3.   1.3. JUAN DE COLOMA   Coloma was born in Borja (Valencia) and died in Zaragoza in 1517. Coloma became secretary to King Juan II of Aragón in 1462 and filled the same office for King Fernando throughout his reign (1479 to 1516). Coloma had represented the monarchs in the negotiations with Columbus and was responsible for the draft wording of the Capitulations (Escudero 1969: 1.13–14; Rumeu de Armas 1985: 28–32). For Coloma's career and fortune see Serrano y Sanz 1918: cxcvii–ccxvii. This biographical essay and Coloma's will, which Serrano published in the appendixes, pp. dxx–dxxii, are based on documents in the Archivo Provincial de Zaragoza.

4.   1.14. CALCENA   Juan Ruiz de Calcena, registrar of the Aragonese royal chancery, was serving as King Fernando's keeper of the privy seal during this biennium. Born in Calatayud, he achieved the post of secretary to the king in 1504 and became a member of the king's council. At the time of Fernando's death in 1516, Calcena had been in the king's service for 36 years (Escudero 1969: 1.34). Nevertheless, this Arago-

nese administrator's name was unfamiliar to the city clerks of Seville who, in 1498, could not decipher his signature and mistakenly transcribed his name as Talzeña.

5. 2. GRANADA CAPITULATIONS   The original document issued to Columbus, which was stamped with the Castilian privy seal, disappeared sometime after 1829. The first transcripts were a notarized copy, not extant, made in La Isabela on the island of La Española, 30 December 1495, and the further expanded version issued by the royal chancery in Burgos, 23 April 1497. Columbus included one copy of the Burgos transcript in the *Book of Privileges*. I have duplicated the Burgos transcript here at the beginning, where the original, had it survived, would appear in chronological order.

6. 2.1. SIR FERNANDO . . . GOCEANO   Royal writs of great solemnity and permanence begin by invoking all the hereditary domains over which the monarchs exercised or claimed sovereignty—the places where the decree would have effect. The Castilian monarchy claimed sovereignty over the southern part of Portugal (the Algarve), in addition to the domains that still form part of modern Spain (Castile, León, Granada, Toledo, Galicia, Seville, Córdoba, Murcia, Jaén, Algeciras, the Canary Islands, Vizcaya, and Molina). They also claimed Gibraltar, of course, which Castile had captured from the Muslims in the fourteenth century and which remained part of the Castilian monarchy until the early eighteenth century.

7. 2.1. ORISTANO AND GOCEANO   The Crown of Aragón in the fifteenth century comprised Aragón, Valencia, Barcelona, the Balearics, and Sicily. The Aragonese monarchs also claimed sovereignty over two seignorial domains (Oristano and Goceano) on Sardinia; two frontier counties (Roussillon and Cerdagne) disputed with France; and two crusader domains (Athens and Neopatria) in Greece that had been conquered by Catalan Companies in the fourteenth century but were now held by the Ottoman Turks.

8. 2.2. PRINCE SIR JUAN . . . ORDERS.   Royal writs of great solemnity and permanence were binding on all Spaniards and residents in Spanish territory, who are addressed in rank order. This first group of addressees comprises the traditional councilors of the monarchy: members of the royal family, nobles, and ecclesiastical hierarchs. Juan, crown prince of Castile and Aragón, was born in 1478 and died in 1497 (Azcona 1964: 289; fig. 9).

9. 2.2. ROYAL COUNCILORS . . . CHANCERY.   This next group of addressees includes those appointed by the monarchy to the highest judicial offices of the realm.

10. 2.2. SUBCOMMANDERS . . . BUILDINGS.   The next group of addressees consists of commanders of royal fortifications.

11. 2.2. ALL MUNICIPAL COUNCILS . . . ACQUIRE.   This next group of addressees comprised all municipal officials and citizens, including officers of the municipal militia. These addressees would have totaled over 95 percent of the Spanish population, since virtually all Spaniards lived in municipalities, the basic administrative units of the monarchy. Castile and Aragón during the reign of Fernando and Isabel comprised more than 32,000 cities, towns, and villages.

12. 2.2. CAPTAINS . . . CREWS   Naval officers and personnel formed the penulti-

mate group of addressees in royal decrees. The standing royal navy consisted of oar-powered galleys that patrolled the Mediterranean shipping lanes to protect against pirates. For oceangoing fleets, the monarchy commissioned private vessels and civilian seamen on an ad hoc basis. As compensation for their obligation to serve the monarchy on demand with ships and crews, seamen on both the Atlantic and Mediterranean coasts enjoyed exemption from royal taxes. Even the lowliest fisherman was tax exempt and, therefore, an hidalgo.

13.   2.2. SUBJECTS . . . FUTURE   The category of royal subjects *(subjetos)* was a small but diverse group. It included all who were Spanish natives but not citizens of municipalities. Of these the most powerful bloc were the clergy, who gave up their municipal citizenship when they took their vows of obedience to the bishop or abbot. The most numerous royal subjects were religious minorities such as Jews and Muslims, who were citizens of their own religious communities.

14.   2.4. CIRCLE OF SIGNATURES   The medieval charter of privilege endorsed by prelates and nobles in a circle (hence *privilegio rodado*) around the royal seal was obsolete by the reign of Fernando and Isabel. In fact, the royal chancery issued the Granada Capitulations as a simple writ. Writs were signed by the monarchs and the royal chancery staff. They were authenticated by a red wax seal, which, however, was visible only as seepage through an embossed patch of paper. Below the signatures, the deputy chancellor dropped a spot of red wax. Over this he placed a small square of paper. Then, with the wax still warm, he embossed the three layers with the privy seal.

15.   2.8. RODERICUS, DOCTOR   Rodrigo Maldonado de Talavera, doctor of laws, held the chair of canon and civil law at the University of Salamanca. He resigned from his teaching position in 1477 to join the royal council and represented Castile in the negotiations that ended the war with Portugal in 1479. In 1487 he was royal judge of the city of Salamanca. As legal counsel to the Castilian monarchy, he checked the legality of most of the royal writs issued for the first, second, and third voyages. In 1515 he testified that he had been present in 1487 when Columbus submitted his proposal to the royal committee that the monarchs appointed to advise them on the project's feasibility. In that testimony, he described himself as a citizen and city councilman of the city of Salamanca, a member of the queen's council, and more than 55 years old. He also claimed that he had known Columbus's son, Diego Colón, for 20 years (*Pleitos* 3.389–392; Varona 1981: 319, 333).

16.   2.9. SEBASTIÁN DE OLANO   Sebastián de Olano was a permanent member of the queen's household staff and, in 1491 and 1492, deputy registrar of the Castilian royal chancery. Olano acted as deputy for the registrar, Dr. Andrés de Villalón, who lived in Valladolid where he was a judge of the royal court of appeals. In the summer of 1493, Olano received an appointment as collector of royal revenues in the Indies. He crossed the Atlantic on Columbus's second voyage, served in La Isabela (the city that Columbus founded on the island of La Española in 1493), returned to Castile in 1495, and reincorporated himself in the royal staff. After Queen Isabel's death in 1504, he became secretary to Queen Juana, a post that he held until his death in 1515.

17. 2.9. FRANCISCO . . . CHANCELLOR   Francisco Ramírez de Madrid, born Francisco Ramírez de Oreña entered the royal chancery staff during the reign of Enrique IV and participated in the war against Granada, becoming noted for his daring and successful feats in battle. He was killed in an ambush in the Sierra Bermeja in 1501. As deputy Castilian chancellor during the biennium 1492–1493, he had responsibility for the final steps in issuing a royal writ, the embossing of the red wax seal (Escudero 1969: 1.32–33).

18. 3.5. FERNÁN ALVAREZ   Born Fernán Alvarez Zapata, this secretary of both monarchs changed his name to Fernán Alvarez de Toledo to signal his birthplace and distinguish himself from a homonym who was also a royal secretary. His brother, Alonso Alvarez, was also a member of the secretariat. Fernán's loyalty and expertise made him the most frequent redactor of important royal documents. He held multiple offices in the chancery: chief clerk of privileges and confirmations, chief notary of the Kingdom of Granada after 1492, and chief notary of privileges. Outside the chancery, he was also auditor of the military order of Santiago (1494–1498). He died about 1504 (Rumeu de Armas 1985: 32–33, 38, 45; on the family see Márquez Villanueva 1960).

19. 5.3. BOUNDARY . . . BELONGS TO US.   The monarchs are referring to the boundary established in their 1479 agreement with Portugal, the Treaty of Alcáçovas. The Portuguese king had relinquished claim to the Canary Islands; Castile had relinquished its claims to all other Atlantic islands already known to Europeans. The Portuguese waters encompassed the sea lanes between their Atlantic islands and the west African coast, so Castilian ships sailing for the Canary Islands had to give advance notice to Portugal. Fernando and Isabel did not notify the Portuguese king that Columbus would be sailing to the Canary Islands.

20. 5.12 PEDRO GUTIÉRREZ   Pedro Gutiérrez, together with Francisco Ramírez de Madrid, was keeper of the seal during the biennium 1492–1493, when the most important Columbian documents were issued (Rumeu de Armas 1985: 46).

21. 5.14. ALFONSO PÉREZ   Alfonso Pérez was on the staff of the chief registrar, Andrés de Villalón. During the early months of 1492, he was residing in Córdoba as registrar of the documents expedited by the royal council and the judges of the royal court. After mid-May, when the monarchs were resident in Córdoba, he served his first term as deputy registrar of royal documents, alternating with other bureaucrats. While Fernando and Isabel traveled from Córdoba to Valladolid with a stopover in Guadalupe, he continued to take turns as deputy registrar. During the royal progress to Barcelona and residence there (October 1492 to November 1493), Alfonso Pérez registered all the Castilian royal documents except those personally registered by the chief registrar, Dr. Villalón. Alfonso Pérez continued on the staff of the royal chancery until 1498, when his name disappears from the records (Rumeu de Armas 1985: 43–45).

CHAPTERS 2.1, 2.2, AND 2.3

1. 6.1 JUAN DE FONSECA   Juan Rodríguez de Fonseca (1451–1523) was born in the city of Toro, son of the lord of the towns of Coca and Alaejos and his second wife.

His career as a churchman was secondary to his many royal administrative posts. In 1491–1492 he formed part of the team that negotiated Aragón's annexation of Roussillon and Cerdagne from France. He was present when Columbus arrived at the royal court in Barcelona to report on his first voyage to America. On 20 May the monarchs appointed Fonseca to create a fleet in Seville for Columbus's second voyage. For the rest of his life, he supervised the peninsular side of the enterprise of the Indies. In 1495 Fonseca established regulations and procedures for trade with the Americas. This trade grew so much that at the beginning of 1503 the monarchs established a Seville branch of the royal treasury, the House of Trade (Casa de la Contratación) to house the customs, mint, navigation, licensing, and judicial offices. After Fonseca's death, Charles V had to create a whole new royal council to carry out all the jobs related to the Indies that Fonseca had done (Alcocer y Martínez 1926; *DHEE* 1987).

2.   6.3. RIGGING   Spanish ship owners completely refitted their oceangoing vessels after each transatlantic round trip by moving the rigging from one ship to another. They stripped all rigging and equipment from a returned ship and sent the hull to be careened for repairs and recaulking. Meanwhile the sails, rigging, and equipment from the returned ship were cleaned, repaired, and fitted to a ship that had returned earlier and already been careened and caulked. The process required months to carry out (Phillips 1986).

3.   7.1. STATUS . . . VASSALS   The chancery here is dividing all residents of Castile into three different legal groups. Royal vassals *(vassallos del rey)* achieved their status by personally taking an oath of vassalage to the monarch. By this oath they submitted to the royal will, giving up the protection of any but royal law codes and courts, and gaining the prospect of bountiful rewards. Royal vassals comprised members of the royal family, the staff of the royal court and government, military professionals in the royal service, and nobles.

4.   7.1. SUBJECTS   This second legal category, royal subjects *(subjetos)* did not take personal oaths of loyalty to the monarchs. They were groups who, though born in Castile, obeyed religious law. Clergy, both regular and secular, became subject to canon law and church courts when they took their clerical vows. They also relinquished their citizenship in their native cities and towns. Jews and Muslims born in Castile, by virtue of their communities' longstanding agreements with the monarchy, lived under their own religious law, administered by their own local judges (rabbis and qadis, respectively).

5.   7.1. CITIZENS   Citizens *(naturales)* comprised the vast majority of Castilians. They were citizens by birth of their native cities, towns, or villages, and subject to municipal law codes and judges. They resorted to royal courts and law codes only in appellate cases or in cases that pitted one municipal code against another.

6.   7.4. THE MINE   In 1480, King João II of Portugal constructed a fortified trading post on the west African coast near a native owned and operated gold mine. He named the fort São Jorge da Mina (Saint George of the Mine).

7.   7.4. OUR BROTHER   Custom required the monarchs to refer to King João II of Portugal as their brother, even though the marriage in 1490 between their daughter

and his son had ended abruptly with the death of the Portuguese bridegroom just eleven months after the marriage.

8. 7.4. OBSERVE . . . AGREED When Castile and Portugal signed the Treaty of Alcáçovas in 1479, the line between their two spheres of influence was drawn so that Portugal would have a monopoly on exploration and trade with the West African coast.

9. 9.1. NOMINATE . . . OFFICE See the second article of the Santa Fe Capitulations.

10. 10.1. ANTONIO DE TORRES Antonio de Torres was on the staff of Isabel's household, and his sister, Juana de La Torre, was governess of Prince Juan's household. Antonio commanded a ship on the outward voyage, with instructions from the monarchs to return in command of several ships to resupply the new colony on La Española. Torres sailed from La Española on 2 February 1494 in command of 12 ships, 26 Indians, and about 30,000 pesos of gold. He arrived at Cádiz on 7 March 1494 and traveled to the royal court in Medina del Campo, where he arrived about 9 April and where he remained until 16 August. His resupply fleet of four caravels left Cádiz in October and arrived in La Isabela in late November. On 24 February 1495, Torres and his four caravels sailed from La Isabela with the only valuable commodities Columbus had acquired during his two years on the island, 500 enslaved Indians. Torres inexplicably chose a southern route that proved inordinately slow. By the time the fleet arrived in Cádiz at the beginning of April, 200 slaves had died. In June 1502, Torres commanded the great gold-bearing fleet that was destroyed by a hurricane off Santo Domingo. He survived to serve a year as governor of the island of Gran Canaria, only to die in a shipwreck in the bay of Cádiz in the autumn of 1503.

11. 10.5. BERNAL DE PISA Bernal Díaz de Pisa was a constable of the royal household and court. He went to La Española on the second voyage, appointed by the monarchs as comptroller to supervise the work of the expedition's accountants. Samuel Eliot Morison claims that "a paper of his full of false charges against the admiral and outlining a plan to seize some of the caravels and return to Spain was discovered in an anchor buoy." Columbus arrested Pisa and sent him back to Spain on the next fleet. Pisa died in 1497 (Navarrete 1825–1837, 2.91–94; Prieto Cantero 1969: 216, 523; Morison 1942: 2.108).

12. 10.5. FRIAR BUYL Bernardo Buyl (also Boil and Buil), captained warships in the Mediterranean for King Fernando of Aragón in 1479, then served as secretary to the king until 1481, when he became a priest and retired to the Benedictine monastery of Montserrat. He again served Fernando as ambassador to France in the negotiations for Rousillon in 1492–1493. In 1493 Pope Alexander VI named him papal representative in the Americas, and Buyl chose several other monks to accompany him on Columbus's second voyage—the first Christian priests to travel on a Columbian voyage to the Americas. Once on La Española, however, Buyl became sharply critical of Columbus's policies and returned to Spain in November 1494, where he continued to serve the king until his death, which most historians place in 1505 (Fita 1891, 1893).

13.   10.7. JUAN DE LA PARRA.   Born in Parra near Zafra, Juan de La Parra was described by one of his contemporaries as "a virtuous man of decent family." He was a member of the queen's staff, working for many years in the office of the queen's personal secretary Fernán Alvarez de Toledo. He achieved the rank of secretary in February 1490 but continued to assist Fernán Alvarez. In 1503 he received a lump sum of 50,000 maravedís as reimbursement for expenses, and as secretary he received an annual salary and allowance of 100,000 maravedís (Rumeu de Armas 1985: 33–34).

14.   12.17. FRANCISCO DÍAZ.   Francisco Díaz held the office of deputy high chancellor of the privy seal at this time. In 1495 he became responsible for drafting the royal tax collection contracts *(encabezamientos),* a task he was still carrying out in 1504, when the monarchs reimbursed him for the wax and paper he had bought during the previous ten years (Prieto Cantero 1969: 109).

15.   13.4. DECEIVED IN ANY WAY   The monarchs were worried that Columbus, whom they had instructed to cooperate with Portuguese mariners, would be deceived by them if he knew of the revised papal decree and let down his guard.

16.   14.2. PEDRO GARCIAS   Garcias, bishop of Arles, was elevated bishop of Barcelona on 14 June 1490. He died 8 February 1505.

17.   14.3. ALEXANDER VI   Pope Alexander VI, born Rodrigo Borja in Játiva near Valencia, in 1431. He rose in the church hierarchy to become cardinal and papal chancellor. While on an embassy to Aragón and Castile in 1472, Borja allied the papacy with the powerful Mendoza family in supporting Isabel's claims as queen of Castile. Although the father of two notorious illegitimate children, Cesare and Lucrezia Borgia, he was elected pope in 1492. He died in Rome in 1503. See fig. 7.

18.   14.6.   Note that the papal chancery does not give Columbus his new honorific of "sir."

19.   14.7. EMBRACE . . . ISLANDS   This, the first mention of conversion in the *Book of Privileges,* occurs in a church decree from the Roman curia rather than a government document from Castile.

20.   14.10. CHRISTMAS . . . BEGINS   European states began the new year on different dates. Several Italian city-states, for example, began the new year on March 15. The papal chancery dated the New Year from Christmas Day. The Castilian and Aragonese chanceries had switched from Christmas to January 1 earlier in the century.

21.   14.10. EFFECTIVE POSSESSION . . . AWAY   Here, of course, the reference is to Portugal's effective possession of Madeira, the Azores, and St. George of the Mine.

22.   14.11. AUTOMATIC EXCOMMUNICATION   *Latae sententiae* is excommunication incurred by reason of the offense itself, as soon as it occurs, without any action by an ecclesiastical court.

23.   14.16. ALFONSO ALVAREZ DE TOLEDO.   Alfonso was a secretary to the Castilian Chancery and a brother of Isabel's secretary Fernand Alvarez de Toledo.

24.   14.19. SIR DIEGO   Diego Hurtado de Mendoza, born in Guadalajara about 1445. Grandson and homonym of the first admiral of Castile, he was the youngest son of the first count and countess of Tendilla, and a nephew of the powerful archbishop

of Toledo and cardinal of Spain, Pedro González de Mendoza. Fernando and Isabel appointed him president of the royal appeals court in Valladolid and commissioned him to draw up new procedures for the court. He succeeded his uncle as archbishop of Seville in 1485, became cardinal of Santa Sabina in 1500, and died in 1502.

25.   14.22. PAPAL NOTARY PUBLIC   The papal chancery administered an examination testing an applicant's ability to draft and correct church documents in Latin. The successful candidate could practice as a papal notary wherever he lived or was posted as a priest.

CHAPTERS 3.1, 3.2, AND 3.3

1.   17.1. OUR TREASURER   In 1497 a Genoese businessman, Bernardo Pinelo, was acting as treasurer in Seville for the royal enterprise of the Indies. He was responsible for disbursing royal funds to purchasing agents and providers of services on the pay vouchers of Fonseca and Columbus. He is most noted for having issued 12,000 maravedís to Columbus's steward and cousin, Juan Antonio Colón, without the admiral's voucher and then not being able to extract an accounting for the expenditure from Juan Antonio or the admiral (Gil and Varela 1986: 2). Columbus's hostility toward the treasurer may have extended to Bernardo's uncle, the royal banker Francisco Pinelo, from whom Columbus previously had received support (Varela 1992: 135–136).

2.   18.1. Document 16 above.

3.   18.5. HUSBANDRY   Plowing depends, of course, on the availability of domesticated animals. There were no domesticated mammals in the Caribbean, so the natives planted their seed by digging with a pointed stick that had been hardened by fire.

4.   18.12. CHEST WITH THREE LOCKS   These chests with multiple locks, each requiring a separate key, were the customary safes or strongboxes of early modern Europe. Whoever was responsible for the chest distributed the three separate keys among trustworthy clergy and officials.

5.   18.16. [. . .]   The space for the name was left blank.

6.   20.2. ALREADY . . . INDIES   We do not know how many Europeans remained on the island of La Española at this time, although it was apparently fewer than 330. Most of the 1,200 who had embarked on the second voyage returned to Spain with the resupply fleets in 1494, 1495, and 1496.

7.   20.2–4.   Elaboration of 18.5.

8.   20.4. BUSINESS   The monarchs still regarded the Indies as a *negocio* or business and the voyages as commercial ventures.

9.   20.5. BARLEY   Spaniards from the Duero River south used mules for plowing and barley as feed, in contrast to northern farmers who plowed with oxen and used grass and hay as feed. Normally, farmers who plowed with mules needed to sow equal amounts of wheat and barley to provide enough bread for themselves and feed for the plow team.

10.   20.6. MATTOCKS . . . CROWBARS   These are the tools used to clear previously uncultivated land.

11.   20.6–7.   The monarchs are introducing metal tools and plow animals experimentally, in order to test them for various types of soil. These tools will belong to the royal stores. To the disgust of the colonists, Columbus later claimed for himself the natural increase in livestock as partial payment of his one-eighth of the profits on provisions.

12.   20.8. OLD CARGO CARRIER   Once again, the monarchs display their famous parsimony in their American enterprise. Also they are imitating the Portuguese king, who was said to have used this method to build the fortified trading post of São Jorge da Mina in West Africa. The Portuguese king did not have a reputation for penny pinching, and it has been suggested that he used this method in order to give credence to Portuguese propaganda that large ships could not return up the African coast.

13.   20.9. HORSE-MILLS   If Columbus could not find a site on the island suitable for a water-powered flour mill, he would have to use horses to turn the millstone. This is indeed what happened at La Isabela, with the result that the cavalry officers successfully petitioned the queen for compensation for the damage incurred by their warhorses from this mill work (Ramos 1979, 1982)

14.   20.15. INDIAN CITIZENS   Here the monarchs refer to the native Americans as Indios, but immediately qualify the term as "citizens of these Indies" *(Yndios naturales de las dichas Yndias)*. This description parallels their usual terminology for taxpaying citizens *(naturales)* of the kingdoms of Castile and Aragón.

15.   20.17. HIGH COMMANDER OF LEÓN   Alonso de Cárdenas, son of the last master of Santiago. After the master's death in 1493, the monarchs discontinued the mastership, leaving the high commandery of León as the highest office in the military order of Santiago.

16.   21.2. BRAZILWOOD   Brazilwood supplied a dye highly prized for textiles. The monarchs included brazilwood in the royal monopoly, along with gold and other precious ores.

17.   21.7. FERNANDO ORTIZ   Fernando Ortiz was a member of the staff of the king's secretary, Gaspar de Gricio. In 1502, Ortiz received a commitment from the monarchs that he would receive the next vacancy as clerk of the royal appeals court in Valladolid. He died before 1515 (Varona 1981: 358).

18.   21.7. REGISTERED: DOCTOR   This is the usual signature of Dr. Andrés de Villalón, chief registrar of the Castilian chancery. In 1470, King Enrique IV appointed Villalón as a judge of the royal council and the royal appeals court in Valladolid, with an annual salary of 30,000 maravedís. Fernando and Isabel confirmed him in both positions, and later appointed him chief registrar. As a member of the royal council he would later receive 100,000 maravedís in salary, and as registrar he received the registration fees established by the chancery ordinances. Because he was based in Valladolid and did not travel with the royal court, his deputies Sebastián de Olano and Alfonso Pérez usually registered royal writs during 1492–1493. When the royal court was in

Medina del Campo, near Valladolid, however, Villalón fulfilled his duties as chief registrar (Rumeu de Armas 1985: 36–38).

19. 23.8. SIR ALVARO Alvaro de Luna, son of Pedro de Luna, illegitimate son of the famous Alvaro de Luna? If so, second lord of Fuentidueña, royal cupbearer, commander of Loja, high commander of Montalbán in the order of Santiago. Died 5 February 1519 (Gutiérrez Coronel 1946: 1. 620; see also autograph documents in Incháustegui 1964: 128, 315).

20. 24.1. COUNT OF CIFUENTES Sir Juan de Silva, count of Cifuentes and royal judge *(asistente)* of Seville from 1482 to 1500. While Silva was a prisoner of war in a Muslim prison during 1487–1488, his functions as royal judge of Seville were carried out by a lieutenant. The prestige and importance of Silva's office are indicated by his salary; the usual royal city judge's salary was about 200 maravedís per day (about 73,000 annually), while Silva's was about 4,000,000, with 187,000 for expenses (Lunenfeld 1987: 83).

21. 24.1. ROYAL JUDGE In Seville, the title of the resident royal judge was "asistente." In other Castilian cities, the title was "corregidor." For each of the Canary islands, it was "gobernador."

22. 24.2. JUSTICES The chancery usually applied the title "justicia" to interim judges. The monarchs transferred the royal appeals court of Cindad Real to the city of Granada in 1505.

23. 32.1. BISHOP OF BADAJOZ Juan Rodríguez de Fonseca.

24. 35.1. ISABELA ESPAÑOLA Our clerk here has conflated the city of La Isabela and the island of La Española.

25. 36.1. Bartolomé Colón, born Bartolomeo Colombo in Genoa about 1455, he joined his older brother's import-export business in Lisbon and remained there while Columbus was in Spain between 1486 and 1490. He apparently had traveled to France on business when Columbus departed Spain on the first and second voyages but joined his brother on La Española with Antonio de Torres's resupply fleet that arrived in La Isabela in November 1494. He died in Santo Domingo in 1514 leaving an illegitimate daughter in Spain who died in poverty (Albònico 1986: 51–70).

26. 36.1. CORTES OF TOLEDO The Cortes (national representative assembly) of the Kingdom of Castile met in the city of Toledo several times during the reign of Queen Isabel: in 1480, 1489, and 1502. This writ refers to the momentous Cortes of 1480, which reorganized the royal administration, judiciary, and treasury (see Azcona 1964: 318–365).

CHAPTERS 3.4 AND 3.5

1. 42.1. SIR GUTIERRE DE TOLEDO Gutierre Gómez de Toledo became bishop of Palencia in 1423, archbishop of Seville in 1439, and archbishop of Toledo in 1442. In 1428, King Juan II appointed him president of the royal appeals court for the usual one-year term. In 1429 he was still serving as president and in 1442 he served in the

presidency once again. Before he died in 1446, he enriched a nephew whose estates would become the seignorial domains of the dukes of Alba (Varona 1981: 46, 111).

2. 42.1. Sir Fadrique   Fadrique Enríquez succeeded his father as admiral of Castile in 1435. That, undoubtedly, was the occasion for Juan II's confirmation of the admiralty.

3. 43.1. Sir Juan.   King Juan II of Castile reigned from 1406 to 1454. He was the father of Queen Isabel. Born 7 March 1405, Juan became king at the age of twenty months. His long minority was dominated by rivalry between his two regents, the widowed Queen Catherine of Lancaster and his uncle Fernando de Antequera. Elected king of Aragón in 1412, Fernando de Antequera used his new kingdom as a base for plundering Castile in order to enrich his sons and daughters, plunging the two kingdoms into prolonged warfare (Suárez Fernández 1959).

4. 43.1. Castile . . . Molina   Juan's domains did not include Granada, of course, because Castile had not yet conquered it. The domains of the king of Aragón, who happened to be Juan's nephew, were not relevant to a Castilian document before the marriage of Fernando and Isabel in 1469.

5. 43.2. My uncle   Custom called for the king to address nobles who were his elders as "uncle," those of his own age as "cousin," and those who were younger as "nephew." The familial relationship between Juan and Alfonso Enríquez was one of distant cousins, at best. Alfonso Enríquez claimed to be the illegitimate nephew of King Enrique II, Juan's great grandfather and founder of the Trastamara dynasty. Though the claim was dubious, Queen Catherine accepted it in order to gain the military support of the powerful Mendoza family, into which Alfonso Enríquez had married (Mitre 1968).

6. 44.1. King Juan   Juan I, King of Castile from 1379 to 1390.

7. 44.1. King Enrique   King Enrique III of Castile, 1390–1406. Note that his regnal dates are sometimes given as 1390–1407, because he died on Christmas Day, which on the calendar of that time was New Year's Day.

8. 45.1. Sir Diego Hurtado de Mendoza   Diego Hurtado de Mendoza (1365–1404) had led the Castilian fleet to victory in three separate naval engagements during the war between Castile and Portugal in 1385. At the time of his death, he was reputed to be the richest man in Castile and left a vast estate to his son Iñigo López de Mendoza, future marquis of Santillana (Nader 1979).

9. 46.7. Including the city of Seville   A previous royal grant that temporarily separated Seville from the admiralty of Castile probably was the precipitating factor in the admiral's request for confirmation of his jurisdiction in Seville.

10. 46.11. Circle of signatures   A *privilegio rodado* was so called because the king's counsellors—members of the royal family, nobles, and prelates—endorsed the document by signing in a circle around the royal seal. The endorsements guaranteed that the most powerful members of society accepted and would enforce the privilege, even if its terms violated the law.

11. 46.13. Queen Catalina   Catherine of Lancaster, widow of King Enrique

III. Catherine was the daughter of John of Gaunt, Duke of Lancaster, and his second wife, Constanza, daughter of King Pedro of Castile (died 1369). Catherine's sister married Juan I of Portugal.

12.   46.14. PRINCE, SIR JUAN   Juan, infante de Castilla, was the king's first cousin, son of Fernando de Antequera. He succeeded his childless brother Alfonso V (1416–1458) as king of Aragón (1458–1479), and was the father of King Fernando the Catholic (king of Aragón 1479–1516 and co-ruler of Castile 1474–1504).

13.   46.15. SIR ENRIQUE   Enrique, infante de Castilla, was the second son of Fernando de Antequera. He died before his eldest brother, King Alfonso V (1416–1458) of Aragón.

14.   46.16. PRINCE, SIR PEDRO   Pedro, the youngest of the infantes de Castilla, died in adolescence.

15.   46.17. SIR LUIS DE GUZMÁN   Luis de Guzmán, elected master of the order of Calatrava at a general chapter held at Cîteaux in 1414.

16.   46.19. SIR LUIS DE LA CERDA   Luis de La Cerda, third count of Medinaceli and lord of the town of Puerto de Santa María, died 1447 (*HGCM* 1946).

17.   46.20. SIR PABLO   Pablo de Santa María, born Salomón ha-Levi (1350–1435). As chief rabbi of the city of Burgos, Salomón ha-Levi acted as appeals judge for most of Castile's Jews. His conversion to Christianity in 1390, after what he later claimed was a serious study of the theology of Thomas Aquinas, set the example for many other Jews to convert in the same and following years. He studied at the University of Paris and went on to practice law in the papal court at Avignon. In 1403, he became bishop of Cartagena, and in 1415 was promoted to bishop of Burgos (*DHEE* 1987).

18.   46.21. SIR LOPE DE MENDOZA   Lope de Mendoza was archbishop of Santiago from 1399 to 1455, having previously been bishop of Mondoñedo. He spent most of his time with the royal court, which had been deeply divided into factions during the minority of Juan II. Nevertheless, he did convene assemblies (synods) of the clergy in his diocese in 1415, 1431, 1435, 1436, 1439, 1451, and 1452 (*DHEE* 1987).

19.   46.22. FRIAR SIR ALFONSO   Not listed in *DHEE* as an archbishop of Santiago. Lope de Mendoza was bishop of Santiago at this date, but spent nearly all the time at the royal court, where he was royal chaplain. Could fray Alfonso have been auxiliary bishop during Lope's absences from Santiago?

20.   46.23. SIR JUAN   Juan Vázquez de Cepeda, born Juan Vázquez de Tordesillas, bishop of Segovia from 1398 until his death in 1437. He founded the Carthusian monastery in Aniago, participated in the ceremony that marked the legal majority of Juan II, and visited the antipope Benedict XIII (Pedro de Luna).

21.   46.24. SIR DIEGO   Diego de Anaya, one of the most revered prelates of Castilian history. He was bishop of Tuy (1384–1390), of Orense (1390–1392), Salamanca (1392–1407), Cuenca (1407–1418), and elevated to archbishop of Seville (1418 until his death, after January 1423). He attended the Council of Constance, where he was

one of the five electors of Pope Martin V. While bishop of Salamanca, he established and endowed the scholarship College of San Bartolomé and his funerary chapel in the old cathedral of Salamanca (*DHEE* 1987).

22. 46.25. SIR GONZALO DE ZÚÑIGA   *DHEE* does not list him as bishop of Palencia in 1416, the year he endorsed the privilege. Instead, it lists Alonso de Argüello, former bishop of León, promoted to Palencia in 1415, and then to Sigüenza in 1418 (*DHEE* 1987).

23. 46.26. SIR DIEGO GÓMEZ DE SANDOVAL   Diego Gómez de Sandoval, first count of Denia and Castrogeriz by privilege of Juan II in 1426; lord of the towns of Lerma, Gumiel, Maderuelo, and Portillo; royal judge of Castile, high chancellor of the privy seal (*HGCM* 1946: 2.328).

24. 46.27. SIR JUAN RAMÍREZ DE ARELLANO   Juan Ramírez de Arellano, lord of Los Cameros, distinguished himself in battle during King Juan I's unsuccessful invasion of Portugal in 1384 (Suárez Fernández 1977: 1.189–194).

25. 46.28. SIR GARCÍA FERNÁNDEZ MANRIQUE   García Fernández Manrique, lord of the towns of Estar, Villanueva, and San Martín de Halinas. In 1395 he married the lady of Aguilar, who brought to the marriage the towns of Aguilar, Bricia, Santa Gadea, Peñamelera, Villalumbroso, and Villatoquite.

26. 46.29. IÑIGO LÓPEZ DE MENDOZA   Iñigo López de Mendoza (1398–1454), first marquis of Santillana (1445), was the son of the previous admiral of Castile, Diego Hurtado de Mendoza (q.v. 45.1). Santillana later in life became one of the leading poets of the Castilian Renaissance (Nader 1979).

27. 47.6. HIGH CHANCELLOR . . . SEALS   Here the monarch addresses the royal officials who travel with the court: the royal counsellors, royal appeals judges, and chancery staff. These officials have access to the original documents and the power to certify copies as authentic.

28. 47.9. QUEEN MARÍA, MY WIFE   In 1420 King Juan II married María de Aragón, daughter of his uncle Fernando de Antequera.

29. 47.13. SIR RUY LÓPEZ DÁVALOS   Ruy López Dávalos (1357–1428), active participant in battles against the Muslims of Granada, royal judge of the cities of Avila and Baeza during the reign of Juan I; chamberlain of King Enrique III, constable of Castile, royal governor of Murcia. Lord of the towns of Dávalos, Lerín, Arjona, Ribadeo, Arenas, Colmenar, and Adrada (Mitre 1968).

30. 47.16. SIR JUAN ALFONSO PIMENTEL   Juan Alfonso Pimentel came to Castile in 1398 as a political refugee from Portugal, where he had been lord of Braganza. Enrique III granted him the border town of Benavente in the same year, and between 1402 and 1405 Pimentel bought small towns all around Benavente (Mitre 1968).

31. 47.19. SIR RODRIGO DE VELASCO   Rodrigo de Velasco became bishop of Palencia on 7 June 1417. He was murdered in 1426 (*DHEE* 1987).

32. 47.21. SIR ALFONSO   Alfonso de Argüello, O.P., in 1402 represented King

Enrique III before the curia of Avignon to deliver Castile's recognition of the antipope Benedict XIII. He was appointed bishop of Palencia in 1417, transferred to Zaragoza in 1419, promoted bishop of Sigüenza on 7 June 1419, the day after he signed this charter. He died in February 1429 (*DHEE* 1987).

33.　47.23. SIR JUAN　Juan Ramírez de Guzmán, abbot of the collegiate church of Santa María in Valladolid, appointed bishop of La Calahorra 1394, promoted bishop of Avila 30 June 1403. He died 6 October 1424 (*DHEE* 1987).

34.　47.24. SIR ALVARO　Alvaro Núñez de Isorna.　Bishop of Mondoñedo since 1400, he was promoted to León in August 1415, then bishop of Cuenca in 1418, then to Santiago 7 April 1445. While bishop of Cuenca he served two terms as president of the royal appeals court. He died 9 February 1449. He participated in the Council of Basel as a representative of Castile (*DHEE* 1987; Varona 1981: 46).

35.　47.25. SIR FERNANDO　Fernando González Deza, bishop of Córdoba from 1398 until his death in 1425 (*DHEE* 1987).

36.　47.27. SIR RODRIGO　Rodrigo Fernández de Narváez, promoted bishop of Jaén on 4 November 1383, died in 1422 (*DHEE* 1987).

37.　48.4. JUDGES OF THE HIDALGOS　Hidalgos, or tax exempt persons, could have their lawsuits heard by judges authorized to preside over cases involving very large sums of money.

38.　50.1. OUR OWN INITIATIVE . . . POWER　Here, for the first time, Fernando and Isabel use their absolute royal power to confirm the heritability of Columbus's royal office of admiral. They strengthened this violation of the fundamental laws of monarchy by marshalling the signatures of three of their legal counsel: doctor Rodericus, doctor Antonius, and doctor Fernand Alvarez. These doctors of law, however, signed without the usual approbation "approved."

39.　51.1. ROYAL ABSOLUTE POWER　The monarch invokes his royal absolute power because, by permanently alienating a royal office, he is violating the fundamental principles of monarchy.

40.　55.1. MAINLAND　Columbus had explored the coasts of modern Venezuela and Central America on the outward voyage earlier in the year. The volume of water pouring out of the Orinoco River delta left no doubt that this was a continent whose existence had never been suspected by Europeans. From this time on, Spaniards referred to this section of the South and Central American coast as Tierra Firme. Columbus referred to it as "another world" and speculated that it might be the terrestial paradise.

41.　55.1. DIEGO DE ALVARADO　Diego de Alvarado, public clerk in Santo Domingo in 1498.

42.　56.2. PEDRO DE TERREROS　Pedro de Terreros, the admiral's butler, went on every one of the admiral's four voyages. He took possession of Paria during the third voyage while the admiral was ill, commanded the caravel *Gallego* on the fourth voyage, receiving an annual captain's salary of 48,000 maravedís, and died 29 May 1504 (Varela 1985: 281).

1.   57. JUANA DE LA TORRE   Sister of royal secretary Pedro de Torres and of Antonio de Torres, Juana de La Torre, also known as Juana Velázquez de La Torre, had been entrusted with the position of *ama* or mistress of the household, of Prince Juan (b. 30 June 1478, d. 4 October 1497). The *ama* managed the housekeeping, possessed all the keys of the household, and supervised the servants. She was not a wet nurse, as some have mistakenly translated this term, and would not have been appointed to her position until the prince had his own household in early adolescence. She received a royal pension of 60,000 maravedíes in Granada on 31 August 1499. Juana de La Torre died before 11 July 1503, when her daughter Isabel de Avila received a dowry of 1,500,000 maravedís from Queen Isabel (Thacher 1967: 2.423).

2.   57.0. OPEN LETTER   In typical Renaissance fashion, Columbus addressed this letter to one person but intended the recipient to make copies available for public consumption. Several copies of this open letter, with only slight variations, survive.

3.   57.2. DARKNESS   A tragic play on words: Columbus had been partially blinded by his physical ailments during the third and fourth voyages.

4.   57.5. NEW HEAVEN AND EARTH   Columbus alludes to the continent of Paria (South America) in millenarian terms.

5.   57.13. SUFFERING . . . THEN   Here, Columbus refers to the final illness of Prince Juan, who died 4 October 1497.

6.   57.15. PEARLS . . . GOLD   Some critics at court charged that Columbus had failed to discover or had withheld notice about the pearls on the Venezuelan coast during his third voyage. A modern historian, Manzano, believes that Columbus did discover and exploit the pearls (but in 1494 on his second voyage) and failed to report them to the monarchs because he was preoccupied with the revolt on La Española (Manzano 1972).

7.   57.18. HOJEDA   Alonso de Hojeda (b. 1466 in Cuenca, d. 1515? on La Española) had received permission from Fonseca to make voyages of discovery and exploration independently of Columbus. Son of Rodrigo de Huete, citizen of Cuenca, he had been on the staff of the duke of Medinaceli. He first went to La Española on Columbus's second voyage, then remained involved in the Indies for twenty years, always exploring new frontiers but with disastrous results. He commanded a fleet, financed by a joint stock company, that departed from Seville on 18 May 1499, one of the "Andalusian Voyages." This fleet returned to Seville 22 October 1500 with 200 enslaved Indians, 32 others having died during the crossing of the Caribbean. The voyage was notable for having carried a passenger, Amerigo Vespucci, who published a narrative account, falsely dated two years earlier without mentioning Hojeda and thus resulting in the name Americas for the western hemisphere. In January 1502 Hojeda commanded another fleet, again financed by a joint stock company, from Cádiz to establish a colony on the northern coast of modern Venezuela, which he had explored on his first voyage. This colony failed largely due to his mismanagement, and

his partners arrested him in May 1502 and sent him to La Española. In 1508, he and Juan de la Cosa organized another voyage, this time a royal project to colonize the coast of Central America, which also failed, with an appalling loss of lives (Bedini 1991; Formisano 1992; Gould 1984; Gil 1985; Vigneras 1976).

8. 57.20. VICENTE YÁÑEZ   Vicente Yáñez Pinzón, who had commanded *Niña* on the outward passage of Columbus's first voyage, had also received royal permission to carry out voyages of discovery and exploration independently of Columbus. He died in 1514 (Manzano 1988: 2.602–603).

9. 57.20. APPELLATE JUDGE   Columbus is referring to the appellate judge he had appointed for the island of La Española, Francisco Roldán. Roldán died at sea in the 1502 hurricane.

10. 57.22. OCCURRED ... INDIES   All the ships in the Indies except *Niña* had been destroyed or seriously damaged by two hurricanes in 1495, after Antonio de Torres sailed for Spain with the resupply fleet.

11. 57.23. ADRIÁN   Adrián de Múgica, one of the colonists who had gone to La Española on the third voyage, joined the rebels who tried to establish a new town on the southwestern peninsula of the island, and later led another rebellion that was put down by Roldán on Columbus's orders.

12. 57.27. RETURN TRIP   Columbus and the colonists managed to patch together a ship, *India,* from the wreckage of the hurricanes. With this and *Niña,* he set sail from La Isabela on 10 March 1496 and arrived in Cádiz on 11 June 1496.

13. 57.31. EXEMPTIONS ... YEARS   Bobadilla announced that anyone could mine gold and pay only 11 percent to the monarchy during the next twenty years. He did not have authority to make this change, which the monarchs annulled in September 1501.

14. 57.33. COMMANDER BOBADILLA   Fernando and Isabel appointed Francisco de Bobadilla as investigative judge of the island of La Española. In Castile, he was commander of several towns belonging to the military order of Calatrava: Auñón, Castellanos, El Collado, Berninches, and Villarrubia de los Ojos. Bobadilla already had a reputation for harshness and had been sued by the citizens of the towns of Auñón and Berninches for malfeasance. He arrived in Santo Domingo on 23 August 1500. During his two years on the island, he thoroughly lived up to his reputation in Spain. He died in the shipwreck by hurricane that destroyed the return fleet in 1502. He is not to be confused with the man of the same name who was a member of the royal staff (Incháustegui 1964).

15. 57.33. LA VEGA   Columbus established a fortified settlement, Concepción de La Vega, in the central valley of the island as a base for gold prospecting.

16. 57.33. INTERIM GOVERNOR   Columbus's brother Bartolomé Colón. Their youngest brother, Diego Colón, remained in Santo Domingo.

17. 57.36. JUDGE   The appellate judge, Francisco Roldán, who was leading the rebellion in Jaraguá.

18. 57.38. FRIARS   Apparently three Franciscans, Juan de Leudelle, Juan de Ro-

bles, and Juan Trasier, who had written to Cardinal Cisneros complaining about Columbus.

19.   57.41. JUAN AGUADO   In April 1495 the monarchs appointed the provisioner of the royal court, Juan Aguado, as investigative judge of La Española. He sailed from Spain with four caravels, arriving with fresh supplies for La Isabela in October 1495. A hurricane wrecked his fleet a few days later, but the Spaniards utilized the remains to build *India*, which, together with *Niña*, arrived in Cádiz in June 1496. He is believed to have been highly critical of the provisioning of the second voyage, but Columbus may not have been aware that Aguado submitted an unfavorable report to the monarchs (Gil 1986: 12; Heers 1991: 353).

20.   57.43. ESTABLISHED RESIDENCE . . . SPADE   The fundamental requirement for clear legal possession of newly cleared land was to cultivate it with plow or spade.

21.   57.58. SONS . . . PAGES   Columbus's sons Diego and Fernando had been appointed pages in the household of Prince Juan. After his death, they moved to the queen's household.

22.   57.73. ARABIA FELIX   Columbus is referring to the sea trade along the south coast of the Arabian Peninsula. Arabia Felix was an ancient Roman name of the southern Arabian peninsula, in the region of modern Yemen.

23.   57.73. LA MEJORADA   Rumeu de Armas believes that, when Columbus gave his recommendation to the monarchs, who were staying at the monastery of La Mejorada for a few days in 1497, on how the Spanish and Portuguese interests in the Ocean Sea should be partitioned, he also requested that he be given lordship over the westernmost Indies from Arabia to Calicut (Rumeu de Armas 1972: 20).

24.   58. CAPITULATION   This document is a copy of the entire text of the Santa Fe Capitulations, signed by the monarchs on April 17, 1492 (see document 1 above).

25.   60.5th art.16. LERCAR . . . ARCHDUCHESS   The writer is referring to the fleet that transported Princess Juana and her entourage to the Netherlands as the bride of Philip, duke of Burgundy. The fleet sailed from Laredo on 22 August 1496. By the time this legal opinion was written, Philip had succeeded his father Maximilian of Habsburg as archduke of Austria; hence Juana had become the archduchess.

26.   60.5th art.18. Document 59 above.

27.   61.6. OUR GOVERNOR   Friar Nicolás de Ovando, high commander of Lares in the military order of Alcántara, was appointed governor of La Española and the Indies on 3 September 1501. He sailed from Cádiz on 13 February 1502, with orders to audit Bobadilla's governorship (Lamb 1977).

28.   61.7. GORBALÁN   Ginés de Gorbalán or Corbalán, captain of one of the ships on Columbus's second voyage, with Alonso de Hojeda led the first expedition inland on La Española during January 1494. When they returned to La Isabela, they reported discovering traces of gold in the interior (Morison 1942: 2.103–104).

29.   61.12. ALONSO SÁNCHEZ DE CARBAJAL   Alonso de Carvajal was also known as Alonso Sánchez de Carvajal and as "Alonso de Carvajal, lord of the town of Jódar." He first appears as a citizen and city councilman of Baeza, and member of the queen's

staff during the war on Granada. Carvajal was the royal provisioner of the second voyage and traveled with the fleet to La Española, where Columbus appointed him to the city council of La Isabela. On the third voyage Carvajal commanded a ship and rotated weekly with the captains of the other three ships as captain-general of the fleet. In 1501 Columbus and the monarchs appointed Carvajal as Columbus's representative (factor) in the Indies. He was in Spain caring for the admiral's business affairs and thus did not participate in the fourth voyage. In Burgos on 6 February 1503 he sold some gold for the admiral's account, then went to La Española, where he submitted Columbus's claims for restitution to the new governor, Ovando. On 27 November 1503 his three servants received permits to sail for Spain, presumably with Carvajal. On 5 March 1504 he sold more gold in Spain for Columbus. The admiral, after he returned to Seville in November 1504, made a copy of Carvajal's account of the gold sales. That copy in Columbus's handwriting is the only surviving example of Carvajal's accounts (Berwick 1892: 21–22). On 6 November 1515 he testified in Madrid on behalf of Admiral Diego Colón. In that testimony he claimed he was 58 years old, that he had gone on the second voyage, and had been in Spain during Columbus's fourth voyage (*Pleitos* 3.43–44). He continued to manage his own affairs actively until early 1524, when he sold his seat on the city council of Baeza.

30. 61.18. GASPAR DE GRICIO   Gaspar de Gricio appears as royal secretary as early as March 1476. He left this post to become secretary to Prince Juan, then returned to the queen's staff after the prince's death in 1497. He was the presiding notary and secretary who recorded Isabel's last will and testament on 12 October 1504 and her codicil on 12 November 1504. After Isabel's death, he became secretary to Fernando during his regency, drafting and signing writs in the name of Queen Juana and sometimes in the name of both the queen and her father. During this time, he was responsible for all despatches concerning the Indies. It is assumed that Gricio died in 1506 or early 1507 (Escudero 1969: 1.21–22; Manzano 1988: 2.106).

31. 62.1. JIMENO DE BRIVIESCA   Jimeno de Briviesca (he also signed Berviesca), comptroller of the royal outfitter of fleets in Seville until 14 February 1503, when the monarchs appointed him clerk and comptroller of the House of Trade (Casa de Contratación) for the Indies. By early 1501, all fleet commanders had to present themselves before Briviesca and another royal official in Seville or Cádiz. Briviesca received his last salary payment (50,333 maravedís for the first eight months of 1506) on 31 August 1506 (Manzano 1988). Briviesca's account ledgers, Libro de Armadas, for 1494 survive and have recently been researched by Eugene Lyon (Lyon 1986) and, most extensively, by Juan Manzano (Manzano 1988).

32. 64.2. OUR SON   The king of Portugal by this time was the son-in-law of Fernando and Isabel.

33. 64.3. SIR FERNANDO   Fernando Colón, Columbus's illegitimate son, was about thirteen years old at this time.

34. 64.8. DOCTOR ANGULO   Doctor Martín Fernández de Angulo, canon of Seville Cathedral since 1495 and later archdeacon of Talavera, became a member of the

royal council in 1500. The monarchs often assigned him to ecclesiastical matters, such as negotiations with the papacy. Angulo was one of the six witnesses to Queen Isabel's will, drafted in Medina del Campo on 12 October 1504.

35. 64.8. LICENTIATE ZAPATA   Licentiate Luis de Zapata, of the king's chamber, advised Fernando on his will in the last days of his life (Bernáldez 1962: 678).

36. 64.9. YOUR SON   The admiral's legitimate son, Diego Colón, was about 22 years old at the time this letter was written.

37. 64.13. MIGUEL PÉREZ DE ALMAZÁN   Born in Calatayud and protegé of Juan de Coloma, Almazán entered the royal service in 1488 as clerk of "mandamiento" in the Aragonese chancery. He served as acting secretary during 1492 while Coloma was away, and received the same office in the Castilian chancery, although he was not officially appointed secretary of Castile with full salary until 31 May 1502. From that time on, he rose in the king's esteem until he became Fernando's preferred confidant and supervisor of the secretarial staff. He not only drafted the royal documents but also wrote letters over his own signature transmitting the king's orders. He received many favors from Fernando and Isabel: lord and baron of Maella, knight of Santiago, commander of Beas and Ricote, elector of Santiago, city councilman of Seville. The monarchs arranged Almazán's marriage to a niece of Isabel's lady in waiting. Almazán died in early 1514 (Rumeu de Armas 1985: 136–138).

38. 65.1. There followed documents 1–59 above.

39. 66. NICOLÒ ODERIGO   Oderigo was Genoese ambassador to the kingdoms of Castile and Aragón.

40. 66. SIR FRANCESCO DE RIVAROLI.   Francisco di Riberol, a Genoese business-man, resided in Seville for many years and carried on trade with the Canary Islands. He probably met Columbus in Granada in early 1492, when Riberol formed a partnership with the Florentine slaver and banker Juanoto Berardi. The partners agreed to finance the conquest of the island of La Palma (Canaries) that the Spaniard Alonso de Lugo had negotiated with Fernando and Isabel. Riberol remained Columbus's closest business associate throughout the admiral's life. He and three other Genoese in Seville—Francisco Doria, Francisco Catanio, and Gaspar de Spínola—formed a partnership with Columbus in 1500 for the purpose of supplying the merchandise that would be carried to Santo Domingo by the new governor Ovando. The Genoese businessmen gained a great potential advantage from the partnership, because it allowed them to participate in the Indies trade on which Columbus had a monopoly. In return for this opportunity, the partners advanced Columbus almost 200,000 maravedís for his expenses in Spain between 1498 and 1501. In 1501, although Riberol was fined for having sent two unauthorized merchant ships to the Indies, he continued to invest in Lugo's conquest of the Canary Islands, acquiring large parcels of land and sugar mills. He must have died before 25 August 1518, when his only child, Marixtina de Riberol, had inherited all his property in the Canaries (Rumeu de Armas 1954: 165–170; Columbus 1984: 309–310; Varela 1992: 136–137).

41. 66. NEW DOCUMENT   The new document was the letter (64) Queen Isabel

wrote in Valencia de La Torre promising Columbus reinstatement and giving him instructions for the fourth voyage.

42.   66. SIR JUAN LUIS   Possibly, this refers to Juan Luis de Mayo or Juan Luis Fiesco.

43.   66. .S. . . . FERENS   Columbus adopted this rubric officially, as he told his son Diego. "Christo ferens" signifies Christ bearer. The other letters in the rubric remain a mystery.

44.   67.1. There follow documents 61–64.

45.   68. REVENUE . . . RECEIVED   Columbus is investing money in shares of the Bank of Saint George. He offers one-tenth of its earnings as charity to reduce the official price of wheat in his native city of Genoa.

46.   71. The chancellor of the Bank of St. George, Antonio Gallo, wrote a letter to Columbus on 8 December 1502, acknowledging receipt of the codices and other documents. Because he knew that Columbus was in the Indies at the time, Gallo enclosed the letter with a letter to Diego. That may explain why Columbus did not find it, even though it was still in the family archive in the early sixteenth century.

47.   71. FRANCO CATANIO   Francisco Cataño, as he was called in Spain, was one of the four Genoese businessmen in Seville who invested in the Ovando fleet in partnership with Columbus.

48.   71. WROTE . . . VOYAGE   His report on the fourth voyage was written one month after he was shipwrecked on Jamaica. An Italian version of the report is known as the *Lettera Rarissima* (Varela 1984: 316).

49.   72. LORENZO ODERICO   Lorenzo was a descendant of Nicolò Oderigo. Both codices that Columbus sent to Genoa had remained in possession of the Oderico family for over a century. In 1670, Lorenzo donated both of the codices to the Genoese Republic, in exchange for a promise that he would receive preferment for government office.

PHILOLOGICAL COMMENTARY

Luciano Formisano

PHILOLOGICAL COMMENTARY

THE TWO REDACTIONS

The so-called *Book of Privileges* is transmitted in the following four codices, listed with their sigla:[1]

1)   *G:* Genoa codex

2)   *P:* Paris codex

3)   *V:* Veragua codex

4)   *W:* Washington codex.

In addition to these codices, which are more or less complete, there are two manuscripts that contain fragmentary extracts:

5)   *H:* Huntington Library codex

6)   *Pr:* Providence codex.

The four principal documents *GPVW* can in turn be separated into two distinct versions:

1) an older and shorter redaction, datable to 1498, today represented only in *V;*

2) a more recent redaction, which completes the first version with the addition of documents that were drawn up after its compilation in 1498. This second redaction was begun on 5 January 1502 and completed after 22 March of that year (cf. XXXVII.ii) and is found in codices *GPW,* particularly in the first two, which in

---

[1] See also Helen Nader's introduction.

completeness and internal arrangement represent the original order found in the newest version of the *Book of Privileges*.

Internal examination of *V* indicates that the earliest redaction was accomplished in two distinct phases:

1) The nucleus is formed of documents I–XXV, all drawn up prior to Columbus's departure on his third voyage (30 May 1498); a copy of this nuclear group of documents was notarized in Seville on 15 March 1498 by the public scribe Martín Rodríguez (cf. Additional Document 2.B.1, which is the formal conclusion of 2.A.2). There is evidence, however, of an internal separation into two sections: the first, consisting of document I, which in itself constitutes a relatively autonomous subsection containing a preliminary list of the privileges granted to the admiral of Castile; and the second, consisting of documents II–XXV, which constitute the Columbian section of this nucleus, that is to say, the *Book of Privileges,* properly speaking. Both sections have been notarized, on the same date and by the same notary,[2] at the end of document I and at the beginning of the following series of documents (cf. Additional Documents 2.A.1 and 2.A.2). Also document I bears the royal provision that instructs Francisco de Soria to direct in Seville a compilation of the privileges granted to Columbus (cf. I.i, dated in Burgos, 23 April 1497).

2) This nucleus was later enriched by the addition of documents XXVI–XXIX, relating to the privileges granted in 1493 and 1494, during Columbus's second voyage;[3] their transcription was authenticated by Diego de Alvarado, scribe and notary public in the city of Santo Domingo (La Española), on 4 December 1498 (cf. Additional Documents 2.B.2 and 2.C). However, taking into consideration the fact that a compilation of privileges is by its very nature a work in progress, the possibility cannot be excluded that other documents had been successively integrated onto the nine folios that originally followed Additional Document 2.C and were later removed. Francisco de Soria's note, now glued to one of the loose and unnumbered parchment sheets which end the codex, could support this hypothesis:[4]

The Capitulations between the Catholic Monarchs and Columbus granted in Burgos in 1497 are missing. Madrid, December, 826.-Soria.

In any case, it does not belong to the codex, properly speaking, the "royal license to establish a *mayorazgo,* granted to Christopher Columbus on 23 April 1497," and transcribed on these same folios.[5]

---

[2] Just as if documents I–XXV had been transcribed in a single day. We are, therefore, dealing with a fictitious date whose purpose is to testify to the authenticity of the entire text.

[3] The justification for these particular insertions has been given by Bustamante, LVIII–LIX.

[4] Cf. Bustamante, LXI.

[5] *Ibid.*

Thus, there are two stages written at two different times and places and supervised by two different notaries, an observation borne out by a precise comparison of the two hands appearing in the manuscript, the second of which is found in folios 34r–36v, where the series Additional Document 2.B.2, XXVI–XXIX begins.[6]

With respect to the first redaction *(V)*, the second *(GPW)* can be considered as a "new enlarged version."[7] In fact, the second version was accomplished in the simplest of ways through the addition of new documents and the elimination of others that were no longer compatible. This operation, again conducted under the supervision of Martín Rodríguez, the notary who in 1498 had been responsible for the Sevillian section of the *Book*,[8] can today be evaluated only by means of a direct comparison between *V* and *GP*, given the reduction accomplished in *W*. It can be summarized as follows:

1) The documents I–XXIX from *V*, which constitute the new nucleus, have been included, while all reference to the two stages of compilation and to the work of two different notaries has been removed (Additional Documents 2.A.2, B.1; 2.B.2, C). In particular, Additional Document 2.A.2 has been reformulated and transferred to the beginning of the codex as a declaration of the circumstances of the new version (cf. document 0). This has the effect of moving document I.i, so that, considering also the elimination of Additional Document 2.A.1, the autonomy of subsection I is greatly reduced.

2) A new nucleus is thus established, and a double series of documents added to it. The first, comprising numbers XXX–XXXV, is formally connected as well to the nucleus, which is referred to in clausula XXXVbis, the completion of the initial notarization (cf. 0). The second, now appearing in documents XXXVI–XL, is separated from the first by XXXVbis, so that it has the appearance of a relatively autonomous, although composite, section, as demonstrated by its further articulation in the following subsections, each of which begins on a new folio:

a) Document XXXVI: transcription of the second version of the bull *Inter coetera*, promulgated 4 May 1493 by Pope Alexander VI (XXXVI.ii.1.1), accompanied by the appropriate certification. The first (XXXVI.ii.2) is dated Barcelona, 19 July 1493; the second (XXXVI.i/iii), is authenticated by the apostolic notary Ruiz Montana and dated Seville, 30 December 1502, thus chronologically and formally distinct from the group of documents I–XXXV, which had been authenticated in the same city, but on 5 January of the same year and by the civil notary Martín Rodríguez. It should be mentioned in addition that in *GP* the Latin section of the document (XXXVI.ii) reveals not only a change of script,[9] but also of hand (cf. *infra*).

---

[6]Cf. Bustamante, LXIV.

[7]*Ibid.*, LIX.

[8]And who again was assisted by the scribe Juan Fernández, while the scribe Diego de la Bastida was replaced by Gómez Nieto.

[9]It is written, in fact, in the humanistic script of the chancellery, while the rest of the two codices is written in *letra cortesana*. (For a discussion of the latter, see Bustamante, p. LXII, where, however, the definition includes the script of *V*, which is less rounded and on the whole more regular and elegant then that of *GP*.) On the hand that transcribed no. XXXVI.ii, cf. note 28.

b) Document XXXVII: a compilation of four distinct documents, arranged roughly in chronological order and authenticated by Martín Rodríguez, as usual, on 22 March 1502 (cf. XXXVII.ii).[10] This is, therefore, a group anterior to XXXVI whose true significance is revealed by the interruption of the chronological order between XXXV and XXXVII.

c) Documents XXXVIII and XXXIX: the autonomy of this section is supported by the assumption of continuity between XXXVII and XXXVIII, which in *GP* were separated by a series of blank folios corresponding to the blank space in the table of contents of *G*.[11] It can be argued that these folios were "reserved for documents that had not at that time been written,"[12] among which were probably the second copy of the *Capitulación* (cf. Additional Document 3) which in *P* opens the series XXXVIII–XXXIX, to which it is also related by content.[13] Furthermore, it is noteworthy that in *G* the conclusion of XXXVII does not entirely fill folio 50v and that also XXXIX (folios [61r]–[65v]) does not immediately follow XXXVIII, which in the codex ends with the last line of folio [60r], while [60v] is left blank.

d) Document XL: letter to Doña Juana de la Torre, governess of the prince Don Juan, placed at the end of *GP*, but not immediately following XXXIX. The text is related only marginally, and negatively at that, to the purpose of the *Book*, giving free rein to the admiral's harsh and bitter outbursts in denouncing Francisco de Bobadilla's usurpation of his privileges.

As for the final statement, which is published as XLbis and is absent from the Paris codex, it is a type of colophon, referring globally to the contents of the Genoa codex.

It goes without saying that of this double series of documents, only the first (I–XXXV) belong to the *Book of Privileges*, properly speaking, as is demonstrated by the authentication supervised by Martín Rodríguez, which follows immediately (XXXVbis) and which completes the proemial statement (o). The second series (XXXVI–XL) can be explained by the necessity of preparing an updated collection that would better respond to the admiral's personal situation during the period immediately preceding his departure on the fourth voyage (9 May 1502).[14] This is an example of the need for completeness that can be observed as well among the previous owners of the individual codices. We have already discussed *V*, which played an im-

[10]But XXXVII.i.3, dated 27 September 1501, should have been placed before the series XXXVII.i.1 (27 September 1501)–XXXVII.i.2 (28 September 1501), immediately followed by XXXVII.i.4 (14 March 1502).

[11]Cf. Additional Document 1.C.

[12]*Raccolta*, XV, referring only to *G*, but applicable also to the related *P* (cf. the following note). That is, of the eight folios which have been left blank in *G*, numbers [53] through [55], all numbered originally, have been successively removed. The numeration today is legible only on folios 51 and 52, but traces of it can be distinguished on the others (56–58: cf. *ibid.*).

[13]In *P* the *Capitulación*, which in *GP* already appears as doc. II.ii, is transcribed on folio LXIII (= 64), at the end of the series of blank folios (LIIII–LXII in the old numeration, corresponding to folios 55–63 of the modern numeration).

[14]Cf. in this regard Bustamante, XLVII–L, and Nader's introduction.

portant role in the *Pleitos Colombinos*.[15] In *G*, in addition to later documents which are still included in the volume (cf. Additional Document 1.A, 1.B), two letters from Columbus to Nicolò Oderico were inserted, to which we will return shortly.[16] As for *W*, we see that the second version of the *Book of Privileges* opens with the bull *Inter coetera* (cf. XXXVI.ii.1.1) and that this is preceded in turn by (and completed by) the later bull *Dudum siquidem,* presented as a letter and added as such to the volume (cf. Additional Document 4); this letter, moreover, is transcribed by an Italian hand, leading to the supposition (which possibly goes too far) that it is "an unofficial transcript sent directly in 1493 from Rome to the Spanish king, either by his agent or by the Vatican authorities."[17]

STEMMA CODICUM

The legal and official character of the documents joined together in the *Book of Privileges* explains the substantial homogeneity of the four principal codices; this is a case in

[15]Cf. Nader's observations. Not the two copyists, but a sixteenth-century owner of *V*, the same person who wrote most of the marginal postils (cf. Bustamante, LXIV), is responsible for the introductory table of the codex, which I transcribe here in an interpretative edition (*ibid., 2*):

En este libro ay los prebilejios siguientes:

Sédula de lo Reyes Católicos don Fernando y doña Ysabel para que Francisco de Soria, teniente de‹› almirante de Castilla, dé un traslado sinado del prebilejio de‹› almirante de Castilla, para que el almirante de las Yndias don Christóval Colón gose todas las preminencias y derechos que el almirante de Castilla gosa; y luego prosigue el dicho prebilejio del almirante de Castilla, todo sinado y autorisado.

Luego se sigue que pide en Sevilla, sábado 15 del mes de março de 1498 años, el almirante don Christóval Colón, ante Martín [deleted word] Rodrigues, escribano público, le den autoriçado los traslados que ubiere menester de dos prebilejios que presenta de los señores Reyes Católicos; y assimesmo otras patentes y sédulas reales prosiguen luego.

Y enpiesa con las capitulasiones que a [*s.l.*] el dicho almirante don Christóval Colón [deleted word] consedieron los Reyes Católicos, siendo secretario Juan Coloma, su data en Santa Fe de la Bega de Granada a 17 de abril de 1492 años; y prosigue el dicho prebilejio confirmándolo en 23 de abril de 1497 años, en Burgos y secretario Fernal [*sic*] Álbares de Toledo.

[16]Cf. *Raccolta,* XV.

[17]Thus Seymour de Ricci in the *expertise* dated 18 February 1931 and today included in the codex, adding that the two folios which contain the letter "were already in the book ca. 1600 when the Spanish archivist wrote the title *Las Bullas*." (He writes later, "I fancy this is—if already written in 1493, as I believe it to have been—the earliest ms. extant record of the Discovery of America.") From the seventeenth-century note of ownership that follows the title ("Es de la cámara del Rey y de conocimiento de La Bribiesca") I do not believe that it is possible to conclude that "the Library of Congress copy is the one sent by Columbus to the Royal Court" (*ibid.*), even in the case that La Bribiesca was a functionary of the court. In fact, this copy, incomplete and without any sign of notarial authentication, does not seem to have been authorized by the admiral.

point in the history of the tradition of vernacular texts, in which the boundaries between transcription and reelaboration are often unstable, above all in the case of prose texts. In fact, fidelity to the first model is such that neither the examples of writing over erasures nor the interlinear additions, carefully listed on p. 258, 85 ff., are found in any of the four exemplars which have come down to us, thus demonstrating the existence of a codex that is now lost and that contained the first version from which certification had been taken.[18] Similarly, the indication "Vala ó dis 'que' escripto sobre raýdo en esta plana" (p. 356, 40–41) and its analogue on p. 358, 121–122 do not refer to any of the codices in question (in this particular case, only *GP*); they must therefore refer to a lost codex of the second redaction.

Even more exemplary is the fact that the homogeneity extends from text to form. The formal, or only graphic, variants are minimal and in every case respect the original linguistic patina, even in the case of a form which had already fallen into disuse such as—to give a morphological example—the analytic conditional *pechar me ýan* (p. 250, 120), which by the time of the document in which it appears (dated 1416) would have been regarded as an archaic usage (or, if one prefers, as a technical archaism of juridical language). This would be a banal observation if the discussion were limited to *GPV*, all of which are authenticated by the signature and by the seal of one scribe and notary public, or, even worse, simply to *GP,* codices which, as we will soon see, are clearly related in physical appearance. In fact, the observation is more significant for a codex like *W,* an incomplete fair copy, which lacks the seal of notarial authentication.[19]

However, in order to explain this phenomenon, I weigh the modes of composition and transmission of the *Book of Privileges* more than the nature of the documents. A series of significant errors common to *V,* on the one hand, and to *GPW,* on the other, shows that the second redaction has been made starting from an exemplar of the first, to be identified with *V* or with one of its relatives. These errors are seen in the following examples:

H (but not *Pr*): I.ii.1.1a', 40; III.ii.1, 92 and 94 (with *VW* which at l. 93 correct, independently, *parescades* to *parescan*); III.ii.2, 73.

Neither *H* nor *Pr:* I.ii.1.2, 24; II.i, 52;[20] V, 22; IX.i, 15; IX.ii, 61; IX.ii, 104; X, 12; XII, 38; XII, 57; XX, 6; XXII, 16; XXII, 53; XXIII, 65; XXIV, 3. But already significant in itself is the space which has been left blank in *GPVW* at VI, 134.

---

[18]And in which must figure the Juan Lopes cited on p. 258, 91, today absent from the *Book*. On the other hand, the examples of writing over erasures and between the lines indicated in Additional Documents 2.A.1 and B.1 have an exact counterpart in the codex, which in fact contains other examples.

[19]Cf. especially XXXVbis 61–68, where only *GP* contain autograph signatures with final notarizations. As for *V,* cf. also the signatures and the seal in Additional Documents 2.A.1 and B.1.

[20]Where the plural agrees with the preceding *reyes* (which explains in turn the erroneous *les* in *HW*,55). The *pertenesçe* of l. 50 does not admit the possibility that *al qual* (l. 49) is a reference to God (cf. also the parallel passage on p. 268, 49 ff.)

While *W* is missing because of a homoeoteleuton: III.ii.2, 79 (*H* = *GPV*).

Particularly interesting is the case of VIII, 19, a point which has eluded all previous editors, where the integration *e ‹diez› ortelanos* explains the 330 people indicated at l. 21, taking into consideration the parallel passage of XVIII, 7 (*çinqüenta labradores, diez ortelanos*).

In considering the question of internal agreement between codices of the second redaction, it is convenient to start with *GP,* that is, with the two exemplars of the *Book* that were sent by Columbus to Genoa to his friend Nicolò Oderigo by means of Francesco Rivarola and Francesco Cattaneo (or Cattani).[21] It is understood that both codices must have remained for a long time within the Spanish milieu—it will be recalled that Oderigo was the ambassador from Genoa to the Spanish Court—as is demonstrated by the late sixteenth-century marginal headings, which, sketched in red, are an integral part of the rich ornamentation that characterizes these two official copies.[22] In particular, as the final clause of *G* is expressly dated "este año de 1502,"[23] we can reject the hypothesis found in the *Raccolta* according to which this codex contains the exemplar sent in 1504,[24] which can, therefore, be identified with *P,* which does not contain the clause. From the textual point of view, the certification found on p. 346, 51–57 (omitted in *W*), argues for a derivation of *P* from *G,* in as much as two of the three rewritings over erasures indicated there and referred to in the same way by both the manuscripts are duplicated exactly in the Genoa codex.[25] The errors which are common to *GP* are found in the following places:[26]

VW: I.ii.1.1.A, 21 (*H* = *VW*); I.ii 1.1.B, 24 (*H* = *VW*); I.ii. 2, 11; III.ii.1, 75; V, 33; VIII, 12; XXVII, 14 (*V* = *W*).

---

[21]The relevant documentation is found in *Raccolta,* X ff.; and see also Additional Document 1.B. The two autograph letters that Columbus sent with the two codices to Oderigo have been republished in Varela-Gil, LXX (481) and LXXXVIII (520).

[22]I note, in any case, that some of these marginal headings are common to the two codices.

[23]Cf. XLbis, 8.

[24]Cf. *Raccolta,* XV, where the only proof offered is the correspondence between the exterior appearance of the codex and the description in the letter to Oderigo on 27 December 1504. This is an inconclusive line of reasoning, in as much as it can be imagined that, being the work of the same copyist, the two codices were originally similar with respect to the containers in which they were placed and the locks placed on their bindings.

[25]The first and the third (cf. folios 2r and 20v, respectively), but not the second, which will be related to the ascendancy of the manuscript, while there is no certification for the other erasures found only here.

[26]Specifying that the error found in *GP* in XL, 108, characterizing at least another version of the document, lies outside the archetype of the *Book:* cf. Varela-Gil, no. XLVIII, p. 432, where the copy of Bartolomé de Las Casas is published.

W but not *V*: XXX, 58; XXX, 106; XXXVI.ii.1.1, 124.

Not *W*: XXXVI.ii.2, 5–6; XXXVI.ii.2, 11; XXXVI.ii.2, 18; XXXVI.ii.2, 37; XXXVII.i.1, 13; XXXVII.i.1, 93; XXXVII.i.4, 52 (corrected by *HPr*); XXXVIII, 64 (*Pr* = *GP*); XL, 134; XL, 197; XL, 217.

On the other hand, G presents a certain number of errors and lacunae not shared by *P*, which is in turn linked to *W* by a series of errors and lacunae absent in *G(V)*:

V: (= G): I.ii.1.1.a', 59; I.ii.1.1.B, 93; I.ii.1.2, 89; II.i, 26 (*H* = *GV*); II.i, 72 (*H* = *GV*); III.i, 29; IX.ii, 114; IX. ii, 123; IX.iii, 17; XII, 23; XIII, 45; XXII, 52; XXVII, 49.

Not *V*: XXX, 110; XXX, 159 (*se cumplan*); XXXVbis, 5; XXXVI.ii.1.1, 48, 100, 113–114, 125, 128, 137.

This is sufficient to reject the hypothesis that *P* is a *descriptus* of *G*, but not that it is derived from an accurately revised copy, from which *W* would also be descended; that is, a copy carefully cleansed of the errors and lacunae belonging to *G*, but responsible for a new series of errors (conjunctive to *PW*), and from which the certification of the rewritings listed on p. 346, 51–57 would not have been eliminated, following phenomenology we have already encountered. Nor can we exclude the possibility that this copy can be identified with one of the exemplars of the *Book of Privileges* enumerated in doc. XLbis, from which, in any case, *W* can be eliminated.[27]

The chronological difference between the two codices is thus confirmed, even though they have in common the principal copyist and the hand which in both manuscripts has added document XXXVI.ii,[28] not to mention the more general affinities between the two codices in physical appearance and ornamentation. In this regard, the autograph letter dated 21 March 1502 from Columbus to Nicolò Oderigo is significant, for we learn from it that when one of the two exemplars was already in the hands

---

[27]That *W* cannot be identified with one of the codices mentioned in the final clausula of *G*, as the editors of the *Raccolta* had hypothesized, is demonstrated by the fact that it is an incomplete copy that bears no autograph notarial authentication. At the time of the publication of the *Raccolta* this was not known, as the manuscript only became available in 1901, at the time of its acquisition by the Library of Congress. As for the three codices recorded in the clausula, the hypothesis must be rejected that the antigraph of *P* is the exemplar of the *Book of Privileges* which in 1502 already was in the Indies (namely, in La Española) in the hands of Alonso Sánchez de Carvajal (cf. XLbis, 8–10).

[28]As was already recognized in the *Raccolta*, XVI–XVII, where the proposition was advanced that the copyist (G folios 43–46, P folios 44–47) was don Fernando.

of Francesco Rivarola, to be sent to Genoa to the very same Oderigo, the other must have still been in the process of transcription.[29]

The intervention of a reviser can be demonstrated by means of the Washington codex in the cases in which a correct reading of *W* opposes a significant error shared by *GPV*.[30] This occurs in the following places:

I.ii.1.1.a', 50–51 (*H = W*); I.ii.1.1.B, 114 (*H = W*); II.i, 18 (*H = GPV*); II.i, 46 (*H = GPV*); II.i, 62 (*H = GPV*); III.i, 18; III.ii.2, 48 (*H = GPV, Pr = W*); IV, 17 (*Pr = GPV*); VI, 8; VI, 23; VI, 62; VI, 63; VI, 89; VI, 126; VI, 129; VI, 130; VIII, 15; IX.i, 20; XIII, 51 and 52; XXII, 50.

If this is the general picture, we can easily explain:

(1) the errors which are found in the second redaction (*GPW*) but not in the first (naturally, where the latter occurs):

V, which gives the correct reading: cf. II.ii, 29 (*HPrP' = V*); III.ii.2, 76; III.iii, 39–40 (*H = V*); XI.ii, 27; XIII, 16; XVI, 4; XIX, 10; XXIII, 26–27 (if, as is likely at this point, the homoeoteleuton goes back to G).

Not *V*: cf. XXX, 77; XXX, 88; XXX, 110; XXXI, 7; perhaps also XXXV, 32. Adding the significant or formal errors of the Latin document XXXVI.ii.1.1: cf. lines 7, 12, 19, 21, 35, 38, 40, 45, 47, 51, 55, 58, 69, 74,[31] 75, 105, 109, 125, 142, 143; perhaps also XXXVI.ii.1.1, 13.

(2) the errors common to *GV*, but not found in *PW*:

[29]Cf. Varela-Gil, 481–482: "El libro de mis escrituras di a miçer Francisco de Ribarol, para que os lo enbíe . . . Otro tal se acabará y se os enbiará por la mesma guisa." But this is analogous to the conclusion that is drawn from the other letter, also autograph, to Oderigo, dated 27 December 1504, and entrusted by Columbus to Francesco Cattaneo, bearer of the second copy of the *Book of Privileges* to the Genoese friend in place of Rivarola (who, on the basis of the letter of 1502, was formerly considered to be a likely bearer of both the volumes). And cf. also the autograph letter to the Banco di San Giorgio of 2 April 1502, where just a single exemplar is mentioned: "Miçer Nicolò de Oderigo sabe de mis fechos más que yo proprio y a él he enbiado el treslado de mis privilegios y cartas, para que los ponga en buena guardia. Folgaría que los viésedes" (*ibid.*, 483).

[30]Therefore, Davenport's affirmation (765–766, referred to also by Bustamante, p. LV) that *W* is derived immediately from *P* which is derived from G is subsequently attenuated.

[31]Not only for *de terream*: given that *fidutiamque* for *fidutiaque* is common to the three codices, it can be imagined that *firmam* for *firma* was also in the antigraph of *W* and that *spem* for *spe* could have been corrected independently by G and by *W*.

I.ii.1.1.a', 18 (*H* = *PW*); II.i, 21 (*H* = *PW*); II.i, 62 (*H* = *GV*); II.ii, 65 (*HPz* = *GV*); II.iii,22 (*H* = *PW*); III.i, 80; III.ii.2, 3 (*H* = *GV*); III.ii. 2, 100 (*H* = *GV*); VI, 121; X, 26–27.

The convergence of *PW* in adiaphorous readings can be listed here:

I.ii.1.1.a, 8 and 19; I.ii.1.2, 84; III.i, 71; III.ii.2, 80; VI, 71; X, 33; XI.ii, 6; XVI, 14; XXI, 12; XXV, 11; XXXV, 41 and 45 (*G* vs. *PW*); XXXVbis, 49 (*G* vs. *PW*); and cf. especially the example of XXXVbis, 63 where the opposition between *Johan Fernandes* (*G*) and *Alfonso Lucas* (*PW*) could be of an editorial nature, a conclusion that has eluded previous scholars.

Naturally, individual corrections of errors common to the two redactions occur both in *P* and in *G;* as for *P* cf. III.i, 79 (an error in *GVW*); XXX, 111 and XXXVI.ii.1.1, 128 (an error in *GW*); as for *G,* cf. IX.iii, 19 (an error of *PVW*). In any case, all of these corrections could easily have been conjectured.

On the whole, reducing the number of *codices interpositi,* the relationships among the four codices can be schematized as follows:

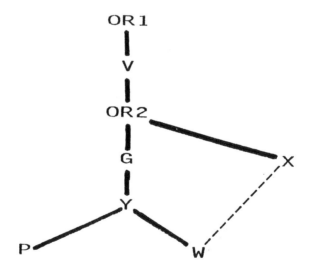

Here *x* represents the exemplar of the collation used by *W* to correct the errors in *G,* and therefore in *Y,* passing into *P,* and from which, perhaps, are derived the adiaphorous readings common to *HVW* (cf. I.ii.1.2, 82; VIII, 35; XI.ii, 2; XIII, 66; XIV, 30). As for the error in *VW* in II.i, 49 (a correct reading in *GHP*) it could be polygenetic or it could have been corrected independently by *G*(*H*) and by *P*.

The picture becomes more complex, however, when the two cases of double translation are taken into consideration (cf. II.ii with Additional Document 3, and I.i with XVII). With regard to these, we can deduce that certain documents must have also circulated autonomously, facilitating the independence of the individual revisers, with the consequent clouding of the overall relations that characterize the *Book of Privileges* in its entirety; this produces as well the uncertain stemmatic position of the fragmentary compilations. Thus *H* contains some errors common to *GPV* (cf. II.i, 18; II.i, 46; II.i, 62, *ellas* for *ella*; III.ii.2, 48), except that then the agreement is restricted just to *GV* at II.i, 62; III.ii.2, 3 and 100 (at II.ii, 65 *H* = *Pr* = *GV*), just to *V* at II.i, 24 and II.i, 52 (which however could have been corrected by *G*). The errors common to *HW* are probably polygenetic, however (cf. I.ii.1.1.a', 138; I.ii.1.1.a', 165–166, where a homoeoteleuton is present); while at I.ii.1.1.a', 115, the correction of *GPV* is somehow automatic.[32] The adiaphorous readings are, on the other hand, in agreement with *VW* (III.ii.1, 10–11 and 85), with *V* (I.ii.1.1.b, 22; III.ii.1, 53; III.ii.1, 60 and 71; III.ii.2, 100; III.ii.2, 114), and with *W* (I.ii.1.1.b, 29; III.ii.1, 35). This produces a certain affinity with *V* and *W,* which could confirm the closeness of the relationship just observed between the two codices.

As for *Pr,* leaving aside the convergence of errors with *HW,* it is sometimes associated with *GPV* (cf. IV, 17), sometimes only with *V* (cf. I.ii.1.1.a', 65; II.i, 48); while *V* is missing, it is linked to *GP* (cf. XXXVIII, 64), but above all it shows an affinity with *P* (cf. XXXVIII, 1, 2, 11, 18, 38, 94, 100; XXXIX, p. 370, 72), supposing that *P* had corrected in itself the error common to *Pr* and *G* noticeable in XXXIX, p. 375, 78. The codex could therefore be associated either with *V* or with *P;* that is, it is contaminated.

It is evident, in any case, that the second redaction originally was entrusted to a greater number of codices than have reached us. Its subsequent updating can probably be recognized in the Paris codex, the only one which repeats the *Capitulación* (cf. Additional Document 3). The physical as well as textual homogeneity of the individual copies is also apparent: the format, the internal articulation of the material in sections introduced by large capital letters, and certain beginnings of paragraphs or blank spaces in *GP* which are found in exactly the same way in *W.*

3. THE PRESENT EDITION

3.1 Establishment of the Text

The present edition proposes the second redaction of the *Book of Privileges,* which in every respect represents the ultimate wish of Columbus. The particular nature and the modes of transmission of the work seem, however, to exclude an edition of the Lachmannian type. There is no authenticated copy which could not have been thoroughly

---

[32]The errors common to *HG* also seem without significance: cf. I.ii.1.1.a', 16; III.ii.1, 29.

revised and which, when it was licensed, represented in every respect the definitive redaction. On the other hand, the existence of contamination does not ensure that the revision was entirely based on the original copies remaining in the admiral's possession. This is all the more true if one considers that some of the particularly interesting documents must have circulated in autonomous form. It is therefore necessary to choose a base text for correction and occasional integration with the help of the other tradition (*V* included), while taking into account the *usus scribendi* (that is, the comparisons within the work) and probabilistic considerations (as in the case of lacunae that are not immediately apparent, but constitute a *lectio singularis* and are therefore highly suspect). *W* is ruled out for the simple reason that it is an incomplete and unauthenticated copy, and the displacement within it of the bull *Inter coetera* indicates an attempt at internal reorganization of the material according to criteria which have nothing to do with the *Book of Privileges*. We may note in favor of text *P* that its second copy of the *Capitulación* could refer to a new redactional stage which we can place in 1504 when the codex was sent to Nicolò Oderigo; on the other hand, in terms of its readings, this codex is often inferior to *G,* which in addition cannot be suspected of contamination and which, thanks to the edition in the *Raccolta,* now forms a sort of *textus receptus,* an essential reference point for Columbian bibliography. I have therefore chosen the Genoa codex, without, however, feeling the need to respect all its *lectiones singulares* when these are obviously erroneous; I have dealt with them according to the criteria stated above.

The base text has been carefully checked against one of the two facsimile reproductions currently available.[33] This has allowed the verification of the diplomatic accuracy of the edition in the *Raccolta,* whose only objective limit was the tradition then known, which included only two complete manuscripts (*GP*) and the *excerpta* provided by *Pr.* The subsequent reappearance of *V* and *W* has permitted the correction of a series of lacunae and errors, which occurred between the first and the second redactions. So, for *PV* I have carried out a collation on the basis of the respective facsimile texts.[34] I have collated *HW,* codices not yet edited, with microfilms; while *Pr* has been directly taken from the diplomatic transcription in the *Raccolta.*[35] In this way the edition offers a text which, if not radically different in its readings from that established just a century ago by Staglieno and Belgrano, nonetheless contains some important new elements, verifiable point by point in the accompanying apparatus, which for the first time draws upon the entire manuscript tradition presently known.

[33]In the case in point, on the facsimile reproduction contained in the *Libro dei Privilegi di Cristoforo Colombo. Carte dei privilegi, cedole ed altre scritture di Don Cristobal Colon, Ammiraglio Maggiore del mare Oceano, Vicerè e Governatore delle Isole e Terraferma,* edited by the Regione Liguria in collaboration with the Comune di Genova, with the Patrocinio della Presidenza del Consiglio dei Ministri (Genova: Edizioni Analisi, 1987). The other reproduction: *Il Codice dei privilegi di Cristoforo Colombo, con tre lettere autografe del medesimo, di proprietà del Municipio di Genova, ed altri documenti riprodotti in fototipia* (Genova: Armanino, 1893).

[34]Cf. Stevens. For *V,* cf. the second volume of Bustamante.

[35]Cf. *Raccolta,* 105–114; facsimile and transcription also in Nader 1992.

The texts belonging to the first redaction but left out of the second or appearing on their own in *P* and *W* have been collected in an interpretative edition in the relevant Additional Documents, except for those texts which do not figure in the *Book of Privileges* proper. On the other hand, Additional Document I, referring particularly to *G,* registers all the texts that are physically present in the codex, even when they are extraneous to the compilation, including the table, which, although forming an integral part of the *Book,* would not have any significance in a critical edition. I have however reproduced alongside the text in an interpretative edition the marginal headings *(didascalyes)* from the base text which have already been reproduced in the *Raccolta,* if for no other reason than that they form part of the later history of the manuscript. Their placement in the margins reflects as closely as possible that of the codex itself, except that in the latter, the addition of these late sixteenth-century *didascalyes* (that is, all the headings except two, here italicized) is made immediately evident by the calligraphic flourishes, colored in red, which starting out from the headings run parallel to the margin in two directions. I have not registered the marginal notations (and any possible *maniculae*) in *HPVW* even when this notation is in a hand contemporary with the main text (as in the case of *H* and *W.*).[36]

To facilitate rechecking of the readings and to give an idea, even if only a rough one, of the physical aspect of the codex I have supplied folio numbers (transliterated into arabic numerals and placed between slashes), inserting in the numeration even the folios that today are missing. I have, however, refrained from reproducing or even noting the presence of crude crosses (mostly at the beginning of a folio) and any signs of a diplomatic or notarial character (whose purpose was to prevent additions at the base of the page) which are found both in the base codex and in the subsequent tradition.

3.2 Numeration of the Documents and Paragraphing

In *G,* as in the other codices, an initial summary articulation of the material is seen in a series of sections of varying length, the incipits of which are separated from the preceding text by a blank space which is further on marked out by the placement of large capital letters, extended over a variable number of lines, often also across more letters, except in the case of XL (which is introduced more modestly by an initial capital letter). In addition, in *GP* the initial capital letters are usually illuminated and decorated with arabesques, with the exception of the initial letters of documents XXXVIII–XXXIX, which conform also in physical appearance to the section of the *Book* transcribed after the group of blank folios (51–58), anticipating the even greater

---

[36]Of the marginal headings in *G,* only two (drawn in black ink) are in the hand of the copyist and therefore reflect the wish of the compiler (cf. in particular, p. 289, where the signature of Martín Rodríguez is autograph). This does not eliminate the possibility that an embryo of marginal notation, normal in works of this type, already had characterized the original.

lack of pretension of the document with which the *Book* is concluded. The following is a complete list of sections, each given with its initial folio number and the number of the corresponding document in our edition:

1r (0), 7v (II), 10r (III), 14v (IV), 15r (V), 15v (VI), 17v (VII), 18r (VIII), 19v (IX), 22r (X), 22v (XI), 24v (XII), 26r (XIII), 27r (XIV), 30r (XXII), 30v (XXIII), 32v (XXVI), 33r (XXVII), 34v (XXIX), 40v (XXXV), 43r (XXXVI, with further division into XXXVI.i, XXXVI.ii.1, XXXVI.ii.1.1, XXXVI.ii.2, all four having incipit with a large capital letter which is not illuminated, although in the first two cases the initial letter is made prominent through the use of yellow ink), 47r (XXXVII), [59r] (XXXVIII), [61r] (XXXIX), [66r] (XL).

There are twenty-five sections, which in turn correspond to one or more documents in our edition; document XXXVI includes a further division introduced by us. Within each section the documents are arranged without interruption, with the exception of the texts introduced by the heading *El Rey e la Reyna,* preceded and followed by a blank space and isolated at the center of the line.

The *Raccolta* edition corresponds to this arrangement of the material, which is followed by Bustamante in his edition of *V.* The present edition proposes a much finer articulation, which through the individuation and the numeration of texts takes into account the additional indications in the table of contents of *G,* where the following numbers are added (parentheses indicate numbers already indicated in the body of the codex):

(0), (II), (III), (IV), (V), (VI), (VII), (VIII), (IX), (X), (XI), (XII), (XIII), (XIV), XV, XVI, XVII, XVIII, XIX, XX, XXI, (XXII), (XXIII), XXIV, XXV, (XXVI), (XXVII), XXVIII, (XXIX), XXX, XXXI, XXXII, XXXIII, XXXIV, (XXXV), (XXXVI), (XXXVII), (XXXVIII), (XXXIX), (XL);

with the clarification that in the same table, document XXXVII is actually represented by the texts identified in our numbering as XXXVII.i.1, XXXVII.i.2, XXXVII.i.3, XXXVII.i.4.[37] On the basis of this further division of the material, I have proceeded to distinguish the documents transcribed (that is cited) in the *Book* from the three authentications of 1502, which constitute a "frame." For this reason I have introduced a document 0 (distinct from I) and a XXXVbis (first frame, corresponding to sections

---

[37]We note further that the numeration of the folios which form the individual sections indicated in the Table does not always correspond to that of the codex: cf. II (7v, not 8), IV (14v, not 15), VI (15v, not 16), VII (17v, not 18), etc. It can be concluded that the Table was based on a codex related, but not identical, to G.

I–XXXV) and have individuated the subsections XXXVI.i and XXXVI.iii (second frame, pertaining to XXXVI), XXXVII.i and XXXVII.ii (third frame, pertaining to XXXVII). For reasons of formal coherence I have identified with number XLbis the final clausula found only in *G*, but which I have separated from the rest of the *Book* by printing it in boldface. For the same reason the two parts of each "frame" are printed in boldface.

A further articulation was applied to the composite documents, which I have carefully divided into components which cannot always be easily numbered without destroying the unity of the whole, for example, document I, whose structure resembles that of a Chinese puzzle.

The individual texts (homogenous documents in their entirety or individual subsections) are in turn subdivided into paragraphs, each of which corresponds to a section of text contained between two periods, but the paragraphing of documents XXXIX and XL is given by the codex itself. Although the bureaucratic and cavilling juridical syntax of the *Book of Privileges* permits internal partitioning of a single paragraph, this system of paragraphs at the very least frees the text from the pagination of the edition. On the other hand, the numbering of lines answers the necessity of furnishing an immediate point of reference for the readings cited in the critical apparatus; therefore, it answers the needs of a restricted group of users, given the nature of the work.

3.3 Questions of Orthography

This edition conserves all the graphic peculiarities[38] of the base text, whose writing is generally clear; the distinction, however, between intervocalic *s* and *z* remains uncertain,[39] so much so that the proposed solutions can diverge substantially from those of the *Raccolta*. In particular, the character of the edition and the peculiarities of the language of the *Book of Privileges* invite the conservation without exception of the numerous graphic archaisms (accordingly, the alternation between *h*- and *f*- and the absence of initial *h*, as well) and the similarly numerous latinized or pseudo-latinized spellings (among which the improper addition of *h*- in *hera* for *era* and the use of *ti* for *ci* in *afetión* and in *peculio profetitio*, which is a true and proper calque of Latin). In addition, I have conserved:

1) the incongruous (and inconsistent) doublings, more or less etymological; traditional is in any case, the use of *-ss* and of *-ll* (for example, *doss* and *mill;* also at the end of a syllable: *húmillment*, where *-ll* is not etymological). I would like also to point out the following spellings: *datta* for *data*, *dottor* for *doctor*, *efetto* for *efe(c)to*, *ratta* for *rata*, *respetto* for *respecto*, *trattar* for *tractar*, which suggest the Italian assimilation of the latinizing nexus *ct* (under the hypothesis that the latinisms *data* and *rata*—in the expression

---

[38]And, of course, the phonetic ones: for example, the metatheses *renumeraçiones* for *remuneraçiones, perlados* for *prelados, presona* for *persona,* and *perrogativas* for *pre(r)rogativas* are phonetic in nature.

[39]Occasional uncertainties exist in distinguishing *c* from *t* and *i* from *e* (especially in superscription, e.g. in *esc(r)evir / esc(r)ivir*).

ratta parte, which is latinizing or Latin—has been incorrectly interpreted as *dacta* and *racta).*

2) the use of *(s)ç* for *c* preceding a palatal vowel, as well as the use of *zç* in *dézçima* (and cf. also *çç* in *Oçéano,* close to *Occéano).*

3) the use of *n* for *m* preceding *p* and *b,* except in places where the nasal is abbreviated, in which case I follow modern usage (but I retain *yten* for *ytem,* in observance of the *usus* of the codex; and *-m* for *-n* in *sandhi).* On the other hand:

1) I distinguish *u* from *v, i* from *j,* while conserving *y* in diphthongs and in contact with consonants, including *n, m,* and *v* (cf. *yndustria, Yndias, ynmunidades, nyn, my, Martýn, Sevylla,* next to *ysla, sygno, asý, sy* conjunction or pronoun, etc.).

2) I transcribe as *r* the *R* or the *rr* of the codex, whether at the beginning of a word or at the beginning of a syllable (for example, *honra, obreçión* and *subreçión, visrey),* with the exception of the cases in which the double *r* is part of Spanish graphic tradition (for example, *arrendar* and its derivations, *corroboraçión, perrogativas* or *pre(r)rogativas, visorrey).*

3) I divide words according to modern usage.

4) I introduce capital letters following modern usage, but I avoid their use to designate titles and offices, so as not to clutter the page. For this reason, I write *Rey* and *Reyna* only when the updating is obvious.

5) I introduce punctuation, trying to reproduce the flow of the phrase, which is particularly slow due to the frequent use of formulas and of interpolated clauses of a juridical nature.

6) I expand abbreviations according to current norms; I make note, however, of the following special cases:

a) I give the abbreviations *no(n)* and *ni(n)* as *non* and *nin;* they are transcribed in the *Raccolta* as *no* and *ni* (but contradictions or errors in reading are frequent), on the hypothesis that the abridgment of nasals had only ornamental, but not phonetic, value. This hypothesis is valid in principle (cf. the examples of *no* and *ni* without *titulus),* but is contradicted in fact in the cases in which *non* and *nin* are written out.

b) I transcribe as *ñ* the abbreviation *n(n),* corresponding to the etymological form, while observing that in a form such as *ynnotas* (written in full, for *ignotas) -nn-* stands for *-n-* (an archaic vulgar restitution of the Latin *-gn-:* cf. *ynorançia* for *ignorancia).*

c) I expand the abbreviation of *per* following current practice, even in the presence of the metathetical forms *presona* and *perrogativas,* which, moreover, alternate with *persona* and *pre(r)rogativas* written in full.

d) I write *Christo* and *Christóval,* even though I am convinced that in vulgar texts the abbreviation of *Chr-* corresponds to a borrowed parasitical feature of Latin writing. Analogously, I always write *sancto* (which alternates with *santo:* cf. p. 291, 102 and 103, where both versions are written out; and cf. also *Sanctiago,* also written out); and I resolve as *Jhesu* the abbreviation which in the Latin texts I render as *Ihesu.*

e) In abbreviated forms, I introduce *ç* even preceding a palatal vowel (for example, *Françisco, liçençia, merçed, serviçio),* following the *usus* of the codex.

f) I always write *previlegio/privilegio* (a form which appears in full eight times and in the title), even though the corresponding abbreviation could be expanded to *previl-*

legio/privillegio (a form that is documented seven times). As for the solution *previllejo/ privillejo* adopted by the *Raccolta,* I concede that this is a rendition which is a priori possible, but which is documented only once, in the *Tavola.*

g) I transcribe as *e* the graphic signs corresponding to the conjunction, which in the *Raccolta* edition are given as *&,* which is indeed consistently used in the Latin section of document XXXVI (where it has been resolved as *et*).

h) As for proper nouns, it is uncertain which is the correct solution: *Martins* or *Martínez (VW),* or *Martines (P).* I have chosen the first, previously adopted in the *Raccolta.* There is no doubt, however, about the form *Pero* (rather than *Pedro,* in the codex abbreviated as *'p(er)o*), which is completely written out and confirmed in *W,* apart from *Peres* (*p(er)es* in the codex).

i) I conserve the abbreviated forms of the honorifics *Rev.mo* and *Su/Sus A.* (next to *S.A.*); I render *eç.a* as *etç.*

3.3.1. *The Spelling of Latin Texts and Citations*

The Latin texts (XXXVI.ii and juridical formulas) deserve to be discussed separately. Given the nature of this type of text, I have introduced, as did the *Raccolta,* the distinction between *u* and *v.* I have conserved the *j* of *jure,* which corresponds to a traditional graphic usage, and the use of *ch* in *bachalaureus;* the *e caudata* has been rendered as *ae.* I have maintained *ti* for *ci* (and vice versa) before vowels, but I have corrected the numerous graphic aberrations, cases of vernacularism or uncertainty arising from ignorance of the language. The conservative attitude adopted in this respect by the *Raccolta* does not seem to me to be justified, because, the agreement in principle among *G, P,* and *W* notwithstanding, in some cases the same codices are self-contradictory in their opposition of correct to incorrect forms. Above all, it is reasonable to wonder if Columbus's legal advisers were really not capable of providing better texts, at least as far as the papal bull is concerned.

3.4 *Diacritical Signs*

The assimilation of *-s* in *sandhi* is indicated, according to the current practice in editing medieval texts by a raised period.

I follow modern usage in the introduction of accent markings, not placing an accent in paroxytonic words (proper nouns included) where *-z* is substituted for *-s.* I write, however, *canibales,* and not *caníbales,* the paroxytonic accent being easily demonstrable on the basis of coeval Italian forms.[40] Finally, I distinguish *ál* ("other") from *al,* tonic *nós/vós* from atonic *nos/vos,* *ó* (UBI) from *o* (AUT), whereas I always write *so* (SUBTUS), and *do* (DE UBI). In *âquellos* the circumflex indicates the crasis *a aquellos.*

[40]Cf. Gianfranco Folena, "Le prime immagini dell'America nel vocabolario italiano," in *Bollettino dell'Atlante Linguistico Mediterraneo,* 13–15: 1971–1973 (= *Studi offerti a Carlo Battisti e Gerhard Rohlfs*) (Firenze: Olschki, 1976): 673–692 (688–689).

3.5 Critical Apparatus

The critical apparatus of this edition is absolutely new. It is positive and aims to be complete, registering all the essential variants (including *lectiones singulares*), with some recognition, where appropriate, of readings which lie on the border between form and substance (as is the case of the graphic aberrations in the Latin texts).

For all documents and subsections, I have indicated the relevant codices. The readings I have accepted from a text are printed in boldface; when immediate identification is not possible, they are followed by the indication, between parentheses, of the reading which follows immediately (or, when it is more economical, which immediately precedes it). In cases in which a variant is common to two or more testimonies, the spelling of the codex that opens the series has been adopted, resolving without fail the abbreviations, unless there are elements which could clarify the etiology or the importance of the variant (for example, the indication of an abridgment of nasals in a finite verb form could display the passage from a plural third to a singular third, not to mention what has already been said about the possibility of a purely "ornamental" or parasitic usage of the *titulus*). I have not registered the rewritings over erasures which are not clearly legible in the microfilm and in the fascimile, but I note *supra lineam* additions.

When the variant refers to an immediately identifiable lemma (as in the majority of cases), *u* is distinguished from *v,* but neither capital letters (when absent in the codex or in the codices of reference) nor accents are introduced. In the apparatus, capital letters, accents, and punctuation are introduced only in the recording of rubrics, that is, in texts of a certain length.

In any case, the apparatus furnishes indications, generally in the form of internal references, which are useful for the evaluation of the adopted or of the rejected readings. Usually it avoids references to the choices, the interpretations, or the misreadings of previous editors.

3.6 Conventional Markings

[ ] in the apparatus indicates one or more deleted letters or words and not numbered folios; a slash / not preceded by a blank indicates the end of a line; a double slash // indicates the end of a page.

‹ › indicates an editor's conjectural addition to the text.

‹***› indicates a conjectural lacuna.

*** indicates a blank space (or a series of blank folios) in the codex or codices of reference.

† indicates a corrupt text.

corr. = an adopted correction.

l.m. = left margin.

r.m. = right margin.

s.l. = *supra lineam.*

CRITICAL EDITION OF THE TEXTS

Luciano Formisano

CARTAS, PREVILEGIOS, ÇÉDULAS, Y OTRAS ESCRITURAS DE DON CHRISTÓVAL COLÓN, ALMIRANTE MAYOR DEL MAR OÇÉANO, VISORREY Y GOVERNADOR DE LAS YSLAS Y TIERRA FIRME

0 (65)

/ 1 recto/

[1] **En la muy noble e muy leal çibdad de Sevilla, miércoles çinco días del mes de enero, año del nasçimiento
de nuestro salvador Jhesu Christo de mill e quinientos e
dos años, en este dicho día a ora de bísperas dichas, poco
más o menos, estando en la posada del señor almirante** 5
**de las Yndias, que es en esta dicha çibdad en la collaçión
de Santa María, ante Estevan de la Roca e Pero Ruys
Montero, alcaldes ordinarios en esta dicha çibdad de
Sevilla por el Rey e la Reyna nuestros señores, e en**

P: Cartas Previlegios / Çédulas y / otras Escrituras / de Don Christóval Colón / Almirante Mayor / del Mar Oçéano Vi-/ sorey y Governador de / las Jslas y Tierra Firme. *W* [*on the parchment cover, written in a seventeenth-century hand*]: Treslado de / Las Bullas del Papa Alexandre 6° de la concessión de / las Indias y los títulos, Privilegios y cédulas Reales que se dieron / a Christóval Colón [*in the same hand follows:* Es de la cámara del Rey y de cono-/cimiento de la bribiesca]. Sources: *GPW. For V cf. the introductory note for I.i. In W it follows document XXXVI.ii.1.1 and is preceded by the marginal heading:* Este es traslado de dos escripturas escriptas en pargamino de cuero, la una abtorizada de çiertas çédulas e cartas e títulos del almirante de las Yndias ante çiertos alcaldes e firmadas e sygnadas de Martín Rodríguez, escrivano público de Sevilla; su thenor de las quales, una en pos de otra, es este que se sygue: 1. **muy noble e** *GP*] *om. W.* 1-2. **miércoles** *GP*] martes *W.* 4-5. **dichas . . . menos** *GP*] *om. W.* 6. **de las Yndias** *GP*] *om. W.* 9. **la** *GP*] por la *W.*

presençia de mí Martín Rodrígues, escrivano público 10
d'esta dicha çibdad de Sevilla, e de los testigos yuso
escriptos, que a ello fueron presentes, pareçió ende presente el muy magnífico señor don Christóval Colón,
almirante mayor del mar Oçéano, visorrey e governador
de las yslas e tierra firme, e presentó ante los dichos 15
alcaldes çiertas cartas e previlegios e çédulas de los dichos Rey e Reyna nuestros señores, escriptas en papel e
pargamino, e firmadas de sus reales nonbres, e selladas
con sus sellos de plomo pendientes en filos de seda a
colores, e de çera colorada en las espaldas, e refrendadas 20
de çiertos ofiçiales de su real casa, segund por ellas e por
cada una d'ellas paresçía; el thenor de las quales, una en
pos de otra, es este que se sigue:

I.i (40)

El Rey e la Reyna

[1] Françisco de Soria, lugarteniente de nuestro almirante
mayor de Castilla: nos vos mandamos que dedes e fagades dar a
don Christóval Colón, nuestro almirante de la mar Oçéano, un
traslado abtorizado en manera que faga fee de qualesquier cartas
de merçed e previlegio e confirmaçiones qu'el dicho almirante 5
mayor de Castilla tiene del dicho cargo e ofiçio de almirante,
por donde él, y otros por él, lieven e cojan los derechos e otras
cosas a ello pertenesçientes con el dicho cargo; porque avemos
fecho merçed al dicho don Christóval Colón que aya e goze de

11. **d'esta** *GP*] de la *W*. **yuso** *GP*] de y. *W*. 12. **que . . . presentes** *GW*] *om. P*. 20. **refrendadas** *GP*]
referendadas *W*. 22. **el** *GP*] su *W*.   Sources: *GHPVW*, *Pr* 1-17 *(complir)*. *Cf. also* n° XVII, *whose variants*
(G'P'V'W') are reported here. This is the first document in V, where it is introduced by the rubric: Este es traslado de
una çédula del Rey e de la Reyna nuestros señores, escripta en papel e firmada de sus reales nonbres, e
ansimesmo de una escriptura escripta en papel e firmada e signada de escrivano e notario público, segund que
por ella paresçía; su thenor de lo qual, uno en pos de otro, es este que se sigue. 3. **de la** *GPPrV*] del *HW*,
G'P'V'W'. 5. **de merçed** *GHPPrV, G'P'V'W'*] e merçedes *W*. **previlegio** *GHPPrV, G'P'V'W'*] previllejos *W*. 6. **mayor** *GHPVW, G'P'V'W'*] *om. Pr*. 7. **cojan** *GHPPrVW*] se c. *G'P'V'W'*. **otras**
GHPPrVW, G'P'V'] *om. W*. 8. **ello** *GHPVW*] ellos *Pr*, el *G'P'V'W'*.

las merçedes e honras e prerrogativas e libertades e derechos e 10
salarios en el almirantadgo de las Yndias, que ha e tiene e goza
el dicho nuestro almirante mayor en el almirantadgo de Castilla. [2] Lo qual fazed e complid luego como fuerdes requerido
con esta nuestra carta, syn que en ello pongáys escusa nin dilaçión alguna; e sy ansí non lo fizierdes e cumplierdes, mandamos 15
al nuestro asistente e otras justiçias de la çibdad de Sevilla que
vos compelan e apremien a lo asý fazer e complir; e non fagades
nin fagan ende ál.
[3] Fecha en la çibdad de Burgos a veynte e tres días del mes de
abril de noventa e siete años. 20

Yo el Rey

Yo la Reyna

[4] Por mandado /1 verso/ del Rey e de la Reyna. Fernand
Álvares.

I.ii.1 (41)

[1] Éste es treslado de una escriptura escripta en papel e sygnada
e firmada de escrivano e notario público, segund por ella paresçía; su thenor de la qual dize en esta guisa:

I.ii.1.1 (42)

[1] En la villa de Valladolid, estando aý la corte e chançillería del
Rey nuestro señor, martes, çinco días del mes de jullio, año del
nasçimiento de nuestro señor Jhesu Christo de mill e quatroçientos e treynta e çinco años: ante los señores oydores del
dicho señor Rey, estando faziendo relaçiones en los palaçios e 5
casas del señor don Gutierre de Toledo, obispo de Palençia,

---

12. **mayor** *GHPVW, G'P'V'W*] *om. Pr.* 15. **e** (sy) *GHPVW, G'P'V'W*] *om. Pr.* **e** *GHPVW, G'P'V'W*]
nin *Pr.* 16. **e** *GHPPrVW, V*] e a *G'P'W'*. 24. **Álvares** *GHPVW*] A. Acordada *G'P'V'W'*.   Sources:
GPVW.   Sources: *GPVW.* 3. **señor** *GPV*] salvador *W.*

oydor de la dicha abdiençia, en el palaçio e logar acostunbrado
adó continuamente se suelen fazer e fasen abdiençia pública e
relaçión, los dichos señores oydores, en presençia de nós Juan
Martíns de León e Pero Garçía de Madrigal, escrivanos del   10
dicho señor Rey e de la su abdiençia e sus notarios públicos en
la su corte e en todos los sus reynos e señoríos, e de los testigos
yuso escriptos, paresçió Gonçalo Fernandes de Medina,
procurador aquí en la corte del dicho señor Rey, en nonbre e
en boz del señor almirante don Fadrique, cuyo procurador se   15
dixo e presentó ante los dichos señores oydores, que fizo leer
por nós e ante nós los dichos escrivanos una carta de previlegio
del dicho señor Rey, rodado, escripto en pergamino de cuero,
e firmado de su nonbre, e sellado con su sello de plomo pendiente en filos de seda; el thenor del qual es este que se sygue: 20

I.ii.1.1.A (43)

[1] Don Juan, por la graçia de Dios rey de Castilla, de León, de
Toledo, de Galizia, de Sevilla, de Córdova, de Murçia, de
Jahén, del Algarbe, de Algesira, e señor de Viscaya e de Molina
a todos los perlados, maestres de las órdenes, duques, condes,
ricos omes, e a los del mi consejo e oydores de la mi abdiençia,   5
e alcaldes, e notarios, e justiçias, e otros ofiçiales de la mi corte
e chançillería e de la mi casa e rastro, e adelantados, e merinos
mayores, cavalleros, escuderos, e a todos los conçejos, regidores, e alcaldes, e alguaziles, merinos, e prestameros, prebostes, e otras justiçias, e ofiçiales qualesquier de la muy noble 10
çibdad de Sevilla e de todas las otras çibdades e villas e logares de
los mis reynos e señoríos, e a los capitanes de la mar, e al mi
armador de la flota, e patrones, e cómitres de las mis galeas, e a
los maestres e marineros e mareantes e otras personas qualesquier que navegaren por la mar e río, e todas las otras e quales-   15
quier personas de qualquier estado e condiçión, preheminençia
o dinidad que sean, a quien atañe o atañer puede lo yuso es-

8. **adó** GPV] adonde W. 13. **yuso** GPV] de y. W.   Sources: GHPVW. 4. **maestres** GPVW] e m. H.
5. **e** (oydores) GHVW] om. P. 11. **e** (villas) GHPV] om. W. 14. **marineros** GHPW] marinos V.   **e mareantes** GPVW] om. H. 15. **e** (qualesquier) GHPV] om. W. 17. **o** (atañer) GHPV] e W. **yuso** GHPV]
ayuso W.

cripto, o a quien esta mi carta de previlegio fuere mostrada, o el
traslado d'ella abtorizado e sygnado de escrivano público, e a
cada uno de vós, salud e graçia. [2] Sepades que vide una carta   20
de previllegio rodada e sellada con mi sello de plomo pendiente, que por mi mandado fue dado a don Alfonso Enriques,
mi tío, mi almirante mayor de la mar, escripta en pargamino de
cuero; su thenor del qual es este que se sygue:

I.ii.1.1.a (44)

[1] En el nombre de Dios, Padre e Fijo e Spíritu Sancto, que
son tres personas e un solo Dios verdadero, que reyna por siempre jamás, e de la bienaventurada Virgen /2 recto/ gloriosa
santa María, Su madre, a quien yo tengo por señora e por
abogada en todos mis fechos, e a honra e serviçio del bienaven-   5
turado apóstol Sanctiago, luz e espejo de todas las Españas e
patrón e guiador de los Reyes de Castilla mis anteçesores e mío,
e de todos los Santos e Santas de toda la Corte Çelestial: e
porqu'es natural cosa todos los que bien sirven a los reyes con
limpia voluntad, en lo qual han grand trabajo y afán, que reçi-   10
ban porende grand galardón d'ello, porque sea grand refrigerio
e consolaçión de sus afanes; e otrosý, porque está bien a los
reyes de dar galardón a los que bien les sirven, lo uno por fazer
lo que deven, lo otro porque sea en enxemplo a·los que lo
supieren e oyeren, porque de mejor miente le·sirvan; el rey que   15
lo faze ha de catar en ello tres cosas: la primera, qué merçed es
aquella que haze; la segunda, quién es aquél a quien la haze e
cómo se la meresçe; e la terçera, qu'es el pro o el daño que le
puede venir, sy la fiziere; e porende, yo, acatando e considerando todo esto, e otrosý los muchos e buenos serviçios que   20
vos don Alfonso Enriques, mi tío e mi adelantado mayor de la
mar, fezistes al Rey don Juan de esclaresçida memoria, my
abuelo, que Dios dé santo Paraýso, e al Rey don Enrique, mi

18. **o** GHPV] *om.* W. **fuere mostrada**] *after* público (19) W. 21. **rodada e sellada** (GP)HVW] e s. e r. W.
rodada HVW] rodado GP (*cf.* p. 254, 94).   Sources: GHPVW. 1. **e** (Fijo) GHPV] *om.* W. **e** (Spíritu)
GHPV] *om.* W. 6. **e** (patrón) GPV] *om.* HW. 8. **toda** GHV] *om.* PW. 13. **les** G] le HPV (le·sirven; *cf.* 15),
om. W. 15. **le** (= les) GHPV] lo W. **el** GHPV] e el W. 19. **e** (porende) GHV] *om.* PW. 21-22. **de la mar**]
s.l. H.

padre e señor, que Dios perdone, e avedes fecho e fazedes a mí
de cada día, e el linaje donde vos venides, e el debdo que con- 25
vusco he e quien vos soys, e por vos dar galardón d'ellos, quiero
que sepan por este mi previlegio todos los omes que agora son,
o serán de aquí adelante, cómo yo don Juan, por la graçia de
Dios rey de Castilla, de León, de Toledo, de Galizia, de Sevilla,
de Córdova, de Murçia, de Jahén, del Algarbe, de Algezira, e 30
señor de Viscaya e de Molina, vi una carta del dicho señor Rey
don Enrique mi padre e mi señor, que Dios perdone, escripta
en papel, e firmada de su nombre, e sellada con su sello en las
espaldas, fecha en esta guisa:

I.ii.1.1.b (45)

[1] Don Enrique, por la graçia de Dios rey de Castilla, de León,
de Toledo, de Galizia, de Sevilla, de Córdova, de Murçia, de
Jahén, del Algarbe, de Algezira, e señor de Viscaya e de Molina,
por fazer bien e merçed a vós don Alfonso Enriques, mi tío, por
los muchos e leales e señalados serviçios que fezistes al Rey don 5
Juan mi padre e mi señor, que Dios perdone, e avedes fecho e
fazedes a mí de cada día, e por vos dar galardón d'ellos, fágovos
mi almirante mayor de la mar, e quiero e es mi merçed que
seades de aquí adelante mi almirante mayor de la mar, segund
que lo solía ser el almirante don Diego Hurtado de Mendoça, 10
qu'es finado; e que ayades el dicho almirantadgo con todas las
rentas e derechos e juridiçiones que le perteneçen e perteneçer
deven en qualquier manera, segund mejor e más complidamente los avía el dicho don Diego Furtado e los otros almirantes que fasta aquí han seýdo. [2] E por esta mi carta mando 15
a todos los perlados e maestres, condes, ricos omes, cavalleros e
escuderos, e a todos los conçejos, e alcaldes, e alguaziles, e
merinos, e prestameros, e prebostes, e otras justiçias qualesquier
de la muy noble çibdad de Sevilla, e de todas las otras çibdades
e villas e logares de los mis reynos e señoríos, e a los capitanes de 20

25. **donde** GHVW] de d. P. **venides** GPVW] venistes H. 28. **o** GHPV] e W.   Sources: GHPVW. 5.
muchos GHPV] m. et buenos W. 11. **almirantadgo** GHPV] mi adelantado W. 12. **e derechos** GPVW]
om. H. 16. **maestres** GHPV] maestre es W.

la mar, /2 verso/ e al mi armador de la flota, e patrones e
cómitres de las mis galeas, e a los maestres e marineros e mareantes e otras personas qualesquier que anduvieren e navegaren por la mar, e a qualquier e qualesquier d'ellos, que vos
ayan e obedezcan a vós el dicho don Alfonso Enriques por mi   25
almirante mayor de la mar en todas las cosas, e cada una d'ellas,
que al dicho ofiçio de almirantadgo pertenesçen, e que vos
recudan e fagan recudir con todas las rentas e derechos que por
razón del dicho ofiçio pertenesçen e pertenesçer vos deven,
bien e complidamente, en guisa que vos non mengue ende cosa   30
alguna, segund que mejor e más complidamente avían e obede-
çían e recudían al dicho almirante don Diego Furtado e a los
otros almirantes que fasta aquí han seýdo. [3] E por esta mi carta
vos dó todo mi poder complidamente para que podades usar e
usedes de la juredição çevil e creminal que al dicho ofiçio de   35
almirantadgo perteneçen e pertenesçer deven en qualquier
manera en todos los derechos de la mar, así para dar cartas de
represarias e judgar todos los pleitos que en ella acaesçieren,
como en los puertos e en los logares d'ellos fasta do entra el agua
salada e navegan los navíos; e que vos el dicho almirante ayades   40
poder de poner e pongades vuestros alcaldes e alguaziles e escrivanos e ofiçiales en todas las villas e logares de los mis reynos
que son puertos de mar, e para que conozcan e libren todos los
pleitos criminales e çeviles que acaesçieren en la mar e en el río
donde llegaren las creçientes e menguare, segund e en la ma-   45
nera que mejor e más complidamente los otros mis almirantes
pasados lo pusieron e pusierdes en la dicha çibdad de Sevilla. [4]
E por esta mi carta mando a los del mi consejo e a los oydores de
la mi abdiençia, e alcaldes de la mi corte, e a todas las otras
justiçias de las dichas villas e logares de los puertos de la mar e de 50
los mis reynos, que se non entremetan de conoçer nin librar los
dichos pleytos, ni perturbar a vós nin a los dichos vuestros ofiçiales de la dicha vuestra juridisçión que pusierdes por vós para
conozçer de los dichos pleitos, en la manera que dicha es. [5] E
sobre esto mando al mi chançiller mayor e notarios e escrivanos   55
e otros ofiçiales qualesquier que están en la tabla de los mis

22. **e** (marineros) *GHPV*] *om. W*. **marineros** *GPW*] marinos *HV* 24. **e** (qualesquier) *GHVW*] o *P*. 29.
pertenesçen *GPV*] vos p. *HW*. 36. **deven** *GHVW*] deve *P*. 37. **de la mar** *GPVW*] *om. H*. 38. **acaesçieren** *GHPV*] conteçieren *W*. 42. **reynos** *GPVW*] r. e señoríos *H*. 45. **menguare** *GHV*] menguaren *P*,
menguantes *W* (*but cf.* p. 249, 101) 51. **nin** *GHVW*] e *P*. 56. **en** *GPVW*] a *H*.

sellos, que vos den e libren e sellen mis cartas de previlegios las
más fuertes e firmes e bastantes e con mayores firmezas que
fueren menester, e segund fueron dadas a los otros almirantes
vuestros anteçesores, o a qualquier d'ellos, que más con-   60
plidamente lo ovieron; e los unos ni los otros non fagades ende
ál por alguna manera, so pena de la mi merçed. [6] E d'esto
mandé dar esta mi carta firmada de mi nombre e sellada con mi
sello de la /3 recto/ poridad.

[7] Dada en la çibdad de Toro, a quatro días del mes de abril,   65
año del nasçimiento de nuestro señor Jhesu Christo de mill e
quatroçientos e çinco años.

[8] Yo Johan Martíns, chançiller del Rey, la fis escrevir por su
mandado.

Yo el Rey   70

[9] Registrada.

I.ii.1.1.a' (46)

[1] E agora el dicho don Alfonso Enriques, mi tío e mi almirante mayor de la mar, pidióme por merçed que le confirmase la dicha carta del dicho Rey mi padre e mi señor, que
Dios perdone, e las merçedes en ella contenidas, e gelas mandase guardar e complir en todo e por todo, segund que en la   5
dicha carta se contiene, mandándole dar mi carta de previlegio
escripta en pargamino de cuero e sellada con mi sello de plomo
pendiente, para que mejor e más complidamente él pudiese
gozar e gozase del dicho ofiçio de almirantadgo e de las dichas
merçedes en la dicha carta del dicho señor Rey mi padre con-   10
tenidas; e otrosý para que le recudiesen con todas las rentas e
derechos e le fuesen guardadas, e oviese todas las juridiçiones e
franquezas e previlegios e libertades que le pertenesçen e perteneçer deven en qualquier manera por razón del dicho almirantadgo, segund que mejor e más conplidamente lo ovieron los   15
otros mis almirantes sus anteçesores, o qualquier d'ellos, ‹e› en

Sources: *GHPVW*, *Pr* 64 (*tengo*) - 87 (*señoríos*), 112 (*e*) - 134 (*es*). *In Pr it is preceded by the rubric:* Traslado
de unos capítulos del previllegio del señor almirante de Castilla e del señor almirante de las Yndias. 3. **mi
. . . señor** *GHPV*] mi s. e mi p. *W*. 4. **e** (gelas) *GHPV*] que *W*. 16. ‹e› *PVW*] *om. GH*.

la dicha carta del dicho señor Rey mi padre e mi señor, que
Dios perdone, se contiene. [2] E yo el sobredicho Rey don
Juan, por fazer bien e merçed al dicho don Alfonso Enriques,
mi tío e mi almirante mayor de la mar, tóvelo por bien e confir- 20
mole la dicha carta del dicho Rey mi padre e las merçedes en
ella contenidas, e mando que valan e que sean guardadas en
todo e por todo, bien e complidamente, segund que en la dicha
carta se contiene. [3] E por este mi previllegio e por el traslado
d'él, sygnado de escrivano público, sacado con abtoridad de 25
jues o de alcalde, mando a todos los perlados, maestres, priores
de las órdenes, e condes, e ricos omes, e comendadores e subcomendadores, cavalleros, escuderos, e a los del mi consejo, e a
los oydores de la mi abdiençia, e alcaldes e alguasyles de la mi
corte, e a todos los conçejos e alcaldes e alguasyles, e merinos e 30
prestameros e prebostes, alcaydes de los castillos e casas fuertes e
llanas, e otras justiçias e ofiçiales e aportellados qualesquier de la
muy noble çibdad de Sevilla e de todas las otras çibdades e villas
e logares de los nuestros reynos e señoríos, e a los capitanes de la
mar e patrones e cómitres e navicheles e maestres de las naos e 35
galeas, e al mi armador de la flota, e a los marineros e mareantes,
e a todos los onbres de la mar e río, e a los pescadores e bar-
queros que navegaren por la mar e río, e a todos los otros que
andan en la mi flota e fuera d'ella en qualquier manera o en
qual‹es›quier navíos que andovieren de aquí adelante, de qual- 40
quier estado e condiçión que sean, que ayades e ayan e reçi-
bades e /3 verso/ reçiban al dicho Alfonso Enriques, mi tío, por
mi almirante mayor de la mar en todas las partes de los dichos
mis reynos e señoríos, e que usedes con él en el dicho ofiçio del
dicho almirantadgo e juridiçión çevil e criminal, e vengáys a sus 45
llamamientos o enplazamientos, o de los qu'él por sí pusiere,
segund que mejor e más complidamente usaron e usastes con
los dichos almirantes que fueron en tiempo de los Reyes donde
yo vengo, o con qualquier d'ellos, e otrosí en la dicha carta del
dicho Rey mi padre e mi señor, que Dios perdone, ‹se con- 50
tiene›; e que recudades e fagades recudir con todas las rentas e

18. **contiene** *HPW*] contiene(n) *GV*. 22. **que** (sean) *GHPV*] *om. W*. 24. **e** *GHVW*] o *P*. 26. **de** (alcalde)
GHPV] *om. W*. 26. **maestres** *GHVW*] e m. *P*. 28. **a los** *GHPV*] *om. W*. 30. **e** (prestameros) *GPVW*] *om.*
H. 35. **e** (maestres) *GHVW* (e [de] *H*)] *om. P*. 37-38. **la mar . . . por la** *GHPV*] *om. W* (*homoeoteleuton*).
40. **qual‹es›quier**] qualquier *GHPVW*. 44. **en el** *GPVW*] *om. H*. 44–45. **del dicho** *GHPV*] de *W*. 46.
o (enplazamientos) *GH*] e *PVW*. **por sí** *GHPV*] *om. W*. 48. **dichos** *GHPW*] otros *V*. 50. **Rey** *GPVW*]
señor e r. *H* 50–51. **‹se contiene›** *HW*] *om. GPV*. 51. **rentas** *GHPV*] dichas r. *W*.

derechos que al dicho ofiçio de almirantadgo pertenesçen e
pertenesçer deven en qualquier manera o por qualquier razón
que sea; e otrosý que lo obedezcades e fagades su mandado así
como de mi almirante mayor de la mar, e como faríades por mi 55
cuerpo mesmo e por mi persona real. [4] E otrosý tengo por
bien e mando que sy alguno o algunos de la mar o de los dichos
ríos fizieren en la mar o en el río o fuera por que menester sea
fazer derecho d'él o justiçia en él o en ellos, o sý les fueren
desobidientes al dicho don Alfonso Enriques, mi tío, o a sus 60
ofiçiales qu'él por sý pusiere en la mar o en el río o en tierra,
qu'el dicho almirante pueda fazer, o mandar fazer, e faga la
justiçia en él o en ellos, e de les dar, o mandar dar, aý la pena o

Nota: por virtud
d'esto perteneçe al
Almirante de las
Indias el terçio d'ellas
y de lo que en ellas se
halla, por ser por él
ganadas como
almirante con la
armada de S. A.
[r. m.]

penas que de derecho meresçieren aver. [5] E tengo por bien
que todas las ganançias qu'el dicho mi almirante mayor oviere o 65
fisiere en la mi flota o por la mar, que aya yo las dos partes e el
dicho almirante la terçia parte, e yendo él por su cuerpo mesmo
en la dicha flota, aunque la dicha flota o parte d'ella se aparte
por su mando o syn su mandado; e otrosý que todas las galeas
que yo mandare armar syn flota para ganar, que de la ganançia 70
que oviere, que aya yo las dos partes e el dicho almirante la
terçia parte. [6] Otrosý tengo por bien e mando que todas las
galeas e naos e galeotas e leños e otras fustas qualesquier que
armaren a otras partes, de que yo aya de aver el quinto, que yo
aya las dos partes d'este dicho quinto e el dicho mi almirante la 75
terçia parte d'él; e otrosý tengo por bien que cada qu'el dicho
mi almirante fiziere armar por mi mandado, que pueda sacar e
saque quatro omes acusados de qualquier malefiçio por que
devan ser condenados de muerte, que estén presos, qualesquier
que fueren o vinieren en la dicha çibdat de Sevilla o otros puer- 80
tos qualesquier de los mis reynos e señoríos, flotados o por flotar, que pueda el dicho mi almirante cargar la terçia parte en él
o en ellos para sí, segund el preçio o preçios que vinieren flota-

---

57. **mar** GHP*V*] dicha m. *W*. 59. **o** (justiçia) GH*VW*] e *P*. **les** GH*V*] le *PW* (le/ *W*). 60. **o** GH*VW*] e *P*.
62. **o** GH*VW*] e *P*. 64. **E tengo**] *in G there is a large hand coming out of a sleeve drawn on the l. m. and
corresponding to the mark in the rubric.* 65. **mi** GHP*VW*] om. *Pr*. **o** GHP*W*] om. *PrV*. 66. **o** GHP*VW*] e *Pr*.
67. **almirante** GHPP*rV*] mi a. *W*. 67-69. **e yendo . . . mandado** GHP*VW*] om. *Pr*. 69. **mando** GHP]
mandado *VW*. 71. **oviere** GHP*W*] ovieren *PrV*. **que** GPP*rVW*] om. *H*. 73. **galeotas** GHPP*rV*] galeotes
W. 75. **d'este** GHPP*rV*] d'el *W*. **mi** GHP*rVW*] om. *P*. 76. **e** GHP*VW*] om. *Pr*. 78. **qualquier malefiçio**
GHP*VW*] qualesquier malefiçios *Pr*. 79. **de** GHP*VW*] a *Pr*. 80. **o** (vinieren) G*VW*] e HP*Pr*. **vinieren**
GHP*rVW*] vivieren *P*. **o** GHP*V*] e *Pr*, o en *W*. 81. **flotados** GP*VW*] fletados H*Pr*. **o** GHPP*rV*] e *W*.
81-82 **flotar** GHP*VW*] fletar *Pr*. 83-84. **flotados** GHP*VW*] fletados *Pr*.

dos o flotare. [7] Otrosý tengo por bien qu'el dicho mi almirante que aya el dicho mi almirantadgo /4 recto/ e avelaje e   85
juridiçión çivil e criminal bien e complidamente en todos los
puertos e logares de todos los mis reynos e señoríos, que sean
puertos de mar, así como la dicha çibdat de Sevilla, con todas las
fuerças e derechos que al dicho ofiçio de almirantadgo pertenesçen e perteneçer deven en qualquier manera; e otrosí que   90
aya e pueda usar e use, él e los que por sí pusiere, de la dicha
juridiçión çevil e criminal en qualquier manera en todos los
dichos puertos de la mar e las villas e logares d'ellos, así para dar
cartas de represarias e judgar todos los pleitos que en la dicha
mar e río acaesçieren, como en los dichos puertos e villas e   95
logares d'ellos, fasta donde entra agua salada o navegan los
navíos; e qu'el dicho almirante ponga sus alcaldes e alguaziles e
escrivanos e ofiçiales en todas las villas e logares de los mis
reynos e señoríos, que son puertos de mar, para que conozcan e
libren todos los pleitos criminales o çeviles que acaesçieren en la   100
mar o en el río por donde llegare la creçiente e menguare, segund e en la manera que mejor e más complidamente los otros
almirantes, o qualquier d'ellos, los pusieron en la dicha çibdat
de Sevilla. [8] E mando a los sobredichos del mi consejo e
oydores de la mi abdiençia e alcaldes de la dicha mi corte, e a   105
todas las otras justiçias de la dichas villas e logares de los dichos
puertos de la mar de los dichos mis reynos, que se non entremetan de conosçer nin librar los dichos pleitos, ni de perturbar ni
perturben al dicho mi almirante ni a los dichos sus ofiçiales
qu'él por sí pusiere para conoçer de los dichos pleitos, en la   110
manera que dicha es, la dicha juredición çivil ni criminal, ni
parte d'ella; e defiendo firmemente que ninguno nin algunos
non sean osados de yr nin pasar contra la dicha carta del dicho
señor Rey mi padre e mi señor, que Dios perdone, ni contra las
merçedes nin franquesas ni libertades en ella e en este dicho mi   115
previlegio contenidas, ni contra parte d'ellas, agora nin de aquí
adelante, para gelos quebrantar o menguar ninguna nin algunas
d'ellas; e qualquier o qualesquier que lo contrario fizieren, o
contra ello o contra parte d'ello fuesen o pasasen, avrían la mi

84. **flotare** *GHPV*] flotaren *W*, fletare *Pr*. 85. **mi** (almirantadgo) *GHPVW*] *om*. *Pr*. 96. **agua** *GPVW*] el a.
H 100. **o** *GHPW*] e *V*. 101. **e** (menguare) *GHPV*] o *W*. **menguare** *GHPW*] menguante *V* (*but cf*. p. 245,
45). 108. **los** *GPVW*] de l. *W*. 113-114. **del . . . perdone** *GHPVW*] *om*. *Pr*. 115. **ni** *GHPVW*] o *Pr*. **en
ella e** *GHPVW*] *om*. *Pr* (*homoeoteleuton*). **e** *GHPPrV*] ni *W*. **este** *GPV*] esto *HPrW*. 115. **mi** *GHPVW*] *om*.
Pr. 117. **algunas** *GHPV*] alguna *PrW*. 118. **fizieren** *GHPVW*] fiziesen *Pr*. 119. **o pasasen** *GHPVW*] *om*.
Pr.

yra e pechar me ýan en pena, por cada vegada que contra ello   120
fuesen o pasasen, dos mill doblas castellanas de fino oro e de
justo peso, e al dicho mi almirante mayor, o a quien sus bos
toviese, todos los daños e menoscabos que porende reçibiesen,
doblados, e demás a los cuerpos e a lo que toviesen me tornaría
por ello. [9] E mando a las dichas justiçias e a cada uno de vós en   125
vuestros logares e juridiçiones que prendades en bienes de aquel
o aquellos que contra ello, o contra parte d'ello, fueren o pa-
saren, o quisieren yr o pasar, por la dicha pena de las dichas dos
mill doblas a cada uno por cada vegada, e las guarden para fazer
de ellas lo que la mi merçed fuere; e otrosý que emendedes e   130
fagades emendar al dicho mi almirante mayor, o a quien la
dicha su boz toviere, de todos los dichos daños e menoscabos
que por la dicha razón reçibiere, /4 verso/ doblados, como
dicho es. [10] E demás, por qualquier o qualesquier por quien
fincare de lo así fazer e complir, mando al ome que este mi   135
previlegio mostrare, o el traslado sygnado, como dicho es, que
vos enplase que parescades ante mí doquier que yo sea, vos los
dichos conçejos por vuestros procuradores e sufiçientes, e uno
o dos de los ofiçiales de cada çibdad o villa do esto acaesçiere,
personalmente, con procuraçión de los otros ofiçiales vuestros   140
compañeros, del día que vos enplazaren en quinze días primeros syguientes, so la dicha pena, a desyr por quál rasón non
complides mi mandado; e mando, so la dicha pena, a qualquier
escrivano público que para esto fuere llamado, que dé ende al
que vos la mostrare, testimonio sygnado con su sygno, porque   145
yo sepa en cómo se cumple mi mandado. [11] E d'esto le
mandé dar al dicho don Alfonso Enriques, mi tío e mi almirante
mayor de la mar, este mi previlegio escripto en pergamino de
cuero, rodado e sellado con mi sello de plomo colgado en filos
de seda.   150
[12] Dada en la villa de Valladolid, diez e syete días de agosto,
año del nasçimiento de nuestro señor Jhesu Christo de mill e
quatroçientos e diez e seys años.
[13] E yo el sobredicho Rey don Juan, reynante en uno con la
Reyna doña Catalina, mi madre e mi señora e mi tuctora e   155

122. **mayor** GHPVW] om. Pr. 125. **uno** GHPVW] una Pr. 127. **o** (contra) GHPVW] e Pr. 128. **o** (pasar)
GHPVW] e Pr. **dos** GHPVW] om. Pr. 129. **a** GHPVW] e Pr. 130. **fuere** GHPVW] fuese(n) Pr. **e**
GHPVW] om. Pr. 131. **mayor** GHPVW] om. Pr. 134. **dicho** GHPVW] dicha Pr. 138. **e** (sufiçientes)
GPV] om. HW. 148. **de la mar** GHPV] om. W. 152. **señor** GPV] salvador HW.

regidora de los mis reynos, e con la ynfanta doña Catalina, mi
hermana, en Castilla e en León e en Toledo e en Galizia e en
Sevilla e en Córdova e en Murçia e en Jahén e en Baeça e en
Badajós e en Algarbe e en Algezira e en Viscaya e en Molina,
otorgo este previlegio e confírmolo.   160

[14] El ynfante don Juan, primo del dicho señor Rey e su
mayordomo mayor, confirma.

[15] Don Enrique, su hermano, primo del dicho señor Rey,
maestre de Santiago, confirma.

[16] El ynfante don Pedro, su hermano, primo del dicho señor   165
Rey, confirma.

[17] Don Luys de Gusmán, maestre de la orden de la cavallaría
de Calatrava, confirma.

[18] Don Pedro, señor de Monte Alegre, vasallo del Rey, confirma.   170

[19] Don Luys de la Çerda, conde de Medinaceli, vasallo del
Rey, confirma.

[20] Don Pablo, obispo de Burgos, chançiller mayor del Rey,
confirma.

[21] Don Lope de Mendoça, arçobispo de Santiago, capellán   175
mayor del Rey, confirma.

[22] Don fray Alfonso, obispo de Santiago, confirma.

[23] Don Johan, obispo de Segovia, confirma.

[24] Don Diego, obispo de Cuenca, confirma.

[25] Don Gonçalo de Çúñiga, obispo de Palençia, confirma.   180

[26] Don Diego Gomes de Sandoval, adelantado mayor de
Murçia, confirma.

[27] Don Johan Ramires de Arellano, señor de los Cameros,
vasallo del Rey, confirma.

[28] Don Garçía Fernandes Manrique, señor de Aguilar, vasallo   185
del Rey, confirma.

[29] Ýñigo Lopes de Mendoça, señor de la Vega, vasallo del
Rey, confirma.

[30] Yo Johan Fernandes de Palençia, escrivano del dicho señor
Rey, fis escrevir por su mandado en el año deseno qu'el dicho   190
señor Rey reynó.

[31] Fernandus, bachalareus en legibus; Alfonsus: registrada.

---

156. **e** *GHPV*] *om. W.* 159. **Algarbe** *GHPV*] *el A. W.* 165-166. **El . . . confirma** *GPV*] *om. HW*
(*homoeoteleuton*). 175. **Santiago** *GHPV*] *blank space in W;* Stevens *corr.* Siguenza (*cf.* p. 255, 127). 184.
vasallo] vasallo[s] *H.* 188. **confirma** *GHPV*] confirme *W.* 192. **en** *GHPV*] in *W.*

[1] E agora el dicho don Alfonso Enriques, almirante mayor de
la mar, pidióme por merçed que le confirmase el dicho previlegio de merçed aquí contenido, e /5 recto/ gele mandase
guardar en todo, bien e complidamente, segund que en él se
contiene. [2] E yo el sobredicho Rey don Juan, por fazer bien e   5
merçed al dicho don Alfonso Enriques, mi tío e mi almirante
mayor de la mar, e acatando al debdo que comigo ha e los
muchos e buenos e señalados serviçios que fizo al Rey don
Johan mi abuelo e al Rey don Enrique, mi padre e mi señor,
que Dios perdone, e faze a mí de cada día, tóvelo por bien. [3]   10
E porende, de mi proprio motuo e çierta sçiençia, es mi voluntad y merçed de confirmar e confírmole el dicho previlegio e
todas las merçedes en él contenidas, e dógelo agora de nuevo en
todo, segund e en la manera que en el dicho previlegio se contiene; e que pueda usar e use del dicho ofiçio de almirantadgo   15
con toda la justiçia e jurediçión alta e baxa, çevil e criminal, e en
el mero mixto imperio, e con todas las otras cosas, e cada una
d'ellas, en la dicha carta de previlegio suso encorporada contenidas, e use d'ello, e de cada cosa d'ello, e los que por sý
pusiere, asý en la mi corte e chançillería e casa e rastro, como   20
fuera d'ella; e pueda fazer e faga él, o los que por sý pusiere,
todas las otras cosas, e cada una d'ellas, contenidas en la dicha
carta de previlegio suso encorporada, las quales yo agora dó e
otorgo con libre e plenaria ju‹re›diçión e poderío e complida
abtoridad, segund que yo la he. [4] E defiendo firmemente por   25
esta mi carta de previlegio e por el treslado sygnado de escrivano público, sacado con abtoridad de juez, o de alcalde, que
de aquí adelante ninguno ni algunos non sean osados de le yr
nin pasar contra el dicho previlegio, ni contra parte d'él, para
gelo quebrantar o amenguar en alguna cosa de lo que en él se   30
contiene; que a qualquier o qualesquier que lo fizieren, o contra él, o contra parte d'él, fuesen o pasasen, avrían la mi yra e
demás pechar me ýan las penas en la dicha carta de previlegio
suso encorporada contenidas, e al dicho don Alfonso Enriques,

---

Sources: *GHPVW*. 3. **gele** *GHVW*] gelo *P*. 7. **e** (acatando) *GPVW*] *om. H*. **al** *GHPV*] el *W*. 16-17.
e en el] *s.l. V*. 21. **o** *GHPV*] e *W*. 24. **ju‹re›diçión** *HVW*] judiçión *GP*. 30. **amenguar** *GPVW*] menguar *H*. 34. **encorporada** *PW*] encorporadas *GHV* (*attraction of* contenidas).

mi tío e mi almirante mayor, o aquel que su boz toviese, todos   35
los daños e menoscabos que porende reçibiese; e esomismo
pagar le ha‹n› diez mill maravedís de pena para su cámara al
dicho don Alfonso Enriques, mi tío e mi almirante; en los
quales dichos diez mill maravedís de pena quiero, e es mi
merçed e voluntad, que cayan por ese mesmo fecho qualquier   40
que viniere o tentare venir contra lo contenido en este mi
previlegio, o contra cosa o parte d'ello, ca yo le fago merçed al
dicho Alfonso Enriques, mi tío e mi almirante mayor, o a quien
él quisiere o por bien toviere. [5] E sobre esto mando a todos los
sobredichos perlados, maestres de las órdenes, e comendadores,   45
e subcomendadores, duques e condes e ricos omes, e a los del
mi consejo e oydores de la mi abdiençia, e alcaldes, e notarios,
e alguaziles, e justiçias, e otros ofiçiales de la mi corte e chançillería e de la mi casa e rastro, e a los mis adelantados e merinos
mayores, cavalleros e escuderos, e a todos los conçejos, e cor-   50
regidores, e alcaldes, e alguasyles, e merinos, e prestameros, e
prebostes, e /5 verso/ otras justiçias, e ofiçiales qualesquier de la
muy noble çibdad de Sevilla e de todas las çibdades e villas e
logares de los mis reynos e señoríos, e a los capitanes de la mar,
e al mi armador de la flota e patrones e cómitres de las mis   55
galeas, e a los maestres e marineros e mareantes e otras personas
qualesquier que andovieren e navegaren por la mar, e a todas las
otras personas de qualquier estado e condiçión o preheminen-
nençia o dignidad que sean, que esta mi carta de previllegio
vieren o el treslado d'ella, sygnado como dicho es, que guarden   60
e cumplan, e fagan guardar e complir al dicho don Alfonso
Enriques, mi tío e mi almirante mayor de la mar, o al que lo
oviere de aver por él, este dicho previlegio e todas las merçedes
en él contenidas, en todo bien e complidamente, segund e en la
manera que en él se contiene; e que le non vayan nin pasen, ni   65
consientan yr nin pasar contra él ni contra parte d'él, en algund
tiempo, nin por alguna razón que sea, so pena de la mi merçed
e de la pena contenida en la dicha carta de previlegio suso encorporada a cada uno por quien fincare de lo asý fazer e complir. [6] E mando al my chançiller mayor del mi sello de la   70
poridad, e a los del mi consejo e oydores de la mi abdiençia, e

37. **ha‹n›** *HPVW*] ha *G*. 40. **cayan** *GHPW*] caya *V*. 41. **o** *GHPW*] e *V*. 44. **o** *GV*] e *HPW*. **todos**
GHPV] *om. W*. 49-51. **e merinos . . . alguasyles** *GHPV*] *om. W (homoeoteleuton)*. 58. **e** *GPV*] o *HW*.

alcaldes, e notarios, e a los mis contadores mayores, e a los mis
ofiçiales e escrivanos que están a la tabla de los mis sellos, que sy
sobre todas las cosas susodichas, o sobre qualquier o qualesquier
d'ellas, el dicho mi almirante, o los qu'él por sý pusiere, les   75
pidieren qualesquier mis cartas e previlegios rodados, o otros
qualesquier, que gelos den e libren e pasen e sellen los más
firmes e bastantes e complidos que pudieren e menester ovieren
para todo lo susodicho, e para cada cosa e parte d'ello, e para la
exsecuçión d'ello, e non fagades ni fagan ende ál, so la dicha   80
pena; e demás por qualquier o qualesquier de vós o d'ellos por
quien fincare de lo así fazer e complir, mando al ome que vos
esta mi carta de previlegio mostrare o el dicho su traslado, sygnado como dicho es, que vos enplaze que parescades ante mí en
la mi corte, los conçejos por vuestros procuradores, e los ofi-   85
çiales e las otras personas syngulares personalmente, del día que
vos enplasaren fasta quinse días primeros syguientes, cada uno a
desyr por quál rasón non complides mi mandado, so la dicha
pena, e a qualquier escrivano público que para esto fuere
llamado, que dé dende al que vos la mostrare testimonio syg-   90
nado con su sygno, porque yo sepa en cómo se cumple mi
mandado. [7] E d'esto le mandé dar al dicho mi almirante, mi
tío, esta mi carta e previlegio, escripta en pargamino de cuero,
firmado de mi nombre, rodado e sellado con mi sello de plomo
pendiente en filos de seda.   95
[8] Dada en la çibdad de Segovia a seys de junio, año del nasçimiento de nuestro salvador Jhesu Christo de mill e quatroçientos e diez e nueve años.

               Yo el Rey

[9] Yo el sobredicho Rey don Juan, reynante en uno con la   100
reyna doña María, mi esposa, e con la ynfanta doña Catalina, mi
hermana, en Castilla e en León e en Galizia e en Toledo e en
Sevilla, /6 recto/ en Córdova e en Murçia e en Jahén e en
Baeça e en Badajós e en el Algarbe e en Algezira e en Viscaya e
en Molina, otorgo este previlegio e confírmolo.   105
[10] El ynfante don Juan, primo del dicho señor Rey, ynfante
de Aragón, maestre de Santiago, confirma.
[11] El ynfante don Pedro, primo del dicho señor Rey, confirma.

72. **e a** GHPV] de W. 77. **e** (libren)] e [p] H. 78. **ovieren** GHPW] oviere V. 87. **enplasaren** GHPV]
enplazare W. 93. **e** GHV] de PW (cf. p. 256, 19-20). 103. **en** (Córdova) GHPV] y en W. 104. **en** (Viscaya)
GPVW] en gallizia e en H; **e** GHPV] om. W.

[12] Don Alfonso Enriques, tío del Rey, almirante mayor de la   110
mar, confirma.

[13] Don Ruy Lopes de Ávalos, conde estable de Castilla, adelantado mayor de Murçia, confirma.

[14] Don Luys de Gusmán, maestre de la orden de ‹la› cavallaría
de Calatrava, confirma.   115

[15] Don Luys de la Çerda, conde de Medinaçeli, vasallo del
Rey, confirma.

[16] Don Juan Alfonso Pimentel, conde de Benavente, vasallo
del Rey, confirma.

[17] Don Pedro, señor de Monte Alegre, vasallo del Rey, con-   120
firma.

[18] Don Lope de Mendoça, arçobispo de Santiago, capellán
mayor, confirma.

[19] Don Rodrigo de Velasco, obispo de Palençia, confirma.

[20] ‹Don Pablo, obispo de Burgos, chançiller mayor del Rey,   125
confirma.›

[21] Don Alfonso, obispo de Çigüença, confirma.

[22] Don Juan, obispo de Segovia, confirma.

[23] Don Juan, obispo de Ávila, confirma.

[24] Don Álvaro, obispo de Cuenca, confirma.   130

[25] Don Fernando, obispo de Córdova, confirma.

[26] Don Gutierre Gomes, administrador de la iglesia de Palençia, chançiller mayor de la Reyna de Castilla, confirma.

[27] Don Rodrigo, obispo de Jahén, confirma.

[28] E yo Juan Fernandes de Guadalajara la fis escrivir por su   135
mandado del Rey nuestro señor.

[29] Fernandus, bachalareus in legibus: registrada.

I.ii.1.2 (48.1-10)

[1] La qual dicha carta de previlegio del dicho señor Rey, pre-
sentada e leýda en la manera que dicha es, el dicho Gonçalo
Fernandes, en nombre del dicho señor almirante, dixo a los
dichos señores oydores que por quanto el dicho señor almirante

---

113. **de Murçia**] *repeated in H.* 114. ‹la› *HW*] *om. GPV.* 125-126. ‹**Don . . . confirma**› *HV*] *om. GPW*
(*homoeoteleuton*). 127. **de** *GPVW*] *om. H.* 137. **registrada** *GPVW*] *om. H.*   Sources: *GPVW.*

entendía e le era neçesario de enbiar la dicha carta de previlegio,   5
e la presentar en algunos logares do complía a serviçio del dicho
señor Rey e del bien común de los sus reynos e señoríos e de los
sus súbditos e naturales d'ellos, e guarda e conservaçión del
dicho almirantadgo e del dicho almirante, e que se reçelava que
la dicha carta de previlegio se podría perder o dañificar, asý por   10
robo como por fuego o por agua o por otra cabsa o caso fortuyto o peligro alguno que podría acaesçer, e d'ello se podría
seguir deserviçio al dicho señor Rey e al dicho señor almirante
recreçer en ello daño; porende dixo que pedía, e pidió, a los
dichos señores oydores en la mejor manera e forma que podía e   15
devía de derecho que de su ofiçio, el qual ynplorava mandasen
e diesen liçençia a nós los dichos Juan Martíns e Pero García,
escrivanos, para que anbos a dos juntamente, como personas
públicas, sacásemos e fiziésemos sacar de la dicha carta e previlegio del dicho señor Rey, original, un treslado o dos o más,   20
quantos cunpliesen e fuesen menester al dicho señor almirante
don Fadrique, e gelos diésemos sygnados de cada uno de nós
juntamente, en manera que fisyesen fee, conçertados con la
dicha carta de previlegio original; e que el tal treslado o treslados, que ansí diésemos sygnados de nuestros sygnos, /6 verso/   25
de la dicha carta de previlegio del dicho señor Rey, al dicho
señor almirante, o al que lo oviese de aver por él. [2] E porque
fuesen más firmes e valederos, pidió a los dichos señores
oydores que diesen e ynterpusiesen a ello, e para ello, su decreto e abtoridad para que de los tales treslado o treslados que   30
nos los dichos escrivanos asý diésemos d'ello, sygnados como
dicho es, valiesen e fiziesen fee doquier que paresçiesen, en
juysio e fuera d'él, asý como valdría e faría fee la dicha carta de
previlegio original suso contenida paresçiendo. [3] E luego los
dichos señores oydores, visto el dicho pedimiento, tomaron la   35
dicha carta de previlegio original en sus manos e vieron e catáronla e exsamináronla, e por quanto al presente no la fallaron
rota ni casa ni chançelada nin sopuntada, ni en alguna parte

---

5. **de** GPV] om. W. 6. **do** GPV] om. W. 8. **sus** GPV] om. W. 10. **podría** PVW] prodria G. **o** GV] e PW.
11. **fuego** GPV] furto W. **o** (por agua) GV] e PW. **o** (por otra) GPV] e W. **o** GPV] e W. 11-12. **fortuyto**
GPV] fortituyto W. 19. **e** (fiziésemos) GVW] o P. **e** GPV] de W (but cf. 254, 93). 23. **fisyesen** GPV]
hiziese W. 24. **el**] al GPVW. 25. **de nuestros sygnos**] repeated in G at the beginning of fol. 6v. **nuestros
sygnos** GPV] nuestro sygno W. 29. **e para ello** GPV] om. W. 33. **valdría** PW] valdrian GV. **faría** PVW]
farian G. 36. **vieron** GP] vieronla VW (attraction of e catáronla e exsamináronla ?).

d'ella dubdosa ni sospechosa, mas antes caresçiente de todo
viçio, porende, acatando lo sobredicho todo, dixeron que man-   40
davan e mandaron e dieron liçençia a nós los dichos Juan Martíns de León e Pero Garçía de Madrigal, escrivanos sobredichos,
para que amos a dos juntamente, como personas públicas,
sacásemos e fiziésemos sacar de la dicha carta de previlegio del
dicho señor Rey original un treslado o dos o más, quantos cun-   45
pliesen e fuesen menester al dicho señor almirante, e gelos
diésemos sygnados con nuestros sygnos, conçertados con la
dicha carta de previlegio original en manera que fisyesen fe; e al
treslado o treslados, que nosotros asý diésemos d'ella al dicho
señor almirante, como dicho es, los dichos señores oydores   50
dixeron que ynterponían, e ynterpusieron, su abtoridad e decreto, sý e en quanto e en la mejor manera e forma que podían
e devían de derecho, para que los tales treslado o treslados que
asý diésemos d'ello sygnados, valiesen e fiziesen fe doquier que
paresçiesen, en juysio e fuera d'él, sý e asý e atán com-   55
plidamente como valdría e faría fe la dicha carta de previlegio
original del dicho señor Rey paresçiendo.

[4] Testigos que fueron presentes a todo lo que dicho es: el
liçençiado Johan Lopes de Miranda e los bachilleres Diego
Muñós, alcaldes de los fijosdalgo, e Luys Rodrigues, e Fernand   60
Matheos, e Alonso Lopes de Sevilla, e Luys Gonzales de Córdova, escrivanos del dicho señor Rey.

[5] E d'esto en cómo pasó, el dicho Gonçalo Fernandes, en
nombre del dicho señor almirante, pidió a nós los dichos escrivanos que le diésemos este treslado de la dicha carta de previ-   65
legio original del dicho señor Rey, con la dicha abtoridad e
decreto, para guarda e conservaçión del dicho almirante e de las
cabsas sobredichas: que fue fecho e pasó día e mes e año ante los
testigos sobredichos de suso escriptos. [6] E nos los dichos Juan
Martíns de León e Pero Garçía de Madrigal, escrivanos sobredi-   70
chos, por virtud de la dicha liçençia e mandamiento a nós fecho
e dado por los dichos señores oydores de la dicha abtoridad e
decreto por ellos asý ynterpuesta, fesymos escrevir e sacar e
sacamos /7 recto/ este treslado de la dicha carta de previlegio
original del dicho señor Rey, amos a dos juntamente, e lo con-   75
çertamos con la dicha carta de previllegio original de verbo ad

---

42. **Madrigal** *GPW*] madril *V*. 44. **e** *GV*] o *PW*. 49. **d'ella** *GPV*] dello/ *W*. 52. **podían** *GPW*] podia *V*.
53. **devían** *GPW*] devia *V*. **treslado** *GPW*] treslados *V*. 74. **este** *GPV*] e. dicho *W*.

verbo, en presençia de los testigos que yuso serán escriptos, que
fueron presentes al dicho conçertamiento e vieron e oyeron
leer e conçertar este dicho traslado con la dicha carta de previlegio original. [7] Los quales dichos testigos que fueron presentes e llamados al dicho conçertamiento, son estos que se
syguen: Francisco Martíns de Villa Anpando, escrivano de la
dicha abdiençia, e Andrés de Valladolid e Fernando de Medina,
fijo de Juan de Medina, criados del dicho Juan Martíns de León.
[8] Va escripto sobre raýdo en un lugar donde dize "porende
grand galardón"; e ó dis "e escripto" entre renglones; e ó dis
"mi" e "escripto" entre renglones, e ó dis "qualquier navío" e
ó dis "en la dicha mar"; e entre renglones ó dis "dicha"; e sobre
raýdo ó dis "público que para"; e entre renglones ó dis "de" e
ó dis "de orgaz"; e escripto sobre raýdo ó dis "tenorio notario";
e entre renglones escripto ó dis "mí" e ó dis "Juan Lopes" non
le enpezca.
[9] E yo el dicho Juan Martíns de León, escrivano e notario
público sobredicho, que a esto que sobredicho es presente fuy
con el dicho Pero García de Madrigal, escrivano, ante los dichos señores oydores, en uno con los dichos testigos que a ello
fueron presentes, e por el dicho mandamiento e liçençia de los
dichos señores oydores, en uno con el dicho Pero García, escrivano, fis escrivir e sacar este treslado de la dicha carta de
previlegio del dicho señor Rey, con la dicha abtoridad, en estas
tres fojas e media de pergamino de cuero, con ésta en que va mi
sygno, e debaxo de cada plana va puesto mi nombre, e conçertado este treslado con la dicha carta de previlegio original del
dicho señor Rey en uno con el dicho Pero García, escrivano,
en presençia de los testigos que en esta escriptura fase mençión,
que fueron presentes al dicho conçertamiento; e porende fis
aquí este mío sygno, qu'es tal, en testimonio de verdad. Juan
Martíns.
[10] E yo el dicho Pero García de Madrigal, escrivano e notario
público susodicho, que a esto que sobredicho es presente fuy
con el dicho Juan Martíns de León, escrivano, ante los dichos
señores oydores, en uno con los dichos testigos que a ello fue-

77. en . . . testigos *GPV*] *om. W.* 81. e *GPV*] *om. W.* 82. **Villa Anpando** *GP*] Villalpando *VW.* 83.
Medina] mº *P.* 84. **fijo . . . Medina** *GPV*] *om. W.* **criados** *GV*] criado *PW.* 86. **e** (escripto) *GVW*] e e
P. **e** *GPV*] *om. W.* 87. (renglones) **e** *GPV*] *om. W.* 89. **ó dis** ("de") *GV*] *om. PW.* 94. **sobredicho** *GPV*]
dicho *W.* 97. **fueron presentes** *GPV*] p. f. *W.* 107. **tal** *GPV*] atal *W.*

ron presentes, e por el dicho mandamiento e liçençia de los
dichos señores oydores, en uno con el dicho Juan Martíns, escrivano, fis escrivir e sacar este traslado de la dicha carta de   115
previlegio del dicho señor Rey, con la dicha abtoridad, en estas
tres fojas e media de pergamino de cuero, e más este pedaço en
que va este mío sygno, e debaxo de cada plana va puesto mi
nonbre, e conçertado este traslado con la dicha carta de previlegio original del dicho señor Rey en uno con el dicho Juan   120
Martíns, escrivano, en presençia de los testigos que en esta escriptura fase minçión e fueron presentes al dicho conçertamiento; e porende fis aquí este mío sygno en testimonio de
verdad. Pero García.

I.ii.2 (48.11-13)

[1] E este traslado fue conçertado con la dicha escriptura original, donde fue sacado, ante los testigos /7 verso/ que a ello
fueron presentes, en viernes, treze días del mes de noviembre,
año del nasçimiento de nuestro salvador Jhesu Christo de mill e
quatroçientos e ochenta e nueve años.   5
[2] Testigos que fueron presentes al leer e conçertar d'este
dicho traslado sacado de la dicha escriptura: Alfonso de Valle e
Diego de Mesa, alcaldes, e Nuño de Mendoça, e Fernando
d'Esquivel, e Juan de Montaños, escrivano del Rey nuestro
señor, e otros.   10
[3] ‹E› yo Gonçalo García de Villamayor, escrivano de nuestro
señor el Rey e su notario público en la su corte e en todos los
sus reynos e señoríos, presente fuy en uno con los dichos testigos a conçertar este dicho traslado con la dicha escriptura
donde fue sacado, el qual fis escrivir; e porende fis aquí este mío   15
sygno atal en testimonio. Gonçalo García, escrivano del Rey.

117. **e** (más) *GV*] con *PW*. 122. **e** *GPV*] que *W*.   Sources: *GPVW*. 7. **Alfonso** *GPV*] Alonso *W*. 9.
Montaños *VW*] montanos *GP*. 11. ‹E› *VW*] *om. GP*. 11-12. **de . . . Rey** *GPV*] del rey nuestro señor *W*.

[1]En el nombre de la Sancta Trenidad y Eterna Unidad, Padre
e Fijo, Spíritu Sancto, tres personas realmente distintas en una
esençia divina, que bive e reyna por syenpre syn fin, e de la
bienaventurada Virgen gloriosa sancta María, nuestra señora,
Su madre, a quien nos tenemos por señora e por abogada en   5
todos los nuestros fechos, e a honra e reverençia Suya e del
bienaventurado apóstol señor Sanctiago, luz e espejo de las Españas, patrón e guiador de los reyes de Castilla e de León, y
asymesmo a onor y reverençia de todos los otros Santos e Santas
de la Corte Çelestial; porque, aunque segund natura non puede   10
el ome complidamente conoçer qué cosa es Dios, por el mayor
conosçimiento que del mundo puede aver, puédeLo conoçer
viendo e contemplando Sus maravillosas obras e fechos que fizo
e faze de cada día, pues que todas las obras por Su poder son
fechas, e por Su saber governadas, e por Su bondad mantenidas.   15
[2] Y así el ome puede entender que Dios es comienço e medio
e fin de todas las cosas, e que en Él se ençierran, y Él mantiene
a cada una en aquel estado que las ordenó, y todas Le han
menester, y Él non ha menester a ellas, y Él las puede mudar
cada que quisiere segund Su voluntad, y non puede caber en Él   20
que Se mude nin Se cambie en alguna manera. [3] ‹E› Él es dicho
Rey sobre todos los reyes, porque d'Él han ellos nonbre, y por
Él reynan, y Él los govierna y mantiene; los quales son vicarios,
cada uno en su reyno, puestos por Él sobre las gentes para los
mantener en justiçia y en virtud tenporalmente. [4] Lo qual se   25
muestra complida-/8 recto/ mente en dos maneras: la una d'e-
llas es spiritual, segund lo mostraron los Prophetas e los Sanctos,
a quien dio Nuestro Señor graçia de saber todas las cosas çiertamente e las fazer entender; la otra manera es segund natura,
asý como lo mostraron los omes sabios que fueron conos-   30
çedores de las cosas naturalmente. [5] Ca los Sanctos dixeron
qu'el rey es puesto en la tierra en el lugar de Dios para complir
la justiçia e dar a cada uno su derecho, y porende lo llamaron

Sources: GHPVW. 2. **Spíritu** GHPV] y e. W. 4. **sancta . . . señora** GHPV] nuestra señora Sancta
maria W. 12. **puede** GHPV] pueda W. 17. **e** (que) GHPV] om. W. 18. **una** W] uno GHPV. **todas**
GPVW] todolas H. 21. ‹E› HPW] om. GV (El = E Él ?): cf. p. 267, 21. 24. **puestos** GPW] puesto HV. 26.
es GHV] om. PW. 33. **y** GPVW] om. H.

coraçón y alma del pueblo: y así como el alma está en el coraçón
del ome, e por él bive el cuerpo y se mantiene, asý en el rey está   35
la justiçia, qu'es vida y mantenimiento del pueblo de su señorío;
y así como el coraçón es uno y por él reçiben todos los otros
mienbros unidad, para ser un cuerpo, bien así todos los del
reyno, maguer sean muchos, son uno, porqu'el rey deve ser, y
es, uno, y por eso deven ser todos uno con él para lo seguir y   40
ayudar en las cosas que ha de faser. [6] Y naturalmente dixeron
los sabios que los reyes son cabeça del reyno, porque, como de
la cabeça naçen los sentidos por que se mandan todos los miembros del cuerpo, bien asý por el mandamiento que naçe del rey,
que es señor y cabeça de todos los del reyno, se deve mandar y   45
guiar y lo obedesçer. [7] Y tan grand es ‹el› dicho del poder de
los reyes, que todas las leyes y los derechos tiénenlo so su poderío, porque aquél non lo han de los omes, mas de Dios, cuyo
lugar tienen en las cosas temporales; al qual entre las otras cosas
prinçipalmente pertenesçe amar e honrar e guardar sus pueblos,   50
y entre los otros señaladamente deve tomar e honrar a los que lo
meresçen por serviçios que le ayan fecho; y porende el rey o el
prínçipe, entre los otros poderes que ha, non tan solamente
puede, mas deve fazer graçias a los que las mereçen por serviçios
que le ayan fecho y por bondad que falle en ellos. [8] Y porque   55
entre las otras virtudes anexas a los reyes, segund dixeron los
sabios, es la justiçia, la qual es virtud e verdad de las cosas, por la
qual mejor e más endereçadamente se mantiene el mundo, y es
asý como fuente donde manan todos los derechos, e dura por
syempre en las voluntades de los omes justos, e nunca desfa-   60
lleçe, e da e reparte a cada uno ygualmente su derecho, e comprehende en sí todas las virtudes prinçipales, y naçe d'ella muy
grand utilidad, porque haze bivir cuerdamente y en paz a cada
uno segund su estado, sy culpa e syn yerro; e los buenos se
hazen por ella mejores, reçibiendo galardones por los bienes   65
que fizieron, e los otros por ella se endereçan e emiendan. [9]

34. **alma** (del) *GHPV*] anima *W*. **alma** (está) *GHPV*] anima *W*. 35. **asý**] asy [est] *H*. 39. **son uno** *GHPV*]
om. W. 40. **eso** *GHV*] esto *PW*. **uno** *GPW*] unos *HV*. 45. **deve** *GHPV*] deven *W*. 46. ‹el› *W*] *om. GHPV*
(*but cf.* p. 268, 46-47). **dicho del** *GHPV* (**d(ic)ho** *GHPV*)] derecho y *W* (*cf.* p. 268, 47, *reading of P*). 47.
los (derechos) *GHPV*] *om. W*. **tiénenlo** *GHPV*] tienen *W* (*but cf.* p. 268, 47). 48. **lo** *GV*] le *HPW*. **han**
GHPV] ha *W*. 49. **tienen** *GHP*] tiene *VW*. 52. **le**] les *GHPVW*. **ayan** *GPW*] aya *HV*. 53. **ha** *GHPV*] han
W. 54. **puede** *GHPV*] pueden *W*. **deve** *GHPV*] deven *W*. 55. **le** *GPV*] les *HW*. **falle** *GHPV*] hallen *W*.
59. **dura** *GHVW*] duran *P*. **por** *GHPV*] *om. W*. 62. **naçe** *PW*] naçen *GHV*. **ella** *W*] ellas *GHPV*. **muy**
GHPV] *om. W*. 63. **haze** *GPVW*] hazen *H*. 65. **bienes** *GHPV*] benefiçios *W* (*but cf.* p. 269, 66).

La qual justiçia tiene en sí dos partes prinçipales: la una /8
verso/ es comutativa, que es entre un ome e otro, e la otra es
distributiva, en la qual consisten los galardones e renumeraçiones de los buenos e virtuosos trabajos e serviçios que los omes   70
fazen a los reyes e prínçipes e a la cosa pública de sus reynos.
[10] Y porque, segund dizen las leyes, dar galardón a los que
bien e lealmente syrven, es cosa que conviene mucho a todos
los omes, mayormente a los reyes e prínçipes e grandes señores
que tienen poder de lo haser, e a ellos es cosa propia honrar e   75
sublimar a aquellos que bien e lealmente les sirven e sus virtudes
e serviçios lo mereçen, en galardonar los buenos fechos los
reyes que lo fazen muestran ser conoçedores de la virtud e otrosý
justiçieros. [11] Ca la justiçia non es tan solamente en escarmentar los malos, mas aun es galardonar los buenos; e demás   80
d'esto, naçe d'ella otra muy grand utilidad, porque da voluntad
a los buenos para ser más virtuosos, e a los malos para emendarse; e quando asý non se fase, podría acaesçer por contrario.
[12] E porque entre los otros galardones e renumeraçiones que
los reyes pueden fazer a los que bien e lealmente les sirven, es   85
honrarlos e sublimarlos entre los otros de su linage, e los ennobleçer e decorar e honrar, e les faser otros muchos bienes e
graçias e merçedes, porende, considerando e acatando todo lo
susodicho, queremos que sepan por esta nuestra carta de previlegio, o por su traslado sygnado de escrivano público, todos los   90
que agora son e serán de aquí adelante, cómo nos don Fernando
e doña Ysabel, por la graçia de Dios rey e reyna de Castilla, de
León, de Aragón, de Seçilia, de Granada, de Toledo, de Valençia, de Galizia, de Mallorcas, de Sevilla, de Çerdeña, de
Córdova, de Córçega, de Murçia, de Jahén, de los Algarbes, de   95
Algezira, de Gibraltar e de las yslas de Canaria, conde e condesa
de Barçelona, señores de Viscaya e de Molina, duques de
Athenas e de Neopatría, condes de Rosellón e de Çerdania,
marqueses de Oristán e de Goçiano, vimos unos capítulos firmados de nuestros nombres e sellados con nuestro sello, fechos   100
en esta guisa:

68. **e** (la) *GPVW*] *om. H.* 70. **buenos** *GHPV*] benefiçios *W* (*but cf.* p. 269, 70). 72. **Y** *GHV*] *om. PW.* 75.
e (a) *GPVW*] *om. H.* 76. **a** *GPVW*] *om. H* (aquellos = a aquellos). **les** *GHV*] los *PW.* 77. **en** *GHPV*] y en
W (*cf.* p. 269, 77-78). **buenos** *GHPV*] benefiçios *W* (*but cf.* p. 269, 78). 79. **es tan** *GHPVW*] *corr.* está (*cf.*
p. 269, 78-79)? 80. **aun es** *GHPV*] en *W* (*cf.* p. 269, 79). **los** *GHPV*] a los *W* (*but cf.* p. 269, 80). 81. **ella**
GHPV] ello *W* (*but cf.* p. 269, 81). 83. **por** *GHV*] por el *P,* al *W* (*but cf.* p. 269, 84). 85. **les** *GHPV*] los *W.*
88. **considerando e acatando** *GHPV*] a. e c. *W* (*but cf.* p. 270, 89). 90. **o** *GPV*] e *HW* (*but cf.* p. 270, 90).
96. **de** (Gibraltar) *GHPV*] e de *W.* 97. **señores** *GPVW*] e s. *H.* 100. **nuestros nombres** *GHPV*] nuestro
nombre *W* (*but cf.* p. 270, 100).

[1] Las cosas suplicadas e que Vuestras Altesas dan e otorgan a
don Christóval Colón en alguna satisfaçión de lo que ha descubierto en las mares Oçéanas e del viage que agora, con la
ayuda de Dios, ha de fazer por ellas en serviçio de Vuestras
Altesas, son las que se syguen: 5

[2] Primeramente, que Vuestras Altesas, como señores que son
de las dichas mares Oçéanas, fazen dende agora al dicho don
Christóval Colón su almirante en todas aquellas yslas e tierras
firmes que por su mano e yndustria se descubrirán o ganarán en
las /9 recto/ dichas mares Oçéanas para durante su vida e, des-   10
pués d'él muerto, a sus herederos e subçesores de uno en otro
perpetuamente, con todas aquellas preheminençias e perrogativas perteneçientes al tal ofiçio, e segund que don Alonso
Enriques, vuestro almirante mayor de Castilla, e los otros
predeçesores en el dicho ofiçio lo tenían en sus distritos.   15

[3] Plaze a Sus Altesas. Johan de Coloma.

[4] Otrosý, que Vuestras Altesas fazen al dicho don Christóval
su visorrey e governador general en todas las dichas yslas e tierras firmes e yslas que, como dicho es, él descubriere e ganare
en las dichas mares, e que para el regimiento de cada una, e   20
qualquier d'ellas, faga eleçión de tres personas para cada ofiçio,
e que Vuestras Altesas tomen e escojan uno, el que más fuere su
serviçio, e así serán mejor regidas las tierras que Nuestro Señor
le dexará fallar e ganar a serviçio de Vuestras Altesas.

[5] Plaze a Sus Altesas. Juan de Coloma.   25

[6] Yten, que todas e qualesquier mercaderías, siquier sean perlas, piedras preçiosas, oro, plata, espeçiería, y otras qualesquier
cosas y mercadurías de qualquier espeçie, nonbre e manera
que sea, que se conpraren, trocaren, fallaren, ganaren e ovieren dentro de los límites del dicho almirantadgo, que dende   30

**Cosas suplicadas y
que Sus Altezas le
concedieron en
conformidad de lo
contenido en los
privilegios al
Almirante Mayor
de Castilla, como
Almirante Mayor
del mar Oçéano, y
algo más, respecto a
lo futuro en el
aquisto de las Yslas
[l. m].**

Sources: GHPPrVW. Cf. also Additional documents 3, pp. 398-400, whose variants (P') are reported here. In
P'Pr the document is preceded by the rubric: La Capitulaçión. 3. la GHPPrVW] el P'. 8-9. **tierras firmes**
GHPPrVW] tierra firme P'. 15. **predeçesores** GHPPrVW (**preçedesores** Pr)] preçesores P'. 18-19. **tier-
ras firmes** GHP(Pr)VW] tierra firme P'. **tierras** GHP(P')VW] otras Pr. 19. **e** (ganare) GPW] o HPrV, P'.
20. **e** (qualquier) GHPVW, P'] o Pr. 21. **faga** GHPPrVW] fagan P'. 24. **dexará** GHPPrVW] dexare P'. **a**
GHPVW, P'] en Pr. **Vuestras Altezas** GHPVW, P'] vuestra alteza Pr. 26. **mercaderías** GPPrW, P']
mercadurias HV. 26-27. **perlas piedras** GHPVW, P'] piedras perlas Pr. 27. **espeçiería** GHPPrV, P'] e e.
W. 28. **mercadurías** GHPV] mercaderias P'PrW. 29. **que sea** G(H)P(Pr)(V)W] om. P'. **sea** GPW] sean
HPrV. **conpraren** HPrV, P'] conpren GPW. **fallaren ganaren** GHPVW, P'] g. hallaren Pr. 30. **los
límites** GHPPrVW] las l. P'.

agora Vuestras Altesas fazen merçed al dicho don Christóval y quieren que aya e lleve para sí la dezena parte de todo ello, quitadas las costas todas que se fizieren en ello, por manera que de lo que quedare limpio e libre aya e tome la déçima parte para sí mismo e faga d'ella a su voluntad, quedando las otras nueve partes para Vuestras Altesas.

[7] Plaze a Sus Altesas. Johan de Coloma.

[8] Otrosý, que sy a cabsa de las mercadurías qu'él traerá de las dichas yslas e tierras que, así como dicho es, se ganaren o descubrieren, o de las que en troque de aquéllas se tomaren acá de otros mercaderes, naçiere pleito alguno en el lugar donde el dicho comerçio e trato se terná e fará, que, sy por la preheminençia de su ofiçio de almirante le perteneçerá conoçer del tal pleito, plega a Vuestras Altesas que él o su theniente, e no otro juez, conozca del tal pleito, e asý lo provean dende agora.

[9] Plaze a Sus Altezas, sy perteneçe al dicho ofiçio de almirante, segund que lo tenía el almirante don Alfonso Enriques y los otros sus anteçesores en sus distritos, e seyendo justo. Juan de Coloma.

[10] Yten, que en todos los navíos que se armaren para el dicho trato e negoçiaçión, cada e quando e quantas vezes se armaren, que pueda el dicho don Christóval Colón, sy quisiere, contribuyr e pagar la ochena parte de todo lo que se gastare en el armazón, e que tanbién aya e lieve del provecho la ochena parte de lo que resultare de la tal armada.

[11] Plaze a Sus Altesas. Juan de Coloma./9 verso/

[12] Son otorgados e despachados con las respuestas de Vuestras Altezas en fin de cada un capítulo en la villa de Sancta Fee de la Vega de Granada, a diez e siete días de abril del año del naçimiento de nuestro salvador Jhesu Christo de mill e quatroçientos e noventa e dos años.

Yo el Rey

Yo la Reyna

---

31. **Vuestras Altesas fazen merçed** *GHPVW, P'*] hazen v. a. m. *Pr.* **Christóval** *GHPVW, P'*] c. colon *Pr.* 33. **las . . . todas** *GPVW*] todas las costas *Pr.* **todas** *GPPrVW*] *om. HP'*. 35. **ella** *GHPPrVW*] ello *P'*. **a** *GHPVW, P'*] *om. Pr* (ella = ella a?). 38. **mercadurías** *GHPPrV, P'*] mercaderias *W*. **traerá** *GPPrVW*] trahere *HP'*. 39. **o** *GPPrVW*. , *P'*] e *H*. 40. **en troque** *GHPVW, P'*] entro que *Pr.* 41. **mercaderes** *GHPW, P'*] mercadores *PrV*. 44. **Vuestras Altesas** *GHPPrVW*] vuestra alteza *P'*. **o** *GPPrVW, P'*] e *H*. **e** *GHPVW, P'*] *om. Pr.* 45. **juez** *GHPVW, P'*] *om. Pr.* **provean** *GHPPrV*] provea *P'W*. 46. **Sus Altezas** *GHPPrVW*] su alteza *P'*. 48. **anteçesores** *GHPVW*] subçesores *P'Pr.* **distritos** *HPPrW, P'*] discritos? *G*, discriptos *V*. 53. **pagar** *GHPVW, P'*] proveer *Pr.* **ochena** *GHPPrV*] ochava *P'W*. 54. **ochena** *GHPPrV*] ochava *P'W*. 56. **Sus Altezas** *GHPPrVW*] su alteza *P'*. 57. **otorgados** *GHPVW*] otorgadas *P'Pr.* **despachados** *GHPVW*] despachadas *P'Pr.* 59. **siete** *GHPVW, P'*] syca *Pr.* 60. **salvador** *GHPVW, P'*] señor *Pr.*

[13] Por mandado del Rey e de la Reyna. Johan de Coloma.
[14] Registrada: Calçena.   65

II.iii (50)

Confirmación de la
merced y
privilegios hechos a
Don Christóval
Colón, con que
passen y se
estableçcan en sí, en
sus hijos, nietos y
descendientes sin
que alguno sea
osado a contravenir
a lo otorgado por
Sus Altezas [*l. m.*].

[1] E agora, por quanto vos el dicho don Christóval Colón,
nuestro almirante del mar Oçéano e nuestro visorrey e governador de la tierra firme e yslas, nos suplicastes e pedistes por
merçed que, porque mejor e más complidamente vos fuese
guardada la dicha carta de merçed a vós e a vuestros fijos e   5
deçendientes, que vos la confirmásemos e aprovásemos e vos
mandásemos dar nuestra carta de previlegio d'ella, o como la
nuestra merçed fuese; e nos, acatando lo susodicho e los muchos e buenos e leales e grandes e continuos serviçios que vos el
dicho don Christóval Colón, nuestro almirante e visorrey e   10
governador de las yslas e tierra firme descubiertas e por descobrir en el mar Oçéano en la parte de las Yndias, nos avedes
fecho e esperamos que nos faréys, espeçialmente en descobrir e
traer a nuestro poder e so nuestro señorío a las dichas yslas e
tierra firme, mayormente porque esperamos que, con ayuda de   15
Dios nuestro señor, redundará en mucho serviçio Suyo e honra
nuestra e pro e utilidad de nuestros reynos e señoríos, porque
esperamos, con ayuda de Dios, que los pobladores Yndios de las
dichas Yndias se convertirán a nuestra sancta fe cathólica, tovímoslo por bien; e por esta dicha nuestra carta de previlegio, o   20
por el dicho su traslado sygnado, como dicho es, de nuestro
propio motuo e çierta sçiençia e poderío real absoluto, de que
en esta parte queremos usar e usamos, confirmamos e
aprovamos, para agora e para siempre jamás, a vós el dicho don
Christóval Colón e a los dichos vuestros fijos, nietos e desçen-   25
dientes de vós e d'ellos, e a vuestros herederos, la sobredicha
nuestra carta suso encorporada e la merçed en ella contenida; e
queremos, e mandamos, e es nuestra merçed e voluntad que
vos vala e sea guardada a vós e a vuestros fijos e desçendientes,
agora e de aquí adelante, inviolablemente, para agora e para   30

---

64. **Por . . . Reyna** *GHPPrVW*] *om. P'.* 65. **Calçena** *PP'W*] Talçeña *GHPrV.*   Sources: *GHPVW.* 2.
del *GHPW*] de la *V.* 12. **el** *GHPV*] la *W.* 17. **e señoríos**] *s.l. V.* 22. **motuo** *HPW*] motiuo *GV.* 25.
nietos *GHPV*] e n. *W.*

syempre jamás, en todo e por todo, bien e complidamente, segund e por la forma e manera que en ella se contiene; y, sy neçesario es, agora de nuevo vos fazemos la dicha merçed, e defendemos firmemente que ninguna, ni algunas personas non sean osadas de vos yr ni venir contra ella, ni contra parte d'ella, por vos la quebrantar ni menguar en tiempo alguno ni por alguna manera. [2] Sobre lo qual mandamos al prínçipe don Juan, nuestro muy caro e muy amado fijo, e a los ynfantes, duques, perlados, marqueses, condes, ricos omes, maestres de las órdenes, priores, comendadores e subcomendadores, e a los del nuestro consejo, oydores de la nuestra abdiençia, alcaldes, alguaziles e otras justiçias qualesquier de nuestra casa e corte e chançillería, e alcaydes de los castillos e casas fuertes e llanas, e a todos los conçejos, asistentes, corregidores, alcaldes, alguaziles, merinos, prebostes, e a otras justiçias de todas las çibdades e villas e logares de los /10 recto/ nuestros reynos e señoríos, e a cada uno d'ellos, que vos guarden e fagan guardar esta dicha nuestra carta de previlegio e confirmaçión e la carta de merçed en ella contenida, e contra el thenor e forma d'ella no vos vayan nin pasen, ni consientan yr ni pasar en tiempo alguno ni por alguna manera, so las penas en ella contenidas. [3] De lo qual vos mandamos dar esta dicha nuestra carta de previlegio e confirmaçión, escripta en pargamino de cuero, e firmada de nuestros nombres, e sellada con nuestro sello de plomo pendiente en filos de seda a colores; la qual mandamos al nuestro chançiller, mayordomo e notario, e a los otros ofiçiales que están a la tabla de los nuestros sellos, que sellen e libren e pasen. [4] Lo qual todo que dicho es en los dichos capítulos suso encorporados y en esta nuestra confirmaçión contenidos, queremos y es nuestra merçed e voluntad que se guarde e cumpla asý, segund que en ellos se contiene; e los unos nin los otros non fagades nin fagan ende ál por alguna manera, so pena de la nuestra merçed e de diez mill maravedís para la nuestra cámara a cada uno que lo contrario fiziere; e demás mandamos al ome que vos esta nuestra carta mostrare, que vos enplase que parescades ante nós en la nuestra corte doquier que nos seamos, del día que vos enplasare fasta quinze días primeros syguientes, so la dicha pena; so la qual

35

40

45

50

55

60

65

---

35. **osadas** *GHPV*] osados *W*. 36. **la** *GHVW*] lo *P*. **ni menguar** *GHPV*] e amenguar *W*. 41. **oydores** *GHPV*] e o. *W*. 41-42. **alguaziles** *GPVW*] e a. *H*. 42. **nuestra** *GHPV*] la n. *W*. 45. **otras** *GHPV*] a o. *W*. 56. **mayordomo** *GHPV* (**mayor°** *V*)] mayor *W*.

mandamos a qualquier escrivano público que para esto fuere
llamado, que dé ende al que gela mostrare testimonio sygnado
con su sygno, porque nos sepamos en cómo se cumple nuestro   70
mandado.

[5] Dada en la çibdad de Burgos a veynte e tres días del mes de
abril, año del nasçimiento de nuestro señor Jhesu Christo de
mill e quatroçientos e noventa e syete años.

Yo el Rey   75
Yo la Reyna

[6] Yo Fernand Álvares de Toledo, secretario del Rey e de la
Reyna nuestros señores, las fis escrivir por su mandado.

[7] Antonius, doctor. Registrada. Doctor Rodericus; doctor
Antonius; doctor Fernand Álvares; Juan Velasques.   80

[8] E en las espaldas de la dicha carta de previlegio estava escripto lo syguiente: "Syn chançillería e syn derechos, por mandado de Sus Altesas".

III.i (4)

[1] En el nombre de la Sancta Trenidad y Eterna Unidad, Padre
e Fijo, Spíritu Sancto, tres personas realmente distintas e una
esençia divina, que bive e reyna por syempre syn fin, e de la
bienaventurada Virgen gloriosa santa María, nuestra señora, Su
madre, a quien nos tenemos por señora e por abogada en todos   5
los nuestros fechos, e a honra e reverençia Suya e del bienaventurado apóstol señor Santiago, lus y espejo de las Españas, patrón e guiador de los reyes de Castilla e de León, e asymismo a
honra e reverençia de todos los otros Sanctos e Sanctas de la
Corte Çelestial; porque, aunque segund natura non puede el   10
ome complidamente conoçer qué cosa es Dios, por el mayor
conosçimiento que del mundo puede aver, puédeLo conoçer
veyendo e contemplando Sus maravillas e obras e fechos que
fizo e fase de cada día, pues que todas las obras por Su poder son
fechas, e por Su saber governadas, e por Su bondad mantenidas.   15

---

73. **señor** *GPV*] salvador *HW*. 79-80. **doctor . . . Antonius** *GHPV*] om. *W* (*homoeoteleuton*). 81. **de la**
. . . de *GHPV*] del dicho *W*.   Sources: *GPVW*, *H* 1-10 (*Çelestial*). 2. **Spíritu** *GHPV*] y espiritu *W*. 3.
syn fin *GPVW*] jamas *H*. 10. **Çelestial** *GPVW*] ç. etc. *H*. 12. **puede** *GPV*] pueda *W*.

[2] Y asý el ome puede entender que Dios es comienço e medio e fin de todas las cosas, e que en Él se ençierran, y Él mantiene a cada una en aquel estado que las ordenó, y todas Le han menester, y Él no ha menester a ellas, y Él las puede mudar cada ves que quisiere, segund Su voluntad, y non puede caber en Él que Se mude ni Se cambie en alguna manera. [3] Y Él es dicho rey sobre todos /10 verso/ los reyes, porque d'Él han ellos nombre, e por Él reynan, y Él los govierna y mantiene; los quales son vicarios Suyos, cada uno en su reyno, puestos por Él sobre las gentes para los mantener en justiçia y en verdad temporalmente. [4] Lo qual se muestra complidamente en dos maneras: la una d'ellas es spiritual, segund lo mostraron los Prophetas y los Sanctos, a quien dio Nuestro Señor graçia de saber las cosas çiertamente e las faser entender; la otra manera es segund natura, asý como lo mostraron los omes sabios que fueron conoçedores de las cosas naturalmente. [5] Ca los Santos dixeron qu'el rey es puesto en la tierra en el lugar de Dios para complir la justiçia e dar a cada uno su derecho, y porende lo llamaron coraçón y alma del pueblo: y asý como el alma está en el coraçón del ome, y por él bive el cuerpo y se mantiene, asý en el rey está la justiçia, qu'es vida e mantenimiento del pueblo de su señorío; y asý como el coraçón es uno e por él reçiben todos los otros miembros unidad, para ser un cuerpo, bien asý todos los del reyno, maguer sean muchos, son uno, porqu'el rey deve ser, y es, uno, y por eso deven ser todos unos con él para lo seguir e ayudar en las cosas que ha de faser. [6] Y naturalmente dixeron los sabios que los reyes son cabeça del reyno, porque, como de la cabeça naçen los sentidos, por que se mandan todos los miembros del cuerpo, bien asý por el mandamiento que naçe del rey, que es señor y cabeça de todos los del reyno, se deven mandar y guiar y lo obedeçer. [7] Y tan grand es el dicho del poder de los reyes, que todas las leyes y los derechos tienen so su poderío, porque aquél non lo han de los omes, mas de Dios, cuyo lugar tienen en las cosas temporales; al qual, entre las otras cosas, prinçipalmente perteneçe amar y

20

25

30

35

40

45

50

18. **una** *W*] uno *GPV*. **aquel** *GPV*] el *W* (*but cf*. 260, 18). 24. **puestos** *GPW*] puesto *V*. **por Él** *GPV*] *om*. *W*. 27. **es** *GPV*] *om*. *W*. 29. **es** *GV*] *om*. *PW* (*but cf*. p. 260, 29). 32. **el** (lugar) *GV*] *om*. *PW* (*but cf*. p. 260, 32). 34. **alma del pueblo** *GPV*] anima/ *W*. **alma** (está) *GPV*] anima *W*. 36. **del pueblo** *GPV*] *om*. *W* (*but cf*. p. 261, 36). 40. **eso** *GPV*] esto *W*. 41. **seguir** *GPV*] servir *W* (*but cf*. p. 261, 40). **las** *GPV*] l. sus *W* (*but cf*. p. 261, 40). 47. **dicho** *GVW* (d(ic)ho *GW*] derecho *P* (*cf*. p. 261, 46, *reading of W*). **del** *GPV*] *om*. *W* (*but cf*. p. 261, 46, *reading of W*). 48. **lo** *GVW*] le *P*.

honrar y guardar sus pueblos, y entre los otros señaladamente deve tomar y honrar a los que lo mereçen por serviçios que le ayan fecho; y porende el rey o el prínçipe, entre los otros poderes que ha, no tan solamente puede, mas deve haser graçias a los que las meresçen por serviçios que le ayan fecho y por 55 bondad que falle en ellos. [8] Y porque entre las otras virtudes anexas a los reyes, segund dixeron los sabios, es la justiçia, la qual es virtud o verdad de las cosas, por la qual mejor e más endereçadamente se mantiene el mundo, y es asý como fuente donde manan todos los derechos, e dura por syempre en las 60 voluntades de los omes justos, e nunca desfalleçe, e da e reparte a cada uno ygualmente su derecho, e comprehende en sí todas las virtudes prinçipales, y naçe d'ella muy grand utilidad, porque fase bevir cuerdamente y en paz a cada uno segund su estado, syn culpa e syn yerro; e los buenos se hasen por ella 65 mejores, reçibiendo galardones por los bienes que fizieron, e los otros por ella se endereçan e emiendan. [9] La qual justiçia tiene en sý dos partes prinçipales: la una es comutativa, que es entre un ome e otro; la otra es distributiva, en la qual consiguen los galardones e renumeraçiones de los buenos e virtuosos trabajos 70 e serviçios que los omes fasen a los reyes e prínçipes, o a la cosa pública de sus reynos. [10] E porque, segund disen las leyes, dar galardón a los que bien e lealmente syrven, es cosa que conviene mucho a todos los omes, y mayormente a los reyes e prínçipes e grandes señores que tienen poder de lo faser, y a 75 ellos es propia cosa honrar e sublimar a aquellos que bien e lealmente les syrven e sus virtudes e serviçios lo meresçen, y en galardonar los buenos fechos los reyes que lo fasen muestran ser conoçedores de la virtud ‹e› otrosý justiçieros. [11] Ca la justiçia non está solamente en escarmentar los malos, mas aun ‹en› 80 galardonar los buenos; y demás d'esto, naçe d'ella otra grand utilidat, porque da voluntad a los buenos para ser más virtuosos, y a los malos para emendarse; y / 11 recto/ quando asý non se hase, podría acaesçer por contrario. [12] Y porque entre los

52. **tomar** GPV] amar W (but cf. p. 261, 51). 53. **o** GPV] y W (but cf. p. 261, 52). 60. **dura** GPW] duran V. 63. **ella**] ella[s] V. 64. **a** GPV] om. W. 69. **e** GPW] a V (but cf. p. 261, 68). **en . . . consiguen** GPV] la qual considera W (but cf. p. 262, 69). 70. **e** (renumerouçiones) GPW] a V. 71. **omes** GV] buenos PW (but cf. p. 262, 70). **o** GV] e PW (but cf. p. 262, 71). 74. **y** GPV] om. W (cf. p. 262, 74). 79. **‹e›** P] om. GVW (but cf. p. 262, 78). **justiçia** GPV] virtud de la j. W (but cf. p. 262, 79). 80. **está** GPW] estan (= es tan) V (cf. p. 262, 80). 80. **‹en›** PW] om. GV; corr. es (cf. p. 262, 80)? 81. **los** GPV] a los W (but cf. p. 262, 80). 82. **virtuosos** GPV] buenos W (but cf. p. 262, 82).

otros galardones y renumeraçiones que los reyes pueden fazer a   85
los que bien e lealmente le·sirven, es honrarlos e sublimarlos
entre los otros de su linaje, e los ennobleçer e decorar e honrar,
e les fazer otros muchos bienes e graçias e merçedes, porende,
considerando e acatando lo susodicho, queremos que sepan por
esta nuestra carta de previlegio, o por su treslado sygnado de   90
escrivano público, todos los que agora son e serán de aquí adelante, cómo nos don Fernando e doña Ysabel, por la graçia de
Dios rey e reyna de Castilla, de León, de Aragón, de Seçilia,
de Granada, de Toledo, de Valençia, de Galizia, de Mallorcas,
de Sevilla, de Çerdeña, ‹de Córdova›, de Córçega, de Murçia,   95
de Jahén, del Algarbe, de Algezira, de Gibraltar e de las yslas de
Canaria, conde e condesa de Barçelona, señores de Viscaya e de
Molina, duques de Athenas e de Neopatría, condes de Rosellón

Que, descubiertas
las Islas y Tierra
firme, sea
Almirante de lo
hallado, y lo
gobierne con título
de Almirante,
Visorey y
Governador de las
Islas y Tierra firme,
y se pueda de allí
adelante llamar y
intitular Don
Christóval Colón; y
assý sus hijos y
subcesores en el
dicho oficio y cargo
se puedan intitular
y llamar Don y
Almirante, Visorey
y Governador de las
Islas y Tierra firme.
Y demás le dan
poderío civil y
criminal para juçgar
y determinar en
qualquiera causa
[r. m.].

e de Çerdania, marqueses de Oristán e de Goçiano, vimos una
carta de merçed firmada de nuestros nombres e sellada con   100
nuestro sello, fecha en esta guisa:

III.ii.1 (2)

[1] Don Fernando e doña Ysabel, por la graçia de Dios rey e
reyna de Castilla, de León, de Aragón, de Seçilia, de Granada,
de Toledo, de Valençia, de Galizia, de Mallorcas, de Sevilla, de
Çerdeña, de Córdova, de Córçega, de Murçia, de Jahén, del
Algarbe, de Algezira, de Gibraltar e de las yslas de Canaria,   5
conde e condesa de Barçelona e señores de Viscaya e de
Molina, duques de Athenas e de Neopatría, condes de Rosellón
e de Çerdania, marqueses de Oristán e de Goçiano: por
quanto vos, Christóval Colón, vades por nuestro mandado a
descobrir e ganar, con çiertas fustas nuestras e con nuestra   10
gente, çiertas yslas e tierra firme en la mar Oçéana, e se espera
que, con la ayuda de Dios, se descubrirán e ganarán algunas de

---

86. le G] les PVW. 88. otros GPW] otro V. 91. e GPW] o V (but cf. p. 262, 91). 95. ‹de Córdova› VW]
om. GP (homoeoteleuton). 96. del Algarbe GPV] de los Algarbes W. 97. señores GPV] e s. W. 99. Çer-
dania GVW] cerdenia P.   Sources: GHPVW, Pr 8 (por) - 11 (Oçéana). 2-8. de Aragón . . . Goçiano
GPVW] etc. H. 3. de Mallorcas GPV] om. W. 4-5. del Algarbe GPV] de los Algarbes W. 6. e (señores)
GPV] om. W. 10-11. nuestra gente GPPr] nuestras gentes HVW. 11. e (tierra) GHPPrW] en V. Oçéana
GHPVW] o. etc. Pr. se GHPV] su W.

las dichas yslas e tierra firme en la dicha mar Oçéana por vuestra
mano e industria; e asý es cosa justa e rasonable que, pues os
ponés al dicho peligro por nuestro serviçio, seades d'ello   15
remunerado; e quiriendos honrar e faser merçed por lo susodicho, es nuestra merçed e voluntad que vos el dicho Christóval Colón, después que ayades descubierto e ganado las dichas
yslas e tierra firme en la dicha mar Oçéana, o qualesquier d'ellas,
que seades nuestro almirante de las dichas yslas e tierra firme   20
que así descubrierdes e ganardes, e seades nuestro almirante e
visorrey e governador en ellas, e vos podades dende en adelante
llamar e yntitular "don Christóval Colón", e asý vuestros fijos
/11 verso/ e subçesores en el dicho ofiçio e cargo se puedan
yntitular e llamar "don" e "almirante" e "visorrey" e "gover-   25
nador" d'ellas; e para que podades usar e exerçer el dicho ofiçio
de almirantadgo con el dicho ofiçio de visorrey e governador
de las dichas yslas e tierra firme que así descubrierdes e ganardes
por vós o por vuestros lugartenientes, e oýr e librar todos los
pleitos e cabsas çeviles e criminales tocantes al dicho ofiçio de   30
almirantadgo e de visorrey e governador, segund fallardes por
derecho, e segund lo acostumbran usar e exerçer los almirantes
de nuestros reynos; e podades punir e castigar los delinqüentes,
e usedes de los dichos ofiçios de almirantadgo e visorrey e
governador, vos e vuestros dichos lugartenientes, en todo lo   35
que a los dichos ofiçios, e a cada uno d'ellos, es anexo e conçer-
niente; e que ayades e levedes los derechos e salarios a los dichos
ofiçios, e a cada uno d'ellos, anexos e conçernientes e perteneçientes, segund e como los lieva e acostumbra llevar el
nuestro almirante mayor en el almirantadgo de los nuestros   40
reynos. [2] E por esta nuestra carta, o por su treslado sygnado de
escrivano público, mandamos al prínçipe don Juan, nuestro
muy caro e muy amado fijo, e a los ynfantes, duques, perlados,
marqueses, condes, maestres de las órdenes, priores, comendadores, e a los del nuestro consejo e oydores de la nuestra   45
abdiençia, alcaldes e otras justiçias qualesquier de la nuestra casa
e corte e chançillería, e a los subcomendadores, alcaydes de los
castillos e casas fuertes e llanas, e a todos los conçejos e asys-

Que goçe los
derechos y salarios
que son anexos,
convenientes y
pertenecientes,
como los lleva y
acostumbra llevar el
Almirante Mayor y
el Almirantadgo de
los Reynos.
   Manda a todo
género de personas
que le conoçcan,
reconoçcan y
obedeçcan por tal,
y después d'él a sus
hijos y subcesor, y
de subcesor en
subcesor para
siempre jamás
[*l. m.*].

---

29. o*PVW*] e *GH*. 34. **e** (visorrey) *GPVW*] e de *H*. 35. **vos** *GHPV*] e v. *W*. **e** *GP*] e los *HVW*. **vuestros dichos** *GPV*] d. v. *HW* (*but cf.* p. 272, 64). 38. **e conçernientes** *GPVW*] *om. H*. **conçernientes** *GPW*] pertenesçientes/ *V*. 38–39. **perteneçientes** *GHPW*] e p. *over an erasure V*. **los**] los/ los *G*. **lieva**] lievan *GHPVW*. **acostumbra** *W* (*but* acostumbran levar *corr. in* acostumbrallevar)] acostumbran *GHPV*. 40. **los** *GHPV*] *om. W*. 44. **maestres**] *in H follows a crossed-out word* (Rricos?). 45. **la** *GHPV*] *om. W*.

tentes, corregidores e alcaldes e alguasyles, merinos, veynte e
quatros, cavalleros, jurados, escuderos, ofiçiales e omes buenos   50
de todas las çibdades e villas e lugares de los nuestros reynos e
señoríos, e de los que vos conquistardes e ganardes, e a los capitanes, maestres, contramaestres e ofiçiales, marineros e gentes
de la mar, nuestros súbditos e naturales, que agora son e serán
de aquí adelante, e a cada uno e qualquier d'ellos, que, syendo   55
por vós descubiertas e ganadas las dichas yslas e tierra firme en la
dicha mar Oçéana, e fecho por vós, o por quien vuestro poder
oviere, el juramento e solepnidad que en tal caso se requiere,
vos ayan e tengan dende en adelante para en toda vuestra vida,
e después de vós a vuestro fijo e subçesor, e de subçesor en   60
subçesor para syempre jamás, por nuestro almirante de la dicha
mar Oçéana, e por visorrey e governador de las dichas yslas e
tierra firme que vos el dicho don Christóval Colón descubrierdes e ganardes; e usen con vós, e con los dichos vuestros
lugartenientes que en los dichos ofiçios de almirantadgo e   65
visorrey e governador pusierdes, en todo lo a ellos conçer-
niente, e vos recudan e fagan recudir con la quitaçión /12
recto/ e derechos e otras cosas a los dichos ofiçios anexas e
pertenesçientes; e vos guarden e fagan guardar todas las honras
e graçias e merçedes e libertades, preheminençias, pre-   70
rrogativas, esençiones e ynmunydades, e todas las otras cosas, e
cada una d'ellas, que por razón de los dichos ofiçios de almirante e visorrey e governador devedes aver e gosar, e vos
deven ser guardadas, en todo bien e complidamente, en guisa
que vos non mengue ende cosa alguna; e que en ello, ni en   75
parte d'ello, embargo ni contrario alguno vos non pongan ni
consientan poner. [3] Ca nos, por esta nuestra carta, desde agora

Lo concedido es
por juro y derecho
hereditario para
siempre jamás
[l. m.].

para entonçes vos fasemos merçed de los dichos ofiçios de almirantadgo e visorrey e governador por juro de heredad para
syempre jamás, e vos damos la posesyón e casi posesyón d'ellos,   80
e de cada uno d'ellos, e poder e abtoridad para lo usar e exerçer,
e llevar los derechos e salarios a ellos, e a cada uno d'ellos,
anexos e pertenesçientes, segund e como dicho es. [4] Sobre lo
qual todo que dicho es, sy neçesario vos fuere, e gelos vos pi-

---

49. **e** (alcaldes) *GPVW*] *om. H.* **e** (alquasyles) *GPVW*] *om. H.* 50. **quatros** *GPVW*] quatro *H.* **jurados**
GHPV] *om. W.* 53. **e** (ofiçiales) *GPW*] *om. HV.* 54. **e** (serán) *GHPV*] o *W.* 57. **o** *PVW*] e *GH.* 60. **a**
GPW] *om. HV (but cf.* p. 274, 39). 71. **esençiones** *GPW*] e e. *HV.* **e** (ynmunydades) *GHPV*] *om. W.* 75.
mengue *HVW*] menguen *GP.* 81. **lo** *GHPV*] los *W.*

dierdes, mandamos al nuestro chançiller e notarios, e los otros   85
ofiçiales qu'están a la tabla de los nuestros sellos, que vos den e
libren e pasen e sellen nuestra carta de previlegio rodado, la más
fuerte e firme e bastante que les pidierdes e ovierdes menester:
e los unos nin los otros non fagades nin fagan ende ál por alguna
manera, so pena de la nuestra merçed e de diez mill maravedís   90
para la nuestra cámara a cada uno que lo contrario fiziere. [5] E
demás, mandamos al ome que vos esta nuestra carta mostrare,
que vos enplaze que parescades ante nós en la nuestra corte,
doquier que nos seamos, del día que vos emplasare a quinze días
primeros syguientes, so la dicha pena, so la qual mandamos a   95
qualquier escrivano público que para esto fuere llamado, que dé
ende al que gela mostrare testimonio sygnado con su sygno,
porque nos sepamos en cómo se cumple nuestro mandado.
[6] Dada en la nuestra çibdad de Granada a treynta días del mes
de abril, año del nasçimiento de nuestro señor Jhesu Christo de   100
mill e quatroçientos e noventa e dos años.

Yo el Rey
Yo la Reyna

[7] Yo Johan de Coloma, secretario del Rey e de la Reyna
nuestros señores, la fis escrivir por su mandado.   105
[8] Acordada en forma: Rodericus, doctor.
[9] Registrada: Sebastián d'Olano; Françisco de Madrid, chançiller.

III.ii.2 (5)

[1] E agora, porque plugo a Nuestro Señor que vos fallastes
muchas de las dichas yslas, e esperamos que con la ayuda Suya
que fallaréys e descobriréys otras yslas e tierra firme en el dicho
mar Oçéano a la dicha parte de las Indias, /12 verso/ nos suplicastes e pedistes por merçed que vos confirmásemos la dicha   5
nuestra carta que de suso va encorporada e la merçed en ella
contenida, para que vos e vuestros fijos e desçendientes e sub-

---

85. **e** (los) *GP*] e a *HVW*. 92. **vos**] les *GHPVW*. 93. **vos**] les *GHPVW*. **parescades** *GHP*] parescan *VW*.
94. **vos**] les *GHPVW*. 99. **la** *GHPV*] *om. W.* 100. **señor** *GHPV*] salvador *W*. 107. **Sebastián** *GHV*]
savastian *PW*.   Sources: *GHPVW*, *Pr* 31 (*E*) - 55 (*porque*). 2. **que** (con) *GHV*] *om. PW.* 3. **e** (tierra) *PW*]
en *GHV*.

Confirma con todas
las facultades,
preheminencias y
prerrogativas que
han sido y son de
los Almirantes,
Visoreyes y
Governadores de
los Reynos de
Castilla y de León
[*l. m.*].

çesores, uno en pos de otro, y después de vuestros días, podades
tener y tengades los dichos ofiçios de almirante e visorrey e
governador del dicho mar Oçéano e yslas e tierra firme que asý   10
avéys descubierto e fallado e descubrierdes e fallardes de aquí
adelante, con todas aquellas facultades e preheminençias e prerrogativas de que han gozado e gozan los nuestros almirantes e
visorreyes e governadores, que han seýdo e son, de los dichos
nuestros reynos de Castilla y de León; e vos sea acudido con   15
todos los derechos e salarios a los dichos ofiçios anexos e perteneçientes, usados e guardados a los dichos nuestros almirantes,
visorreyes e governadores, o vos mandemos proveer sobr'ello
como la nuestra merçed fuese. [2] E nos, acatando el arrisco e
peligro en que por nuestro serviçio vos posistes en yr a catar e   20
descobrir las dichas yslas, e en el que agora vos pornéys en yr a
buscar e descobrir las otras yslas e tierra firme, de que avemos
seýdo e esperamos ser de vós muy servidos, e por vos faser bien
e merçed, por la presente vos confirmamos a vós e a los dichos
vuestros fijos e desçendientes e subçesores, uno en pos de otro,   25
para agora e para syempre jamás, los dichos ofiçios de almirante
del dicho mar Oçéano e de visorrey e governador de las dichas
yslas e tierra firme que avéys fallado e descubierto, e de las otras
yslas e tierra firme que por vós o por vuestra yndustria se fallaren e descubrieren de aquí adelante en la dicha parte de las   30
Yndias. [3] E es nuestra merçed e voluntad que ayades e tengades vos e, después de vuestros días, vuestros fijos e deçendientes e subçesores, uno en pos de otro, el dicho ofiçio de
nuestro almirante del dicho mar Oçéano, qu'es nuestro, que
comiença por una raya, o liña, que nos avemos fecho marcar,   35
que pasa desde las yslas de los Açores a las yslas de Cabo Verde,
de setentrión en abstro, de polo a polo, por manera que todo lo
que es allende de la dicha liña al oçidente es nuestro e nos perteneçe; e ansí vos fazemos e criamos nuestro almirante, e a
vuestros fijos e subçesores, uno en pos de otro, de todo ello para   40
siempre jamás, e asimismo vos fazemos nuestro visorrey e
governador, e, después de vuestros días, a vuestros fijos e
deçendientes e subçesores, uno en pos de otro, de las dichas

8. **y** *GHPV*] *om. W.* 17. **e guardados**] *repeated in G.* 20. **catar** *GHPV*] buscar *W.* 21. **pornéys** *GHPV*]
poneys *W.* 27. **de** (visorrey) *GHPV*] *om. W.* 29. **o** *GHPV*] e *W.* 35. **o** *GHP*] e *PrVW.* 37. **setentrión**
GHPPrV] sententrion *G.* **de** *GHPPrV*] y de *W.* 40. **de** *GHPVW*] *om. Pr.* 43. **deçendientes e subçesores**
GHPVW] s. e d. *Pr.*

yslas e tierra firme, /13 recto/ descubiertas e por descobrir, en
el dicho mar Oçéano a la parte de las Yndias, como dicho es; e   45
vos damos la posesyón e casi posesión de todos los dichos ofiçios de almirante e visorey e governador para syenpre jamás, e
poder e facultad para qu'e‹n› las dichas mares podades usar e
usedes del dicho ofiçio de nuestro almirante en todas las cosas,
e en la forma e manera, e con las perrogativas e preheminençias   50
e derechos e salarios segund e como lo usaron e usan, gozaron e
gozan los nuestros almirantes de las mares de Castilla e de León.
[4] E para en la tierra de las dichas yslas e tierra firme que son
descubiertas e se descubrieren de aquí adelante en la dicha mar
Oçéana en la dicha parte de las Yndias, porque los pobladores   55
de todo ello sean mejor governados, vos damos tal poder e
facultad para que podades, como nuestro visorrey e governador, usar por vós e por vuestros logartenientes e alcaldes e alguaziles e otros ofiçiales que para ello pusierdes, la jurisdiçión
çevil e criminal, alta e baxa, mero mixto ymperio; los quales   60
dichos ofiçios podades amover e quitar, e poner otros en su
lugar, cada e quando quisierdes e vierdes que cunple a nuestro
serviçio; los quales puedan oýr e librar e determinar todos los
pleitos e cabsas çeviles e criminales que en las dichas yslas e
tierra firme acaesçieren e se movieren, e aver e llevar los dere- 65
chos e salarios acostumbrados en nuestros reynos de Castilla e
de León a los dichos ofiçios anexos y perteneçientes; e vos, el
dicho nuestro visorrey e governador, podades oýr e conoçer de
todas las dichas causas, e de cada una d'ellas, cada que vos quisierdes, de primera ynstançia, por vía de apellaçión o por simple 70
querella, e las ver e determinar e librar como nuestro visorrey e
governador; e podades fazer e fagades, vos e los dichos vuestros
ofiçiales, qualesquier pesquisas a los casos de derecho premisos,
e todas las otras cosas a los dichos ofiçios de visorrey e governador perteneçientes e que vos e vuestros lugarestenientes e ofi-   75
çiales que para ello pusierdes entendierdes que cumple a nuestro serviçio e a exsecuçión de nuestra justiçia. [5] Lo qual todo
podades e puedan hazer e exsecu‹t›ar e llevar a devida exsecu-

44. **tierra firme** *GHPVW*] tierras firmes *Pr.* 45. **a** *GHPVW*] en *Pr.* 48. **qu'e‹n›** *PrW*] que *GHPV.* 49.
usedes *GHPPrV*] excerçer e u. *W.* 50. **en la** *GHPVW*] *om. Pr.* **perrogativas e preheminençias**
GHPVW] preheminençias e p. *Pr.* 52. **las** *GHPPrV*] los *W.* 53. **tierra** *GHPPrV*] dicha t. *W.* **dichas**
GHPPrV] *om. W.* 54. (adelante) **en** *GHPVW*] a *Pr.* **dicha** *GHPVW*] *om. Pr.* 61. **ofiçios** *GHPV*] ofiçiales
(*over* ofiçios *?*) *W.* 65. **llevar**] llevar [e] *H.* 66. **en** *GHPV*] de *W.* 70. **por** (vía) *GHPV*] e p. *W.* 73.
premisos] premisas *GHPVW.* 76. **entendierdes** *V*] e e.*GHPW.* 77. **a** *GHPV*] *om. W.* 78-79. **hazer
. . . podrían** *GHPV*] *om. W* (*homoeoteleuton*). 78. **exsecu‹t›ar** *HPVW*] exsecuar *G.*

çión con efetto, bien asý como lo faría‹n› e podrían fazer si por
nós mismos fuesen los dichos ofiçiales puestos; pero es nuestra   80
merçed e voluntad que las cartas e provisiones que dierdes, sean
e se espidan e libren en nuestro nombre, diziendo: "Don Fernando e doña Ysabel, por la graçia de Dios rey e reyna de Castilla, de León, etc.", e sean selladas con nuestro sello, que nos
vos mandamos dar, para las dichas yslas y tierra firme. /13   85
verso/ [6] E mandamos a todos los vesynos e moradores e a
otras personas que están e estovieren en las dichas yslas e tierra
firme, que vos obedescan como a nuestro visorrey e governador d'ellas; e a los que andovieren en las dichas mares suso declaradas, vos obedezcan como a nuestro almirante del dicho   90
mar Oçéano; e todos ellos cumplan vuestras cartas e mandamientos, e se junten con vós e con vuestros ofiçiales para
exsecutar la nuestra justiçia, e vos den e fagan dar todo el favor
e ayuda que les pidierdes e menester ovierdes, so las penas que
les pusierdes; las quales nos por la presente les ponemos e   95
avemos por puestas, e vos damos poder para las executar en sus
personas e bienes. [7] E otrosý es nuestra merçed e voluntad
que si vos entendierdes ser complidero a nuestro serviçio e a
exsecuçión de nuestra justiçia, que qualesquier personas que
están e estovieren en las dichas Yndias e tierra firme, salgan   100

Que pueda empedir
la entrada y estar en
las Yslas y Tierra
firme a quien le
pareciere sin
apellación y
consulta en
contrario [l. m.].

d'ellas e que non entren nin estén en ellas, e que vengan e se
presenten ante nós, que lo podáys mandar de nuestra parte e los
fagáys salir d'ellas; a los quales nos por la presente mandamos
que luego lo fagan e cumplan e pongan en obra, syn nos requerir nin consultar en ello, nin esperar ni aver otra nuestra carta   105
nin mandamiento, non enbargante qualquier apellaçión o su-
plicaçión que del tal vuestro mandamiento fizieren e
ynterpusieren. [8] Para lo qual todo que dicho es, e para las otras
cosas devidas e perteneçientes a los dichos ofiçios de nuestro
almirante e visorrey e governador, vos damos todo poder con-   110
plido, con todas sus ynçidençias e dependençias e mergençias,
anexidades e conexidades; sobre lo qual todo que dicho es, sy
quisierdes, mandamos al nuestro chançiller, e notarios, e a los
otros ofiçiales que están en la tabla de los nuestros sellos, que
vos den e libren e pasen e sellen nuestra carta de previlegio   115

---

79. **faría‹n›**] faria *GHPV*. **podrían** *GP*] podria *HV*. **si** *GHPV*] como sy *W*. 80. **mismos** *GHV*] *om. PW*.
90. **vos** *GHPV*] que v. *W*. 100. **Yndias** *GPW*] yslas *HV*. **tierra firme** *PW*] tierras firmes *GHV*. 102. **que**
GHVW] se *P*. 104. **luego** *GHPV*] *om. W*. 110. **e** (visorrey) *GHPV*] *om. W*. 114. **en** *GPV*] a *HW*.

rodado, la más fuerte e firme e bastante que les pidierdes e menester ovierdes; e los unos nin los otros non fagades nin fagan
ende ál por alguna manera, so pena de la nuestra merçed e de
dies mill maravedís para la nuestra cámara a cada uno que lo
contrario fiziere. [9] E demás, mandamos al ome que vos esta   120
nuestra carta mostrare, que vos enplase que parescades ante nós
en la nuestra corte, doquier que nos seamos, del día que vos
enplasare fasta quinse días primeros syguientes, so la dicha pena,
so la qual mandamos a qualquier escrivano público que para
esto fuere llamado, que dé ende al que gela mostrare testimonio   125
sygnado con su sygno, porque nos sepamos en cómo se cunple
nuestro mandado.

[10] Dada en la çibdad de Barçelona a veynte e ocho días del
mes de mayo, año del nasçimiento de nuestro señor Jhesu
Christo de mill e quatroçientos e noventa e tres años.   130

Yo el Rey

Yo la Reyna

[11] Yo Fernand Álvares de Toledo, secretario del Rey e de la
Reyna nuestros señores, la fis escrivir por su mandado.

[12] Pero Gutierres, chançiller.   135

[13] Derechos del sello e registro: nichil.

[14] En las espaldas: "Acordada, Rodericus doctor. Registrada:
Alonso Peres".

III.iii (51)

[1] E agora, por quanto vos el dicho don Christóval Colón,
nuestro almirante del mar Oçéano e nuestro visorrey e governador de la tierra firme e yslas, nos suplicastes e pe-/14 recto/
distes por merçed que, porque mejor e más complidamente vos
fuese guardada la dicha carta de merçed a vós e a vuestros fijos   5
e desçendientes, que vos la confirmásemos e aprovásemos, e vos
mandásemos dar nuestra carta de previlegio d'ella o como la
nuestra merçed fuese, e nos, acatando lo susodicho e los mu-

---

116. **rodado** GHPV] rodada W. **fuerte e** GHPW] firme V. 118. **de la** . . . **e** GHPV] om. W (homoeoteleuton). 121. **vos** W] los GHPV (Raccolta: qu'él os). 129. **señor** GHPV] salvador W. 136. **Derechos** GHPW]
derecho V. **registro** GHPV] de r. W. 137. **En** GHPV] y en W.   Sources: GHPVW.

chos e buenos e leales e grandes e continuos serviçios que vos el
dicho don Christóval Colón, nuestro almirante e visorrey e   10
governador de las Yndias e tierra firme descubiertas e por descobrir en el mar Oçéano en la parte de las Yndias, nos avedes
fecho e esperamos que nos faréys, espeçialmente en descobrir e
traer a nuestro poder e so nuestro señorío las dichas yslas y tierra
firme - mayormente porque esperamos que, con ayuda de Dios   15
nuestro señor, redundará en mucho serviçio Suyo e honra
nuestra e pro e utilidad de nuestros reynos, porque esperamos
que los pobladores Yndios de las dichas Yndias se convertirán a
nuestra santa fe cathólica -, tovímoslo por bien; e por esta dicha
nuestra carta de previlegio, o por el dicho su traslado sygnado,   20
como dicho es, de nuestro propio motuo e çierta sçiençia e
poderío real absoluto, de que en esta parte queremos usar e
usamos, confirmamos e aprovamos para agora e para siempre
jamás a vós el dicho don Christóval Colón e a los dichos vuestros fijos e nietos e desçendientes de vós e de vuestros herederos   25
la sobredicha nuestra carta suso encorporada e la merçed en ella
contenida, e queremos e mandamos e es nuestra merçed e
voluntad que vos vala e sea guardada a vós e a los dichos vuestros fijos e desçendientes agora e de aquí adelante ynviolablemente, para agora e para syenpre jamás, en todo e por todo,   30
bien e complidamente, segund e por la forma e manera que en
ella se contiene. [2] Y sy neçesario es, agora de nuevo vos fazemos la dicha merçed e defendemos firmemente que ninguna ni
algunas personas non sean osadas de vos yr ni venir contra ella,
ni contra parte d'ella, por vos la quebrantar nin menguar en   35
tiempo alguno nin por alguna manera; sobre lo qual mandamos
al prínçipe don Juan, nuestro muy caro e muy amado fijo, e a
los ynfantes, duques, perlados, marqueses, condes, ricos omes,
maestres de las órdenes, priores, comendadores ‹e subcomendadores›, e a los del nuestro consejo, oydores de la nuestra ab-   40
diençia, alcaldes, alguaziles e otras justiçias qualesquier de la
nuestra casa e corte e chançillería, e alcaydes de los castillos e
casas fuertes e llanas, e a todos los conçejos e asystentes, corregidores, alcaldes, alguasyles, merinos, prebostes, e otras jus-

10. **e** (visorrey) *GHPV*] *om. W.* 14. **señorío** *GHPW*] serui(çi)o *V.* 17. **e utilidad** *GHPV*] *om. W.* 25. **de**
(vuestros) *GPW*] de los *HV.* 33. **que** *GPVW*] *om. H* (firmemente/). 34. **osadas** *GHPV*] osados *W.* 35.
nin *GPVW*] o *H.* 39-40. ‹**e subcomendadores**› *HV*] *om. GPW.* 43. **e** (asystentes) *GHPV*] *om. W.* 44.
alcaldes *GHPV*] e a. *W.* **alguasyles** *GHPV*] e a. *W.* **merinos** *GHPV*] *om. W.*

tiçias de todas las çibdades e villas e logares de los nuestros 45
reynos e señoríos, e a cada uno d'ellos, que vos guarden e fagan
guardar esta dicha nuestra carta de previlegio e confirmaçión, e
la carta de merçed en ella contenida, e contra el thenor e forma
d'ella non vos vayan nin pasen, nin consientan yr nin pasar, en
tiempo alguno ni por alguna manera, so las penas en ellas con- 50
tenidas. [3] De lo qual vos mandamos dar esta dicha nuestra
carta de previlegio e confirmaçión, escripta en pargamino de
cuero e firmada de nuestros nonbres e sellada con nuestro sello
de plomo pendiente en filos de seda a co-/14 verso/ lores; la
qual mandamos al nuestro chançiller mayor e notario e a los 55
otros ofiçiales que están a la tabla de los nuestros sellos, que
sellen e libren e pasen; e los unos ni los otros non fagades nin
fagan ende ál por alguna manera, so pena de la nuestra merçed
e de dies mill maravedís para la nuestra cámara a cada uno que
lo contrario fiziere. [4] E demás, mandamos al ome que vos esta 60
nuestra carta mostrare, que vos enplase que parescades ante nós
en la nuestra corte, doquier que nos seamos, del día que vos
emplasare fasta quinse días primeros syguientes, so la dicha
pena, so la qual mandamos a qualquier escrivano público que
para esto fuere llamado, que dé ende al que gela mostrare testi- 65
monio sygnado con su sygno, porque nos sepamos en cómo se
cunple nuestro mandado.
[5] Dada en la çibdad de Burgos a veynte e tres días del mes de
abril, año del nasçimiento de nuestro salvador Jhesu Christo de
mill e quatroçientos e noventa e syete años. 70
Yo el Rey
Yo la Reyna
[6] Yo Fernand Álvares de Toledo, secretario del Rey e de la
Reyna nuestros señores, la fis escrevir por su mandado.
[7] Rodericus, doctor; Antonius, doctor; Fernand Álvares; 75
Johan Velasques; Antonius, dottor. Conçertado.
[8] Y en las espaldas del dicho previlegio desýa: "Registrada:
Doctor".

---

51. **nuestra** GHPV] om. W. 55. **nuestro** GHPV] dicho n. W.

El Rey e la Reyna

[1] Por quanto en la capitulaçión e asyento que por nuestro
mandado se hizo e tomó con vós don Christóval Colón, nuestro almirante del mar Oçéano en la parte de las Yndias, se contiene que vos ayáys de aver çierta parte de lo que se oviere e
truxiere de las dichas Yndias, sacando primeramente las costas e   5
gastos que en ello se ovieren fecho e fizieren, como más largamente en la dicha capitulaçión se contiene; e porque fasta
agora vos avéys trabajado mucho en descobrir tierra en la dicha
parte de las Yndias, de cuya cabsa non se ha avido mucho ynterese d'ellas, aunque se han fecho algunas costas y gastos, y   10
porque nuestra merçed y voluntad es de vos fazer merçed, por
la presente queremos y mandamos que las costas y gastos que
fasta aquí se han fecho en los negoçios tocantes a las dichas
Yndias, e se fizieren en este viaje que agora /15 recto/ mandamos fazer e armar para las dichas Yndias, fasta que sean llega-   15
dos a la ysla Ysabella Española, que non se os demande cosa
alguna d'ella‹s›, ni vos seáys obligado a contribuyr en ellas cosa
alguna demás de lo que posistes al tiempo del primer viaje; con
tanto que vos non pidáys ni llevéys cosa alguna de lo que fasta
aquí se ha traýdo de las dichas yslas, por razón del diezmo, nin   20
del ochavo, que vos el dicho almirante avéys de aver de las cosas
muebles de las dichas yslas, nin por otra rasón alguna, de lo que
avéys avido fasta aquí vos fasemos merçed. [2] E porque vos el
dicho almirante desýs que de lo que aquí adelante se oviere de
las dichas yslas se ha de sacar primeramente el ochavo, y de lo   25
que restare se han de sacar las costas e despúes el diesmo; e
porque, por la orden e thenor de la dicha capitulaçión, pareçe
que se deven sacar primero las costas e despúes el diezmo, e

Sources: GPPrVW. 5. **truxiere** GPV] traxiere PrW. 5-6. **las costas e gastos** GPVW] los g. e c. Pr.
6. **ovieren** GPVW] oviere Pr. **e** GPVW] o Pr. 10. **costas** GPVW] cosas Pr. 11-18. **en . . . alguna** GPVW]
cosa alguna en ellas Pr. 12. **costas** GPVW] cosas Pr. 13-15. **las . . . para** GPPrW] om. W (homoeoteleuton).
17. **ella‹s›** W] ella GPPrV. 23. **aquí** GPVW] q(ue) Pr. 24. **aquí . . . oviere** GPPrV] se oviere d'aqui
adelante W. 26. **restare** PPrVW] resultare G. 28. **deven** GPW] deve PrV. **sacar primero** GPPrV]
p. s. W.

Que por tres años
se saque primero el
ochavo para el
Almirante sin costa
alguna, y después se
saquen las costas, y
de lo que resultare
se saque el diezmo
para el Almirante
[r. m.].

después el ochavo, e non está por agora averiguado cómo esto
se ha de hazer, es nuestra merçed, por hazer merçed a vós el   30
dicho almirante, que por tres años se saque primero el ochavo
para vós syn costa alguna, e después se saquen las costas, y de lo
que restare se saque el diezmo para vós el dicho almirante; pero,
pasado el dicho tiempo, que se aya de sacar el dicho diezmo e
las costas e ochavo, segund en la dicha capitulaçión se contiene;   35
e que por esta merçed que vos fazemos por el dicho tiempo,
non se os dé nin quite más derecho del que tenéys por virtud de
la dicha capitulaçión; antes, aquella quede en su fuerça e vigor
para adelante, pasado el dicho tiempo.
[3] Fecha en la villa de Medina del Campo a dose días de junio   40
de noventa e syete años.

Yo el Rey
Yo la Reyna

[4] Por mandado del Rey e de la Reyna. Fernand Álvares.
[5] E en las espaldas d'esta carta dezía: "Acordada".   45

V (33)

[1] Don Fernando e doña Ysabel, por la graçia de Dios rey e
reyna de Castilla, de León, de Aragón, de Seçilia, de Granada,
de Toledo, de Valençia, de Galizia, de Mallorcas, de Sevilla, de
Çerdeña, de Córdova, de Córçega, de Murçia, de Jahén, de los
Algarbes, de Algezira, de Gibraltar e de las yslas de Canaria,   5
conde e condesa de Barçelona, señores de Viscaya e de Molina,
duques de Athenas e de Neopatría, condes de Rosellón e de
Çerdania, marqueses de Oristán e de Goçiano: por quanto al
tiempo que don Christóval Colón, nuestro almirante de la mar
Oçéano, fue a descobrir las yslas y tierra firme que, por graçia   10
de Dios nuestro señor, él halló e se le descubrieron en el dicho
mar Oçéano a la parte /15 verso/ de las Yndias, se asentó con
él que oviese e llevase para sý çierta parte de aquello que se
hallase, e agora por su parte nos es suplicado que, porque mejor
e más complidamente lo suso dicho se guardase e cunpliese, que   15

31. **primero** GPVW] primeros Pr. 32. **costa** GPVW] cosa Pr. 33. **restare** PPrVW] resultare G. **el** (dicho)
PPrVW] al G? 45. **dezía** GPVW] om. Pr.   Sources: GPVW.

Que el Almirante
pueda nombrar una
persona, o personas,
que entiendan en la
negoçiaçión de las
Yndias juntamente
con las personas
que están puestas
por Sus Altezas
[*l. m.*].

a Nuestra Merçed pluguiese mandar que toda la negoçiaçión e
cosas que se oviesen de fazer e proveer en estos nuestros reynos
tocantes a la dicha negoçiaçión de las dichas Yndias, que se
oviesen de fazer e fiziesen por una persona o personas nuestras,
con poder nuestro, que en ello entendiesen, e por él, o por   20
quien su poder oviese, juntamente, porque asý se podría
mejor saber lo que resultará de los gastos e pro e utilidad de la
dicha negoçiaçión, para que se le pudiese a él acudir con aquella
parte que por los dichos asientos le perteneçe e de que nos le
fezimos merçed, o sobre ello proveyésemos como la nuestra   25
merçed fuese; e nos tovímoslo por bien, e por esta nuestra carta
mandamos a las personas que por nuestro mandado tienen o
tovieren cargo de entender en lo susodicho, de aquí adelante
que lo fagan e negoçien juntamente con la persona o personas
qu'el dicho almirante, o quien su poder oviere, pusiere o nom-   30
brare para ello, e non en otra manera. [2] Lo qual se entienda,
teniendo el dicho almirante de las Yndias diputadas e nonbradas
persona o personas que por su parte, o con su poder, en ello
entiendan, e seyéndonos fecho saber cómo las tales personas
están diputadas e nombradas por el dicho almirante, para en-   35
tender por su parte en la dicha negoçiaçión; de lo qual vos
mandamos dar la presente firmada de nuestros nonbres e sellada
con nuestro sello.
[3] Dada en la villa de Medina del Canpo a treynta días del mes
de mayo, año del nasçimiento de nuestro señor Jhesu Christo   40
de mill e quatroçientos e noventa e syete años.

Yo el Rey

Yo la Reyna

[4] Yo Fernand Álvares de Toledo, secretario del Rey e de la
Reyna nuestros señores, la fis escrevir por su mandado.   45
[5] E en las espaldas d'esta dicha carta desýa: "En la forma, acordada: Rodericus, doctor. Registrada: Alonso Peres; Françisco
Dias, chançiller".

17-18. que se . . . Yndias] *repeated in G.* 20. poder nuestro *GPV*] n. p. *W.* 21. podría *GPW*] podia *V.*
22. resultará] resultaua *GPVW.* gastos *GPV*] dichos g. *W.* 33. o (personas) *VW*] e *GP.* 36. por su parte
GPV] con su poder *W.* 40. señor *GPV*] salvador *W.* 46. espaldas *GPVW*] e. del original *V.* dicha *GPW*]
om. V.

El Rey e la Reyna

[1] Don Christóval Colón, nuestro almirante, visorrey e governador del mar Océano: las cosas que nos pareçen que, con
ayuda de Dios nuestro señor, se deven e han de hazer e complir
para la poblaçión de las Yndias e tierra firme descubiertas e
puestas so nuestro señorío /16 recto/ e de las que están por   5
descobrir a la parte de las Yndias en el mar Oçéano, e de la
gente que por nuestro mandado allá está e ha de yr e estar de
aquí adelante, demás e allende de lo que, por otra ynstruçión
nuestra, vos y el obispo de Badajós avéys de proveer, es lo siguiente: 10

[2] Primeramente, que como seáys en las dichas Yndias, Dios
quiriendo, procuréys con toda deligençia de animar e traer a los
naturales de las dichas Yndias a toda paz e quietud; e que nos
ayan de servir e estar so nuestro señorío e subjeçión be-
gninamente; e principalmente, que se conviertan a nuestra   15
sancta fee cathólica, y que a ellos e a los que han de yr a estar en
las dichas Yndias, sean administrados los sanctos sacramentos
por los religiosos e clérigos que allá están e fueren, por manera
que Dios nuestro señor sea servido y sus conçiençias se seguren.
[3] Yten, que por esta ves, en tanto que nos mandamos más   20
proveer, ayan de yr e vayan con vós el número de las trezientas
e treynta personas, quales vos eligierdes de la calidad e ofiçios, e
segund se contiene en la dicha ynstruçión; pero, sy a vós pareçiere que algunos de aquéllos se deven mudar, acreçentando o
amenguando de unos ofiçios en otros e de la calidad de unas   25
personas en otras, que vos, o quien vuestro poder oviere, lo
podáys fazer e fagáys, segund e en la manera e forma, e en el
tiempo, o tiempos, que vierdes e entendierdes que cumple a
nuestro serviçio e al bien e utilidad de la dicha governaçión de
las dichas Yndias.   30

Sources: *GPVW*. 4. **Yndias** *GPV*] yslas *W*. 8. **ynstruçión** *W*] ynstituçion *GPV*. 12. **procuréys** *GPV*]
proveays *W*. **traer** *GPW*] atraer *V*. 18. **están e fueren** *GPV*] f. y e. *W*. 21. **vayan** *GPV*] vaya *W*. 22. **e**
GPV] *om*. *W*. 23. **ynstruçión** *W*] ynstituçion *GPV*. 24. **o** *GPV*] e *W*. 29. **dicha** *GPV*] *om*. *W*.

[4] Yten, que quando seáys en las dichas Yndias, Dios quiriendo, que ayáys de mandar hazer, y que se haga, en la ysla
Española una otra poblaçión o fortaleza, allende de la que está
fecha, de la otra parte de la ysla çercana al minero del oro,
segund, en el logar e de la forma que a vós bien visto fuere.   35

[5] Yten, que cerca de la dicha poblaçión, o de la que agora está
fecha, o en otra parte qual a vós os paresca dispuesto, se aya de
hazer e asentar alguna labrança e criança, para que mejor e a
menos costa se puedan sostener las personas que están, o estarán, en la dicha ysla; e que, porque esto se pueda mejor hazer, se   40
aya de dar e dé a los labradores que agora yrán a las dichas
Yndias, del pan que allá se enbiare, fasta çincüenta cahizes de
trigo e çevada prestados para lo sembrar, e fasta veynte yuntas
de vacas e yeguas o otras bestias para labrar; e que los tales labradores que así reçibieren el dicho pan, lo labren e syembren,   45
e se ayan de obligar de lo bolver a la cosecha e pagar el diezmo
de lo que cogieren; e lo restante, que lo puedan vender a los
christianos a como mejor pudieren, tanto que los preçios non
exçedan en agravio de los que lo compraren, porque en tal caso
vos el dicho nuestro almirante, o quien vuestro poder oviere, lo   50
avéys de tasar e moderar./16 verso/

[6] Yten, qu'el dicho número de las dichas trezientas e treynta
personas que han de yr a las dichas Yndias, se les aya de pagar e
pague el sueldo de los preçios, segund que fasta aquí se les ha
pagado; e en logar de mantenimiento que se les suele dar, se les   55
aya de dar y dé del pan que mandamos allá enbiar, a cada persona, una fanega de trigo cada mes e doze maravedís cada día,
para que ellos conpren los otros mantenimientos neçesarios, los
quales se les aya de librar por vós el dicho nuestro almirante e
por vuestro logarteniente e por los ofiçiales de nuestros con-   60
tadores mayores que en las dichas Yndias están e estovieren; e
que por vuestras nóminas, libramientos e çédulas en la forma
susodicha les aya de pagar e pague nuestro thesorero que estoviere en las dichas Yndias.

[7] Yten, que sy vos el dicho almirante vierdes e entendierdes   65

---

33. **una** *GPV*] *om. W.* **o** *GPV*] e *W.* 34. **la** (ysla)] las *W.* 35. **en** *GPV*] e/ en *W.* **e . . . forma** *GPV*] *om.*
W. 37. **os** *GPV*] *om. W.* 38. **e criança** *GPV*] *om. W.* 39-40. **o estarán** *GPV*] *om. W.* 40. **porque** *GPV*]
por *W.* **se** (aya) *V*] e se *GPW.* 43. **prestados** *GPV*] prestado *W.* **lo** *GPV*] los *W.* 44. **yeguas** *GPV*] de y.
W. **o** *GPV*] e *W.* **para** *GPV*] pa/ *W.* 50. **nuestro** *GPV*] *om. W.* 54. **ha** *GPV*] han *W.* 55. **de** *GPV*] del
W. 59. **aya** *GPV*] ayan *W.* 60. **por** (vuestro) *GPV*] *om. W.* 62. **que** *W*] por que *GPV.* 63. **aya** *W*] ayan
GPV. 65. **dicho** *GPV*] d. nuestro *W.* **vierdes e** *GPV*] *om. W.*

que cumple a nuestro serviçio que, allende de las dichas trezientas e treynta personas, se deve creçer el número d'ellas, lo podáys fazer, fasta llegar a número de quinientas personas por
todas; con tanto que el sueldo e mantenimiento que las tales
personas acreçentadas ovieren de aver, se pague de qualesquier   70
mercaderías e cosas de valor que se hallaren e ovieren en las
dichas Yndias, syn que nos mandemos proveer para ello de otra
parte.

[8] Yten, que a las personas que han estado y están en las dichas
Yndias, se les aya de pagar e pague el sueldo que les es e fuere   75
devido por nóminas, e segund e en la manera que de suso se
contiene; e algunos que non llevaron sueldo, se les pague su
serviçio segund que a vós bien visto fuere, e a los que han servido por otros ansymismo.

[9] Yten, que a los alcaydes e otras personas prinçipales e ofi-   80
çiales que allá han estado e servido e syrven, se les aya de acreçentar e pagar, y acreçienten y paguen, sus tenençias e salarios e
sueldos que ovieren de aver, segund que a vós el dicho nuestro
almirante paresçiere que se deve faser, avida consyderaçión a la
calidad de las personas y a lo que cada uno ha servido e syrviere,   85
porque demás d'esto, quando a Dios plega que aya de que ha-
serles merçedes en las dichas Yndias, nos avremos memoria para
se las faser; lo qual se aya de asentar ante los dichos nuestros
ofiçiales, e que se les aya de librar e pagar en la forma susodicha.

[10] Yten, paresçiendo herederos del abad Gallego e Andrés de   90
Salamanca que murieron en las dichas Yndias, se les deve pagar
el valor de los toneles e pipas que se les gastaron e tomaron, por
aver ydo a las dichas Yndias contra nuestro defendimiento.

[11] Yten, en lo que toca al descargo de las ánimas de los que en
las dichas Yndias han fallesçido e falleçieren, nos pareçe que se   95
deve /17 recto/ guardar la forma que está en el capítulo de
vuestro memorial que sobre esto nos distes, que es el siguiente:

[12] "Muchos estrangeros y naturales son muertos en las
Yndias, e yo mandé, por virtud de los poderes que de Vuestras
Altesas tengo, que diesen los testamentos e se cunpliesen; e d'el-   100
los di cargo a Escobar, vezino de Sevilla, e a Juan de León,

71. **ovieren** *GV*] oviere *PW*. 80-81. **e ofiçiales** *GPV*] *om. W.* 81. **e** (servido) *GPW*] o *V.* **aya** *GPV*] ayan
W. 82. **acreçienten** *GPW*] acreçient(e) *V.* **paguen** *GPW*] pague *V.* 89. **aya** *W*] ayan *GPV.* 97. **que** (es)
GPV] e *W.* 99. **e** *GPV*] *om. W.* **mandé** *GPV*] mando *W.* 99-100. **Vuestras Altesas** *GPW*] Vuestra Alteza
V. 100-101. **ellos** *GPV*] ello *W (in the text?).*

vezyno de la Ysabela, que bien e fielmente procurasen todo
esto, asý en pagar lo que devían, sy sus albaçeas no lo oviesen
pagado, como en recabdar todos sus bienes e sueldo; e que esto
todo pasase por ante justiçia e escrivano público, y que todo lo   105
que recabdasen fuese puesto en una arca que toviese tres llaves,
e que ellos toviesen la una llave e un religioso otra e yo otra; e
que estos dichos sus dineros fuesen puestos en la dicha arca, e
estoviesen allá fasta tres años, porque entretanto oviesen logar
sus herederos de lo venir o enbiar requerir; y sy en este tiempo   110
non requiriesen, que se destribuyese en cosas por sus ánimas."
[13] Asymismo, nos paresçe qu'el oro que oviere en las dichas
Yndias, se acuñe e faga d'ello moneda de exçelentes de la
Granada, segund nos avemos ordenado que se haga en estos
nuestros reynos, porque en esto se evitará de haser fraudes e   115
cautelas del dicho oro en las dichas Yndias. [14] E para labrar la
dicha moneda, mandamos que llevéys las personas e cuños e
aparejos que ovierdes menester, ca para ello vos damos poder
complido, con tanto que la moneda que se hiziere en las dichas
Yndias, sea conforme a las ordenanças que nos agora mandamos   120
fazer sobre la lavor de la moneda, e los ofiçiales que la ovieren
de labrar guarden las dichas ordenanças, so las penas en ellas
contenidas.
[15] Yten, nos pareçe que los Yndios con quien está conçertado
que ayan de pagar el tributo ordenado, se les aya de poner una   125
pieça e señal de moneda de latón o de plomo que trayga‹n› al
pescueço; y esta tal moneda se le mude la figura o señal que
toviere, cada vez que pagare, porque se sepa el que no viniere a
pagar, e que cada e quando se hallaren por la ysla personas que
‹non› truxieren la dicha señal al pescueço, que sean presos e se   130
les dé alguna pena liviana.
[16] Yten, porque en el coger e recabdança del dicho tributo
será menester proveer de persona deligente e fiable que en ello
entienda, e es nuestra merçed e mandamos que ★★★ tenga el
dicho cargo e que del tributo e mercadurías que asý recabdare e   135
cogiere e fisiere e pagare, aya e lleve para sí çinco pesos o medi-

103. **asý** GPV] e a. W. 107. **la** GPV] om. W. 110. **o** GPV] e W. **requerir** GPV] a r. W. 114. **haga** GPV]
hagan W. 115. **evitará** GV] evitaran P, evitan W. 121. **la** (ovieren) PW] lo GV. 126. **e** GPV] o W.
trayga‹n› W] trayga GPV. 129. **cada** W] queda GPV. **hallaren** GVW] fallare P. **personas**] repeated in W.
130. **‹non›** W] om. GPV. 132. **porque** GPV] que porque W. 134. ★★★] blank space in GPVW. 135. **recabdare** GPV] recabdaren W. 136. **cogiere** GPV] cogieren W. **e fisiere** GV] om. PW. **pagare** GPV] pagaren
W. **o** GPV] e W.

das o libras por çiento, que es la veyntena /17 verso/ parte de lo que asý recabdare e fiziere coger e recabdar.

Yo el Rey

Yo la Reyna   140

[17] Por mandado del Rey e de la Reyna. Fernand Álvares de Toledo.

[18] Acordada.

VII (25)

[1] Don Fernando e doña Ysabel, por la graçia de Dios rey e reyna de Castilla, de León, de Aragón, de Seçilia, de Granada, de Toledo, de Valençia, de Galizia, de Mallorcas, de Sevilla, de Çerdeña, de Córdova, de Córçega, de Murçia, de Jahén, de los Algarbes, de Algezira, de Gibraltar, de las yslas de Canaria,   5
conde e condesa de Barçelona, señores de Viscaya e de Molina, duques de Athenas e de Neopatría, condes de Rosellón e de Çerdania, marqueses de Oristán e de Goçiano: al nuestro jus-tiçia mayor e a los del nuestro consejo, oydores de la nuestra abdiençia, alcaldes e alguasyles de la nuestra casa e corte e chan-   10
çillería, e a todos los corregidores, asistentes, e alcaldes, e al-guaziles, e otras justiçias qualesquier de todas las çibdades e villas

Que las cosas como mercadurías, mantenimientos, provissiones y aparejos que ha de comprar en los Reynos, y qualesquier otras cosas, no se escusen de venderlas por encarecerlas: se vendan al Almirante por precio raçonable y conforme se suelen pagar [l. m.].

e logares de los nuestros reynos e señoríos, e a cada uno e qual-quier de vós en vuestros logares e juridiçiones a quien esta nuestra carta fuere mostrada, o su traslado d'ella, sygnado de   15
escrivano público, salud e graçia. [2] Sepades que para la pobla-çión de las yslas e tierra firme descubiertas e puestas so nuestro señorío a la parte de las Yndias en el mar Oçéano, será menester comprar en estos dichos nuestros reynos, para llevar a ellas, al-gunas mercaderías e mantenimientos e provisiones e aparejos e   20
ferramientas e toneles e vasijas e otras cosas, lo qual ha de com-prar la persona que por nós e por don Christóval Colón, nues-tro almirante del dicho mar Oçéano, tiene o diere cargo d'ello.

[3] E porque nos es fecha relación que las personas que tienen

138. **recabdare** GPV] recavdaren W. **fiziere** GPV] fizieren e fisieren W.   Sources: GPVW. 5. **de** (las) GPV] e de W. 6. **señores** GPV] e s. W. 9. **oydores** GPV] e o. W. 12. **e** (villas) GPV] om. W. 15. **mostrada** GVW] mostrado P. 18. **Yndias** GPV] yslas V. 23. **dicho** GPV] om. W.

las dichas mercaderías e otras cosas se escusan de lo vender por   25
lo encareçer más, lo qual sería en nuestro deserviçio, nuestra
merçed e voluntad es que lo que de lo susodicho se comprare
sea por los presçios e segund suele valer: porende nos vos mandamos que a las personas nuestras e del dicho nuestro almirante
que las cosas susodichas, o otras qualesquier, que compraren   30
para la abitaçión e proveymiento de las dichas Yndias e para el
navegar a ellas, gelo fagáys dar por preçios razonables e segund
que suelen valer en esas dichas çibdades e villas e logares entre
los vesynos d'ellas, syn encareçer más; e non fagades ende ál por
alguna manera, so pena de la nuestra merçed e de diez mill   35
maravedís a cada uno de vós que lo contrario fizierdes, para la
nuestra cámara. [4] E demás, por / 18 recto/ qualquier o qualesquier de vós las dichas justiçias por quien fincare de lo asý fazer
e cumplir, mandamos al ome que esta nuestra carta mostrare,
que vos emplase que parescades ante nós en la nuestra corte,   40
doquier que nos seamos, del día que vos emplasare fasta quinse
días primeros syguientes, so la dicha pena; so la qual mandamos
a qualquier escrivano público que para esto fuere llamado, que
dé ende al que vos la mostrare testimonio sygnado con su signo,
porque nos sepamos en cómo se cumple nuestro mandado.   45
[5] Dada en la çibdad de Burgos a veynte e tres días del mes de
abril, año del nasçimiento de nuestro señor Jhesu Christo de
mill e quatroçientos e noventa e syete años.

Yo el Rey

Yo la Reyna   50

[6] Yo Fernand Álvares de Toledo, secretario del Rey e de la
Reyna nuestros señores, las fis escrevir por su mandado.

[7] Acordada: Rodericus, doctor.

[8] Registrada: Alonso Peres; Françisco Dias, chançiller.

---

25. **lo** *GPV*] las *W*. 30. **o** *GPV*] e *W*. **que** *GPW*] om. *V*. 41. **doquier** *GPV*] adoquier *W*.

El Rey e la Reyna

*Esta carta de
instruçión no pareçió
originalmente ante los
alcaldes que aquí
dieron su abtoridad,
salvo ante mí el dicho
escrivano que la vi, de
lo qual doy fe.
    Martín Rodrigues
[l. m.]*

Çédula de memoria
de las cosas que se
deven llevar a las
Yndias [r. m.].

Privilegio de la
eleçión de las
personas que se han
de llevar [r. m.].

Véase la carta de
Sus Alteças a ojas
.XXVIII. en fin de
las espaldas [l. m.].

[1] Don Christóval Colón, nuestro almirante del mar Oçéano,
visorrey e governador de la tierra firme e yslas de las Yndias, e
Antoño de Torres, contino de nuestra casa: las cosas que nos
pareçen que, con ayuda de nuestro señor Dios, se deven proveer e enbiar a las Yndias para la governaçión e mantenimiento   5
de las personas que allá están e han de yr, para las cosas que allá
se han de haser conplideras a serviçio de Dios y nuestro, son las
siguientes:

[2] Primeramente, en este primer viage, y en tanto que nos
mandamos proveer, ayan de yr a estar en las dichas Yndias   10
número de trezientas e treynta personas de la suerte, calidad e
ofiçios que de yuso serán ‹declaradas›, contando el dicho
número de las dichas trezientas e treynta personas con las que
agora están e quedaron en las dichas Yndias. [3] Las quales
dichas trezientas e treynta personas han de ser elegidas por vós   15
el dicho nuestro almirante, o por quien vuestro poder oviere; e
han de ser repartidas en esta manera: quarenta escuderos, çient
peones de guerra, treynta marineros, treynta grumetes, veynte
labradores /18 verso/ de oro, çinqüenta labradores e ‹diez›
ortelanos, veynte ofiçiales de todos ofiçios, e treynta mugeres,   20
así que son el número de las dichas trezientas e treynta personas.

[4] Las quales ayan de yr a estar en las dichas Yndias quanto su
voluntad fuere, por manera que sy algunas de las personas que
están en las dichas Yndias se quisieren e ovieren de venir, ayan
de quedar, e quede en ellas, asý de las que agora están, como de   25
las que agora fueren, el dicho número de las dichas trezientas e
treynta personas; pero sy a vós el dicho almirante pareçiere
qu'es bien e provecho de la negoçiaçión de mudar el dicho

Sources: *GPVW. Marginal heading: autograph signature preceded by a sigla.* 4. **pareçen** *GPV*] pareçe *W.* 9.
Primeramente] *in the middle of the line in GPVW.* 11. **calidad** *GPV*] e c. *W.* 12. ‹**declaradas**› *V*] *om. GP,*
contenidas *W.* 15. **elegidas** *W*] elegidos *GPV* (*but cf.* 17 repartidas). 19. ‹**diez**›] *om. GPVW* (*but the number
of people should come to 330 and cf. p. 315, 7.* 22. **Las** *GPV*] los *W.* 24. **venir** *GPV*] vebir *with b over n V.* 25.
quede *GPV*] queden *W.*

número de personas, quitando de los unos ofiçiales e pro- 30
veyendo otros en su lugar, que lo podades fazer, tanto que non
pase el número de las personas que en las dichas Yndias han de
estar de las trezientas e treynta personas, e non más.

[5] Yten, que para mantenimiento de vós el dicho almirante e
de vuestros hermanos e otros ofiçiales, personas prinçipales, que
con vós han de yr a estar en las dichas Yndias, e para las dichas 35
trezientas e treynta personas, e para labrar e senbrar, e para el
govierno de las bestias que allá llevardes, se ayan de llevar e
lleven quinientos e çinqüenta cahizes de trigo, e más çinqüenta
cahizes de çevada; los quales se ayan de proveer e provan del
pan a nós pertenesçiente de las terçias del arçobispado de Sevilla 40
e obispado de Cadis del año pasado de noventa e seys años,
segund se contiene en las cartas de libramiento que sobr'ello
mandamos dar.

[6] Yten, que se ayan de enbiar a las dichas Yndias las he-
rramientas e aparejos que pareçiere a vós el dicho almirante, 45
para labrar en las dichas Yndias, e asimesmo açadones e açadas e
picos y almádanas y palancas que convinieren para las dichas
Yndias.

[7] E asimesmo, que sobre las vacas e yeguas qu'están en las
dichas Yndias, se ayan de complir número de veynte yuntas de 50
vacas e yeguas e asnos, con que puedan labrar en las dichas
Yndias, segund a vós el dicho almirante pareçiere.

[8] E asimesmo, nos pareçe que será bien que se compre una
nao vieja en que vayan los mantenimientos e cosas susodichas
que copieren en ella, porque de la tablazón e madera e clavazón 55
d'ella se podría aprovechar para la población que agora nuevamente se ha de hazer en la /19 recto/ otra parte de la ysla Española çerca de las minas; pero, sy a vós el dicho almirante
paresçiere que non es bien llevarse la dicha nao, que non se
lleve. 60

[9] Otrosý, se deven llevar a las dichas Yndias çinqüenta cahizes
de harina e fasta mill quintales de viscocho, para en tanto que se
provee de hazer molinos e atahonas; e para los hazer, se deven
llevar de acá algunas piedras y otros aparejos de molinos.

[10] Yten, se deven llevar a las dichas Yndias dos tiendas de 65
campo que cuesten fasta veynte mill maravedís.

---

32. **las** GPV] om. W. 35. **a** GP (cf. p. 294, 44)] e VW (cf. p. 291, 69). 49. **E** GPV] om. W. 64. **llevar** GPV]
de ll. W.

[11] Yten, para lo que toca a los otros mantenimientos e proveymientos que sean neçesarios llevarse a las dichas Yndias para el mantenimiento e vestido de los que allá han de yr e estar, nos pareçe que se deve tener la forma siguiente: 70

[12] Que busquen algunas personas llanas e abonadas, la quales dis que vos el dicho almirante dis que tenéys casi conçertadas, que ayan de cargar e llevar a las dichas Yndias los dichos mantenimientos e otras cosas allá neçesarias; para lo qual se les aya de dar y dé de los maravedís que nos mandamos librar para esto, lo 75 que a vós paresçiere, y que ellos den seguridad por los maravedís que así reçibieren. [13] Los quales ayan de enplear en los dichos mantenimientos, e cargarlos, e llevarlos a su costa a las dichas Yndias, e que vaya a nuestro riesgo e a ventura de la mar, e que llegando allá, Dios quiriendo, ayan de vender e vendan 80 los dichos mantenimientos: el vino a quinse maravedís el açumbre, e la libra de toçino e carne salada a ocho maravedís, e los otros mantenimientos e legumbres a los preçios que vos el dicho almirante, o vuestro logarteniente, les pusierdes, de manera que ellos ayan alguna ganançia e non pierdan en ello, e 85 a la gente non se les haga agravio. [14] E que de los maravedís que la tal persona o personas reçibieren de los dichos mantenimientos que asý vendieren, ayan de dar e pagar, e den e paguen, allá al nuestro thesorero que es o estoviere en las dichas Yndias, los dichos maravedís que les dierdes, que así se les han 90 de dar para comprar los dichos mantenimientos, para que d'ellos paguen el sueldo de la gente; pero sy la dicha gente tomaren los dichos mantenimientos para en cuenta de su sueldo, séanles reçebidos en cuenta, mostrando conosçimiento de lo que reçibieron, por donde el dicho thesorero e los ofiçiales de 95 cuenta se lo carguen en cuenta de su sueldo, e las dichas personas den seguridad; e obligándose de lo asý hazer e complir segund dicho es, se les ayan de dar e den las dichas contías de maravedís que asý vos paresçiere./19 verso/

[15] Yten, se deve procurar que vayan a las dichas Yndias al- 100 gunos religiosos e clérigos, buenas personas, para que allá administren los santos sacramentos a los que allá estarán, e procuren de convertir a nuestra sancta fee católica a los dichos

69. **vestido** GPV] vestidos W. 71. **Que** GPW] q. se V. 72. **dis que** (vos) GPV] om. W. 74. **aya** GPW] ayan V. 76. **y** GVW] om. P. 89. **al** GPV] a W. 90. **que** (así) GPV] e a. W. 91. **dar** GPV] d. et pagar W. 102. **e** GPV] que W.

Yndios naturales de las dichas Yndias, e lleven para ello los
aparejos e cosas que se requieran para el serviçio del culto   105
divino e para la administraçión de los sus sacramentos.

[16] Asimesmo, deve yr un físico e un boticario e un ervolario,
e algunos ynstrumentos e músicas para pasatiempo de las gentes
que allá han de estar.

[17] Otrosý, agora mandamos librar çierta contía de maravedís   110
para este viage que agora avéys de hazer vos el dicho almirante:
nos vos mandamos que aquéllos se gasten segund va por una
relaçión firmada del comendador mayor de León, nuestro contador mayor, e del doctor Rodrigo Maldonado, del nuestro
consejo, e de Fernand Álvares, nuestro secretario. [18] Por que   115
vos mandamos que lo así fagáys guardar e cumplir e poner en
obra segund que de suso se contiene, en lo qual plaser e serviçio
nos faréys, ca para ello vos damos poder complido con todas sus
ynçidençias e dependençias, anexidades e conexidades.

[19] Fecha en la villa de Medina del Canpo a quinse días del mes   120
de junio, año del nasçimiento de nuestro señor Jhesu Christo de
mill e quatroçientos e noventa e syete años.

Yo el Rey

Yo la Reyna   125

[20] Por mandado del Rey e de la Reyna. Fernand Álvares.

[21] Acordada: Rodericus, doctor.

IX.i (12.1)

[1] Don Fernando e doña Ysabel, por la graçia de Dios rey e
reyna de Castilla, de León, de Aragón, de Seçilia, de Granada,
de Toledo, de Valençia, de Galizia, de Mallorcas, de Sevilla, de
Çerdeña, de Córdova, de Córçega, de Murçia, de Jahén, de los
Algarbes, de Algezira, de Gibraltar e de las yslas de Canaria,   5
conde e condesa de Barçelona e señores de Viscaya e de
Molina, duques de Athenas e de Neopatría, condes de Rosellón
e de Çerdania, marqueses de Oristán e de Goçiano: por quanto

104. **ello** GPW] ellos V. 106. **sus** GPV] s(an)tos W (in the text?). 108. **pasatiempo** GPW] pasar tienpo V.
110. **contía** GV] quantia PW. 112. **aquéllos** GPW] aquello V. **gasten** GPW] gaste V. 121. **señor** GPV]
salvador W.   Sources: GPVW. 4. **de Córçega** GPV] om. W. 6. **e** (señores) GPV] om. W.

al tiempo que don Christóval Colón, nuestro almirante del mar
Oçéano, fue a descobrir tierra a la dicha mar Oçéana por nues-   10
tro mandado, se tomó con él çierto asiento; e después, quando
el primer viage vino de descobrir e fallar, segund que por la
graçia e /20 recto/ ayuda de Dios nuestro señor falló, las dichas
Yndias e tierra firme, le confirmamos e aprovamos el dicho
asiento e conçierto ‹que› con él por nuestro mandado ‹se›   15
tomó, e de nuevo le dimos e mandamos dar çiertos privilegios e
merçedes, segund que en el dicho asyento e cartas e privilegios
se contiene; e agora el dicho don Christóval, nuestro almirante
del dicho mar Oçéano, nos fizo relaçión que después acá nos
mandamos dar una carta nuestra para provisión, encorporados   20
en ella çiertos capítulos, el thenor de la qual es este que se sygue:

IX.ii (12.1-17)

[1] Don Fernando e doña Ysabel, por la graçia de Dios rey e
reyna de Castilla, de León, de Aragón, de Seçilia, de Granada,
de Toledo, de Valençia, de Galizia, de Mallorcas, de Sevilla, de
Çerdeña, de Córdova, de Córçega, de Murçia, de Jahén, de los
Algarbes, de Algezira, de Gibraltar e de las yslas de Canaria,   5
conde e condesa de Barçelona, señores de Viscaya e de Molyna,
duques de Athenas e de Neopatría, condes de Rosellón e de
Çerdania, marqueses de Oristán e de Goçiano: por quanto a nós

es fecha relaçión que algunas personas, vesynos e moradores en
algunas çibdades e villas e logares e puertos de nuestros reynos e   10
señoríos, nuestros súbditos e naturales, querrían yr a descobrir
otras yslas y tierra firme a la parte de las Yndias en el mar
Oçéano, demás de las yslas e tierra firme que por nuestro mandado se han descubierto en la dicha parte del mar Oçéano; e
asimesmo otros querrían yr a bevir e morar a la ysla Española   15
que está descubierta e fallada por nuestro mandado, sy por nós
les fuesse dada liçençia para ello e fuesen ayudados con mantenimientos por çierto tiempo, e que dexan de hazerlo por el

9. almirante GPV] a. mayor W. 15. ‹que›] om. GPVW. ‹se›] om. GPVW. 17. cartas e GPV] om. W. 20.
provisión W] promision GPV (but cf. p. 293, 1). encorporados] encorporada GPVW.   Sources:
GPVW. 13. firme GPW] om. V. 14. del GPW] de la V.

vedamiento que por nuestro mandado fue puesto para que ninguna persona fuese a las Yndias syn nuestra liçençia e mandado,　20
so çiertas penas; lo qual por nós visto, e acatando que sy descu-
briesen las dichas tierras e yslas, e resgatar en ellas e poblar dexá-
‹se›mos la dicha ysla Española que está descubierta, qu'es serviçio de Dios nuestro señor, porque la conversación d'ellos
podría atraer a los que abitan en la dicha tierra en conos-　25
çimiento de Dios nuestro señor e arreduzirlos a nuestra sancta
fee cathólica; otrosý qu'es serviçio nuestro, e bien e pro común
de nuestros reynos e señoríos e de nuestros súbditos e naturales;
acordamos de mandar dar, e por la presente damos e con-
çedemos, la dicha liçençia a los dichos nuestros súbditos e natu-　30
rales, para que vayan a las dichas yslas e tierra firme, e a desco-
brirlas e contratar en ellas, con las condiçiones e segund e en la
manera que en esta nuestra carta serán contenidas e declaradas
en esta guisa:

[2] Primeramente, que todos los navíos que ovieren de yr a la　35
parte de las dichas yslas en qualquier de las maneras que de yuso
en esta nuestra /20 verso/ carta serán contenidas, ayan de partir
desde la çibdad de Calis y no de otra parte alguna; e que antes
que partan, se presenten allý ante los ofiçiales que estovieren
puestos por nós, o por quien nuestro poder oviere, para que　40
sepan los que van a las dichas Yndias; e ayan de conplir e guardar cada uno en su caso lo que de yuso en esta nuestra carta será
contenido.

[3] Que qualesquier personas que quisieren yr a bivir e morar
en la dicha ysla Española syn sueldo, puedan yr e vayan li-　45
bremente, e que allá serán francos e libres, e que non paguen
derecho alguno, e ternán para sí e por suyo propio e para sus
herederos, e para quien d'ellos oviere cabsa, las casas que hizie-
ren e las tierras que labraren e las heredades que plantaren, segund que allá en la dicha ysla les serán señaladas tierras e logares　50
para ello por las personas que por nós tienen e tovieren cargo; e
que a las tales personas que así bivieren e moraren en la dicha
ysla Española e non llevaren sueldo nuestro, como dicho es, se
les dará mantenimiento por un año. [4] E demás, queremos e es
nuestra merçed que, yendo con liçençia de los que nuestro　55

---

35. **navíos** _GPW_] nouiçios _V._   40. **oviere** _GPW_] toviere _V._   45. **la dicha** _GPW_] la[s] dicha[s] _V._   47.
ternán _GPV_] tener/ _W._   50. **les** _GV_] le _PW_ (les serán le·serán).   53. **e** _GPW_] _om. V._ **llevaren** _GPW_] llevare
_V._

poder tovieren e ovieren para ello a la dicha ysla Española, ayan
para sí la terçia parte del oro que hallaren e cogieren en la dicha
ysla, tanto que non sea por resgate, e las otras dos terçias partes
sean para nós; con las quales recudan al ofiçial que por nós estoviere en la dicha ysla. [5] E demás d'esto, yendo con liçençia,   60
aya‹n› para sý todas las mercaderías e otras qualesquier cosas que
hallaren en la dicha ysla, dando el diezmo d'ello a nós, o a quien
nuestro poder oviere para lo reçebir, eçebto el oro, de que nos
han de dar las dos partes, como dicho es; lo qual todo ayan de
resgatar en la dicha ysla Española ante los nuestros ofiçiales, e   65
pagar a nuestro reçebtor que por nós lo oviere de aver, las dos
terçias partes del oro e la dicha diezma parte de todas las otras
cosas que hallaren, como dicho es.

[6] Yten, que qualesquier personas, nuestros súbditos e naturales, que quisieren, puedan yr de aquí adelante, en quanto   70
nuestra merçed e voluntad fuere, a descobrir yslas e tierra firme
en la dicha parte de las dichas Yndias, asý a las que están descubiertas fasta aquí, como a otras qualesquier, e resgatar en ellas,
tanto que non sea en la dicha ysla Española; que puedan comprar de los christianos que en ella están, o estovieren, quales-   75
quier cosas e mercaderías, con tanto que non sea oro. [7] Lo
qual puedan fazer y fagan con qualesquier navíos que quisieren,
con tanto que al tiempo que partieren de nuestros reynos, partan desde la dicha çibdad de Calis e allí se presenten ante nuestros ofiçiales; e porque desde allí han de /21 recto/ llevar en   80
cada uno de los tales navíos una o dos personas que sean nombradas por los nuestros ofiçiales ante quien asý se presentaren, e
más han de llevar la diezma parte de las toneladas del porte de
los tales navíos de cargazón nuestra, syn que por ello les aya de
ser pagado flete alguno; e lo que asý llevaren nuestro, lo descar-   85
gen en la dicha ysla Española e lo entreguen a la persona o
personas que allá tovieren cargo de lo reçebir por nuestro mandado de lo que de acá se enbíe, tomando conosçimiento suyo
de cómo lo reçibe.

[8] E queremos e es nuestra merçed que de lo que las dichas   90
personas fallaren en las dichas yslas e tierra firme, ayan para sí las
nueve partes e la otra dezena parte sea para nós; con la qual nos
ayan de recudir al tiempo que bolvieren a estos nuestros reynos,

---

61. aya‹n›] aya *GPVW*. 67. **dicha** *GPV*] d. nuestra *W*. 73. **e** *GPV*] a *W*. 80. **allí** *GPV*] alla *W*. 83.
toneladas *GPV*] tonelas *W*. 87. **tovieren** *GVW*] estovieren *P*. **lo** *GPW*] *om*. *V*.

en la dicha çibdad de Calis, donde han de bolver primeramente
a lo pagar a la persona que allí toviere cargo por nós de lo   95
reçebir; e después de así pagado, se puedan yr a sus casas, o
donde quisieren, con lo que asý troxieren; e al tiempo que partieren de la dicha çibdad de Calis, ayan de dar seguridad que lo
cunplirán asý.

[9] Yten, que qualesquier personas que quisieren llevar quales-   100
quier mantenimientos para la dicha ysla Española, o para otras
qualesquier yslas que por nuestro mandado estovieren pobladas
de las dichas Yndias, lo puedan llevar e vender allá francamente
e por los preçios que seygnalaren con los conpradores, los
quales les paguen allá en mercadurías o en otro de lo que allá   105
tovieren; e que si todo el dicho mantenimiento o parte d'ello
vendieren a nuestros ofiçiales que allá estovieren para los bastimentos de la gente que aý nos sirven, lo ayan de pagar e
paguen allá, como dicho es, o les den çédulas para que acá se les
paguen. [10] Con las quales çédulas nos les çertificamos que les   110
será pagado, con tanto que al tiempo que partieren los dichos
navíos en que fueren los dichos mantenimientos, ayan de partir
de la dicha çibdad de Calis, para que allí se presenten ante los
dichos nuestros ofiçiales, e lleven syn flete la dézçima del porte
de los tales navíos de la cargazón que nos mandáremos llevar   115
para la dicha ysla, segund de suso dize, e se obliguen de pagar la
déçima parte de lo que de allá truxieren, resgatándose segund la
capitulaçión que de suso se contiene; e a la buelta sean thenidos
de venir a la dicha çibdad de Calis para lo pagar, como dicho es.

[11] Otrosý, por quanto nos ovimos fecho /21 verso/ merçed a   120
don Christóval Colón, nuestro almirante de las dichas Yndias,
qu'él pudiese cargar en cada uno de los dichos navíos que
fuesen a las dichas Yndias la ochava parte del porte d'ellos, es
nuestra merçed que con cada syete navíos que fueren a las dichas Yndias, pueda el dicho almirante, o quien su poder oviere,   125
cargar uno para fazer el dicho resgate.

[12] Lo qual todo que dicho es, e cada una cosa e parte d'ello,
mandamos que se guarde e cumpla en todo e por todo, segund

95. **la persona** GPV] las personas W. **que** GVW] om. P. **toviere** GPV] tovieren W. 101. **ysla** GPV] om.
W. 104. **seygnalaren** (= **señalaren**)] se ygualaren GPVW. 105. **mercadurías** GPV] mercaderias W.
108. **nos** GVW] no P (nos sirven› no·sirven). 110. **les** (çertificamos) GPV] le/ W. **les** GPV] se les W. 113.
presenten GVW] presente P. 114. **del porte** GV] om. PW. 115. **mandáremos** GPV] mandamos W.
117. **de** (allá) GPW] om. V. 118. **thenidos** GPW] thenudos V. 123. **del porte** GV] om. PW. 126. **resgate**
GVW] resgato P.

de suso en esta nuestra carta se contiene; e porque venga a notiçia de todos, segund de suso se contiene, mandamos que sea   130
apregonada por las plaças e mercados e otros lugares acostumbrados de todas las çibdades e villas e logares e puertos del Andaluzía, e otras partes de nuestros reynos donde conviniere, y
dar el traslado d'ella a qualesquier personas que lo quisieren.
[13] De lo qual mandamos dar e dimos esta nuestra carta fir-   135
mada de nuestros nombres e sellada con nuestro sello.
[14] Dada en la villa de Madrid a diez días del mes de abril, año
del nasçimiento de nuestro salvador Jhesu Christo de mill e
quatroçientos e noventa e çinco años.

Yo el Rey   140
Yo la Reyna

[15] Yo Fernand Álvares de Toledo, secretario del Rey e de la
Reyna nuestros señores, la fis escrevir por su mandado.
[16] Acordada: Rodericus, doctor.
[17] Registrada: Doctor; Françisco Dias, chançiller.   145

IX.iii (34)

[1] La qual dicha nuestra carta de provisión e lo en ella contenido, el dicho almirante don Christóval Colón dize que fue
dada en perjuyzio de las dichas merçedes que de nós tiene e de
las facultades que por ellas le dimos; e nos suplicó e pidió por
merçed que çerca d'ello mandásemos proveer de remedio, o   5
como la nuestra merçed fuese. [2] E porque nuestra yntinçión
nin voluntad non fue ni es perjudicar en cosa alguna al dicho
don Christóval Colón, nuestro almirante del mar Oçéano, nin
que se vaya nin pase contra los dichos asyentos e previlegios e
merçedes que le fezimos, antes, por los serviçios que nos ha   10
fecho, le entendemos de hazer más merçedes; por esta nuestra
carta, sy neçesario es, confirmamos e aprovamos los dichos
asyentos e previlegios e merçedes por nós al dicho almirante
fechas, e es nuestra merçed e mandamos que en todo e por todo

131. **apregonada** GPW] apregonado V. 138. **salvador** GVW] señor W. 145. **Registrada: Doctor** GPV]
om. W (homoeoteleuton).   Sources: GPVW. 6-7. **yntinçión nin** GPV] merçed e W. 7. **perjudicar**
GPV] de p. W.

le sean guardadas e complidas segund que en ellas se contiene. 15
[3] E defendemos firmemente que alguna nin algunas personas
non sean osadas de yr nin pasar contra ellas nin contra parte
d'ellas en tiempo alguno ni por alguna manera, so las penas en
ellas contenidas; e sy el thenor e forma d'ella, o parte d'ello, en
algo perjudica la dicha provisión que asý mandamos dar, que de 20
suso va encorporada, por la presente la revocamos, e queremos
e mandamos /22 recto/ que non aya fuerça nin efecto alguno
en tiempo alguno nin por alguna manera, en quanto es en perjuyzio del dicho almirante e de lo que así tenemos otorgado e
confirmado. [4] De lo qual mandamos dar la presente firmada 25
de nuestros nombres e sellada con nuestro sello.
[5] Dada en la villa de Medina del Campo a dos días del mes de
junio, año del nasçimiento de nuestro salvador Jhesu Christo de
mill e quatroçientos e noventa e siete años.

Yo el Rey 30
Yo la Reyna
[6] Yo Fernand Álvares de Toledo, secretario del Rey e de la
Reyna nuestros señores, la fis escrevir por su mandado.
[7] Acordada: Rodericus, doctor.
[9] Registrada: Alonso Peres; Françisco Dias, chançiller. 35

X (26)

Para que las cosas
que llevará el
Almirante a las
Yndias y las que
traerá de allá no
paguen derecho ny
alcabala alguna,
tanto en la carga
como en descarga
[r. m.].

[1] Don Fernando e doña Ysabel, por la graçia de Dios rey e
reyna de Castilla, de León, de Aragón, de Seçilia, de Granada,
de Toledo, de Valençia, de Galizia, de Mallorcas, de Sevilla, de
Çerdeña, de Córdova, de Córçega, de Murçia, de Jahén, de los
Algarbes, de Algezira, de Gibraltar e de las yslas de Canaria, 5
conde e condesa de Barçelona, señores de Viscaya e de Molina,
duques de Athenas e de Neopatría, condes de Rosellón e de
Çerdania, marqueses de Oristán e de Goçiano: a vós los nuestros almoxarifes e recabdadores e arrendadores e fieles e cogedores, e otras personas que tenedes e tovierdes cargo de coger e 10
de recabdar en renta o en fieldad, o en otra qualquier manera,

17. **nin pasar** GV] om. PW. 19. **o** G] om. PVW. 28. **de** (nuestro) GPV] del W. Sources: GPVW. 10.
e (tovierdes) GPV] o W. e GPV] o W.

las rentas e almoxarifadgo‹s› e alcavalas de las çibdades de Sevilla
e Calis, este presente año de la datta d'esta nuestra carta e los
años venideros, tanto quanto nuestra voluntad fuere, e a cada
uno e qualquier de vós, salud e graçia. [2] Sepades que nuestra   15
merçed e voluntad es que todos los mantenimientos e otras
cosas que por nuestro mandado e de don Christóval Colón,
nuestro almirante del mar Oçéano en la parte de las Yndias, se
cargaren para llevar a ellas, e otrosý de lo que se truxiere de las
dichas Yndias a esas dichas çibdades e sus puertos, non se ayan   20
de pagar nin paguen por la primera venta d'ello almoxarifadgo
nin alcavala nin otro derecho alguno, este presente año ni
dende en adelante quanto nuestra merçed e voluntad fuere. [3]
Por que vos mandamos a todos e a cada uno de vós que asý lo
guardéys e cumpláys como de suso en esta nuestra carta se con- 25
tiene, e en guardándolo e cumpliéndolo non pidáys nin demandéys ni llevéys almoxarifadgo nin alcavala nin otros derechos
algunos por la primera venta /22 verso/ e carga e descarga de
qualesquier mercaderías e mantenimientos, e otras cosas que
paresçiere por fe de nuestros ofiçiales e del dicho almirante e   30
personas que tienen o tovieren cargo de la dicha carga e descarga que se carga para las dichas Yndias e se descarga trayén-
dolo d'ellas en las dichas çibdades e puertos, e cada una d'ellas,
este dicho año e de aquí adelante quanto nuestra merçed e
voluntad fuere. [4] E sy asý non lo fizierdes e cunplierdes, por   35
esta nuestra carta mandamos a qualesquier nuestras justiçias que
vos costringan e apremien a lo asý hazer e cumplir; e los unos
nin los otros non fagades nin fagan ende ál por alguna manera,
so pena de la nuestra merçed e de diez mill maravedís a cada
uno por quien fincare de lo así fazer e cumplir; e demás, man-   40
damos al ome que vos esta nuestra carta mostrare que vos enplaze que parescades ante nós en la nuestra corte, doquier que
nos seamos, del día que vos enplazare fasta quinse días primeros
siguientes, so la dicha pena; so la qual mandamos a qualquier
escrivano público que para esto fuere llamado, que dé ende al   45
que la mostrare testimonio signado con su signo, porque nos
sepamos en cómo se cunple nuestro mandado.

---

12. **almoxarifadgo‹s›**] almoxarifadgo *GPVW*. 20. **esas** *GPW*] estas *V*. 21. **paguen** *GPV*] pague *W*.
26-27. **demandéys** *PW*] demandays *GV*. 32. **que se carga** *GV*] om. *PW*. **carga**] descarga *GV*. **para las**
dichas] *repeated in P*. 32. **descarga** *GPW*] carga *V*. 33. **e** (cada) *GPW*] e en *V*. 36. **nuestra** *GV*] n. dicha
P, dicha n. *W*. 44. **siguientes** *GVW*] sygnase *P*.

[5] Dada en la muy noble çibdad de Burgos a veynte e tres días del mes de abril, año del nasçimiento de nuestro señor Jhesu Christo de mill e quatroçientos e noventa e siete años.   50

Yo el Rey

Yo la Reyna

[6] Yo Fernand Álvares de Toledo, secretario del Rey e de la Reyna nuestros señores, la fis escrevir por su mandado.

[7] Acordada: Rodericus, doctor.   55

[8] Registrada: Alonso Peres; Françisco Dias, chançiller.

XI.i (27)

[1] Don Fernando e doña Ysabel, por la graçia de Dios rey e reyna de Castilla, de León, de Aragón, de Seçilia, de Granada, de Toledo, de Valençia, de Galizia, de Mallorcas, de Sevilla, de Çerdeña, de Córdova, de Córçega, de Murçia, de Jahén, de los Algarbes, de Algezira, de Gibraltar e de las yslas de Canaria,   5
conde e condesa de Barçelona, señores de Viscaya e de Molina, duques de Athenas e de Neopatría, condes de Rosellón e de Çerdania, marqueses de Oristán e de Goçiano: a los corregidores, alcaldes, alguaziles, regidores, cavalleros, escuderos, ofiçiales, omes buenos de las /23 recto/ çibdades de Sevilla e   10
Calis, e de las villas e logares e puertos de su arçobispado e obispado, e a vós los arrendadores e recabdadores, almoxarifes e portadgueros e aduaneros e dezmeros, e otras personas que tenéys e tovierdes cargo de coger e recabdar en renta o en fieldad, o en otra qualquier manera, las rentas de las alcavalas e   15
almoxarifadgos e portadgos e almirantadgo de las dichas çibdades e villas, e a cada uno de vós, salud e graçia. [2] Sepades que para la poblaçión de las yslas e tierra firme descubiertas e puestas so nuestro señorío e por descobrir en el mar Oçéano en la parte de las Yndias, será menester traer a vender d'ellas a estos   20
nuestros reynos algunas mercadurías y otras cosas, y llevar a ellas de acá mantenimientos y otras provisiones e cosas, e para el resgate de las dichas Yndias e para otras cosas que allá son e serán

Sources: *GPVW*. 10. **omes** *GPV*] e o. *W*. 14. **recabdar** *GPV*] de r. *W*. 19. **el** *GPV*] la *W*. 21. **mercadurías** *GPV*] mercaderias *W*.

menester para sustentaçión e mantenimiento de las personas que allá están y avrán de estar, y para sus biviendas e labranças. 25
[3] E porque nuestra merçed e voluntad es que de las cosas que asý se traxieren a estos nuestros reynos de las dichas Yndias non se pague derecho alguno, antes se descarguen libremente, e que d'el descargo d'ellas non se pague derecho alguno de almoxarifadgo nin aduana, nin portadgo, ni almirantadgo, nin 30 otro derecho alguno, nin alcavala de la primera venta que d'ellas se fiziere; e asimismo que los que compraren qualesquier cosas para enbiar e llevar a las dichas Yndias para proveymiento e sostenimiento d'ellas e de las gentes que en ellas estovieren, non paguen derecho de almoxarifadgo nin aduana, nin por- 35 tadgo, ni almirantadgo, nin otro derecho por el cargar d'ellas: mandamos dar esta nuestra carta para vós en la dicha rasón; por la qual vos mandamos a todos e a cada uno de vós, cada e quando se truxieren y descargaren de las dichas Yndias quales- quier cosas a estos nuestros reynos, que, en quanto nuestra 40 merçed e voluntad fuere, los dexéys e consintáys descargar las tales cosas que así truxieren, libremente, syn les llevar almoxa- rifadgo mayor nin menor, nin aduana, ni almirantadgo, nin portadgo, ni otros derechos algunos, nin alcavala de la primera venta que se fiziere de las tales cosas que asý truxieren de las 45 dichas Yndias, mostrándovos carta firmada de don Christóval Colón, nuestro almirante de las dichas Yndias, o de la persona que toviere para ello su poder, e de la persona o personas que por nós, o por nuestros contadores mayores en nuestro nombre estovieren en las dichas Yndias, como aquellas cosas se cargaron 50 en las dichas Yndias para estos nuestros reynos. [4] E asymismo dexéys libremente cargar, en quanto nuestra merçed e voluntad fuere, qualesquier cosas que se llevaren a las dichas Yndias para proveymiento e sostenimiento d'ellas e de las gentes que en ellas estovieren, syn les demandar nin llevar derechos algunos 55 de almoxarifadgo mayor nin menor, ni aduana, ni /23 verso/ almirantadgo, ni portadgo, ni otros derechos algunos; lo qual hazed e complid asý mostrándovos carta firmada del dicho don Christóval Colón, almirante de las dichas Yndias, o de quien su poder oviere, e de la persona e personas que por nós e por 60 nuestros contadores mayores en nuestro nonbre estovieren en la çibdad de Calis para entender en las cosas de las dichas

34. **sostenimiento** GPV] mantenimiento W. 38. **a** (cada) GPV] om. W. 62. **çibdat** GPV] dicha ç. W.

Yndias. [5] E sy algunas personas descargaren las dichas cosas que vinieren de las dichas Yndias, sin mostrar la dicha carta del dicho almirante, o de quien su poder oviere, e de la persona o personas que por nós e por los nuestros contadores mayores estovieren en las dichas Yndias, como aquellas cosas se cargaron en ellas para estos dichos nuestros reynos, o cargaren de estos nuestros reynos para las dichas Yndias, syn llevar carta del dicho almirante, o de quien su poder oviere, e de la persona o personas que por nós e por los dichos nuestros contadores mayores estovieren en la dicha çibdad de Calis, como aquellas cosas se cargan e llevan para las dichas Yndias, que las ayan perdido e pierdan. [6] E por la presente damos poder e facultad a la persona o personas que por nós o por los dichos nuestros contadores mayores están e estovieren nombradas para lo susodicho en la dicha çibdad de Calis, o a la persona qu'el dicho almirante asimismo allí tiene o toviere, que les tomen las tales mercaderías e otras cosas que así truxieren de las dichas Yndias o cargaren para ellas syn mostrar las dichas cartas firmadas en la manera que dicha es, e las tengan en depósito fasta que nos mandemos fazer d'ellas lo que fuere justiçia e nuestra merçed e voluntad sea. [7] E otrosý mandamos que los dichos tenientes e ofiçiales tomen seguridad que lo que asý se cargare para llevar a las dichas Yndias, se llevará a ellas e non a otra parte alguna; e los ofiçiales que estovieren en las dichas Yndias tomen asymesmo seguridad que lo que así cargaren en las dichas Yndias se descargará en estos nuestros reynos e non en otra parte alguna, y se presentarán con ello en la dicha çibdad de Calis ante los ofiçiales que allí estovieren por nós e por el dicho almirante de las Yndias, porque no pueda yntervenir fraude ni cautela alguna; e mandamos a vós las dichas nuestras justiçias que asý lo fagáys e cumpláys, e se faga e cumpla lo en esta nuestra carta contenido, en quanto nuestra merçed e voluntad fuere, como dicho es. [8] E porque lo susodicho venga a notiçia de todos e d'ello no pueda ninguno pretender ynorançia, mandamos que esta nuestra carta sea pregonada por la plaças e mercados e otros lugares acostumbrados d'esas dichas çibdades de Sevilla e Calis, e de los puertos d'esa comarca; e mandamos a los nuestros contadores

65

70

75

80

85

90

95

Se publique por pregón para noticia de todos [*l. m.*].

65. **o** (personas) *GPV*] e *W*. 67. **estovieren** *GPV*] que e. *W*. 69. **nuestros** *GPV*] *om*. *W*. **llevar** *GVW*] llenar *P*. 70. **e** *GPW*] o *V*. 72. **estovieren** *GPV*] que e. *W*. 84-86. **seguridad . . . asymesmo** *GPV*] *om*. *W* (*homoeoteleuton*). 87. **que** *GPW*] de *V*. 88. **estos** *GPW*] esto *V*.

mayores que tomen el traslado d'esta nuestra carta e lo pongan   100
e asyenten en los nuestros libros, e sobre escrivan /24 recto/
esta carta original en las espaldas, e la tornen al dicho don Christóval Colón, nuestro almirante de las Yndias, e que con los
arrendamientos que fizieren de aquí adelante, en quanto nuestra merçed e voluntad fuere, de los nuestros almoxarifadgos e   105
alcavalas e portadgos e aduanas e otros nuestros derechos, pongan por salvado lo contenido en esta nuestra carta; e los unos ni
los otros non fagades nin fagan ende ál por alguna manera, so
pena de la nuestra merçed e de diez mill maravedís para la nuestra cámara a cada uno que lo contrario fiziere. [9] E demás,   110
mandamos al ome que esta nuestra carta mostrare que vos enplaze que parescades ante nós en la nuestra corte, doquier que
nos seamos, del día que vos enplazare fasta quinze días primeros
siguientes, so la dicha pena; so la qual mandamos a qualquier
escrivano público que para esto fuere llamado, que dé ende al   115
que vos la mostrare, testimonio signado con su signo, porque
nos sepamos en cómo se cumple nuestro mandado.
[10] Dada en la çibdad de Burgos, seys días del mes de mayo,
año del nasçimiento de nuestro salvador Jhesu Christo de mill e
quatroçientos e noventa e siete años.   120

Yo el Rey

Yo la Reyna

[11] Yo Fernand Álvares de Toledo, secretario del Rey e de la
Reyna nuestros señores, la fis escrevir por su mandado.
[12] En la forma acordada: Rodericus, doctor.   125
[13] Registrada: Alonso Peres; Francisco Dias, chançiller.

XI.ii (28)

[1] Corregidores, alcaldes, alguaziles, regidores, cavalleros, escuderos, ofiçiales, omes buenos de las çibdades de Sevilla e
Calis, e de las villas e logares de los puertos de su arçobispado e
obispado, e arrendadores e recabdadores, almoxarifes e portadgueros, aduaneros e dezmeros, e las otras personas en esta   5

117. **en** *GPW*] *om. V.* 125. **acordada** *GPW*] dada *V.*   Sources: *GPVW.* 2. **omes** *GP*] e o. *VW.*

carta del Rey e de la Reyna nuestros señores d'esta otra parte
escripta contenidas: ved esta dicha carta de Sus Altesas e com-
plidla en todo e por todo, segund e por la forma e manera que
en ella se contiene e Sus Altesas por ella lo mandan; e sea entendido que todas las mercaderías que fueren del Andaluzía, o de   10
otros qualesquier puertos gozando d'esta dicha franqueza para
las dichas Yndias, han de dar seguridad que traerán testimonio e
fe del dicho almirante, o de quien su poder oviere, e de la persona que por Sus Altesas o los dichos sus contadores mayores
para ello ovieren señalado; e esomesmo las liçençias e fees que   15
se han de llevar a las Yndias o traer d'ellas de las cosas que se
llevaren e truxieren, han de ser firmadas del dicho almirante, o
de quien su poder oviere, e de la persona que Sus Altesas e sus
contadores mayores nonbraren: de ambos, e non del uno syn el
otro. [2] E asymismo se entienda que por lo en esta dicha carta   20
contenido non se ha de reçebir en cuenta maravedís nin otras
cosas algunas a los arrendadores e recabdadores mayores, e almoxarifes e otras personas que tienen o tovieren cargo de coger
/24 verso/ e recabdar las rentas a nós pertenesçientes en el
dicho arçobispado de Sevilla e obispado de Calis, este dicho   25
año, nin dende en adelante en ningund año, quanto fuere la
‹merçed e› voluntad de Sus Altesas que dure e se guarde lo en
esta dicha su carta contenido; e como quiera que dize que esta
dicha franqueza se ha de guardar desde este dicho presente año,
sea entendido que ha de ser guardada desde primero día de   30
enero del año venidero de noventa e ocho años, e dende en
adelante, segund dicho es, e non antes.
[3] Mayordomo Juan Lopes; Fernand Gomes; Juan Hurtado;
Montoro; Luys Peres; Pedro de Arbolancha.

XII (22)

[1] Don Fernando e doña Ysabel, por la graçia de Dios rey e
reyna de Castilla, de León, de Aragón, de Seçilia, de Granada,

6. **otra** *GV*] *om.* PW. 11. **esta** *GVW*] esa *P.* 13. **o** *GPV*] e *W.* 14. **por** *GPVW*] *but cf.* 18-19. 15. **e**
(esomesmo) *GPV*] *om. W.* 17. **e** *GPV*] o *W.* 18. **e** (sus) *GPW*] o *V (cf.* 14). 20. **E** *GPV*] *om. W.* 27.
‹**merçed e**› *V*] *om. GPW.* 29. **dicho** *GPW*] *om. V.* 30. **de** (enero) *GPV*] del mes de *W.*   Sources:
GPVW.

de Toledo, de Valençia, de Galizia, de Mallorcas, de Sevilla, de
Çerdeña, de Córdova, de Córcega, de Murçia, de Jahén, de los
Algarbes, de Algezira, de Gibraltar e de las yslas de Canaria, 5
conde e condesa de Barçelona, señores de Viscaya e de Molina,
duques de Athenas e de Neopatría, condes de Rosellón e de
Çerdania, marqueses de Oristán e de Goçiano: a los del nuestro
consejo, oydores de la nuestra abdiençia, alcaldes e alguasyles de
la nuestra casa e corte e chançillería, e a todos los conçejos e 10
justiçias, regidores, cavalleros, escuderos, ofiçiales e omes
buenos de todas las çibdades e villas e logares de los nuestros
reynos e señoríos, asý realengos como abadengos, e hórdenes e
behetrías e otras qualesquier personas, nuestros vasallos, súbditos e naturales a quien toca e atañe lo en esta nuestra carta 15
contenido, e a cada uno e qualquier de vós a quien esta nuestra
carta fuere mostrada, o el traslado d'ella sygnado de escrivano
público, salud e graçia. [2] Sepades que nos avemos mandado a
don Christóval Colón, nuestro almirante de la mar Oçéano,
que buelva a la ysla Española e a las otras yslas e tierra firme que 20
son en las dichas Yndias, e entienda en la conversión e poblaçión d'ellas, porque d'esto Dios nuestro señor es servido e Su
sancta fe acreçentada, e nuestros reynos e señoríos ensanchados;
e para ello avemos mandado armar çiertos navíos e caravelas en
que va çierta gente pagada por çierto tiempo, e bastimentos e 25
mantenimientos para ella; /25 recto/ e por quanto aquello non
puede bastar para que se faga la dicha poblaçión como cumple a
serviçio de Dios e nuestro, sy non van otras gentes que en ellas
estén e bivan e sirvan a sus costas, e nos queriendo proveer
sobre ello asý por lo que cumple a la dicha conversión e pobla- 30
ción, como por usar de clemençia e piedad con nuestros súbditos e naturales, mandamos dar esta nuestra carta en la dicha
rasón. [3] Por la qual de nuestro propio motuo e çierta sçiençia
queremos e ordenamos que todas e qualesquier personas, varones e mugeres, nuestros súbditos e naturales, que ovieren 35
cometido, fasta el día de la publicaçión d'esta nuestra carta, qualesquier muertes e feridas, e otros qualesquier delitos de qualquier natura e calidad que sean, eçebto la eregía, o *lese magesta-*

3-4. **de Çerdeña** GPV] *om. W.* 6. **conde e condesa** GPV] condes/ *W.* 9. **oydores** GPV] e o. *W.* 19.
de la GPV] del *W.* 23. **e señoríos** GV] *om. PW.* 26. **ella** GPW] alla (= allá) *V.* 27. **la . . . poblaçión**
GPV] *om. W* (faga/). 33. **de** GPV] e de *W.* 38. **lese**] lege GPVW.

Perdón general a
los delinqüentes
que yrán a servir a
la ysla Española a
sus propias costas,
por dos años los
que merecieren
muerte y por uno
los que mereçieren
menos [*l. m.*].

tis, o *perdulionis*, o trayçión, o aleve, o muerte segura o fecha
con fuego o con saeta, o crimen de falsa moneda, o de sodomía, 40
o ovieren sacado moneda o oro o plata, o otras cosas por nós
vedadas, fuera de nuestros reynos, que fueren a servir en persona a la ysla Española, e syrvieren en ella a sus propias costas, e
sirvieren en las cosas qu'el dicho almirante les dixere e mandare
de nuestra parte, los que meresçieren pena de muerte por dos 45
años, e los que meresçieren otra pena menor que no sea muerte,
aunque sea perdimiento de miembro, por un año, sean per-
donados de qualesquier crímines e delitos de qualesquier natura
e calidad e gravedad que sean, que ovieren fecho e cometido,
fasta el día de la publicación de esta nuestra carta, eçebto los 50
casos susodichos, presentados ante el dicho don Christóval
Colón, nuestro almirante del mar Oçéano, ante escrivano público, desde oy de la datta d'esta nuestra carta fasta en fin del mes
de setienbre primero que viene, para que puedan yr con el
dicho almirante a la dicha ysla Española e a las otras yslas e tierra 55
firme de las dichas Yndias, e servir en ellas por todo el dicho
tiempo en lo qu'el dicho almirante les mandare complidero a
nuestro serviçio, como dicho es, e asý presentados fueren a las
dichas yslas e tierra firme, e estovieren en el dicho serviçio continuamente por todo el dicho tiempo, trayendo carta patente 60
firmada del dicho almirante e sygnada de escrivano público, en
que den fe como syrvieron los tales delinqüentes en las dichas
yslas o en qualquier d'ellas, por todo el dicho tiempo, sean per-
donados. [4] E por la presente de nuestro propio /25 verso/
motuo e çierta sçiençia los perdonamos de todos los dichos 65
delitos que asý ovieren fecho e cometido fasta el día de la publicación de esta dicha nuestra carta, como dicho es; e que
dende en adelante non puedan ser acusados por los dichos delitos, nin por ninguno d'ellos, nin se proçeda nin pueda ser
proçedido contra ellos, nin contra sus bienes, por nuestras jus- 70
tiçias a crimen nin a pena alguna çevill nin criminal a pedimiento de partes, nin de su ofiçio, nin de otra manera alguna;
nin puedan ser exsecutadas en ellos, nin en sus bienes, las sentençias que contra ellos son o fueren dadas; las quales nos, por

---

39. **perdulionis** (= **perduellionis**) *GPW*] perduliçiones *V*. 41. **ovieren** *GPV*] oviere *W*. 48. **delitos**
GPW] d. e *V*. **qualesquier** *GVW*] qualquier *P*. 49. **e** (calidad) *GPV*] o *W*. **e** (gravedad) *GPV*] o *W*. **e**
GPW] o *V*. 50. **fasta** *GPW*] e f. *V* (*but cf.* 66–67). 53. **oy** *GPV*] oy dia *W*. 57. **complidero**] complideras
GPVW (*but cf.* p. 315, 14; 325, 22). **a** *GPV*] al *W*. 74. **contra** *GPV*] en *W*.

esta nuestra carta, revocamos e damos por ningunas e de nin- 75
gund efecto e valor, complido el dicho serviçio. [5] E mandamos al dicho almirante de las Yndias, e a otras qualesquier
personas que por nós estovieren en las dichas Yndias, que dexen
libremente venir a los que asý ovieren servido el tiempo que
son obligados de servir, segund el thenor d'esta nuestra carta, e 80
que non los detengan en manera alguna. [6] E por esta nuestra
carta mandamos a los del nuestro consejo e oydores de la nuestra abdiençia, alcaldes de la nuestra corte e chançillería, e a
todos los corregidores e otras justiçias qualesquier de todas las
çibdades e villas e logares de los nuestros reynos e señoríos, que 85
esta nuestra carta de perdón e remisión, e lo en ella contenido,
e cada una cosa e parte d'ello, guarden e cunplan, e fagan guardar e complir, en todo e por todo, segund que en ella se contiene; e en guardándola e cunpliéndola, non procedan contra
los tales que asý ovieren servido en las dichas Yndias, por nin- 90
gund delito que ovieren fecho nin cometido, eçebto en las
cosas susodichas, a pedimiento de parte, nin de su ofiçio, nin de
otra manera alguna, e nin las exsecuten en sus personas nin
bienes, por razón de los tales delictos. [7] E sy algunos proçesos
contra ellos están fechos, o sentençias dadas, lo revoquen o den 95
por ningunas, que nos, por la presente, de la dicha nuestra çierta
sçiençia desde agora para entonçes lo revocamos, cassamos e
anullamos, e damos por ningunos, e restituymos a los dichos
delinqüentes en su buena fama e en el punto e estado en que
estavan antes que oviesen fecho e cometido los dichos delictos. 100
[8] E porque lo susodicho sea notorio e ninguno d'ello pueda
pretender ynorançia, mandamos que sea pregonado pú-
blicamente por las plaças e mercados e otros lugares acostumbrados; e los unos nin /26 recto/ los otros non fagades nin fagan
ende ál por alguna manera, so pena de la nuestra merçed e de 105
diez mill maravedís para la nuestra cámara a cada uno que lo
contrario fiziere. [9] E demás, mandamos al ome que esta nuestra carta mostrare, que vos emplase que parescades ante nós en
la nuestra corte, doquier que nos seamos, del día que vos enplazare fasta quinse días primeros syguientes, so la dicha pena; 110
so la qual mandamos a qualquier escrivano público que para
esto fuere llamado, que dé ende al que vos la mostrare testi-

89. **e cunpliéndola** GPV] om. W (guardandola/). 91. **ovieren** GPV] oviere W. 93. **e** GPV] om. W. 97.
cassamos GPW] tasamos V. 112. **vos** GPV] ge W.

monio sygnado con su sygno, porque nos sepamos en cómo se
cunple nuestro mandado.

[10] Dada en la villa de Medina del Campo a veynte e dos días   115
del mes de junio, año del nasçimiento de nuestro salvador Jhesu
Christo de mill e quatroçientos e noventa e syete años.

Yo el Rey

Yo la Reyna

[11] Yo Fernand Álvares de Toledo, secretario del Rey e de la   120
Reyna nuestros señores, la fis escrevir por su mandado.

[12] Acordada: Rodericus, doctor.

[13] Registrada: Doctor; Françisco Dias, chançiller.

XIII (23)

[1] Don Fernando e doña Ysabel, por la graçia de Dios rey e
reyna de Castilla, de León, de Aragón, de Seçilia, de Granada,
de Toledo, de Valençia, de Galizia, de Mallorcas, de Sevilla, de
Çerdeña, de Córdova, de Córçega, de Murçia, de Jahén, de los
Algarbes, de Algezira, de Gibraltar e de las yslas de Canaria,   5
conde e condesa de Barçelona, señores de Viscaya e de Molina,
duques de Athenas e de Neopatría, condes de Rosellón e de
Çerdania, marqueses de Oristán e de Goçiano: a todos los corregidores, asistentes, alcaldes, alguasyles, e otras justiçias qualesquier de todas las çibdades e villas e logares de los nuestros   10
reynos e señoríos, a quien esta nuestra carta fuere mostrada, o su
traslado sygnado de escrivano público, salud e graçia. [2]
Sepades que nos avemos mandado a don Christóval Colón,
nuestro almirante de las Yndias del mar Oçéano, que buelva a la
ysla Española e a las otras yslas e tierra firme qu'es en las dichas   15
Yndias, a entender en la ‹conversión e› poblaçión d'ellas, e para
ello nos le mandamos dar çiertas naos e caravelas e que vaya
çierta gente pagada por çierto tiempo e bastimentos e mantenimientos para ella; e porque aquélla non puede bastar para
que se faga la dicha poblaçión como cunple a serviçio de Dios e   20
nuestro, sy non van otras gentes que en ellas estén e bivan e

Sources: *GPVW*. 3-4. **de Çerdeña** *GPV*] *om. W*. 4. **de Córçega** *GPV*] *om. W*. 14. **del mar Oçéano**
GPV] *om. W*. 16. ‹**conversión e**› *V*] *om. GPW*.

syrvan a sus costas, acordamos de mandar dar esta nuestra carta
para vós e para cada uno de vós en la dicha rasón. [3] Por que
vos mandamos que cada e quando alguna o algunas /26 verso/

Carta a las Justiçias
para que los que
mereçieren ser
desterrados de los
Reynos por algunos
delitos, o
condenados a
algunas yslas o para
labrar o servir en los
metales, se
destierren para la
ysla Española
[*l. m.*].

personas, así varones como mugeres, de nuestros reynos ovie-   25
ren cometido e cometieren qualquier delicto o delitos por que
merezcan o devan ser desterrados, segund derecho e leyes de
nuestros reynos, para alguna ysla o para labrar e servir en los
metales, que los desterréys que vayan a estar e servir en la dicha
ysla Española en las cosas qu'el dicho nuestro almirante de las   30
Yndias les dixere e mandare, por el tiempo que avían de estar
en la dicha ysla e labor de metales; e asymesmo todas las otras
personas que fueren culpantes en delitos que non merescan
pena de muerte, seyendo tales los delitos que justamente se les
pueda dar destierro para las dichas Yndias, segund la calidad de   35
los delitos, los condenéys e desterréys para la dicha ysla Española, para que estén allí e fagan lo que por el dicho almirante
les fuere mandado por el tiempo que a vosotros paresçiere. [4] E
a los que fasta aquí tenéys condenados e condenardes de aquí
adelante para yr a las dichas yslas, e los tovierdes presos, los   40
enbiéys presos e a buen recabdo a una de las nuestras cárçeles de
las nuestras abdiençias de Valladolid o Çibdad Real, o a la cárçel
real de Sevilla; e los entreguen, los que los llevaren a las dichas
chançillerías, a los nuestros alcaldes d'ellas; e los que se llevaren
a la cárçel de Sevilla, se entreguen al nuestro asistente d'ella, a   45
costa de los tales condenados, sy tuvieren bienes, e sy bienes
non tuvieren, se paguen a costa de los maravedís de las penas de
nuestra cámara. [5] E mandamos a las dichas nuestras justiçias
que asý lo fagan e cumplan, segund de suso se contiene, e a los
consejos de todas las çibdades e villas e logares de nuestros   50
reynos, que vos den para ello todo el favor e ayuda que menester ovierdes; e sy otras algunas personas ovieren cometido e
cometieren delitos por que devan ser desterrados fuera d'estos
dichos nuestros reynos, los desterréys para la dicha ysla en la
manera syguiente: los que ovieren de ser desterrados per-   55

Limitaçión de la
cantidad del tiempo
que han de estar
desterrados [*l. m.*].

petuamente de los dichos nuestros reynos, los desterréys para
la dicha ysla por diez años, e los que ovieren de ser desterrados
por çierto tiempo fuera de los dichos nuestros reynos, que sean

---

30. **nuestro** *GPV*] *om. W.*   38. **vosotros** *GVW*] vos e otros *P.*   39. **e** *GPV*] o *W.*   41. **e** *GPV*] *om. W.*   45.
d'ella *GV*] *om. PW.*   51. **vos** *W*] les *GPV.*   52. **ovierdes** *W*] ovieren *GP,* oviere *V.* **e** (cometicren) *GPW*]
o *V.*   58. **que** *GPV*] *om. W.*

desterrados para la dicha ysla por la mitad del dicho tiempo que
avían de ser fuera d'estos nuestros reynos; e los unos nin los   60
otros non fagades nin fagan ende ál por alguna manera, so pena
de la nuestra merçed e de diez mill maravedís para la nuestra
cámara a cada uno que /27 recto/ lo contrario fisiere. [6] E
demás, mandamos al ome que esta nuestra carta mostrare que
vos enplase que parescáys ante nós en las nuestra corte, doquier   65
que nos seamos, del día que vos enplasare a quinse días primeros
syguientes, so la dicha pena; so la qual mandamos a qualquier
escrivano público que para esto fuere llamado, que dé ende al
que vos la mostrare testimonio sygnado con su sygno, porque
nos sepamos en cómo se cumple nuestro mandado.   70
[7] Dada en la villa de Medina del Campo a veynte e dos días
del mes de junio, año del nasçimiento de nuestro salvador Jhesu
Christo de mill e quatroçientos e noventa e syete años.

Yo el Rey

Yo la Reyna   75

[8] Yo Fernand Álvares de Toledo, secretario del Rey e de la
Reyna nuestros señores, la fis escrevir por su mandado. Don
Álvaro.

[9] Acordada: Rodericus, doctor.

[10] Registrada: Doctor; Françisco Dias, chançiller.   80

XIV (24)

El Rey e la Reyna

Carta para que se
entreguen al
Almirante los presos
desterrados para la
ysla Española
[r. m.].

[1] Conde de Cifuentes, nuestro alferes mayor e asistente en la
çibdad de Sevilla: nos enbiamos mandar a las justiçias de nuestros reynos que todas las personas que ovieren de desterrar e
desterraren para yslas, o para fuera de los dichos nuestros
reynos, los destierren para la ysla Española, e que los enbíen a   5
esa nuestra cárçel de Sevilla. [2] Porende nos vos mandamos

---

64. **que** (esta) *GPV*] q. vos *W*. 66. **a** *GP* (*cf.* p. 273, 94)] fasta *VW* (*cf.* p. 299, 43). 72. **salvador** *GPV*] señor
W. 80. **Doctor**] dottor *G*?   Sources: *GPVW*. 4. **o** *GPV*] e *W*. 5. **que** *GPV*] *om. W*.

que, cada e quando vos fueren enbiados los tales condenados
por los nuestros presidentes e oydores e alcaldes de las nuestras
chançillerías de Valladolid e Çibdat Real, e por qualesquier
otros corregidores e justiçias de los dichos nuestros reynos, que   10
los reçibáys e los tengáys presos a buen recabdo fasta que los
entreguéys a nuestro almirante de las Yndias del mar Oçéano o,
en su absençia, a la persona que por nós toviere cargo del
proveymiento de las cosas de las dichas Yndias, e a la persona
que para ello estoviere puesta por el dicho almirante, los quales   15
vos requerirán por ellos al tiempo que tovieren prestos los
navíos para partir e faser su viage a las dichas Yndias. [3] Al qual
dicho tiempo vos gelos dad e entregad dentro en los dichos
navíos en la dicha çibdad de Sevilla o en la çibdad de Calis, /27
verso/ dondequiera que los dichos navíos estuvieren prestos   20
para partir, presos e a buen recabdo por ante escrivano e testigos, reçibiendo conosçimiento e seguridad de los maestres de
los tales navíos, que los llevarán asý presos e a buen recabdo fasta
los entregar al dicho almirante, o a la persona qu'él nombrare
para los reçibir dentro en la dicha ysla Española, e que traerán   25
fee e testimonio de como los llevó e entregó e quedaron en la
dicha ysla. [4] E la costa que se fiziere fasta los entregar en los
dichos navíos, fazed complir e pagar de los bienes de los tales
condenados; e sy no tovieren bienes, fazedlo complir e pagar de
los nuestros maravedís de las penas de nuestra cámara; e non   30
fagades ende ál.
[5] Fecha en la villa de Medina del Campo a veynte e dos días
del mes de junio de noventa e syete años.

Yo el Rey
Yo la Reyna   35

[6] Por mandado del Rey e de la Reyna. Fernand Álvares.

---

8. **nuestros** GPV] om. W. 9. **e** (por) GPV] o W. 10. **e** GPV] o W. **nuestros** GVW] om. P. 12. **a** GPV] al
W. **o** GPW] e V. 20. **dondequiera** PVW (dondequier P)] dondequiera(n) G. 23. **fasta** GPV] e f. V. 25.
los GVW] lo P. **e**] e / e V. 26. **de** GPV] om. W. 27. **ysla** GPV] y. Española W. 30. **nuestros** GP] om. VW
(*cf.* p. 309, 47-48).

El Rey e la Reyna

Carta para que pueda tomar y fletar navíos a precio raçonable sin que se le haga dificultad ni empedimiento [*l. m.*].

[1] Para la poblaçión de las yslas e tierra firme descubiertas en el mar Oçéano, e para llevar mantenimiento a las personas que allá están e ovieren de estar, e para descobrir otras tierras e traer de allá qualesquier mercadurías que se fallaren, será menester fleytar algunas naos e caravelas e otros navíos; e porque los maestres e dueños d'ellos, por aventura, se escusarían de los fleytar, o demandarán mayores fletes de los que acostumbran llevar e deven aver justamente, lo qual sería en deserviçio nuestro e daño e estorvo de los viages que se han de fazer a las dichas Yndias, porende nos vos encargamos e mandamos que quando el nuestro almirante de las Yndias no hallare los navíos que oviere menester, o, hallándolos, non quisieren yr con él, e vos demandare qualesquier navíos e caravelas e otras fustas para los tales viages, que vos veades los navíos e fustas que oviere menester, e dedes forma con los dueños d'ellos que gelos fleyten a preçios razonables, segund a vós pareçiere que justamente gelos deven fleytar, e tengáys manera que los dueños e maestres d'ellos vayan con los dichos navíos /28 recto/ lo más syn agravio e perjuysio de las partes que ser pueda; que por la presente vos damos para ello poder complido.

[2] Fecha en la villa de Medina del Campo a veynte e dos días del mes de junio de mill e quatroçientos e noventa e syete años.

Yo el Rey
Yo la Reyna

[3] Por mandado del Rey e de la Reyna. Fernand Álvares.

5

10

15

20

25

Sources: *GPVW*. 1. **Para**] *a blank half line precedes in GPVW.* 3. **e** (traer) *GVW*] o *P*. 4. **mercadurías** *GPV*] mercaderias *W*. 5. **fleytar** *GPV*] freytar *W* (*Western form?*). **e** (caravelas) *GPV*] o *W*. 6. **ellos** *GPV*] ellas *W*. **escusarían GPV**] escusara(n) *W*. 7. **demandarán** *GV*] demandar *P*, demandarian *W*. 13. **e** (caravelas) *GPV*] o *W*. 16. **gelos** *GPW*] gelas *V*.

El Rey e la Reyna

Carta para que
pueda el Almirante
libremente
proveherse y cargar
trigo y cebada para
bastimento y
proveymiento de las
yslas de las Yndias
[r. m.].

[1] Alcaldes de sacas e cosas vedadas, dezmeros e portadgueros e guardas del arçobispado de Sevilla e del obispado de Cádiz, e a cada uno de vós: nos vos mandamos que del pan que nos tenemos en ese dicho arçobispado ‹e obispado›, de las terçias a nós pertenesçientes, dexedes e consintades libremente sacar e cargar por la mar a don Christóval Colón, nuestro almirante de las Yndias, o a la persona qu'él enbiare con su carta firmada de su nombre, quinientos e çinqüenta cahises de trigo e çinqüenta cahises de çevada para bastimento e proveymiento de las yslas de las Yndias. [2] El qual dicho pan le dexad sacar dentro de çinco meses primeros syguientes, contando desde oy día de la fecha d'esta nuestra çédula, en quantos caminos él quisyere dentro del dicho término, tanto que en cada camino aya de registrar e registre por ante un alcalde e dos de vosotros e de un escrivano, en las espaldas d'esta nuestra çédula, lo que sacare, porque non puedan sacar más de los dichos quinientos e çinqüenta cahises de trigo e çinqüenta cahises de çevada; del qual dicho pan vos mandamos que non le demandedes nin llevedes derechos algunos de saca, nin otros derechos algunos, por quanto nuestra merçed e voluntad es que los non pague, porque el dicho pan es nuestro e lo mandamos llevar para cosas de nuestro serviçio. [3] Lo qual vos mandamos que lo fagades e cumplades asý, syn le poner embargo nin contrario alguno; e non fagades ende ál, so pena de la nuestra merçed e de diez mill maravedís para la nuestra cámara e fisco a cada uno que /28 verso/ lo contrario fiziere. [4] Fecha en la villa de Medina del Campo a veynte e dos días del mes de junio de noventa e siete años.

5

10

15

20

25

Yo el Rey
Yo la Reyna   30

Sources: GPVW. 2. **del** (obispado) GPV] om. W. 4. ‹**e obispado**› V] om. GPW. 7. **qu'él** GVW] que en el P. 13. **dentro** GPV] e d. W. 14. **e** (dos) GPW] o V. **de** (un) GV] om. PW. 19. **nin . . . algunos** GVW] om. W. 23. **contrario** GPW] contrallo V.

[5] Por mandado del Rey e de la Reyna. Fernand Álvares.
[6] Acordada.

XVII (38)

El Rey e la Reyna

Çédula para el
Tiniente del
Almyrante de
Castilla para que dé
auténtico traslado
del privilegio del
Almirantadgo al
Almirante de las
Yndias [*l. m.*].

[1] Françisco de Soria, lugarteniente de nuestro almirante
mayor de Castilla: nos vos mandamos que dedes e fagades dar a
don Christóval Colón, nuestro almirante del mar Oçéano, un
treslado abtorizado en manera que faga fee de qualesquier cartas
de merçed e previlegio e confirmaçiones qu'el dicho almirante   5
mayor de Castilla tiene del dicho cargo e ofiçio de almirante,
por donde él, y otros por él, lleven e se cojan los derechos e
otras cosas a él pertenesçientes con el dicho cargo; porque
avemos fecho merçed al dicho don Christóval Colón que aya e
gose de las merçedes e honras e perrogativas e libertades e dere-   10
chos e salarios en el almirantadgo de las Yndias, que ha e tiene
e goza el dicho nuestro almirante mayor en el almirantadgo de
Castilla. [2] Lo qual fazed e conplid luego como fuerdes
requerido con esta nuestra carta, syn que en ello pongáys escusa
nin dilaçión alguna; e sy así non lo fisierdes e cumplierdes, man-   15
damos al nuestro asistente e a otras justiçias de la çibdad de
Sevilla que vos compellan e apremien a lo asý faser e complir; e
non fagades nin fagan ende ál.
[3] Fecha en la çibdad de Burgos a veynte e tres días del mes de
abril de noventa e syete años.   20

Yo el Rey
Yo la Reyna
[4] Por mandado del Rey e de la Reyna. Fernand Álvares.
[5] Acordada.

Sources: *GPVW. For the apparatus cf.* I.i.

El Rey e la Reyna

Carta a Don
Christóval Colón
para que pueda
tomar y asentar a
sueldo hasta 330
personas [*r. m.*].

Véase la ynstruçión
a ojas .XVI. [*r. m.*].

[1] Por la presente damos liçençia e facultad a vós don Christóval Colón, nuestro almirante del mar Oçéano, para que podáys
tomar /29 recto/ e toméys a sueldo fasta en número de trezientas e treynta personas, para que estén en las Yndias, de los
ofiçios e forma siguiente: quarenta escuderos, cient peones de   5
guerra e de trabajo, treynta marineros, treynta grumetes, veynte
labradores de oro, çinqüenta labradores, diez ortelanos, veynte
ofiçiales de todos ofiçios, treynta mugeres: que son todas las
dichas trezientas e treynta personas; la quales hagáys pagar
sueldo segund se contiene en la ynstruçión que çerca d'ello   10
mandamos dar; e sy alguno de los dichos ofiçios e gente fuere
neçesario mudarse o creçer en el número de los unos, abaxando
en los otros, lo podáys fazer, segund vierdes e entendierdes ser
complidero a nuestro serviçio, e con tanto que non sean más,
por todos, de las dichas trezientas e treynta personas.   15
[2] Fecha en la çibdad de Burgos a veynte e tres días del mes de
abril de mill e quatroçientos e noventa e syete años.

Yo el Rey
Yo la Reyna

[3] Por mandado del Rey e de la Reyna. Fernand Álvares.   20
[4] Acordada.

Sources: *GPVW*. 5. **forma** *GPV*] fama *W*. 11. **e** (gente) *GPW*] o *V*.

El Rey e la Reyna

Orden para que el
Tesorero de la
haçienda pague el
sueldo a las
personas según las
çédulas que
presentarán
firmadas de Don
Christóval Colón
Almyrante [r. m.].

[1] Nuestro thesorero de la hasyenda e cosas a nós pertenesçientes de las yslas e tierra firme descubiertas e puestas so nuestro señorío en el mar Oçéano en las partes de las Yndias: nos vos
mandamos que del oro e mercaderías e otras cosas que se ovieren en las dichas Yndias, dedes y paguedes a las personas que   5
ovieren de aver de nós qualquier salario e sueldo e otros
maravedís que ayan de aver por fletes de navíos e marineros, e
para las otras cosas que sean neçesarias para la habitaçión e poblaçión de la gente que está e oviere de yr a las dichas Yndias,
‹e› por sueldo e salario a la gente que nos oviere servido el   10
tiempo pasado lo que asý oviere de aver e les fuere devido segund se vos diere por nóminas e çédulas e libramientos firmadas
de sus nombres de don Christóval Colón, nuestro almirante,
visorrey e governador de las dichas Yndias, o su lugarteniente, y
los ofiçiales de nuestros contadores mayores que en las dichas   15
Yndias están e estovieren. [2] Con los quales recabdos e nóminas, e con cartas de pago de las partes, /29 verso/ mandamos
que vos sean reçebidos en cuenta los dichos maravedís que asý
libraren el dicho almirante e ofiçiales, e dierdes e pagardes
como dicho es; e non fagades ende ál.   20
[3] Fecha en la çibdad de Burgos a veynte e tres días del mes de
abril de mill e quatroçientos e noventa e syete años.

Yo el Rey

Yo la Reyna

[4] Por mandado del Rey e de la Reyna. Fernand Álvares.   25
[5] Acordada.

Sources: *GPVW*. 1. **Nuestro]** *a blank space precedes in GV*. 3. **las partes** *GPV]* la parte *W*. 7. **por** *GPV]*
om. W. 10. ‹e› *V] om. GPW*. **a** *GPV]* e *W*.

El Rey e la Reyna

Carta para que los
deudores del
Almirante paguen
lo que le deven
[*l. m.*].

[1] Nuestros contadores mayores e vuestros logartenientes e
ofiçiales: don Christóval Colón, nuestro almirante del mar
Oçéano, nos fiso relaçión qu'él ha prestado e presta a algunas de
las personas que están en las Yndias algunas contías de maravedís, las quales dis que le han de ser pagadas del sueldo e man- 5
tenimiento que han de aver de nós las dichas personas, ‹e› nos
suplicó vos mandásemos que gelas librásedes en los maravedís
que las tales personas ovieren de aver de nós. [2] Porende nos
vos mandamos que, mostrándovos el dicho almirante, o quien
su poder oviere, en forma bastante de derecho, como los tales 10
maravedís le son devidos por las tales personas, gelos libréys en
el nuestro thesorero o en su lugarteniente de las dichas Yndias,
para que gelos paguen de lo que ovieren de dar e pagar a las tales
personas que asý las devieren al dicho almirante.
[3] Fecho en Burgos a nueve días de mayo de noventa e syete 15
años.

Yo el Rey

Yo la Reyna

[4] Por mandado del Rey e de la Reyna. Fernand Álvares.

[5] Acordada. 20

Sources: *GPVW*. 3. **presta** *GVW*] prestan *P*. a *GPW*] *om. V* (algunas = a algunas). 4. **contías** *GPV*]
quantias *W*. 6. ‹e›] *om. GPVW* (*in V* personas nos suplico *over an erasure*). 15. a *GPV*] *om. W*. 19. **Por**
. . . **Álvares** *GVW*] *om. V*.

El Rey e la Reyna

Liçençia para tomar
a sueldo más gente,
si el Almirante
quisiere [*l. m.*].

[1] Por la presente damos liçençia e facultad a vós don Christóval Colón, nuestro almirante del mar Oçéano, para que sy
vierdes que conviene a nuestro serviçio que se tomen a sueldo
más número de personas de las que agora mandamos yr a las
Yndias a estar en ellas, las podáys tomar e tener fasta llegar a   5
número de quinientas personas por todas, por el tiempo e segund que a vós bien visto fuere, con tanto que el sueldo e mantenimiento que las tales personas que acreçentardes ovieren de
aver, se les pague de qualquier mercaduría e otras cosas de valor
/ 30 recto/ que se oviere en las dichas Yndias, syn que nos man-   10
damos proveer para ello de otra parte.
[2] Fecha en la çibdad de Burgos a veynte e tres días del mes de
abril de mill e quatroçientos e noventa e syete años.

Yo el Rey

Yo la Reyna   15

[3] Por mandado del Rey e de la Reyna. Fernand Álvares.
[4] Acordada.

XXII (21)

[1] Don Fernando e doña Ysabel, por la graçia de Dios rey e
reyna de Castilla, de León, de Aragón, de Seçilia, de Granada,
de Toledo, de Valençia, de Galizia, de Mallorcas, de Sevilla, de
Çerdeña, de Córdova, de Córcega, de Murçia, de Jahén, de los
Algarbes, de Algezira, de Gibraltar e de las yslas de Canaria,   5
conde e condesa de Barçelona, señores de Viscaya e de Molina,
duques de Athenas e de Neopatría, condes de Rosellón e de

Sources: *GPVW*. 5. **las** *GPV*] *om. W.* 8. **ovieren** *GPW*] oviere *V.* 9. **mercaduría** *GPV*] mercaderia
W. 12. **tres** *GV*] dos *PW.*   Sources: *GPVW.* 6. **señores** *GPV*] e s. *W.*

Çerdania, marqueses de Oristán e de Goçiano: por quanto por
parte de algunas personas que están avezindadas en la ysla Española e de otras que se quieren avezindar en ella, nos fue su-   10
plicado les mandásemos dar e señalar en la dicha ysla tierras en
que ellos pudiesen sembrar pan e otras semillas, e plantar huertas e algodones e linares e viñas e árboles e cañaverales de açúcar, e otras plantas, e faser e hedificar casas e molinos e engenios
para el dicho açúcar, e otros hedifiçios provechosos y neçesarios   15
para su bivir, lo qual es serviçio nuestro e bien e utilidad común
de los moradores de la dicha ysla; porende, por la presente
damos liçençia e facultad a vós don Christóval Colón, nuestro
almirante de la mar Oçéana e nuestro visorrey e governador en
la dicha ysla, para que en todos los términos d'ella podades dar   20
e repartir, e dedes e repartades, a las tales personas e a cada uno
d'ellos que agora biven e moran en la dicha ysla, e a los que de
aquí adelante fueren a bivir e morar en ella, las tierras e montes
e aguas que vos vierdes que a cada uno d'ellos se deven dar e
repartir, segund quien fuere e lo que nos oviere servido e la   25
condiçión e calidad de su persona e bivir, e limitando e amojonando a cada uno lo que ansý le dierdes e repartierdes para que
aquello aya e tenga e posea por suyo e como suyo, e lo use e
plante e labre e se aproveche d'ello, con facultad de lo poder
vender e dar e donar e trocar e canbiar e enagenar e enpeñar e   30
fazer d'ello e en ello todo lo que quisiere e por bien toviere
como de cosa suya propia avida, de justo e derecho título,
obligándose las tales personas de tener e mantener vezindad con
su casa /30 verso/ poblada en la dicha ysla Española por quatro
años primeros syguientes contados desde el día que les dierdes e   35
entregardes las tales tierras e faziendas, e que farán en la dicha
ysla casas e plantarán las dichas viñas e huertas en la manera e
cantidad que a vós bien visto fuere; con tanto que en las tales
tierras e montes e aguas que asý dierdes e repartierdes, las tales
personas non puedan tener nin tengan juridiçión alguna çivil   40
nin criminal, nin cosa acotada nin dehesada, nin término
redondo más de aquello que tovieren çercado de una tapia en
alto, e que todo lo otro desçercado, cogidos los frutos y esquil-

Facultad al
Almirante para que
pueda dar y repartir
en todos los
términos de la ysla
Española tierras a
los moradores que
van y allá han ydo,
para edificar casas y
molinos, cultivar y
sembrar
[r. m.].

16. **común** (*corr.* Bustamante)] como *GPVW*. 19. **de . . . Oçéana** *GV*] del . . . oçeano *PW*. 24. **deven**
GPV] deve *W*. 26. **e** (limitando) *GPW*] *om. V*. 26-27. **amojonando** *GVW*] amojando *P*. 30. **canbiar e**
enagenar *GVW*] e. e c. *P*. 32. **avida** *GPV*] e a. *W*. **e** *GPV*] *om. W*. 36-37. **la dicha ysla** *GPV*] las dichas
yslas *W*. 41. **acotada** *GPV*] a dottada *W*.

Reservándose los
Reyes el oro, plata,
brasil y otros
metales que se
hallaren en las
tierras repartidas
[*l. m.*].

mos d'ello, sea pasto común e baldío a todos. [2] Asimesmo reservamos para nós el brasil e qualquier metal de oro e plata e otro metal que en las tales tierras se hallare; e asymesmo que las tales personas a quien dierdes e repartierdes las dichas tierras, non puedan faser nin fagan en ellas, nin en parte d'ellas, cargo nin descargo alguno de metal, nin de brasil, nin de otra cosa alguna que a nós pertenesçe e de que por nuestro mandado se ha de hazer cargo e descargo; e que solamente ellos puedan sembrar e coger e llevar e gosar los frutos e pan e semillas e árboles e viñas e algodonales e ‹lo› que en las dichas tierras sembraren e cogieren, como dicho es. [3] E queremos e mandamos que las tierras que les vos dierdes e repartierdes en la manera que dicha es, ningunas nin algunas personas non gelas tomen ni ocupen, nin les pongan en ellas, ni en parte d'ellas, embargo nin empedimiento alguno, mas libremente gelas dexen tener e poseer e usar e gozar d'ellas, segund que en esta nuestra carta se contiene. [4] E los unos nin los otros non fagan ende ál por alguna manera, so pena de la nuestra merçed e de diez mill maravedís a cada uno que lo contrario fiziere, para la nuestra cámara.

[5] Dada en la villa de Medina del Campo a veynte e dos días del mes de jullio, año del nasçimiento de nuestro salvador Jhesu Christo de mill e quatroçientos e noventa e syete años.

Yo el Rey

Yo la Reyna

[6] Yo Juan de la Parra, secretario del Rey e de la Reyna nuestros señores, la fis escrevir por su mandado.

[7] E en las espaldas de la dicha carta desýa: "Acordada: Rodericus, doctor; Fernand Órtix, por chançiller. Registrada: Doctor".

45

50

55

60

65

70

---

44. **ello** *GPV*] ellos *W.* 46. **hallare** *GPV*] hallare(n) *W.* 49-50. **otra . . . que** *GPW*] otras cosas algunas de las que *V.* 50. **pertenesçe** *W*] pertenesçen *GPV.* 52. **gosar** *GV*] gastar *PW.* 53. **‹lo›** (*corr.* Bustamante)] *om. GPVW.* 65. **de** (nuestro) *GPV*] del *W.*

El Rey e la Reyna

[1] Don Fernando e doña Ysabel, por la graçia de Dios rey e
reyna de Castilla, de /31 recto/ León, de Aragón, de Seçilia, de
Granada, de Toledo, de Valençia, de Galizia, de Mallorcas,
de Sevilla, de Çerdeña, de Córdova, de Córçega, de Murçia, de
Jahén, de los Algarbes, de Algezira, de Gibraltar e de las yslas   5
de Canaria, conde e condesa de Barçelona, señores de Viscaya e
de Molina, duques de Athenas e de Neopatría, condes de Rosellón e de Çerdania, marqueses de Oristán e de Goçiano: porque
a los reyes e prínçipes es propia cosa de honrar e sublimar e fazer
merçedes e graçias a los sus súbditos e naturales, espeçialmente   10
âquellos que bien e lealmente los sirven, lo qual por nós visto, e
considerando los muchos e buenos e leales serviçios que vos don
Bartolomé Colón, hermano de don Christóval Colón, nuestro
almirante del mar Oçéano e visorrey e governador de las yslas
nuevamente halladas en las Yndias, nos avedes fecho e fazedes de   15

Merçed del
Adelantado de las
Yndias a Don
Bartolomé Colón,
hermano del
Almirante [r. m.].

cada día e esperamos que nos faréys de aquí adelante, tenemos
por bien e es nuestra merçed e voluntad que de aquí adelante vos
lламéys e yntituléys "Adelantado" de las dichas yslas nuevamente halladas en las dichas Yndias, e podades usar e exerçer e
fazer en las dichas yslas, e en cada una d'ellas, todas las cosas que   20
los otros adelantados de los dichos nuestros reynos pueden faser;
e que ayades e gozedes e vos sean guardadas todas las honras e
graçias e merçedes e preheminençias e perrogativas que son
devidas e se deven faser e guardar, segund las leyes por nós fechas
en las cortes de Toledo, e las otras leyes de nuestros reynos, a los   25
otros nuestros ‹adelantados d'ellos, e segund se guardan e las han
e gozan los otros› adelantados de los dichos nuestros reynos, asý
en sus adelantamientos como fuera d'ellos. [2] E por esta nuestra
carta, o por su treslado sygnado de escrivano público, mandamos
al yllustríssimo prínçipe don Juan, nuestro muy caro e muy   30

Sources: *GPVW*. *Rubric*: **El . . . Reyna** *GP*] *om. VW*. 2. **Castilla de**] *repeated in G at the beginning of the document*. 6. **señores** *GPV*] e s. *W*. 11. **âquellos** *GPV*] a aquellos *W*. 26-27. ‹**adelantados . . . otros›** *V*] *om. GPW (homoeoteleuton)*.

amado fijo, e a los ynfantes, perlados, duques, marqueses, condes
e adelantados e ricos omes, maestres de las órdenes, priores,
comendadores e subcomendadores, e a los del nuestro consejo e
oydores de la nuestra abdiençia, alcaldes e alguaziles e otras justiçias qualesquier de la nuestra casa e corte e chançillería, e a   35
todos los conçejos, justiçias, regidores, cavalleros, escuderos,
ofiçiales e omes buenos de las çibdades e villas e logares de los
dichos nuestros reynos e señoríos, e al dicho nuestro almirante,
visorrey e governador de las dichas yslas, e a los vesynos e moradores, e a la otra gente que en ellas están e estovieren de /31   40
verso/ asiento o en otra qualquier manera, que de aquí adelante
vos yntitulen e llamen e vos ayan e tengan por adelantado de las
dichas yslas e tierra firme, e vos guarden e fagan guardar todas las
dichas honras e preheminençias, prerrogativas e inmunidades
que segund las dichas leyes vos deven ser guardadas, e vos recu-   45
dan e fagan recudir con los derechos e salarios al dicho ofiçio de
nuestro adelantado anexos e pertenesçientes, bien e complidamente, en guisa que vos non mengue ende cosa alguna: ca
nos por esta nuestra carta vos criamos e fasemos adelantado de las
dichas yslas e tierra firme, que asý nuevamente se han fallado e   50
descubierto en las Yndias, e vos reçebimos e avemos por
reçebido al dicho ofiçio e al uso e exerçiçio d'él, e mandamos
que en ello, ni en parte d'ello, embargo ni empedimiento alguno
vos non pongan nin consientan poner. [3] E sy d'esto que dicho
es quisierdes nuestra carta de previlegio, mandamos al nuestro   55
chançiller e notarios e a los otros ofiçiales que están a la tabla de
los nuestros sellos, que vos lo den e pasen e sellen, e los unos nin
los otros non fagan ende ál por alguna manera, so pena de la
nuestra merçed e de dies mill maravedís a cada uno que lo contrario fiziere, para la nuestra cámara. [4] E demás, mandamos al   60
ome que les esta nuestra carta mostrare que los enplase que
parescan ante nós en la nuestra corte, doquier que nos seamos,
del día que los enplasare fasta quinse días primeros syguientes, so
la dicha pena; so la qual mandamos a qualquier escrivano público que para esto fuere llamado, que dé ende al que gela mos-   65
trare testimonio sygnado con su signo, porque nos sepamos en
cómo se cumple nuestro mandado.

34. **e** (alguaziles) *GPV*] *om. W.* 36. **escuderos** *GPW*] e e. *V.* 39. **visorrey** *GPW*] e v. *V.* 40. **de**] de // de
G. 44. **inmunidades** *GVW*] ymmdades *P.* 47. **anexos** *GVW*] inexos *P.* 48. **ende** *GPV*] *om. W.* 65.
gela] gelo *GPVW.*

[5] Dada en la villa de Medina del Campo a veynte e dos días
del mes de jullio, año del nasçimiento de nuestro salvador Jhesu
Christo de mill e quatroçientos e noventa e syete años.   70

Yo el Rey
Yo la Reyna

[6] Yo Juan de la Parra, secretario del Rey e de la Reyna nuestros señores, la fis escrevir por su mandado.

[7] Y en las espaldas de la dicha carta desýa: "Acordada: 75
Rodericus, doctor; Fernando Órtix, por chançiller. Registrada:
Doctor".

XXIV (37)
/32 recto/

El Rey e la Reyna

Carta para que el
Almirante pueda
pagar la gente que
ha estado y está en
las Indias a sueldo
[r. m.].

[1] Por la presente damos liçençia e facultad a vós don Christóval Colón, nuestro almirante del mar Oçéano e del nuestro
consejo, para que podades pagar e pagués a las personas que han
estado e están e estovieren de aquí adelante, conforme a la ynstruçión que de nós tenéys del número de la gente que ha de   5
estar en las dichas Yndias, e a las personas e dueños de navíos
que han llevado e llevaren mantenimientos e otras cosas a las
dichas Yndias, todos los maravedís que se les deven e devieren
de aquí adelante de qualesquier sueldos e mantenimientos e
fleytes de navíos, seyendo aquello primeramente averiguado lo   10
que acá se oviere de pagar por el obispo de Badajós e por vós, e
lo que oviere de pagar en las Yndias por vós e por el logarteniente de nuestros contadores mayores que allá residen,
dando a cada uno lo que justamente se le deve e deviere; lo qual
les ayáys de pagar e paguéys de qualesquier mercaderías e otras   15
cosas que en las dichas Yndias se ovieren, con tanto que la paga
o librança que les fizierdes sea señalada del dicho logarteniente

---

Sources: GPVW. 3. **pagués**] paguen GPVW. 9. **e** (fleytes) GPV] de W. 12. **oviere** GPVW] corr. ‹se› o.
(cf. 11)? 15. **mercaderías** GPV] mercadurias W.

de nuestros contadores mayores e asentada en los nuestros libros: para lo qual vos damos poder complido.

[2] Fecho en la villa de Alcalá de Henares a veynte e tres días del   20
mes de diziembre de noventa e syete años.

Yo el Rey
Yo la Reyna

[3] Por mandado del Rey e de la Reyna. Fernand Álvares.

[4] Acordada.   25

XXV (32)

El Rey e la Reyna

Autoridad para que
en compañía del
Obisbo de Badajoz
pueda tasar el
precio de los
mantenimientos
que se han de llevar
a las Indias [*r. m.*].

[1] Reverendo yn Christo Padre, obispo de Badajós, e don
Christóval Colón, almirante del mar Oçéano, ambos del nuestro consejo: vimos una vuestra letra, y çerca de lo que desýs que
non se ha proveýdo cosa alguna fasta agora en lo de los mantenimientos que han de yr a las Yndias, a cabsa que no halláys   5
persona que los tome a cargo por los preçios /32 verso/ que de
acá fueron tasados en las ynstruçiones que vos el dicho almirante levastes, porque dis que valen los dichos mantenimientos a mayores preçios que acá se tasaron, y pues asý es, nos vos
mandamos y encargamos que amos a dos juntamente lo veáys, y   10
busquéys personas fiables que lo tomen, y taséys el preçio que
justo fuere e vos paresçiere que se les deve dar, aviendo respetto
al valor de los dichos mantenimientos; e sy non fallardes tales
personas, lo proveáys como a vosotros mejor paresçiere, por
manera que non se detenga la partida de vós el dicho almirante,   15
ca para ello vos damos poder complido.

[2] Fecho en la villa de Alcalá de Henares a veynte e tres días del
mes de diziembre de noventa e syete años.

Yo el Rey
Yo la Reyna   20

20. **Fecho** GPV (*cf.* p. 324, 17)] fecha *W.* **días** GPW] *om. V.*   Sources: GPVW. 11. **fiables** GV] fieles
PW.

[3] Por mandado del Rey e de la Reyna. Fernand Álvares.
[4] E en las espaldas desýa: "Acordada".

XXVI (11)

[1] Don Fernando e doña Ysabel, por la graçia de Dios rey e
reyna de Castilla, de León, de Aragón, de Seçilia, de Granada,
de Toledo, de Valençia, de Galizia, de Mallorcas, de Sevilla, de
Çerdeña, de Córdova, de Córçega, de Murçia, de Jahén, de los
Algarbes, de Algezira, de Gibraltar, de las yslas de Canaria,   5
condes de Barçelona e señores de Viscaya e de Molina, duques
de Athenas e de Neopatría, condes de Rosellón e de Çerdania,
marqueses de Oristán e de Goçiano: a vós los cavalleros e escuderos, ofiçiales e omes buenos e otras qualesquier personas de
qualquier estado o condiçión que soys, que por nuestro man-   10
dado fuystes e estáys e estovierdes de aquí adelante en las yslas
por nuestro mandado descubiertas e por descobrir en el mar

Carta para que los
de las Indias
obedeçcan al
Almirante como a
Visorrey y
Governador d'ellas,
y cumplan a sus
mandados [l. m.].

Oçéano en la parte de las Yndias, e a cada uno e qualquier de
vós, salud e graçia. [2] Bien sabéys cómo don Christóval Colón,
nuestro almirante de las dichas Yndias del dicho mar Oçéano,   15
es nuestro visorrey e governador d'ellas por virtud de nuestras
cartas de poderes que para ello le mandamos dar e dimos; e
porque nuestra merçed e voluntad es qu'el dicho almirante
tenga el dicho cargo de nuestro visorrey e governador e que lo
/33 recto/ use e exerçite en las dichas yslas, e que todos fagáys   20
e cumpláys todo lo que él de nuestra parte vos mandare y en-
tendiere ser complidero a nuestro serviçio, nos vos mandamos a
todos e a cada uno de vós que asý lo cumpláys y exsecutéys, e
que todos vos conformés con él e fagades e cumplades todo lo
qu'él de nuestra parte vos mandare, como sy nos en persona vos   25
lo mandásemos, so las penas que vos pusiere o mandare poner
de nuestra parte, las quales por la presente vos ponemos e
avemos por puestas: para las exsecutar en los que lo contrario
fiziéredes, damos poder complido al dicho almirante don

---

22. desýa GPW] om. V.   Sources: GPVW.   5. de (las) GPV] e de W.   6. condes GPV] conde e condesa
W.   11. las yslas GVW] la ysla P.   19. tenga GPW] traga V. lo GPV] el W.   26. o GPV] e W.   27. por la
presente GPV] de nuestra parte W.   28. para GPVW] corr. ‹e› p. (Bustamante)?

Christóval Colón o a quien su poder oviere, e los unos ni los   30
otros non fagades nin fagan ende ál por alguna manera, so pena
de la nuestra merçed e de diez mill maravedís para la nuestra
cámara a cada uno de los que lo contrario fizierdes.
[3] Dada en la çibdad de Segovia a diez e seys días del mes de
agosto, año del nasçimiento de nuestro señor Ihesu Christo de   35
mill e quatroçientos e noventa e quatro años.

Yo el Rey
Yo la Reyna

[4] Yo Fernand Álvares de Toledo, secretario del Rey e de la
Reyna nuestros señores, la fis escrevir por su mandado.   40
[5] E en las espaldas de la dicha carta estava escripto esto que se
sygue: "Registrada: Alonso Peres; Pero Gutierres, chançiller".

XXVII (7)

[1] Don Fernando e doña Ysabel, por la graçia de Dios rey e
reyna de Castilla, de León, de Aragón, de Seçilia, de Granada,
de Toledo, de Valençia, de Galizia, de Mallorcas, de Sevilla, de
Çerdeña, de Córdova, de Córçega, de Murçia, de Jahén, del
Algarbe, de Algezira, de Gibraltar e de las yslas de Canaria,   5
conde e condesa de Barçelona e señores de Viscaya e de
Molina, duques de Athenas e de Neopatría, condes de Rosellón
e de Çerdania, marqueses de Oristán e de Goçiano: a todos e
qualesquier capitanes, maestres, e patrones, e contramaestres, e
marineros de naos e caravelas e otras fustas, e a otras qualesquier   10
personas de qualquier condiçión que sean, / 33 verso/ nuestros
vasallos, súbditos e naturales, a quien lo de yuso en esta nuestra
carta contenido atañe o atañer pueda, e a cada uno e qualquier
de vós a quien esta nuestra carta fuere mostra‹da›, o el traslado
d'ella sygnado de escrivano público, salud e graçia. [2] Sepades   15
que nos avemos mandado a don Christóval Colón, nuestro
almirante del mar Oçéano e nuestro visorrey e governador de
las yslas e tierra firme del dicho mar Oçéano a la parte de las

42. **Peres** GPW] peres. Registro e Sello nichil V.   Sources: GPVW. 4-5. **del Algarbe** GPV] de los
Algarbes W. 5. **de** (Gibraltar) GPW] e de V. 10. **a** GPV] om. W. 13. **pueda** GPV] puede W. 14. **mostra‹da›** VW] mostra GP.

Yndias, que con çiertas naos e caravelas e otras fustas, como
nuestro capitán, vaya a las dichas Yndias e tierra firme que son   20
a la dicha parte de las Yndias descubiertas e por descobrir. [3]
Porende, por la presente mandamos a todos e a cada uno de vós
los dichos maestres e capitanes e patrones e contramaestres e
compañas de las dichas naos e caravelas e otras fustas, e a todas
las compañas que en ellas e en cada una d'ellas navegaren, que   25

tengades e tengan por nuestro capitán general de las dichas
naos e fustas e caravelas al dicho don Christóval Colón, nuestro
almirante, visorrey e governador del dicho mar Oçéano, e le
obedescades e tengades por nuestro capitán general, e fagades e
cumplades e pongades en obra todo lo que por él de nuestra   30
parte vos fuere dicho e mandado, e cada cosa e parte d'ello,
segund e como e en la forma e manera e a los tiempos e so las
penas que él de nuestra parte vos mandare, syn poner en ello
escusa nin dilaçión alguna, bien asý e atán complidamente
como sy nos en persona vos lo mandásemos; ca nos por la pre-   35
sente le hazemos nuestro capitán general de los dichos navíos e
caravelas e otras fustas, e le damos poder e facultad para las mandar e governar como nuestro capitán general e para exsecutar
en la compaña d'ellas qualesquier penas en que cayeren e yn-
currieren por non complir e obedeçer sus mandamientos,   40
como dicho es. [4] Pero es nuestra merçed e voluntad que el
dicho nuestro capitán general don Christóval Colón, nuestro
almirante e visorrey e governador, nin vosotros, ni alguno de
vós, non vayades a la Mina ni al trato d'ella que tiene el Sereníss-
simo Rey de Portogal, nuestro hermano, porque nuestra   45
voluntad es de guardar e que se guarde por nuestros súbditos e
naturales lo que çerca de la dicha Mina tenemos capitulado e
asentado /34 recto/ con el dicho Rey de Portogal; lo qual vos
mandamos que así fagáys e cumpláys, so pena de la nuestra
merçed e de confiscaçión de vuestros bienes para la nuestra   50
cámara e fisco.
[5] Dada en la çibdad de Barçelona a veynte e ocho días del mes
de mayo, año del nasçimiento de nuestro señor Jhesu Christo
de mill e quatroçientos e noventa e tres años.

Yo el Rey   55
Yo la Reyna

21. a GPV] en W.   28. **visorrey** GPV] e v. W.   31. **cada** GPV] a c. W.   32. **e** (en) GPV] om. W.   34. **atán**
GPV] tan V.   49. **fagáys e** GV] om. PW.   53. **señor** GPV] salvador W.

[6] Yo Fernand Álvares de Toledo, secretario del Rey e de la Reyna nuestros señores, la fis escrivir por su mandado.

[7] E en las espaldas de la dicha carta estava escripto lo que se sygue: "Acordada: Rodericus, doctor. Registrada: Alonso 60 Peres; Pero Gutierres, chançiller".

XXVIII (8)

El Rey e la Reyna

Para que el Almirante pueda dexar persona que selle las cartas y trate en su nombre las cosas de la Indias [*r. m.*].

[1] Por quanto en el poder que mandamos dar e dimos a vós don Christóval Colón, nuestro almirante de las yslas e tierra firme que se han descubierto e se han de descobrir en el mar Oçéano a la parte de las Yndias, e nuestro visorrey e governador de las dichas yslas e tierra firme, se contiene que vos ayáys de 5 librar las cartas e provisiones patentes que se ovieren de hazer e espedir en las dichas Yndias e tierra firme en nuestro nombre "por don Fernando e doña Ysabel, etç.", las quales han de yr selladas con nuestro sello que para ello vos mandamos que lleváledes, e podría acaesçer que vos no estoviédes en las di- 10 chas Yndias e tierra firme, porque convernía que fuédes a descobrir otras yslas o tierra firme, o hazer otras cosas compli-deras a nuestro serviçio, de cuya cabsa avréys de dexar en vues-tro lugar alguna persona que entienda e provea en las cosas de las dichas Yndias e tierra firme en vuestra absençia, el qual non 15 podría entender nin proveer en ello, dando las dichas nuestras cartas e provisiones en nuestro nombre syn aver para ello nues-tro poder e abtoridad; porende, por la presente damos poder e facultad a la persona que en vuestra absençia vos nombrardes para quedar en las dichas yslas e tierra firme, para que pueda 20 librar e espedir los negoçios e cabsas que allí ocurrieren, dando

---

60. **doctor** *GPV*] *om. W; in V followed by* derecho de sello e rregistro nichil.   Sources: *GPVW.* 2. **yslas**] yndias *GPVW; cf.* 4 a la parte de las Yndias, 5 de las dichas yslas, 15 yslas *V.* 3. **han** (descubierto) *GPV*] ha *W.* **han** *GPV*] ha *W.* 12. **o** (tierra) **GP**] e *VW.* **o** *GPV*] e *W.* 13. **avréys** *GPV*] aveys *W.* 15. **Yndias** *GPW*] yslas *V* (*cf. supra* 2).

las dichas provisiones e cartas en nuestro nombre e sellándolas
/34 verso/ con nuestro sello, segund que vos lo podríades hazer
seyendo presente en las dichas yslas e tierra firme, por virtud de
los dichos nuestros poderes que tenés. [2] De lo qual mandamos   25
dar la presente firmada de nuestros nombres.
[3] Fecha en Barçelona a veynte e ocho días de mayo de
noventa e tres años.

Yo el Rey
Yo la Reyna   30

[4] Por mandado del Rey e de la Reyna. Fernand Álvares.
[5] E en las espaldas desýa: "Acordada".

XXIX (9)

El Rey e la Reyna

Facultad para que el
Almirante ponga
todas las tres
personas del
regimiento [*l. m.*].

[1] Por quanto segund el asiento que nos mandamos fazer con
vós don Christóval Colón, nuestro almirante del mar Oçéano e
nuestro visorrey e governador de las yslas e tierra firme del
dicho mar Oçéano que son a la parte de las Yndias, entre otras
se contiene que para los ofiçios de governaçión que oviere de   5
aver en las dichas yslas e tierra firme, vos ayáys de nombrar tres
personas para cada ofiçio e que nos nombremos e proveamos al
uno d'ellos del tal ofiçio, y al presente no se puede guardar el
dicho asiento por la brevedad de vuestra partida para las dichas
yslas, confiando de vós el dicho nuestro almirante, visorrey e   10
governador, que lo proveerés fiablemente e como cumple a
nuestro serviçio e a la buena governaçión de las dichas yslas, por
la presente vos damos poder e facultad para que en tanto quanto
fuere nuestra merçed e voluntad, podáys proveer de los dichos
ofiçios de governaçión de las dichas yslas e tierra firme a las   15
personas e por el tiempo e en la forma e manera que a vós bien
visto fuere; a los quales que asý por vós fueren proveýdos, les
damos poder e facultad para usar de los dichos ofiçios, segund e

---

22. **provisiones e cartas** *GPV*] c. e p. *W* (*cf.* 6).   Sources: *GPVW.* 11. **a** *GPW*] al *V.* 13. **poder** *GV*]
licencia p. *PW* (*Raccolta*). **quanto** *GPV*] que *W.*

por la forma e manera que en vuestras provisiones que de los
dichos ofiçios les diéredes será contenido.   20

[2] Fecha en la çibdad de Barçelona a veynte e ocho días de
mayo de mill e quatroçientos e noventa e tres años.

Yo el Rey

Yo la Reyna

[3] Por mandado del Rey e de la Reyna. Fernand Álvares.   25

[4] Acordada.

XXX (39)

[1] Don Fernando e doña Ysabel, por la graçia de Dios rey e
reyna de Castilla, de León, de Aragón, de Seçilia, de Granada,
/35 recto/ de Toledo, de Valençia, de Galizia, de Mallorcas, de
Sevilla, de Çerdeña, de Córdova, de Córçega, de Murçia, de
Jahén e de los Algarbes, de Algezira, de Gibraltar e de las yslas   5
de Canaria, conde e condesa de Barçelona e señores de Viscaya
e de Molina, duques de Athenas e de Neopatría, condes de
Rosellón e de Çerdania, marqueses de Oristán e de Goçiano:
por quanto vos don Christóval Colón, nuestro almirante, viso-

Facultad para que | rrey e governador del mar Oçéano, nos suplicastes e pedistes   10
pueda hacer y | por merçed que vos diésemos nuestro poder e facultad para
estableçer de sus | faser e estableser de vuestros bienes, vasallos e heredamientos,
bienes, o oficios, | ofiçios perpetuos, uno o dos mayoradgos porque quede per-
perpetuos dos | petua memoria de vós e de vuestra casa e linage, e porque los
mayoradgos, | que de vós vinieren sean honrados; lo qual por nós visto, e   15
porque quede | considerado que a los reyes e prínçipes es propia cosa honrar e
perpetua memoria | sublimar a sus súbditos e naturales, espeçialmente a aquellos que
d'él, de su casa y de | bien e lealmente lo·syrven; e porque en se faser los tales mayo-
su linage [r. m.]. | radgos es honra de la Corona Real de estos nuestros reynos e
pro e bien d'ellos; e acatando los muchos buenos e leales e   20
grandes e continuos serviçios que vos el dicho don Christóval
Colón, nuestro almirante, nos avedes fecho e fasedes de cada
día, espeçialmente en descobrir e traer a nuestro poder e se-

26. **Acordada** GPW] E en las espaldas dezia acordada V.   Sources: GPW. 5. **e** (de los) GP] om. W. 11.
que GP] om. W. 17. **a** GW] om. P (aquellos = a aquellos). 18. **lo** G] los P, nos W. 23. **espeçialmente** GP]
e e. W.

ñorío las yslas e tierra firme que descobristes en el dicho mar
Oçéano - mayormente porque esperamos que, con ayuda de   25
Dios nuestro señor, redundará en mucho serviçio Suyo e honra
nuestra, e pro e utilidad de nuestros reynos, e porque se espera
que los pobladores de las dichas Yndias se convertirán a nuestra
santa fee católica -, tovímoslo por bien; e por esta nuestra carta,
de nuestro propio motuo e çierta sçiençia e poderío real ab-   30
soluto, de que en esta parte queremos usar e usamos como rey
e reyna e señores non reconosçientes superior en lo temporal,
vos damos liçençia e facultad para que cada e quando vos quisierdes e por bien tuvierdes, asý en vuestra vida por symple
contrato e manda, como por donaçión entre bivos, como por   35
vuestro testamento e postrimera voluntad e por cobdeçildo, o
en otra manera qualquier que quisierdes e /35 verso/ por bien
tovierdes, podades fazer e fagades mayoradgo, o mayoradgos,
por una, o dos, o tres escripturas, o por muchas, tantas quantas
veses y en la manera que quisierdes e bien visto vos fuere; e   40
aquél o aquéllos o qualquier cosa o parte d'ellos podades revo-
car, testar e emendar e añadir e quitar e menguar e acreçentar
una e dos e tres veses e quantas más veses e como e en la manera
que quisierdes e bien visto vos fuere; e que el dicho mayoradgo,
o mayoradgos, podades fazer e fagades en don Diego Colón,   45
vuestro hijo mayor legítimo, o en qualquier de vuestros fijos
herederos que oy día tenéys o tovierdes de aquí adelante, e, en
defecto e falta de hijos, en uno o dos de vuestros parientes, o
otras personas que vos quisierdes e bien visto vos fuere; e que lo
podáys fazer e fagáys de qualesquier vasallos, e juridiçiones, e   50
casas, e tierras, e heredamientos, e molinos, e dehesas, e otros
qualesquier heredamientos e bienes, e de qualesquier ofiçios
que vos de nós tengáys de juro e de heredad, e de todo lo
susodicho, e cada cosa e parte d'ello, que oy día tenedes e po-
seedes e vos perteneçe aver e tener fasta aquí, e tovierdes e   55
poseyerdes de aquí adelante, asý por merçed e donadíos, como
por renunçiaçiones e compras e troques e cambios e premutaçiones, o por otros qualesquier títulos onorosos o lucrativos, o en
otra qualquier manera, o por qualquier cabsa o razón que sea.
[2] El qual dicho mayoradgo, o mayoradgos, podades fazer e   60

27. **utilidad** GP] auctoridad W. 33. **vos** (quisierdos) GP] que v. W. 43. **e** (dos) GP] o W. **e** (tres) GP] o
W. 47. **o tovierdes**] *repeated in* G. 48. **o** (otras) GP] e W. 57. **e** (premutaçiones)] e / e G. 58. **lucrativos**
W] latrativos GP.

fagades a toda vuestra voluntad e libre querer e dispusiçión, asý
de los dichos vuestros bienes e cosas, entera e complidamente
syn diminuçión alguna, como de qualquier parte o partes d'e-
llos, para que ynviolablemente queden los dichos vuestros
bienes e qualquier cosa e parte d'ellos por mayoradgo en el   65
dicho don Diego Colón, vuestro fijo, e en los dichos vuestros
fijos e desçendientes en quien quisierdes fazer e fizierdes el
dicho mayoradgo, o mayoradgos, con las condiçiones e limita-
çiones, cargos, vínculos e firmezas, instituçiones e sostituçiones,
modos, reglas e penas e submisiones que vos quisierdes e por   70
bien tovierdes, e con qualesquier hordenanças e mandas e pac-
tos e /36 recto/ convenençias, e segund e por la forma e manera
que vos vinculardes e mandardes e dispusierdes e otorgardes,
por una o por muchas escripturas, como dicho es. [3] Lo qual
todo, e cada cosa e parte d'ello, aviéndolo aquí por expresado e 75
declarado, como sy de palabra a palabra aquí fuesse puesto e
expeçificado, nos desde agora para entonçes, de la dicha nuestra
çierta sçiençia e propio motuo e poderío real absoluto, de que
en esta parte queremos usar e usamos, lo loamos e aprovamos,
confirmamos e ynterponemos a ello, e a cada cosa e parte d'ello, 80
nuestro decreto e abtoridad real; e mandamos que vos vala e sea
guardado todo, e cada cosa e parte d'ello, ynviolablemente,
para agora e para syempre jamás, aunque aquello, e cada cosa e
parte d'ello, sea contra expresso derecho e contra toda forma e
orden d'él, e sea tal e de tal manera que de neçesario se deviesse 85
haser expresa e espeçial minçión en esta nuestra carta e que non
pudiesse ser comprehendido so la generalidad d'ella; e que sea
guardado bien, asý e atán complidamente como sy sobre cada
cosa e parte e artículo d'ello oviese nuestra aprovança e liçençia
e mandado, como e segund e por la forma que en la dicha   90
vuestra dispusiçión, o dispusiçiones, se contuviere. [4] Lo qual
todo es nuestra merçed que se faga asý, non enbargante que los
otros vuestros fijos herederos e los otros vuestros parientes e
debdos e desçendientes e transversales sean agraviados en su
legítima e alimentos que les pertenesçen, e qu'el dicho don   95
Diego Colóm, vuestro fijo, e aquél, o aquéllos, en quien fizierdes el dicho mayoradgo, o mayoradgos, o manda, o me-
joría, lieven o ayan muy grand e notable demasía de lo que,

---

67. **fizierdes** *GP*] fagades *W*. 75. **aviéndolo** *GP*] aviendo *W*. 77. **expeçificado** (*corr. Raccolta*)] ex-
paçificado *GPW*. 87. **ella** *GW*] ello *P*. 88. **guardado**] guardada *GPW*. 96. **en** *GP*] a *W*.

segund derecho e leyes del fuero, les podedes dexar en vuestro testamento e postrimera voluntad, e dar por donadíos entre 100 bivos o en otra qualquier manera. [5] Los quales dichos bienes que ansý yncluyerdes e pusierdes en el dicho vuestro mayoradgo, o mayoradgos, queremos e es nuestra merçed que sean ymprestibles y ynpartibles para syempre jamás, e que la persona, o personas, en quien fizierdes el dicho mayoradgo, o mayo- 105 radgos, o que, segund vuestra dispusiçión, le oviere, o los oviere, non los pueda vender, nin dar, nin donar, ni enagenar, nin dividir, ni apartar, nin los pueda perder, ni pierda, /36 verso/ por ninguna debda que deva, nin por otra razón ni cabsa, nin por ningund delicto nin crimen nin excesso que cometa, 110 salvo crimen *lese magestatis* o *perdulionis*, o trayçión, o crimen de eregía. [6] Lo qual queremos e es nuestra merçed que se guarde, non enbargante las leyes que se contienen que los mayoradgos no ayan logar, aunque se fagan por virtud de qualesquier cartas e rescritos que sobr'ello se den; e otrosý non enbargante quales- 115 quier leyes e fueros, e derechos, ordenamientos, usos e costumbres, estilos e fazañas, asý communes e muniçipales de los reyes nuestros anteçesores, que en contrario de lo susodicho sean o ser puedan; ni las leyes e derechos que dizen que cosa fecha en perjuyzio de terçero o contra los buenos usos e costumbres, en 120 que la parte entiende ser lepsa e dañificada, que non vale; e la ley que dize que los derechos proybitivos non pueden ser revocados; e las leyes que dizen que las cartas dadas contra ley, fuero e derecho, deven ser obedesçidas e non complidas, aunque contengan en sí qualesquier cabsas derogativas e otras 125 firmezas e nonobstançias; e la ley que dize que la defensa de la parte es prometida de derecho natural, e que aquélla non puede ser quitada nin revocada, e que las leyes e fueros e derechos valederos non pueden ser revocados, salvo por cortes, ni otra qualquier cosa, efecto, calidad, vigor, misterio que en contra de 130 lo susodicho sea, o ser pueda, aunque sea urgente o neçesario o mixto, o en otra qualquier manera: ca de la dicha nuestra çierta sçiençia e propio motuo e poderío real absoluto, de que en esta parte queremos usar e usamos, como reyes e soberanos señores non reconosçientes superior en lo temporal, aviéndolo aquí por 135

---

100. **e** (postrimera) *GP*] o *W.* 106. **le** *GP*] lo *W.* **oviere** *W*] ovieren *GP.* 108. **pierda** *PW*] pierda(n) *G.* 109. **deva** *PW*] deva(n) *G.* 110. **nin excesso** *G*] *om. PW.* **cometa**] cometan *GPW.* 111. **lese** *P*] legi *G*, lege *W.* 123. **leyes** *GW*] *om. P.* 128. **e** (fueros) *GP*] *om. W.* 130. **contra** *GP*] contrario *W.*

expresado e declarado, como sy de palabra a palabra aquí fuesse puesto e expresado, dispensamos con ello e lo abrogamos e derogamos, e quitamos e admovemos, en quanto a esto toca e atañe e atañer puede d'esta nuestra carta e de lo en ella contenido, toda obreçión e subreçión e todo otro ostáculo o en-/ 37 recto/ pedimento, e suplimos qualesquier defectos e otras qualesquier cosas que de fecho e de derecho, de sustançia o de solepnidad sean neçesarias e provechosas de suplir para validaçión e corroboraçión d'ello. [7] E mandamos al yllustríssimo prínçipe don Juan, nuestro muy caro e muy amado hijo, e a los ynfantes, perlados, duques, condes, marqueses, ricos ombres, maestres de las hórdenes, priores, comendadores e subcomendadores, e a los alcaydes de los castillos e casas fuertes e llanas, e a los del nuestro consejo e oydores de la nuestra abdiençia e chançillería, alcaldes e alguaziles de la nuestra casa e corte e chançillería, e a todos los corregidores, asystentes, alcaldes, alguaziles, merinos, prebostes, regidores, cavalleros, escuderos, ofiçiales e omes buenos de todas las çibdades e villas e logares d'estos nuestros reynos e señoríos, que agora son, o serán de aquí adelante, que vos guarden e fagan guardar esta merçed que vos fasemos, en todo e por todo, segund que en ella se contiene, e que vos non vayan nin pasen contra ella, nin contra parte d'ella en tiempo alguno, nin por alguna manera, nin por qualquier cabsa, nin rasón que sea o ser pueda; e que cumplan e que exsecuten e lleven a devida exsecuçión con efetto la dispusiçión e dispusiçiones que fizierdes del dicho mayoradgo, o mayoradgos, manda o mejorías, segund e por la forma e manera que en ellas, e en cada una d'ellas, se contenga e contuviere, syn atender nin esperar para ello otra nuestra carta, nin mandamiento, nin segunda nin terçera jusión. [8] De lo qual todo mandamos al nuestro chançiller mayor e notarios e otros ofiçiales que están a la tabla de los nuestros sellos, que vos libren e pasen e sellen nuestra carta de privilegio, la más firme e bastante que para ello menester ovierdes; e los unos nin los otros non fagades nin fagan ende ál por alguna manera, so pena de la nuestra merçed e de dies mill maravedís para la nuestra cámara a cada

140-141. **o enpedimento**] o en// o enpedimento G. 142. **o** GP] e W. 149. **e** (oydores) GP] *om. W.* 151. **asystentes** GP] e a. W. 153. **e** (omes) GP] *om. W.* 154. **o** GP] e W. 155. **e . . . guardar** GP] *om. W.* 156. **ella** GW] ellas P. 157. **ella** GP] ello W. 158. **ella** GP] ello W. 159. **cumplan** G] se c. PW. **que** G] *om. PW.* 161. **e** GP] o W.

uno por quien fincare de lo así fazer e cunplir. [9] E demás, mandamos al ome que vos esta carta mostrare, que vos emplase que parescades ante nós /37 verso/ en la nuestra corte, doquier que nos seamos, del día que vos enplazare fasta quinze días 175 primeros siguientes, so la dicha pena; so la qual mandamos a qualquier escrivano público que para esto fuere llamado, que dé ende al que gela mostrare testimonio signado con su signo, porque nos sepamos en cómo se cumple nuestro mandado.

[10] Dada en la çibdad de Burgos a veynte e tres días del mes de 180 abril, año del nasçimiento de nuestro señor Jhesu Christo de mill e quatroçientos e noventa e syete años.

Yo el Rey

Yo la Reyna

[11] Yo Fernand Álvares de Toledo, secretario del Rey e de la 185 Reyna nuestros señores, la fis escrevir por su mandado.

[12] Y en las espaldas de la dicha carta estava escripto lo siguiente: "En forma: Rodericus, doctor. Registrada: Alfonso Peres, e sellada".

XXXI (3)

El Rey e la Reyna

Çédula mensagera en que S. A. le mandan venir [*l. m.*].

[1] Don Christóval Colóm, nuestro almirante del mar Oçéano, e visorrey y governador de las yslas que se han descubierto en las Yndias: vimos vuestras letras y ovimos mucho plazer en saber lo que por ellas nos escrevistes, y de averos dado Dios tan buen fin en vuestro trabajo y encaminado bien en lo 5 que començastes, en que Él será mucho servido, y nosotros assimismo, y nuestros reynos reçibir‹án› tanto provecho; plazerá a Dios que, demás de lo que en esto Le servís, por ello reçibirés de nós muchas merçedes, las quales creed que se vos harán como vuestros serviçios e trabajos lo meresçen. [2] Y porque 10 queremos que lo que avéys començado con el ayuda de Dios se

Sources: *GPW*. 4. **escrevistes** *GP*] escrevis *W*. 7. **reçibir‹án›**] reçibir *GPW*. 10. **serviçios** *GP*] previllejos *W*.

continúe y lleve adelante, y desseamos que vuestra venida
fuesse luego, porende por serviçio nuestro que dedes la mayor
priessa que pudierdes en vuestra venida, porque con tiempo se
provea todo lo que es menester. [3] Y porque, como vedes, el   15
verano es entrado, y non se pase el tiempo para la yda allá, ved
sý algo se puede adereçar en Sevilla, o en otras partes, para vuestra tornada a la tierra que avéys hallado; y escre-/38 recto/ vid-
nos luego con esse correo que ha de bolver presto, porque
luego se provea como se haga en tanto que acá vos venís y   20
tornáys, de manera que quando bolvierdes de acá, esté todo
aparejado.
[4] De Barçelona, a treynta días de março de noventa e tres
años.

Yo el Rey   25
Yo la Reyna
[5] Por mandado del Rey e de la Reyna. Fernand Álvares.
[6] E en las espaldas desýa: "Por el Rey e la Reyna, a don
Christóval Colón, su almirante de la mar Oçéano, e visrey e
governador de las yslas que se han descubierto en las Yndias."   30

XXXII (13)

La Reyna

Çédula de mensage
sobre el traslado del
libro que le embía
S. A. para la
participación con
los Portugueses
[r. m.].
[1] Don Christóval Colón, mi almirante del mar Oçéano,
visorrey e governador de las yslas nuevamente falladas en las
Yndias: con este correo vos embío un traslado del libro que acá
dexastes, el qual ha tardado tanto porque se escriviesse se-
cretamente, para que éstos que están aquí de Portogal ni otro   5
alguno non supiesse d'ello; y a cabsa d'esto, porque más presto
se fiziesse, va de dos letras, segund veréys. [2] Çiertamente, segund lo que en este negoçio acá se ha platicado y visto, cada día
se conosçe ser muy mayor y de grand calidad y sustançia, y que

19. **esse** GP] este W.   20. **acá vos** GP] v. a. W.   29. **de la** G] del PW.   Sources: GPW.   1. **mi** GP]
nuestro W.

vos nos avéys en ello mucho servido, y tenemos de vós grand 10
cargo, y assí esperamos en Dios que demás de lo asentado con
vós que se ha de fazer e cumplir muy enteramente, que vos
reçibiréys de nós mucha más honra, merçed y acreçentamiento,
como es razón y lo adeudan vuestros serviçios e meresçimiento.

Compuso el
Almirante una carta
de marear, y la
Reyna le escrive
que, si está acabada,
la embíe luego
[*r. m.*].

[3] La carta del marear que avíades de fazer, sy es acabada, me 15
embiad luego, y por serviçio mýo deys grand priessa en vuestra
partida, para que aquélla, con la graçia de Nuestro Señor, se
ponga en obra syn dilaçión alguna, pues vedes quanto cumple al
bien del negoçio; y de todo de allá nos escrivid y fazed syempre
saber, que de acá de todo lo que oviere vos avisaremos e vos lo 20
faremos saber. [4] En el negoçio de Portogal no se ha tomado
con estos que aquí están determinaçión; aunque yo creo qu'el
Rey se llegará a razón en ello, querría que pensásedes lo contrario, porque /38 verso/ por ello non vos descuydéys ni dexéys
de yr sobre aviso al recabdo que cumple, para que en manera 25
alguna non podáys reçebir engaño.

[5] De Barçelona, a çinco días del mes de setiembre de noventa
e tres años.

Yo la Reyna

[6] Por mandado de la Reyna. Juan de la Parra. 30

[7] E en las espaldas desýa: "Por la Reyna, a don Christóval
Colón, su almirante del mar Oçéano y visorrey y governador
de las yslas nuevamente halladas en las Yndias".

XXXIII (10)

El Rey e la Reyna

Conoce S. A. la
grandeza de las
obras y servicios del
Almirante, y manda
que embíe Bernal
de Pisa [*l. m.*].

[1] Don Christóval Colón, nuestro almirante del mar Oçéano
y nuestro visorrey y governador de las yslas nuevamente falladas
en las partes de las Yndias: vimos las cartas que nos embiastes
con Antonio de Torres, con las quales ovimos mucho plazer, y

---

15. **me** *GP*] nos *W.* 16. **en** *GP*] a *W* (*but cf.* p. 336, 14). 19. **todo** *GP*] t. lo *W.* 25. **aviso** *GW*]
om. P. 31. **desýa** *GP*] d. lo siguiente *W.*   Sources: *GPW.*

damos muchas graçias a nuestro señor Dios que tan bien lo ha 5
fecho y en averos en todo tan bien guiado. [2] En mucho cargo
y serviçio vos tenemos lo que allá avéys fecho y trabajado con
tan buena orden y proveymiento, que non puede ser mejor; y
asimesmo oýmos al dicho Antonio de Torres y reçebimos todo
lo que con él nos embiastes, y non se esperava menos de vós, 10
segund la mucha voluntad y afetión que de vós se ha conosçido
y cognosçe en las cosas de nuestro serviçio. [3] Sed çierto que
nos tenemos de vós por mucho servidos y encargados en ello
para vos fazer merçedes y honra y acreçentamiento como vuestros grandes serviçios lo requieren y adeudan; y porque el dicho 15
Antonio de Torres tardó en venir aquí fasta agora y non avíamos visto vuestras cartas, las quales non nos avía embiado por
las traer él a mejor recabdo y por la priessa de la partida d'estos
navíos que agora van (los quales, a la ora que lo aquí supimos,
los mandamos despachar con todo recabdo de las cosas que de 20
allá embiastes por memorial e quanto más complidamente se
pudiesse fazer syn detenerlos, y assí se fará e /39 recto/ complirá
en todo lo otro qu'él traxo a cargo, al tiempo y como él lo
dixere), non ha lugar de vos responder como quisiéramos: pero,
quando él vaya, plaziendo a Dios, vos responderemos y man- 25
daremos proveer en todo ello, como cumple. [4] Nos avemos
avido enojo de las cosas que allá se han fecho fuera de vuestra
voluntad, las quales mandaremos bien remediar e castigar. [5]
En el primero viaje que para acá se fiziere, embiad a Bernal de
Pisa, al qual nos embiamos mandar que ponga en obra su 30
venida, y en el cargo qu'él lleva entienda en ello la persona que
a vós y al padre frey Buyl paresçiere, en tanto que de acá se
provee; que por la priessa de la partida de los dichos navíos non
se pudo agora proveer en ello, pero en el primero viaje, sy plaze
a Dios, se proveerá de tal persona qual conviene para el dicho 35
cargo.
[6] De Medina del Campo, a treze de abril de noventa e quatro.

Yo el Rey

Yo la Reyna

[7] Por mandado del Rey e de la Reyna. Juan de la Parra. 40
[8] E en las espaldas desýa: "Por el Rey e por la Reyna, a don

---

10. **esperava** *GP*] espera *W*. 16. **non**] *s.l. W*. 16-17. **avíamos** *GW*] avemos *P*. 29. **para** *GP*] *om. W*. 30.
que *GW*] *om. P*. 31. **qu'él lleva** *GP*] q(ue) lleuo *W*. 37. **treze** *GP*] xviij° *W*. **quatro** *GP*] q. años *W*. 41.
desýa *GP*] d. lo siguiente *W*.

Christóval Colón, su almirante del mar Oçéano e su visorrey y
governador en las yslas nuevamente falladas en las partes de las
Yndias''.

XXXIV (15)

El Rey e la Reyna

Muestran S. A. el
gusto de leer las
cartas del
Almirante, alaban
su servicio, y le
mandan que dé
noticia de todas las
cosas y de las
condiciones de los
tiempos del año, y
embíe las
diferencias de las
aves, deseando
verlas [*r. m.*].

[1] Don Christóval Colón, nuestro almirante mayor de las
yslas de las Yndias: vimos vuestras letras e memoriales que nos
enbiastes con Torres, y avemos avido mucho plaser de saber
todo lo que por ellas nos escrevistes, y damos muchas graçias a
Nuestro Señor por todo ello, porque esperamos que con Su   5
ayuda este negoçio vuestro será causa que nuestra santa fee
cathólica sea mucho más acreçentada; e una de las prinçipales
cosas por que esto nos ha plazido tanto, es por ser ynventada,
prinçipiada e avida por vuestra mano, trabajo e yndustria; y
paréçenos que todo lo que al prinçipio nos dexistes que se   10
podría alcançar, por la mayor parte todo ha salido /39 verso/
çierto, como sy lo oviérades visto antes que nos lo dixéssedes:
esperança tenemos en Dios que en lo que queda por saber assí se
continuará, de que por ello vos quedamos en mucho cargo para
vos fazer merçedes de manera que vos seáys muy bien con-   15

Prométenle muchas
mercedes y tantas
que quede mui
contento [*l. m.*].

tento. [2] Y visto todo lo que nos escrivistes, como quiera que
assaz largamente dezís todas las cosas que es mucho gozo e
alegría leerlas, pero algo más querríamos que nos escriviéssedes
assí en que sepamos quántas yslas fasta aquí se han fallado, y, a las
que avéys puesto nombres, qué nombre tiene cada una, porque,   20
aunque nombráys algunas en vuestras cartas, non son todas, y a

Que dé noticia de
los nombres de los
lugares i de las
distancias que ay de
una tierra a otra
[*l. m.*].

las otras, los nombres que les llaman los Yndios, y quánto ay
de una a otra, e todo lo que avéys hallado en cada una d'ellas, y
lo que disen que ay en ellas, y en lo que se ha sembrado después
que allá fuestes qué se ha avido, pues ya es passado el tiempo   25

Sources: *GPW*. 1. **nuestro** *GP (s.l. G)] om. W*. 4. **ellas** *GP*] ella/ *W*. 5. **esperamos que** *GP*] *om. W*
(*homoeoteleuton*). 12. **lo**] *s.l. W*. 17. **que** *GP*] de q. *W*. 24. **sembrado** *GP*] enbiado *W*.

que todas las cosas sembradas se han de coger. [3] Y prinçipalmente desseamos saber todos los tiempos del año qué tales son allá en cada mes por sý, porque a nós pareçe que en lo que dezís que ay allá, ay mucha diferençia en los tiempos a los de acá; algunos quieren desyr sý en un año ay allá dos ynviernos y dos veranos: todo nos lo escrevid por serviçio nuestro, y embiadnos todos los más halcones que de allá se pudieren embiar, y de todas las aves que allá ay y se pudieren aver, porque querríamos las ver todas. [4] Y quanto a las cosas que nos embiastes por memorial que se proveyesse y enbiasse de acá, todas las mandamos proveer, como del dicho Torres sabréys y veréys por lo que él lleva; querríamos, sy os parece, que asý para saber de vós y de toda la gente que allá está, como para que cada día pudiéssedes ser proveýdos de lo que fuesse menester, que cada mes viniesse una caravela de allá y de acá fuesse otra, pues que las cosas de Portogal están asentadas y los navíos podrán yr e venir seguramente: vedlo, y, sy os paresçiere que se deve hazer, hazedlo vos, y escrividnos la manera que vos paresçiere que se deve embiar de acá. [5] Y en lo que toca a la forma que allá devéys tener con la gente que allá tenéys, bien nos paresçe lo que fasta agora avéys prinçipiado, y así lo devéys continuar, dándoles el más contentamiento que ser pueda, /40 recto/ pero no dándoles lugar que exçedan en cosa alguna en las cosas que devieren hazer y vos les mandardes de nuestra parte; y quanto a la poblaçión que hezistes, en aquello no ay quien pueda dar regla çierta ni emendar cosa alguna desde acá: porque allá estaríamos presentes, y tomaríamos vuestro consejo y parecer en ello, quanto más en absençia; por eso a vós lo remitimos. [6] A todas las otras cosas contenidas en el memorial que traxo el dicho Torres, en los márgenes d'él va respondido lo que convino que vos supiéssedes la respuesta: a aquello vos remitimos. [7] Y quanto a las cosas con Portogal, acá se tomó çierto assiento con sus embaxadores, que nos pareçía que era más syn ynconviniente; y porque d'ello seáys bien ynformado largamente, vos enbiamos el traslado de los capítulos que sobre ello se fizieron; y por esso aquí non conviene alargar en ello, syno que vos mandamos y encargamos que aquello guardéys enteramente e hagáys que por todos sea guardado así como en

Nota la gran confiança que los Reyes tenían en el Almirante [*r. m.*].

30
35
40
45
50
55
60

30–31. **y . . . veranos** GP] *om. W.* 31. **serviçio nuestro** GP] n. s. *W.* 53. **eso a** GP] esto *W.* 55–56. **convino** GP] conviene *W.* 56. **a aquello** GP] aquello *W.* **vos** *W*] nos GP.

los capítulos se contiene. [8] Y en lo de la raya, o límite, que se
ha de hazer, porque nos pareçe cosa muy dificultosa y de   65
mucho saber y confiança, querríamos, sy ser pudiesse, que vos
os hallássedes en ello y la hiziéssedes con los otros que por parte
del Rey de Portugal en ello han de entender; y sy ay mucha
difficultad en vuestra yda a esto, o podría traer algund ynconviniente en lo que ende estáys, ved sý vuestro hermano, o otro   70
alguno tenéys ende que lo sepan, y ynformadlos muy bien por
escripto y por palabra y aun por pintura y por todas las maneras
que mejor pudieren ser ynformados, y embiádnoslos acá luego
con las primeras caravelas que vinieren, porque con ellos enbiaremos otros de acá para el tiempo que está asentado; y, quier 75
ayáys vos de yr a esto o non, escrividnos muy largamente todo
lo que en esto supierdes y a vos pareçiere que se deve hazer para
nuestra enformaçión y para que en todo se provea como cumple a nuestro serviçio; y hazed de manera que vuestras cartas y
los que avéys de embiar vengan presto, porque puedan bolver   80
adónde se ha de hazer la raya, antes que se cumpla el tiempo
que tenemos asentado con el Rey de Portugal, como veréys por
la capitulaçión.
[9] De Segovia, a /40 verso/ diez e seys de agosto de noventa e
quatro.   85

Yo el Rey
Yo la Reyna

[10] Por mandado del Rey e de la Reyna. Fernán Álvares.
[11] E en las espaldas desýa: "Por el Rey e la Reyna, a don
Christóval Colón, su almirante mayor de las yslas de las   90
Yndias".

XXXV (6)

Carta de poder y
licencia para armar
navíos al Almirante
y al Obispo Don
Juan de Fonseca
[*l. m.*].

[1] Don Fernando e doña Ysabel, por la graçia de Dios rey e
reyna de Castilla, de León, de Aragón, de Seçilia, de Granada,
de Toledo, de Valençia, de Galizia, de Mallorcas, de Sevilla, de
Çerdeña, de Córdova, de Córçega, de Murçia, de Jahén, del

---

74. **ellos** *GP*] ellas *W*. 80. **los** *GW*] las *P*. 85. **quatro** *GP*] iiij° años *W*.   Sources: *GPW*. 4-5. **del Algarbe** *GP*] de los Algarves *W*. 5. **de** (las) *GP*] e de *W*.

Algarbe, de Algesyra, de Gibraltar, de las yslas de Canaria,   5
conde e condesa de Barçelona, señores de Viscaya e de Molina,
duques de Athenas e de Neopatría, condes de Rosellón e de
Çerdania, marqueses de Oristán e de Goçiano: a vós don Christóval Colóm, nuestro almirante de las nuestras yslas e tierra
firme que por nuestro mandado se han descubierto e se han de   10
descobrir en el mar Oçéano en la parte de las Yndias, e a vós
don Juan de Fonseca, arçediano de Sevilla, del nuestro consejo,
salud e graçia. [2] Sepades que nos avemos acordado de mandar
que se haga çierta armada de algunos navíos e fustas para enbiar
a las dichas Yndias, asý para señorear e poseer las dichas yslas e   15
tierra firme de que en nuestro nombre está tomada posesyón,
como para descobrir otras; y porque para faser y peltrechar la
dicha armada y la proveer de todas las cosas a ella neçesarias e
complideras es neçesario que nos nombremos e diputemos personas que en ello entiendan e lo pongan en obra, confiando de   20
vosotros, que soys tales que guardaréys nuestro serviçio e bien e
fiel e diligentemente faréys lo que por nós vos fuere mandado e
encomendado, mandamos dar esta nuestra carta para vosotros
en la dicha rasón, por la qual vos mandamos que vades a las
çibdades de Sevilla e Cadis e otras qualquier çibdades e villas e   25
lugares e puertos de mar de su arçobispado e obispado /41
recto/ donde entendierdes que cumple, e fagáys fletar e comprar, e compréys e fletéys, qualesquier navíos e naos e caravelas
e fustas que vierdes e entendierdes que cumplen e son convinientes para la dicha armada, de qualesquier persona o per-   30
sonas; e sy por esta vía non las pudierdes aver, las podades tomar
e tomedes, aunque estén fletados, a qualesquier personas, lo más
syn daño que ser pudiere. [3] E mandamos a los dueños de las
dichas naos e navíos e fustas e caravelas que vos las den e entreguen e vendan o afleten, pagándoles el presçio que por voso-   35
tros fueren comprados o afletados e que ovieren de aver segund
los contratos e asyentos que con vosotros fizieren o asentaren; e
asý compradas e fletadas las dichas naos e navíos e caravelas e
fustas, las podades armar e pertrechar e basteçer de armas e peltrechos, e bastescáys de las armas e peltrechos e bastimentos e   40

6. **señores** GP] e s. W. 10. (e) **se** (han)] *in G added at the end of the line in a different ink with a long s because of lack of space.* 32. **fletados** GPW] *corr.* fletadas (*or agreement with 28 navíos ?*). 34. **las** GP] los W. **e** GP] o W. 35. **e** GP] o W. **afleten** GP] fleten W. 36. **afletados** GP] fletados W. **e** GP] o W. 37. **o** GP] e W. 38-39. **caravelas e fustas** GP] f. e c. W.

tiros de pólvora e gentes e marineros e aparejos de marear e
ofiçiales que menester fueren e vosotros vierdes e entendierdes
que cumple. [4] Lo qual podades tomar, e tomedes, de qualesquier lugares e partes navíos donde los fallardes, pagando a los
dueños d'éllos los preçios rasonables que por ellos devan aver; e   45
asymismo podades costreñir e apremiar a qualesquier ofiçiales
de qualesquier ofiçios que son convinientes para yr en la dicha
armada e entendierdes que cumple que vayan en ella, a los
quales será pagado el sueldo e salario rasonable que por ello
devan aver, e para que çerca d'ello podades otorgar e otor-   50
guedes qualquier seguridad en nuestro nombre que convenga e
menester sea. [5] Para lo qual todo que dicho es, e para que
çerca d'ello podades fazer e fagades todas las prendas, premias,
prisiones e esecuçiones, e remates e vençiones de bienes que
convengan e menester sean, con todas sus ynçidençias e depen-   55
dençias, anexidades e conexidades, vos damos poder complido
por esta nuestra carta; pero es nuestra merçed e mandamos que
de todo lo susodicho se tenga rasón e cuenta para quando nos la
quisyéremos mandar ver, que se asiente en los nuestros libros
que tienen los nuestros contadores mayores, e que qualquier   60
cosa de las susodichas tocante a la dicha armada se haga e pase
ante Juan de Soría, secretario del prínçipe don Juan, nuestro
muy caro e muy amado hijo, que va por lugarteniente de los
dichos nuestros contadores mayores, e /41 verso/ con su poder
e non en otra manera alguna. [6] E otrosý es nuestra merçed e   65
mandamos que todo lo que toca a las compras de armas e pel-
threchos e mantenimiento e otras cosas, e flete de navíos e otros
gastos de la dicha armada, se haga e pase ante el lugarteniente de
nuestro escrivano que agora nombramos para esta armada, juntamente con el dicho Juan de Soría, teniente de nuestros con-   70
tadores mayores; y asimesmo porque en el sueldo que se oviere
de pagar a la gente que fuere a la dicha armada non aya fraude
nin encubierta alguna, es nuestra merçed que las presentaçiones
e alardes de la dicha gente se haga ant'el teniente del dicho
nuestro escrivano, e que por fe suya firmada de su nombre fagan   75
la librança de todo lo susodicho los dichos almirante e don Juan
de Fonseca; e el dicho teniente de nuestros contadores mayores

41. **aparejos** G] aparejo *PW*. 43. **e** G*W*] o *P*. 44. **navíos** G*P*] puertos *W*. 45. **devan** G] deven *PW*.
60-61. **qualquier cosa** G*P*] qualesquier cosas *W*. 68. **haga** G*P*] faga(n) *W*. **pase** G*P*] passen *W*. 69. **agora**
G*P*] de a. *W*.

firme en los dichos libramientos porque él tenga la rasón e cuenta d'ellos, por manera qu'el que lo oviere de pagar non pague cosa alguna syn carta o nómina de los dichos almirante e 80 don Juan de Fonseca e firmada del dicho teniente de nuestros contadores mayores. [7] E sy para haser e complir e poner en obra lo susodicho, o qualquier parte d'ello, menester ovierdes favor e ayuda, por esta dicha nuestra carta mandamos a qualesquier conçejos, asystentes, corregidores, alcaldes, alguasyles, 85 regidores, cavalleros, escuderos, ofiçiales, e omes buenos, e maestres de navíos e fustas, e otras qualesquier personas que para ello fueren requeridos, que vos lo den e fagan dar por bien e complidamente, e que en ello, ni en parte d'ello, enbargo ni contrario alguno vos non pongan nin consyentan poner, so 90 pena de la nuestra merçed e de privaçión de los ofiçios e de confiscaçión de todos sus bienes a cada uno de los que lo contrario fizieren. [8] E demás, mandamos al ome que vos esta nuestra carta mostrare que vos emplase que parescades ante nós en la nuestra corte, doquier que nos seamos, del día que vos 95 enplasare fasta quinse días primeros syguientes, so la dicha pena; so la qual mandamos a qualquier escrivano público que para esto fuere llamado, que dé ende al que vos la mostrare testimonio sygnado con su sygno, porque nos sepamos en cómo se cumple nuestro mandado. 100

[9] Dada en la çibdad de Barçelona a veynte e quatro días del mes de mayo, año del nasçimiento de nuestro señor Jhesu Christo de mill e quatroçientos /42 recto/ e noventa e tres años.

Yo el Rey 105
Yo la Reyna

[10] Yo Fernand Álvares de Toledo, secretario del Rey e de la Reyna nuestros señores, la fise escrevir por su mandado.
[11] E en las espaldas dezía: "Registrada en forma: Rodericus, dottor; Pero Gutierres, chançiller; e sellada". 110

86. **e** (omes) *GP*] *om. W.* 88. **por** *GP*] *om. W.*

[1] E asý presentadas ante los dichos alcaldes en la manera que dicha es, dixo a los dichos alcaldes el dicho señor
almirante susodicho que por quanto él ha menester de
llevar e presentar los dichos previlegios e çédulas e cartas
originales de suso encorporados a muchas partes e   5
lugares do a su derecho convenía, e que se temía e
reçelava que, llevándolas o presentándolas, que se le per-
derían o rasgarían o acaesçería en ellas, o en alguna
d'ellas, algund caso fortuyto, e que, por evitar los dichos
ynconvinientes, pedía, e pidió, a los dichos alcaldes e a   10
cada uno d'ellos que amos ‹a dos› juntamente viesen e
exsaminasen los dichos previlegios e cartas e çédulas que
ante ellos presentava, e mandasen a mí el dicho escrivano que sacase o fiziese sacar un traslado o dos o
más, los que menester oviese; en el qual dicho traslado   15
o traslados ellos ynterpusiesen su abtoridad e decreto
judiçial para que fagan entera fe, doquier que paresçiesen, asý como valen e fazen fe los dichos previlegios
e cartas e çédulas originales susodichos e firmados de sus
nombres; e otrosý firmados e sygnados de mí el dicho   20
escrivano, gelos mandase dar para guarda de su derecho;
sobre lo qual dixo que, sy neçesario era, ymplorava, e
ymploró, el noble ofiçio de los dichos alcaldes. [2] E
luego los dichos alcaldes, visto el dicho pedimiento, tomaron las dichas cartas e privilegios e çédulas originales   25
en sus manos e leyeron por ellas, ellos e cada uno d'ellos;
e porque las vieron sanas e non rotas, nin cançelladas nin
en alguna parte sospechosas, porque de derecho non
deviessen valer, antes caresçientes de todo viçio e suspi-
çión, dixeron amos juntamente que mandavan, e man-   30
daron, a mí el dicho escrivano que sacase o fiziese sacar
de las dichas cartas e privilegios e çédulas un traslado o

Sources: *GPW*. 5. **encorporados** G] encorporadas *PW*. 9. **fortuyto** *GP*] fortituyto *W*. 11. ‹a dos›
PW] *om*. G (*but cf*. p. 257, 43; 324, 10). 13. **mandasen** *GW*] mandase *P*. 16. **ynterpusiesen** *GP*] pusiesen
W. 17-18. **paresçiesen** G] pareçiere *P*, paresçiere(n) *W*. 21. **mandase** *PW*] mandasen G. 23-24. **E . . .
alcaldes** *GW*] *om. P*.

dos o más, los qu'el dicho señor almirante me pidiese e
oviese menester, e gelos diese e entregase firmados de
sus nombres e firmados e sygnados de mí el dicho es-   35
crivano, a los quales, e a cada uno d'ellos, ellos, e cada
uno d'ellos, ynterponían, e ynterpusieron, su /42 verso/
abtoridad e decreto para que valiesen e fiziesen fe en
juyzio e fuera d'él, en todo tiempo e lugar do paresçiesen, bien asý e atán complidamente como valdrían e   40
farían fee las dichas cartas e previlegios e çédulas originalmente paresçiendo. [3] E de todo esto en como pasó,
el dicho señor almirante dixo que gelo diesse por fe e
testimonio para guarda de su derecho; e yo dile ende
éste, el qual va firmado de los dichos alcaldes e de cada   45
uno d'ellos, e firmado e sygnado de mí el dicho escrivano público; e fue fecho e sacado e corregido e conçertado con los dichos originales e con cada uno d'ellos
en la dicha çibdad de Sevilla e en el dicho día e mes e año
susodichos.   50
[4] Va escripto sobre raýdo ó dis "fágovos mi almirante
mayor de la mar e quiero e es mi merçed que seades de
aquí adelante mi almirante mayor de la mar, segund que
lo solía ser el almirante don Diego Hurtado de Mendoça
qu'es finado, e que ayades el dicho almirantadgo"; e ó   55
dis "e otros e yo" e ó dis "e non llevaren sueldo nuestro,
como dicho es, se les" vala e non le enpesca.

> Ruys Montero, alcalde
> Estevan de la Roca, alcalde

[5] Yo Gomes Nieto, escrivano de Sevilla, fuy presente   60
a la abtoridad e mandamiento de los dichos alcaldes, e só
testigo.
[6] Yo Johan Fernandes, escrivano de Sevilla, fuy presente a su abtoridad e mandamiento de los dichos alcaldes, e soy testigo.   65

36-37. d'ellos . . . uno GP] om. W (homoeoteleuton). 42. en GW] om. P. 45-46. firmado de . . . sygnado
G] firmado e signado de los dichos alcaldes e W. firmado de . . . d'ellos G(W)] om. P (homoeoteleuton). 47.
e (fue) GP] que W. 49. e (en) G] om. PW. 51-57. Va . . . enpesca GP] om. W. 58-59. Ruys . . . alcalde
GP] Pero Ruyz W. 58. Ruys . . . alcalde] in GP a sigla precedes and follows. 59. Estevan . . . alcalde] in
GP a sigla precedes and follows. 60-68. Yo . . . testigo] in GP autograph signatures followed by a sigla, which in
G fill the lower half of fol. 42v. 63. Johan Fernandes G] Alfonso Lucas PW. 64. su G] la dicha P, la W.

[7] E yo Martín Rodrigues, escrivano público de Sevilla, fuy presente a la dicha abturidad e fis aquí mío signo e só testigo.

XXXVI.i (14.1)

/43 recto/

Traslado de una
bula de nuestro
muy Santo Padre
Alexandro .VI.
[r. m.].

[1] In Dei nomine, amen: éste es traslado bien e fiel-
mente sacado de una escriptura escripta en pergamino
de cuero en lengua latina e sellada con un sello de çera
colorada, metido en una caxa de madera, pendiente en
una çinta de seda verde e sygnada e firmada de çierto   5
notario apostólico, segund por ella paresçía, el thenor de
la qual *de verbo ad verbum* **es este que se sygue:**

XXXVI.ii.1 (14.2-3)

[1] Petrus Garsie, Dei et Apostolice Sedis gratia Episcopus Barchinoniensis, regius auditor et consiliarius, universis et singulis
presentes litteras sive presens publicum instrumentum visuris,
lecturis pariter et audituris, salutem in Domino sempiternam et
prosperos advoca succesus.   5
[2] Vobis et cuilibet vestrum notum facimus per presentes,
quod nos in nostris manibus habuimus, tenuimus, palpavimus,
vidimus et diligenter inspeximus sanctissimi in Christo patris et
domini nostri Alexandri, divina providentia Pape, sexti, litteras
apostolicas eius vera bulla plumbea in filis sericis rubei cro-   10

66. **E** GP] om. W. 67. **fuy** GP] fize escrevir estas escripturas e f. W. **abturidad** GP] a. y mandamiento de
los dichos alcaldes W. **signo**] sig no *with notarization inserted* GP. **e** GW] e d'ello P. **testigo**] W *ends here, and
the rest of fol.* (42v) *has been left blank and is followed by four more blank fols.* (43-46), *which, however, are ruled; the
sign of the owner appears on fol.* 46v: Ferdinando Becheroni Portiere di Casa il / Duca di Albanieche; *and below:*
Sig.e Luigi Cacciatore.   Sources: GP. Sources: GP. 2. **auditor**] audictor GP. 6. **notum**] noctum GP.
10. **filis sericis**] filiis sericiis GP.

ceique coloris more Romane Curie impendente, sanas siquidem et integras, non viciatas, non chancellatas, nec in aliqua sui
parte suspectas, sed omnimoda suspitione carentes, ut in eis ap-
parebat; quarum quidem harum tenor et continentia de verbo
ad verbum sequitur, et est talis: 15

XXXVI.ii.1.1 (14.4-15)

[1] Alexander Episcopus, servus servorum Dei, carissimo in
Christo filio Fer‹di›nando Regi et carissime in Christo filie Elisabeth Regine Castelle, Legionis, Aragonum, Sicilie, Granatae,
illustribus, salutem et apostolicam benedictionem. [2] Inter ce-
tera Divine Maiestati bene placita opera et cordis nostri   5
desiderabilia, illud profecto potissimum existit, ut fides catholica ‹et› christiana /43 verso/ religio nostris presertim temporibus exaltetur et ubilibet amplietur et dilatetur, anima-
rumque salus procuretur ac barbare nationes deprimantur et ad
fidem ipsam reducantur; unde cum ad hanc sacram Petri   10
sedem, divina favente clementia, meritis licet imparibus,
evocati fu‹er›imus, cognoscentes vos tanquam veros catholicos
reges et principes, quales semper fuisse novimus et a vobis pre-
clare gesta toti pene iam orbi notissima demostrant, nedum id
exoptare, sed omni conatu, studio et diligentia, nullis laboribus,   15
nullis impensis nullisque parcendo periculis, etiam prop‹r›ium
sanguinem effundendo, efficere ac omnem animum vestrum
omnesque conatus ad hoc iam dudum dedicasse, quemad-
modum recuperatio regni Granate a tira‹n›nide Saraceno‹rum›
‹h›odiernis temporibus per vos cum tanta divini nominis gloria   20
facta testatur, digne ducimur non ‹in›merito et debemus illa
vobis etiam sponte et favorabiliter concedere, per que huiusmodi sanctum et laudabile ac inmortali Deo acceptum proposi-

---

13. **suspitione**] suspetione *GP*.   Sources: *GPW. Cf. also Raccolta, Parte III, vol. II, pp. 8-11 (= R, which
we report only in case of an adiaphorous reading or of an error common to GPW that can not be corrected immediately);
ibidem, pp. 5-7, version of 3 May 1493 (= R').* 2. **Fer‹di›nando** *W (= R)*] Fernando *GP*. 5. **Divine** *GP*]
divini *W*. **Maiestati**] magestati *GPW*. 6. **profecto**] proffeto *GPW*. 7. ‹et› *R*] *om. GPW*. 8. **ubilibet** *GP*]
ubel(ib)et *W*. 12. **fu‹er›imus** *R*] fuimus *GPW*. 13. **vobis** *R*] nobis *GP, W*? 15. **conatu**] cognatu *GPW*.
17. **sanguinem** *GP*] saguinem *W*. 18. **conatus**] cognatus *GPW*. 19. **Saraceno‹rum›** *R*] sarraceno & *
GPW*. 21. ‹in›**merito** *R*] merito *GPW*.

tum in dies ferventiori animo ad ipsius Dei honorem et imperii
christiani propagationem prosequi valeatis. [3] Sane accepimus   25
quod vos, qui dudum animo proposueratis aliquas insulas et
terras firmas remotas et incognitas ac per alios hactenus non
repertas querere et invenire, ut illarum incolas et habitatores ad
colendum Redemptorem nostrum et fidem catholicam profitendam reduceretis, hactenus in expugnatione et recuperatione   30
ipsius regni Granate plurimum occupati, huiusmodi sanctum et
laudabile propositum vestrum ad optatum finem perducere ne-
quivistis; sed tandem, sicut Domino placuit, regno predicto
recuperato, volentes desiderium adimplere vestrum, dilectum
filium Christoforum Colon, virum utique /44 recto/ ‹dignum›   35
et plurimum co‹m›mendandum ac tanto negotio aptum, cum
navigiis et hominibus ad similia instru‹c›tis, non sine maximis
laboribus et periculis ac expensis, destina‹s›tis, ut terras firmas et
insulas remotas et incognitas huiusmodi per mare ubi hactenus
navigatum non fuerat, diligenter inquirere‹n›t. [4] Qui tandem,   40
divino auxilio, facta extrema diligentia, in mari Occeano navi-
gantes, certas insulas remotissimas et etiam terras firmas quae
per alios hactenus reperte non fuerant, invenerunt; in quibus
quamplurime gentes pacifice viventes et, ut asseritum, nudi in-
cedentes nec carnibus vescentes, inhabitant; et, ut prefati nuncii   45
vestri possunt opinari, gentes ipse in insulis et terris predictis
habitantes credunt unum Deum creatorem in celis esse, ac ad
fidem catholicam amplexandum et bonis moribus imbuendum
satis apti videntur, spesque habetur quod si erudirentur, nomen
salvatoris domini nostri Ihesu Chrysti in terris et insulis predic-   50
tis facile induceretur. [5] Ac prefatus Christophorus in una ex
principalibus insulis predictis iam unam turrim satis munitam,
in qua certos christianos, qui secum iverant, in custodiam, et ut
alias insulas et terras firmas remotas et incognitas inquirerent,
posuit, construi et edificari fecit; in quibus quidem insulis et   55
terris iam repertis aurum, aromata et alie quamplurime res
preciose diversi generis et diverse qualitatis reperiuntur; unde
omnibus diligenter et presertim fide‹i› exaltatione catholicae et
dilatatione, prout decet catholicos reges et principes, considera-

29–30. **profitendam**] proffitendam *GPW*. 35. **utique** *R*] utaque *GPW*. ‹**dignum**› *R*] *om. GPW*. 38.
destina‹s›tis *R*] destinatis *GPW*. 40. **fuerat** *R*] fuit *GPW*. **inquirere‹n›t** *R*] inquireret *GPW*. 45. **vescentes** *R*] vestentes *GPW*. **prefati**] prefacti *GPW*. 47. **credunt** *R*] credum *GPW*. 48. **bonis moribus** *G*]
moris bonibus *PW*. 51. **Ac** *R*] at *GPW*. **prefatus**] prefactus *GPW*. 55. **edificari** *R*] edificare *GPW*. 57.
preciose (preciose *W*)] preciosse *GP*. 58. **presertim**] pressertim *G*, presertum *W*. **fide‹i›** *R*] fide *GPW*.

tis, more progenitorum vestrorum clare memorie Regum, ter-   60
ras firmas et insulas predictas illarumque incolas et habitatores
vobis, divina favente clementia, subicere et ad fidem catholicam reducere proposuistis. [6] Nos igitur huiusmodi vestrum
sanctum et laudabile propositum plurimum in Domino co‹m›-
mendantes, ac cupientes ut illud ad debitum finem perducatur   65
et ipsum nomen Salvatoris nostri in partibus illis inducatur,
hortamur /44 verso/ vos plurimum in Domino et per sacri
lavacri susceptionem, qua mandatis apostolicis obligati estis, et
viscera misericordie domini nostri Ihesu Christi attente requiri-
mus ut, cum expeditionem huiusmodi omnino persequi et as-   70
sumere prona mente orthodoxe fidei zelo intendatis, populos in
huiusmodi insulis et terris degentes ad christianam religionem
suscipiendam inducere velitis et debeatis, nec pericula nec
labores ullo unquam tempore vos deterreant, firma spe fidutiaque conceptis quod Deus omnipotens conatus vestros felici-   75
ter prosequetur. [7] Et ut tanti negotii provintiam, apostolice
gratie largitate donati, liberius et audatius assumatis, motu
prop‹r›io, non ad vestram vel alterius pro vobis super hoc nobis
oblate petitionis instantiam, sed de nostra mera liber‹ali›tate et
certa scientia ac de apostolice potestatis plenitudine, omnes in-   80
sulas et terras firmas inventas et inveniendas, detectas et detegendas, versus occidentem et meridiem, fabricando et constituendo unam lineam a polo ar‹c›tico, scilicet septentrione, ad
polum antarcticum, scilicet meridiem, sive terre firme et insule
invente et inveniende sint versus Indiam aut versus aliam   85
quamcumque partem; que linea distet a qualibet insularum que
vulgariter nuncupantur "de los Açores et Cabo Verde" centum
leucis versus occidentem et meridiem, ita quod omnes insule et
terre firme reperte et reperiende, detecte et detegende, a prefata
linea versus occidentem et meridiem, per alium regem aut   90
principem christianum non fuerint actualiter posse‹s›se usque
ad diem nativitatis domini nostri Ihesu Christi proxime preteri-
tum, a quo incipit annus presens millesimus quadringentesimus

62-63. **catholicam** *GP*] catholica *W*. 66. **nomen** *W*] nomem *GP*. 69. **viscera** *GP*] vicera *W*. **attente** *R*]
hactenter *GPW*. 70. **expeditionem**] expiditionem *GPW*. 73. **suscipiendam** *GP*] suscipienda *W*. 74.
ullo *GP*] ullos *W*. **deterreant** *R*] de terream *GPW*. **firma** *W*] firma(m) *GP*. **spe** *GW*] spem *P*. 74-75.
fidutiaque *R*] fidutia(m)que *GPW*. 75. **conatus**] cognatus *GPW*. 76. **prosequetur** *R*] prosequitur
GPW. 79. **liber‹ali›tate** *R*] libertate *GPW*. 83. **septentrione** *P*] steptentrione *G*, septemtriom *W*. 84.
antarcticum *GP*] am/tarticum *W*. 86. **quamcumque partem** *GP*] quacumq(ue) *W*. 88. **insule** *GPW*]
over insull *W*. 89. **detecte** *GP*] dececte *W*. **prefata**] prefacta *GPW*. 90. **aut** *GP*] ad *W*. 93. **annus** *GP*]
annis *W*. **quadringentesimus**] quadragentesimus *W*.

nonagesimus tertius, quando fuerunt per nuntios et capitaneos vestros invente alique predictarum insularum, auctoritate omnipotentis Dei nobis in beato Petro concessa ac vicariatus Ihesu Christi, qua fungimur in terris, cum omnibus illarum dominiis, civitatibus, castris, locis et villis iuribusque et iurisditionibus ac pertinentiis universis, vobis heredibusque /45 recto/ et subcessoribus vestris, Castelle et Legionis regibus, in perpetuum, tenore presentium, donamus, concedimus et assignamus, vosque et heredes ac subcessores prefatos illarum dominos cum plena, libera et omnimoda potestate, auctoritate et iurisdi‹c›tione facimus, constituimus et deputamus, decernentes nichilominus per huiusmodi donationem, concessionem et assignationem vestram nulli christiano principi qui actualiter prefatas insulas aut terras firmas possederit usque ad predictum diem nativitatis domini nostri Ihesu Christi, ius quesitum sublatum intelligi ‹posse› aut auferri debere. [8] Et insuper mandamus vobis in virtute sancte obedientie ut, sicut etiam pollicemini, et non dubitamus pro vestra maxima devotione et regia magnanimitate vos esse facturos, ad terras firmas et insulas predictas viros probos et Deum timentes, doctos, peritos et expertos ad instruendum incolas et habitatores prefatos in fide catholica et in bonis moribus imbuendum destinare debeatis, omnem debitam diligentiam im premissis adhibentes; ac quibuscumque personis cuiuscumque dignitatis, etiam imperialis et regalis, status, gradus, ordinis vel conditionis, sub excommunicationis late sententie pena, quam eo ipso, si contrafecerint, incurrant, districtius inhibemus ne ad insulas et terras firmas inventas et inveniendas, detectas et detegendas versus occidentem et meridiem, fabricando et constituendo lineam a polo ar‹c›tico ad polum antar‹c›ticum, sive terre firme et insule invente et inveniende sint versus Indiam aut versus aliam quamcumque partem, que linea distet a qua‹li›bet insularum que vulgariter nuncupantur "de los Açores et Cabo Verde" centum leucis versus occidentem et meridiem, ut prefertur, pro mercibus habendis

95

100

105

110

115

120

125

99. **vobis** GP] nobis W? 100. **Legionis** G] legionibus PW. **perpetuum**] perpectuum GP. 102. **prefatos**] prefactos GPW. 103-104. **iurisdi‹c›tione**] iuriiditione GP, iurisditione W. 104. **facimus**] fatimus GP. 105. **per** R] et p. GPW. 106-107. **prefatas**] prefactas GPW. 109. ‹**posse**› R] om. GPW. **auferri**] aufferri GP, afferi W. 113-114. **peritos . . . habitatores** G (= R)] om. PW. 114. **prefatos** (prefattos W)] prefactos GP. 119. **eo** W] co GP. **contrafecerint** GP] contra fecerunt W. 122. **polo**] pollo GPW. 124. **sint** GW] sunt P. **quamcumque** GP] quacumque W. 125. **linea** G] lineam PW. **qua‹li›bet** W] quabet GP. **insularum que** R] insula h(oc)oq(ue) GPW.

vel quavis alia de causa accedere presumant absque vestra ac
heredum et successorum vestrorum predictorum licentia
spetiali, /45 verso/ non obstantibus constitutionibus et ordina-   130
tionibus apostolicis ceterisque contrariis quibuscumque, in Illo
a quo imperia et dominationes ac bona cuncta procedunt con-
fidentes quod, dirigente Domino actus vestros, si huiusmodi
sanctum et laudabilem propositum prosequamini, brevi tem-
pore, cum felicitate et gloria totius populi christiani, vestri   135
labores et conatus exitum felicissimum consequentur. [9]
Verum, quia difficile foret presentes litteras ad singula queque
loca in quibus expediens fuerit deferri, volumus, ac motu et
scientia similibus decernimus, quod illarum transumptis, manu
publici notarii inde rogati subscriptis et sigillo alicuius persone   140
in ecclesiastica dignitate constitute, seu curie ecclesiastice,
munitis, ea prorsus fides in iuditio et extra ac alias ubilibet adhibeatur que presentibus adhiberetur, si esse‹n›t exhibite vel ostense. [10] Nulli ergo omnino hominum liceat hanc paginam
nostre commendationis, hortationis, requisitionis, donationis,   145
concessionis, assignationis, constitutionis, deputationis, decreti,
mandati, inhibitionis et voluntatis infringere vel ei ausu teme-
rario contra ire: si quis autem hoc attentare presumpserit, in-
di‹g›nationem omnipotentis Dei ac beatorum Petri et Pauli
apostolorum Eius se noverit incursurum.   150

[11] Datum Rome apud Sanctum Petrum, anno incarnationis
dominice millesimo quadringentesimo nonagesimo tertio,
quarto Nonas Maii, pontificatus nostri anno primo.

[12] Gratis, de mandato sanctissimi domini nostri Pape, p.
rev.mo A. de Mucciallis, pro. Jo. Lur. A. Consenino, L. Podo-   155
chatharus, D. Gallectus.

[13] Registrata in Camera Apostolica: Amerinus.

---

128. **quavis** *P*] qua(m)vis *GW*. **vestra** *G*] vestram *PW*. 129. **licentia** *GP*] licentiam *W*. 132. **procedunt**
GP] procedum *W*. 136. **felicissimum**] fellicissimum *GP*, fellississimum *W*. 137. **difficile**] difficille *GPW*.
ad *G*] ac *PW*. 142. **ea** *R* (*cf.* p. 353, 11)] et *GPW*. **prorsus**] prorssus *GP*. **alias** *R*] alios *GPW*. 143. **esse‹n›t**
R (*cf.* p. 353, 13)] esset *GPW*. 148. **autem**] auctem *GPW*. **attentare**] actentare *GPW*. 154-157. **Gratis**
. . . **Amerinus** *GPW*] om. *RR'*. 155. **Mucciallis** *GP*] Mucialis *W*. **Lur.**] Lur(um) *GPW*. 157. **Amerinus**
GP] Amerimus *W*.

[1] Quibus quidem litteris diligenter, ut prefertur, per nos inspectis, ad requisitionem honorabilis viri Alfonsi Alvares de Toledo, Domus Regie ⟨H⟩ispanie continui familiaris, per notarium publicum infrascriptum, in vim clausule in fine prefatarum litterarum apostolicarum superius insertarum apposite, que talis est:/46 recto/"Verum, quia difficile foret presentes litteras ad singula queque loca in quibus expediens fuerit deferri, volumus, ac motu et scientia similibus decernimus, quod illarum transumptis, manu publici notarii inde rogati subscriptis et sigillo alicuius persone in ecclesiastica dignitate constitute, seu curie ecclesiastice, munitis, ea prorsus fides in iuditio et extra ac alias ubilibet adhibeatur que presentibus adhiberetur, si essent exhibite vel ostense," ipsas exemplari mandavimus et transumi ac in publicam formam redigi, decernentes et volentes ut huic presenti transumpto publico, sive exemplo, plena fides deinceps adhibeatur ubilibet in locis omnibus et singulis quibus fuerit opportunum, ipsumque transumptum fidem faciat et illud stetur ac si originales ipse littere apparerent, producerentur et presentarentur; quibus omnibus et singulis auctoritatem nostram ordinariam interposuimus, interponimusque pariter et decretum per presentes, et, ad ampliorem et clariorem evidentiam premissorum, sigillum nostrum presentibus, una cum infrascripti notarii signo et subscriptione impendenti, duximus apponendum.

[2] Acta fuerunt hec Barchinone, in domo habitationis nostre, in Camera nostra, die veneris, decima nona mensis Iulii, sub anno a nativitate Domini millesimo quadringentesimo nonagesimo tertio, pontificatus eiusdem sanctissimi in Christo patris domini nostri domini Alexandri, divina providentia Pape, sexti, anno primo, presentibus ibidem venerabilibus et providis viris Nicholao Pillicer, nostre Ecclesie Barchinoniensis canonico, et Petro Joanne Vayo ac Michaele Ginnous, clericis,

5

10

15

20

25

30

Sources: GP. 1. **prefertur**] preffertur GP. 3. ⟨H⟩ispanie] Ispannie GP. 5. **prefatarum**] prefactarum GP. 5-6. **apposite**] apposite(m) GP. 11. **munitis**] munitatis GP. 14. **transumi**] transsumi GP. **redigi**] redigii GP. 15. **transumpto**] transsumpto GP. 18. **illud**] ille GP. 20. **interposuimus**] interpossuimus G, interpussuimus P. 26. **Iulii**] iullii GP. 27. **quadringentesimo** G] quadragesimo P.

presbyteris, ca‹p›pellanis et familiaribus nostris, testibus ad pre-
missa vocatis et rogatis.

[3] Et ego Alvarus Peres del Villar, sancte ecclesie Compostel-   35
lane canonicus, notarius apostolicus, rev.mi domini Didaci
Hispalensis ‹Epis›copi sectarius, quia premissis litterarum apostolicarum preinsertarum presentationi, receptioni, requisitioni,
visioni, dictusque interpositioni, exemplationi, omnibusque
aliis et singulis, dum, sicut premittitur, fierent, agerentur et   40
dicerentur, una cum prenominatis testibus presens /46 verso/
interfui, eaque omnia et singula sic fieri vidi, audivi et in notam
suprascripsi; ex qua presens instrumentum per alium, me aliis
occupato negotiis, fideliter scriptum de mandato prefati domini
Episcopi extraxi prefatasque litteras apostolicas superius insertas   45
exemplavi ac auscultavi cum prop‹r›iis originalibus, et concor-
datur de verbo ad verbum; signoque et nomine meis solitis et
consuetis signavi in fidem et testimonium omnium et sin-
gulorum premissorum, rogatus et requisitus.

XXXVI.iii (14.20-22)

[1] El qual dicho traslado fue corregido e concertado por
mí el notario infra escripto con la dicha escriptura original onde fue sacado, en la muy noble e muy leal çibdad
de Sevilla jueves treynta días del mes de diziembre, año
de la natividad del nuestro señor Jhesu Christo de mill e   5
quinientos e dos años. [2] Testigos que fueron presentes
a vella corregir con el original: los honrados e discretos
varones Gomes Nieto, escrivano, e Martín de Ayamonte, e Juan Gonçales Contero, vezinos de la dicha
çibdat de Sevilla para esto llamados e rogados. Ruys   10
Montana, notario.

[3] Yo Pero Ruys Montana, clérico de Córdova, notario
público apostólico, que a todo e cada cosa de lo con-

37. ‹Epis›copi (corr. Raccolta)] copi GP. 38. preinsertarum G] prensertarum P. 39. dictusque]
dectusque GP. 43. alium G] aliam P.   Sources: GP. 10-19. Ruys . . . notario] in GP autograph. 10-11. Ruys
. . . notario] in GP written in the notarization. 11. Montana G] Montaña P. notario G] n. apostolico
P. 13. público G] om. P.

tenido en esta escritura de pargamino del nuestro muy
santo Padre, en uno con los dichos testigos, presente fui   15
e lo vy e oý e por otro fielmente lo fis escrevir, ‹ocupado
de otros negoçios›, e de este mi acostumbrado siño lo
subsiné en fe e testymonio de verdad, rogado e
requerido. Pero Ruys Montana, notario.

XXXVII.i (67)

/47 recto/
[1] Éste es treslado bien e fielmente sacado de una declaratoria e dos çédulas e una carta mensagera del Rey e
de la Reyna nuestros señores, escriptas en papel e firmadas de sus reales nombres, segund por ellas paresçía;
su thenor de las quales, una en pos de otra, es este que   5
se sigue:

XXXVII.i.1 (61)

El Rey e la Reyna

*Muy agraviado es el
Almirante en esta
declaratoria, la qual es
muy al contrario de
las merçedes y
promessas que S. A.
le han fecho, como se
muestra en los
privilegios y cartas
d'este libro [r. m.].*

*Declaratoria que
llevó Caravajales
[sic], en que S. A.
mandan volver sus
bienes al Almirante
[r. m.].*

[1] Lo que nos declaramos e mandamos que se faga en las cosas
de fazienda tocantes a don Christóval Colón, nuestro almirante
del mar Oçéano:
[2] Primeramente, que en lo que toca a la contribuçión de la
ochava parte de las mercaderías que nos agora mandamos enbiar   5
a las dichas yslas e tierra firme e las que yrán de aquí adelante,
qu'el dicho almirante, poniendo la ochava parte de las tales
mercaderías o dando la estimaçión d'ellas, sacadas primero las

16. **oý** G] en nota lo reçeby P. 16-17. ‹ocupado . . . negoçios› P] *om.* G. 19. **Pero . . . notario**] *a sigla
precedes and follows in GP, where the rest of the fol. is blank.*   Sources: GP. 1-2. **una declaratoria . . .
mensagera** P] tres çedulas G. 5. **es este** P] son estas G. 6. **sigue** P] syguen G.   Sources: GP.

costas e gastos que en ello se fizieren, aya para sý la ochava parte
del provecho que de las dichas mercaderías se oviere, conforme   10
a la capitulaçión que con él está fecha, que sobre esto dispone.
[3] Otrosý, por quanto el comendador Bovadilla tomó en sí
çierto oro e joyas e otros bienes muebles e raýses e semovientes
qu'el dicho almirante tenía en la ysla Española, porque aquello
es fructo e renta de las dichas Yndias, mandamos que ante de   15
todas cosas se pague de las dichas cosas que le fueron tomadas,
las costas e gastos e sueldos que fueren devidos e se ovieren
fecho desde qu'el dicho almirante postrimera vez fue a las
Yndias el año de noventa e ocho, desque fue llegado en la ysla
Española; porque, aunque aquello, por la capitulaçión, es a   20
cargo del dicho almirante, pero entiéndese para que lo aya de
pagar de lo que de las dichas Yndias se adquiriese, e de lo que
restare, pagado lo susodicho, se faga una suma, e fechas diez
partes, las nueve serán para nós e la dezena parte para el dicho
almirante; e de las dichas nueve partes nos paguemos los sueldos   25
e costas e gastos que se han fecho e se devieren fasta el dicho
viage que se fiso el año de noventa e ocho, qu'el almirante fue
en la dicha ysla /47 verso/ Española, por quanto nos le fezimos
merçed de la parte que le cabía de los dichos gastos, e el dicho
almirante de la dicha desena parte pague lo que se averiguare   30
que deviere particularmente a algunas personas como almirante.
[4] Yten, que en quanto a los ganados que de acá se han llevado
a nuestra costa, como quiera que, segund la dicha capitulaçión,
se avían de sacar las costas e gastos que en ello se han fecho, e de   35
lo restante el dicho almirante avía de aver la desena parte, por le
faser merçed mandamos que syn sacar las dichas costas e gastos
le sea acudido con la desena parte de los dichos ganados e partos
e pospartos que d'ello se han avido; e las nueve partes queden e
finquen para nós. (Vala ó dis "que" escripto sobre raýdo en esta   40
plana).
[5] Yten, mandamos que le sean tornados e restituydos todos los
atavíos de su persona e casa e bastimentos de pan e vino que el
dicho comendador Bovadilla le tomó, o su justa estimaçión, syn
que nos ayamos de aver parte alguna d'ello.   45
[6] Yten, que por quanto el dicho comendador Vobadilla, entre
otras cosas que tomó al dicho almirante, le tomó çierta cantidad

13. **semovientes**] somonientes *GP.* 44. **dicho** *G*] *om. P.* 46. **Vobadilla** *G*] Bobadilla *P.*

de piedras que eran del nasçimiento donde naçe el oro, que
tienen parte de oro, mandamos al nuestro governador de las
dichas yslas que reçiba declaraçión del dicho comendador   50
Bovadilla con juramento quantas e que tamañas eran, e gelas
fagan restituyr para que se partan e devidan en la manera que
dicha es.

[7] Yten, mandamos que sean restituydas al dicho almirante dos
yeguas con sus crías, qu'el dicho almirante compró de un labra-   55
dor en las Yndias, e dos cavallos qu'el dicho almirante tenía:
uno que compró de Gorvalán, e otro que ovo de sus yeguas,
que le tomó el dicho comendador Bovadilla, o su justa estimaçión, syn que nos aya de dar parte alguna d'ello.

[8] Yten, por quanto el dicho almirante dize que resçibe agravio   60
en non proveer él de capitanes e ofiçiales de los navíos que nos
agora mandamos yr a la ysla Española, que segund la dicha
capitulaçión él dise que avía de proveer, desymos que, porque
ya está proveýdo por nuestro mandado los dichos capitanes e
ofiçiales, que adelante mandaremos que se provea conforme a la   65
dicha capitulaçión.

[9] Yten, declaramos y mandamos qu'el dicho almirante pueda
traher /48 recto/ de aquí adelante cada año de la ysla Española
çiento e honze quintales de brasil por razón de la desena parte
que ha de aver a respetto de los mill quintales de brasil que se   70
han de dar cada año por nuestro mandado a los mercaderes con
quien está fecho asiento sobre ello, porque por el asyento que se
tomó con los dichos mercaderes está eçebtada su parte de lo
qual gose el dicho almirante por el tiempo contenido en el
dicho asyento de los dichos mercaderes e después de la dezena   75
parte de lo que se sacare.

[10] Yten, que por quanto el almirante dise qu'el comendador
Bovadilla ha pagado algunas debdas de sueldo e otras cosas en la
dicha ysla Española a algunas personas a quien non se devía
sueldo nin otra cosa alguna, segund parescerá por los libros de   80
los dichos ofiçiales e se podrá provar e mostrar, mandamos que
sy oviere pagado a personas a quien non se devía sueldo nin
cosa alguna, qu'el dicho almirante non sea obligado a pagar lo
semejante.

[11] Yten, por quanto el dicho comendador Bovadilla tomó a   85
los hermanos del dicho almirante çierta cantidad de oro e joyas,
porque aquello fue adquirido por ellos como por quien tenía
governaçión de las dichas Yndias, de todo aquello se fagan diez
partes, e la desena parte aya el almirante, e las nueve queden e

finquen para nós; e que en quanto a los atavíos e mantenimien- 90
tos e conucos e casas que tenían, e el oro que ovieron de cosas
que avían vendido suyas, próvandolo que fue d'esta condiçión,
que, aunqu'e‹n› aquello tengamos algund derecho, nos les fazemos merçed de todo ello, para que fagan d'ello como de cosa
suya propia. 95

[12] Yten, es nuestra merçed e voluntad qu'el dicho almirante
tenga en la dicha ysla Española persona que entienda en las cosas
de su fazienda e reçiba lo qu'él oviere de aver, e que sea Alonso
Sanches de Carvajal, contino de nuestra casa, e qu'el dicho
Alonso Sanches de Carvajal por parte del dicho almirante esté 100
presente con nuestro veedor a ver fundir e marcar el oro que en
las dichas yslas e tierra firme se oviere, e con nuestro factor
entienda en las cosas de la negoçiaçión de las dichas mercaderías; e mandamos al nuestro governador e contador e justiçias
e ofiçiales que agora son o fueren de las dichas yslas e tierra 105
firme, que cumplan e fagan guardar lo susodicho en quanto
nuestra merçed e voluntad fuere, e que, mostrando el dicho
Alonso /48 verso/ Sanches de Carvajal poder bastante del dicho
almirante, le acudan con la parte del oro que le pertenesçiere
por razón del diezmo en la dicha ysla, sacadas las costas e gastos, 110
e con el provecho de mercadurías por el ochava parte que mostrare el dicho almirante aver puesto en la costa d'ello.

[13] Yten, por quanto el dicho almirante ovo arrendado los ofiçios de alguaziladgo e escrivanía de la dicha ysla Española por
çierto tiempo, mandamos que los maravedís e lo que los dichos 115
ofiçios avrán rentado e valido se hagan diez partes: las nueve
sean para nós e la una para el dicho almirante, sacando primeramente las costas e gastos de los dichos ofiçiales; e porque el que
tenía la dicha escrivanía no estava obligado a dar por ello cosa
çierta, mandamos que, satisfecho de su trabajo, acuda con todo 120
lo que ha avido, para que se parta como dicho es. (Vala ó dis
"por el", que va escripto sobre raýdo en esta plana).

[14] Yten, que le buelvan los libros e escripturas que le fueron
tomados, e sy de algunos d'ellos oviere neçesydad para la
negoçiaçión, se saque un traslado sygnado de escrivano público 125
e se le entreguen los originales como dicho es.

[15] Yten, que en lo que toca al flete e mantenimientos, gose el

---

93. **aunqu'e‹n›**] aunq(ue) *GP.*

dicho Carvajal de todo ello segund e como gosaren los otros
nuestros ofiçiales.

[16] Lo qual todo que dicho es, e cada cosa e parte d'ello, man-   130
damos a vós el nuestro governador e nuestro contador e otros
ofiçiales e justiçias e personas de la dichas yslas e tierra firme que
asý fagáys e cumpláys en todo e por todo como de suso se contiene; e en cumpliéndolo, deys e entreguéys al dicho almirante
e sus hermanos, e a quien su poder oviere, las cosas susodichas,   135
syn que en ello le sea puesto ympedimiento alguno, e non
fagades ende ál.

[17] Fecha en Granada a veynte e syete días de setiembre de mill
e quinientos e uno años.

Yo el Rey   140
Yo la Reyna

[18] Por mandado del Rey e de la Reyna. Gaspar de Grizio.

XXXVII.i.2 (63)

El Rey e la Reyna

Cédula para el
Comendador de
Lares [*l. m.*].

[1] Comendador de Lares, nuestro governador de las Yndias:
nos /49 recto/ avemos mandado e declarado la orden que se ha
de tener en lo que se ha de fazer con don Christóval Colón,
nuestro almirante del mar Ocçéano, e sus hermanos çerca de las
cosas qu'el comendador Bovadilla les tomó, e sobre la forma   5
que se ha de tener en el acudir al dicho almirante con la parte
del diezmo e ochavo que ha de aver de los bienes muebles de las
yslas e tierra firme del dicho mar Occéano, e de las mercaderías
que nos de acá enbiaremos, segund veréys por la dicha nuestra
declaración e mandamiento firmado de nuestros nonbres que   10
sobre ello les mandamos dar; porende nos vos mandamos que
veáys la dicha declaración e conforme a ella les fagáys entregar
los dichos sus bienes e acudir al dicho almirante con lo que le

---

132. **tierra firme** G] tierras firmes P.   Sources: *GP*. 7. **ha** P] han G.

perteneçe de lo susodicho, por manera qu'el dicho almirante e
sus hermanos, o quien su poder oviere, sean de todo ello en-   15
tregados; e sy el oro e otras cosas que asý el dicho comendador
Bovadilla les tomó, los oviere gastado o vendido, vos mandamos que gelo fagáys luego pagar: lo que fuere gastado en
nuestro serviçio, se les pague de nuestra fazienda, e lo qu'el
dicho comendador Bovadilla oviere gastado en sus cosas   20
propias, se les pague de los bienes e fazienda del dicho comendador, e non fagades ende ál.

[2] Fecha en Granada a veynte e ocho días del mes de setiembre
de mill e quinientos e uno años.

Yo el Rey   25
Yo la Reyna

[3] Por mandado del Rey e de la Reyna. Gaspar de Grizio.

XXXVII.i.3 (62)

El Rey e la Reyna

[1] Ximeno de Briviesca: nos avemos mandado tomar asiento
con don Christóval Colón, nuestro almirante del mar Ocçéano,
que en todas las mercaderías que se llevaren a las Yndias ponga
la ochava parte e gose de la ochava parte que se ganare en ellas,
segund veréys por un asiento que se ha tomado con él, firmado   5
de nuestros nombres; porende nos vos mandamos que le deys
rasón e copia de todo lo que montan las mercaderías que agora
mandamos llevar a las dichas Yndias, para que, sy quisiere,
ponga en ellas la dicha ochava parte. [2] La qual reçebid vos en
nuestro nombre del dicho almirante, o de quien su poder   10
oviere, e le dad carta de pago d'ello, e reçebildo en dinero o en
las mercaderías que a él, o a quien su poder oviere, le pareçiere;
e sy en dinero lo pagare, tened en vós los maravedís que en ello
montare, para que acudáys con ellos a quien nos vos mandáremos, e a-/49 verso/ sentad la razón de todo ello en los   15

18. **fuere** G] fue P.   Sources: GP.

libros que vos tenéys, para que allí se averigue lo que oviere de
aver del provecho, e non fagades ende ál.

[3] Fecha en Granada a veynte e syete días del mes de setiembre
de mill e quinientos e uno años.

Yo el Rey   20
Yo la Reyna

[4] Por mandado del Rey e de la Reyna. Gaspar de Grizio.

XXXVII.i.4 (64.1-14)

El Rey e la Reyna

[1] Don Christóval Colón, nuestro almirante de las yslas e tierra
firme que son en el mar Occéano a la parte de las Yndias: vimos
vuestra letra de veynte e seys de febrero e las que con ella enbiastes y los memoriales que nos distes, y a lo que dezís que para
este viage a que vays querríades pasar por la Española, ya vos   5
deximos que, porque no es razón que para este viage a que
agora vays se pierda tiempo alguno, en todo caso vays por este
otro camino; que a la buelta, plaziendo a Dios, sy os paresçiere
que será neçesario, podéys bolver por allí de pasada, para
deteneros poco, porque, como vedes, converná que, buelto vos   10
del viage que agora vays, seamos luego ynformados de vós en
presona de todo lo que en él ovierdes fallado y fecho, para que
con vuestro pareçer y consejo proveamos sobre ello lo que más
cumpla a nuestro serviçio y las cosas neçesarias para el resgate de
acá se proveen.   15
[2] Aquí vos enbiamos la ynstructión de lo que, plaziendo a
Nuestro Señor, avéys de fazer en este viage; e a lo que desýs de
Portogal, nos escrivimos sobre ello al Rey de Portogal, nuestro
hijo, lo que conviene, y vos enbiamos aquí la carta nuestra que
desýs para su capitán, en que le fasemos saber vuestra yda hazia   20
el poniente y que avemos sabido su yda hazia el levante: que sy

Sources: *GP*, *H* 43 (*Quanto*) - 72 (*Almaçán*), *Pr* 43 (*Quanto*) - 68 (*años*). 9. **podéys** *G*] podres *P*. 11. **que**
G] a q. *P*.

en camino os topardes, vos tratéys los unos a los otros como
amigos e como es rasón de se tratar capitanes y gente de reyes
entre quien ay tanto debdo, amor y amistad, diziéndole que lo
mesmo avemos mandado a vós, y procuraremos qu'el Rey de   25
Portugal, nuestro fijo, escriva otra tal carta al dicho su capitán.
[3] A lo que nos suplicáys que ayamos por bien que llevéys con
vós este viage a don Fernando vuestro fijo, e la ración que se le
da, que dé a don Diego vuestro hijo, a nós plase d'ello.
[4] A lo que desýs que querríades llevar uno o doss que sepan   30
arávigo, a nós plase d'ello, con tal que por ello no os deten-
gáys./50 recto/
[5] A lo que dezís que qué parte de la ganançia se dará a la gente
que va con vós en esos navíos, desymos que vayan de la manera
que han ydo los otros.   35
[6] Las diez mill pieças de moneda que desýs, se acordó que no
se fiziesen por este viage fasta que más se vea.
[7] De la pólvora e artillería que demandáys, vos avemos ya
mandado proveer, como veréys.
[8] Lo que desýs que no podistes fablar al doctor Angulo e al   40
liçençiado Çapata a cabsa de la partida, escrivídnoslo muy larga
e particularmente.
[9] Quanto a lo otro contenido en vuestros memoriales y letras
tocante a vós y a vuestros fijos y hermanos, porque, como
vedes, a cabsa que nos estamos en camino, y vos de partida, no 45
se puede entender en ello fasta que paremos de asiento en alguna parte, y sy esto oviésedes de esperar, se perdería el viage a
que agora vays, por esto es mejor que, pues de todo lo neçesario
para vuestro viage estáys despachado, vos partáys luego, syn
detenimiento alguno, y quede a vuestro fijo el cargo de sol‹i›çi- 50
tar lo contenido en los dichos memoriales. [10] Y tened por
çierto que de vuestra prisión nos pesó mucho, y bien lo vistes
vos, y lo conoçieron todos claramente, pues que luego que lo
supimos, lo mandamos remediar; y sabéys el favor con que os
avemos mandado tratar siempre, y agora estamos mucho más en 55
vos honrar y trattar muy bien; y las merçedes que vos tenemos

22. **a** G] e P. 23. **gente** G] gentes P. 28. **vós** G] *om. P.* 33. **que qué** GP] *corr.* que (*Raccolta*)? 43. **Quanto**]
in H preceded by the rubric: Traslado del capítulo de la carta de Valençia de la Torre, en que el Rey e la Reyna
prometen al almirante de poner a su fijo en la posesyón de la governación de las Yndias y guardalle sus
previ(legio)s. *In Pr preceded by the rubric:* Éste es traslado de un capítulo de una carta que Su A. mandó escrevir
al señor almirante al tiempo de su partida del viaje donde agora viene. 50-51. **sol‹i›çitar** HPr] solçitar GP.
56. **muy** GHP] *om. Pr.*

fechas, vos serán guardadas enteramente segund forma y tenor
de nuestros privilegios que d'ellas tenéys, syn yr en cosa contra
ellas, y vos y vuestros fijos gozaréys d'ellas, como es rasón, e sy
neçesario fuere confirmarlas de nuevo, las confirmaremos, e a   60
vuestro fijo mandaremos poner en la posesyón de todo ello.
[11] Y en más que esto, tenemos voluntad de vos honrar y fazer
merçedes, y de vuestros fijos y hermanos nos ternemos el
cuydado que es razón; y todo esto se podrá fazer yéndovos en
buen ora y quedando el cargo a vuestro hijo, como está dicho;   65
y así vos rogamos que en vuestra partida non aya dilaçión.
[12] De Valençia de la Torre a quatorze días de março de quinientos e doss años.

Yo el Rey

Yo la Reyna   70

[13] Por mandado del Rey e de la Reyna. Miguel Peres de
Almaçán.
[14] E en las espaldas de la /50 verso/ dicha carta estava escripto
lo siguiente: "Por el Rey e la Reyna, a don Christóval Colón,
su almirante de las yslas e tierra firme que son en el mar Oc-   75
céano a la parte de las Yndias".

XXXVII.ii (64.15-18)

**[1] Este traslado fue conçertado con las dichas declara-
toria e çédulas e carta originales onde fue sacado ante los
escrivanos públicos de Sevilla, que lo sygn‹ar›on e firmaron de sus nombres en testimonio, en la dicha çibdad
de Sevilla, a veynte e dos días del mes de março, año del   5
nasçimiento de nuestro salvador Jhesu Christo de mill e
quinientos e doss años.**
[2] Yo Gomes Nieto, escrivano de Sevilla, só testigo.
[3] Yo Alonso Lucas, escrivano de Sevilla, só testigo.
[4] Yo Martýn Rodrigues, escrivano público de Sevilla,   10

67. **a** *GHP*] *om. Pr.* 71. **Miguel Peres de** *GP*] *om. H.*   Sources: *GP.* 2. **ante** *G*] en presençia *P.* 3.
sygn‹ar›on *P*] sygno *surmounted by the titulus G.* 8. **testigo**] *in G a sigla follows.* 9. **testigo**] *in G a sigla
follows.* 10-11. **Yo . . . testigo**] *in GP autograph.*

fys escrevir este traslado y fys aquí mío signo, y só testigo.

⋆　⋆　⋆

XXXVIII (59)

/59 recto/

[1] Lo que se declara que perteneçe e pertenecer puede e deve al señor almirante, visorrey y governador de las Yndias por el Rey e la Reyna nuestros señores, es lo siguiente:

[2] Muy claro pareçe por la capitulaçión fecha con Sus Altesas e firmada de sus reales nombres, que S. A. otorgan e conçeden al 5 dicho almirante de las Yndias todas las preheminençias e perrogativas que ha e tiene el almirante de Castilla; al qual por su previlegio pareçe perteneçelle la terçia parte de todo lo que ganare, e por consiguiente el almirante de las Yndias deve aver la terçia parte de todo lo que ha ganado de las yslas e tierra firme 10 que ha descubierto e queda por descobrir, porque *relatum me est in referente*, y tanbién ha de aver el diezmo e ochavo, como pareçe en el terçero e quinto capítulo de la dicha capitulaçión.

[3] Y sy alguno quisiere argüyr que la terçia parte conçedida al almirante de Castilla se deve entender de lo mueble que ganare 15 por la mar e que, por ser las dichas yslas tierra firme, que, aunque sean ganadas por la mar, no perteneçe el terçio d'ellas al dicho almirante, por ser cosa ynmutable: a esto responde el dicho almirante e dise que se deve mirar que por la dicha capitulaçión el dicho almirante de Castilla es nombrado al- 20

---

11. **signo**] sig no *with notarization inserted in GP; in G (where the second half of fol. 50v has been left blank) eight blank fols. followed, three of which (53-55) were subsequently removed, while the numeration of fols. 56-58 has been erased; in P the document ends fol. 54 (modern numeration): 7 blank fols. (55-62) follow in addition to the recto of fol. 63, while in 63v the document here published as* Appendix III *is transcribed.* Sources: GPPr. 1-3. **Lo . . . siguiente**] *in Pr written as a rubric.* 1. **se . . . que** G] *om.* PPr. **e . . . deve** G] *om.* PPr. 2. **señor** G] *om.* PPr. **governador** GP] guardador Pr. 3. **es lo siguiente** GP] *om.* Pr. 5. **nombres** GP] manos e n. Pr. 10. **yslas** GP] yndias Pr. 11. **queda** G] quedan PPr. 11. **me est** GPr] *om.* P. 13. **terçero** GP] terçio Pr. 15. **deve** GP] d. de Pr. 16. **yslas** GP] y. e Pr. 18. **cosa** G] tierra PPr. **ynmutable** GPr] ynumerable P. *The rest of the line is blank in GPPr, where* a esto responde . . . *is written at the head after a double space.*

mirante de la mar, por la qual causa le es otorgada la terçia parte
de lo que ganare por la mar, porque en otra parte non le es dado
juridiçión nin ofiçio; e fuera mucho ynconviniente e cosa no
rasonable dalle parte fuera de su ofiçio, como se dise, *"quia
propter offitium datum beneficium"* (porque el benefiçio ha y deve   25
aver rexpecto al ofiçio, e non fuera d'ello). [4] Pero el almirante
de las Yndias ha seýdo constituydo e nombrado, según el
thenor de la dicha capitulaçión, por almirante no de la mar, mas
expressamente de las Yndias e tierra firme descubiertas y por
descobrir en el mar Oçéano, por lo qual muy justamente le   30
perteneçe la terçia parte de las dichas yslas e tierra firme que ha
ganado exerçitando e usando de su ofiçio de almirante, e asý se
deve entender e ynterpretar el privillegio del dicho almirante
de Castilla e el capítulo que a él se refiere; ca muy manifiesto es
que toda cosa se deve entender *secundum subiectam materiam et*   35
secundum qualitatem personarum, e dándole otra ynteligençia, no
sirviría nada el dicho privilegio e capítulo al dicho almirante de
las Yndias, porque, no llevando el terçio de las dichas Yndias,
de donde él es almirante, e no seyendo constituydo almirante
de la mar, non /59 verso/ podría tanpoco llevalle de lo que   40
ganase por la mar, por ser fuera de su jurisdiçión e ofiçio, de
manera que no aprovecharía nada el dicho capítulo e constitu-
çión: y tal cosa non es de desyr, porque cada palabra puesta en
un contrato deve obrar e non deve ser ynterpretada super-
flamente, quanto más en este caso de tanta ynportançia e utili-   45
dad e gloria de Sus Altesas, avida con muy poca costa e syn
ningund peligro de honra, ni de personas, nin de bienes, e con
grandíssimo peligro, como era común opinión, de la vida, e no
syn mucha costa del dicho almirante; por la qual rasón sería
reputado por muy poca cosa solamente la déçima parte (no ha-   50
syendo minçión de la ochava, porque aquella le perteneçe por
respecto de la costa de su ratta parte), e muy poca parte sería
para tan grand serviçio tan pequeña merçed; e bien viene a
propósito lo que disen las sagradas leyes: *"quia benefitia principum*
sunt latissime interpretanda"; e pues las merçedes fechas por los   55

21. **le** GPr] les P. 22. **ganare** GP] gane Pr. 24. **quia** GPr] om. P. 25. **datum beneficium** GP] etc. Pr.
datum] dactum GP. 27. **las Yndias** GP] castilla Pr. 29. **expressamente** G] espresa e señaladamente PPr
(but cf. p. 375, 67). 38. **no** G] om. PPr. 40. **tanpoco** GP] tener poco Pr. 46. **Sus Altesas** GP] su alteza Pr.
50-52. **(no . . . parte)**] textual parentheses in G. 52. **costa** GP] cosa Pr. **sería** GP] seria(n) Pr. 54. **prin-**
cipum GP] p(ri)nçipun Pr. 55. **interpretanda**] interpetranda GPPr.

príncipes se deven entender amplíssimas e muy complidas, mayormente de los príncipes exçelentíssimos e altos como Sus A., de quien más que de otros ningunos se esperan amplíssimas merçedes. [5] E por esto la dicha tercia parte, aunque pareçe mínima, le perteneçe al dicho almirante, ca veemos que en las compañías que entre mercaderes se fasen, que en tanto grado es reputada e tenida la yndustria e aviso de un compañero, e tanta parte le perteneçe, como al otro que puso dineros, sy por cabsa de aquélla, aun‹que› de los mesmos dineros del otro, resulta la ganançia: quanto más en este caso del almirante, el qual ha obrado yndustria admirable e yncreýble, e con grande costa e peligro de su persona e de sus hermanos e criados; por lo qual tanto más de rasón ha de aver el terçio de todo, como verdaderamente fue la yntinçión de Sus A.; e que esto sea verdad, veemos que Sus Altesas dan a los que van a las Yndias de las seys partes las çinco, e a los que menos de las çinco partes, las quatro, e governaçión de tierra syn ningund peligro, abierto el camino e asegurado e aclarado a todos. [6] E para confirmaçión de lo que digo, como se contiene en muchos privilegios del dicho almirante de las Yndias, el dicho almirante fue por mandado de Sus Altesas a ganar no naos, nin fustas, ni cosa alguna de la mar, mas expressamente yslas e tierra firme, /60 recto/ como señaladamente se dize en el privilegio, que más se puede desyr merçed, en .XI. fojas, en fin de la foja e prinçipio del privilegio, en que dise asý: "e porque vos Christóval Colón vades por nuestro mandado a descobrir e ganar yslas e tierra firme, etç."; y, pues, sy la ganançia avía de ser yslas e tierra firme, nesçesidad es que la terçia parte sea de la ganançia, e seyendo el terçio de la ganançia, notoria cosa es qu'el terçio de las yslas e tierra firme ganadas perteneçen al dicho almirante; e syn dubda se deve creer que sy al prinçipio oviera pedido el dicho almirante mayor parte, le fuera otorgada, seyendo todo de su ganançia, e de cosa que no avía ninguna esperança nin notiçia, e cosa que era fuera de la memoria e señorío de Sus Altesas: asý que complida y claramente se responde a los que contra esto dixieren, y justa y claramente pareçe perteneçer la terçia parte de las dichas Yndias y tierra firme al dicho almirante.

56. **amplíssimas** *GP*] cu(m)plisymas *Pr*. 58. **de** (otros) *GP*] *om. Pr.* 64. **aun‹que›**] aun *GPPr*. 70. **veemos** *GP*] veamos *Pr*. **Sus Altesas** *GP*] su a(lteza) *Pr*. 74. **del dicho** *GP*] de *Pr*. 81. **e ganar** *GP*] *om. Pr.* 86. **que** *GP*] e *Pr*. 91. **dichas** *GPr*] *om. P.*

[7] Y porqu'el diezmo es claríssimo, acerca del ochavo, el qual
aunque tanbién es muy claro, quiero desyr. [8] Sy contra él se
dixesse que no ha de aver el dicho ochavo de las mercaderías e   95
cosas llevadas e traýdas en los navíos que han ydo a descobrir e
los que fueron a las Perlas e a otras partes de su almirantadgo, en
tanto qu'él estava en la ysla Española en serviçio de Sus A.,
diziendo que no contribuyó el dicho almirante en el armazón
d'ellas, respóndese que a él no se le notificó la yda de tales   100
navíos, nin al tiempo de la partida fue requerido nin avisado; y
por esto, como *de jure* al ynorante que pueda pretender ynorançia de algund fecho no le corre tiempo, mas antes la ynorançia syn ninguna dubda da legítima escusaçión, e antes res-
tituçión por entero, e asý se deve reduzir e desyr por este caso   105
qu'el almirante satisfase ofreçiéndose a contribuyr por su parte
al presente: ni puede ser él culpado, mas antes los que no le han
notificado lo que eran obligados, etç.

XXXIX (60)

/61 recto/
[0] La declaraçión de lo que perteneçe e perteneçer puede e
deve al señor almirante de las Yndias por virtud de la capitulaçión e asiento que con S. A. fizo, qu'es el título e derecho que
tiene el dicho almirante e sus desçendientes a las yslas e tierra
firme del mar Oçéano, es esta que se sigue: 5

El primero capítulo
[1] Primeramente, por el primero capítulo S. A. le fizieron su
almirante de las yslas e tierra firme descubiertas e por descobrir
en el mar Oçéano, con las preheminençias e segund e en la
manera que el almirante de la mar de Castilla ha e tiene su   5
almirantadgo en su distrito.

94. **quiero desyr** G] pero *PPr.* **Sy**] *at the head in* G. 97. **a** (otras) *GPr*] *om.* P. 99. **el** (dicho) *GP*] al *Pr.* 100.
d'ellas *GP*] della *Pr.* **respóndese** G] responde *PPr.* 102. **al** *GP*] e al *Pr.* 103. **antes** *GPr*] *om.* P. 105. **e
desyr** *GP*] *om. Pr.* 108. **etç.** *GP*] *om. Pr; in* G *it ends the last line of fol.* [60r], *while fol.* [60v] *has been left blank.*
Sources: *GPPr.* 1. **e** (perteneçer) *GP*] p(er) *Pr.* 3. **e** (asiento) *GP*] o? *Pr.* 5. **esta** *GP*] este *Pr.*

[2] Para declaración d'esto, es de notar qu'el almirante de Castilla tiene por su privilegio la terçia parte de lo que se gana o él
ganare en la mar, por que, por esta razón, el almirante de las
Yndias deve aver la terçia parte d'ellas y de lo que en ellas se   10
gana.

[3] Ca puesto qu'el almirante de Castilla no aya el terçio, salvo
de lo que se gana por la mar de donde él es almirante, el almirante de las Yndias deve aver el terçio d'ellas y de todo lo que
por tierra en ellas se gana.   15

[4] La razón es porque Sus A. yslas e tierra firme le mandaron
ganar, y d'ellas señaladamente le titularon almirante, y d'ellas y
en ellas deve aver el galardón, como quien es almirante d'ellas y
con mucho peligro, contra la opinión de todo el mundo, las
ganó.

Capítulo segundo

[1] Por el segundo capítulo Sus A. le fizieron su visorey y
governador general de todas las dichas yslas y tierra firme, con
facultad que oviese todos los ofiçios que perteneçen a la governaçión, eçebto que de tres S. A. pudiesen nombrar el uno; y   5
después Sus A. le fizieron nueva merçed de los dichos ofiçios en
los años de .LXXXXII. y .XCIII. por privillegio otorgado, syn
la dicha condiçión.

[2] La declaración d'esto es que al dicho almirante perteneçen
los dichos ofiçios de visorrey e governador, con facultad de   10
poner todos los ofiçiales en los ofiçios y magistratos de las dichas
/61 verso/ Yndias, porque Sus A. en galardón y casi pago de su
trabajo y costa que el dicho almirante fizo en descobrir y ganar
las dichas Yndias, le fizieron merçed de los dichos ofiçios y
governaçión con la dicha facultad.   15

[3] Ca muy çierta cosa es que al prinçipio el dicho almirante no
se dispusiera nin persona alguna se oviera dispuesto a tanto
riesgo e aventura, sy en galardón y pago de tal enpresa S. A. no
le otorgaran los dichos ofiçios y governaçión.

[4] Los quales Sus A. justamente le otorgaron, porque fuese de   20

---

10. **ellas** GP*r*] ella P. **lo** GP*r*] to P. 12-13. **salvo de lo** GP*r*] salvos lo (lo *with a tilde over* o) P*r*. 13-14. **el
almirante** GP*r*] *om*. P. 16. **La** GP] e la P*r, where line 16 is a continuation of line 15.* 17. **ellas** (señaladamente)
GP] ella P*r*. 17-18. **y . . . ellas** GP] *om*. P*r*. 18. **almirante** GP] el a. P*r*. **d'ellas** GP] *om*. P*r*. 6. **Sus** GP] su
P*r*. 11. **en** GP*r*] de P. 16. **que** GP] ca P*r*. 17. **a tanto** GP*r*] acatando P. 18. **en** GP] el P*r*.

aquello con que tan señalado serviçio les fazía el dicho almirante, antes que otrie, aprovechado, honrado e sublimado.

[5] Ca muy poca honra, o casi ninguna, resçibiera el dicho almirante, aunque otro pago oviera, sy en aquella tierra por él con tanta pena ganada S. A. pusieran otro superior; e pues por tan justas causas fue d'ellos proveýdo, justamente perteneçen al dicho almirante los dichos ofiçios y governaçión.

[6] Y porque agora el dicho almirante, estando paçíficamente en serviçio de S. A. exerçitando los dichos ofiçios en las dichas Yndias, le desapoderaron de la posesión d'ellos ynjustamente y contra toda razón y derecho, syn ser llamado, ni oýdo, ni vençido, de lo qual dise que reçibió el dicho almirante grandíssimo agravio y grand desonor en su persona y menoscabo en sus bienes; y según el dicho capítulo, claramente pareçe por las razones siguientes:

[7] Porque el dicho almirante no pudo ser despojado ni desapoderado de los dichos sus ofiçios, pues nunca cometió ni fizo ningund caso contra Sus A., por que de derecho deviese perder sus bienes; y puesto que cabsa oviera, lo que Dios no quiera, que primero avía de ser el dicho almirante çitado e llamado, oýdo e vençido por derecho.

[8] Y en desapoderalle syn justa cabsa, grand agravio reçibió el dicho almirante y grand injustiçia se le fizo, y aun de derecho Sus A. non lo podían fazer.

[9] Porque Sus A. le dieron los dichos ofiçios y governaçión de la dicha tierra en satisfaçión del serviçio y costa que el dicho almirante fizo en ganalla, de donde consiguió justo ynterese y perpetuo título a los dichos ofiçios; y pues ynjustamente fue d'ellos desapoderado, el dicho almirante, ante de todas cosas, deve ser restituydo en los dichos ofiçios y en su onor y estado.

[10] Y en quanto al daño que ha reçebido, qu'el dicho almirante dise /62 recto/ qu'es en gran cantidad, porque con su yndustria de cada día fallava y descobría en las dichas Yndias mucho oro, perlas e espeçiería y otras cosas de grand valor, qu'el dicho almirante faga juramento y declare la cantidad del ynterese, y aquello de derecho le deve ser satisfecho.

22. **otrie** *GPr* (otri *Pr*)] antes *P.* 25. **superior e** *GPr*] en su lugar *P.* 30. **ynjustamente** *GP*] justamente *Pr.* 32. **qual** *GP*] q(ue)l *Pr.* 39. **que** (cabsa) *GP*] *om. Pr.* 41. **oýdo** *GP*] e o. *Pr.* 47. **donde** *GP*] do *Pr.* 48. **perpetuo . . . ynjustamente** *GPr*] *om. P.* 49. **d'ellos desapoderado** *G(P)*] d. d'e. *Pr.* **desapoderado** *GPr*] adespoderado e los dichos titulos y pues justamente fue dellos desapoderado *P.* 50. **deve** *GP*] d. de *Pr.* **ser restituydo** *GP*] r. s. *Pr.* **ofiçios** *G*] sus o. *PPr.* 52. **qu'es** *GPr*] es *P.* 55. **del** *GP*] de *Pr.*

[11] La satisfaçión d'esto le deve fazer aquel que ynjustamente le desapoderó de todos sus bienes, porque aquél, segund ley divina e umana, como quien traspasó los límites del poder de Sus A., es obligado a ello. 60

[12] Y tanto más presto le deve ser fecha la satisfaçión e reyntegraçión de los dichos ofiçios, bienes y honra al dicho almirante, quanto menos justiçia ovo para ser d'ellos despojado.

[13] Ca muy yncreýble cosa y no digna de creer es que ayan por bueno Sus A. que un varón tan yndustrioso, que de tan longuíssima tierra vino a haser tan señalado y alto serviçio a Sus A. 65 como fizo con su yndustria y persona, por que meresçió ser digno de muy mayor feliçidad, fuesse por cabsa de enbidiosos y maliçias del todo punto destruydo, deviendo estar de razón tan conjunto en amor de Sus A. y tan asentado en sus magnánimas 70 entrañas, qu'el dicho almirante y todo el mundo creýa que ningunos detractores le pudieran hazer ageno del merescimiento de grandes merçedes, quanto más yndignar el coraçón de Sus A. para le fazer perder lo que tan servido y meresçido tenía; con que de cada día el dicho almirante esperava mucho servir y 75 servía a S. A., procurando con su yndustria el provecho presente de las dichas Yndias y governando con sus ofiçios para la poblaçión e abmentaçión d'ellas.

[14] Lo qual otro alguno no hiziera ni hará, porque, demás de avello todo desamparado sy él no governara en el tiempo 80 remoto, los que agora governaren con cobdiçia de se aprovechar durante su governaçión no proveerán en lo porvenir como el dicho almirante, a quien tocava el ynterese perpetuo, que con esperança de la honra y provecho advenidero, después de aver bien regido e conservado los Yndios, qu'es la riqueza de 85 aquella tierra, y reformado y sojudgado el señorío d'ella, no tenía en nada lo del tiempo de agora.

---

58. **todos** G] to todos P, t. los dichos Pr. 61. **fecha** GP] fecho Pr. 62. **bienes** GPr] bien P. 66. **Sus** GP] su Pr. 69. **deviendo**] *begins a new paragraph in* G. 69-70. **tan conjunto** GPr] tanto junto P. 70. **Sus** GP] su Pr. 72. **detractores** G] detradores PPr. 73. **Sus** GP] su Pr. 75. **mucho** GPr] m. mas P. 78. **poblaçión** GP] poblazo(n) Pr. 80. **todo** GP] *om.* Pr. 82. **en** GP] ni(n) Pr. 86. **reformado** GPr] reformando P. **sojudgado** GPr] sojusgando P.

/62 verso/

[1] Por el terçero capítulo S. A. le fizieron merçed de la dezena parte de todo lo que se comprase, fallase e oviese dentro de los límites del dicho almirantado, sacando las costas.

[2] Esto se entiende de manera qu'el dicho almirante ha de aver 5 el diezmo de lo que se oviere e fallare en las dichas Yndias e tierra firme del mar Oçéano por qualesquier personas de todo juntamente, agora sea para provecho de Sus A. o de otras qualesquier personas por merçed que d'ello o de parte d'ello les ayan fecho, sacando las costas que las tales personas o S. A. en 10 ello fizieren.

[3] Y S. A. de justiçia en perjuyzio del dicho diezmo no pueden fazer merçed de todo, ni de parte alguna del provecho de las dichas Yndias a ninguna persona, syn que primeramente aya de pagar e pague d'ello enteramente el diezmo al dicho almirante. 15

[4] Ca por faser Sus A. las tales merçedes, desfasen, o menoscaban, la que ya tienen fecha al dicho almirante, y dexan muy diminuyda, o desmembrada, su devida satisfaçión.

[5] Porque la merçed fecha al dicho almirante del dicho diezmo fue antes primeramente que las dichas Yndias descubriese, y 20 dado y otorgado para ayuda al galardón y pago que por tal serviçio meresçía; y por ello el dicho diezmo es ramo prinçipal de su líquido ynterese.

[6] Y aun sy Sus A. por conçierto, o condiçión, o en otra qualquier manera dieren la meytad, o otra qualquier parte, a quales- 25 quier personas que se dispusieren al trabajo y costa del tal provecho, también deve aver el dicho almirante el diezmo de lo que resultare y no se consumiere de la parte de las tales personas, como de la prinçipal de Sus A., pues lo uno y lo otro es verdadera y prinçipal ganançia y resulte de las Yndias de su 30 almirantadgo.

Quarto capítulo

[1] Por el quarto capítulo Sus A. conçedieron al dicho almirante la juridiçión çevill e criminal de qualesquier pleitos tocantes a

---

1. **Terçero** GP] el t. *Pr.* 3. **comprase** GPr] comprare P. 4. **límites** GP] dichos l. *Pr.* 7. **todo** GPr] todos P. 12. **S.** (= **Sus**) GP] su *Pr.* 14. **a . . . persona** GP] *om. Pr.* 15. **el** GP] el dicho *Pr.* 16. **Ca** GPr] que P. 20. **descubriese** GP] descubriese(n) *Pr.* 24. **Sus** GP] su *Pr.* 30. **y** (resulte) GPr] *om.* P.

las dichas Yndias, e que pudiese conosçer d'ellos acá en las
partes y lugares donde comprehende la juridiçión del almirante 5
de Castilla, seyendo justo.

[2] Para declaraçión de la justiçia que tiene el dicho almirante,
dise que a él perteneçe el dicho judgado, por ser una de las
prinçipales preheminençias y casy braço del cuerpo de su almirantamiento, syn el qual a gran pena se podría señorear el 10
dicho al-/63 recto/ mirantadgo, antes quedaría yermo,
porqu'el dicho judgado es el prinçipal esfuerço que honra,
anima y sostiene todas las otras partes del cuerpo del dicho almirantamiento.

[3] Y que le perteneçe el tal conosçimiento en los puertos y 15
abras de acá, bien asý como en las mesmas yslas e tierra firme de
donde él es el almirante, porque, sy en el tronco de allá solamente toviese el dicho judgado, syn comprehender acá las cabsas emanantes, que por ser los contrayentes naturales d'esta
tierra y todo el trato y negoçiaçión d'ella, que su juridiçión casy 20
sería ninguna; porque los que van a las dichas Yndias, van para
solamente negoçiar, y acá quedan las ligaturas de las compañías
y posturas que de buelta engendran los pleitos, seyendo las cabsas de los tales pleitos de las que desvaran de la negoçiación y
trato que tovieron dentro en su almirantamiento. 25

[4] Lo otro, que, aunque el dicho capítulo no oviera en que
expresamente se fiziera minçión del dicho judgado, que la ora
que Sus A. estableçieron el dicho ofiçio de almirantadgo y fizieron d'él merçed al dicho almirante con las mesmas preheminençias del almirantadgo de Castilla, que conjuntamente al 30
dicho almirantamiento le avían fecho merçed del dicho judgado con la dicha comprehensión, porqu'el almirante de la mar de
Castilla tiene por prinçipal preheminençia de su almirantadgo el
judgado de todos los pleitos çeviles e criminales a él tocantes,
que comprehende en todos los puertos y abras d'esta tierra, 35
aunque son fuera de su almirantadgo.

[5] Y en quanto a ser justamente d'él proveýdo, dise el dicho
almirante que S. A. justamente le pudieron d'él proveer, como
reyes e señores soberanos que para todo tienen poder absoluto,
a quien solamente pertenesçía la tal provisión. 40

---

7. **Para** GP] p. la *Pr.* 8. **dise** GPr] disen *P.* 9. **y** GP] o *Pr.* 9-10. **almirantamiento** GP] almirantadgo *Pr.*
12. **que** GP] e *Pr.* 13-14. **almirantamiento** GP] almirantadgo *Pr.* 16. **en** GP] *om. Pr.* 19. **emanantes**
GP] e manantes *Pr.* 22. **de las compañías** GPr] *om. P.* 24. **de las** GPr] *om. P.* 25. **almirantamiento** G]
almirantadgo *PPr.* 28. **y** GP] *om. Pr.* 32. **de la** GPr] del *P.* 33. **de su** GP] del *Pr.* 35. **comprehende** GPr]
comprehenden P (*Raccolta*). 37. **Y** GP] *om. Pr.* 39. **tienen poder** GP] p. t. *Pr.*

[6] Y Sus A., en proveer al dicho almirante del dicho ofiçio con la dicha comprehensyón, no hizieron agravio a persona alguna, ni les toca ynterese, por ser el dicho su almirantadgo y judgado d'él y las yslas y tierras donde es ynstituydo, nueva y milagrosamente halladas, conjuntas y traýdas al señorío de Castilla. 45
[7] Lo otro, que los pleitos emanantes del dicho almirantadgo a cabsa de la grand distançia e apartamiento de la tierra donde es ynstituydo, y por ser muy alongada de do confluyen los mareantes d'esta tierra, serán muy agenos, divididos y apartados de los pleitos acá tocantes, y en apartar y dividir el conosçimiento 50 d'ellos no se sygue a ninguna juridiçión agravio.
[8] Y pues Sus A. syn agravio de persona alguna y con poder soberano /63 verso/ justamente proveyeron, es muy çierto que en la tal provisyón no yntervino ynjustiçia, ca dos contrarios naturalmente no pueden señorear un subjeto, antes tanto 55 rehuyen y se enagenan de consistir en una cosa, que por la espeçie del uno venimos en conosçimiento de la calidad del otro: de donde se concluye que la dicha provisión es justa.
[9] Y aun de la persona del dicho almirante proçede ser justa la dicha provisión, porque segund la calidad de las dichas Yndias 60 oçidentales a todo el mundo ynnotas, de neçesydad se avía de poner acá jues de çierta yspirençia para dar justa sentençia; pues ¿quien las avría más experimentado, nin ternía más çierto conosçimiento de la calidad de los pleitos d'ellas, qu'el tal almirante que continuamente en ellas ha resydido y mila- 65 grosamente con su mucha sotileza y çiençia de la mar, corriendo mucho peligro, del mismo mar las sacó?

Quinto capítulo

[1] Por el quinto capítulo Sus Altesas conçeden al dicho almirante que pueda contribuyr en la ochava parte de qualesquier armadas que se fagan para el trato e negoçiación de las yslas y tierra firme de su almirantadgo, e que tanbién aya la ochava 5 parte de lo que resultare de la tal armasón.
[2] El verdadero entendimiento d'esto es qu'el dicho almirante

---

41. **Sus** GP] su Pr. 43. **el** GP] al Pr. **almirantadgo** G] almirantamiento PPr. 44. **y las** GP] om. Pr. **yslas** PPr] yndias G. **y** (tierras) GP] o Pr. **es** G] el es PPr (dondel es Pr). 51. **sygue** GP] sygue(n) Pr. 52. **Sus** GP] su Pr. 54. **ynjustiçia** GPr] justiçia P. 56. **enagenan** GPr] agenan P. **consistir en una** GP] consintir ni(n)g(un)a Pr. 58. **concluye** GPr] c. en P. 60-61. **Yndias oçidentales** GP] yslas yçidentales Pr. 3. **pueda** GPr] puedan P. 4. **y** GP] de Pr. 7. **d'esto** GP] om. Pr.

deve aver el ochavo de qualesquier cosas que en qualquier manera en las dichas Yndias se aya, agora sea para provecho de Sus A., o de otras qualesquier personas, sacando el ochavo de la costa d'ello, por rata. 10

[3] Porque en la primera armada de que resultó las dichas Yndias, es a saber la ganançia que d'ellas proçede, el dicho almirante contribuyó en su ochava parte, y aun çerca de la meytad de la costa; de donde consiguió perpetuo título al dicho 15 ochavo, por ser el resulte de la dicha armada sempiterno.

[4] Lo otro, que, pues al prinçipio señaladamente yva a ganar yslas y tierra firme, qu'es cosa ynmutable, no se entendiera poder traer ganançia, para aver d'ella el ochavo, sy por lo mueble d'ellas como verdadero resulte y fin de la tal armasón no 20 fuera entendido.

[5] Y aunqu'el dicho almirante de la primera armada no traxo lo mueble de las dichas Yndias, que era el resulte y ganançia d'ella, /64 recto/ que pues él metió las dichas yslas e tierra firme de baxo del poder de Sus A., y allá paçíficamente como suyas las 25 dexó, que asymesmo se entiende aver apoderado y dado a S. A. todo lo mueble d'ellas que en ellas a la sasón y en qualquier tiempo se oviese; pues quietamente dende en adelante podían enbiar S. A. por todo ello, como por cosa suya, a quien quisiesen. 30

[6] Lo otro, que puesto que por contribuyr en la primera armada no oviera el dicho almirante conseguido perpetuo derecho al dicho ochavo, que pues Sus A. forçosamente han de armar para gosar de la ganançia de las dichas Yndias, que de justiçia no le pueden vedar qu'él no contribuya en la costa 35 d'ellas y llevar el ochavo del resulte, y porque las armadas han de ser continuas, por ser el resulte de las Yndias continuo, que perpetuamente le perteneçe el dicho ochavo.

[7] Y aunque se diga que solamente del resulte de mercadería le perteneçe el tal ochavo, porque dise en el capítulo del trato e 40 negoçiaçión que dis que se entiende "mercadería", la verdad es que generalmente perteneçe al dicho almirante el dicho ochavo de todo el mueble de las dichas Yndias, porque los dichos voca-

9. **aya** GP] haga Pr. 10. **Sus** GP] su Pr. **el** GP] lo dicho Pr. 11. **d'ello por** GP] dellos Pr. 16. **resulte** GP] resulto Pr. 17. **que** GPr] om. P. 23. **d'ella** GP] dello Pr. 27. **y** GPr] om. P. 29-30. **quisiesen** GP] quisiese Pr. 34. **de la ganançia** GP] de las armadas Pr. 35. **le** GP] la Pr. **qu'él no contribuya** GP] que lo contribuya(n) Pr. 37. **continuo** GP] perpetuo Pr. 38. **dicho** GP] om. Pr. 39. **resulte** GP] resulto Pr. 43. **porque** GPr] p. en P.

blos "trato", "negoçiación" comprehenden todo género de
cosa que en qualquier manera y tiempo se aya. 45

[8] Ca el dicho vocablo "trato" es astuçia, o la deligençia que se
pone para conseguir el fin de la negoçiación, y finalmente el
trato, o modo, que el dicho almirante avía de tener con los
poseedores de las dichas Yndias que yva a ganar para conseguir
el fin, que era ganallas, y pues las ganó, lo que d'ellas resulta es 50
lo que justamente se deve partir, como verdadero resulte de la
tal negoçiación.

[9] Y este otro vocablo "negoçiación" se deriba de "negoçio",
que se entiende "nega oçio", *quia "negotium" est quasi "nega*
otium", de manera que su entendimiento es general para en 55
qualquier género de cosa; e por ello se comprehende a qualquier género de cosa mueble que en las dichas Yndias se falle.

[10] Y puesto qu'el dicho vocablo no fuera equívoco e que
tuviera líquida determinaçión de "mercadería", que /64 verso/
pues las dichas Yndias y tierra firme, espeçialmente la Española, 60
avía ganado el dicho almirante más por dádivas de mercaderías
que por fuerça de armas, que justamente las dichas Yndias y
todas las cosas d'ellas se pueden desyr "mercadas", y por ello
"mercadería", porque de "mercar" se deriba el dicho vocablo
"mercadería". 65

[11] Lo otro, que aunque por fuerça de armas oviera ganado el
dicho almirante las dichas Yndias y Sus A. expresamente a mer-
cadear le ovieran enbiado, que por eso no çesava de aver d'ellas
el dicho su ochavo, porque lo mueble que en ellas se falla, así
como oro, perlas, espeçiería e otras cosas, pura e prinçipalmente 70
es mercadería; ca toda cosa mueble que se puede comprar,
eçebto consagrada, se deve llamar "mercadería", segund las
leyes que disen *"quod omnia sunt in commertio nostro"*.

[12] Lo otro, que por qualquier forma que oviese conseguido el
fin de la yntinçión del armada, que era la ganançia de las dichas 75
Yndias, perteneçía al dicho almirante el dicho su ochavo,
porque las ganançias de la mar y los casos d'ellas son muy varios,
afortunados, ynçiertos e ynopinados, y lo que d'ellas resulta
para por todos partirse, tanto monta aver seýdo cortado por

---

44. **comprehenden** GPr] conprehende P. 53. **vocablo** PPr] vacablo G. 54. **nega oçio** GP] ne/goçio Pr.
negotium GP] negutium Pr. 54-55. **quasi . . . otium** GP] casy negacio(n) Pr. 58. **equívoco** GP]
equivoca Pr. **que** GP] om. Pr. 59. **que** PPr] que // q(ue) G. 61. **ganado . . . almirante** GP] el dicho
almirante ganado Pr. 64. **vocablo** GP] v. de Pr. 68. **çesava** GPr] çesa P. 73. **quod** GP] quot Pr. **omnia**
GP] o. que Pr. **nostro** GP] nuestro Pr. 77. **d'ellas** GP] della Pr. 78. **d'ellas** P] dellos GPr.

fuerça, como desatado por arte; ca éste es el común estilo de   80
todos los armadores para lo qual ay ynfinitos exemplos.

[13] Ca muy çierto es que, sy algunos mercaderes armasen en
compañía para solo trato de mercadería, e por ventura se con-
çertasen con el patrón qu'él pudiese contribuyr en alguna parte
del armasón porque también oviese aquella parte del resulte,   85
que, aunque fuera de mercadería ganase alguna çibdad o sueldo
o navíos de enemigos, que tanbién le perteneçía la parte de la tal
ganançia, como de derecho avía de aver de la mercadería,
porque, aunque fue ganado fuera de mercadería, es verdadero
resulte avido a cabsa de la tal armada.   90

[14] Y sy por caso un factor de alguna otra compañía, nego-
çiando en algund reyno, se fisyese muy parçial del rey de
aquella tierra, syrviéndole con enpréstidos o con vendelle mercaderías a menos preçio, e por caso después de desatada la compañía, aquel rey, por contemplaçión del amistad le fiziese a él   95
merçed de alguna cosa, es obligado a partir con sus compañeros
enteramente como de verdadero resulte avido a cabsa de la tal
/65 recto/ compañía, aunque ya oviese grand tiempo que fuese
desligada, porque en todas partes asý se judga, y asý lo disponen
las leyes d'estos reynos de S. A..   100

[15] Y en Portugal ha muy poco que acaesçió lo semejante a un
florentín, factor de una gruesa compañía de Florentia, que por
aver mucho servido al rey de aquella tierra con enpréstidos y
otras cosas de sus mercaderías, fue costreñido a dar parte a sus
compañeros de una merçed qu'el rey le fizo por contemplaçión   105
del amistad a él propio, después de dada cuenta y desligada la
compañía, como de verdadero resulte emanante d'ella.

[16] Y aun aquel patrón Lercar a quien Sus A. fizieron merçed
por contenplaçión del serviçio que les fizo en el pasaje del Ar-
çiduquesa y en alguna satisfaçión de la carraca que perdió en los   110
bancos, fue en Genua por justiçia costreñido a dar parte a sus
compañeros como de resulte verdadero, y solamente le quedó
lo que le perteneçía como patrón por rata.

[17] Y aun sy por caso a un fijo se fase alguna donaçión por
algund grand amigo de su padre, aunque todas las otras dádivas   115
se atribuyan a peculio, no menos ‹ésta› se deve asygnar a peculio
profetitio, porqu'el fin proçede del padre. [18] Y otras muchas

---

87. **navíos** GP] navio P. 99. **todas partes** G] toda parte PPr. 102. **gruesa** GP] grand Pr. 106. **propio**
GPr] proproprio P. **cuenta** GP] cont(r)a Pr. 107. **de** GP] om. Pr. 108. **fizieron** GP] le f. Pr. 111. **por**
justiçia GP] om. Pr. 114. **alguna** GP] una Pr. 116. **atribuyan** GPr] contribuya P. **a** GP] al Pr. ‹**ésta**› PPr]
om. G.

cosas continuamente acaesçen que al propósito se podrían
desyr, pero, dexando aquello, baste que de todo lo susodicho se
colige que al dicho almirante perteneçe justamente el terçio de   120
las dichas Yndias e tierra firme, e ochavo e diezmo de todas las
cosas muebles que en ellas y dentro de su almirantadgo en qualquier tiempo y por qualesquier personas y en qualquier manera
se halle, como de verdadero resulte de la dicha su primera armada, aunque en las otras no aya contribuydo, porque tocante   125
a esto farto se ha dicho en otro escripto.

[19] Quedava por desyr a Sus A. que fizieron merçed al almirante de todos los ofiçios como los tiene el almirante de la
mar de Castilla, y qu'él podía dar el alguaziladgo y escrivanías o
mandallo·servir en su nombre; y pues esto es asý, que tanbién   130
los podía arrendar y llevar las rentas asý como lleva un cavallero
a quien Sus A. ayan fecho merçed de una tenençia o de un
ofiçio, como se vee en muy muchos en Castilla que ellos se
llevan las rentas y fasen servir el dicho cargo a uno suyo, o se
conçiertan con una persona y /65 verso/ le dan una çierta parte   135
de la renta; y asý lo suplica a S. A. que le desagravien y le dexen
usar de sus ofiçios y reçebir el benefiçio, pues que asý fue por
capitulaçión y merçed.

XL (57)

/66 recto/

[0] Treslado de una carta mensagera qu'el almirante escrivió al
ama del prínçipe don Juan, que gloria aya, el año de 1500, viniendo preso de las Yndias.

121. **Yndias** G] yslas PPr. 127. **Sus** GP] vuestras Pr. 130. **mandallo (mandallos servir > mandallo·ser-
vir)** GPr] mandallos P. 131. **las rentas** G] la renta PPr. **cavallero** GP] cavallo Pr. 132. **Sus A**. G] vuestras
altezas P, vuestra a. Pr. **ayan** GP] aya Pr. 134. **las rentas** G] la renta PPr. 135. **conçiertan** GP] conçierta
Pr. 136. **S**. (= **Sus**) GP] su Pr. 138. **merçed**] *In GPPr the rest of the page has been left blank; on the next page of
Pr a cataloger added, in a more modern hand, the following text*: Habiendo descubierto Don Christóval Colón las
islas de tierra firme en el mar Occéano, le hacen varias mercedes cuya copia simple certificada, e entre ellas
escaeçer [*sic*] offiçio de Almirante y Virrey de lo descubierto y que fuere descubriendo, con más otros
derechos que más largamente aquí se contienen; *written vertically on the page:* Capytulaçyon del almyrante
colon / .XXXVIII. [*shelving number*]   Sources: GP; *for a different version cf. the transcription of Las Casas
published by* Varela-Gil, pp. 430-437, n° XLVIII; *cf. also Nuova Raccolta*, vol. III, t.II, pp. 183-203, n° XXIV.
  1. **mensagera** G] *om. P*. **almirante escrivió** G] a. de las Yndias embio P. 1-2. **al ama** G] al ma P. 2. **que
. . . aya** G] de Castilla P.

[1] Muy virtuosa Señora ★★★, sy mi quexa del mundo es nueva, su uso de maltratar es de muy antiguo: mill combates me ha dado, y a todos resistí fasta agora, que non me aprovechó armas ni avisos. [2] Con crueldad me tiene echado al fundo. [3] La esperança de Aquel que crió a todos me sostiene; Su socorro fue siempre muy presto: otra vez, y non de lexos, estando yo más baxo, me levantó con Su braço derecho, diziendo: "O ombre de poca fee, levántate, que Yo soy; non ayas miedo".

[4] Yo vine con amor tan entrañable a servir a estos Prínçipes y he servido de serviçio de que jamás se oyó ni vido.

[5] Del nuevo çielo e tierra que hazía Nuestro Señor, escriviendo sant Juan el *Apocalís*, después de dicho por boca de Ysaýas, me hyzo d'ello mensagero y amostró a quál parte. [6] En todos ovo yncredulidad, y a la Reyna, mi señora, dió d'ello el spíritu de ynteligençia y esfuerço grande, y le hizo de todo eredera como a cara y muy amada fija. [7] La posessión de todo esto fue yo a tomar en su real nombre; la ynorançia en que avían estado todos, quisieron emendalle traspasando el poco saber a fablar en ynconvinientes y gastos: S. A. lo aprovava, al contrario, y lo sostuvo fasta que pudo.

[8] Syete años se pasaron en la plática y nueve exsecutando. [9] Cosas muy señaladas y dignas de memoria se pasaron en este tiempo: de todo non se hizo conçepto. [10] Llegué yo, y estoy que non ha nadie tan vil que no piense de ultrajarme: por virtud se contará en el mundo a quien puede no consentillo.

[11] Sy yo robara las Yndias o tierra que jaz haze ellas, de que agora es la fabla, del altar de Sant Pedro y las diera a los Moros, no pudieran en España amostrarme mayor enemiga. [12] ¿Quién creyera tal adonde ovo siempre tanta nobleza? /66 verso/

[13] Yo mucho quisiera despedir del negoçio, si fuera onesto para con mi Reyna: el esfuerço de Nuestro Señor y de Su A. hizo que yo continuase, y, por aliviarle algo de los enojos en que a causa de la muerte estava, cometí viage nuevo al nuevo çielo e mundo que fasta entonçes estava oculto; y sy no es tenido allí en estima así como los otros de las Yndias, no es maravilla, porque salió a pareçer de my yndustria.

[14] A sant Pedro abrasó el Spíritu Santo, y con él otros doze, y

---

4. **Señora**] *in GP a blank space follows between* / /. 11. **ayas** G] ayays P. 29. **haze** GP] *corr.* hacia? Varela-Gil: ia[n]faze. 34. **despedir** G] me d. P. 36. **yo** G] *om.* P.

todos combatieron acá, y los trabajos y fatigas fueron muchas: en fin, de todo llevaron la vitoria.

[15] Este viage de Parya creý que apaziguaría algo por las perlas y la fallada del oro en la Española: las perlas mandé yo ayuntar e pescar a la gente con quien quedó el conçierto de mi buelta por ellas y, a mi compreender, a medida de fánega; sy yo non lo escriví a Sus A., fue porque asý quisiera aver fecho del oro antes.

[16] Esto me salió como otras cosas muchas: non las perdiera, ni mi honra, sy buscara yo mi bien propio y dexara perder la Española, o se guardaran mis privilegios y asientos; y otro tanto digo del oro que yo tenía agora junto, que con tantas muertes y trabajos por virtud divinal he llegado a perfecto.

[17] Quando yo fue de Paria, hallé casi la mitad de la gente en la Española alçados, y me han guerreado fasta agora como a moro, y los Yndios, por otro cabo, gravemente. [18] En esto vino Fojeda y provó a echar el sello: dixo que S. A. le enbiavan con promesas de dádivas y franquezas y paga; allegó grand quadrilla, que en toda la Española muy pocos ay salvo vagamundos, y ninguno con muger y fijos. [19] Este Fojeda me trabajó harto: fuele neçesario de se yr, y dexó dicho que luego sería de buelta con más navíos y gente, y que dexava la real presona de la Reyna, nuestra señora, a la muerte. [20] En esto llegó Vinçentiañes con quatro caravelas: ovo alboroto y sospecha, mas non daño. [21] Los Yndios dixeron de otras muchas a los Canibales y en Parya, /67 recto/ y después una nueva de seys otras caravelas que traýa un hermano del Alcalde: mas fue con maliçia. [22] Esto fue ya a la postre, quando ya estava muy rota la esperança que Sus A. oviesen jamás de enbiar navío a las Yndias, ni nos esperarlos, y que vulgarmente desýan que S. A. era muerta.

[23] Un Adrián en este tiempo provó a alçarse otra ves como de antes, mas Nuestro Señor non quiso que llegase a efecto su mal próposito. [24] Yo tenía propuesto en mí de non tocar el cabello a nadie, y a éste, por su ingratitud, con lágrimas non se pudo guardar asý como yo lo tenía pensado: a mi hermano non hiziera menos, sy me quisiera matar y robar el señorío que mi Rey e Reyna me tenían dado en guarda.

[25] Este Adrián, segund se muestra, tenía enbiado a don Fernando a Xoraguá a allegar a algunos sus secaçes, y allá ovo debate con el Alcalde, adonde naçió discordia de muerte, mas non

63-64. **Vinçentiañes** G] Viçentianes P. 79. **a** (algunos) G] om. P.

llegó a efecto: el Alcalde le prendió, y a parte de su quadrilla, y el caso era qu'él los justiçiara sy yo non lo proveyera. [26] Estovieron presos esperando caravela en que se fuesen: las nuevas de Fojeda, que yo dixe, fizieron perder la esperança, que ya no vernía.

[27] Seys meses avía que yo estava despachado por venir a S. A. con las buenas nuevas del oro y fuyr de governar gente disoluta que non teme a Dios, nin a su Rey ni Reyna, llena de achaques y de maliçias.

[28] A la gente acabara yo de pagar con seysçientas mill, y para ello avía quatro cuentos de diezmos, e alguno syn el terçio del oro.

[29] Antes de mi partida, supliqué tantas veses a S. A. que enbiasen allá a mi costa a quien toviesse cargo de la justiçia; y después que fallé alçado el Alcalde, se lo supliqué de nuevo o por alguna gente, o al menos un criado, con cartas, porque mi fama es tal que, aunque yo faga iglesias y ospitales, syempre serán dichas espeluncas para ladrones.

[30] Proveyeron ya al fin, y fue muy al contrario de lo que la negoçiaçión demandava: ¡vaya en buen ora, pues que fue a su grado!

[31] Yo estuve allá dos años syn poder ganar una provisión de favor por mí, nin por los que allá fuesen, y éste llevó una /67 verso/ arca llena: sy pararán todos a su serviçio, Dios lo sabe; ya, por comienço, ay franquesas de veynte años, que es la hedad de un onbre, y se coge el oro, que ovo persona de çinco marcos en quatro oras, de que diré después más largo.

[32] Si pluguiese a S. A. de desfazer un ⁺vulgo⁺ de los que saben mis fatigas, que mayor daño me ha fecho el maldesyr de la gente, que no me ha aprovechado el mucho servir y guardar su fazienda y señorío, sería limosna y yo restituydo en mi honra y se fablaría d'ello en todo el mundo, porque el negoçio es de calidad, que cada día ha de ser más sonado y en alta estima.

[33] En esto vino el comendador Bovadilla a S. Domingo: yo estava en la Vega, y el Adelantado en Xoraguá, adonde este Adrián avía fecho cabeça, mas ya todo era llano y la tierra rica y en paz todos. [34] El segundo día que llegó, se crió governador, y fizo ofiçiales y exsecutiones, y apregonó franquezas del oro y

85

90

95

100

105

110

115

96. **un** G] algund P.   104. **pararán** G] pariran P.   108. **+vulgo+** GP] *also in* Varela-Gil.   109-110. **la gente**] las gentes P.   117. **en paz todos** G] t. e. p. P.

diezmos, y generalmente de toda otra cosa, por veynte años, que, como digo, es la hedad de un onbre, y que venía para pagar todos, bien que non avían servido llenamente fasta ese día; y publicó que a mí me avía de enbiar en fierros y a mis hermanos, asý como ha fecho, y que nunca más bolvería yo allí, ni otrie de mi linage, diziendo de mí mill desonestas y descorteses cosas. [35] Esto todo fue el segundo día que llegó, como dixe, y estando yo lexos absente, syn saber d'él nin de su venida. [36] Unas cartas de S. A. firmadas en blanco, de que él llevava una cantidad, escrivió y enbió al Alcalde y a su compaña, con favores y encomiendas; a mí nunca me enbió carta ni mensagero, ni me ha dado fasta oy. [37] Piense Vuestra Merçed qué pensaría quien toviera mi cargo: ¡honrar y favoreçer a quien provó a robar a S. A. el señorío y ha fecho tanto mal y daño, y arrastrar a quien con tantos peligros se lo sostuvo! [38] Quando yo supe esto, creý que esto sería como lo de Hojeda o uno de los otros: templóme que supe de los frayles que ‹de çierto› S. A. le enbiavan. [39] Escrevíle yo que su venida fuesse en buen ora, y que yo estava despachado para yr a la Corte y fecho almoneda de quanto yo tenía, y que en esto de las franque-/68 recto/ zas que no se açelerase, que esto y el govierno que yo se lo daría luego tan llano como la palma; y así lo escreví a los religiosos. [40] Ni él ni ellos me dieron respuesta, antes se puso él en son de gerra y apremiava a quantos allí yvan que le jurasen por governador, dixéronme que por veynte años. [41] Luego que yo supe d'estas franquezas, pensé de adobar un yerro tan grande y qu'él sería contento, las quales dió syn neçesidad ni causa de cosa tan gruesa, y a gente vagamunda, que fuera demasiado para quien truxiera muger y fijos: publiqué por palabra y por cartas que él non podía usar de sus provisiones, porque las mías eran las fuertes, y les mostré las franquesas que llevó Juan Aguado. [42] Todo esto que yo hize era por dilatar, porque S. A. fuesen sabidores del estado de la tierra y oviesen logar de tornar a mandar en ello lo que fuese su serviçio. [43] Tales franquezas escusado es de las apregonar en las Yndias: los vesynos que han tomado vezindad es logro, porque se les dan las mejores tierras y, a poco valer, valerán dozientas mill al

---

120. **como digo** G] *om. P.* 121. **todos** G] a t. *P.* 125. **llegó** G] allego *P.* 128. **escrivió** G] enchio *P.* 130. **Vuestra Merçed** G] *om. P.* 132. **el señorío** G] *om. P.* 134. **esto**] este *GP.* 136. **‹de çierto›** P] *om. G.*

cabo de los quatro años que la vezindad se acaba, syn que den una açadonada en ellas. [44] Non diría yo asý sy los vezinos fuesen casados, mas non ay seys entre todos que non estén sobre el aviso de ayuntar lo que pudieren y se yr en buen ora: de Castilla sería bien que fuesen, y aun saber quién y cómo, y se poblase de gente honrada.

[45] Yo tenía asentado con estos vesynos que pagarían el terçio del oro y los diezmos, y esto a su ruego, y lo reçibieron en grand merçed de S. A.: reprendílos quando yo oý que se dexavan d'ello, y esperava qu'el Comendador faría otro tanto, mas fue al contrario.

[46] Yndignólos contra mí diziendo que yo les quería quitar lo que S. A. les davan, y trabajó de me los echar a cuestas, y lo hizo, y que escriviesen a S. A. que no me enbiasen más al cargo (y asý se lo suplico yo por mí e por toda cosa mía, en quanto non aya otro pueblo); y me ordenó él con ellos pesquisas de maldades, que al ynfierno nunca se supo de las semejantes. [47] Allí está Nuestro Señor que escapó a Daniel y a los tres mochachos, con tanto saber y fuerça como /68 verso/ tenía y con tanto aparejo, sy Le pluguiere, como con Su gana.

[48] Supiera yo remediar todo esto y lo otro de que está dicho y ha pasado después que estoy en las Yndias, sy me consintiera la voluntad a procurar por mi bien propio y me fuera onesto; mas el sostener de la justiçia y acreçentar el señorío de S. A. fasta agora me tiene al fondo. [49] Oy en día que se falla tanto oro, ay división en qué aya más ganançia: yr robando o yr a las minas; por una muger tanbién se falla çient castellanos, como por una labrança; y es mucho en uso, y ay hartos mercaderes que andan buscando muchachas: de .IX. a .X. son agora en preçio; de todas hedades ha de tener un bueno.

‹[50] Digo que la fuerça del maldesyr de desconçertados me ha más dañado que mis servicios fecho provecho: mal exemplo es por el presente y por lo futuro; fago juramento que cantidad de onbres han ydo a las Yndias que non meresçían el agua para con Dios y con el mundo, y agora buelven allá y se les consiente›.

[51] Digo que en desyr yo qu'el Comendador no podía dar franquezas, que hize yo lo que él deseava, bien que yo a él

160. **pudieren** G] pudiere *P*. 182. **ganançia** G] g. o *P*. 187-191. ‹**Digo . . . consiente›** *P*] *om.* G. 187. **maldesyr** G] mar desyr *P*.

dixese que era para dilatar fasta que S. A. toviesen el aviso de la
tierra y tornasen a ver y mandar lo que fuese su serviçio. 195
[52] Enemistólos a ellos todos conmigo, y él pareçe, segund se
ovo y segund sus formas, que ya lo venía; y bien entendido es,
que se dize que ha gastado mucho por venir a este negoçio. [53]
Non sé d'ello más de lo que oygo: yo nunca oý qu'el pesquisidor allegase los rebeldes y los tomase por testigos contra aquel 200
que govierna, a ellos, ni a otros syn fe ny dignos d'ella.
[54] Sy S. A. mandasen faser una pesquisa general allí, vos digo
que se vería la maravilla como la ysla non se funde.
[55] Yo creo que se acordará Vuestra Merçed quando la tor-
menta syn velas me echó en Lisbona, que fuy acusado fal- 205
samente que avía yo ydo allá al Rey para darle las Yndias; después supieron Sus A. el contrario y que todo fue con maliçia.
[56] Bien que yo sepa poco, no sé quién me tenga por tan turpe
que yo non conozca que, aunque las Yndias fuesen mías, que
yo non me pudiera sostener syn ayuda de prínçipe. 210
[57] Sy esto es asý, ¿adonde pudiera tener yo mejor arrimo y
seguridad de non ser echado d'ellas del todo que en el Rey e
Reyna nuestros señores, que de nada me han puesto /69 recto/
en tanta honra y son los más altos prínçipes, por la mar y por la
tierra, del mundo? [58] Los quales tienen que yo les aya servido 215
y me guardan mis privilegios y merçedes; y sy alguien me los
quebranta, S. A. me los acreçienta‹n› con aventaja, como se
vido en lo de Juan Aguado, y me mandan haser mucha honra;
y, como dixe, ya S. A. reçibieron de mí serviçio y tienen a mis
fijos sus criados, lo que en ninguna manera pudiera esto llegar 220
con otro prínçipe, porque adonde non ay amor, todo lo otro
çesa.
[59] Dixe yo agora ansí esto contra un maldesyr con maliçia y
contra mi voluntad, porque es cosa que ni en sueño deviera
llegar a memoria; porque las formas y fechos del comendador 225
Bovadilla con maliçia las quiere alumbrar en esto: mas yo le faré
ver con el braço ysquierdo que su poco saber y grand cobardía
con desordenada codiçia le ha fecho caer en ello.
[60] Ya dixe como yo le escreví y a los frayles; y luego partí, asý

---

195. ver y G] om. P. 197. entendido Varela-Gil] ençendido o GP. 202. digo G] d. yo P. 203. se . . .
maravilla G] verian por grand maravilla P. 212. de . . . todo G] om. P. 215. Los G] y l. P. 217.
acreçienta‹n›] acreçienta GP. 224. sueño G] sueños P.

como le dixe, muy solo, porque toda la gente estava con el 230
Adelantado, y tanbién por le quitar de sospecha. [61] Él,
quando lo supo, echó a don Diego preso en una caravela, car-
gado de fierros, y a mí, en llegando, hizo otro tanto, y después
al Adelantado, quando vino: nin le fablé más, ni consintió que
fasta oy nadie me aya fablado; y fago juramento que non puedo 235
pensar por qué sea yo preso.

[62] La primera deligençia qu'él fizo, fue a tomar el oro, el qual
ovo syn medida nin peso, e, yo absente, dixo que quería él
pagar d'ello a la gente, y, segund oý, para sý hizo la primera
parte, y enbía por rescate rescatadores nuevos. [63] D'este oro 240
tenía yo apartado çiertas muestras, granos muy gruesos, como
huevos de ánsara, de gallina y de pollas, y de otras muchas fe-
churas, que algunas personas tenían cogido en breve espaçio,
con que S. A. se alegrasen y por ello comprehendiesen el
negoçio, con una cantidad de piedras grandes llenas de oro: éste 245
fue el primero a se dar con maliçia porque S. A. non tengan este
negoçio en algo fasta que él tenga fecho el nido; de que se da
buena priesa.

[64] El oro que está por fundir mengua al fuego: unas /69
verso/ cadenas que pesarían fasta veynte marcos nunca se han 250
visto.

[65] Yo he seýdo muy agraviado en esto del oro, más ‹aún› que
de las perlas, porque non lo he traýdo yo a S. A..

[66] El Comendador, en todo lo que le pareçió que me dañaría,
luego fue puesto en obra: ya dixe con seysçientas mill pagara a 255
todos syn robar a nadie, y que avía más de quatro cuentos de
diezmos y alguaziladgo, syn tocar en el oro. [67] Hizo unas
larguezas que son de risa, bien que creo que començó en sí la
primera parte: allá lo sabrán Sus A. quando le mandarán tomar
cuenta, en espeçial sy yo estoviese a ella. [68] Él no hase syno 260
desyr que se deve grand suma, y es la que yo dixe, y non tanto:
yo he seýdo muy mucho agraviado en que se ayan enbiado
pesquisidores sobre mí que sepan que, sy la pesquisa qu'él enbiare fuera muy grave, que él quedará en el govierno.

[69] Pluguiera a Nuestro Señor que S. A. le enbiaran a él o a 265

---

234. **más** G] m. a el P. 242. **ánsara** G] a. e P. 244. **S. A. se alegrasen** G] se a. S. A. P. 246. **tengan** G]
toviesen P. 249. **unas** G] una P. 252. ‹**aún**› P] *om.* G. 253. **yo** G] *om.* P. 258. **començó** G] encomenço
P. 259. **mandarán** G] mandaren P. 262. **muy** G] *om.* P. 263. **pesquisidores** G] pesquisidor P. **sepan** G]
sepa P.

otro dos años ha, porque ‹sé que› yo fuera ya libre de escándalo y disfamia, y non se me quitara mi honra, ‹n›y la perdiera: Dios es justo y ha de haser que se sepa por qué y cómo. [70] Allí me judgan como a governador que fue a Çiçilia o a çibdad o villa puesta en regimiento y adonde las leyes se pueden guardar por entero, syn temor que se pierda todo: yo reçibo grande agravio. 270

[71] Yo devo de ser judgado como capitán que fue d'España a conquistar fasta las Yndias a gente belicosa y mucha, y de costumbres y seta a nós muy contraria, los quales biven por syerras y montes syn pueblo asentado (ni nosotros), y adonde, por voluntad divina, he puesto so el señorío del Rey e de la Reyna, nuestros señores, otro mundo, y por donde la España, que hera dicha pobre, es la más rica. 275

[72] Yo devo ser judgado como capitán que de tanto tiempo fasta oy trae las armas a cuestas syn las dexar una ora, y de cavalleros de conquistas y del uso, y non de letras, salvo sy fuesen de Griegos o de Romanos, o otros modernos, de que ay tantos y tan nobles en España; ca, de otra guisa, reçibo grande agravio, porque en las Yndias non ay /70 recto/ pueblo ni asyento. 280

[73] Del oro y perlas ya está abierta la puerta, y cantidad de todo, piedras preciosas y espeçiería y de otras mill cosas se pueden esperar firmemente; y nunca más mal me viniese, como, con el nonbre de Nuestro Señor, le daría el primer viage, asý como diera la negoçiación del Arabia Felís fasta la Meca, como yo escriví a S. A. con Antonio de Torres en la respuesta de la repartiçión del mar e tierra con los Portogueses, y después viniera a lo de Colocuti, asý come le dixe y di por escripto en el monesterio de la Mejorada. 285 290

[74] Las nuevas del oro que yo dixe que yo diría, son que día de Nabidat, estando yo muy aflegido, guerreado de los malos christianos y de Yndios, en término de dexar todo y escapar, sy pudiese, la vida, me consoló Nuestro Señor milagrosamente y dixo: "Esfuerça, non desmáy‹es›te nin temas: Yo proveeré en todo; los syete años del término del oro non son pasados, y en ello y en lo otro te daré remedio". 295 300

[75] Ese día supe que avía ochenta leguas de tierra, y, en todo cabo d'ellas, minas (el pareçer agora es que sea toda una). [76]

266. ‹sé que› P] om. G. 267. disfamia G] de d. P. ‹n›y P] y G. 269. a (çibdad) G] om. P. 279. devo G] d. de P. 283. ca G] o P. 288. le G] que le P. 290. Antonio G] Antoño P. 292. Colocuti P] colo arti G. 294. diría G] daria P. 298. non desmáy‹es›te nin G] no P. 299. todo G] todos P.

Algunos han cogido .CXX. castellanos en un día, otros .XC., y
se ha llegado fasta .CCL.: de çinqüenta fasta .LXX., otros muchos de .XV. fasta .L., es tenido buen jornal, y muchos lo con-   305
tinúan; el común es de seys fasta dose, y quien de aquí abaxa,
non es contento. [77] Pareçe tanbién que estas minas son como
las otras, que responden en los días non ygualmente: las minas
son nuevas, y los cogedores. [78] Al pareçer de todos es que
aunque vaya allá toda Castilla, que, por turpe que sea la presona,   310
que non abaxará de un castellano o dos cada día: y agora es esto
asý en fresco; es verdad que tienen algund Yndio, mas el
negoçio todo consiste en el christiano. [79] Ved qué discriçión
fue de Bovadilla: dar todo por ninguno y quatro cuentos de
diezmos syn cabsa nin ser requerido, syn primero lo notificar a   315
S. A.; y el daño non es éste solo. [80] Yo sé que mis hierros non
han seýdo con fin de fazer mal, y creo que S. A. lo creen asý
como yo lo digo, y sé y veo que usan de misericordia con quien
maliçiosamente les desyrve. /70 verso/ [81] Yo creo y tengo
por muy çierto que muy mejor y más piedad avrán comigo que   320
caý en ello con ynorançia y forçosamente, como sabrán despúes
por entero, ‹y el qual soy su fechura›, y mirarán a mis serviçios
y conoçerán de cada día que son muy aventajados; todo pornán
en una balança, asý como nos cuenta la Sacra Escriptura que
será el bien con el mal el día del Juyzio.   325
[82] Sy todavía mandan que otrie me judgue, lo qual non es-
pero, y que sea por pesquisa de las Yndias, muy húmillmente les
suplico que enbíen allá dos personas de conçiençia y honrados,
a mi costa, los quales creo que fallarán de ligero agora que se
falla el oro çinco marcos en quatro oras: con esto e syn ello, es   330
muy neçesario que lo provean.
[83] El Comendador, en llegando a Santo Domingo, se apo-
sentó en mi casa, e asý como la falló, asý dió todo por suyo:
¡vaya en buen ora, que, quiçá, lo avía menester! (¡cosario nunca
tal usó con mercader!) [84] De mis escripturas tengo yo mayor   335
quexa, que asý me las ayan tomadas, que jamás se le pudo sacar
una, y aquellas que más me avían de aprovechar en mi desculpa,
ésas tenía más ocultas: ¡ved qué justo y onesto pesquisydor! [85]
Cosas de quantas él aya fecho, me dizen que ha seýdo con tér-

---

305. **es** P] y es G. 306. **es** G] va P. 310. **turpe** G] torpe P. 313. **todo** G] *om.* P. 317. **creen** G] tienen P.
318. **de** G] *om.* P. 322. ‹**y . . . fechura**› P] *om.* G. 331. **muy** G] *om.* P. 333. **e** G] om. P. 336. **ayan
tomadas** G] aya tomado P. 337. **que . . . en** G] de mas P. 339. **Cosas** G] cosa P. **ha** G] aya P.

mino de justiçia, salvo absolutamente Dios nuestro señor está   340
con Sus fuerças y saber, como solía, y castiga en todo cabo, en
espeçial la yngratitud de ynjurias.

XLbis (70)

/71 recto/

[1] **Los originales d'estos privillegios y cartas y çédulas, y otras muchas cartas de Sus Altezas e otras escripturas tocantes al señor almirante están en el monesterio de Sancta María de las Cuevas de Sevilla.**

[2] **Otrosý está en el dicho monesterio un libro traslado   5 de los previlegios e cartas susodichos, semejante que éste.**

[3] **Otro traslado levó este año de .MDII. y tiene Alonso Sanches de Carvajal a las Yndias, escripto en papel e abtorizado.   10**

[4] **Otro treslado en pergamino, tal como éste.**

Source: G.

ADDITIONAL DOCUMENTS

Luciano Formisano

I

Genova Codex

1.A

The codex, strictly speaking, is preceded by two pages bound in before fol. 1. The text on the recto reads: Lettera di Filippo secondo Re di / Spagna rallegrandosi col Ser.mo / Ottavian Oderigo per esser stato creato / Duce della Rep.a Ser.ma. *The verso is left blank. A letter follows; on the recto, the address:*

Al Ill.mo fiel y amado nuestro Octaviano Gentil de Odorico Dux de Génova.

On the verso: Don Phelippe por la gracia de Dios Rey d'España, de las dos Sicilias, de Hierusalén.

[1] Ill.mo y bien amado nuestro: por aviso del Embaxador Figueroa avemos entendido la eléction que se ha hecho de vuestra persona para Dux d'essa Ill.ma République y holgado mucho d'ella, porque con las buenas partes que nos ha scripto que en vós concurren es de esperar que la governaréis como al bien d'ella conviene. [2] El qual yo deseo tan de veras, que, por este respecto y por lo que a vós os toca en particular, escrivo y embío a mandar al dicho mi Embaxador que se alegre con vós de mi parte, y os visite y diga lo demás que d'él oyréis, y assí os ruego le deis entera fee y creencia, teniendo por cierto que en todo lo que occurriere y tocare a essa République nos emplearemos siempre con la buena voluntad que por lo passado, porque tenemos de sus cosas el mismo cuydado que de las nuestras, como hasta aquí lo avréis podido conosçer y os lo dirá más largo nuestro Embaxador, a quien nos remitimos.

[3] De Madrid a VI de Noviembre .M.D.LXVI.

Yo el Rey
G.º Pérez

/ 1 verso/

Questo con l'altro simile libro, che ambi contengono i Privileggi concessi dal Re Ferdinando di Spagna e Regina Isabella, sua consorte, a Cristoforo Colombo, furono donati alla Rep.^{ca} da Lorenzo Oderici, come dal attestato e grazioso Decreto accordatogli da Ser.^{mi} Colleggi li 10 Genaro 1670, che vedesi annesso ad altro simil Decreto concesso al M.^{co} Gio. Paulo Oderico, figlio del detto Lorenzo, a¹ 29 Genaro del 1700, ambi infilzati nel Fogliaccio de' Privileggi Onorifici.

1.C (73)

/ 3 recto-verso/

Ihesus

TABLA de las cartas y previlegios y çédulas y otras escripturas que ay en este libro.

---

1. **a** *over other writing.*

★★★

---

1. **de** repeated. 2. *Nine blank lines follow.*

Treslado de una carta mensagera que enbió el Almirante al ama del prínçipe don
Juan, viniendo preso de las Yndias. f. LXVI

2
Veragua Codex
2.A (between I.ii.2 and II.i)

2.A.1 (53)

fol. 7 verso; Bustamante 26.5–25.

[1] E este traslado fue sacado e conçertado con la dicha çédula
de Sus Altezas e escriptura oreginal, donde fue sacado, ante los
escrivanos públicos de Sevilla que lo firmaron e signaron de sus
nombres en testimonio en la çibdad de Sevylla.

[2] Este traslado fue corregido e conçertado con la dicha çédula 5
original de Sus Altesas e escriptura original, onde fue sacado,
ante los escrivanos públicos de Sevilla, que lo firmaron e signaron de sus nombres en testimonio, en la dicha çibdad de
Sevilla, quinze días del mes de março, año del nasçimiento de
nuestro salvador Jhesu Christo de mill e cuatroçientos e 10
noventa e ocho años. [3] Va escripto sobre raýdo ó dis "e notario público", e ó diz "que dedes e fagades dar a don Christóval", e ó dis "d'esto le mande dar al dicho"; e entre renglones
ó dis "e en el"; e sobre raýdo ó dis "e chançillería e casa e
rastro", e ó dis "quales dichos", e ó dis "qualesquier que an- 15
dovieren e navegaren por la mar e a todas las otras personas de
qualquier estado e condiçión e preheminençia o dignidad que
sean qu'esta mi carta de previlegio vieren o el traslado d'ella,
signado como dicho es, que guarden"; e ó dis "vasallo del rey"
e ó dis "almirante" vala e no le empezca. 20

[4] Yo Diego de la Bastida, escrivano de Sevilla, só testigo
d'este traslado.

[5] Yo Iohan Fernández, escrivano de Sevilla, só testigo d'este
traslado.

4. **Sevylla**] *the rest of the line and the following line have been left blank.* 20. **empezca**] *a sigla follows.* 21-26. **Yo**
. . . testigo] *autograph signatures.* 22. **traslado**] *a sigla follows.* 24. **traslado**] *a sigla follows.*

[6] Yo Martýn Rodrigues, escrivano público de Sevilla, fys es- 25
crevir este traslado e fis aquí mio signo e só testigo.

2.A.2 (52)

fol. 8 recto; Bustamante 27.1-28.28.

Capitulaciones
entre los Señores
Reyes y Christóval
Colón [*l.m.*]

[1]En la muy noble e muy leal çibdad de Sevilla, sábado
quinze días del mes de março, año del nasçimiento de nuestro
salvador Jhesu Christo de mill e quatroçientos e noventa e ocho
años, estando dentro en las casas donde posa el muy magnífico
señor don Christóval Colón, almirante mayor de la mar   5
Oçéano, visorrey e governador de las yslas de las Yndias e tierra
firme por el Rey e la Reyna, nuestros señores, e su capitán
general de la mar, que son en esta çibdad en la collaçión de
Sanct Bartolomé, estando aý presente el dicho señor almirante y
en presençia de mí Martín Rodrigues, escrivano público de la   10
dicha çibdad, e de los escrivanos de Sevilla que a ello fueron
presentes, e luego el dicho señor almirante presentó ante los
dichos escrivanos dos cartas de previlegios del Rey e de la
Reyna, nuestros señores, escriptas en pargamino de cuero e selladas con su sello de plomo pendiente en filos de seda a colores   15
diversas, e firmadas de sus reales nonbres e de los del su consejo
e de sus contadores mayores e de otros ofiçiales, e asimismo
otras cartas patentes firmadas de sus reales nonbres e selladas con
su çera colorada a las espaldas de las dichas cartas, y otras çédulas
de Sus Altezas firmadas de sus reales nonbres, los quales dichos   20
previlegios e cartas e çédulas serán de yuso escriptas e nonbradas. [2] E porque dixo que si él las oviese de llevar por la mar
a las Yndias o a otras partes, que se reçelava que por fuego, o
por agua, o por otros casos fortuytos, o llevándolas, gelas furtarían, de que su derecho pereçería y Sus Altezas serían deser-   25
vidos, porque los dichos previllegios e cartas e çédulas rellevan
al serviçio de Sus Altezas: porende dixo que pedía, e pidió, a
nós, los dichos escrivanos, que sacásemos un traslado, o dos, o

25. **Yo**] *a sigla follows.* 26. **signo**] sig no *with notarization inserted.* **testigo**] *two sigla follow.* 3. **ocho**] *over an
erasure.*

más, de los dichos previlegios e cartas e çédulas, corrigiéndolos
con los dichos originales bien e fielmente, en manera que fi-   30
ziese fee para guarda de su derecho del sobredicho señor almirante. [3] Los quales dichos previlegios e cartas e çédulas, uno
en pos de otro, son estos que se siguen.

2.B (between XXV and XXVI)

2.B.1 (54)

fol. 33 verso; Bustamante 103.12–104.32.
[1] Este traslado fue corregido e conçertado con las dichas dos
cartas de previlegios e con las dichas cartas patentes e con todas
las otras çédulas de suso encorporadas originales onde fue
sacado ante los escrivanos públicos de Sevilla, que lo firmaron e
signaron de sus nombres en testimonio que fue fecho e sacado   5
en la dicha çibdad de Sevilla en el dicho día e mes e año susodicho. [2] Va escripto sobre raýdo ó dis "ocho", e ó dis "los del su
consejo" e "de sus", e ó dis "acaesçer por contrario", e ó dis
"yslas que", e ó dis "grandes", e ó dis "mos", e ó dis "mandamos al prínçipe don Juan", e ó diz "qual se muestra", e ó dis   10
"e pertenesçientes", e ó dis "e después de vuestros días", e ó dis
"oviere", e ó dis "en", e ó dis "el flete", e ó dis "con", e ó dis
"don", e ó dis "dri", e ó dis "ni almirantadgo", e ó dis "del
dicho", e ó dis "e desmeros e las otras", e ó dis "por lo", e ó dis
"contra ellos están", e ó dis "re", e ó dis "el dicho pan", e ó dis   15
"que lo contrario hiziere". [3] E en la çédula que habla con
Françisco de Soria, va una raya de tinta e va escripto sobre
raýdo ó dis "personas nos suplicó", e ó dis "dichos nuestros"
vala e non enpezca.
[4] Yo, Diego de la Bastida, escrivano de Sevilla, só testigo   20
d'este traslado.
[5] Yo, Iohán Fernandes, escrivano de Sevilla, só testigo d'este
traslado.

20–25. **Yo . . . testigo**] *autograph signatures.* 21. **traslado**] *a sigla follows.* 23. **traslado**] *a sigla follows.*

[6] Yo, Martýn Rodrigues, escrivano público de Sevilla, fis escrevir este treslado, e fis aquí mío signo, e só testigo. 25

2.B.2 (55)

fol. 34 recto; Bustamante 104.1-105.31.

[1] En la villa de Santo Domingo, que es en las Yndias en la ysla
Española, martes quatro días del mes de dizienbre, año del nasçimiento de nuestro señor Jhesu Christo de mill e quatroçientos
e noventa e ocho años, estando dentro en las casas donde posa
el muy magnífico señor don Christóval Colóm, almirante 5
mayor del mar Oçéano, visorrey e governador de las yslas de las
Yndias e tierra firme por el Rey e la Reyna, nuestros señores, e
su capitán general de la mar, que son en esta dicha vylla de
Santo Domingo, estando aý presente el dicho señor almirante, e
en presençia de mí, Diego de Alvarado, escrivano público del 10
Rey e de la Reyna, nuestros señores, e luego el dicho señor
almirante presentó ante mí el dicho escrivano algunas cartas
patentes del Rey e de la Reyna, nuestros señores, escritas en
papel e selladas con su sello de çera colorada en las espaldas, e
otras çédulas de Sus Altezas firmadas de sus reales nonbres, las 15
quales dichas cartas e çédulas serán de yuso escritas e nonbradas.
[2] E porque dixo que sy él las oviese de llevar o enbiar por la
mar a los reygnos de Castilla o a otras partes, que se reçélava que
por fuego, o por agua, o por otros casos fortuytos, o llevándolas,
gelas furtarían, de que su derecho pereçería y Sus Altezas serían 20
deservidos, porque las dichas cartas e çédulas relevavan al serviçio de Sus Altezas: porende dixo que pedýa, e pedió, a mí, el
dicho escrivano, que sacase un treslado, o dos, o más, de las
dichas cartas e çédulas, corregiéndolas con las dichas oreginales
byen e fielmente, en manera que feziese fe para guarda de su 25
derecho del sobredicho señor almirante. [3] Las quales dicha
cartas e çédulas, una en pos de otra, son estas que se siguen.

25. **signo**] sig no *with notarization inserted.* **testigo**] *two sigla follow.* 19. **fortuytos**] fortituytos.

2.C (56)
(after XXIX, at the end of the Book)

fol. 36 verso; Bustamante 111.21-35.

[1] Fecho e sacado fue este treslado de las dichas cartas e çédulas originales de Sus Altezas en la dicha villa de Santo Domingo, martes quatro días del mes de dezienbre, año del nasçimiento de nuestro señor Jhesu Christo de mill e quatrocientos e noventa e ocho años.

[2] Testigos que fueron presentes a ver, ler e conçertar las dichas cartas e çédulas oreginales con los dichos treslados: Pedro de Terreros, e Diego de Salamanca, e Lope Muñoz; las quales van çiertas e conçertadas.

[3] E yo el dicho Diego de Alvarado, escrivano e notario público susodicho, presente fuy a todo lo que dicho es en uno con los dichos testigos, e por mandado del dicho señor almirante estos treslados saqué de las dichas cartas e çédulas oreginales, las quales van çiertas e conçertadas; e porende fis aquí este mío sygno atal, en testimonio de verdad.

                                  Diego de Alvarado
                                  escrivano público

3 (58)
Paris Codex (between XXXVII and XXXVIII)

fol. 63 recto-verso (= 64 recto-verso), after a series of blank folios; *Raccolta* 87.1-88.15.

La Capitulaçión

[1] Las cosas suplicadas e que Vuestras Altesas dan e otorgan a don Christóval Colón en alguna satisfaçión de lo que ha descubierto en las mares Oçéanas e del viaje que agora, con el

---

6. **ler**] Bustamante *corr.* le‹e›r. 15. **sygno**] syg no *with notarization inserted.* 16-17. **Diego . . . público**] *between two sigla; two other sigla follow at the end of fol., at present the end of the codex, but originally followed by 9 other fols. which were removed. Cf. also* II.ii.

ayuda de Dios, han de faser por ellas en serviçio de Vuestras
Altesas, son las que se siguen: 5
[2] Primeramente, que Vuestras Altesas, como señores que son
de las dichas mares Oçéanas, fasen dende agora al dicho don
Christóval Colón su almirante en todas aquellas yslas e tierra
firme que por su mano e yndustria se descubrirán o ganarán en
las dichas mares Oçéanas para durante su vida e, después d'él   10
muerto, a sus herederos e subçesores de uno en otro perpetuamente, con todas aquellas preheminençias e prerrogatyvas
perteneçientes al tal ofiçio e según que don Alonso Enriques,
vuestro almirante mayor de Castilla, e los otros preçesores en el
dicho ofiçio lo tenían en sus distritos.   15
[3] Plase a Sus Altesas. Juan de Coloma.
[4] Otrosý, que Vuestras Altezas hasen al dicho don Christóval
Colón su visorrey e governador general en todas las dichas yslas
e tierra firme e yslas que, como dicho es, él descubriere o
ganare en las dichas mares, e que para el regimiento de cada   20
una, e qualquier d'ellas, fagan eleçión de tres personas para cada
ofiçio, y que Vuestras Altesas tomen y escojan uno, el que más
fuere su serviçio, e asý serán mejor regidas las tierras que Nuestro Señor le dexare fallar e ganar a serviçio de Vuestras Altesas.
[5] Plase a Sus Altesas. Juan de Coloma.   25
[6] Yten, que todas e qualesquier mercaderías, syquier sean perlas, piedras preçiosas, oro, plata, espeçiería, y otras qualesquier
cosas e mercaderías de qualquier espeçie, nombre e manera que
se compraren, trocaren, fallaren, ganaren e ovieren dentro de
las límites del dicho almirantadgo, que dende agora Vuestras   30
Altesas fasen merçed al dicho don Christóval y quieren que aya
y lieve para sý la desena parte de todo ello, quitadas las costas
que se hisieren en ello, por manera que de lo que quedare
lynpio e libre aya e tome la déçima parte para sý mismo e faga
d'ello a su voluntad, quedando las otras nueve partes para Vues-   35
tras Altesas.
[7] Plase a Sus Altesas. Juan de Coloma.
[8] Otrosý, que sy a cabsa de las mercadurías que él trahere de
las dichas yslas e tierra que, asý como dicho es, se ganaren o
descubrieren, o de las que en troque de aquéllas se tomaren acá   40
de otros mercaderes, naçiere pleito alguno en el logar donde el
dicho comertio e trato se terná e fará, que, sy por la preheminençia de su ofiçio de almirante le perteneçerá conoçer del tal
pleito, plega a Vuestra Altesa que él o su teniente, e non otro
jues, conosca del tal pleito, e asý lo provea dende agora.   45

[9] Plase a Su‹s› Altesa‹s›, sy perteneçe al dicho ofiçio de almirante, según que lo tenía el almirante don Alonso Enriques e los otros sus subçesores en sus distritos, e seyendo justo. Juan de Coloma.

[10] Yten, que en todos los navíos que se armaren para el dicho   50
trato e negoçiaçión, cada e quando e quantas veses se armaren, que pueda el dicho don Christóval Colón, sy quisyere, contribuir e pagar la ochava parte de todo lo que se gastare en el armasón, e que tanbién aya e lieve del provecho la ochava parte de lo que resultare de la tal armada.   55

[11] Plase a Su‹s› Altesa‹s›. Juan de Coloma.

[12] Son otorgadas e despachadas con las respuestas de Vuestras Altesas en fin de cada un capítulo, en la villa de Santa Fe de la Vega de Granada, a dies e syete días de abril del año del naçimiento de nuestro salvador Jhesu Christo de mill e quatroçien-   60
tos e noventa e dos años.

Yo el Rey
Yo la Reyna

[13] Juan de Coloma.

[14] Registrada: Calçena.   65

4

Washington Codex

Two pages folded and addressed as a letter, inserted before fol. 1, on which document XXXVI.ii.1.1 follows.

/a recto/

[1] Alexander Episcopus, servus servorum Dei, carissimo in Christo filio Ferdinando Regi et carissime in Christo filie Elisabeth Regine Castelle, Legionis, Aragonum et Granate, illustribus, salutem et apostolicam benedictionem. [2] Dudum siquidem omnes et singulas insulas et terras firmas inventas et   5
inveniendas versus occidentem et meridiem, que sub actuali dominio temporali aliquorum dominorum christianorum constitute non essent, vobis heredibusque et subcessoribus vestris Castelle et Legionis regibus im perpetuum motu proprio et ex certa sciencia ac de apostolice potestatis plenitudine donavi-   10
mus, concessimus et a‹s›signavimus, vosque ac heredes et suc-

cessores prefatos de illis investivimus, illarumque dominos cum
plena, libera et omnimoda potestate, auctoritate et iurisdictione
constituimus et deputavimus, prout in nostris inde confectis litteris, quarum tenores, ac si de verbo ad verbum presentibus 15
insererentur, haberi volumus pro sufficienter expressis, plenius
continetur: cum autem contingere posset quod nuntii et capita-
nei aut vassalli vestri versus occidentem et meridiem navi-
gantes, ad partes orientales applicarent, ac insulas et terras firmas, que inde fuissent vel essent, reperirent, nos, volentes etiam 20
vos favoribus prosequi gratiosis, motu et sciencia ac potestatis
‹apostolice› plenitudine similibus, donationem, concessionem,
assignationem et litteras predictas, cum omnibus et singulis in
eisdem litteris contentis clausulis, ad omnes et singulas insulas et
terras firmas inventas et inveniendas, /a verso/ ac detectas et 25
detegendas, que, navigando aut itinerando versus occidentem
aut meridiem, huiusmodi sint vel fuerint aut apparuerint, sive
in partibus occidentalibus vel meridionalibus et orientalibus et
Indie exsistant, auctoritate apostolica, tenore presentium in
omnibus et per omnia, perinde ac si in litteris predictis de eis 30
plena et expressa mentio facta fuisset, extendimus pariter et am-
pliamus; vobis ac heredibus et successoribus vestris predictis per
vos, vel alium seu alios, corporalem insularum ac terrarum predictarum possessionem propria auctoritate libere apprehendendi ac perpetuo retinendi, illasque adversus quoscumque im- 35
pedientes etiam defendendi, plenam et liberam facultatem con-
cedentes, ac quibuscumque personis, etiam cuiuscumque dignitatis, status, gradus, ordinis vel condicionis, sub
excomunicacionis late sentencie pena, quam contrafacientes eo
ipso incurrant, districtius inhibentes ne ad partes predictas ad 40
navigandum, piscandum, vel inquirendum insulas vel terras firmas, aut quovis alio respectu seu colore, ire, vel mittere
quoquomodo presumant absque expressa vel speciali vestra ac
heredum et successorum predictorum licencia, non obstantibus
constitucionibus et ordinationibus apostolicis, ac quibusvis 45
donacionibus, concessionibus, facultatibus et a‹s›signationibus
per nos vel predecessores nostros quibuscunque regibus vel

---

12. **investivimus**] investimus *R*. 15. **tenores**] tenorem *R*. 18. **versus**] verssus. 20. **inde** *R*] Indie. **reperirent**] repperirent. 22. **‹apostolice›** *R*] *om.* 34-35. **apprehendendi**] i *over* um. 35. **adversus**] adverssus.
40. **inhibentes**] -tes *over other writing*. 41. **piscandum**] i *su* e. **inquirendum**] u *over another letter*. 43.
vestra] v *over another letter*. 47. **nostros** *R*] vestros.

principibus, infantibus, aut quibusvis aliis personis, aut or-
dinibus et miliciis de predictis partibus, maribus, insulis atque
terris, vel aliqua /b recto/ eorum parte, ex quibusvis causis,   50
etiam pietatis vel fidei aut redemptionis captivorum, et aliis
quantumcumque urgentissimis, et cum quibusvis clausulis
etiam derogatoriarum derogatoriis, fortioribus, efficacioribus et
insolitis, etiam quascumque sententias, censuras et penas in se
continentibus, que suum per actualem et realem possessionem   55
non essent sortite effectum, licet forsan aliquando illi quibus
donationes et concessiones huiusmodi facte fuissent, aut eorum
nuntii, ibidem navigassent. [3] Quos tenores illarum etiam presentibus pro sufficienter expressis et insertis habentes, motu,
sciencia et potestatis ‹apostolice› plenitudine similibus omnino   60
revocamus, ac quoad terras et insulas per eos actualiter non pos-
sessas pro infectis haberi volumus, necnon omnibus illis que in
litteris predictis voluimus non obstare, ceterisque contrariis
quibuscumque.

[4] Datum Rome apud Sanctum Petrum, anno incarnacionis   65
dominice millesimo quadringentesimo nonagesimo tercio,
sexto Kalendas Octobris, pontificatus nostri anno secundo.

[5] Gratis, de mandato sanctissimi domini nostri Pape, Jo.
Nolis, P. Gormaz.

/b verso/

Carissimo in Christo filio Fer/dinando Regi et Cari/ssime in   70
Christo filie Elisabeth / Regine Castelle Legionis / Aragonum
et Granate illus/tribus.

---

52. **urgentissimis** R] urgentissimus. 56. **forsan**] forsam. 58. **Quos** R] quas. 60. ‹apostolice›] *om. also* R, *but cf.* 21-22. 66. **quadringentesimo nonagesimo**] quadringentessimo nonagessimo.

APPENDICES

Helen Nader

APPENDIX A

Codices and Editions of the Privileges

Codex	Editions
Veragua	1951 *Libro de los privilegios del almirante don Cristóbal Colón (1498)*. Ed. Ciriaco Pérez-Bustamante. 2 vols. Madrid: RAH.
Washington	
Genoa	1823 *Codice diplomatico colombo-americano, ossia Raccolta di documenti originali e inediti spettanti a Cristoforo Colombo, alla scoperta ed al governo dell'America*. Ed. G. B. Spotorno. Genoa: Ponthenier.
	1823 *Memorials of Columbus: or a collection of authentic documents of that celebrated navigator, now first published from the original manuscripts, by order of the decurions of Genoa: preceded by a memoir of his life and discoveries. Translated from the Spanish and Italian*. London: Treuttel and Wurtz.
	1867 *Códice diplomático-americano de Cristóbal Colón. Colección de cartas de privilegios, cédulas y otras escripturas del grande descubridor del Nuevo Mundo*. Habana: El Iris.
	1894 *Il codice dei privilegi di Cristoforo Colombo: edito secondo i manoscritti di Genova, di Parigi e di Providence*. Ed. L. T. Belgrano and M. Staglieno, Raccolta 2:2.
Paris	1893 *Christopher Columbus, His Own Book of Privileges, 1502*. . . . Transliteration and translation by George F. Barwick. Intro. by Henry Harrisse. Comp. and ed. with preface by Benjamin Franklin Stevens. London: B. F. Stevens.
Providence, R.I.	*Rights of Discovery: Christopher Columbus's Final Appeal to King Fernando*. Transcription, translation, and edition by Helen Nader of The John Carter Brown Library's Spanish Codex 1. Cali, Colombia: Carvajal.
Huntington Library	

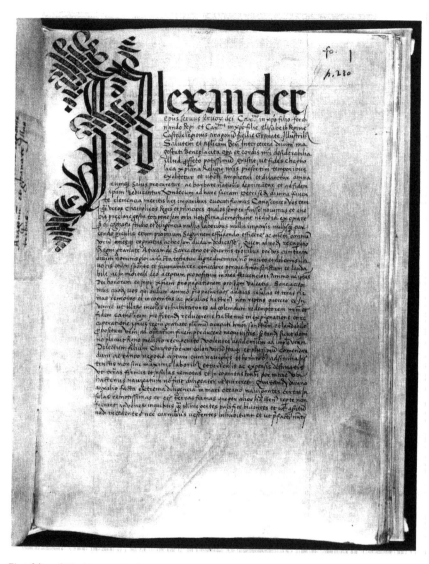

First folio of Washington Codex. (From the collections of the Library of Congress)

APPENDIX B

Collation of Documents in the Codices

Nader/Genoa (Document)	Paris (Document)	Veragua (Folio)	Washington (Folio)	Huntington (Folio)	Providence (Page)
1 Santa Fe 17/4/1492	2	9–10	9–12v		1–2
2 Granada 30/4/1492	3	11v–12v	12v–17v		3
3 Barcelona 30/3/1493	31		38–38v		
4 Barcelona 28/5/1493	3	10v–11v	12v		
5 Barcelona 28/5/1493	3	13–14	17–17v		
6 Barcelona 24/5/1493	34		40v–41v		
7 Barcelona 28/5/1493	27	35v–36	34v–35v		
8 Barcelona 28/5/1493	28	36	35v		
9 Barcelona 28/5/1493	29	36–36v	35v–36		
10 Barcelona 13/4/1494	33		30–39v		
11 Segovia 16/8/1494	26	34–35	34–34v		
12 Madrid 10/4/1495	9	21–23	24		
13 Barcelona 5/9/1493	32		38v–39		
14 Rome 6/1493	36		2–3v		
15 Segovia 16/8/1494	34		39v–40v		

Nader/Genoa (Document)	Paris (Document)	Veragua (Folio)	Washington (Folio)	Huntington (Folio)	Providence (Page)
16 Burgos 23/4/1497	18	29v–30	31		
17 Burgos 23/4/1497	19	30–3v	31–31v		
18 Burgos 23/4/1497	6	16–18	18v–20v		
19 Burgos 23/4/1497	21	30v–31	32		
20 Medina del Campo 15/6/1497	8	18v–20v	21–22v		
21 Medina del Campo 22/7/1497	22	31–32	32v–33		
22 Medina del Campo 22/6/1497	12	25v–27	27v–28v		
23 Medina del Campo 22/6/1497	13	27–28	28v–29v		
24 Medina del Campo 22/6/1497	14	28–28v	29v–30		
25 Burgos 23/4/1497	7	18–18v	20v–21		
26 Burgos 23/4/1497	10	23–23v	25–25v		
27 Burgos 6/5/1497	11	23v–25	25v–27v		
28 Burgos 6/5/1497		25–25v	27v–28		
29 Medina del Campo 22/6/1497	15	29v–29	30		
30 Burgos 9/5/1497	20	30v	31v–32		
31 Medina del Campo 22/6/1497	16	29–29v	30v		
32 Alcalá de Henares 23/12/1497	25	33	34		

Nader/Genoa (Document)	Paris (Document)	Veragua (Folio)	Washington (Folio)	Huntington (Folio)	Providence (Page)
33 Medina del Campo 30/5/1497	5	15v–16	18–18v		
34 Medina del Campo 2/6/1497	9	20v	23–25		
35 Medina del Campo 12/6/1497	4	14–15	17v–18		4
36 Medina del Campo 22/7/1497	23	32–33	33–33v		
37 Alcalá de Henares 23/12/1497	24	33	33v–34		
38 Burgos 23/4/1497	17	29v	30v–31		
39 Burgos 23/4/1497	30		36–38		
40 Burgos 23/4/1497	1	1	3	1	2
41 Burgos 23/4/1497	1	1			
42 Valladolid 5/7/1435	1	1–1v	4		
43 Valladolid 5/7/1435	1	1v	5	1–1v	'
44 Valladolid 17/8/1416	1	1v–2	6	1v	
45 Toro 4/4/1405	1	2–3	7–10	2–2v	
46 Valladolid 17/8/1416	1	3–4v	10–15	2v–5	2–3
47 Segovia 6/6/1419	1	4v–6	15–21		
48 Valladolid 12/11/1489	1	6–7v	21–25	7–8v	
49 Burgos 23/4/1497	2	8–9	9v–12v		
49b Santa Fe 17/4/1497		9–10		8v–9	1
50 Burgos 23/4/1492	2	10–10v		9–10	

Nader/Genoa (Document)	Paris (Document)	Veragua (Folio)	Washington (Folio)	Huntington (Folio)	Providence (Page)
51 Burgos 23/4/1497	3	14–15		13v–14v	
52 Seville 15/3/1498	10	8			
53 Seville 15/3/1498	35	7v	33v		
54 Seville 15/3/1498		33v			
55 Santo Domingo 4/12/1498		34			
56 Santo Domingo 4/12/1498		36			
57 Granada 1500	44				
58 Santa Fe 17/4/1492	41				
59 Granada 1501	43		8–15		8–15
60 Granada 1501	42		5–8		5–8
61 Granada 27/9/1501	37				
62 Granada 27/9/1501	38				
63 Granada 28/9/1501	39				
64 Valencia de la Torre 14/3/1502	40				
65 Seville 5/1/1502	1		3–9v	14v	
66 Seville 21/3/1502					
67 Seville 22/3/1502					4–5
66 Seville 2/4/1502					
69 Seville 30/12/1502					
70 Seville 12/1502					
71 Seville 27/12/1504					

Nader/Genoa (Document)	Paris (Document)	Veragua (Folio)	Washington (Folio)	Huntington (Folio)	Providence (Page)
72 Genoa 10/1/1670					
73 Genoa 1670					

GLOSSARY
Helen Nader

AZUMBRE	Liquid measure equivalent to four pints.
CAHIZ	The *cahiz* (plural *cahices*) was a dry measure of volume, divisible into 12 *fánegas*.
EXCELENTE	A new gold coin made possible by the gold acquired in the conquest of Granada. It was equivalent to 11 *reales* and one *maravedí*, or 375 *maravedís*, and was popularly called a ducat.
FÁNEGA	Dry measure of volume equivalent to about 1½ bushels (the modern American bushel is 35.2 liters). Weight varied, depending on item measured, and on region. The average fanega in Andalusia was 55.5 liters, in Toledo 44 liters. One *fánega* was divisible into 12 *celemines*; 12 *fánegas* made a *cahiz*.
HIDALGO	A lay person who was tax-exempt. Exemption *(hidalguía)* could be acquired by several means, including birth, but usually by entering royal service. In the sixteenth century, the monarchs sold the status of hidalgo. They also granted exempt status to parents of very large families and emigrants to the Spanish Indies.
MAINLAND	When the monarchs used the term "mainland" *(tierra firme)*, they were hoping that Columbus would be able to establish Castilian sovereignty on some portion of the Asian coast. In this, they were trying to imitate the Portuguese, who in 1480 acquired permission from local rulers in west Africa to establish a trading post under Portuguese sovereignty, the fortress they called São Jorge da Mina. In Italy, the term "terra firme" referred to that portion of the Italian Peninsula conquered by the island Republic of Venice.
MARAVEDÍ	The smallest unit of money of account, just as the cent is our smallest unit of money. Three hundred seventy-five *marave-*

dís were equivalent to one ducat. The coin itself was no longer in circulation in the fifteenth century.

SUBJETOS — A legal category of royal subjects who did not take personal oaths of loyalty to the monarchs. They were groups who, though born in Castile, obeyed religious law and were subject to religious law courts. Clergy, both regular and secular, became subject to canon law and church courts when they took their clerical vows. Muslims and Jews also lived under their own religious laws, administered by the elders of their own communities. *Subjetos,* because they did not live under the municipal laws, were not citizens (*vecinos*) of the municipalities where they resided.

TERCIAS — Since the thirteenth century, most Spanish farm land was subject to a church tithe on agricultural products. The tithe was ten percent of the crop in theory, but usually between three and five percent in fact. The Castilian monarchy had negotiated with the papacy the right to collect for itself two-ninths of the tithe. This royal share of the tithe was called the royal thirds *(tercias).*

VASALLO — Any and all subjects of the monarch, including both tax payers and tax exempt. Subjects of a noble or ecclesiastical lord were *vasallos* of both the monarch and their lord.

VASALLOS DEL REY — Royal vassals who achieved their status by personally taking an oath of vassallage to the monarch. By this oath they submitted to the royal will, giving up the protection of the law and gaining the prospect of bountiful rewards. Royal vassals comprised members of the royal family, the staff of the royal household, court, and chancery, military professionals in the royal service, and nobles.

LIST OF WORKS CITED

Albònico, A. 1986	Bartolomeo Colombo, adelantado mayor de las Indias. In *La presenza Italiana in Andalusia nel basso medioevo,* ed. Alberto Boscolo and Bibiano Torres. Bologna: Cappelli.
Alcocer y Martínez, M. 1926	*D. Juan Rodríguez de Fonseca: Estudio crítico-biográfico.* Valladolid: Casa Social Católica.
Aldea, Quentín, et al. 1987	*Diccionario de Historia Ecclesiástica de España.* 5 vols. Madrid: CSIC.
Altolaguirre, A. 1926	La real confirmación del mayorazgo fundado por d. Cristóbal Colón. *Boletín de la Real Academia de Historia* 88: 330–55. Rpt. Madrid: Tip. de Archivos, Bibliotecas, y Museos, 1926.
1901	Estudio jurídico de la capitulación y privilegios de Cristóbal Colón. *BRAH* 38: 279–94.
Assereto, U. 1904	La data della nascità di Colombo accertata da un documento nuovo. *Giornale Storico e Letterario della Liguria* 1–2.
Ayala, J. de. 1965	*A Letter to Ferdinand and Isabella, 1503.* Trans. and ed. Charles E. Nowell. Minneapolis: University of Minnesota Press.
Azcona, T. 1964	*Isabel la católica: Estudio crítico de su vida y su reinado.* Madrid: Editorial Católica.
Battlori, M. 1976	The Papal Division of the World and Its Consequences. In *First Images of America,* ed. Fredi Chiappelli, I:211–220. Berkeley: University of California Press.
Bedini, S. 1991	*The Christopher Columbus Encyclopedia.* 2 vols. New York: Simon and Schuster.

Belgrano, L.T. and Staglieno, M. 1894 — *Il Codice dei privilegi di Cristoforo Colombo edito secondo i manoscritti di Genova, di Parigi, e di Providence.* Raccolta, 2: 2.

Bernáldez, A. 1962 — *Memorias del reinado de los reyes católicos.* Ed. Manuel Gómez-Moreno and Juan de Mata Carriazo. Madrid: CSIC.

Berwick, M.R. 1892 — *Autógrafos de Cristóbal Colón y papeles de América.* Madrid: Sucesores de Rivadeneyra.

1902 — *Nuevos autógrafos de Cristóbal Colón y relaciones de ultramar.* Madrid: Berwick.

Blake, J. W. 1969 — *European Beginnings in West Africa 1454–1578.* Westport, Conn.: Greenwood Press. Vol. 1.

Cadiñanos Bardeci, I. 1989 — *El adelantamento de Castilla, partido de Burgos: Sus ordenanzas y archivo.* Madrid: ANABAD.

Casas, B. 1986 — *Historia de las Indias.* 3 vols. Ed. André Saint-Lu. Caracas: Biblioteca Ayacucho.

1951 — *Historia de las Indias.* Ed. Agustín Millares Carlo. Introduction by Lewis Hanke. Mexico City and Buenos Aires: Fondo de Cultura Económica. 3 vols.

Chiappelli, F., ed. 1976 — *First Images of America: The Impact of the New World on the Old.* Berkeley and Los Angeles: University of California Press.

Colomer Montset, J. 1952 — Las Capitulaciones de Santa Fé registradas en el archivo de la Corona de Aragón en Barcelona. *Studi Colombiani.* 2: 391–97.

Colón, F. 1959 — *The Life of the Admiral Christopher Columbus by His Son, Ferdinand.* Trans. Benjamin Keen. New Brunswick, N. J.: Rutgers University Press.

Columbus, C. 1991 — *The* Libro de las profecías *of Christopher Columbus.* Ed. and trans. August Kling and Delno C. West. Gainesville: University of Florida Press.

1989 — *Libro copiador de Cristóbal Colón: Correspondencia inédita con los Reyes Católicos sobre los viajes a América: Estudio histórico-crítico y edición.* Ed. Antonio Ruméu de Armas. Madrid: Ministerio de Cultura/Testimonio Compañía Editorial. Vol. 1.

1988 — *The Diario of Christopher Columbus's First Voyage to America, 1492–1493.* Ed. Oliver Dunn and James E. Kelley, Jr. Norman, Oklahoma: University of Oklahoma Press.

1984	*Textos y documentos completos: Relaciones de viajes, cartas, y memoriales.* Ed. Consuelo Varela. Madrid: Alianza.
Copilación 1989	*Copilacion de leyes del reino de Alfonso Díaz de Montalvo.* Ed. Emiliano González Díez. Valladolid: Editorial Lex Nova.
Davenport, F. G. 1917	*European Treaties bearing on the History of the United States and its Dependencies to 1648.* Washington, D.C.: Carnegie Institution.
1909	Text of Columbus's Privileges. *AHR* 14: 764–76.
Dickerson, R. 1986	*The Fundamentals of Legal Drafting.* 2nd ed. Boston: Little, Brown.
Escudero, J.A. 1969	*Los secretarios de estado y del despacho.* 4 vols. Madrid: Instituto de Estudios Administrativos.
Fernández, R. D. 1987	*Capitulaciones colombinas (1492–1506).* Zamora, Michoacán (Mexico): Colegio de Michoacán.
Fernández Armesto, F. 1991	*Columbus.* Oxford: Oxford University Press.
Fernández de Oviedo, G. 1959	*Historia general y natural de las Indias.* Ed. Juan Pérez de Tudela Bueso. Madrid: Ediciones Atlas.
Ferro, G. 1984	*Le navigazioni lusitane nell'Atlantico e Cristoforo Colombo in Portogallo.* Milan: Mursia.
Fita, F. 1891	Fray Bernal Buyl y Cristóbal Colón. Nueva colección de cartas reales, enriquecida con algunas inéditas. *BRAH* 19: 173–233.
1893	Fray Bernaldo Buyl. Documentos inéditos. *BRAH* 22:373–78.
Floyd, T. 1973	*The Columbus Dynasty in the Caribbean, 1492–1526.* Albuquerque: University of New Mexico Press.
Fonseca, L. A. 1987	*O essencial sobre Bartolomeu Dias.* Lisbon: Imprenta Nacional-Casa de Moneda.
1978	*Navegación y corso en el Mediteráneo occidental: los portugueses a mediados del siglo XV.* Pamplona: Ediciones Universidad de Navarra.
Formisano, L. 1992	*Letters from the New World. Amerigo Vespucci's Discovery of America.* Ed. L. Formisano. Foreword by G. Wills. Tran. D. Jacobson. New York: Marsilio, 1992.

Franco Silva, A.   *La esclavitud en Andalucía, 1450–1550*. Granada: Universidad de
1992   Granada, Biblioteca del Bolsillo, 13.

1985   *La esclavitud en Andalucía al término de la edad media*. Madrid: Marcial
                  Pons.

1980   *Los esclavos de Sevilla.* Seville: Diputación Provincial de Sevilla, Co-
                  lecciones paralelas, Historia, 1.

1979a   *La esclavitud en Sevilla y su tierra a fines de la edad media*. Seville:
                  Diputación Provincial de Sevilla.

1979b   *Regesto documental sobre la esclavitud sevillana (1453–1513)*. Seville:
                  Publicaciones de la Universidad de Sevilla, Anales de la Univer-
                  sidad Hispalense, Serie Filosofía y Letras, 46\46.

García Gallo, A.   *Las bulas de Alejandro VI y el ordenamiento jurídico de la expansión
1958   portuguesa y castellana en Africa y Indias.* Madrid: Instituto Nacional
                  de Estudios Jurídicos.

1957–1958   Las bulas de Alejandro VI y el ordenamiento jurídico de la expan-
                  sión portuguesa y castellana en Africa e Indias. *AHDE* 24–28: 480–
                  500, 501–532, 589–610, 721–736.

1944   Los orígenes de la administración territorial en las Indias. *AHDE*
                  15.

García Martínez, R.   Ojeada de las capitulaciones para la conquista de América. *RHA*
1970   69: 1–40.

Gibson, C.   *Tlaxcala in the Sixteenth Century*. New Haven: Yale University
1952   Press.

Gil, J. and C. Varela   *Temas colombinos*. Seville: EEHAS.
1986

Gil, J.   *Mitos y utopias del descubrimiento*. Madrid: Alianza.
1989

1984   Las cuentas de Cristóbal Colón. *AEA* 41: 425–511.

Gil, J. and C. Varela   *Cartas de particulares a Colón y relaciones coetáneas*. Madrid: Alianza.
1984

Giménez Fernández, M.   *Las Cortes de La Española in 1518*. Seville: *AUH*
1954

1946   *Algo más sobre las bulas alejandrinas de 1493 referentes a las Indias*. Se-
                  ville: La Gavidia.

1944a	*Nuevas consideraciones sobre la historia, sentido, y valor de las bulas alejandrinas de 1493 refrentes a las Indias.* Seville: EEHAS.
1944b	Nuevas consideraciones sobre la historia y el sentido de las letras alejandrinas de 1493 referentes a las Indias. *AEA* 1:173–259.
Gioffré, D. 1971	*Il mercato degli schiavi a Genova nel secolo XV.* Genoa: Fratelli Bozzi.
González Gallego, I. 1974	El Libro de los Privilegios de la Nación Genovesa, in *Historia. Instituciones. Documentos* 1: 275–358.
Gould, A. 1984	*Nueva lista documentada de los tripulantes de Colón en 1492,* Ed. José de la Peña y Camara. Madrid: RAH.
Gutiérrez Coronel, D. 1946	*Historia genealógica de la casa de Mendoza.* Ed. Angel González Palencia. 2 vols. Madrid, CSIC.
Hanke, L. 1959	*Aristotle and the American Indians: A Study in Race Prejudice in the Modern World.* Chicago: H. Regnery Co.
Harrisse, H. 1884	*Christophe Colomb, son origine, sa vie, ses voyages, sa famille, & ses descendants, d'après des documents inédits tirés des archives de Gênes, de Savone, de Séville et de Madrid.* 2 vols. Paris: E. Leroux.
1866	*Bibliotheca Americana Vetustissima: A Description of Works Relating to America Published between the Years 1492 and 1551.* New York: G. P. Philes. Newest edition, updated by Carlos Sanz. *Bibliotheca Americana Vetustissima; comentario crítico e índice general cronológico de los seis volúmenes que componen la obra.* Madrid: Suárez, 1960.
Heers, J. 1981a	*Christophe Colomb.* Paris: Hachette.
1981b	*Esclaves et domestiques au Moyen Age dans le monde méditerranéen.* Paris: Fayard.
1957	Le royaume de Grenade et la politique marchande de Gênes en Occident (XVe siècle). *Moyen Age:* 87–121.
Henige, D. 1991	*In Search of Columbus.* Tucson: University of Arizona Press.
Incháustegui, J.M. 1964	*Francisco de Bobadilla: Tres homónimos, y un enigma colombino descifrado.* Madrid: Cultura Hispánica.
Irving, W. 1828	*A History of the Life and Voyages of Christopher Columbus.* 4 vols. New York: Carvill.

Jiménez de Cisneros, F.   *Memorial de Zamora sobre las Indias.* Ed. Demetrio Ramos Pérez.
1981   Zamora: Fundación Ramos de Castro para el Estudio y Promoción
                           del Hombre.

Jos, E.   *El plan y la génesis del descubrimiento colombino.* Ed. Demetrio
1980   Ramos. Valladolid: Casa-Museo de Colón.

Lamb, U.   *Frey Nicolás de Ovando, gobernador de las Indias, 1501–1509.* Santo
1977   Domingo: Editora de Santo Domingo.

Liss, Peggy K.   *Isabel the Queen. Life and Times.* New York: Oxford University
1992.   Press.

Lunenfeld, M.   *Isabella I of Castile, 1474–1504.* Cambridge: Cambridge University
1987   Press.

Lyon, E.   Fifteenth-Century Manuscript Yields First Look at Niña. *National
1986   Geographic,* 601–5.

Manzano Manzano, J.   *Los Pinzones y el descubrimiento de América.* 3 vols. Madrid: Ediciones
1988   Cultural Hispánica.

1972   *Colón descubrió América del Sur en 1494.* Caracas: Academia Nacional
                           de la Historia

1964   *Cristóbal Colón. Siete años decisivos de su vida, 1485–1492.* Madrid:
                           Cultura Hispánica.

Provost, F.   *Columbus: An annotated Guide to the Scholarship on His Life and Writ-
1991   ings, 1750–1988.* Providence, R.I.: The John Carter Brown Li-
                           brary/ Detroit: Omnigraphics.

Márquez Villanueva, F.   *Investigaciones sobre Juan Alvarez Gato: Contribución al conocimiento de
1960   la literatura castellana del siglo XV.* Madrid: S. Aguirre Torre.

Martini, D. G.   *Cristoforo Colombo tra ragione e fantasia.* Genoa: Edizioni Culturali
1987   Internazionali.

Meisnest, F.   The Lost Book of Privileges of Columbus Located and Identified.
1949   *Huntington Library Quarterly* 12: 401–407.

Memorials of Columbus.   *Memorials of Columbus; or a Collection of Authentic Documents of that
1823   Celebrated Navigator.* London: Treuttel and Wurtz.

Milhou, A.   *Colón y su mentalidad mesiánica, en el ambiente franciscanista español.*
1983   Valladolid: Casa-Museo de Colón, Seminario Americanista de la
                           Universidad de Valladolid.

Mitre Fernández, E. 1968	*Evolución de la nobleza en Castilla bajo Enrique III, 1396–1406*. Valladolid: Universidad de Valladolid.
Morales Padrón, F. 1955	Descubrimientos y toma de la posesión. *AEA* 12: 321–80.
Morison, S.E. 1942	*Admiral of the Ocean Sea: A Life of Christopher Columbus*. 2 vols. Boston: Little, Brown and Company.
Moya Pons, F. 1986	*El pasado dominicano*. Santo Domingo: Fundación J.A. Caro Alvarez.
1982	*Historia Dominicana*. 2 vols. Santo Domingo: Caribe Grolier.
1977	*Historia colonial de Santo Domingo*. Santiago, Dominican Republic: Universidad Católica Madre Maestra.
Muro Orejón, A. 1964–89	*Pleitos colombinos*. 5 vols. Seville: EEHAS.
1951	*El original de la capitulación de 1492 y sus copias contemporáneas*. Seville: EEHAS.
1947	La primera capitulación con Vicente Yáñez Pinzón para descubrir las Indias, 6 junio 1499. *AEA* 4.
Nader, H. 1992	*Rights of Discovery: Christopher Columbus's Final Appeal to King Fernando*. Cali (Colombia): Carvajal.
1990	*Liberty in Absolutist Spain: The Habsburg Sale of Towns 1516–1700*. Baltimore: The Johns Hopkins University Press.
1979	*The Mendoza Family in the Spanish Renaissance 1350–1550*. New Brunswick (New Jersey): Rutgers University Press.
Navarrete, M. F. 1825–37	*Colección de los viajes y descubrimientos que hicieron por mar los Españoles*. 5 vols. Madrid: Imprenta Real.
Parry, J. 1984	*New Iberian World: A Documentary History of the Discovery and Settlement of Latin America to the Early 17th Century*. Ed. John H. Parry and Robert G. Keith. 6 vols. New York: Times Books/ Hector and Rose.
Pérez-Bustamante, C. 1951	*Libro de los privilegios del almirante don Cristóbal Colón (1498)*. Madrid: RAH.
Phillips, C.R. 1986	*Six Galleons for the King of Spain: Imperial Defense in the Early Seventeenth Century*. Baltimore and London: Johns Hopkins University Press.

Phillips, W. and C.R.
1992

The Worlds of Christopher Columbus. New York: Cambridge University Press.

Pike, R.
1966

Enterprise and Adventure: Genoese in Seville and the Opening of the New World. Ithaca, N.Y.: Cornell University Press.

Prieto Cantero, A.
1969

Casa y descargos de los reyes católicos. Valladolid: Instituto "Isabel la Católica" de Historia Eclesiástica.

Provost, F.
1991

Columbus. An Annotated Guide to the Scholarship on His Life and Writings, 1750 to 1988. Detroit: Omnigraphics for the John Carter Brown Library.

Ramos Pérez, D.
1986

La primera noticia de América. Valladolid: Casa de Colón.

1982

Las variaciones ideológicas en torno al descubrimiento de América: Pedro Mártir de Anglería y su mentalidad. Valladolid: Casa-Museo de Colón, Seminario Americanista de la Universidad de Valladolid.

1981

Audacia, negocios, y política en los viajes españoles de 'descubrimiento'. Valladolid: Casa-Museo Colón.

1979

Colón y el enfrentamiento de los caballeros: un serio problema del segundo viaje que nuevos documentos ponen al descubierto. *Revista de Indias* 39: 9–87.

Restrepo Uribe, F.
1987

Gonzalo Fernández de Oviedo, primer cronista de Indias. *Boletín de Historia y Antigüedades* 74.757: 245–57.

Rodríguez Demorizi, E.
1984

Colón en Española: Itinerario y bibliografía. Santo Domingo: Academia Dominicana de la Historia.

1942

Relaciones históricas de Santo Domingo. Ciudad Trujillo: Editora Montalvo. Vol. 1.

Rouse, I.
1992

The Taino: Rise and Decline of the People Who Greeted Columbus. New Haven: Yale University Press.

Rumeu de Armas, A.
1985

Nueva luz sobre las capitulaciones de Santa Fe de 1492 concertadas entre los reyes católicos y Cristóbal Colón: Estudio institucional y diplomático. Madrid: CSIC.

1982

El "Portugués" Cristóbal Colón en Castilla. Madrid: Cultura Hispánica.

| 1974 | *Itinerario de los reyes católicos, 1474–1516.* Madrid: CSIC. |

1973   *Hernando Colón, historiador del descubrimiento de América.* Madrid: Cultura Hispánica.

1972   *Un escrito desconocido de Cristóbal Colón: El memorial de La Mejorada.* Madrid: Cultura Hispánica.

1969   *La política indigenista de Isabel la Católica.* Valladolid: Instituto "Isabel la Católica" de Historia Eclesiástica.

1954   *Alonso de Lugo en la corte de los reyes católicos: 1496–1497.* Madrid: CSIC.

1953   *Código del trabajo del indígena Americana.* Madrid: Cultura Hispánica.

Russell, J. B.
1991   *Inventing the Flat Earth: Columbus and Modern Historians.* New York: Praeger.

Salinero, G.
1602   *Annotationes Iulii Salinerii iures consulti savonensis ad Cornelium Tacitum.* Genoa: Apud Josephum Pavonem.

Schaefer, E.
1935   *El consejo real y supremo de las Indias; su historia, organización y labor administrativa hasta la terminación de la casa de Austria.* Castilian translation by the author. Seville: Imp. M. Carmona. Vol. 1.

Schoenrich, O.
1949–1950   *The Legacy of Christopher Columbus. The Historic Litigations Involving His Discoveries, His Will, His Family, and His Descendants . . . Resulting from the Discovery of America.* 2 vols. Glendale, Calif.: A. H. Clark Co.

Serrano y Sanz, M.
1918   Los amigos y protectores aragoneses de Cristóbal Colón. In *Orígenes de la dominación española en América: Estudios históricos.* Madrid: Bailly/Bailliere.

Spotorno, G. B.
1823   *Codice diplomatico colombo-americano, ossia Raccolta di documenti originali e inediti spettanti a Cristoforo Colombo, alla scoperta ed al governo dell'America.* Genoa: Ponthenier.

Suárez Fernández, L.
1977   *Historia del reinado de Juan I de Castilla.* Madrid: Universidad Autónoma.

1962   *El canciller Pedro López de Ayala y su tiempo, 1332–1407.* [Vitoria]: Diputación Foral de Alava. Consejo de Cultura.

1960   *Castilla, el cisma y la crisis conciliar, 1378–1440.* Madrid: CSIC.

1959   *Navegación y comercio en el Golfo de Vizcaya*. Madrid: CSIC.

Sued-Badillo, J.   *Cristóbal Colón y la esclavitud de los Indios en las Antillas*. San Juan:
1983   Fundación Arqueológica, Antropológica, Histórica de Puerto
    Rico.

Tejada y Sainz, J.   *Spanish and English legal and commercial dictionary, a revision and en-*
1945   *largement of the Law translator's reference glossary*. Santa María del Ro-
    sario, Cuba: Editorial Var-I-Tek.

Thacher, J. B.   *Christopher Columbus: His Life, His Work, His Remains as Revealed*
1967.   *by Original Printed and Manuscript Records.* . . . 3 vols. [New York
    and London: G.P. Putnam's Sons, 1903–04] Reprinted New
    York: Kraus Reprint.

Van der Linden, H.   Alexander VI and the Demarcation of the Maritime and Colonial
1922   Domains of Spain and Portugal, 1493–94. *AHR* 22: 1–20.

Varela, C.   *Cristóbal Colón: Retrato de un hombre*. Madrid: Alianza.
1992

1988   *Colón y los florentinos*. Madrid: Alianza.

1985   El rol del cuarto viaje colombino. *AEA* 47: 243–295.

1984   El entorno florentino de Cristóbal Colón. In *Colloquia sulla pre-*
    senza italiana in Andalusia nel basso medioeve. Ed. Alberto Boscolo
    and Bibiano Torres. Rome: Cappelli.

Varona García, M. A.   *La chancillería de Valladolid en el reinado de los Reyes Católicos*. Val-
1981   ladolid: Universidad de Valladolid.

Vignaud, H.   *Le vrai Christophe Colomb et la légende*. Paris: Picard.
1921

1920   *The Columbian Tradition on the Discovery of America and of the Part*
    Played Therein by the Astronomer Toscanelli. Oxford: Clarendon.

1905   *Etudes critiques sur la vie de Colomb avant ses découvertes*. Paris: Welter.

Vigneras, L.   *The Discovery of South America and the Andalusian Voyages*. Chicago:
1976   University of Chicago Press for the Newberry Library.

Watts, P.   Prophecy and Discovery: On the Spiritual Origins of Christopher
1985   Columbus's "Enterprise of the Indies." *AHR* 90: 73–102.

INDEX

negotiations between Columbus and, xix, xviii, 5–6, 8, 17–19, 40–41
the new world and, xviii
orders to royal judge of Seville to deliver prisoners to serve time in La Española, 116–117
papal decree granting American sovereignty to, 37–38, 93–98
in partnership with Columbus, 3–4, 16, 19–21, 48–49, 49–51
permission to convicted criminals to settle on La Española granted by, 112–114
permission to increase Columbus's personnel granted by, 108
permission to persons other than Columbus to explore and colonize La Española granted by, 88–91
powers and privileges granted to Columbus by, 63–66, 66–69, 169–170, 172–179
reign of, 4
reimbursement to Columbus for cash advances to colonists, 124
restriction of permission to persons other than Columbus to explore and colonize La Española, 128–129
second-voyage objectives of, 30–31, 32
security provided for crew by, 27
seizure of supply ships for colonies by, 123–124
spelling of name of, xix–xx
tax exemption to Spanish colonists granted by, 119–120, 120–122, 122–123
transcripts of documents sent to Columbus by, 132–133
upgrading of Granada Capitulations by, 28–29, 70–72, 73–75
warrant empowering Columbus to outfit the second voyage, 79–82
warrant to deliver a statement of privileges to Columbus, 138
wheat ordered delivered to colonists by, 124–125
writ authorizing payment of colonists' wages from royal assets, 132

writ concerning the duties of Columbus, 83–84
writ for payment of wages, 105
writ on appointing Columbus's officers, 84–85
writ on using La Española as a place of banishment, 115–116
writ ordering provisions for the Indies at customary prices, 118–119
writ to ascertain Columbus's profit share, 127–128
Fernando the Catholic, King, 208n. See also Fernando, King
Fernandus, charters registered by, 145, 148
Field, Arthur, 38n
Fiesco, Juan Luis, 216n
First Letter from America, 36–37
versions of, 37
First voyage, 17–29
crew recruited for, 26–27
documents empowering Columbus for, 63–75
documents in Book of Privileges relating to, 63–75
duration of, 26–27
financial failure of, 30–31, 40
payment to Columbus for, 49
provisioning of, 26–27
route of, 27–28
secrecy of, 25
Fonseca, Juan Rodríguez de, 80illus., 200–201n. See also Badajoz, bishop of
exploratory voyages to the Americas under captains other than Columbus authorized by, 49
maximum prices of provisions set by, 49
organization of second voyage by, 31, 32, 79–82
sale of native American slaves by, 35
tax exemptions for colony provisions and, 48
Foods
controlling costs of, 48–49
taxes paid by native Americans in the form of, 47
Formisano, Luciano, xvii
Fourth voyage, 55–58
addition to Veragua Codex of instructions for, 56–57
arrival of Columbus at Santo Domingo after, 57
Columbus's family business and, 56–58

creation of the final version of the Book of Privileges and, 56–57
destruction of most of the fleet during, 57
disillusionment of Columbus after, 57–58, 161–169
documents in Book of Privileges relating to, 161–194
motivation behind, 55–56
organization of, 56
royal instructions for, 184–186
France, Aragonese rivalry with, 20
Frank, Dr. William, 12n
Free trade, as instituted in Spanish colonies, 45, 57–58

Galicia, recruitment of colonists from, 52–53
Gallectus, D., 97
Gallego, Abbot, 107
Gallego, 210n
Gallo, Antonio, 216n
Garcias, Pedro, 38, 203n
as transcriber of papal decree, 93
Genoa
Columbus as native of, 50
destruction of notarial documents of, 51
Genoa Codex, 216n
appearance of, 15
creation of, 11, 57
inventory of, 193–194
provenance of, 14
receipt from Lorenzo Oderico of, 192–193
Genoese merchants
business dealings of, 22
in Seville, 11
Ginnous, Michele, notarization of papal decree by, 98
Goceano, 198n
God
as the source of all things, 70–71
relationship of philosophers to, 71
Gold, 211n
conversion into coinage of, 107
restitution of Columbus and his brothers' stolen, 181
royal share of, 89, 112, 163, 165, 166–167, 168, 181–182
Gold mining
at La Española, 44, 47, 48, 53, 89, 106, 162, 167–168, 212n
in Portugal, 201n

Made in the USA
Middletown, DE
27 August 2021